INTELLECTUAL PROPERTY, INNOVATION AND ECONOMIC INEQUALITY

While growing disparities in wealth and income are well-documented across the globe, the role of intellectual property rights is often overlooked. This volume brings together leading commentators from around the world to interrogate the interrelationship between intellectual property and economic inequality. Interdisciplinary and globally oriented by design, the book features economists, legal scholars, policy analysts, and other experts. Chapters address the impact of intellectual property rights on economic inequality, the effect of economic inequality on the protection and enforcement of these rights, and the potential use of innovation law and policy to help reduce economic inequality. The volume also tackles timely issues such as race and gender disparities and the North–South divide in innovation. This book is available as Open Access on Cambridge Core.

Daniel Benoliel is Professor of Law at the University of Haifa Faculty of Law and Director of the Haifa Center of Law and Technology.

Peter K. Yu is Regents Professor of Law and Communication and Director of the Center for Law and Intellectual Property at Texas A&M University.

Francis Gurry is an Australian lawyer who served as the Director General of the World Intellectual Property Organization from 2008 to 2020.

Keun Lee is Distinguished Professor of Economics at Seoul National University. He is also a fellow of the Canadian Institute for Advanced Research (CIFAR), an editor of *Research Policy*, and a regular writer for Project Syndicate.

Intellectual Property, Innovation and Economic Inequality

Edited by

DANIEL BENOLIEL

University of Haifa

PETER K. YU

Texas A&M University

FRANCIS GURRY

World Intellectual Property Organization

KEUN LEE

Seoul National University

CAMBRIDGE
UNIVERSITY PRESS

CAMBRIDGE
UNIVERSITY PRESS

Shaftesbury Road, Cambridge CB2 8EA, United Kingdom

One Liberty Plaza, 20th Floor, New York, NY 10006, USA

477 Williamstown Road, Port Melbourne, VIC 3207, Australia

314–321, 3rd Floor, Plot 3, Splendor Forum, Jasola District Centre, New Delhi – 110025, India

103 Penang Road, #05-06/07, Visioncrest Commercial, Singapore 238467

Cambridge University Press is part of Cambridge University Press & Assessment, a department of the University of Cambridge.

We share the University's mission to contribute to society through the pursuit of education, learning and research at the highest international levels of excellence.

www.cambridge.org
Information on this title: www.cambridge.org/9781108841702

DOI: 10.1017/9781108894722

When citing this work, please include a reference to the DOI 10.1017/9781108894722

First published 2024

A catalogue record for this publication is available from the British Library

Library of Congress Cataloging-in-Publication Data
NAMES: Benoliel, Daniel, 1972- editor. | Yu, Peter K., 1971- editor. | Gurry, Francis, 1951- editor. | Lee, Keun, 1960- editor.
TITLE: Intellectual property, innovation, and economic inequality / edited by Daniel Benoliel, University of Haifa; Peter K. Yu, Texas A&M University; Francis Gurry, World Intellectual Property Organization; Keun Lee, Seoul National University.
DESCRIPTION: Cambridge, United Kingdom ; New York, NY : Cambridge University Press, 2024.
IDENTIFIERS: LCCN 2023057316 (print) | LCCN 2023057317 (ebook) | ISBN 9781108841702 (hardback) | ISBN 9781108795227 (paperback) | ISBN 9781108894722 (epub)
SUBJECTS: LCSH: Intellectual property. | Technological innovation–Law and legislation. | Income distribution–Law and legislation. | Economic development–Law and legislation.
CLASSIFICATION: LCC K1401 .I556545 2024 (print) | LCC K1401 (ebook) | DDC 346.048–dc23/eng/20231214
LC record available at https://lccn.loc.gov/2023057316
LC ebook record available at https://lccn.loc.gov/2023057317

ISBN 978-1-108-84170-2 Hardback

Contents

Figures

Tables

Contributors

EDITORS

Daniel Benoliel is a law professor at the University of Haifa Faculty of Law and the Director of the Haifa Center of Law and Technology in Israel. His main fields of expertise include intellectual property, law and economics, and technology entrepreneurship law. He published numerous books, including *Patent Intensity and Economic Growth* (Cambridge University Press, 2017), its Chinese edition (Cambridge University Press and Intellectual Property Publishing House, 2023), and *Líderes improváveis: A batalha dos países em desenvolvimento pelo acesso a medicamentos patenteados* [*Improbable Leaders: The Battle of Developing Countries for Access to Patented Medicines*] (with Bruno M. Salama, FGV University Press, 2017) (in Portuguese). He holds a J.S.D. from UC Berkeley School of Law and has been a John M. Olin Research Fellow with the John M. Olin Center for Law and Economics at UC Berkeley and an alumnus of the Information Society Project at Yale Law School.

Francis Gurry is an Australian lawyer who served as the Director General of the World Intellectual Property Organization (WIPO) from 2008 to 2020

Keun Lee is Distinguished Professor at Seoul National University in the Republic of Korea. He is a Fellow of the Canadian Institute for Advanced Research (CIFAR). He serves as an editor of *Research Policy* and is a regular writer for Project Syndicate. He won the 2014 Schumpeter Prize, the 2019 Kapp Prize from the European Association for Evolutionary Political Economy, and the EBES Fellow Award 2023 from the Eurasia Business and Economics Society. He served as the President of the International Schumpeter Society. He holds a Ph.D. from the University of California, Berkeley.

Peter K. Yu is Regents Professor of Law and Communication and Director of the Center for Law and Intellectual Property at Texas A&M University in the United States. The university recently awarded him the title of University Distinguished Professor, its highest faculty award. Born and raised in Hong Kong, he previously held the Kern Family Chair in Intellectual Property Law at Drake University Law School and was Wenlan Scholar Chair Professor at Zhongnan University of Economics and Law in Wuhan, China. He served as a visiting professor of law at Bocconi University, Hanken School of Economics, Hokkaido University, Tel Aviv

University, the University of Haifa, the University of Helsinki, the University of Hong Kong, and the University of Strasbourg.

CONTRIBUTORS

Frederick M. Abbott is Edward Ball Eminent Scholar Professor of Law at Florida State University College of Law in the United States. He has served as expert consultant or legal representative for international and regional organizations, governments, and nongovernmental organizations, mainly in the fields of intellectual property, public health, technology transfer, competition, trade, and sustainable development. The author of many books and articles, he chairs the Technical Advisory Group on Local Production and Technology Transfer (TAG) of the World Health Organization (WHO). He also serves as a consultant to the WIPO Global Challenges Division and the U.N. Development Programme and as co-chair of the Committee on Global Health Law of the International Law Association. In addition, he has served as counsel to governments in dispute settlement proceedings at the World Trade Organization (WTO), as well as in national court proceedings. He sits on the editorial board of the WIPO–WTO Colloquium Series. More information about him is available on his website, frederickabbott.com.

Flor Brown is a professor at the Graduate Faculty of Accounting and Business Economics at Universidad Autónoma de Querétaro in Mexico. A Level III member of the Mexican National System of Researchers (SNI), she has published thirteen books, nearly fifty articles in academic journals, and thirty book chapters. Her research has dealt with industrial organization, technical change, productivity, economics of gender, and labor transitions. Among her recent publications are "Do Male and Female Labor Market Transition Patterns Differ in Mexico?" "Innovative Factors Affecting the Diffusion of the New Nanotechnology Paradigm, 1983–2013," and "Objective and Subjective Variables behind the Working Conditions of Tertiary-Educated Mexican Migrants in the USA." She holds a Ph.D. in Economics from Universidad Autónoma Metropolitana.

Thomas Cottier is Professor Emeritus of European and International Economic Law at the University of Bern in Switzerland. He is the founder and was the managing director and a senior research fellow of the World Trade Institute, where he served from 1993 to 2015. He was a legal advisor to the Swiss Department of Foreign Economic Affairs and the Deputy Director General of the Swiss Intellectual Property Office at the Department of Justice. He served on the Swiss negotiating team of the Uruguay Round of Multilateral Trade Negotiations, including as the chief negotiator on the Agreement on Trade-Related Aspects of Intellectual Property Rights. He has been a frequent member or chair of panels established at the General Agreement on Tariffs and Trade and the WTO and currently sits in the pool of appeal arbitrators under the WTO's Multi-Party Interim Appeal Arbitration Arrangement. His main research interests are in international economic law (including intellectual property), general principles of law (in particular, the functions of equity), constitutional theory of international law, and multi-level governance.

Marliese Dalton is a recent graduate of the University of Virginia School of Law in the United States. After graduation, she clerked for Judge John K. Bush of the U.S. Court of Appeals for the Sixth Circuit and Judge Mark S. Davis of the U.S. District Court for the Eastern District of Virginia.

Rochelle C. Dreyfuss is Pauline Newman Professor of Law Emerita at New York University School of Law. She is a member of the American Law Institute and a co-reporter for its project on "Intellectual Property: Principles Governing Jurisdiction, Choice of Law, and Judgments in Transnational Dispute." She clerked for Judge Wilfred Feinberg of the U.S. Court of Appeals for the Second Circuit and Chief Justice Warren Burger of the U.S. Supreme Court. She served or consulted on the National Academies' Committee on Science, Technology, and Law; the Department of Health and Human Services' Advisory Committee on Genetics, Health, and Society; the Federal Courts Study Committee; and the Presidential Commission on Catastrophic Nuclear Accidents. She co-authored *A Neofederalist Vision of TRIPS: The Resilience of the International Intellectual Property Regime* (Oxford University Press, 2012) with Professor Graeme Dinwoodie She co-edited *Balancing Wealth and Health: The Battle Over Intellectual Property and Access to Medicines in Latin America* (Oxford University Press, 2014) with Professor César Rodríguez-Garavito and *The Oxford Handbook of Intellectual Property Law* (Oxford University Press, 2017) with Professor Justine Pila.

Carsten Fink is the Chief Economist of WIPO. Before joining the organization, he was Professor of International Economics at the University of St. Gallen. He also held the positions of Visiting Professor at the Fondation Nationale des Sciences Politiques (Sciences Po) in Paris and Visiting Senior Fellow at the Group d'Economie Mondiale, a research institute at Sciences Po. Prior to his academic appointments, he worked for more than ten years at the World Bank. His research, which focuses on intellectual property, innovation, and international trade, has been published in academic journals and books. He holds a Ph.D. in Economics from the University of Heidelberg in Germany and an M.S. in Economics from the University of Oregon.

Alenka Guzmán is a full-time research professor in the Department of Economics at Universidad Autónoma Metropolitana Iztapalapa in Mexico. She teaches in the Master's and Doctorate in Social Studies – in the Social Economy Line (Social Innovation Laboratory) – and the Integrated Program for Master's and Doctorate in Economic Sciences. She has supervised theses in both programs. A Level II member of the SNI, she has published books, articles in refereed and indexed academic journals, and book chapters. Her work focuses on innovation, intellectual property, productivity and competitiveness, and economic growth, particularly in relation to the steel, pharmaceutical, biopharmaceutical, and nanotechnology sectors. She has presented papers at national and international conferences and is currently developing research projects relating to intellectual property, sectoral innovation, technological specialization and economic growth between countries, and Latin American scientific migration (including gender issues). She earned her Ph.D. in Industrial Economics from Sorbonne Nouvelle University (Paris III) in 1999.

George B. Haringhuizen is a consultant in medical and public health law to governments, international organizations, and academic research projects. From 2001 to 2006, he led the task force for revising the Dutch national infrastructure for infectious disease control. He co-drafted the Dutch Public Health Act (2008) and was responsible for the legal implementation of the International Health Regulations in the Netherlands and the Caribbean Overseas Territories. Until mid-2023, he was chief legal advisor to the director of the Dutch National Center for Infectious Disease Control at Rijksinstituut voor Volksgezondheid en Milieu (RIVM), with which he is still affiliated. Since 2022, he has been a member of the International Health Regulations' Review Committee of the WHO. He published on law and infectious disease control, European comparative public health law, and privacy and global data sharing. He received an M.A. in Behavioral Sciences from the University of Amsterdam in 1983 and an LL.M from the Open University of the Netherlands in 2001.

Lital Helman is Senior Lecturer at the Ono Academic College Faculty of Law in Israel. Her research focuses on intellectual property law and law and technology. At the Israeli Ministry of Justice, she is responsible for developing intellectual property and law-and-technology policies. She is the co-founder and board member of GradTrain.com, an artificial intelligence–driven platform for international students worldwide. She holds an S.J.D. from the University of Pennsylvania Law School, which she pursued as a J. William Fulbright scholar. She also served as a Fellow with the Kernochan Center for Law, Media and the Arts at Columbia Law School and the Engelberg Center on Innovation Law and Policy at New York University School of Law.

Yotam Kaplan is Professor of Law at the Faculty of Law of the Hebrew University of Jerusalem in Israel. His research focuses on private law remedies and the law of unjust enrichment. He was awarded a European Research Council grant to explore the use of unjust enrichment doctrine as a vehicle for public interest litigation and as a governance mechanism for addressing broad societal issues. This project investigates contemporary crises, including climate change, the opioid pandemic, and the proliferation of disinformation online. His work on these topics has been published in or are forthcoming from leading journals, such as the *Cornell Law Review*, the *Georgetown Law Journal*, the *Vanderbilt Law Review*, and the *Journal of Legal Studies*. His work has been recognized with numerous awards and research grants, including the Polonsky Prize for Best Tort Law Article from Tel Aviv University, the Outstanding Lecturer Award and the Junior Scholar Cheshin Award for Academic Excellence in the Field of Law from Bar Ilan University, and grants from the Israel Science Foundation and the German Israel Foundation. He received his S.J.D. from Harvard Law School and clerked for Chief Justice Dorit Beinish of the Israeli Supreme Court.

Miriam Marcowitz-Bitton is a full professor at Bar Ilan University Faculty of Law in Israel. She teaches and writes in the fields of intellectual property law, property, and law and technology. Her recent work deals with the gender gap in intellectual property law. She graduated from the University of Michigan Law School and was a Microsoft research fellow at UC Berkeley School of Law.

Keith E. Maskus is Arts and Sciences Professor of Distinction in Economics at the University of Colorado, Boulder, in the United States. He was Chief Economist of the U.S. Department of State from 2016 to 2017 and a Lead Economist at the World Bank from 2001 to 2002. He is a Research Fellow at the Peterson Institute for International Economics and a consultant for international organizations. He has written extensively about various aspects of intellectual property rights, international trade and investment, and technology. His most recent book is *Private Rights and Public Problems: The Global Economics of Intellectual Property in the 21st Century* (Peterson Institute for International Economics, 2012).

Emily Michiko Morris holds the David L. Brennan Endowed Chair and is Associate Director of the Center for Intellectual Property Law and Technology at the University of Akron School of Law in the United States. She is also Senior Fellow of Life Sciences at the Center for Intellectual Property x Innovation Policy at George Mason University. She specializes in patent law, particularly as it relates to biotechnology and university research. She is also an expert on intellectual property and regulatory issues related to the pharmaceutical industry. Her research focuses on comparative law and comparative intellectual property law. She has published book chapters and articles in leading journals, including the *Connecticut Law Review*, the *Stanford Technology Law Review*, and the *Harvard Journal of Gender and Law*. She clerked for Judge Bruce M. Selya of the U.S. Court of Appeals for the First Circuit and practiced for three years as an associate in the Issue and Appeals Group in the Washington, DC, office of Jones Day. She holds an A.B. from Harvard University and a J.D. from the University of Michigan.

Ernest Miguelez is a research scientist at the Institute of Public Goods and Policies (IPP) at the Spanish National Research Council (CISC). Before joining the Council in 2023, he worked as a tenured scientist at the French National Centre for Scientific Research (CNRS), attached to the Bordeaux School of Economics at the University of Bordeaux. His research interests cover economic geography, innovation economics, migration, intellectual property, and, more recently, the diffusion or adoption of green technologies and products.

Dotan Oliar is Professor of Law at the University of Virginia School of Law in the United States. His research focuses on how the law affects what people create. He teaches intellectual property law, entrepreneurship, art law, Internet law, and law and economics. He writes on these topics and their intersection with empirical and behavioral methods, legal history, property theory, and technological progress. His academic articles were published in major legal journals and covered a wide variety of topics, including first possession in intellectual property law, copyright registrations at the U.S. Copyright Office, the interaction between expressive creativity and technological change, the scope of Congress's intellectual property power under the U.S. Constitution, and social norms concerning joke ownership among standup comedians. He earned his S.J.D. from Harvard Law School and M.A. in Economics from the University of Virginia. He is admitted to practice law in New York and Israel.

Julio Raffo is the Head of the Innovation Economy Section of the Department for Economics and Data Analytics at WIPO. Before joining WIPO, he conducted research at the École Polytechnique Fédérale de Lausanne (EPFL) in Switzerland, the Institut Français des Relations Internationales (IFRI) in France, the Pan-American Health Organization in the United States, and the Red Iberoamericana/Interamericana de Indicadores de Ciencia y Tecnología (RICYT). He holds a bachelor's degree in Economics from the University of Buenos Aires, a master's degree in Industrial Organization, Innovations and International Strategy, and a Ph.D. in Economics from the Université de Paris Nord. His main research interests are in the economics and metrics of innovation and intellectual property, with a particular focus on their intersection with socioeconomic development.

Jerome H. Reichman is Bunyan S. Womble Professor of Law Emeritus and the Co-Director of the Center for the Study of the Public Domain at Duke University School of Law in the United States. He previously taught at Vanderbilt Law School and Ohio State University College of Law, after a Fulbright Scholarship to India in 1958. From 1976 to 1979, he was Senior Editor at the Directorate of Operations in the International Trade Center (U.N. Conference on Trade and Development/General Agreement on Tariffs and Trade). He currently serves on the Editorial Advisory Board of the *Journal of International Economic Law*. He was a consultant to the National Academy of Sciences Panel to Improve the Transfer of Technology from Federal Laboratories (2019–2021); a member of the Board of Advisors of the Center for Transnational Intellectual Property, Media and Technology Law and Policy at Bucerius Law School in Hamburg, Germany; and a Lecturer at the WIPO LL.M. in Intellectual Property Program in Turin, Italy. At Max Planck Institute for

Innovation and Competition, he served on the Steering Committee for the Declaration on Basic Principles of International Patent Law (2011–2016) and the Advisory Committee on Drafting an International Instrument on Permitted Uses of Copyright Law (2013–2016). He has published more than eighty articles. In 2019, his life's work was celebrated at a conference at Harvard Law School featuring distinguished intellectual property scholars. He received his J.D. from Yale Law School, where he served as a comment editor of the *Yale Law Journal*.

Carolina dos S. Ribeiro has been a senior policy advisor at the Dutch National Centre for Infectious Disease Control at RIVM since 2016. She combines policy analysis with scientific research and has participated in international projects. As a member of the Dutch delegation, she negotiated at international fora, such as the WHO and the Convention on Biological Diversity. Her main field of work is global health security, more specifically related to multi-stakeholder collaboration and the sharing of outbreak-related resources, such as data, materials, and countermeasures. Her research covers topics such as ethical, legal, governance, and economic aspects of international collaboration and sharing, including initiatives such as the One Health approach. She received her Ph.D. cum laude from the Athena Institute at the Faculty of Sciences of Vrije Universiteit Amsterdam in the Netherlands in 2022. Her dissertation is entitled "Global Health Security, Multi-Stakeholder Collaboration, and Pathogen Sharing: Building a New Microbial Commons." She holds a Master of Science in Global Health from Vrije Universiteit Amsterdam in 2016 and a bachelor's degree in veterinary medicine (BVetMed) from the Federal University of Goiás (UFG) in Brazil in 2010.

Paul F. Uhlir is a consultant in information policy and management to governments, international organizations, and universities. He founded the Board on Research Data and Information at the National Academy of Sciences (NAS) in Washington, DC, which he directed from 2008 to 2015. Since joining the NAS in 1985, he has served as a senior staff officer for the Space Studies Board, where he worked on solar system exploration and environmental remote sensing studies for the National Aeronautics and Space Administration (NASA). He then served as Associate Executive Director of the Commission on Physical Sciences, Mathematics, and Applications. He directed the Office of International Scientific and Technical Information for eight years after that. Before joining the NAS, he worked in the General Counsel's Office at the National Oceanic and Atmospheric Administration of the U.S. Department of Commerce. He has written numerous books and articles and speaks worldwide on data issues. He holds a J.D. and an M.A. in International Relations from the University of San Diego. More information about his professional activities is available on his website, www.paulfuhlir.com.

Shlomit Yanisky-Ravid is the Founder and Head of the graduate law program for "law and technology" at Ono Academic College Faculty of Law in Israel, where she also directs the Shalom Comparative Legal Research Institute Eliyahu Law and Tech Center. An authority in intellectual property and artificial intelligence (AI), she specializes in intricate challenges posed by AI, cyberspace, and privacy. She has been a visiting professor at Fordham University School of Law since 2012 and has been affiliated with the Information Society Project at Yale Law School since 2011. At an event organized by the Copyright Society of the U.S.A., Judge Katherine Forrest lauded her as the foremost thinker on AI and copyright. She contributed to the international project for securing recognition of the AI system "DABUS" as an inventor by patent offices, led by Professor Ryan Abbott. She recently authored a Supreme Court amicus brief in the case of *Thaler v. Vidal*, supported by distinguished professors, including Professor Lawrence Lessig of Harvard Law School. The influence of her numerous publications on AI and intellectual property has extended to top academic institutions and international bodies like WIPO. She holds a Ph.D. from the Hebrew University of Jerusalem.

Lior Zemer is Dean and Professor of Law at Harry Radzyner School of Law, Reichman University (IDC) in Herzliya, Israel. He is the founder and director of the M.A. Program in Law, Technology and Business Innovation, an innovative and multidisciplinary program bridging law, science, technology, and business innovation for both law and non-law graduates. He held academic positions at the faculties of law of the University of Leicester, the University of Birmingham, and University College London and visiting professorships at Osgoode Hall Law School, York University in Toronto, and Boston University School of Law. Prior to joining legal academia, he served as an assistant lawyer to Judge J.D. Cooke at the European Court of First Instance and Judge S. von Bahr at the European Court of Justice in Luxembourg. His scholarship focuses on intellectual property, jurisprudence, and European Union Law. He is the author of *The Idea of Authorship in Copyright* (Ashgate 2007), arguing for a more inclusive approach to the public in the creative process. He has published several edited collections in the field of intellectual property and numerous articles in leading law reviews, including the *Georgetown Law Journal*, the *Boston University Law Review*, the *Utah Law Review*, and *Harvard Journal of Law and Public Policy*. He has supervised numerous Ph.D. and LL.M. students in Canada, the United States, the United Kingdom, and Israel.

Introduction

Daniel Benoliel and Peter K. Yu

I.1 UNDERSTANDING ECONOMIC INEQUALITY

I.1.1 *The Scale of the Problem*

Since the mid-1970s, it has been generally believed that reasonable inequality is the price for a vibrant economy. Today, however, disparities in income and wealth are increasingly perceived as a threat. Indeed, issues about economic inequality have now moved to the center of national and global policy debates.

The *World Inequality Report 2022*, spearheaded by Thomas Piketty and compiled by his collaborating team, finds that "[t]he richest 10% of the global population currently takes 52% of global income, whereas the poorest half of the population earns 8.5% of it."[1] The report states further that "[o]n average, an individual from the top 10% of the global income distribution earns … USD 122,100 … per year, whereas an individual from the poorest half of the global income distribution makes … USD 3,920 … per year" – only slightly over 3 percent of what the top decile makes.[2] The report continues: "The poorest half of the global population barely owns any wealth at all, possessing just 2% of the total. In contrast, the richest 10% of the global population own 76% of all wealth."[3] Based on purchasing power parity estimates, on average the poorest half of the population owns US$4,100 per adult, while the top 10 percent own US$771,300 per adult.[4]

[1] Lucas Chancel, Thomas Piketty, Emmanuel Saez & Gabriel Zucman, World Inequality Report 2022, at 10 (2022).
[2] *Id.*
[3] *Id.*
[4] *Id.*

Another report, released by Oxfam, indicates that the number of billionaires has doubled to over 2,000 over the past decade.[5] In 2019, these billionaires "had more wealth than 4.6 billion people."[6] As if all of these statistics were not depressing enough, the *World Inequality Report 2022* states that the year 2020 "marked the steepest increase in global billionaires' share of wealth on record."[7] In the words of *The Guardian*, "the billionaire class has added $308bn to its wealth in four weeks – even as a record 26 million people lost their jobs."[8] Whether directly or not, the world's richest has benefited from the COVID-19 pandemic.

In his seminal work *Capital in the Twenty-First Century*, Piketty describes the historical trends of wealth concentration, with a focus on developed countries.[9] He shows that wealth concentration in these countries has steadily risen in the past few decades of the twentieth century, after declining between the 1930s and the 1960s. Consider the United States for instance. Between 1978 and 2015, "the bottom 50 percent income share in the United States [dropped] from 20 percent to 12 percent of total income, while the top 1 percent income share rose from 11 percent to 20 percent."[10]

Given the high income and wealth inequality at both the national and global levels, it is no surprise that the United Nations Development Programme has worked closely with other U.N. agencies to eradicate poverty, reduce inequalities, and foster sustainable development.[11] Sustainable Development Goal 10, one of the seventeen goals adopted by the United Nations in December 2015, specifically calls for reducing "inequality within and among countries." Other organizations, such as the World Bank and the International Monetary Fund, have also viewed inequality alleviation as a central development policy challenge in the twenty-first century.[12]

5 Clare Coffey, Patricia Espinoza Revollo, Rowan Harvey, Max Lawson, Anam Parvez Butt, Kim Piaget, Diana Sarosi & Julie Thekkudan, Time to Care: Unpaid and Underpaid Care Work and the Global Inequality Crisis 21 (2020).

6 *Id.* at 9.

7 Chancel et al., *supra* note 1, at 15.

8 Dominic Rushe & Mona Chalabi, *"Heads We Win, Tails You Lose": How America's Rich Have Turned Pandemic into Profit*, Guardian (Apr. 26, 2020), www.theguardian.com/world/2020/apr/26/heads-we-win-tails-you-lose-how-americas-rich-have-turned-pandemic-into-profit.

9 Thomas Piketty, Capital in the Twenty-First Century (Arthur Goldhammer trans., 2014).

10 Facundo Alvaredo, Lucas Chancel, Thomas Piketty, Emmanuel Saez & Gabriel Zucman, *Global Inequality Dynamics: New Findings from WID.world*, 107 Am. Econ. Rev. 404, 406 (2017).

11 For example, International Labour Organization, Global Wage Report 2016/17: Wage Inequality in the Workplace (2016); U.N. Department of Economic and Social Affairs, World Social Report 2020: Inequality in a Rapidly Changing World (2020); U.N. Development Programme, Human Development Report 2019: Beyond Income, Beyond Averages, Beyond Today: Inequalities in Human Development in the 21st Century (2019); UNESCO, World Social Science Report 2016: Challenging Inequalities: Pathways to a Just World (2016).

12 For example, International Monetary Fund, Fiscal Monitor October 2017: Tackling Inequality (2017); World Bank, Poverty and Shared Prosperity 2016: Taking on Inequality (2016).

I.1.2 *Types of Economic Inequality*

As the previously cited reports and data have shown, there are many types of economic inequality and different possible taxonomies. In *An Agenda for Equality* released at the U.N. Summit for the Adoption of the Post-2015 Development Agenda, the former U.N. High Commissioner for Human Rights Zeid Ra'ad Al Hussein identified three types of inequality: horizontal, vertical, and global.[13] For illustrative purposes, this subsection discusses each type in turn.

The first type is horizontal inequality, which covers "inequalities between social, ethnic or other population groups."[14] Examples include inequalities based on race, color, gender, sexuality, language, religion, political affiliation, national or social origin, wealth, or health status. Such inequalities raise concerns about the exclusion of the disadvantaged, vulnerable, and marginalized from political, economic, social, cultural, and technological opportunities.[15] Although these inequalities are often the result of past and current discrimination, other factors have played contributing roles.[16] In recent years, horizontal inequalities, especially those relating to gender and race, have garnered growing attention in the intellectual property field – from the World Intellectual Property Organization (WIPO),[17] national intellectual property agencies,[18] and academic commentators.[19]

[13] Zeid Ra'ad Al Hussein (U.N. High Commissioner for Human Rights), *An Agenda for Equality*, Statement at the Summit for the Adoption of the Post-2015 Development Agenda – Interactive Dialogue (Sept. 25, 2015), www.ohchr.org/en/2015/09/agenda-equality-zeid-raad-al-hussein-united-nations-high-commissioner-human-rights [hereinafter *An Agenda for Equality*].

[14] *Id.*

[15] Sakiko Fukuda-Parr, *Keeping Out Extreme Inequality from the SDG Agenda – The Politics of Indicators*, 10 Glob. Pol'y 61, 63 (2019); Gillian MacNaughton, *Emerging Human Rights Norms and Standards on Vertical Inequalities*, *in* Human Rights and Economic Inequalities 33, 37 (Gillian MacNaughton, Diane F. Frey & Catherine Porter eds., 2021).

[16] Gillian MacNaughton, *Vertical Inequalities: Are the SDGs and Human Rights up to the Challenges?*, 21 Int'l J. Hum. Rts. 1050, 1051 (2017).

[17] World Intell. Prop. Org., The Global Gender Gap in Innovation and Creativity: An International Comparison of the Gender Gap in Global Patenting over Two Decades (2023); *Intellectual Property, Gender, and Diversity*, World Intell. Prop. Org., www.wipo.int/women-and-ip/en/ (last visited May 11, 2023).

[18] For example, U.S. Copyright Off., Women in the Copyright System: An Analysis of Women Authors in Copyright Registrations from 1978 to 2020 (2022); U.S. Patent & Trademark Office, Office of the Chief Economist, Progress and Potential: A Profile of Women Inventors on U.S. Patents (2019); U.S. Patent & Trademark Office, Office of the Chief Economist, Progress and Potential: 2020 Update on U.S. Women Inventor-Patentees (2020); U.K. Intellectual Property Office, Gender Profiles in Worldwide Patenting: An Analysis of Female Inventorship (2016).

[19] For example, Jessica C. Lai, Patent Law and Women: Tackling Gender Bias in Knowledge Governance (2022); Colleen V. Chien, *The Inequalities of Innovation*, 72 Emory L.J. 1 (2022); Paul R. Gugliuzza & Rachel Rebouché, *Gender Inequality in Patent Litigation*, 100 N.C. L. Rev. 1683 (2022); W. Michael Schuster, Miriam Marcowitz-Bitton & Deborah R. Gerhardt, *An Empirical Study of Gender and Race in Trademark Prosecution*, 94 S. Cal. L. Rev. 1407 (2021); S. Sean Tu, Paul R. Gugliuzza & Amy Semet, *Overqualified and*

The second type of inequality is vertical inequality,[20] which "refers to inequalities of wealth, income or social outcome, including inequalities in health, education, housing and political power."[21] Many of the figures cited earlier in this chapter concern this type of inequality. Although vertical inequalities have been under-explored in international policy debates, they are staples in domestic political debates, especially during elections.

The third type of inequality is global inequality,[22] or what commentators and the U.N. Sustainable Development Goals have referred to as "inequality among countries." The North–South divide frequently discussed in relation to the Agreement on Trade-Related Aspects of Intellectual Property Rights (TRIPS Agreement) and other international intellectual property agreements provides a textbook example of global inequality in the intellectual property context.

Although these three types of inequality deserve separate theoretical, empirical, and policy attention, they can also provide useful insights when examined alongside each other. For instance, Branko Milanovic reminds us that although the inequality among Asian countries has been narrowing, with their average incomes slowly converging, such narrowing may "give relatively greater salience to inequalities within nations."[23] Likewise, François Bourguignon notes our tendency to conclude that the recent acceleration of globalization was responsible for the rise in national inequality even though "globalization has *also contributed* to a drop in international inequalities."[24] In the future, we may face a world where there is shrinking global inequality but rising national inequality. It will therefore be instructive to develop a better understanding of the relationship between the two.

I.1.3 *Research on Economic Inequality*

Beginning in the 1950s, economics has been dominated by the idea that inequality diminishes as countries become more technologically developed and as more people take advantage of the opportunities generated by such development. This idea was first formulated by Nobel laureate Simon Kuznets.[25] Named after him, the Kuznets curve hypothesizes that inequality increases with economic development at first before eventually declining. Building on his seminal work, a myriad of studies

Underrepresented: Gender Inequality in Pharmaceutical Patent Law, 48 BYU L. REV. 137 (2022).

20 *An Agenda for Equality*, *supra* note 13.

21 MacNaughton, *supra* note 16, at 1051.

22 *An Agenda for Equality*, *supra* note 13.

23 BRANKO MILANOVIC, GLOBAL INEQUALITY: A NEW APPROACH FOR THE AGE OF GLOBALIZATION 5 (2018).

24 FRANÇOIS BOURGUIGNON, THE GLOBALIZATION OF INEQUALITY 3 (Thomas Scott-Railton trans., 2017).

25 Simon Kuznets, *Economic Growth and Income Inequality*, 45 AM. ECON. REV. 1 (1955).

on income inequality and growth have found evidence confirming the Kuznets curve.[26]

In recent years, however, commentators have started to question the Kuznets curve hypothesis. Among the critics were distinguished economists such as Piketty, Joseph Stiglitz, and Erik Brynjolfsson.[27] For example, in *The Second Machine Age*, Brynjolfsson and Andrew McAfee declare that "the main driver [of inequality] is exponential, digital, and combinatorial change in the technology that undergirds our economic system," especially after the 2008 global economic crisis.[28] There is indeed mounting evidence showing how modern capitalism has increased income and wealth inequality. This evidence brings to the forefront an important question concerning the role of law and policy in the debate on economic inequality. If law and policy has exacerbated such inequality, what adjustments can we make to provide redress?

Thus far, policymakers have attributed economic inequality and income and wealth concentration to financial deregulation, tax benefits for high-income individuals and households as well as corporations, and underinvestment in public services such as healthcare and education, among others. One field that has not been explored much is intellectual property. What role does intellectual property law and policy play in the debate on economic inequality? This volume seeks to fill this void.

Has intellectual property law and policy – and, more broadly, law and policy in the innovation area – contributed to income and wealth inequality? If so, how significant is its contribution? Has the inequality generated by such law and policy affected certain segments of the population more than the others? Do the adverse impacts break down according to gender, race, wealth, level of education, or other factors? Will the analysis vary from industry to industry? Relatedly, are some forms of intellectual property rights more harmful to certain groups – if so, what are they, to what extent, and why?

Looking at economic inequality at the global level, does intellectual property law affect certain countries more than the others? For instance, shortly after the end of the TRIPS transition period for developing countries, the World Bank released a study estimating that the adoption of the TRIPS Agreement has resulted in rent transfers of more than twenty billion U.S. dollars from developing countries "to major technology-creating countries – particularly the United States, Germany, and

26 For example, Jeffrey G. Williamson, Did British Capitalism Breed Inequality? (1985); Gene M. Grossman & Alan B. Krueger, *Economic Growth and the Environment*, 110 Q.J. Econ. 353 (1995).

27 Erik Brynjolfsson & Andrew McAfee, The Second Machine Age: Work, Progress, and Prosperity in a Time of Brilliant Technologies (2014); Piketty, *supra* note 9; Joseph E. Stiglitz, The Great Divide: Unequal Societies and What We Can Do about Them (2015).

28 Brynjolfsson & McAfee, *supra* note 27, at 133.

France – in the form of pharmaceutical patents, computer chip designs, and other intellectual property."[29] Intergovernmental bodies, policymakers, and commentators have also widely lamented the deleterious effects of TRIPS-plus bilateral, regional, and plurilateral trade agreements.[30] Based on these critiques, can we draw at least some preliminary conclusions about the negative relationship between intellectual property and economic inequality? If so, was the inequality confronting the Global South caused by intellectual property rights or by inappropriate standards for protecting and enforcing those rights? In addition, will the analysis differ depending on whether the focus is on copyrights, patents, trademarks, trade secrets, geographical indications, or other forms of intellectual property rights?

What about emerging economies? Countries such as Brazil, China, and India seem to have successfully played economic and technological catch-up, notwithstanding the relatively high TRIPS standards imposed upon them since the mid-1990s. What explains their ability to persevere and their subsequent innovative turn? Did high intellectual property standards provide at least some benefits to these countries? Did these emerging countries succeed by embracing only some but not all of TRIPS standards – or practicing what several commentators have termed "selective adaptation"?[31] In addition, amid the emerging countries' impressive economic and technological gains, has the inequality within these countries worsened as a result? If so, what is the relationship between national inequality and global inequality? Is the former the price for reducing the latter?

All of these important questions deserve scholarly and policy attention. They have been underexplored, if at all, in existing intellectual property literature. We hope that this volume will add to this literature and get the debate on intellectual property, innovation, and economic inequality started.

I.2 THE STRUCTURE OF THE VOLUME

The research in this volume is situated in the broader literature crossing the fields of intellectual property law and economic inequality theory. While the book focuses specifically on the interrelationship between intellectual property and economic inequality, it also intersects with the literature on intellectual property and development, intellectual property and poverty, intellectual property issues relating to

[29] World Bank, Global Economic Prospects and the Developing Countries 2002: Making Trade Work for the World's Poor, at xvii (2001).

[30] For example, Mary Robinson (U.N. High Commissioner for Human Rights), *The Impact of the Agreement on Trade-Related Aspects of Intellectual Property Rights on Human Rights*, para. 27, U.N. Doc. E/CN.4/Sub.2/2001/13 (June 27, 2001); Peter K. Yu, *The Non-multilateral Approach to International Intellectual Property Normsetting*, *in* International Intellectual Property: A Handbook of Contemporary Research 83, 92–97 (Daniel J. Gervais ed., 2015).

[31] Peter K. Yu, *TRIPS and Its Contents*, 60 IDEA 149, 207–15 (2020).

gender and race, the need for access to intellectual property–based goods and services, and intellectual property rights as social, economic, and cultural rights.

Interdisciplinary by design, this volume features economists, legal scholars, policy analysts, and other intellectual property experts. The chapters were written by a geographically diverse group of scholars based in East Asia, Europe, the Middle East, and North and Latin America. To strengthen the project, the chapters were presented at two workshops: the "Intellectual Property, Innovation and Global Inequality" Workshop at the Faculty of Law at the University of Haifa on December 10–12, 2018, and the "Inequality through IP: A New Policy Lever?" Workshop organized online by the Oxford Intellectual Property Research Centre at the University of Oxford on May 26–27, 2021.

The entire volume contains fifteen chapters. The remainder of this book is grouped into three parts, as detailed later. Each of the ensuing chapters aims to address one or more of the following questions: (1) What impact does the intellectual property law and policy have on economic inequality? (2) What impact does economic inequality have on the creation of intellectual property, the protection and enforcement of intellectual property rights, and the development of intellectual property law and policy? Finally, can intellectual property law and policy, whether alone or in conjunction with other policies, be used as a tool to help reduce economic inequality?

I.2.1 *Theoretical, Empirical, and Policy Issues*

The first part examines broad theoretical, empirical, and policy issues relating to the interrelationship between intellectual property and economic inequality. The chapters in this part focus on both national and global inequalities.

Opening this part is "Intellectual Property Rights and Inequality: Economic Considerations." Written by Keith Maskus, one of the world's foremost economists in the intellectual property field, this chapter reviews, with an emphasis on international comparisons, available economic theories and empirical evidence concerning the role played by intellectual property rights in increasing or reducing income and wealth inequality. Although the past twenty-five years have seen a simultaneous increase in both economic inequality and intellectual property protection in many countries, and there has been growing convergence in average incomes in developed and emerging economies, the linkage between the two remains inconclusive. Indeed, systematic evidence has been scarce. As the author points out, the role played by intellectual property protection in the emergence of inequality has been "[a]lmost completely unstudied" by economists. The interrelationship between the two – in particular, whether any causality exists – therefore deserves urgent scholarly attention.

The next chapter, "The Unequal Geographical Distribution of Innovative Activity: Implications for Income Inequality and Innovation Policies," was written by Carsten Fink, Ernest Miguelez, and Julio Raffo. Fink and Raffo are WIPO's lead economists. Drawing on more than forty years of data from international patent applications and scientific articles, this chapter examines the unequal geographical distribution of innovation at both the national and subnational levels. As the authors point out, countries, and regions within them, innovate at different rates. Even the world's most innovative countries face the challenge of unequal distribution of innovation, having hotspots and niche clusters. It is therefore worthwhile to explore why innovation has been unequally distributed and what consequences such unequal distribution has on income inequality. Notably, this chapter shows how innovation has been more geographically skewed than other economic activities at both the national and subnational levels. It further interrogates the role innovation policies can play in increasing knowledge acquisition and diffusion while changing the technological trajectory of countries and their subnational regions. As the authors remind us, the continuous increase in technological development, interconnectivity, and innovation concentration has instilled both optimism and pessimism.

Joining the theme of inequality in subnational regions is "Intellectual Property, Global Inequality, and Subnational Policy Variations," written by one of us (Yu). This chapter points out that the arrival of middle-income countries, such as Brazil, China, and India, has called into question the old North–South debate – a recurring theme in a number of chapters in this volume. Taking note of the wide geographic, sectoral, and income inequalities in these emerging countries and the growing literature on inequality *within* countries, as opposed to *among* countries, this chapter explains why such inequality in the intellectual property context deserves both scholarly and policy attention. It further proposes interventions in three areas: international norm-setting, national policymaking, and academic and policy research. This chapter underscores the need for policymakers and commentators to explore the feasibility and benefits of using subnational variations in intellectual property policies to combat national inequality.

As far as success in using innovation policies to generate economic growth and increase technological capabilities is concerned, there are no better examples than latecomer economies. Our coeditor, Keun Lee, is one of the leading scholars on this particular subject. His chapter, "Is IPR a Facilitator of, or a Barrier to, Catch-Up by Latecomers? Implications for Global Inequality," explains the important roles played by innovation and innovation policies in enabling countries to play catch-up and to avoid what commentators have referred to as the "middle-income trap." Drawing on experience from his home country, South Korea, and his decades-long research, this chapter explores the roles played by different forms of intellectual property rights in promoting innovation. It further discusses the impact strong intellectual property protection in the Global North has on the Global South's exports to the Global North. This discussion is particularly important considering the high intellectual property standards imposed on developing countries by the

TRIPS Agreement; agreements administered by WIPO; and subsequent bilateral, regional, and plurilateral trade agreements. This chapter concludes by discussing how latecomer countries have successfully overcome intellectual property–related barriers to leapfrog their economy, often with local firms moving into new areas and products ahead of incumbents from the Global North. The key takeaway of this chapter is that enhancing innovation capabilities and economic growth will be key to reducing global inequality.

Closing out the first part is a chapter written by one of us (Benoliel) and Rochelle Dreyfuss, a frequent commentator on patent law and international intellectual property law. "Patents and Economic Inequality" examines the roles innovation and international intellectual property protection have played within the theory of economic inequality. This chapter further discusses how the demands of the Global North for ever-stronger patent and patent-like protections have exacerbated the problem of technological inequality. To mitigate this problem, the chapter suggests ways to restructure the patent system to better enable local inventors to avail themselves of the global knowledge base while also enhancing incentives for those innovators who fulfill the needs of the Global South. Suggested reforms include altering the landscape of prior art and recalibrating the inventive step to domestic capabilities. Specifically, the authors advocate the introduction of a relative novelty standard that includes only locally available technology in the prior art and that considers domestic innovators' capacity in determining inventiveness. In the authors' view, ensuring technological self-sufficiency and reducing intellectual property–based inequality are key steps toward mitigating the problem of income and wealth inequality.

I.2.2 *Intellectual Property and National Inequality*

The second part highlights the challenges national inequalities have posed to the intellectual property and innovation systems. Among the wide variety of contributing factors – or the "horizontal inequalities" explored earlier – the chapters in this part focus primarily on gender and, to a lesser extent, race.

Opening this part is a study conducted by Dotan Oliar, a law professor at the University of Virginia, and his collaborator Marliese Dalton. "Are Men and Women Creating Equal? Contextualizing Copyright and Gender in the United States" focuses on the gender gap in copyright registrations. It explores whether structural, systemic, industry-specific, or other barriers exist to prevent women from participating in the copyright system at the same rates as men. This chapter reviews a wide variety of factors, including data based on work type, trends in patent and trademark ownership, and gender-linked differences in other forms of property such as home and corporate ownership. The chapter further interrogates the extent to which the gender disparity in copyright registration based on work type reflects inequality within the creative professions, such as publishing, music, film, theater, art, dance, and architecture. While the available data suggest that the gender gap in copyright registration may reflect more general social realities, such as inequitable patterns of property ownership by women, it is impossible to rule out the possibility that the U.S. copyright system, along with the creative industries that it supports, may have a discriminatory effect on women's incentives to create. This study is interesting in terms of both its findings and methodology.

In "Building Innovation Skills to Overcome Gender Inequality: Mexico, India, and Brazil," Alenka Guzmán and Flor Brown, both economists in Mexico, examine gender inequality in inventive activities through a comparative study of Brazil, India, and Mexico. This chapter outlines the factors impeding women's ability to demonstrate their inventive capabilities. It further discusses the policies implemented by these emerging countries to reduce gender inequalities in education, science, and technological knowledge. Drawing on data provided by the U.S. Patent and Trademark Office on patents granted in Brazil, India, and Mexico and an empirical project that the authors have conducted to examine the dynamics of female inventive activities in these emerging countries, the chapter presents the project's findings and offers policy recommendations on how to boost female participation in inventive activities.

Also focusing on gender inequality is the third chapter in this part, "Unregistered Patents and Gender Equality: A Global Perspective." Written by a team of legal scholars in Israel and the United States – Miriam Marcowitz-Bitton, Yotam Kaplan, and Emily Michiko Morris – this chapter proposes a novel regime for automatic, unregistered patent rights. Complementing extant patent rights, the proposed rights would cover inventions that meet the standard substantive requirements for patentability but that have not gone through the expensive, complicated, and time-consuming patent examination process. Lasting for only a limited period of time, the proposed unregistered patents would protect only against the direct and knowing copying of the patented invention. Because the patent examination process has posed significant barriers to women inventors, the authors believe that this proposal would help reduce the gender gap in the patent system while also making that system more inclusive and egalitarian.

Another chapter targeting inequality in the patent system – in particular, its bias against women, racialized minorities, and small start-ups – is "Can Decentralization Encourage Equality in the Patent System?" Written by Lital Helman, this chapter builds on her earlier proposal for replacing the patent agency's central record with a decentralized database. Supported by blockchain or other innovative technology, this new database would provide more information about the invention as well as updates on the invention's additional functions. Under the proposal, inventors would submit patent applications to a shared record that can be updated during the patent examination process and throughout the duration of the patent. Such updates would allow third parties to submit prior art, scientists to weigh in on obviousness, patentees to offer licenses, and courts to list outstanding cases that pertain to the patent. In the author's view, the proposal would improve accessibility, affordability, and equality. It would also turn the extant patent record into an effective platform for learning about inventions and finding ways to commercialize them at affordable prices.

Closing this part is "Inequality and Asymmetry in the Making of Intellectual Property a Constitutional Right," written by Lior Zemer, a law professor who has published extensively on intellectual property clauses in national constitutions. This chapter explores whether countries could reduce inequalities in the innovation system by adopting intellectual property rights as socio-economic rights in their constitutions. Drawing on an original data set that includes all intellectual property clauses in national constitutions since the beginning of the nineteenth century, the chapter shows that the inclusion of an intellectual property–related clause in a constitution does not always lead to stronger intellectual property protection and enforcement. Instead, such inclusion may reflect the external demands from powerful trading partners and the power asymmetry between these partners and the country introducing a new constitutional clause. In view of this somewhat counter-intuitive finding, the author calls for greater scholarship on intellectual property constitutionalism.

I.2.3 *Intellectual Property and Global Inequality*

The final part of this volume covers global inequality, or inequality among countries. Opening this part is "Inequality and Intellectual Property: Equity, Innovation, and Creative Imitation," written by Thomas Cottier, one of the world's foremost trade experts and a negotiator for Switzerland during the Uruguay Round of Multilateral Trade Negotiations. This chapter examines the potential for taking income and wealth distribution into consideration when interpreting international trade and intellectual property rules. It further explores the relationship between innovation and creative imitation. Recognizing that the latter is an important driver of development and has helped decrease inequality, the author calls for a better balance between the two by conceptualizing intellectual property as a means to stimulate and protect human investment. He also discusses the need to limit exclusive rights and protection to appropriate returns and reasonable profits. To exclude unwarranted economic rents, he argues that the international minimum standards in the TRIPS Agreement and subsequent TRIPS-plus bilateral, regional, and plurilateral agreements should be complemented by the graduation of obligations and the introduction of ceilings and maximum periods of protection for all forms of intellectual property rights. These maximum periods are particularly important for rights unlimited in time, such as trademarks, trade secrets, and geographical indications. In the author's view, equity and the principle of unjust enrichment can provide important tools for shaping the scope and duration of intellectual property rights.

The next chapter is "Managed Trade and Technology Protectionism: A Formula for Perpetuating Inequality?" written by Frederick Abbott, a noted commentator on international intellectual property, health, and trade law. This chapter examines how the recent trend toward "economic nationalism," localization of production, and preference for power diplomacy may affect the ability of low- and middle-income countries (LMICs) to develop and implement new technologies. Such development and implementation, in turn, would improve the economic performance of these countries vis-à-vis the dominant national or regional economies. This chapter laments how the existing international trade and investment agreements have favored high-income countries, making it difficult for LMICs to use foreign-owned technology to climb the innovation curve. To help the latter, the chapter identifies several policy options, including the creation of new, locally developed technical solutions to leapfrog stages of technological development and the creation of a more attractive environment for foreign investment. The chapter reminds us that there is no magic bullet for addressing the marked global disparity in income and wealth.

"Sharing Pathogen Sequence Data for Global Scientific Research under the Nagoya Protocol to the Convention on Biological Diversity" was written by a team of experts who have closely studied governance issues relating to genetic sequence data. In this chapter, Jerome Reichman, Carolina dos Santos Ribeiro, George Haringhuizen, and Paul Uhlir use the specific example of pathogen sequence data to advance a proposal to tackle the challenges posed by the uncertain coverage of what the Nagoya Protocol to the Convention on Biological Diversity has termed "digital sequence information." Aiming to restore the balance between provider and user countries, the protocol requires prior informed consent, mutually agreed terms, and access and benefit sharing. As well intended as they may be, these requirements could harm cross-border scientific research and the promotion of global public health when they overprotect genetic sequence data and create impenetrable transaction costs. To strike an appropriate balance, this chapter calls for the development of an agreed waiver for pathogen sequence data used for upstream scientific research. Such development would not compromise the duty of users to share monetary benefits from commercial applications with provider countries. Instead, the proposed waiver would help alleviate the problems of definition and subject-matter coverage that have stymied multilateral action in this area. It would also help address global inequality by protecting the interests of provider countries, usually in LMICs. The authors believe that their proposal could provide a model for other biodiversity data in the future.

Also highlighting the promise of international initiatives but taking a more forward-looking approach is the last chapter in this volume, "Distributive Justice beyond Intellectual Property Laws: An International Perspective." Written by Shlomit Yanisky-Ravid, an expert on artificial intelligence and blockchain technology, this chapter calls for a new and broader understanding of intellectual property rights that internalizes equality and distributive justice considerations, especially at the global level. In the author's view, such an approach is particularly important in what she has called the "digital 3A" era of automated, autonomous, and advanced technologies. To illustrate how such an approach could help address the problem of global inequality, the chapter identifies three services WIPO has developed to provide support to those in need, wherever they may be geographically. WIPO Proof, which has now been discontinued, provided each submitted file with a time-stamped digital fingerprint to prove its existence at a specific point in time. WIPO Match is a free online matching tool that enables those having specific intellectual property–related development needs to find providers of the needed resources. WIPO Re:Search is a global public–private consortium that brings together collaborators to accelerate research and development on the pharmaceuticals, vaccines, and diagnostics needed to treat neglected infectious diseases.

I.3 FINAL WORDS AND ACKNOWLEDGMENTS

Because of the interdisciplinary nature of this volume, each chapter provides citations in the format that is widely used in the author's or authors' discipline. Although the editors and the publisher have made some effort to ensure consistency, this book recognizes the diversity of disciplinary norms and preferences.

A book project of this scale cannot be completed without the support of many individuals and institutions. Such support becomes even more important amid the COVID-19 pandemic. The editors would like to thank, first and foremost, all chapter contributors for their support, encouragement, and patience during the production process and Lauren Crais, a DPhil student at the University of Oxford, for her superb editorial assistance. They are also grateful to the Faculty of Law at the University of Haifa for holding the 2018 workshop and the Oxford Intellectual Property Research Centre for hosting the 2021 workshop. In addition, they want to thank Matt Gallaway, Jadyn Fauconier-Herry, Balamuthukumaran Pasupathy, and other editors at Cambridge University Press and Straive for their guidance and assistance with the acquisition and production processes. Matt, it has always been a pleasure working with you and your team. It goes without saying that the academic editors of this volume are deeply grateful for the support provided by their home institutions, the Faculty of Law at the University of Haifa, the Department of Economics at Seoul National University, and Texas A&M University School of Law.

Finally, the editors would like to thank the University of Haifa Research Authority for providing generous support to make this volume available under an open-access arrangement. In our continuous effort to combat economic inequality – whether at the national or global level – there is nothing more important than making knowledge and academic research freely available. So, thank you. Todá rabá!

PART I

Theoretical, Empirical, and Policy Issues

1

Intellectual Property Rights and Inequality

Economic Considerations

Keith E. Maskus

INTRODUCTION

Growing economic inequality in many countries, perhaps especially in the United States, has become a central issue for scholarly analysis and policy debates. Numerous important treatises analyze the dimensions of the problem, ranging from educational inadequacies to tax and subsidy policies biased toward favoring the wealthy.[1] Concerns about the potential effects of income and wealth inequality include social stratification, a reduction in intergenerational economic mobility, diminished incentives to invest in innovation and human capital, and possibly violent political polarization. Elements of such factors loomed large in the U.S. presidential election of 2020 and similar elections elsewhere.

There are multiple and interrelated sources of inequality, which vary with national and local circumstances, making it a highly complex issue that defies straightforward categorization. Numerous determinants have been identified, including the following primary factors. First, economic globalization through trade and investment liberalization, falling trade costs, and offshoring of jobs through supply chains has placed considerable downward pressure on the real wages of lower-skilled workers in the advanced economies, exemplified most starkly in the impacts of the so-called China Shock in the United States.[2] Second, technological progress in automation and robotics has displaced workers performing relatively routine tasks, even if these workers are relatively skilled.[3] This is just one form, among many, of "skill-biased technical changes" that have increased wage gaps

1 See, for example, Goldin and Katz (2008) and Piketty (2014).

2 The phrase comes from Autor et al. (2013), who document these and other effects, kicking off a large literature on the labor-market impacts of low-wage imports.

3 See Brynjolfsson and MacAfee (2011) for a strong statement of this thesis.

between the college-educated and others in advanced economies.[4] Third, the degree of unionization has fallen considerably in the United States and similar countries, reducing the workers' bargaining power and wages. Fourth, market concentration has increased markedly across most industries, raising the pricing power of the largest producers and generating above-normal profits that find their way into higher wages for managers and skilled workers while supporting increases in stock valuations. This outcome is consistent with the emergence of "superstar managers" in certain countries who command exceptionally high compensation packages.[5] Finally, at least in the United States, educational attainment has lagged the demand for technical skills, raising the relative wages of technical workers (Goldin and Katz, 2008).

Almost completely unstudied, at least by economists, have been the roles played by intellectual property (IP) protection in the emergence of inequality. It is easy to make intuitive claims about this question. For example, it is reasonable to argue that the exclusivity rights in IP raise the returns to invention, innovation, and creativity, all of which tend to be skill intensive. Moreover, patents, copyrights, and trade secrets have the potential to establish temporary but significant market power in specific industries and products, which seems correlated with rising market concentration, profit shares, and manager salaries. In these ways, strengthening IP rights ought to be a force for growing income and wealth inequality. There are offsetting factors, however. For example, to the extent that IP protection increases the rate of product innovation and encourages the diffusion of new goods and technologies, consumers benefit from greater variety and lower average prices. Such outcomes can be intricately linked to other policies, such as market opening and research and development (R&D) support. Whether these outcomes increase or decrease inequality is an empirical question about which we have little information. It is also important to note that inequality may be a determinant of innovation incentives, lending a two-way relationship between distributional disparities and support for IP rights. In brief, the entire question of how inequality interacts with IP is open for much-needed economic research.

These issues are addressed in this chapter, which proceeds as follows. The next section offers a brief overview of trends in basic data regarding inequality and IP rights across countries, followed by a review of extant empirical analysis of correlations between them. The second section elucidates the potential theoretical relationships between IP and inequality, moving from intuitive to subtle. It also considers recent microeconomic empirical studies of such questions, which are informative but far from definitive. The final section concludes with a call for additional work in this nascent area.

4 Acemoglu (2002) offers a seminal discussion of the sources of accelerating skill bias in technology over prior decades.

5 Piketty (2014) emphasizes this factor.

1.1 BASIC DATA ANALYSIS

1.1.1 *Statistical Overview*

Begin with a simple look at primary data on within-country income distributions across a large sample of countries at varying levels of development. The most common measure is the Gini coefficient, constructed to capture how unequally income is distributed across households. The coefficient runs, in principle, from zero (which means that all households have an identical share of national income) to 100 (which means that just one household captures all the income). The higher the Gini coefficient, the less equal the income distribution.[6] Historically, such coefficients were infrequently and intermittently estimated for different countries, making statistical analysis difficult. However, a current project has compiled and published annual Gini coefficients for many countries to facilitate cross-country comparisons.[7]

Table 1.1 shows the evolution of these measures from 1990 to 2015 for a selection of ninety-seven countries with data broken into income groups identified by the World Bank as of 1999. Two Gini coefficients are reported: the Gini Market, which is the coefficient based on incomes before taxes and transfers, and the Gini Disposable, which is the coefficient after such transfers are made. The difference between them indicates how much the income-transfer system in each country offsets (or reinforces) inequities established by the markets. Listed are simple averages within each country group and weighted averages, with the weights based on within-group populations. The countries are listed in Appendix Table A1.1.

These data suggest that there has been a steady but modest increase in inequality when all countries are averaged equally. Among the high-income countries (HICs), the average coefficient rose by two points using after-transfer income (around 7 percent) and by nearly four points using market incomes (almost 9 percent). The other income groups with rising coefficients were the lower-income countries (LICs) and lower-middle-income countries (LMICs). Interestingly, there was little net change in inequality in the upper-middle-income countries (UMICs) over the period. Presumably, this reflected a balance between higher inequality from technological change and lower inequality from the ability of lower-wage workers to gain from exporting labor-intensive goods, among other factors.

6 Formally, the coefficient is proportional to the area between the diagonal of a box measuring total national income and the Lorenz Curve below the diagonal, where the Lorenz Curve traces the cumulative distribution of income from the lowest households to the highest. A sharply bowed curve implies a less equal distribution and a higher Gini coefficient.

7 The project is the Standardized World Income Inequality Database, available at https://dataverse.harvard.edu/dataset.xhtml?persistentId=doi:10.7910/DVN/LM4OWF. For details, see Solt (2019).

TABLE 1.1 *Gini coefficients across country groups, 1990–2015*

Income group	Gini Disposable: simple average					Gini Market: simple average				
	1990	2000	2010	2015	Percent change	1990	2000	2010	2015	Percent change
High (28)	28.8	30.0	30.7	30.8	6.9	42.9	45.3	46.7	46.7	8.9
Upper-Middle (12)	38.5	39.4	38	37.4	−2.9	48.2	49.8	49.4	48.6	0.8
Lower-Middle (35)	37.3	40.1	38.6	37.7	1.1	43.3	45.7	44.5	43.7	0.9
Lower (22)	40.1	42.3	42.5	42.1	5.0	45.2	46.7	46.6	46.2	2.2
All (97)	35.6	37.6	37.1	36.7	3.1	44.2	46.3	46.2	45.7	3.4
United States	34.6	35.8	37	38.2	10.4	46.6	47.7	50.7	50.9	9.2
China	32.2	38.6	43	41.1	27.6	34.7	40.8	46.7	46.9	35.2

Income group	Gini Disposable: pop-weighted average					Gini Market: pop-weighted average				
	1990	2000	2010	2015	Percent change	1990	2000	2010	2015	Percent change
High (28)	30.4	31.8	33.0	33.5	10.2	43.8	45.8	48.0	48.1	9.8
Upper-Middle (12)	48.0	48.5	45.4	44.5	−7.3	54.3	54.9	52.8	51.3	−5.5
Lower-Middle (35)	34.4	39.5	41.6	40.5	17.7	37.9	42.6	45.5	45.4	19.8
Lower (22)	37.1	40.0	43.8	44.0	18.6	41.4	43.7	46.6	46.6	12.6
All (97)	35.6	39	41.2	40.8	14.6	41.3	44.5	46.9	46.7	13.1

Source: Standardized World Income Inequality Database and author's calculations

TABLE 1.2 *Pretax income shares of top 10 percent*

	HI (26)	UMI (8)	LMI (17)	LI (11)	ALL (62)	USA	China
1990	31.0	35.0	36.4	54.5	37.2	38.9	30.4
2000	33.7	39.7	41.3	52.9	40.0	44.0	35.6
2010	34.2	41.1	41.4	52.2	40.2	45.8	42.6
2015	34.7	42.0	41.0	50.7	40.2	47.3	41.4

Source: World Inequality Database and author's calculations

Unweighted averages can be misleading, however, as measures of inequality faced by large aggregations of households. The growth in the population-weighted average coefficients was considerably larger (though it declined in the UMICs), largely because of the significant increases in the United States (HI) and China (LMI). As shown, these two behemoths saw exceptionally large increases in both pretransfer and posttransfer household income inequality during this period of rapid globalization and technical change. In this context, those nations bear a significant share of the observed inequality.

It should be noted that the Gini coefficient may not be an accurate measure of rising inequality if that process is skewed toward higher incomes of the richest households. The way such coefficients are calculated gives small weights to households at the extremes (because there are not many in those ranges) and high weights to those in the middle ranges (where there are many). In consequence, if the top earners gain a disproportionate share of income within the distribution, the Gini may not go up by much, despite the rising disparities. Thus, Table 1.2 lists the pretax and pretransfer income shares (including capital gains) of the top 10 percent of households in a smaller sample of countries.[8] This measure offers readier evidence of rising inequality at the top, except for the LICs, where the highest households already captured more than 50 percent of income in 1990. The highest earners gained 3.7 points of income shares in the HICs, 7 points in the UMICs, and 4.6 points in the LMICs. Again, the United States and China were the largest contributors to these trends, with the top share in China rising by a remarkable 11 percentage points.

These figures show that there has been a marked rise in income disparities in the last thirty years, though some of that increase is concentrated in specific large countries. The question for this chapter is the degree to which stronger IP rights may be a factor. This is an exceptionally difficult question to answer statistically for many reasons that will be brought out in the text. For now, however, Table 1.3 demonstrates that there has been a marked increase in the strength of legalized patent rights over the same period. Listed are changes in the average Ginarte–Park

[8] These data are available from the World Inequality Database, available at https://wid.world/data.

TABLE 1.3 *GP indexes across country groups, 1990–2015*

	GP: simple average				
Income group	**1990**	**2000**	**2010**	**2015**	**Percent change**
High (28)	3.26	4.27	4.32	4.31	32.2
Upper-Middle (9)	1.98	3.49	3.97	4.01	102.5
Lower-Middle (34)	1.29	2.99	3.42	3.64	182.2
Lower (18)	1.59	2.46	2.98	3.03	90.6
All (89)	2.1	3.36	3.7	3.78	80.0

Calculations use World Bank 2020 income classifications

Source: Data from Walter G. Park and author's calculations

(GP) index of patent strength across another subsample of our main sample.[9] This index notes whether a country has a law or regulation offering various elements of patent scope across five categories: coverage, membership in international conventions, patent duration, the possibility of losing patent rights, and enforcement. These component scores are added, and the final index ranges, in principle, from zero to five.[10]

As seen in Table 1.3, the average index grew in all income groups during this period, reflecting a combination of unilateral reforms, adherence to standards required in the Agreement on Trade-Related Aspects of Intellectual Property Rights (TRIPS) of the World Trade Organization (WTO), additional standards negotiated within regional trade agreements, and other factors. At the beginning of the period, the HICs already had strong protection on this measure and did not have to change their patent laws much over the period.[11] The eye-opening feature is the substantial increase in protection in emerging and developing countries (EDCs). The index doubled in the UMICs and nearly tripled in the LMICs while growing sharply even in the LICs. As described elsewhere, the period since 1990 ushered in the most remarkable transformation of global IP policies in history (Maskus, 2012).

An obvious question for this chapter is, how well did the IP reforms track changes in income inequality? Did countries with relatively stronger increases in the patent index see greater increases in inequality, at least as measured by the Gini coefficients? The evidence provided in Table 1.4 suggests the answer is "not much." The right-most panel depicts a growing but weakly positive correlation between the GP index and the market-based Gini coefficients in the HICs, consistent with higher inequality in more strongly protected jurisdictions. However, the correlation is negative in those countries using the posttransfer Gini measures, suggesting that

9 See Ginarte and Park (1997) for the original index and construction details.

10 Maskus (2012) reviews the index in detail and its growth across all countries in the GP sample.

11 Of course, the relatively small increase in the GP index for the HICs is something of an artifact because the index is capped at 5.

TABLE 1.4 *Correlations between GP indexes and Gini coefficients, 1990–2015*

	GP with Gini Disposable				GP with Gini Market			
Income group	1990	2000	2010	2015	1990	2000	2010	2015
High (28)	−0.27	−0.22	−0.28	−0.08	0.14	0.35	0.31	0.42
Upper-Middle (9)	−0.1	0.09	−0.62	−0.29	0.25	0.27	−0.26	0.06
Lower-Middle (34)	0.03	−0.26	−0.49	−0.07	0.01	−0.16	−0.11	0.16
Lower (18)	0.26	0.25	0.21	0.2	0.12	0.11	0.1	0.13
All (89)	−0.44	−0.51	−0.59	−0.4	−0.03	−0.01	0.01	0.18

Source: prior databases and author's calculations

whatever contribution IP may have made to inequality was more than offset by redistribution policies. A similar process may exist in the UMICs. Otherwise, there is little evidence of any relationship between measured patent rights and household income inequality.

1.1.2 *Econometric Analyses*

Computing simple correlations does little to sort out potential relationships and says nothing about any causal impact of IP protection on inequality. The standardized database of Gini coefficients offers some scope for econometric analysis, however, and two studies have estimated the impact of IP protection on inequality using such data. Because these studies paint a consistent picture, it is worth reviewing their findings before asking if they are reliable.

The first paper was by Adams (2008), who sought to fit IP rights empirically into a selection of determinants of inequality. The author acquired Gini coefficients from the World Bank for intermittent years between 1985 and 2001 for a sample of sixty-two developing countries and regressed them on various independent variables that were lagged to try to reduce reverse causality problems. Specifically, the model related the Gini coefficients to various macroeconomic globalization and policy variables, including trade openness, the degree of incoming foreign direct investment (FDI), the GP index as a measure of IP rights, secondary education rates, government consumption, a measure of institutional quality, and GDP per capita. The estimation found a consistently positive and significant effect of the GP index on subsequent inequality, with the primary coefficient suggesting that a one-unit increase (e.g., from two to three) in the patent index would increase the average Gini coefficient by around 1.2 points, in a scale between 0 and 100. A stronger institutional environment tends to reduce inequality, indicating that if a country plans to strengthen its patents and is concerned about impacts on income distribution, it may wish to complement that policy with a more secure set of rules governing investment.

A second study was by Saini and Mehra (2018). The question they posed was whether strengthened IP rights in the post-TRIPS era had affected income inequality, using a sample of sixty-five developing and developed countries over the period 1995–2009. These authors used the Gini coefficients from the Standardized World Income Inequality Database (reviewed earlier) as the dependent variable in a panel regression highly similar to that in Adams (2008). Specifically, using five-year averages of most data, they regressed the posttransfer Gini measures on the GP index, openness to imports, inward FDI, GDP growth, and an indicator of political stability. The patent index interacted with the economic growth measure to assess whether faster-growing economies had a larger or smaller effect of IP on inequality. Similarly, it interacted with a dummy variable for developed countries to see if that relationship varied among poorer countries. They estimated a random-effects model because of the wide heterogeneity in country characteristics in conjunction with the higher dimensionality of countries than time periods.

Remarkably, the findings were completely at odds with Adam's (2008) findings. In particular, the authors estimated that increases in the GP index tended to reduce the average Gini coefficient in developing countries, suggesting that stronger patent protection reduced income inequality. The authors speculated that this outcome reflected that stronger IP rights tend to attract more inward technology transfer, which could raise the relative wages of lower-skilled workers in labor-abundant countries. The coefficient on the interaction term of the patent index and GDP per capita was significantly positive, implying that the inequality reduction was lower in rich nations. Indeed, the relationship could be positive for countries above a threshold income level, implying higher inequality with strengthened patent rights in developed economies. They interpreted this outcome to suggest that stronger patent laws may induce innovation in the latter group of countries, with rents to that activity favoring those with more technical and managerial skills. Unfortunately, the authors did not attempt to subject these broad conclusions to further empirical testing.

These results are intriguing because, for now, they stand as the only cross-country estimates available of the potential impacts of IP protection on internal income distribution. However, they find distinctly opposite impacts, suggesting that the correlation between the legal determinants of patent scope and inequality, as measured by Gini coefficients, is ambiguous. Its estimation may depend on the data used and the specifications set out.

Moreover, such results are not likely to be reliably robust for further study, given the nature of the analysis. Using national macroeconomic data to assess complex relationships is fraught with risks and subject to fragile interpretations, as shown in prominent debates over the macroeconomic sources of economic growth.[12] Both studies rely on reduced-form specifications that do not emerge from any particular

[12] See Levine and Renelt (1992) for an early critique, among many.

theory other than what may seem to be common sense, and neither worries about general equilibrium and feedback effects among the different variables employed. Their regressions are subject to omitted variable bias, meaning that both inequality and IP rights could be driven higher by excluded variables, leading to spurious positive correlations. Similarly, the GP index is highly correlated with other measures of institutional quality and property rights, raising questions about whether it is really IP or something else that may raise inequality.

All of which suggest that further analysis is needed to sharpen predictions and improve confidence in such estimates. The remarkable element is that so little sound empirical analysis of the underlying questions exists. For that purpose, cross-national macroeconomic studies are unlikely to provide much utility. Rather, the emphasis must be placed on clear theoretical approaches that make detectable predictions about the microeconomic aspects of IP rights and inequality, measured perhaps through wage differentials between skilled and unskilled workers. A literature of this kind is now emerging, as described in the next section.

1.2 ECONOMIC THEORY AND MICROECONOMETRIC ANALYSIS

As mentioned, the literature analyzing the determinants of within-country income and wealth inequality is deep and rapidly expanding. Surprisingly, IP protection has been virtually ignored in this context, except via informal and intuitive statements about raising returns to R&D investments, which filter through to higher wages for skilled and technical workers. In this context, IP rights are facilitating mechanisms for skill-biased technical change (SBTC). They are also viewed as devices for generating and protecting monopoly rents, which go disproportionately to entrepreneurs, managers, high-skilled workers, and shareholders.

1.2.1 *IP Protection and Effects on Inequality*

These are reasonable propositions, even if the mechanisms involved are understudied. They find some explanation and support in scarce theoretical and empirical studies. For example, Chu (2010) studied the impact of stronger patent scope on economic growth and inequality in a single-economy model. The theoretical foundation is the "quality ladders" model, in which a continuous innovation process generates products of increasing quality that displace those previously at the top of the ladder.[13] The canonical model assumes individuals share identical and homothetic preferences, implying that income distribution does not matter for innovation

[13] The "quality ladders" model is a workhorse of modern growth theory in which innovation is a purposeful and endogenous process and becomes the primary engine of growth. Its roots are described in Romer (1994), and it was refined by Grossman and Helpman (1991) and Aghion and Howitt (1992).

and growth, nor is it affected by growth outcomes. Chu extended the model to an environment where households have different wealth profiles. How much to work in the labor market depends on savings and consumption decisions. His model is limited in assuming the distribution of assets among rich and poor households is unchanged in all steady-state equilibrium growth paths.

In this environment, a policy raising the scope of patents increases wealth and income inequality by raising R&D, which enhances the growth rate and raises the interest rate. In turn, asset returns rise, disproportionately favoring the rich, who own more assets. Furthermore (and somewhat counterintuitively), because the higher interest rate raises savings and reduces consumption, it induces households to spend more time at work. This factor also generates relatively higher income for the rich, further expanding income inequality. However, because consumption is reduced by relatively less among the poor, the outcome of stronger patents may be reduced consumption inequality. The author noted that these results are consistent with macroeconomic data in the United States in the 1980s and 1990s when there was a sharp rise in wealth and income inequality but a much smaller rise in consumption inequality. Because this model is highly stylized and does not fit detailed data, it is impossible to determine how much stronger patent scope in this era contributed to inequality via this mechanism. Still, it offers an interesting mechanism for further study.

The paper just described posits a heterogeneous and unchanging asset distribution between rich and poor, without explaining why households might vary that way while arguing that investment returns drive changes in inequality. It does not consider the skill bias of patent-induced innovation. A model doing so is set out by Pan et al. (2015). The model is based on the idea of "directed technological change," also a fundamental model in modern growth theory.[14] This approach argues that investments in new technology depend on numerous factors, including relative factor costs. In skill-abundant countries, such as the United States, such investments tend to reduce demand for low-skilled labor (which is expensive relative to other countries) and raise demand for high-skilled labor. This R&D-skill complementarity, found clearly in information technologies, is one basis for the predominance of SBTC.

In the model by Pan et al., R&D investments predominantly seek new technical solutions in higher-skilled industries, raising the demand for skills and, in turn, increasing wage inequality. Patents may be gained in new technologies complementary to either low-skilled or high-skilled workers. The key assumption is that skill-intensive industries increase returns to scale, lowering costs and raising productivity as output expands. Thus, in countries with abundant skills, it is optimal to scale a patent policy to favor the latter. The optimal patent policy then favors broader breadth to encourage scale economies. The result is a "skill-biased patent policy," which raises wage inequality. It also imparts a clear bias between countries: Skill-abundant nations

[14] Directed technological change is an old concept but found its primary formalization in Acemoglu (1998).

prefer broader patents, and labor-abundant nations prefer narrower protection. This paper offers no empirical analysis, so it cannot assess the validity of its key assumptions or the contribution of patent policy to growth and inequality. Again, however, it offers a useful perspective on which to build further analysis.

If theory suggests that strong IP protection supports wage inequality based on skills, entrepreneurship, or other worker characteristics, an empirical analysis should gravitate toward considering micro data on wage gaps across regions or within firms. This approach is natural because a patent exists at the firm level in specific locations, suggesting that carefully specified analysis could trace the impacts of patenting on wage inequality within the enterprise.

Two recent papers of note take this approach. First, Aghion et al. (2019) analyzed state-level panel data in the United States to study whether "top income inequality" is caused to some degree by innovation. Top income inequality refers to increases in the income shares of the top 1 percent of households. The paper sets out a model of endogenous innovation by incumbents (who own patents and enjoy monopoly markups) and entrants (who innovate to gain patents). Innovation by either group raises the income shares of entrepreneurs and generates more top income inequality. But only investments by entrants increase social mobility, meaning the ability to enter the top income level. Entry may be blocked through high innovation costs, including extant patents. Such blockages slow mobility into the top tier. Regrettably, the model does not explicitly consider the role of stronger patent scope. Presumably, it has offsetting effects. On the one hand, patents should raise the returns on innovation and increase the top income shares. On the other, blocking entry should reduce the inequality associated with more rapid entry into entrepreneurship.

These predictions were tested using state-level panel data from 1975 to 2010. They gathered data on the top 1 percent and top 10 percent of income shares in all fifty states plus Washington, DC. Top income shares rose in every state, from an unweighted average of 8 percent in 1975 to a peak of 21 percent in 2007, before falling during the financial crisis. Moreover, there was increased variability across states, with the highest shares going toward states with stronger patent profiles. Additional data suggested that income from entrepreneurship (patent rents in the model) was disproportionately high in the top income group in such states.[15] The income figures were combined with state-level patenting data from the U.S. Patent and Trademark Office, including patent citations to construct quality measures. The cross-state variation in patenting was markedly high, generating scope for identification. The authors regressed the top income shares across states on lagged patents and patent quality, controlling for business conditions, the prevalence of the financial sector, state GDP, and population, plus state and year fixed effects. In ordinary least

[15] These data were taken from the World Top Income Database. See Alvaredo et al. (2014). This database is now called the World Inequality Database, available at http://wid.world/data, as mentioned *supra* note 9.

squares (OLS) regression, they found consistently positive and significant effects of patents and patent quality on the top 1 percent of incomes.

To control for the endogeneity of patents, they included each state's representation on Congressional Appropriations Committees and other factors as instrumental variables. These regressions reported similar impacts of patents on top income shares. In particular, in the preferred specification, they found that a 1 percent rise in patents per capita raised a state's top income share by 0.17 percent. That is, patenting alone could explain 17 percent of the rise in the top-level income proportion across states. This effect was even greater in high-patent states such as California. Put differently, if a state were to move from the bottom quartile of patents to the top quartile in 2000, the coefficients would imply an increase in its top income share of about 1.5 percentage points, a substantial increase. The authors argued that this calculation underestimated because it failed to account for the possibility that a successful inventor in a low-patent state would likely move to a high-patent state and other factors. Their results were robust to using other measures of top income inequality.

A second study of note is by Bhattacharya et al. (2022). Briefly, these authors took advantage of implementing a new Indian patent law between 2002 and 2005 to analyze whether the gap between manager wages and other wages within firms varied by whether those firms had patents before and after the legal implementation. They found strong evidence of an increase in these wage gaps, which was more pronounced in high-technology sectors. This evidence shows that firms do transfer patent rents disproportionately to skilled and managerial workers within firms, tending to raise wage inequality.

Studies using such microeconomic data are instructive and suggest that patenting and patent reforms can contribute to income and wage inequality through expected channels. The literature would benefit from considerably more such analyses, using other databases across countries, industries, and firms. It would be equally useful to quantify, with microdata, how patents and patent laws contribute to growing intra-industry market concentration and monopoly power within and across countries and how those rents have been distributed.

1.2.2 *Alternative Perspectives*

Even less studied by economists is the novel idea that inequality itself may be a determinant of innovation and the growth effects of IP protection. Put differently, while IP may generate higher growth and inequality, causation may also run from inequality to innovation and growth.[16] Mendez (2002) noted that in an economy

[16] A large antecedent literature was concerned with how concentrated market structures affected innovation. The seminal contribution was Kamien and Schwartz (1982). More broadly, Murphy et al. (1989) argued that for a country to transition from an agricultural base to industrialization required both a large market size and a sufficiently wide sharing of income to support demand for industrial goods.

with a dual labor market, where some workers are paid efficient wages and others competitive wages, even neutral technological change can further increase wage inequality, as can globalization.

Newer literature is emerging and needs much fuller development. However, two papers illustrate how certain mechanisms could link inequality and innovation. First, Weinhold and Nair-Reichert (2009) asked whether income inequality differences help explain innovation performance across countries.[17] There are two potential mechanisms identified. First, countries with large and growing middle classes (and therefore more limited inequality) should see political pressure raised for stronger governance institutions, including IP rights, which could increase innovation. Second, a larger middle class may offer more entrants into sufficiently skilled labor categories that raise the supply of innovation while increasing the demand for innovation through preferences for new goods. There are multiple relationships here to sort out through data analysis.

For this purpose, they used patenting data from the World Intellectual Property Organization (WIPO) database as measures of innovation, distinguishing between resident patent applications and foreign patent applications within each country.[18] They regress patenting on the size of each country's middle class and the GP index as a measure of patent strength, instrumenting the latter with various structural and geographic factors. The argument is that if the income distribution affects innovation only through institutional reforms (the first channel), it should not significantly affect the regression when IP rights are included. However, if it influences innovation directly through supply and demand factors (the second channel), it should be independently significant. Further, its effects should vary between domestic patents (with a positive impact) and foreign patents (with little or no impact). They estimate a cross-section model, averaging national data from 1994 to 2000, leaving just fifty-three observations across countries. Most regressions found a positive and significant coefficient on the instrumented GP variable in explaining domestic patent applications, supporting the institutional channel. More importantly, they found consistently positive and significant estimates of the size of a country's middle-income class on resident patenting, suggesting that more income equality is pro-innovation. In contrast, these variables had little effect on foreign patenting, which depended more on population, market size, and other macroeconomic factors.

This result is interesting but suffers from the usual concerns about cross-country econometric analysis with national data. The paper could be usefully extended, at

17 A large literature has addressed the relationship between inequality and growth, failing to find robust evidence. See Lundberg and Squire (2003). However, there is stronger evidence that a large middle class could increase long-run growth through institutional quality enhancements, as noted in Persson and Tabellini (1994).

18 The WIPO database is suspect for numerous reasons, suggesting this analysis should be updated with data from the European Patent Office's Worldwide Patent Statistical Database (PATSTAT) or related sources.

least through industry patenting data, in which comparisons are made between the technological orientation of industries. It would also be useful to see if explicit measures of income inequality would demonstrate negative impacts on innovation through the identified channels.

A second paper, by Kiedaisch (2021), offers a theoretical model aimed at the related but deeper question of whether the impact of IP rights on economic growth depends on the level of economic inequality. The author studied this possibility in a "product variety" model of endogenous growth.[19] In this model, innovators seek to develop new varieties of existing products across industries, responding to the idea that consumers prefer diverse choices and will pay a premium for such decisions. The economy's growth rate depends on the pace of new product development. Kiedaisch introduces inequality into the model by assuming that rich and poor consumers have different preferences. Specifically, richer households both consume a greater number of varieties and prefer more innovative or complex goods. Thus, in the model, the pace and nature of innovation in a country depend on income distribution. Along a balanced growth path, countries with more unequal distributions in the sense of relatively more rich people would have longer patent duration to incentivize more new products. In this sense, inequality increases expected growth.

The model has many more dimensions but, importantly for this chapter, establishes a theoretical mechanism that helps explain why countries with relatively larger rich groups (or more concentration of income and wealth at the top) prefer stronger IP protection, which in turn implies faster economic growth. The model has not yet been subjected to empirical analysis but doing so would be instructive. For example, while it seems intuitive and consistent with the casual observation that higher top incomes should push for stronger IP rights, the idea that such economies should grow faster clashes with the recent convergence in incomes between rich and emerging countries. Presumably, there is more to inequality across countries than can be explained in a single-country approach, as discussed in the following section.

1.3 INNOVATION, DIFFUSION, AND CROSS-COUNTRY INEQUALITY

The prior sections argued that the impact of IP protection on internal inequality within countries is difficult to conceptualize and demonstrate empirically, though the emerging literature is promising. It is also important to consider another form of inequality across countries. As noted, many EDCs have seen faster economic growth than the HICs over the past twenty-five years. Have IP rights played a role in this process? While this question has not been studied directly, there is considerable indirect evidence that the expansion of IP protection in EDCs has facilitated this convergence of incomes. In brief, the channel through which this happened is that

[19] This is the second workhorse model of endogenous growth and appears often in the literature. For an early explication, see Grossman and Helpman (1992).

TABLE 1.5 *GDP-weighted average annual growth rates in GDP per capita, 1990–2015*

Income group	1990–2000	2000–2010	2010–2015	1990–2015
High (83)	2.31	1.26	0.70	1.93
Low (29)	−1.27	3.80	1.54	1.57
Lower-Middle (70)	0.96	4.96	2.01	3.88
Upper-Middle (45)	2.03	6.67	2.25	5.83

GDP per capita is in 2017 U.S. dollars, at purchasing power parity

Source: World Bank, World Development Indicators, 2020 income classification

stronger IP rights, in conjunction with trade liberalization, have accelerated the international diffusion of technological information and knowledge, even to the point of shifting R&D resources to select EDCs.

1.3.1 *Stylized Facts*

To put this claim in perspective, consider the simple data in Table 1.5. These figures show, over certain subperiods and the full period, average annual growth in real GDP per capita, measured in 2017 U.S. dollars at purchasing power parity (PPP) exchange rates.[20] Such exchange rates are appropriate for focusing on changes in actual living standards.[21] Again, the data are broken down into income groups, but now using the 2020 classifications established by the World Bank. In particular, China is now considered a UMIC, and India is an LMIC. This updated breakdown is more appropriate for analyzing income convergence. The comprehensive samples, rather than limited to those nations with available Gini coefficients as above, paint a complete picture. Finally, they are weighted by consistently measured GDP totals, capturing actual growth experiences in the income groupings more accurately.

It is readily seen in Table 1.5 that the HICs saw their growth rates fall from 2.3 percent in the 1990s to 1.3 percent in the following decade, before the stagnation following the financial crisis of 2008–2010. The 1990s were a period of slow growth for both the LICs and LMICs, though both saw substantial increases in growth in the 2000s. For both the LMICs and UMICs, the 2000s were a period of extremely rapid growth in real consumption standards. This was a period of great convergence in real incomes between EMCs and the HICs.[22] Over the entire period, the UMICs

[20] Available at the World Bank World Development Indicators database, at https://datacatalog.worldbank.org/dataset/world-development-indicators.

[21] PPP exchange rates are defined as those currency values that would equalize the cost of a basket of goods and services in local currencies across countries. By neutralizing exchange-rate differences associated with other factors, they reflect the actual ability of local incomes to purchase goods and services.

[22] For extended analysis and data, see Baldwin (2016).

grew their consumption abilities sharply compared with the HICs, resulting in marked reductions in poverty and improvements in health and education status.[23] In contrast, the LICs remained in relative stagnation.

There are, therefore, the following stylized facts. From 1990 to the present, the UMICs and LMICs considerably expanded their legal IP rights, as shown in Table 1.3, while experiencing significantly faster economic growth than the rich world. The LICs also adopted stronger laws, though these remained well behind those of the other groups while stagnating in relative terms. In short, the period was one of both extensive IP reforms and notable "conditional convergence" in living standards. Again, it would be difficult to argue and not credible to demonstrate with macroeconomic data that the former caused the latter. This is because many other factors could have driven both upward, with no necessary relationship between IP protection and growth.[24]

While that claim is largely correct, it is misleading in at least one important context. Economic logic and evidence both suggest that, at a microeconomic level, IP reforms in EDCs have attracted more technology flows, raising productivity. The next two subsections develop that argument. At this point, it is important to note that higher real incomes in EDCs do not necessarily imply more equal internal income distributions, as the gains may have been acquired largely by the already well-off. Put differently, the growth impacts of IP reforms may not trickle down into widespread income gains.

1.3.2 *The Economics of IP Rights and Technology Development*

How can IP reforms in EDCs raise domestic incomes, at least in the aggregate? The economics literature has emphasized three factors. First is the possibility that stronger home patent rights may directly raise domestic innovation.[25] This question lies outside the scope of this chapter, and, in any case, the linkages from innovation to inequality remain unexplored in those countries.[26] Briefly, the literature suggests that strengthening domestic IP rights can stimulate innovation, typically measured by future patent applications at home or abroad. This conclusion, however, must be strongly conditioned. It holds largely for higher-income emerging economies with, among other things, large domestic markets, adequate supplies of human capital,

[23] For such social indicators, see Radelet (2015).

[24] Maskus (2012), for example, shows that the growth rates in IP rights and patents were essentially uncorrelated with economic growth in a basic data review.

[25] This literature has focused entirely on patent protection, to the exclusion of copyrights, trademarks, and trade secrets, all of which may affect innovation of new products and services. This reflects primarily both data shortages – measuring copyrights and trade secrets is essentially impossible, while patents data are ubiquitous – and conceptual difficulties in relating these IP rights to invention incentives.

[26] Readers seeking reviews of this literature may consult Maskus (2012, 2022).

robust market competition, and sound policy governance. Countries lacking in such dimensions do not become markedly more innovative after patent reforms, highlighting the complexity of effective innovation systems. Specifically, there is little evidence that formal innovation is responsive to patent reforms in the poorest countries simply because the promise of domestic patents is a small incentive in weak economic environments. A corollary is that stronger patent rights likely do not diminish formal domestic innovation in poor countries, a frequently heard concern. Regrettably, there is no systematic evidence about how IP reforms may influence informal (unmeasured) innovation or competition through local imitation in poor countries. It is likely that domestic firms engaged in imitation and counterfeit production may be forced out of the market after significant reforms. Still, shortcomings in economic surveys have defied the systematic linkage of firm exits with IP policy. This remains a significant shortcoming in the economics literature.

A further important qualification is that even in dynamic emerging economies, undertaking extensive upgrades of IP protection may not be advisable in the medium term. The reason is that local firms in those countries, while undertaking R&D programs and exhibiting some innovativeness, may still rely on imitative technical change, often borrowing foreign technologies and making minor adaptations. In this regard, significant IP reforms may discourage local innovation and economic development by securing, often on behalf of foreign inventors, strong exclusionary rights that raise the costs of imitative and adaptive innovation (Kim et al., 2012).

1.3.3 *Trade-Induced Innovation*

Trade liberalization and skill-biased technological change are commonly thought to be the primary sources of income and wealth inequality across countries, including in the developing world. This is largely true regarding SBTC, as noted earlier. Reductions in trade and investment barriers, however, have complex impacts and may reduce inequality in developing countries. The standard reason is that integration with the global economy offers more export opportunities for industries that rely on labor-intensive production, tending to raise the real wages of low-skilled workers. At the same time, it encourages more imports of capital-intensive and skill-intensive goods, diminishing those incomes.[27] Similarly, inward FDI into developing countries tends to be labor-seeking, raising local wages.

This tendency toward diminished inequality is far from certain, however. For example, current trade theory emphasizes that market opening pushes resources into the most efficient enterprises, which raises labor productivity and wages in general

[27] Readers may recognize this claim as the Stolper–Samuelson Theorem, which is foundational in international economics. A good explanation is in Feenstra and Taylor (2017). Evidence of this factor-based wage sorting in Mexico is presented in Chiquiar (2008).

but could raise the wages of those with greater skills.[28] Moreover, when global trade is liberalized, firms that start exporting generally must adopt globally efficient techniques, which tend to raise the relative wages of the most productive workers, who have higher skills even within occupational classes.[29] This logic helps explain why exporting firms and multinational enterprises (MNEs) in manufacturing and services tend to pay significantly higher wages in EDCs than local firms, enhancing this form of cross-firm inequality.[30]

An exceptional form of this process emerged sharply in the 1990s and 2000s, the era of rapid growth in offshoring through vertical production networks (Baldwin, 2016). The ability of multinational firms to fragment their production into lower-skilled activities (resource extraction, intermediate input production, and product assembly) and higher-skilled activities (design, marketing, R&D, and other headquarter services) and to transfer production of the former to developing markets was driven by cuts in trade costs and improvements in information and communication technologies. With lower transport costs and extremely low taxes on trade, parts and semi-finished goods could be shipped across borders multiple times in the production of final goods, a process exemplified by the proliferation of automobile production and trade within North America after the implementation of the North American Free Trade Agreement. The deployment of information and communication technologies permitted efficient inventory and shipping logistics management among nodes within production networks, greatly raising international trade in intermediate inputs.[31]

This fragmentation led to the rapid offshoring of lower-skilled and medium-skilled jobs from the United States, Europe, and other high-wage nations to a limited group of "globalizers" among EDCs, especially China (Baldwin, 2016). The harmful effects on low-skilled manufacturing and service jobs in these rich countries are widely identified as a source of inequality (Autor et al., 2013). Less widely appreciated, however, is that offshoring also may serve to increase inequality in recipient countries. The reason is that the transferred jobs, while coming from the low and medium ends of the skill distribution in, say, the United States, tend to require skills and commitment to formal employment at higher ends in EDCs.[32] Thus, recent globalization, at least within vertical production networks, has been a source of growing inequality in the HICs and EDCs. Recall, however, the earlier discussion of how trade liberalization could raise the demand for low-skilled labor in

[28] The basis for this theory is in Melitz (2003).

[29] Evidence for this outcome in Brazil is presented in Helpman et al. (2017).

[30] The empirical evidence for this claim is deep and robust. See, for example, Brown et al. (2003), Hijsen (2008), and Javorcik (2015). Note that this fact does not imply that inward FDI reduces domestic wage inequality; rather, the opposite is more likely to be true.

[31] Feenstra and Taylor (2017) explain such processes in detail.

[32] Again, see Feenstra and Taylor (2017).

EDCs through the comparative advantage channel. These counterbalancing impacts make the overall effects ambiguous.

Foreign direct investment and offshoring are important forms of trade-induced innovation because they generate new and more efficient forms of production processes in recipient countries. However, trade liberalization through tariff cuts and joining free trade agreements may also raise innovation on the part of domestic enterprises. As suggested earlier, firms must lower costs to compete with more efficient imports or develop new products to enter export markets.[33] Both processes require investments in R&D, new capital goods, and better management techniques. Initial evidence for this spur to innovation in the wake of trade opening is in Bustos (2011), who found that Argentinean firms experiencing relatively larger cuts in Brazilian tariffs after the foundation of MERCOSUR invested relatively more in upgraded technology.[34] However, this happened primarily among firms at the upper reaches of productivity within Argentinean firms, not among lower-productivity and inefficient firms. A second important study is by Aghion et al. (2018), who developed a theoretical model in which greater access to export markets changes the incentives of domestic firms to innovate. Specifically, high-productivity firms have the resources to invest more in R&D and develop new products, while competition forces low-productivity enterprises to reduce innovation spending. These predictions were borne out using exporting and patenting data from French firms from 1994 to 2012.

The relationships between trade and investment liberalization and innovation are considerably more complex than suggested here. Much depends on local circumstances in each country. The broad view, however, posits that increasing global integration has encouraged more innovation, at least in developed and higher-income emerging economies. Because these innovation responses are concentrated in high-productivity enterprises, they likely have contributed to higher wage inequality across skill classes and across (and even within) firms within occupational groups. These issues will continue to attract scholarly attention for years.

It is worth noting an additional complication involving trade and IP rights. Emerging and developing countries that seek to export higher-technology products to developed countries may encounter import barriers. Many advanced economies have laws blocking imports that violate patents or trademarks in the importers. A well-known example is section 337 of the U.S. Tariff Act of 1930. Shin et al. (2016) found evidence that the operation of such import restraints reduces the exports of more sophisticated products from emerging countries.

33 In this "sorting" process, less productive domestic firms are pressured to shut down, as found in Chile by Pavcnik (2002).

34 MERCOSUR (Southern Common Market) is a trade agreement among Argentina, Brazil, Paraguay, Uruguay, and Venezuela, founded in 1991.

While important background for this chapter, none of the prior reviews directly implicated IP rights and how they interact with globalization to affect inequality. At this stage, the best guess is indirect: To the extent that stronger IP protection has causally attracted more trade, FDI, and offshoring, it presumably has contributed to those sources of inequality within nations. And here, the evidence is clear, as developed in the next subsection.

1.3.4 *Technology Transfer and Income Convergence*

Massive literature is now studying how IP reforms affect international flows of technical information through high-technology trade, FDI, offshoring, and licensing. Reviewing that literature is beyond the scope of this subsection.[35] Rather, the intention here is to discuss three observations about how such flows could affect international inequality, defined as divergence or convergence in international living standards, as described empirically in Table 1.5. These issues can be subtle and counterintuitive, making it important to draw lessons from economic theory and empirical work.

1.3.4.1 Product-Cycle Dynamics

The first point is that divergence or convergence over time is a dynamic question requiring extended analysis. To some degree, cross-country income movements depend on relative trends in factor endowments. Emerging countries with high saving and investment rates, strong human capital and skills growth, and sound economic infrastructure and governance grow faster than others, including developed countries. This is a large part of the story in China and the rest of East Asia in recent decades. However, resource accumulation alone tends to run into diminishing returns, slowing down convergence after a time.

Sustained relative income growth requires continued increases in productivity from technological change, which, broadly put, can be driven by continuous domestic innovation or technology acquisition from abroad. Economists frequently study these processes through the lens of the dynamic product-cycle model, in which countries reside in an innovative North and an imitative South.[36] The simplest notion is that firms in the North develop new products or technologies, on which they have a temporary monopoly so long as the technical knowledge is not copied in the South. As soon as new technology is copied, however, production shifts to the South, and the product is exported back to the North, where firms devote resources to the next stages of innovation. What emerges is a continuous

[35] For reviews, see Park (2008) and Maskus (2012, 2022).

[36] The product-cycle model was first explicated by Vernon (1966) and is a workhorse model in trade and global business studies.

cycle of Northern innovation and Southern imitation, the primary form of technology diffusion.

From the standpoint of global income distribution, the relative rates of innovation and diffusion matter.[37] An exogenous rise in the rate of innovation generates a broader swath of Northern monopoly rents, which are paid as higher wages there. In contrast, an exogenous rise in the rate of imitation weakens those monopolies and transfers production more rapidly to the South, raising wages there. The key variable in such models, the ratio of Northern to Southern wages, rises with innovation and falls with imitation. If innovation is sufficiently slow and imitation sufficiently fast, this ratio could approach unity, implying full income convergence. It is evident that IP rights play a straightforward role in this dynamic. Stronger IP in the North expands innovation and protects wages there. Stronger IP in the South raises imitation costs, slowing imitation and reducing wages there. Unambiguously, then, increases in global IP protection would worsen international income inequality in the basic model.

It is fair to say that this simple proposition lies at the heart of concerns in developing countries and among development economists about the potential impacts of IP reforms associated with TRIPS at the WTO.[38] This view formed the essence of the first model translating the product-cycle dynamics into an endogenous growth framework through purposeful innovation and technology transfer, set out by Helpman (1993). He developed a "quality ladders" model, in which Northern innovation could be displaced by Southern imitation, resulting in instantaneous technology transfer and narrowing the North–South wage gap. In this framework, stronger IP protection in the South would sustain Northern technological monopolies for longer periods, leading to reduced rates of both imitation and innovation and limiting economic growth. This prediction suggested the policy harmonization demanded by TRIPS would be a dynamic mistake.

This result inspired lengthy literature extending the endogenous product-cycle model and IP rights in important directions. Most prominently, subsequent models by Lai (1998), Glass and Saggi (2002), and Yang and Maskus (2001) posited that there are two channels of technology diffusion from North to South: imitation and purposeful information transfers through FDI and licensing. Investment is sensitive to IP protection, especially in high-technology manufacturing and services, because multinational firms feel more confident that they can transfer advanced information and know-how without losing them to local imitation. Licensing should expand with IP protection for similar reasons and because enforceable domestic patent

[37] The canonical model is in Krugman (1979). This model and others following it posited identical consumers (workers) in each country, so that internal inequality was not an issue to be studied.

[38] Maskus (2012) discusses these concerns and the evolution of the IP system after TRIPS. For an extended critique of TRIPS and the broader complications with IP rights, see Stiglitz and Charlton (2005).

rights can reduce the costs of reaching mutually acceptable contracts. In turn, FDI and licensing flows increase Northern profits and speed up technology diffusion, raising Southern wages.

Moreover, liberating Northern labor from production permitted more resources to be devoted to innovation. Depending on model parameters, innovation may rise or fall while technology transfer is enhanced. In this context, stronger IP protection in the South has offsetting effects: It slows down uncompensated imitation but enhances market-oriented technology transfer through FDI and licensing. The impact on the North–South income gap depends on circumstances.

In consequence, how IP reforms affect income divergence or convergence is an empirical question. To date, there are no solid econometric studies of this issue for reasons already mentioned. However, there is substantial and consistent evidence that broader patent scope tends to attract more FDI, licensing, and offshoring to those EDCs that can deploy such information effectively into domestic production.[39] The implication is that stronger IP protection, at least in those countries, has accelerated technology transfer and encouraged income convergence by shifting employment abroad from the HICs. Thus, the extensive global IP enhancement period since TRIPS has almost surely reduced relative wages between the rich countries and the emerging countries through enhanced technology transfer. This conclusion may come as a surprise to rich-country politicians who enthusiastically support such reforms. The extent to which such reforms may be credited with this outcome, as opposed to other economic factors, is unclear but surely significant.

Again, it should be noted that this convergence is conditional: There is scant evidence of it in the LICs after their IP reforms. The best conclusion here is that IP rights are insufficient to attract greater technology flows. Countries need to complement those reforms with stronger investment climates, reduced corruption, better human capital, and the like.

1.3.4.2 The Property Rights Approach to Offshoring

There is a second theoretical framework in which stronger IP rights in the South can increase the incomes of local workers and input suppliers. The so-called property rights approach posits that foreign investors and domestic network partners, particularly in an international outsourcing context, operate as principals (the multinational) and agents (the local contractor).[40] The parent firm and the local input contractor must bargain over how they will share the profits from production within the network. The contractor pays lower wages than the parent firm in its location,

[39] Again, see Maskus (2012) for an extensive discussion.

[40] The property rights analysis of principal–agent problems was pioneered by Hart and Moore (1990) and Williamson (1985). It is a fundamental theory of the boundaries of a firm, analyzing conditions under which a firm would produce inputs in-house or outsource them to a contractor. It was extended to international outsourcing and IP rights by Antras (2003, 2005).

which is the incentive for offshoring. However, once the contract is signed, the supplier might choose to save costs through shirking, which is more likely if the parent firm cannot enforce its contract. The cheating may be through not producing the required volumes, but it also could involve stealing know-how or diluting the parent firm's trademark and reputation. It follows that stronger IP rights in the supplier's country would diminish the likelihood of shirking, making outsourcing more likely.

The empirical prediction is that countries with a reasonable ability to produce high-quality inputs are more likely to be invited into a production network if their governments offer enforceable contract rights, including in IP. Again, the evidence suggests that this is the case, for outsourcing locations at different stages of production, other things equal, are sensitive to local IP rights. This also applies to the recent emergence of R&D networks across countries within multinational firms.[41] Again, the implication is that EDCs with transparent IP rights are more likely to become nodes in vertical networks, a force for international wage convergence.

These broad perspectives may be usefully qualified. For example, the R&D spending of MNEs on local affiliates abroad may be either asset-exploiting or asset-augmenting, as discussed by Dunning and Narula (1995). The former case involves local R&D to adapt existing technologies to conditions in recipient markets, tending to lock in competitive advantages of the foreign firm and potentially reducing convergence. Patel and Vega (1999) studied patenting trends in the United States of major global firms, finding evidence that firms generally engaged in local R&D in technological areas where they were strong at home.

In the latter case, local R&D is devoted to acquiring new knowledge-based assets or creating new technologies that may support domestic production and even exports of novel goods. Much of the recent growth in R&D spending by foreign multinationals in China has been asset-augmenting, taking advantage of engineering skills and other Chinese factors. This process is more likely to raise the demand for skilled workers in recipient countries, tending toward international income convergence.

The net impact of international R&D programs within multinational firms on global convergence remains unclear and worthy of additional and deeper research.

1.3.4.3 Technology Spillovers

The third important element in the convergence story is the possibility that capital imports, FDI, and outsourcing contracts entering EDCs result in what economists call productivity spillovers or technology spillovers.[42] High-technology imports and FDI generally embody more advanced technical information and knowledge than

[41] See Branstetter and Maskus (2022) for further discussion.

[42] This is also a large literature. For a comprehensive review, see Keller (2010).

domestic production in lagging countries.[43] Incorporated into domestic production, they directly raise productivity within the firm or local contractor. However, those direct gains are typically paid for. Spillover occurs when a domestic firm or customer gains greater productivity without paying for the economic value of that improvement.

There are several channels through which such productivity spillovers operate. One is direct imitation as local firms observe the operations of MNE affiliates or contractors and figure out how to implement them into their facilities. Another is the practice of skilled engineers and managers to leave employment at an affiliate and take the knowledge learned there to another firm or start-up. A third is reverse engineering of high-technology imported inputs. Perhaps most important are backward and forward spillovers. A backward spillover occurs when a domestic input producer gains higher efficiency through supplying an affiliate of a global firm. This is most likely the result of the MNEs showing how to produce a higher-quality input, which the international firm requires to meet global standards. This ability to produce better inputs becomes a spillover when the input supplier uses it to expand sales to other purchasers. A forward spillover transpires when domestic purchasers of the goods and services produced by local affiliates of MNEs gain greater efficiency, which again permits them to expand sales generally.[44]

Technology spillovers gained through international trade and FDI are the primary source of measured productivity increases and economic growth in most developing countries.[45] Accordingly, the role of various policies and economic characteristics looms large in determining how rapidly such countries may grow relative to the advanced economies. In this context, IP rights again matter considerably, at least among those EDCs in a position to attract inward FDI and licensing. Here, the promise of IP rights is cross-cutting. Stronger patents and trade secrets protection should reduce the scope of uncompensated imitation, learning, and mobility of skilled labor from MNEs to domestic firms, suggesting again that IP rights could diminish growth in EDCs.

On the other hand, the greater volumes of inward technology flows associated with stronger IP protection generate more opportunities for spillovers through backward and forward linkages. Moreover, a policy might follow an intermediate track. China, for example, pursued for some years a regime in which multinationals in designated technology-oriented sectors were encouraged to invest in local joint ventures but under the expectation that the parent companies ultimately would

43 In fact, the existence of multinational production is typically based on the decisions of parent companies to deploy more efficient technologies across production locations and stages, as analyzed in Markusen (2002).

44 Evidence suggests that backward spillovers are common in EDCs, while forward spillovers are less frequently observed (Keller, 2010).

45 For elaboration and quantification of this point, see Keller (2004).

share their key IP with their local partners.[46] Success in deploying such policies is not much in evidence elsewhere among EDCs.

Thus, the question of whether stronger or weaker IP rights raise technology spillovers ultimately is empirical, and data may be marshaled to support either conclusion. To date, there are no systematic econometric studies of this central issue in the debate over global IP requirements, a considerable missing element that should attract more study going forward. For this chapter, the lesson is that IP reforms have attracted considerably more technology transfer through formal channels to select EDCs, particularly the UMICs. It is likely that some domestic firms have suffered from this competition, either shutting down or losing market shares, but evidence on this point is scarce. For these economies, the balance of effects likely has supported income convergence toward the levels of the HICs. In contrast, IP reforms likely have not contributed to such convergence among the LICs.

CONCLUDING REMARKS

This chapter has reviewed the available economic theory and evidence about the potential impacts of IP rights on income and wealth inequality, emphasizing international comparisons. This is a critical question, particularly in light of the simultaneous increase in the scope and international application of IP rights and the growth of inequality across many countries. It is tempting in this context to assign causal importance to the former in explaining the latter.

However, an essential lesson is that establishing such causality is challenging, and systematic evidence is scarce. Cross-country macroeconomic regressions of Gini coefficients on available measures of IP protection, most readily the GP index of patent rights, suggest a correlation between inequality and IP. However, such evidence is surely fragile and should be treated with considerable caution. At the same time, micro-econometric evidence is emerging that firms engaged in more global patenting tend to have more unequal internal wages, even within occupational categories. These findings are suggestive but a long way from establishing a firm and generalizable relationship. Far more analysis is needed.

The chapter also pointed out that IP reforms may accompany trade and investment liberalization, contributing to internal inequality, especially in EDCs. However, while the channels through which globalization, involving trade, FDI, and outsourcing through production networks, can affect inequality are well understood and supported by systematic evidence, there has been almost no empirical study of how IP rights may contribute. This is surely a large gap in our

[46] This and related industrial policies formed the basis of the Section 301 case against China by the Trump Administration in 2018, ultimately launching the bilateral trade war. Maskus (2012) describes the essential characteristics of China's policies.

understanding and needs to be rectified with additional study. However, working out the appropriate frameworks and data to achieve it will again be challenging.

Finally, there is strong evidence that IP reforms in the past twenty years have contributed significantly to increased flows of market-mediated technology transfer from technologically advanced countries to select EDCs. Because these flows embody knowledge that can raise local productivity and generate industrial transformations, IP rights likely have had an indirect but substantially positive effect on raising average incomes in recipient EDCs relative to those in rich countries. However, such flows have not increased much in poorer countries, whose incomes continue to stagnate in relative terms. This process, called conditional convergence, is a first-order outcome of the globalized IP system but remains underappreciated and insufficiently studied.

REFERENCES

Acemoglu, Daron. 1998. "Why Do New Technologies Complement Skills? Directed Technological Change and Wage Inequality." *Quarterly Journal of Economics* 115: 1055–1090.

2002. "Technical Change, Inequality, and the Labor Market." *Journal of Economic Literature* 40: 7–72.

Adams, Samuel. 2008. "Globalization and Income Inequality: Implications for Intellectual Property Rights." *Journal of Policy Modeling* 30: 725–735.

Aghion, Philippe, Ufuk Akcigit, Antonin Bergueard, Richard Blundell, and David Hemous. 2019. "Innovation and Top Income Inequality." *Review of Economic Studies* 86: 1–45.

Aghion, Philippe, Antonin Bergeaud, Matthieu Lequien, and Marc J. Melitz. 2018. "The Impact of Exports on Innovation: Theory and Evidence." National Bureau of Economic Research Working Paper No. 2600.

Aghion, Philippe, and Peter Howitt. 1992. "A Model of Growth through Creative Destruction." *Econometrica* 60: 323–351.

Alvaredo, Facundo, Anthony B. Atkinson, Thomas Piketty, and Emmanuel Saenz. 2014. The World Top Incomes Database. www.parisschoolofeconomics.eu/en/news/the-top-incomes-database-new-website/.

Antras, Pol. 2003. "Firms, Contracts, and Trade Structure." *Quarterly Journal of Economics* 118: 1375–1418.

2005. "Incomplete Contracts and the Product Cycle." *American Economic Review* 95: 1054–1073.

Autor, David H., David Dorn, and Gordon H. Hanson. 2013. "The China Syndrome: Local Labor Market Effects of Import Competition in the United States." *American Economic Review* 103: 2121–2168.

Baldwin, Richard. 2016. *The Great Convergence: Information Technology and the New Globalization*. Cambridge, MA: Belknap Press.

Bhattacharya, Sourav, Pavel Chakraborty, and Chirantan Chatterjee. 2022. "Intellectual Property Regimes and Wage Inequality." *Journal of Development Economics* 154: 1–32.

Branstetter, Lee, and Keith E. Maskus, 2022. "Global Knowledge Flows, Absorptive Capacity, and Capability Acquisition: Old Ideas, Recent Evidence, and New Approaches." In *Trade in Knowledge: Intellectual Property, Trade and Development in a Transformed*

Global Economy, edited by Antony Taubman and Jayashree Watal. Cambridge: Cambridge University Press.

Brown, Drusilla K., Alan V. Deardorff, and Robert M. Stern. 2003. "The Effects of Multinational Production on Wages and Working Conditions in Developing Countries." National Bureau of Economic Research Working Paper No. 9669.

Brynjolfsson, Erik, and Andrew MacAfee. 2011. *Race against the Machine: How the Digital Revolution is Accelerating Innovation, Driving Productivity, and Irreversibly Transforming Employment and the Economy*. Lexington, MA: Digital Frontier Press.

Bustos, Paula. 2011. "Trade Liberalization, Exports, and Technology Upgrading: Evidence on the Impact of MERCOSUR on Argentinian Firms." *American Economic Review* 101: 304–340.

Chiquiar, Daniel. 2008. "Globalization, Regional Wage Differentials, and the Stolper–Samuelson Theorem: Evidence from Mexico." *Journal of International Economics* 74: 70–93.

Chu, Angus C. 2010. "Effects of Patent Policy on Income and Consumption Inequality in a R&D Growth Model." *Southern Economic Journal* 77: 336–350.

Dunning, John H., and Rajneesh Narula. 1995. "The R&D Activities of Foreign Firms in the United States." *International Studies of Management and Organization* 25: 39–73.

Feenstra, Robert C., and Alan M. Taylor. 2017. *International Trade*, 4th ed. New York: Worth Publishers.

Ginarte, Juan-Carlos, and Walter G. Park. 1997. "Determinants of Patent Rights: A Cross-National Study." *Research Policy* 26: 283–301.

Glass, Amy J., and Kamal Saggi. 2002. "Intellectual Property Rights and Foreign Direct Investment." *Journal of International Economics* 56: 387–410.

Goldin, Claudia, and Lawrence F. Katz. 2008. *The Race between Education and Technology*. Cambridge MA: Belknap Press.

Grossman, Gene M., and Elhanan Helpman. 1991. "Quality Ladders in the Theory of Growth." *Review of Economic Studies* 58: 43–61.

1992. *Innovation and Growth in the Global Economy*. Cambridge, MA: MIT Press.

Hart, Oliver, and John Moore. 1990. "Property Rights and the Nature of the Firm." *Journal of Political Economy* 98: 1119–1158.

Helpman, Elhanan. 1993. "Innovation, Imitation, and Intellectual Property Rights." *Econometrica* 61: 1247–1280.

Helpman, Elhanan, Oleg Itskhoki, Marc-Andreas Muendler, and Stephen Redding. 2017. "Trade and Inequality: From Theory to Estimation." *Review of Economic Studies* 84: 357–405.

Hijsen, Alexander. 2008. "Do Multinationals Promote Better Pay and Working Conditions?" In *OECD Employment Outlook*, 263–331. Paris: Organization for Economic Cooperation and Development.

Javorcik, Beata. 2015. "Does FDI Bring Good Jobs to Host Countries?" *World Bank Research Observer* 30: 74–94.

Kamien, Morton I., and Nancy L. Schwartz. 1982. *Market Structure and Innovation*. Cambridge: Cambridge University Press.

Keller, Wolfgang. 2004. "International Technology Diffusion." *Journal of Economic Literature* 42: 752–782.

2010. "International Trade, Foreign Direct Investment, and Technology Spillovers." In *Handbook of the Economics of Innovation*, edited by Bronwyn Hall and Nathan Rosenberg. Vol. 1. Amsterdam: Elsevier.

Kiedaisch, Christian. 2021. "Growth and Welfare Effects of Intellectual Property Rights When Consumers Differ in Income." *Economic Theory* 72: 1121–1170.

Kim, Yee Kyoung, Keun Lee, Walter G. Park, and Kineung Choo. 2012. "Appropriate Intellectual Property Protection and Economic Growth in Countries at Different Levels of Development." *Research Policy* 41: 358–375.

Krugman, Paul R. 1979. "A Model of Innovation, Technology Transfer, and the World Distribution of Income." *Journal of Political Economy* 87: 253–265.

Lai, Edwin L.-C. 1998. "International Intellectual Property Rights Protection and the Rate of Product Innovation." *Journal of Development Economics* 55: 133–153.

Levine, Ross, and David Renelt. 1992. "A Sensitivity Analysis of Cross-Country Growth Regressions." *American Economic Review* 82: 942–963.

Lundberg, Mattias, and Lyn Squire. 2003. "The Simultaneous Evolution of Growth and Inequality." *Economic Journal* 113: 326–344.

Markusen, James R. 2002. *Multinational Firms and the Theory of International Trade*. Cambridge, MA: MIT Press.

Maskus, Keith E. 2012. *Private Rights and Public Problems: The Global Economics of Intellectual Property in the 21st Century*. Washington, DC: Peterson Institute for International Economics.

2022. "The International IP System from an Economist's Perspective." In *Intellectual Property Ordering beyond Borders*, edited by Henning Gross Russe-Khan and Axel Metzger. Cambridge: Cambridge University Press.

Melitz, Marc J. 2003. "The Impact of Trade on Intra-Industry Reallocations and Aggregate Industry Productivity." *Econometrica* 71: 1695–1725.

Mendez, Rodrigue. 2002. "Creative Destruction and the Rise of Inequality." *Journal of Economic Growth* 7: 259–281.

Murphy, Kevin M., Andre Shleifer, and Robert Vishny. 1989. "Income Distribution, Market Size, and Industrialization." *Quarterly Journal of Economics* 104: 537–564.

Pan, Shiyuan, Tailong Li, and Heng-fu Zou. 2015. "Patent Protection, Technological Change, and Wage Inequality." China Economics and Management Academy Working Paper No. 537. https://ideas.repec.org/p/cuf/wpaper/537.html.

Park, Walter G. 2008. "Intellectual Property Rights and International Innovation." In *Intellectual Property, Growth and Trade*, edited by Keith E. Maskus. Amsterdam: Elsevier North-Holland.

Patel, Pari, and Modesto Vega. 1999. "Patterns of Internationalization of Corporate Technology: Location vs Home-Country Advantages." *Research Policy* 28: 145–155.

Pavcnik, Nina. 2002. "Trade Liberalization, Exit, and Productivity Improvement: Evidence from Chilean Plants." *Review of Economic Studies* 69: 245–276.

Persson, Torsten, and Guido Tabellini. 1994. "Is Inequality Harmful for Growth?" *American Economic Review* 84: 600–621.

Piketty, Thomas. 2014. *Capital in the 21st Century*. Cambridge, MA: Harvard University Press.

Radelet, Steven. 2015. *The Great Surge: The Ascent of the Developing World*. New York: Simon & Schuster.

Romer, Paul M. 1994. "The Origins of Endogenous Growth." *Journal of Economic Perspectives* 8: 3–22.

Saini, Swati, and Meeta K. Mehra. 2018. "The Impact of Strengthening the Intellectual Property Rights Regime on Income Inequality: An Econometric Analysis." *Economics Bulletin* 38: 1703–1719.

Shin, Wonkyu, Keun Lee, and Walter G. Park. 2016. "When an Importer's Protection of IPR Interacts with an Exporter's Level of Technology: Comparing the Impacts on the Exports of the North and South." *The World Economy* 39: 772–802.

Solt, Frederick. 2019. The Standardized World Income Inequality Database, Version 8, Harvard Dataverse. https://doi.org/10.7910/DVN/LM4OWF.

Stiglitz, Joseph E., and Andrew Charlton. 2005. *Fair Trade for All: How Trade Can Promote Development*. Oxford: Oxford University Press.

Vernon, Raymond. 1966. "International Investment and International Trade in the Product Cycle." *Quarterly Journal of Economics* 80: 190–207.

Weinhold, Diana, and Usha Nair-Reichert. 2009. "Innovation, Inequality, and Intellectual Property Rights." *World Development* 37: 889–901.

Williamson, Oliver E. 1985. *The Economic Institutions of Capitalism*. New York: Free Press.

Yang, Guifang, and Keith E. Maskus. 2001. "Intellectual Property Rights, Licensing, and Innovation in and Endogenous Product-Cycle Model." *Journal of International Economics* 53: 169–187.

APPENDIX

TABLE A1.1 *Countries in the Gini coefficient sample*

HI	UMI	LMI	LI
Australia	Argentina	Belarus	Armenia
Austria	Brazil	Bolivia	Bangladesh
Belgium	Chile	Bulgaria	Botswana
Canada	Croatia	China	Cote d'Ivoire
Cyprus	Czech Rep	Colombia	Gambia
Denmark	Greece	Costa Rica	Georgia
Finland	Hungary	Dom Rep	Ghana
France	Malaysia	Ecuador	Honduras
Germany	Mexico	Egypt	India
Hong Kong	Slovenia	El Salvador	Kenya
Iceland	South Africa	Estonia	Kyrgyzstan
Ireland	Uruguay	Guatemala	Malawi
Israel		Indonesia	Mauritania
Italy		Iran	Niger
Japan		Jamaica	Pakistan
Korea		Jordan	Rwanda
Luxembourg		Kazakhstan	Sri Lanka
Netherlands		Latvia	Tajikistan
New Zealand		Lithuania	Tanzania
Norway		Moldova	Uganda
Portugal		Morocco	Vietnam
Singapore		Panama	Zambia
Spain		Paraguay	
Sweden		Peru	
Switzerland		Philippines	
Taiwan		Poland	
UK		Romania	
USA		Russia	
		Slovakia	
		Thailand	
		Tonga	
		Tunisia	
		Turkey	
		Ukraine	
		Venezuela	

2

The Unequal Geographical Distribution of Innovative Activity

Implications for Income Inequality and Innovation Policies[*]

Carsten Fink, Ernest Miguelez, and Julio Raffo

INTRODUCTION

Innovation is at the core of economic development, growth, and structural change. This has been well demonstrated previously by scholars both theoretically and empirically (WIPO, 2015). Yet, it does not spur in nor flow to all corners of the world. Not all countries innovate at the same rate; within these, not all regions either. Not even in the most innovative countries is innovation equally distributed or seamlessly flows from national championing areas to the rest of the country.

To a great extent, such unequal innovation distribution mirrors the continuing wide differences in per capita incomes across and within different countries (Crescenzi et al., 2019). Indeed, many economists argue that differences in technology diffusion go a long way in explaining income differences (e.g., Comin and Mestieri, 2018). Worldwide rankings of innovation and income per capita are, however, not necessarily written in stone. Some Asian countries – and several regions within these – were able to achieve remarkable industrial development during the past forty years. Today these regions host companies that compete at the world's technology frontier.

How has this unequal distribution of innovation evolved across and within countries? Does innovation concentrate more than other economic activities? What are the consequences of this concentration for territorial income inequality?

[*] **Disclaimer:** The views expressed in this chapter are the authors' own and do not necessarily reflect the views of WIPO or its member states.

Acknowledgments: We are deeply grateful to Christian Chacua, Massiliano Coda-Zabetta, Francesco Lissoni, and Yin Deyun for our joint research on the topic of geography of innovation, which has contributed greatly to this chapter. We are also thankful for comments from the editors, as well as Kevin Lee and Francesco Lissoni. Ernest Miguelez acknowledges financial support from the French National Research Agency (TKC project – reference: ANR-17-CE26-0016).

Can policy actions do something about this? We aim to answer these questions using patent and publication data for more than forty years, and reviewing the relevant literature.

Understanding where most of innovation happens across and within countries is of foremost importance for innovation and intellectual property (IP) policymaking. Reviewing the successful technological trajectories and the less successful ones can be informative of the paths to follow. A natural question to ask is what role public policies can play in changing the technological trajectory of countries and regions. Given the many market failures associated with knowledge acquisition and knowledge diffusion, it is also pertinent to ponder what IP policy can do specifically.

This chapter is divided into two main sections. The first section reviews and describes empirically the uneven geographical distribution of innovation and its dynamics, at both the national and subnational levels. It also compares such distribution in relation to other indicators of economic activity. The second section examines the potential consequences of such unequal distribution, particularly for its possible influence on inter-regional income inequality, and discusses how inevitable they might be. In light of available evidence, it explores what the role of policy could be.

2.1 INNOVATION'S UNEVEN GEOGRAPHICAL DISTRIBUTION

During much of the past century, knowledge was produced mostly in a few wealthy countries, in particular the United States, Japan, and some Western European economies. What is often much less appreciated is how concentrated this phenomenon is, even within these wealthy nations.[1]

The academic literature has investigated several reasons behind such concentration. Many have to do with the virtuous cycle of national innovation systems (NIS) (Edquist, 1997) and, within these, the cycles of the local innovation ecosystems (Asheim and Gertler, 2005). Long and stable positive economic cycles explain how the best higher-education and research institutions appear and consolidate in certain regions of the world. The same applies to the private sector, where research- and technology-intensive companies flourish in such conditions. The reverse causality also applies: The liveliest NIS of today are more likely to spur innovation and consequent economic growth of tomorrow. For many reasons, these research and development (R&D) intensive companies will prefer to perform their research operations and collaborate with knowledge-intensive partners close to their headquarters (Castellacci and Archibugi, 2008; Chaminade et al., 2016; Patel and Pavitt, 1991). The two directions of causality can generate virtuous and vicious cycles, perpetuating the differences across economies.

[1] This section relies substantially on the research performed in Miguelez et al. (2019) and WIPO (2019). Please refer to them for further details.

National interactions are only part of the successful cycles, the other part being the interactions within the network of successful locations (Crescenzi et al., 2019; WIPO, 2019: ch. 1). It is often argued that the concentration of innovation production can be compensated with a spread of knowledge flows in all directions. Advocates of knowledge spillovers and knowledge as a public good would argue that knowledge diffuses from the innovation production center to the less innovative neighboring countries and regions. However, there is a known imperfect diffusion of knowledge, as information does not diffuse as freely or as fast everywhere, nor is the ability to fully exploit information flows – that is, the absorptive capacity – equally distributed around the world.[2] In this sense, the choice of knowledge connections is affected by the aforementioned virtuous cycles – that is, both economic and innovative – in each of the potential locations. The motivations for these connections can be of various nature: Multinational companies (MNCs) seek knowledge strategically (Castellani and Zanfei, 2006, 2007); supply and value chains reshape their structure globally (Bathelt et al., 2004; Dunning, 1998); decentralized interpersonal networks shine where there is professional talent (Lorenzen and Mudambi, 2013); and scientists, innovators, and entrepreneurs move where there are economic and innovation opportunities (Breschi et al., 2017; Franzoni et al., 2012; Saxenian, 2002, 2006). Chaminade et al. (2016) summarize these different interactions as global innovation networks (GINs) aiming to collectively produce and disseminate new knowledge.[3]

Undoubtedly, innovation eventually diffuses to less innovative regions and countries (Comin and Mestieri, 2018). But the rate at which innovation flows from and to a country might be very different depending on the country's position in the GINs. Successful companies in equally successful countries are also likely to increase their multinational activity overseas, but these countries may also attract other foreign companies. Indeed, it is not surprising that the majority of the MNCs have either spawned in the United States, Japan, or Western Europe or moved their headquarters there. Over the past century, these MNCs have increasingly operated in foreign countries and, lately, have increased their international R&D operations and the geographical diversity of their locations. Yet, many scholars argue that technology transfer to foreign economies – especially developing ones – is imperfect. Most of MNC's overseas R&D activities in developing economies before the turn of the

[2] In the spirit of Marshall (Ellison et al., 2010; Marshall, 1920), arguably the barriers to perfect knowledge diffusion relate to the cost of moving goods, people, and ideas that carry the knowledge in a physical, codified, or tacit manner. These costs can arise from not only economic forces but also national and international legal frameworks. Hence, the legal frameworks regulating the trade of goods and services, the mobility of workers, or the transfer of IP rights could have an impact on the rate of knowledge diffusion.

[3] The GINs framework covers several related approaches, such as Coe and Bunnell's (2003) "transnational innovation networks."

century were confined to market adaptation, with limited production of new knowledge (Gerybadze and Merk, 2014; Krishna et al., 2012).

Was this virtuous cycle unattainable for the rest of the world? The pattern over the past thirty years has shown us otherwise. The last part of the past century and the early years of the twenty-first century display several East Asian and other economies emerging as innovation hubs (Branstetter et al., 2014). Several factors explain this rise. MNCs increasingly redirect foreign investment to gain access to specialized knowledge (Amendolagine et al., 2019; Reddy, 1997). High-skilled professionals and talented entrepreneurs coming from these areas move and connect across the globe, building unprecedented international knowledge pipelines (Foley and Kerr, 2013; Saxenian, 2006; Useche et al., 2020). As a result, China, India, and some other economies have created over that period the environment not only to induce inward R&D activities by MNCs but also to spawn their own local stakeholders (Awate et al., 2012; Branstetter et al., 2014).[4] Analyzing the early technological developments of Chinese clusters, Zhou and Xin (2003) found that local firms in tech clusters benefit from collaborating with MNCs, which provides them with vital technology and organizational training, in turn vastly increasing their innovative capacity.

In the following paragraphs, we make use of patent and scientific publication data to describe empirically the patterns and trends portrayed in the innovation literature earlier. We use scientific publication data from Clarivate's Web of Science (WoS) and Science Citation Index Expanded (SCIE), and patent data from EPO's Patstat, World Intellectual Property Organization (WIPO), and other patent data sources.[5]

2.1.1 A *Slow Pattern of Knowledge Internationalization?*

For the past decades, only three economies – namely the United States, Japan, and Germany – accounted for the majority of scientific and technological (S&T) production (Figure 2.1). Within these two indicators, patents' concentration is always more geographically skewed than scientific articles. Simply adding France, Italy, Switzerland, and the United Kingdom increases the concentration of patents during the second half of the past century to roughly 90 percent.

[4] During this period, several of these economies benefited from less restrictive IP frameworks, making some scholars claim a causality. Yet, many other countries – from the same and other regions – also had equally less stringent national IP laws but did not observe the same innovation boom. We discussed elsewhere (Fink and Raffo, 2019) that "[i]n the end, similar to other hypothesized determinants of industrial development and growth, we are doubtful that there is an unambiguous effect of 'IP strength' waiting to be discovered. This is not only because of the varying role of different IP policies in different sectors, but also because IP policies interact with other elements of the broader innovation ecosystem." In Chapter 1 in this volume, Keith Maskus indicates a similar reservation about the potential causality between growth of inequality and IP rights.

[5] For more details on the sources and methodology, see Miguelez et al. (2019) and WIPO (2019: technical annex).

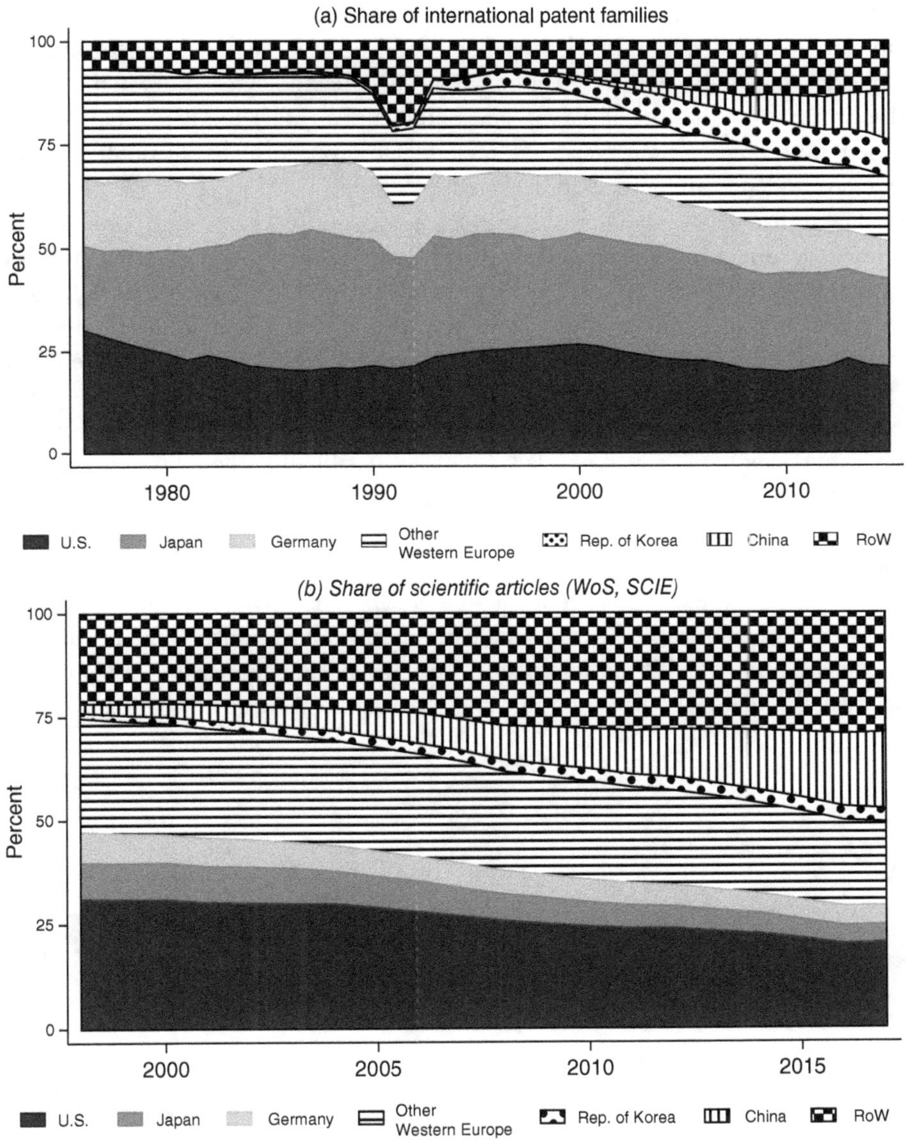

FIGURE 2.1 Evolution of (a) patenting and (b) scientific publication concentration by few economies

Source: Miguelez et al. (2019). Notes: RoW = Rest of the World. See WIPO (2019), technical notes (www.wipo.int/wipr).

These data also show that the distribution of new S&T outputs changed by the turn of the century. The growth of the Republic of Korea and China – but also the other economies grouped as a whole – has outperformed that of the United States, Japan, and Western European countries as a block. Outside of China and the

Republic of Korea, fastest innovation economies are also found in Asia. In particular, India, Iran, Israel, Singapore, and Turkey stand out. The geographical spread is more noticeable in scientific outputs than technological ones. In the rest of the world, Australia, Brazil, Egypt, and South Africa gather the lion's share of the scientific output in their respective regions. However, virtually all nontraditional regions evidence an increase in the scientific output share.

There has been, therefore, some spreading out of knowledge production. However, except for the Republic of Korea first and then China, the hierarchy of innovativeness (and income per capita) has not changed to a great extent (Kemeny, 2011), as high-income countries have managed to keep their positions through sustained innovation, and innovation of higher quality and complexity (Crescenzi et al., 2019). Moreover, the entry of these new players has not necessarily translated into a reduction of geographical concentration. Indeed, among other factors, the extremely rapid emergence of a few countries, notably the Republic of Korea and China, had recently resulted in a reconcentration phenomenon (see Figure 2.2).

By all quantitative accounts, the production of innovation remains more concentrated than other economic activities. At the country level, this is quite apparent. Figure 2.2 reports the country concentration index – Herfindahl–Hirschman Index – for a series of internationally comparable economic indicators over time. In addition to the scientific articles and international patents already discussed in the previous section, this figure also presents indicators for trade (total exports, U.S. dollars PPP),

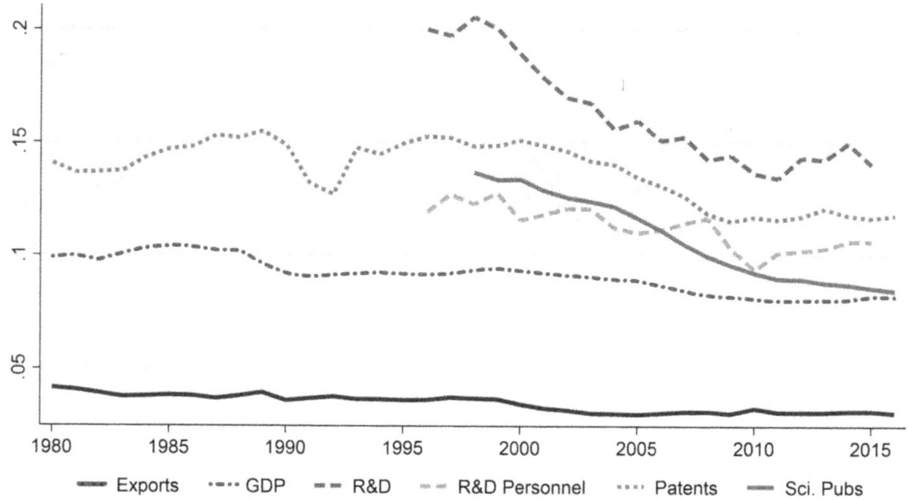

FIGURE 2.2 Innovation is more concentrated than other economic activities
Herfindahl–Hirschman index, selected innovation and economic indicators, 1980–2016.
Source: Authors based on PATSTAT, PCT, and Web of Science data. R&D and R&D personnel are retrieved from the UNESCO Institute for Statistics, while exports and GDP data from the World Development Indicators, the World Bank.

GDP (U.S. dollars PPP), R&D investments (GERD, U.S. dollars PPP), R&D personnel (FTE), and population.

These indicators suggest quite clearly that innovation-related activities are geographically more concentrated than economic ones, such as trade and GDP. The concentration of scientific articles has been declining close to the levels observed for the concentration of GDP. By contrast, R&D expenditures have observed an increase in concentration similar to that for patents since the mid-2000s. The fact that R&D investments are more concentrated than R&D personnel implicitly indicates that R&D budgets per researcher differ substantially across countries. Typically, R&D in richer countries is far more capital intensive, which translates into higher R&D labor productivity. This is in line with the differences in innovation output concentration and also their quality.[6]

What do the data tell us about S&T collaboration? The broad context is that the overall S&T collaboration – that is, local, national, and international altogether – is increasing. Within this increase in collaboration, the share of international scientific collaboration has also been steadily rising (WIPO, 2019). On the contrary, the share of international technological collaboration – as measured in international coinventions – exhibits a substantially lower and less stable pattern. Peaking at almost 11 percent in the 2000s, the share of international coinventorship came a long way from low single digits in the 1970s. Since the 2010s, however, the share of international coinventorship has plateaued and, lately, decreased – mostly explained by the declines in international coinventorship observed in the United States, China, France, and India.

Does knowledge flow globally? The majority of international S&T collaborations occur between and within the United States and Western Europe. The rest of the world is increasingly collaborating internationally, but when it does, it almost always selects a partner from the United States or Western Europe. Interestingly, both international S&T collaboration between other countries – that is, outside the United States and Western Europe – has been increasing for the last two decades but remains small in comparison. In the period 2011–2015, Western Europe gathered 49 percent and 41 percent of all international S&T collaboration, respectively. In the same period, the United States gathered 13 percent and 27 percent for the same indicators (WIPO, 2019). Nevertheless, over the years, the U.S. connections with China and India have become equally or more important than those between the United States and individual Western European countries. This is particularly the case for international coinventorships. Despite being quite advanced, established non-Western economies such as Japan, the Republic of Korea, and Australia, and emerging economies such as China, India, Singapore, and Brazil mostly collaborate

6 Indeed, more valuable patents and scientific outputs – as measured by citations – show Herfindahl-Hirschman Index values even higher than all the indicators reported in Figure 2.2 (see Miguelez et al., 2019).

with the United States and Western Europe. In sum, while collaboration in S&T has increased and, in turn, has contributed to knowledge diffusion – especially from more to less developed countries – it remains quite skewed, and the number of emerging countries entering the global network is still limited.

2.1.2 *Within Countries, Innovation Is Unevenly Localized in a Few Regions*

Be it in the traditional technologically leading countries, or the newly emerged ones, knowledge production does not take place in a spatial vacuum. The multiple sources of knowledge behind the invention, commercialization, and adoption of new products, processes, services, and social practices originate in specific locations within countries and diffuse unevenly across them.

In particular, as most economic activities, innovation benefits from economies of agglomeration (Crescenzi et al., 2019; WIPO, 2019: ch. 1). Scientists, technologists, entrepreneurs, students, and other actors seeking ideas, expertise, and education realize gains when they are colocated, as this increases the probability of recognizing opportunities and solving problems and of lowering all types of search costs. Innovation generated in large agglomerations tends to be of higher quality and more unconventional (Berkes and Gaetani, 2021). Firms, especially innovation-centered ones, are inevitably attracted to innovation clusters by the possibility to access a large and diverse supply of labor (especially labor markets for qualified workers) and of intermediate goods (especially knowledge-intensive ones) but also by the faster flow of ideas.[7] They also allow interacting and learning from peers, favoring localized knowledge spillovers (LKS) (Jaffe et al., 1993). Agglomerations are homes and hosts of multinational enterprises (MNEs) and the true beneficiaries of globalization, being centers of political influence, corporate decision-making and control, knowledge generation and exchange, skills, and jobs (Crescenzi et al., 2019; Feldman et al., 2021). Similarly, skilled workers, students, and entrepreneurs looking for jobs, knowledge, and business opportunities move to the same centers, giving rise to nonnegligible internal and international migration flows (Breschi et al., 2020). Thus, the typical innovative urban agglomeration relies heavily on the external knowledge flows channeled from the national system of innovation, the local MNC's headquarters or subsidiaries, the international science networks, and the

[7] Ellison et al. (2010) summarize Marshall's (1920) economies as "the cost of moving goods, people, and ideas that can be reduced by industrial agglomeration. … Firms … in Silicon Valley, locate near one another to learn and to speed their rate of innovation." According to Ellison and his coauthors' review, in industrial and high-density human-capital concentrations, workers learn skills quicker from each other and businesses exchange more information and benefit more from specialized networks, ultimately speeding up the flows of ideas within the cluster.

mobility of talented people and skilled workers (Bathelt et al., 2004; Lorenzen and Mudambi, 2013; Moreno and Miguélez, 2012).[8]

While both the economic and geography literatures stress the importance of agglomerations for innovative activities, their identification remains an open challenge. At the beginning of the past century, Alfred Marshall already discussed why industries agglomerate and defined the industries concentrating in Birmingham, Bedfordshire, Buckinghamshire, Manchester, or Sheffield as *districts* (Marshall, 1920). More recently, scholars have argued that innovation flourishes in dense urban areas, where knowledge spillovers can flow within and across industries (Glaeser et al., 1992; Jacobs, 1969; Porter, 2000). Indeed, several *Marshallian districts* can coexist and benefit each other in an innovative large metropolitan area. These global innovation hotspots spawn new ideas and technologies faster than other locations, thanks to the agglomeration of capital, skills, entrepreneurship, and the supporting scientific institutions (Engel, 2015; Engel and del-Palacio, 2009; WIPO, 2019: ch. 1). Porter (2000) defines as *clusters* the spatial units that concentrate geographically and thematically a whole series of private and public organizations – and the people therein – that compete and cooperate to achieve innovation. Other terminology ranges from "tech clusters" (when wishing to stress their peculiarities vis-à-vis industrial clusters; Kerr and Robert-Nicoud, 2020) to "innovation hubs" (where the emphasis is placed on cities and knowledge exchanges between them; Nijkamp and Kourtit, 2013) as well as "hotspots," which is more neutral and used interchangeably with the former two. Other approaches, instead, identify "global cities" based on their population and economic activity, and then move on to quantify the innovation they produce (Barca et al., 2012; Castellani, 2018).

Figure 12 by Miguelez et al. (2019) shows the global distribution of international patents and scientific articles by the smallest available administrative area within each country. We observe instantly in this figure that both S&T outputs are sternly skewed to a few locations in the world. Not surprisingly, these locations are mostly confined to the same regions we have been discussing earlier, namely the United States, Western Europe, and East Asia. Within the United States, the main cities on the two coasts – such as Boston, New York, and San Francisco – stand out. In East Asia, Beijing, Seoul, Shanghai, Shenzhen, and Tokyo are among the densest S&T agglomerations. Western Europe shows a more uniform geographical distribution,

[8] Despite the sizeable evidence on the benefits of tech clustering for innovation activities, research has also found that, under certain circumstances, locating out of clusters may bring benefits to innovative firms. Oakey and Cooper (1989) find that the peripheral location of high-technology firms can be driven by the benefits from high natural amenities. Suarez-Villa and Walrod (1997) find that, in the case of Los Angeles advanced electronic sectors, "non-clustered locations may have . . . become attractive alternatives to clusters for many firms, and particularly so with respect to R&D, where privacy is usually regarded as a major concern. Not locating in a cluster may have also been an advantage in its own right, as some firms sought to maintain some independence and secrecy for their R&D activities."

yet cities in France, Germany, Northern Italy, and the United Kingdom agglomerate more S&T outputs.

Yet, using administrative areas for worldwide analysis is problematic. Efforts to map innovation agglomerations, especially at the international level, should not rely on fixed spatial boundaries, such as administrative or political units (Carlino and Kerr, 2015). This practice suffers from both a "modifiable area unit problem" (the unit size may vary across countries, thus making quantitative comparisons impossible) and a "border effect" problem (the unit boundaries may either cut across a cross-border agglomeration or – in case of large units – include two distinct agglomerations).[9] In this chapter, we will adopt the term "innovation-dense areas," which will be proxied by the spatial boundaries computed in Miguelez et al. (2019) and WIPO (2019). In a nutshell, based on the coordinates assigned to each patent and publication (based on inventors' and scientists' addresses), the authors apply a clustering algorithm to identify a multitude of agglomerations worldwide. These are separately identified as "global innovation hotspots" (GIHs) and "niche clusters" (NCs), though for simplicity we analyze them together under the label *innovation-dense areas*.

According to WIPO (2019), the United States hosts most of the main innovation-dense areas of the world (25 percent of all), followed by Germany (12.9 percent), Japan (9.4 percent), China (6.8 percent), the United Kingdom (4.9 percent), and France (4.3 percent).[10] By continent, Europe concentrates 40.5 percent of the most innovation-dense areas, followed by North America (28 percent), Asia (25 percent), Latin America (2.9 percent), Oceania (2.7 percent), and Africa (1 percent).

Figure 2.3 depicts the share of patents and publications produced in the innovation-dense areas of the United States, Japan, Germany, the United Kingdom, the Republic of Korea, China, India, and Brazil, and the population residing in these countries. Several patterns arise from analyzing the innovation-dense areas of these countries. First, in all cases, they account for a disproportionate amount of the S&T output with respect to population. Clearly, in all countries shown here, science and innovation are substantially more concentrated than

[9] In Krugman's (1991: 483) words,

> one of the most remarkable things about the United States is that in a generally sparsely populated country, much of whose land is fertile, the bulk of the population resides in a few clusters of metropolitan areas; a quarter of the inhabitants are crowded into a not especially inviting section of the East Coast. It has often been noted that nighttime satellite photos of Europe reveal little of political boundaries but clearly suggest a center-periphery pattern whose hub is somewhere in or near Belgium.

Indeed, many clusters fall in the definition of *transnational innovation systems*, particularly in Europe (Chaminade and Nielsen, 2011).

[10] For all the quantitative discussion in this section, we use WIPO's (2019) definition of the 487 most innovation-dense areas of the world (GIHs and NCs), which are the densest agglomeration of innovation activities as measured by scientific publications and international patent families by km². Most of the statistics discussed would show little variation with other definitions, and much less differences on the substance discussed.

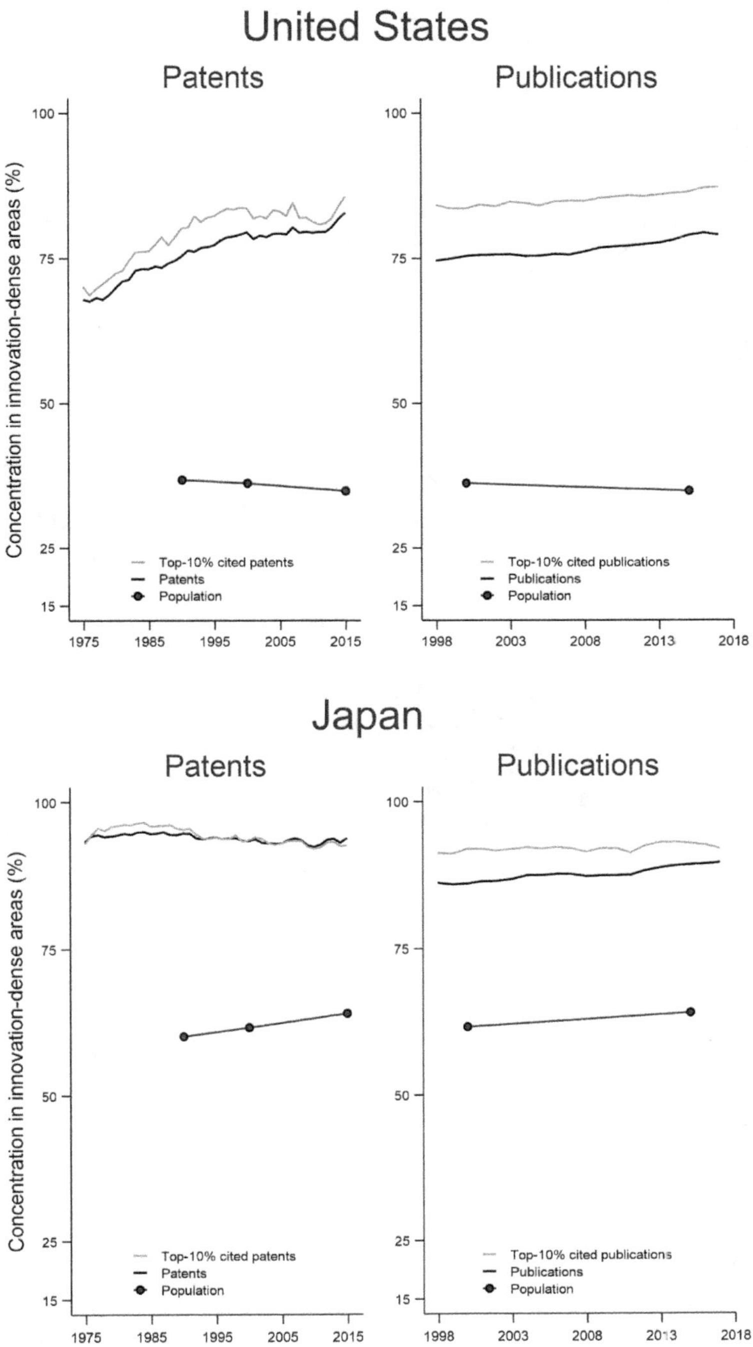

FIGURE 2.3 Share of patenting and scientific publishing in innovation-dense areas, by selected countries

Note: largest innovation-dense areas follow WIPO (2019), www.wipo.int/wipr.

Source: Miguelez et al. (2019).

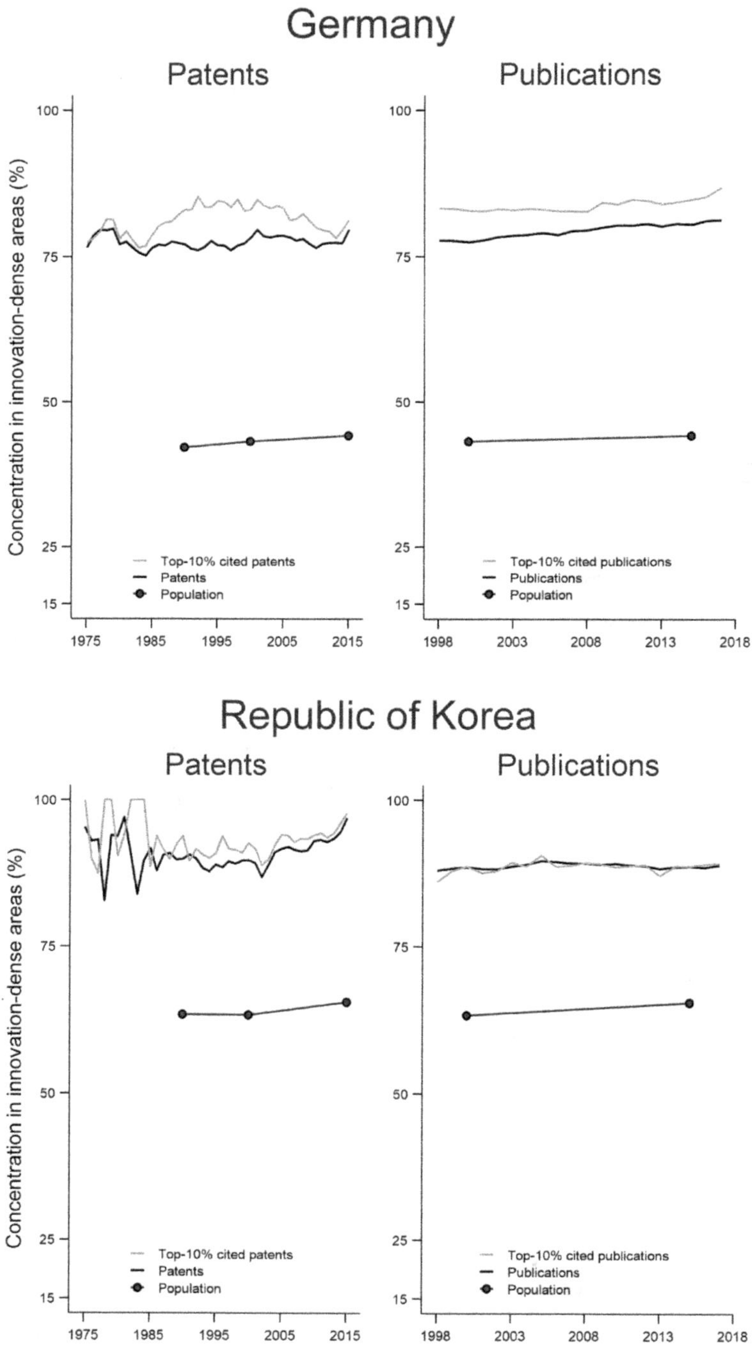

FIGURE 2.3 *(cont.)*

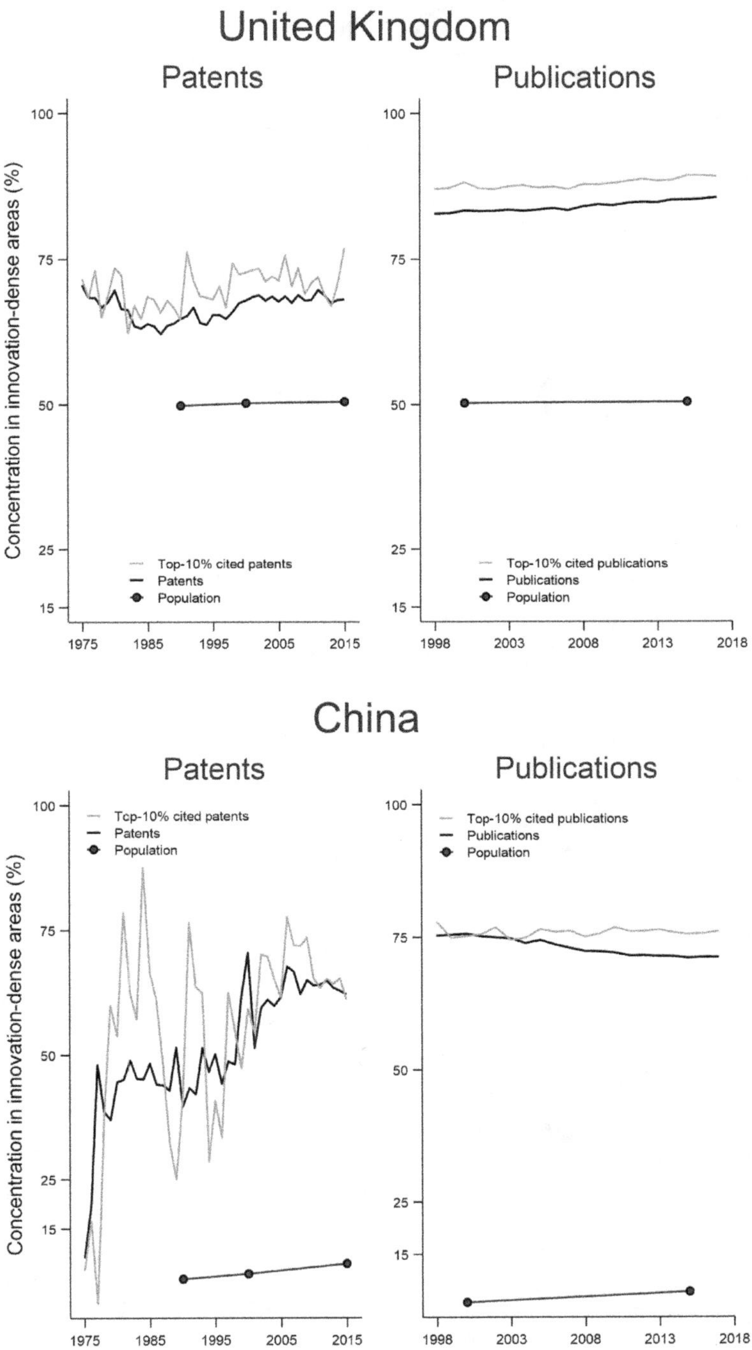

FIGURE 2.3 *(cont.)*

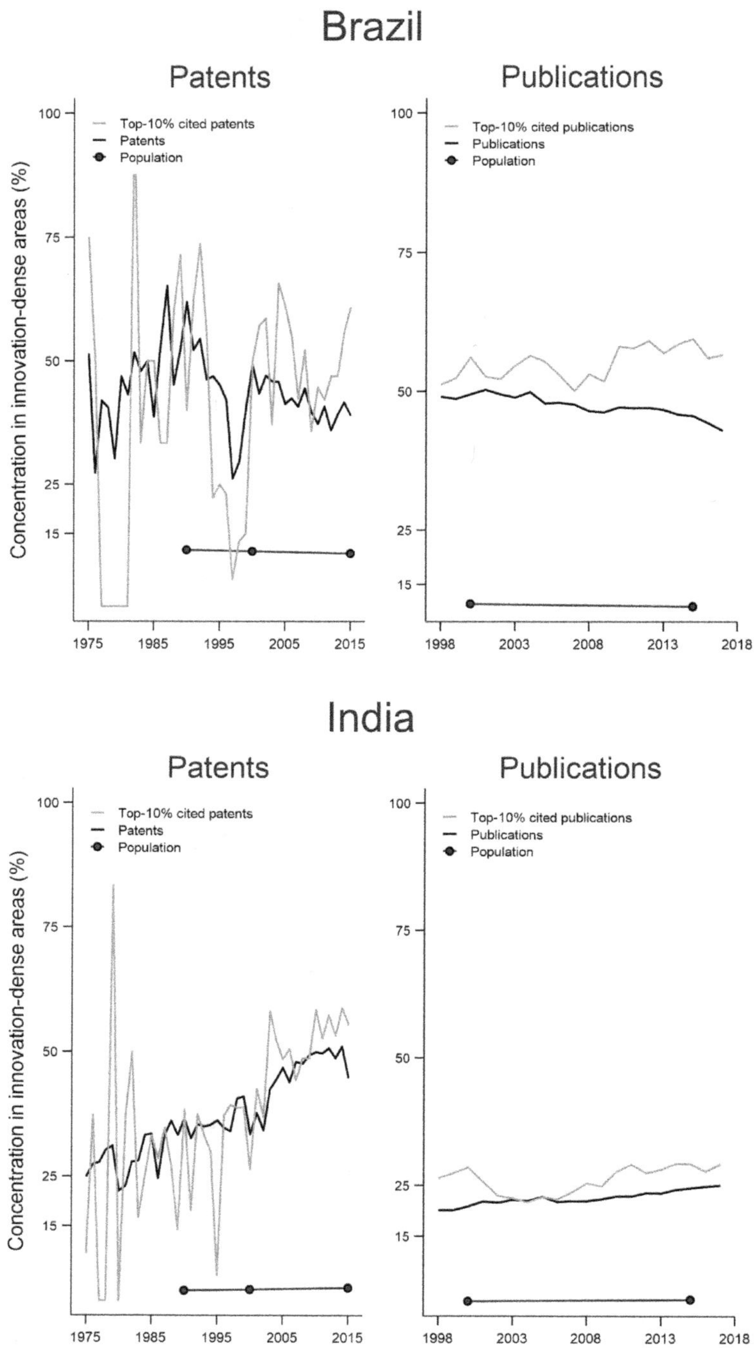

FIGURE 2.3 *(cont.)*

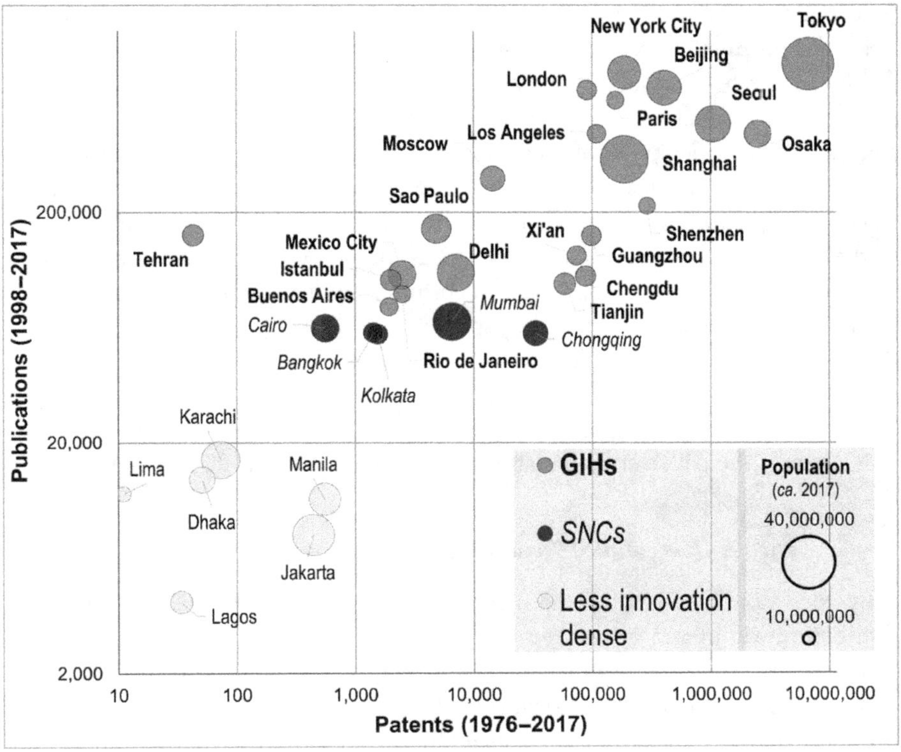

FIGURE 2.4 Population density does not ensure high innovation density
Patents and scientific articles in the top thirty-five largest cities, 1980–2016.
Source: WIPO (2019) based on PATSTAT, PCT, and Web of Science data, and top cities from The City Mayors Foundation (September 2019). Notes: Size of bubble refers to the metropolitan area population (circa 2017). Axis in logarithmic scale. Due to low scientific publication or patent values, Kinshasa and Shijiazhuang are omitted from the chart area.

population, indicating that concentration of population only partially explains the geographical concentration of innovation. Second, the most valuable S&T output – as proxied by the top ten cited patents and publications – is typically more concentrated than the rest. Third, in general, the concentration trends are stable over time. However, we observe some increases in subnational concentration in Figure 2.3. Such increases are found more often in patents than scientific articles.

Yet, while innovation tends to concentrate in large metropolitan areas, not all urban agglomerations concentrate on the equivalent level of innovation-related activities. Figure 2.4 displays the top thirty-five most-populated metropolitan areas in the world and their S&T outputs. Only twenty-two cities out of these are innovation-dense areas. The top-right quadrant shows that Beijing, London, Los Angeles, New York, Osaka, Paris, Seoul, and Tokyo concentrate a large amount of both patents and scientific publishing. In comparison, Shanghai is only less populated than Tokyo but has fewer patents and scientific publications than all of them.

A second-tier group of innovation-dense areas include the metropolitan areas of cities such as Buenos Aires, Delhi, Istanbul, Mexico City, Moscow, São Paulo, and Tehran. Despite their large populations, they concentrate much fewer scientific publications and patents. Other densely populated cities such as Cairo, Bangkok, Kolkata, and Chongqing have only enough innovation density in some specialized scientific or technological fields. Last, in the bottom-left quadrant, Dhaka, Jakarta, Karachi, Lagos, Lima, and Manila do not have an innovation density corresponding to their highly populated metropolitan areas, despite concentrating most of their respective national S&T output. As noted, innovation is even more concentrated than general economic activity and population.

Nevertheless, the lack of innovation-dense output in otherwise economically dense agglomerations is not exclusive to less developed economies. Even within high-income countries, the agglomeration of innovation activities seems to follow only partially the pattern of population and economic activity agglomeration.

2.1.3 A *Concentrated Network of a Few* Innovation-Dense Areas

Why does more collaboration not necessarily lead to less inequality in innovation distribution within and across countries?

The rising concentration of science and innovation production in innovation-dense areas, and the parallel global spreading out of innovation and international team formation, characterizes a globalized hub-to-hub system, which links national and regional systems of innovation and global firms through a spiky geography of knowledge creation (Crescenzi et al., 2019). Many of these hubs are better connected to one another than to their neighboring areas inside their countries. The collaborative scientific communities, the talented migrants, the supply chains, and the knowledge-seeking MNCs give rise to global innovation-dense "hotspots" around the world. The successful regions discussed earlier cannot rely uniquely on the local innovation ecosystem they form – whether private companies, higher-education or research institutions, etc. – but they build national and international links to complementary pools of knowledge abroad (Awate and Mudambi, 2017; Bathelt et al., 2004; Lorenzen and Mudambi, 2013; Turkina and Van Assche, 2018).

Figure 17 by Miguelez et al. (2019) depicts the global network of highly connected innovation-dense areas. As expected, this network is denser within and between a few agglomerations in the United States, the United Kingdom, Germany, France, Japan, the Republic of Korea, China, and India. The United States, Germany, Japan, and the Republic of Korea also show thick national networks.

Even in these countries hosting most of the world's innovation output, we observe that just a few innovation-dense areas concentrate most of the international connections. A handful of cities, mostly on the two coasts of the United States, account for much of the U.S. international coinventorship. Similarly, Western European innovation agglomerations connect mostly nationally to Paris, London, Frankfurt, and

Berlin. Figuratively, these European innovation hubs mediate most of the other European international connections, as if they are Europe's international "gatekeepers." The same pattern happens in Asia, where Tokyo, Seoul, Beijing, Shanghai, Mumbai, and Bengaluru are the key gateways for international coinventions. The same analysis for scientific outputs would cast a much denser network but with an equivalent underlying pattern of concentration of international ties in a few hubs. In sum, S&T outputs are more likely to connect international partners if produced within these already concentrated innovation hotspots. The bias is even more apparent when focusing on the most valuable S&T output (Miguelez et al., 2019).

As a result, these global networks favor a few innovation-dense areas that concentrate the knowledge flows. This is a double-edged sword: While these areas spread knowledge, they do so mostly among themselves. The resulting GINs, in turn, cement the innovation "hotspot" advantages.

2.2 CONSEQUENCES OF THE UNEQUAL INNOVATION DISTRIBUTION AND POSSIBLE POLICY ACTIONS

We have just shown that the global production of innovation is extremely concentrated in a few areas of the world. Moreover, it is even more concentrated than other economic activities. Does this concentration pose a problem? What does it mean for economic and innovation policymaking? We attempt to answer these questions in three parts. First, we rely on the economic geography literature to explore in which ways this unequal distribution of innovative activity relates to one of the biggest challenges of present times, namely growing income inequality (Piketty and Saez, 2003). In particular, we will focus our attention on the relationship between innovation concentration and territorial income inequality. Second, we discuss if this unequal distribution of innovation (and income) across and within countries is inevitable. Last, we conclude by revisiting the role of policy in the light of our discussion.

2.2.1 *Does the Unequal Distribution of Innovative Activity Really Matter?*

Despite the global spread of knowledge production and the emergence of new local innovation giants (in both developed and developing countries), there remain high levels of within (and between) country concentration of innovation. Before diving into the role of policy, it is pertinent to ask if this is a problem that policy has to address.

In a simplified economic view, innovation and the knowledge to produce it have the characteristics of a public good (Arrow, 1962). Many individuals, firms, and regions can use at the same time the knowledge produced by others somewhere else, without rivaling the use by the originators. Indeed, artificial intelligence emerged from a limited number of scientific organizations in a few regions of the world, and today a large number of companies and individuals employ the underlying science for a wide variety of innovative applications around the world. A similar point can be made for mobile communications technology, which has flown to remote corners of the world.

In this sense, if innovation were a pure global public good, it would not necessarily matter where innovative activity takes place. In such a scenario, innovation would flow without attrition benefiting all regions equally. Moreover, there would be strong arguments in favor of agglomerating resources in a few regions to benefit from economies of scale, which will eventually flow to all regions in the world. The "new economic geography" (NEG) school of thought made a strong case that geographical concentration of economic activities is inevitable and even desirable. Regional concentration happens in an iterative manner, where regions progressively attract productive companies and skilled labor, which in turn makes them more attractive for new companies and workers to join the same region. The key to this school of thought is that circumstantial regional advantages in productivity can trigger divergent geographical concentration paths. This simple mechanism can explain how agglomerations emerge but also how existing ones can strengthen their position to the detriment of the outer regions (Krugman, 1991). In this scenario, mainstream theories predict that processes of inter-regional labor mobility, knowledge diffusion, and trickle-down effects will occur, and income convergence will follow. Thus, policy intervention to favor disadvantaged areas is not necessary (World Bank, 2009). This theoretical framework, implicitly, concerns innovation activities. too. While NEG early proponents dismissed high-tech sectors as a particular case, empirical evidence largely found that concentration is particularly salient in knowledge- and innovation-based economic activities (Audretsch and Feldman, 1996), which was largely attributed to the importance of LKS as a localization force (Jaffe et al., 1993; Krugman, 2010).

But several recent economic studies suggest that converging mechanisms might not be working as predicted (Hope and Limberg, 2022; Iammarino et al., 2019). If the benefits of successful innovations depend on the location of innovation, patterns of agglomeration have a direct effect on spatial economic development outcomes, and while the concentration of innovation in a few places may benefit the worldwide rate of innovation, it also hinders the innovative prospects of other areas.

If innovation is indeed "sticky," it is not a pure public good.[11] Why might this be the case? Beyond market size and talent availability, there are notable positive agglomeration externalities arising from knowledge spillovers (Jaffe et al., 1993; Krugman, 2010). The tacit nature of knowledge makes the colocation of innovative

[11] Exclusive IP rights may also erode the notion of innovation as a pure public good. However, IP rights do not turn knowledge into an eternal private good. They are territorial in nature and time bound; most patents, in particular, are only registered in selected high-income economies, and they only last for a maximum of twenty years. Even while they are protected, patents can be licensed, thus enabling knowledge adoption by others. Finally, the patent system offers incentives for knowledge disclosure, which ultimately promotes dissemination. The full effectiveness of IP as means of diffusion is still argued in the innovation economic literature, yet several studies have found evidence of patents being an effective source of knowledge. See, among others, Cohen et al. (2002), Denicolò and Franzoni (2003), Graham et al. (2009), Jaffe et al. (2000), and Moser (2011).

firms, academic centers, and talented human resources a more effective environment for these externalities to arise (Crescenzi et al., 2019; WIPO, 2019: ch. 1). Information may flow relatively free over the geographical space, but knowledge flows are far less fluid. Trade flows, for instance, may help diffuse routinized and codified information, but knowledge that is not economically ubiquitous generates innovative rents to specific geographical locations (Feldman et al., 2021). When the codification of knowledge is difficult – that is, knowledge is more tacit – organizations and, especially, individuals have to physically move with the knowledge embedded in themselves to realize these knowledge flows. Movement of and interactions between individuals and organizations are invariably easier in close proximity. Global networks, such as GINs, while allegedly a mechanism of knowledge diffusion, end up reinforcing concentration effects, as different types of workers are differently exposed to offshoring and outsourcing (Autor and Handel, 2013; Gagliardi et al., 2021). A similar pattern holds for highly skilled migrants holding science and technology jobs, who tend to concentrate in innovative cities (Coda-Zabetta et al., 2022).

As a consequence of the above, some scholars argue that the uneven distribution of science and technology, as well as skilled labor, has translated into rising levels of income inequality (Iammarino et al., 2019). This phenomenon occurs both inside highly innovative superstar cities, and between them and the rest of the country – the "Left Behind Regions" (Rodríguez-Pose, 2018). Starting in many developed countries from around 1980, this process of economic divergence is known as "the great inversion" (Crescenzi et al., 2019; Florida, 2017; Kemeny and Storper, 2020). Moreover, superstar cities and innovation-dense areas tend to host highly skilled, nonroutinized employment but also attract low-skilled, nonroutinized jobs. In such a scenario, inter-regional migration does not occur, either because of high housing costs in superstar cities, unaffordable for medium- and low-skilled workers, or simply because "skill requirements in these superstar cities tend to be both high and specific" (Kemeny and Storper, 2020: 27). Meanwhile, this technological change also reduces employment in many previously dominant manufacturing sectors through automation (Iammarino et al., 2019).

Another related trend is growing evidence of falling R&D productivity. Recent empirical studies indicate that current technological progress is requiring increasingly more innovation investments (Bloom et al., 2020). This is apparent in the information and communication technology (ICT) industries, for example, where continuously achieving Moore's law – that is, doubling the number of transistors on a computer chip every two years – requires eighteen times more researchers than it did in the early 1970s. Other industries evidence a similar pattern: Increases in life expectancy or crop yields require much more investments in medical or agricultural R&D. The innovation frontier problems to be solved seem to be increasingly complex and, thus, requiring increasingly larger research teams and specialization (Hidalgo, 2021; WIPO, 2019: ch. 2). These R&D productivity trends have subsequent negative effects on overall productivity. Some economic scholars have indeed argued that current innovations boost economic productivity to a much smaller extent than the innovations associated with the Second Industrial Revolution (Gordon, 2018).

How does falling R&D productivity relate to geographical inequality? Falling R&D productivity makes a strong case for pooling resources to optimize the local knowledge spillovers. It might be socially desirable to concentrate innovation resources in a few hotspots in the world, but this may generate, again, a whole set of regional imbalances to be sorted out by policymakers. Regardless of which region or country emerges as the concentration champion, any resulting concentration implies a transition period during which large transfers of resources – including human capital – from noninnovation-dense areas occur. These transitions are usually – if not always – socially costly. There are also within-region imbalances. A side effect of innovation agglomeration is the centrifugal forces pushing less innovative firms and unskilled labor to the periphery of the innovation-dense areas. This is unquestionably one of the causes behind the rising housing prices and widening income disparities in Silicon Valley and more recently in Tel Aviv (Srivastava, 2018).

2.2.2 *Can Diverging Innovation Paths in Economies and Regions Be Changed? Lessons from Asia*

We discussed in the previous sections how the geographical concentration of innovation can be instrumental for both regional and economy-wide development outcomes. We also pointed to the social costs associated with such concentration, mainly in terms of not all countries benefiting from the spread of the knowledge economy, and inter-regional income inequality rising even in highly innovative economies. We now turn to evidence on past geographical trends and discuss if and how policy may have played a role.

The global spread of knowledge production documented earlier, the existence of GINs, and the international flows of knowledge were probably necessary but not sufficient conditions for countries to successfully ignite economic development through technological change. Indeed, national innovation strategies and policies played a critical role in making this happen (Crescenzi et al., 2019). The most successful examples of technological catch-up are found in Asia. The spread of knowledge production and global networks toward these countries has coincided with the emergence of strong NIS in them. In turn, public R&D spending and public incentives to private spending, among other things, may have played a role in the development of these NIS (Archibugi and Filippetti, 2018).

In what follows, we first focus on GDP and innovation concentration across countries, where more evidence and policy discussion have consistently emerged.

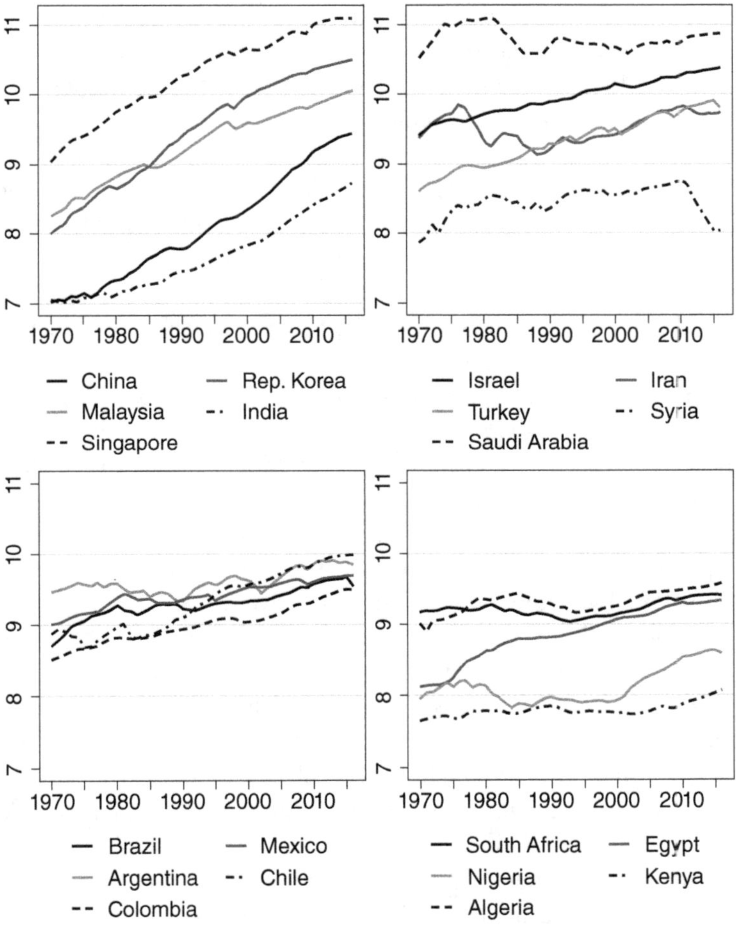

FIGURE 2.5 Diverging growth paths
Real GDP per capita in 2011US$ (logs), selected economies
Sources: Maddison Project Database, version 2018. Bolt et al. (2018)

In terms of overall development, there is still considerable variation in GDP per capita levels and growth across countries and within regions of the world. Asia as a region has the highest income per capita outside the Western world. Latin America, Africa, and, to some extent, the Middle East observe a less remarkable evolution (Figure 2.5).

More recently, the evolution in GDP per capita has correlated with the increase in S&T outputs. Since the 2000s, Asia has increased its share of total patenting from 32 percent to 48 percent and its share of total scientific publishing from 17 percent to 36 percent. This reflects the rise of China and the Republic of Korea and comes despite the relative decline of Japan's share of patents and publications.

Furthermore, considering their low starting point, most selected Asian economies have seen a remarkable increase in their share of S&T outputs in a few decades (Table 2.1). Within these economies, Turkey, Israel, India, Singapore, and Iran stand out as the largest innovating economies.

However, this does not mean that all cities from successful East Asian economies have followed the same pattern. Table 2.2 looks at the top three innovation-dense areas for selected countries in two different periods and the share of patenting and scientific publication they account for in their respective countries. First, the list of top innovation-dense areas per country barely differs in time and between patents and scientific publications, showing the stability of the concentration phenomenon. Second, in all countries shown, the share of the top three is quite high, ranging from around 20 percent up to more than 100 percent.[12] With the exception of Chinese and Indian patenting, the share of the top three patenting and publishing hotspots decreases over time, showing that, within countries, S&T activities seem to be spreading geographically. However, overall, the concentration of S&T output remains relatively high. China and India also show some dispersion trends in scientific publications, but their top three hotspots still hold about a quarter and a third of all national scientific publications, respectively.

Did national and regional policies play a role in such divergent economic performance? At the national level, economic scholars are still quite divided. There is not even full consensus on the source of the divergent paths. Development economists enumerate, among the possible sources of diverging economic performance, insufficient capital accumulation (Young, 1995, 2000a,2000b), a distorted size of the natural resource sector (Sachs and Warner, 1995), and declining terms of trade for low value-added goods (Prebisch, 1962). Alternative theories give more prominence to the role of institutions in economic growth (North, 1990) and their capacity to absorb new technologies (Nelson and Pack, 1999).

Historically, several policies to solve a suspected *natural resource disadvantage* and *declining terms of trade* have been suggested, mostly based on import substitution and state-led industrialization (e.g., Prebisch, 1962; Singer, 1950). They coincided with high sustained returns to capital investment in Asia, with the capacity of absorbing new technologies playing a crucial role (Nelson and Park, 1999), which in turn set the grounds for rapid capital accumulation. As a synthesis, institutional characteristics related to innovation such as education, R&D, S&T infrastructure, and science–industry linkages can go a long way in explaining why some Asian economies outperformed the rest of the developing world (Freeman, 1995).

[12] Singapore innovation agglomeration exceeds the national boundaries.

TABLE 2.1 *Evolution of patenting and scientific publishing, by selected countries*

	Patents							Publications			
Country	1970–1979	1980–1989	1990–1999	2000–2004	2005–2009	2010–2014	2015–2017	2000–2004	2005–2009	2010–2014	2015–2017
China	0.007%	0.064%	0.275%	1.313%	4.043%	8.164%	13.671%	2.446%	4.370%	7.848%	12.011%
Rep. of Korea	0.014%	0.308%	2.579%	5.212%	7.562%	8.506%	8.368%	1.389%	2.003%	2.679%	3.157%
Malaysia	0.005%	0.007%	0.027%	0.078%	0.148%	0.169%	0.115%	0.076%	0.092%	0.181%	0.435%
India	0.031%	0.034%	0.114%	0.533%	0.997%	1.358%	1.334%	1.942%	2.033%	2.635%	3.164%
Singapore	0.005%	0.015%	0.118%	0.308%	0.358%	0.372%	0.343%	0.302%	0.428%	0.474%	0.495%
Israel	0.239%	0.312%	0.576%	0.931%	1.148%	1.083%	1.047%	0.930%	0.908%	0.763%	0.615%
Iran	0.006%	0.003%	0.005%	0.007%	0.017%	0.023%	0.053%	0.116%	0.258%	0.817%	1.555%
Turkey	0.003%	0.005%	0.017%	0.064%	0.168%	0.262%	0.363%	0.587%	0.979%	1.544%	1.671%
Syria	0.001%	0.001%	0.002%	0.002%	0.002%	0.002%	0.001%	0.009%	0.010%	0.011%	0.014%
Saudi Arabia	0.003%	0.007%	0.009%	0.014%	0.031%	0.103%	0.166%	0.165%	0.137%	0.122%	0.305%
Brazil	0.067%	0.093%	0.122%	0.169%	0.245%	0.281%	0.271%	1.110%	1.454%	1.963%	2.325%
Mexico	0.077%	0.048%	0.063%	0.091%	0.107%	0.123%	0.149%	0.442%	0.514%	0.576%	0.593%
Argentina	0.050%	0.042%	0.057%	0.059%	0.056%	0.041%	0.038%	0.461%	0.475%	0.433%	0.456%
Chile	0.006%	0.006%	0.011%	0.018%	0.033%	0.056%	0.053%	0.170%	0.196%	0.221%	0.254%
Colombia	0.007%	0.006%	0.008%	0.015%	0.021%	0.032%	0.038%	0.042%	0.053%	0.091%	0.141%
South Africa	0.224%	0.196%	0.195%	0.211%	0.167%	0.131%	0.098%	0.375%	0.329%	0.351%	0.404%
Egypt	0.002%	0.003%	0.005%	0.013%	0.026%	0.026%	0.021%	0.245%	0.266%	0.294%	0.395%
Nigeria	0.001%	0.001%	0.001%	0.002%	0.002%	0.003%	0.002%	0.081%	0.072%	0.131%	0.128%
Kenya	0.002%	0.001%	0.002%	0.004%	0.003%	0.005%	0.004%	0.040%	0.033%	0.038%	0.043%
Algeria	0.000%	0.001%	0.001%	0.003%	0.003%	0.003%	0.003%	0.029%	0.043%	0.078%	0.105%

Source: Miguelez et al. (2019).

TABLE 2.2 *Top innovation-dense Asian agglomerations and national concentration of S&T outputs, 1991–1995 and 2011–2015, selected economies*

	Patents				Publications			
Country	1991–1995	%	2011–2015	%	2001–2005	%	2011–2015	%
China	Shenzhen-Hong Kong Beijing Shanghai	48.5	Shenzhen-Hong Kong Beijing Shanghai	51.0	Beijing Shanghai Nanjing	43.9	Beijing Shanghai Nanjing	35.8
India	Bengaluru Mumbai Delhi	41.5	Bengaluru Hyderabad Delhi	46.2	Delhi Mumbai Bengaluru	27.7	Delhi Mumbai Kolkata	24.6
Iran	ND	ND	ND	ND	Tehran	57.6	Tehran	46.1
Israel	Tel Aviv Haifa Jerusalem	85.6	Tel Aviv Haifa Jerusalem	82.3	Tel Aviv Jerusalem Haifa	86.4	Tel Aviv Haifa Jerusalem	86.1
Rep. of Korea	Seoul Daejeon Icheon-si	75.8	Seoul Daejeon Beolgyo	70.3	Seoul Daejeon Busan	71.3	Seoul Daejeon Busan	69.9
Malaysia	Kuala Lumpur	61.5	Kuala Lumpur	58.0	Kuala Lumpur	51.4	Kuala Lumpur	59.4
Saudi Arabia	Dammam	42.4	Dammam	38.8	Dammam	21.0	Dammam	7.8
Singapore	Singapore	100.8	Singapore	100.3	Singapore	100.0	Singapore	100.0
Turkey	Istanbul Ankara	59.1	Istanbul Ankara	38.8	Ankara Istanbul	46.5	Ankara Istanbul	42.8

Source: Miguelez et al. (2019).
Notes: Up to three top innovation-dense agglomerations displayed per country, in case of more than one found by the algorithm. Some agglomerations may exceed the national borders (e.g., Singapore). "ND" = No data available.

2.2.3 *What Is the Role for Policy?*

In the context of an uneven geographical distribution of innovation, the relevant question for policymakers is what type of policies can stimulate the institutional environment that better attracts external innovation – that is, technological absorption – and, in turn, better generates new technologies. Traditionally, this question was often simplified as to either favor market liberalizing policies or government interventionist ones.[13]

When it comes to dealing with the unequal distribution of innovation and income, in both developed and developing countries, a similar trade-off arises between efficiency and equity (Iammarino et al., 2019). Efficiency reasons may suggest allowing market forces to generate as many agglomerations as possible, which might be the most efficient for the whole economy, with spatial equity occurring through a trickle-down process – for example, through labor mobility (Glaeser, 2011; World Bank, 2009). Equity concerns may call for greater intervention to directly achieve some redistribution, even at the expense of damaging national champions and overall economic growth. The chosen approach to solving problems of between- and within-country income inequality may determine the chosen type of policies, too: spatially blind policies versus spatially based ones. Again, the former advocates for policies that apply to all locations, without accounting for space and the local context (e.g., regulations ensuring market efficiency), as spatially targeted approaches may deter growth coming from agglomerations (mostly represented by the World Bank's (2009) report, focused on developing countries). The latter prefers policies highly contingent on context, rooted in the local community and local stakeholders (Barca et al., 2012). One approach is based on the need for full-fledged market forces to let Schumpeter's creative destruction of firms and sectors to take place. The other bases its logic on the existence of negative externalities hampering the development of such innovative capacity, which only government policy can overcome. Both underlying economic theories are sound, but the practical policy setups can easily differ.

Arguably, any past policy successes in boosting national technological capacity might not be as relevant in the current context. As innovation is increasingly fragmented in innovation-dense metropolitan areas, which astonishingly are more globally interconnected, a different policy toolbox may be necessary. Likewise, the increasing international interconnectivity of innovation hotspots is also the result of national and multilateral policies promoting openness and international cooperation. The institutional setup favoring openness and cooperation should not be taken for granted, as recently public perception has become more skeptical of the benefits of openness (WIPO, 2019: ch. 5).

[13] World Bank (1993) and Amsden (1994) are samples of these rivaling perspectives.

Any reduced openness of innovation ecosystems will likely affect the rate of knowledge diffusion. Knowledge may not flow across borders as much if researchers cannot move around the world or access scientific journals and patent documents published elsewhere. Limitations to international trade can also impact innovation openness, as a substantial part of technological flows happens through imported parts and components.

However, there are also limits to how widely knowledge can be shared. In fact, we have discussed in Section 2.1 how concentrated the production of new S&T knowledge is within and across countries. Still there are mutual gains for openness, if outward knowledge flows increase economic benefits abroad without reducing the local use. But several opinions perceive innovation as a zero-sum game, where breakthrough innovation can provide a competitive advantage to regions or countries. In the long run, this perspective has little base, as both winning and losing economies will find new equilibria where they are better off. Nevertheless, there are extreme scenarios where such "zero-sum" outcomes could happen (Grossman and Helpman, 1991).

In the short run, things might be different. As discussed earlier, regional differences in productivity and innovativeness can lead to divergent paths of geographical distribution within countries of incomes, technology production, high-skilled employment, and wages. Regional competitive advantages can have profound negative effects for some regions in the short run, as it takes time to reconvert human capital to new industrial needs. Indeed, in the United States, as mentioned earlier, regional divergence started to accelerate in the 1980s and 1990s, after decades of postwar convergence (Ganong and Shoag, 2017). The same applies to the European context since the great recession in 2008 (Alcidi et al., 2018). Moreover, such inequality is also likely to sprout within successful regions. Vibrant innovation hotspots may produce spiked salaries of highly skilled workers, putting upward pressure on local prices, especially for housing, and directly affecting the disposable income of low-skilled workers (see WIPO, 2019: chs. 1 and 5).

How to address such rising regional imbalances is probably one of the most challenging questions that regional policymakers face in current times. Counterweighing the agglomeration forces of the main national innovation hubs might not be the best policy strategy, as it might affect the national innovation outcomes. More importantly, being realistic, it might not even be possible. Similarly, redirecting inward the international connections of the globally successful regions may not have the desired effect and risks slowing down the technological diffusion toward all hubs in the country.

The key problem might be clear, but its solutions are probably not. Labor, capital, and the companies containing these only gradually move from lingering regions to successful innovation agglomerations. Accelerating the structural transformation of economic activity might reduce imbalances, but the social impact might leave long-lasting scars. Individuals, in particular, are geographically bounded, as they may not have the capacity or willingness to move. Public and other supporting institutions – government agencies, schools, transport, etc. – are also extremely hard to transplant geographically.

Alternatively, policy can be directed to mitigate the agglomeration forces by simply financially supporting declining regions. The beneficial social contention of these policies is without question here, but the long-lasting economic results have less consensus. Yet, there are some relevant lessons worth having in mind when designing such policies (Foray, 2015; Rodríguez-Pose, 2018). First, any regional development policy should aim at enhancing existing local advantages by investing in infrastructure, education, and technology. Second, the process of identifying existing capabilities has to rely on inputs from a broad array of local stakeholders. Regional advantages can take several forms – for example, relatively cheap land or labor, existing industrial capabilities, or reputational assets – but, by all means, they have to avoid formulaic solutions transposed from unalike regions.[14] Third, any implemented policies should be assessed regularly. By policy design, distortions will arise if the policies are successful, which inevitably imply that there will be winners and losers within the targeted region.

Is there a specific role for IP policies? History and the rather limited empirical evidence suggest that policies related to IP strengthening played a side part in the industrial development process of countries, and even more of regions.[15] What could be the channel where IP – especially patents – could affect innovation geographical concentration and spread? This is not as straightforward as many would think about it.

In most cases, IP rights have a national jurisdiction, which can be extended to other national jurisdictions. With a valid IP right within a country, right holders could use their IP to exclude the access of competitors to the technology or brand as much inside a cluster than in the neighboring areas outside the cluster. Internationally, holders can, and often do, use their IP to exclude competitors to produce in or export to protected jurisdictions. Still, there is no evidence of the reciprocal being clearly the case. Patent protection for technologies is low in many jurisdictions, yet these technologies do not diffuse to all countries and regions equally. In other words, the fact that large proportions of patented technologies do not have enforceable rights in other countries does not necessarily generate technological diffusion. This is mostly a result of the different local innovation capabilities to exploit the existing technologies, regardless of whether they are publicly available or not.

Overall, there is ample theoretical and empirical literature on how different standards of IP protection affect technology transfer, foreign direct investment

[14] History provides a vast collection of failed "new" Silicon Valleys, while there are several examples of regions specializing "smartly" in a given technology exploiting their relative knowledge and natural advantages. See several examples for Latin American–specific clusters in Pietrobelli and Rabellotti (2006).

[15] See footnote 4.

(FDI), trade flows, and domestic innovation in developing economies, which Keun Lee's chapter in this volume discusses in further detail (see Chapter 4). Two elements are however worth recalling: (i) most patent rights are not protected in poorer economies because of a lack of imitative threat, and (ii) those economies (notably China and the Republic of Korea) that successfully integrated in GINs did so through firms that pro-actively built up patent portfolios (mostly in relation to information technology), mainly to be able to export to rich country markets.

This is not to say that IP cannot be a useful policy instrument to overcome market failures related to knowledge as a public good. Indeed, all the core innovation hotspots show an intensive use of the IP system, both nationally and internationally.

It is also important to mention that IP policies always interact with other public policy tools – namely public funding of R&D activities and infrastructure – aiming at stimulating innovation activity in the private sector. Interestingly, outside the core innovation countries and regions of the world, we do observe a promising increase in scientific activity, but we fail to observe the equivalent use of the patent system. Indeed, in these peripheral regions, most of the patenting results from research produced in universities and research institutions, which are largely publicly funded. It is not always clear to what extent patented inventions are then transformed into commercialized products.

Innovation policies – and IP policies within these – that stimulate the participation of the private sector in the creation of new knowledge and technologies could go a long way toward improving the local innovation ecosystem of these economies. Embedding IP into the targeted regional capability-enhancing policies described earlier is certainly a complementary and feasible strategy. Policymakers should be actively conscious of any cumbersome IP procedures or other barriers preventing local entrepreneurs and companies from using the IP system efficiently. They should also be realistic about policy priorities, as in many cases innovation is hampered by other more pressing matters than IP.

2.3 CONCLUSIONS

In this chapter, we have revisited empirically the unequal geographical distribution of innovation by exploiting rich data from international patent applications and scientific articles.

Despite some new countries – notably in Asia – joining the traditional core economies in the production of new S&T outputs, the global spread of innovation remains limited. Our analysis also shows that, within these economies, the production of innovation is unevenly concentrated in large metropolitan areas.

The secular trends offer some room for optimism, especially if the technologies reducing the cost and enhancing the quality of interconnectivity keep progressing. Our analysis supports in part such optimism. Innovation-related collaboration, in general, and international collaboration, in particular, are mostly increasing. The challenges observed relate to who would reap more benefits from such enhanced connectivity. Indeed, our analysis also shows that, in the current form, the global network of S&T flows is largely concentrated as well. Only a few economies, and a few hotspots within these, represent the bulk of the connections.

There is also some room for pessimism. Recent years show some increase in innovation concentration. Indicators of R&D investments and international patents – especially those highly cited or relating to high-tech or complex technologies – evidence a reconcentration pattern since the second half of the 2000s. Hopefully, this process may just be the result of a new cycle of breakthrough innovation, led by more technologically advanced countries and regions (Kemeny and Storper, 2020). If this is the case, we expect that technological diffusion – and the associated geographical innovation spread – will resume shortly. Nonetheless, it is also apparent in our analysis that only a few countries and regions will act as the main gateways to access the new technology.

Part of the unequal geographical distribution of innovation seems unsolvable by itself, as the economic benefits of agglomeration go far beyond innovation. Nevertheless, we have also documented that innovation is much more geographically skewed – both nationally and subnationally – than other economic activities. This increases the challenge faced by policymakers. National policymakers around the world are already struggling with the problems that regional disparities of income, unemployment, or infrastructure convey. More skewed innovation outputs and flows just make their tasks even harder.

Last, we give some thoughts about what policy consensus the innovation and economic geography literatures can offer. We make the case for national and regional innovation policies that are balanced and attainable. It is always a good practice to acknowledge that these policies are likely to have distributional consequences within countries and regions.

In the context of growing skepticism toward multilateralism after the Great Recession, we also discuss the benefits of openness, as it should not be taken for granted. Certain signs of globalization reversal – or *slowbalization* – are troubling. The increasing self-sufficiency of the largest innovation hotspots and their isolation in an exclusive innovation network could be really bad news for economies and regions aspiring to catch up technologically and, in turn, economically.

REFERENCES

Alcidi, C., J. Núñez Ferrer, M. Di Salvo, M. Pilati, and R. Musmeci. 2018. "Income Convergence in the EU: A Tale of Two Speeds." www.ceps.eu/ceps-publications/income-convergence-eu-tale-two-speeds/.

Amendolagine, V., C. Chaminade, J. Guimón, and R. Rabellotti. 2019. "Cross-Border Knowledge Flows through R&D FDI: Implications for Low- and Middle-Income Countries." In *Trade in Knowledge: Intellectual Property, Trade and Development in a Transformed Global Economy*, edited by Antony Taubman and Jayashree Watal, 352–375. Cambridge: Cambridge University Press.

Amsden, A.H. 1994. "Why Is Not the Whole World Experimenting with the East Asian Model to Develop? Review of the East Asian Miracle." *World Development* 22(4): 627–633.

Archibugi, D., and A. Filippetti. 2018. "The Retreat of Public Research and Its Adverse Consequences on Innovation." *Technological Forecasting and Social Change* 127: 97–111.

Arrow, K.J. 1962. "The Economic Implications of Learning by Doing." *Review of Economic Studies* 29: 155–173.

Asheim, B.T., and M.S. Gertler. 2005. "The Geography of Innovation: Regional Innovation Systems." In *The Oxford Handbook of Innovation*, edited by Jan Fagerberg and David C. Mowery, 291–317. Oxford: Oxford University Press.

Audretsch, D.B., and M.P. Feldman. 1996. "R&D Spillovers and the Geography of Innovation and Production." *American Economic Review* 86(3): 630–640.

Autor, D.H., and M.J. Handel. 2013. "Putting Tasks to the Test: Human Capital, Job Tasks, and Wages." *Journal of Labor Economics* 31(2): S59–S96.

Awate, S., M.M. Larsen, and R. Mudambi. 2012. "EMNE Catch-Up Strategies in the Wind Turbine Industry: Is There a Trade-Off between Output and Innovation Capabilities?" *Global Strategy Journal* 2(3): 205–223.

Awate, S., and R. Mudambi. 2017. "On the Geography of Emerging Industry Technological Networks: The Breadth and Depth of Patented Innovations." *Journal of Economic Geography* 18(2): 391–419.

Barca, F., P. McCann, and A. Rodríguez-Pose. 2012. "The Case for Regional Development Intervention: Place-Based versus Place-Neutral Approaches." *Journal of Regional Science* 52(1): 134–152.

Bathelt, H., A. Malmberg, and P. Maskell. 2004. "Clusters and Knowledge: Local Buzz, Global Pipelines and the Process of Knowledge Creation." *Progress in Human Geography* 28(1): 31–56.

Berkes, E., and R. Gaetani. 2021. "The Geography of Unconventional Innovation." *Economic Journal* 131: 1466–1514.

Bloom, N., C.I. Jones, J. Van Reenen, and M. Webb. 2020. "Are Ideas Getting Harder to Find?" *American Economic Review* 110(4): 1104–1144.

Bolt, J., R. Inklaar, H. de Jong, and J.L. van Zanden. 2018. "Rebasing 'Maddison': New Income Comparisons and the Shape of Long-Run Economic Development." Groningen Growth and Development Centre Research Memorandum No. 174. University of Groningen. www.rug.nl/ggdc/html_publications/memorandum/gd174.pdf.

Branstetter, L., G. Li, and F. Veloso. 2014. "The Rise of International Coinvention." In *The Changing Frontier: Rethinking Science and Innovation Policy*, edited by Adam B. Jaffe and Benjamin F. Jones, 135–168. Chicago: University of Chicago Press.

Breschi, S., C. Lawson, F. Lissoni, A. Morrison, and A. Salter. 2020. "STEM Migration, Research, and Innovation." *Research Policy* 49(9): 104070.

Breschi, S., F. Lissoni, and E. Miguelez. 2017. "Foreign-Origin Inventors in the USA: Testing for Diaspora and Brain Gain Effects." *Journal of Economic Geography* 17(5): 1009–1038.

Carlino, G., and W.R. Kerr. 2015. "Agglomeration and Innovation." In *Handbook of Regional and Urban Economics*, edited by Gilles Duranton, J. Vernon Henderson, and William Strange, 349–404. Amsterdam: Elsevier.

Castellacci, F., and D. Archibugi. 2008. "The Technology Clubs: The Distribution of Knowledge across Nations." *Research Policy* 37(10): 1659–1673.

Castellani, D. 2018. "The Changing Geography of Innovation and the Multinational Enterprise." In *The Routledge Companion to the Geography of International Business*, edited by Gary Cook, Jennifer Johns, Frank McDonald, Jonathan Beaverstock, and Naresh Pandit, 454–474. Abingdon: Routledge.

Castellani, D., and A. Zanfei. 2006. *Multinational Firms, Innovation and Productivity*. Cheltenham: Edward Elgar Publishing.

2007. "Multinational Companies and Productivity Spillovers: Is There a Specification Error?" *Applied Economics Letters* 14(14): 1047–1051.

Chaminade, C., C. De Fuentes, G. Harirchi, and M. Plechero. 2016. "The Geography and Structure of Global Innovation Networks: Global Scope and Regional Embeddedness." In *Handbook on the Geographies of Innovation*, edited by Richard G. Shearmur, David Doloreux, and Christophe Carrincazeaux, 370–381. Cheltenham: Edward Elgar Publishing.

Chaminade, C., and H. Nielsen. 2011. "Transnational Innovation Systems." Serie Estudios y Perspectivas No. 133. ECLAC, Mexico.

Coda-Zabetta, M., C. Chacua, F. Lissoni, E. Miguelez, J. Raffo, and D. Yin. 2022. "The Missing Link: International Migration in Global Clusters of Innovation." In *Cross-Border Innovation in a Changing World: Players, Places, and Policies*, edited by Davide Castellani, Alessandra Perri, Vittoria G. Scalera, and Antonello Zanfei, 82–109. Oxford: Oxford University Press.

Coe, N.M., and T.G. Bunnell. 2003. "'Spatializing' Knowledge Communities: Towards a Conceptualization of Transnational Innovation Networks." *Global Networks* 3(4): 437–456.

Cohen, W.M., A. Goto, A. Nagata, R.R. Nelson, and J.P. Walsh. 2002. "R&D Spillovers, Patents and the Incentives to Innovate in Japan and the United States." *Research Policy* 31: 1349–1367.

Comin, D., and M. Mestieri. 2018. "If Technology Has Arrived Everywhere, Why Has Income Diverged?" *American Economic Journal: Macroeconomics* 10(3): 137–178.

Crescenzi, R., S. Iammarino, C. Ioramashvili, A. Rodríguez-Pose, and M. Storpe. 2019. "The Geography of Innovation: Local Hotspots and Global Innovation Networks." WIPO Economic Research Working Paper No. 57.

Denicolò, V., and L.A. Franzoni. 2003. "The Contract Theory of Patents." *International Review of Law and Economics* 23: 365–380.

Dunning, J.H. 1998. "Location and the Multinational Enterprise: A Neglected Factor." *Journal of International Business Studies* 29(1): 45–66.

Edquist, C. 1997. "Systems of Innovation: Approaches – Their Emergence and Characteristics." In *Systems of Innovation: Technologies, Institutions and Organizations*, edited by Charles Edquist, 1–35. Abingdon: Routledge.

Ellison, G., E.L. Glaeser, and W.R. Kerr. 2010. "What Causes Industry Agglomeration? Evidence from Coagglomeration Patterns." *American Economic Review* 100(3): 1195–1213.

Engel, J.S. 2015. "Global Clusters of Innovation: Lessons from Silicon Valley." https://journals.sagepub.com/doi/abs/10.1525/cmr.2015.57.2.36.

Engel, J.S., and I. del-Palacio. 2009. "Global Networks of Clusters of Innovation: Accelerating the Innovation Process." *Business Horizons* 52(5): 493–503.

Feldman, M., F. Guy, and S. Iammarino. 2021. "Regional Income Disparities, Monopoly and Finance." *Cambridge Journal of Regions, Economy and Society* 14(1): 25–49.

Fink, C., and J. Raffo. 2019. "What Role for Intellectual Property in Industrial Development?" In *Intellectual Property and Development: Understanding the Interfaces*, edited by Carlos Correa and Xavier Seuba, 119–136. Singapore: Springer.

Florida, R. 2017. *The New Urban Crisis: How Our Cities Are Increasing Inequality, Deepening Segregation, and Failing the Middle Class – And What We Can Do about It*. New York: Basic Books.

Foley, C.F., and W.R. Kerr. 2013. "Ethnic Innovation and U.S. Multinational Firm Activity." *Management Science* 59(7): 1529–1544.

Foray, D. 2015. *Smart Specialisation: Opportunities and Challenges for Regional Innovation Policy*. London: Routledge.

Franzoni, C., G. Scellato, and P. Stephan. 2012. "Foreign Born Scientists: Mobility Patterns for Sixteen Countries." National Bureau of Economic Research Working Paper No. 18067.

Freeman, C. 1995. "The 'National System of Innovation' in Historical Perspective." *Cambridge Journal of Economics* 19(1): 5–24.

Gagliardi, L., S. Iammarino, and A. Rodríguez-Pose. 2021. "Exposure to OFDI and Regional Labour Markets: Evidence for Routine and Non-routine Jobs in Great Britain." *Journal of Economic Geography* 21(5): 783–806.

Ganong, P., and D. Shoag. 2017. "Why Has Regional Income Convergence in the US Declined?" *Journal of Urban Economics* 102: 76–90.

Gerybadze, A., and S. Merk. 2014. "Globalisation of R&D and Host-Country Patenting of Multinational Corporations in Emerging Countries." *International Journal of Technology Management* 64: 148–179.

Glaeser, E. 2011. *Triumph of the City: How Our Greatest Invention Makes US Richer, Smarter, Greener, Healthier and Happier*. New York: Penguin Books.

Glaeser, E.L., H.D. Kallal, J.A. Scheinkman, and A. Shleifer. 1992. "Growth in Cities." *Journal of Political Economy* 100(6): 1126–1152.

Gordon, R.J. 2018. "Why Has Economic Growth Slowed When Innovation Appears to Be Accelerating?" National Bureau of Economic Research Working Paper No. 24554.

Graham, S.J., R.P. Merges, P. Samuelson, and T. Sichelman. 2009. "High Technology Entrepreneurs and the Patent System: Results of the 2008 Berkeley Patent Survey." *Berkeley Technology Law Journal* 24(4): 1255–1327.

Grossman, G., and E. Helpman. 1991. *Innovation and Growth in the Global Economy*. Cambridge: MIT Press.

Hidalgo, C.A. 2021. "Economic Complexity Theory and Applications." *Nature Reviews Physics* 3: 92–113.

Hope, D., and J. Limberg. 2022. "The Economic Consequences of Major Tax Cuts for the Rich." *Socio-Economic Review* 20(2): 539–559.

Iammarino, S., A. Rodríguez-Pose, and M. Storper. 2019. "Regional Inequality in Europe: Evidence, Theory and Policy Implications." *Journal of Economic Geography* 19(2): 273–298.

Jacobs, J. 1969. *The Economy of Cities*. New York: Vintage Books.

Jaffe, A.B., M. Trajtenberg, and M.S. Fogarty. 2000. "Knowledge Spillovers and Patent Citations: Evidence from a Survey of Inventors." *American Economic Review* 90(2): 215–218.

Jaffe, A.B., M. Trajtenberg, and R. Henderson. 1993. "Geographic Localization of Knowledge Spillovers as Evidenced by Patent Citations." *Quarterly Journal of Economics* 108(3): 577–598.

Kemeny, T. 2011. "Are International Technology Gaps Growing or Shrinking in the Age of Globalization?" *Journal of Economic Geography* 11(1): 1–35.

Kemeny, T., and M. Storper. 2020. "Superstar Cities and Left-Behind Places: Disruptive Innovation, Labor Demand, and Interregional Inequality." LSE International Inequalities Institute Working Paper No. 41. London School of Economics and Political Science.

Kerr, W.R., and F. Robert-Nicoud. 2020. "Tech Clusters." *Journal of Economic Perspectives* 34(3): 50–76.

Krishna, V.V., S.K. Patra, and S. Bhattacharya. 2012. "Internationalisation of R&D and Global Nature of Innovation: Emerging Trends in India." *Science, Technology and Society* 17(2): 165–199.

Krugman, P. 1991. *Geography and Trade*. Cambridge: MIT Press.

2010. "The New Economic Geography, Now Middle-Aged." *Regional Studies* 45(1): 1–7.

Lorenzen, M., and R. Mudambi. 2013. "Clusters, Connectivity and Catch-up: Bollywood and Bangalore in the Global Economy." *Journal of Economic Geography* 13(3): 501–534.

Marshall, A. 1920. *Principles of Economics*, Abridged ed. New York: Cosimo Classics.

Miguelez, E., J. Raffo, C. Chacua, M. Coda-Zabetta, D. Yin, F. Lissoni, and G. Tarasconi. 2019. "Tied In: The Global Network of Local Innovation." WIPO Economic Research Working Paper No. 58.

Moreno, R., and E. Miguélez. 2012. "A Relational Approach to the Geography of Innovation: A Typology of Regions." *Journal of Economic Surveys* 26(3): 492–516.

Moser, P. 2011. "Do Patents Weaken the Localization of Innovations? Evidence from World's Fairs." *Journal of Economic History* 71: 363–382.

Nelson, R.R., and H. Pack. 1999. *The Asian Miracle and Modern Growth Theory. Economic Journal* 109: 416–436.

Nijkamp, P., and K. Kourtit. 2013. "The 'New Urban Europe': Global Challenges and Local Responses in the Urban Century." *European Planning Studies* 21: 291–315.

North, D.C. 1990. *Institutions, Institutional Change and Economic Performance*. Cambridge: Cambridge University Press.

Oakey, R.P., and S.Y. Cooper. 1989. "High Technology Industry, Agglomeration and the Potential for Peripherally Sited Small Firms." *Regional Studies* 23(4): 347–360.

Patel, P., and K. Pavitt. 1991. "Large Firms in the Production of the World's Technology: An Important Case of 'Non-Globalisation.'" *Journal of International Business Studies* 22(1): 1–21.

Pietrobelli, C., and R. Rabellotti, eds. 2006. *Upgrading to Compete: Global Value Chains, Clusters, and SMEs in Latin America*. Cambridge: Inter-American Development Bank.

Piketty, T., and E. Saez. 2003. "Income Inequality in the United States, 1913–1998." *Quarterly Journal of Economics* 118(1): 1–41.

Porter, M.E. 2000. "Location, Competition, and Economic Development: Local Clusters in a Global Economy." *Economic Development Quarterly* 14(1): 15–34.

Prebisch, R. 1962. "The Economic Development of Latin America and Its Principal Problems." *Economic Bulletin for Latin America* 7(1): 1–22.

Reddy, P. 1997. "New Trends in Globalization of Corporate R&D and Implications for Innovation Capability in Host Countries: A Survey from India." *World Development* 25(11): 1821–1837.

Rodríguez-Pose, A. 2018. "The Revenge of the Places That Do Not Matter (and What to Do about It)." *Cambridge Journal of Regions, Economy and Society* 11(1): 189–209.

Sachs, J.D., and A.M. Warner. 1995. "Natural Resource Abundance and Economic Growth." National Bureau of Economic Research Working Paper No. 5398.

Saxenian, A. 2002. "Silicon Valley's New Immigrant High-Growth Entrepreneurs." *Economic Development Quarterly* 16(1): 20–31.

2006. *The New Argonauts: Regional Advantage in a Global Economy*. Cambridge, MA: Harvard University Press.

Singer, H.W. 1950. "The Distribution of Gains between Investing and Borrowing Countries." *American Economic Review* 40(2): 473–485.

Srivastava, M. 2018. "Israel's Tech Expansion Stokes Glaring Inequality in Tel Aviv." *Financial Times*, December 10. www.ft.com/content/9836aa92-f235-11e8-ae55-df4bf40f9d0d.

Suarez-Villa, L., and W. Walrod. 1997. "Operational Strategy, R&D and Intra-Metropolitan Clustering in a Polycentric Structure: The Advanced Electronics Industries of the Los Angeles Basin." *Urban Studies* 34(9): 1343–1380.

Turkina, E., and A. Van Assche. 2018. "Global Connectedness and Local Innovation in Industrial Clusters." *Journal of International Business Studies* 49: 706–728.

Useche, D., E. Miguelez, and F. Lissoni. 2020. "Highly Skilled and Well Connected: Migrant Inventors in Cross-Border M&As." *Journal of International Business Studies* 51: 737–763.

World Bank. 1993. *The East Asian Miracle: Economic Growth and Public Policy*. Washington, DC: World Bank.

2009. *World Development Report: Reshaping Economic Geography*. Washington, DC: World Bank.

World Intellectual Property Organization (WIPO). 2015. *World Intellectual Property Report 2015: Breakthrough Innovation and Economic Growth*. Geneva: World Intellectual Property Organization.

2019. *World Intellectual Property Report 2019: The Geography of Innovation: Local Hotspots, Global Networks*. Geneva: World Intellectual Property Organization.

Young, A. 1995. "The Tyranny of Numbers: Confronting the Statistical Realities of the East Asian Growth Experience." *Quarterly Journal of Economics* 110: 641–680.

2000a. "Gold into Base Metals: Productivity Growth in the People's Republic of China during the Reform Period." National Bureau of Economic Research Working Paper No. 7856.

2000b. "The Razor's Edge: Distortions and Incremental Reform in the People's Republic of China." *Quarterly Journal of Economics* 115(4): 1091–1135.

Zhou, Y., and T. Xin. 2003. "An Innovative Region in China: Interaction between Multinational Corporations and Local Firms in a High-Tech Cluster in Beijing." *Economic Geography* 79(2): 129–152.

3

Intellectual Property, Global Inequality, and Subnational Policy Variations

Peter K. Yu[*]

INTRODUCTION

The North–South divide has been frequently invoked in the debate on intellectual property, innovation, and global inequality. While the Global North complained about the inadequate protection and enforcement of intellectual property rights in developing countries, the Global South lamented the unfair distribution of benefits within the international intellectual property regime.[1] Developing countries were also frustrated that they bore the brunt of globalization and the detrimental effects of strong intellectual property protection and enforcement.

The arrival of middle-income countries, in particular those with considerable and ever-growing strengths in the intellectual property area, has called into question the North–South debate. First, that debate is both dated and oversimplified. It overlooks the many complications raised by Brazil, China, India, and other fast-growing emerging countries. With increasing abilities to compete effectively against developed countries, these middle-income countries have now taken policy positions that do not always align with the Global South.[2] Second, by emphasizing global inequality (inequality *among* countries), the North–South debate steers policy and scholarly attention away from many important policy challenges posed by widening national inequality (inequality *within* countries). Although these challenges have received some attention from trade and development economists, they have been largely ignored in intellectual property literature.

* This chapter draws on research the author conducted for earlier articles in *IDEA* and the *Washington and Lee Law Review* and for book chapters published by Cambridge University Press and Edward Elgar Publishing. The author is grateful to Daniel Benoliel, Thomas Cottier, Henning Grosse Ruse-Khan, and Keun Lee for valuable comments and suggestions.

1 Peter K. Yu, *TRIPs and Its Discontents*, 10 Marq. Intell. Prop. L. Rev. 369, 379–86 (2006).

2 Peter K. Yu, *TRIPS and Its Contents*, 60 IDEA 149, 219 (2020).

This chapter begins by revisiting the North–South debate on intellectual property, innovation, and global inequality. It explains why the arrival of middle-income countries has called into question this old binary debate. The chapter then moves from the widely studied subject of global inequality to the underexplored topic of national inequality. Focusing on the intellectual property context, the discussion highlights the considerable subnational variations in the economic and technological conditions of middle-income countries. To combat national inequality, this chapter concludes by recommending interventions in three areas: (1) international norm-setting, (2) national policymaking, and (3) academic and policy research.

3.1 INEQUALITY AMONG COUNTRIES

3.1.1 *The North*

The proponents of strong intellectual property rights often start the international law and policy debate by underscoring the need for international harmonization and effective global and national protections for creators and inventors. A strong international intellectual property regime helps ensure the adequate protection of valuable intellectual assets, most of which reside in the Global North.[3] As stated in its preamble, the Agreement on Trade-Related Aspects of Intellectual Property Rights (TRIPS Agreement) of the World Trade Organization (WTO) lays out the "adequate standards and principles concerning the availability, scope and use of trade-related intellectual property rights."[4] This Agreement further provides "effective and appropriate means for the enforcement of trade-related intellectual property rights, taking into account differences in national legal systems."[5]

Although the TRIPS negotiators in the Global North recognized that developing countries might not receive the same distribution of benefits, they readily asserted that strong intellectual property rights would, on balance, benefit the Global South. These rights, they claimed, would help developing countries attract foreign direct investment, increase trade flows, generate jobs and tax revenues, build up human capital, and promote technology transfer and diffusion.[6] To many policymakers and commentators in developed countries, the TRIPS Agreement could be analogized to painful medicine that would provide long-term gains but short-term discomfort. As Daniel Gervais recounted, during the TRIPS negotiations, developing countries

3 Frederick M. Abbott, *Protecting First World Assets in the Third World: Intellectual Property Negotiations in the GATT Multilateral Framework*, 22 VAND. J. TRANSNAT'L L. 689 (1989).

4 Agreement on Trade-Related Aspects of Intellectual Property Rights pmbl., recital 2(b), Apr. 15, 1994, Marrakesh Agreement Establishing the World Trade Organization, Annex 1C, 1869 U.N.T.S. 299 [hereinafter TRIPS Agreement].

5 *Id.* pmbl., recital 2(c).

6 Peter K. Yu, *The Comparative Economics of International Intellectual Property Agreements*, *in* COMPARATIVE LAW AND ECONOMICS 282, 286 (Theodore Eisenberg & Giovanni B. Ramello eds., 2016).

"were told to overlook the distasteful aspects of introducing or increasing intellectual property protection and enforcement in exchange for longer-term economic health."[7]

3.1.2 *The South*

Unlike those in the Global North, policymakers and commentators in the Global South remain skeptical of the benefits provided by strong intellectual property rights, especially in the short term. In the early days of the WTO, many commentators expressed concern that the TRIPS Agreement would lead to a massive outflow of valuable resources from developing countries to their wealthier counterparts. As Jagdish Bhagwati emphatically declared, "TRIPS does not involve mutual gain; rather, it positions the WTO primarily as a collector of intellectual property–related rents on behalf of multinational corporations."[8] Likewise, World Bank economist Michael Finger estimated that the total rent transfer from the Global North to the Global South could go as high as US$60 billion per year.[9] It is, therefore, no surprise that development economist Ha-Joon Chang famously observed that developed countries sought to use the international trading and intellectual property systems to "'kick away the ladder' by which they have climbed to the top."[10]

In the area of intellectual property enforcement, for instance, higher standards will require developing countries to divert scarce resources away from other equally important, if not more important, needs – such as the provision of clean drinking water, food, shelter, electricity, schools, and basic healthcare.[11] As Keith Maskus reminded us:

> A reasonable … estimate [based on figures the U.N. Conference on Trade and Development provided on setup and training costs in relation to TRIPS implementation] is that [the] average operating costs of an effective system might be perhaps $2.5 million per year for 10 years postreform in those countries that upgrade most rapidly and $1.5 million per year for 20 years in the others. These figures imply that, discounted at 3 percent per annum, the net present value of investment costs in effective enforcement in the developing world would be $4.1 billion over 20 years.[12]

[7] Daniel J. Gervais, *The TRIPS Agreement and the Doha Round: History and Impact on Economic Development*, in 4 Intellectual Property and Information Wealth: Issues and Practices in the Digital Age 23, 43 (Peter K. Yu ed., 2007).

[8] Jagdish Bhagwati, *What It Will Take to Get Developing Countries into a New Round of Multilateral Trade Negotiations*, *in* Department of Foreign Affairs & International Trade, Trade Policy Research 2001, at 19, 21 (2001).

[9] J. Michael Finger, *The Doha Agenda and Development: A View from the Uruguay Round* 9 (Asian Development Bank, Economics and Research Department, Working Paper No. 21, 2002).

[10] Ha-Joon Chang, Kicking away the Ladder: Development Strategy in Historical Perspective 10 (2002).

[11] Peter K. Yu, *Enforcement, Economics and Estimates*, 2 WIPO J. 1, 2 (2010).

[12] Keith E. Maskus, Private Rights and Public Problems: The Global Economics of Intellectual Property in the 21st Century 227 (2012).

Given the developing countries' continuous socio-economic plight and their admittedly more limited benefits from the international intellectual property regime, it is understandable why these countries and their supportive intergovernmental and nongovernmental organizations have been quite vocal about the detrimental effects of the TRIPS-based international intellectual property regime,[13] especially after the expiration of the transition period for developing countries on December 31, 1999. It is also unsurprising to find these countries demanding continuous systemic pro-development adjustments at the WTO, the World Intellectual Property Organization (WIPO), and other international fora.[14]

In November 2001, the Global South pushed for the establishment of the Doha Development Round of Trade Negotiations at the WTO. Although this round of negotiations is currently at a standstill, developing countries managed to amend the TRIPS Agreement to allow countries with insufficient or no manufacturing capacity to import generic versions of patented pharmaceuticals.[15] These countries also successfully secured repeated extensions of the transition period for least developed countries, which will last until July 1, 2034.

At WIPO, developing countries, with the support of civil society organizations, managed to establish a development agenda. Adopted in September 2007, the forty-five recommendations for the WIPO Development Agenda covered a wide range of issues, including the transfer of technology, response to the digital divide, protection of genetic resources and traditional knowledge, and preservation of the public domain.[16]

Notwithstanding these pro-development efforts, developed countries' active push for new bilateral, regional, and plurilateral agreements since the early 2000s has led to the adoption of even higher international standards for intellectual property protection and enforcement. Not only do these standards go beyond what many developing countries find suitable, but they are created through nontransparent, power-driven processes with limited voice and representation for the Global South.[17] Among the more controversial negotiations were those surrounding the Anti-Counterfeiting Trade Agreement, the Trans-Pacific Partnership (TPP) – which has now become the Comprehensive and Progressive Agreement for Trans-Pacific Partnership – and the Regional Comprehensive Economic Partnership (RCEP).

[13] U.N. High Commissioner for Human Rights, *The Impact of the Agreement on Trade-Related Aspects of Intellectual Property Rights on Human Rights*, ¶¶ 24–26, U.N. Doc. E/CN.4/Sub.2/2001/13 (June 27, 2001).

[14] Peter K. Yu, *A Tale of Two Development Agendas*, 35 Ohio N.U. L. Rev. 465, 511–40 (2009).

[15] TRIPS Agreement, *supra* note 4, art. 31*bis*.

[16] Peter K. Yu, *Intellectual Property Training and Education for Development*, 28 Am. U. Int'l L. Rev. 311, 312–13 (2012).

[17] David S. Levine, *Transparency Soup: The ACTA Negotiating Process and "Black Box" Lawmaking*, 26 Am. U. Int'l L. Rev. 811 (2011); Peter K. Yu, *Six Secret (and Now Open) Fears of ACTA*, 64 SMU L. Rev. 975, 998–1019 (2011).

3.1.3 *The Middle*

Just as the Global South has become increasingly frustrated by the Global North's incessant demands for higher international intellectual property standards, a group of middle-income countries seemed to have found a formula for success. Since the beginning of the twenty-first century, these countries have selectively adapted international intellectual property standards, to the extent allowed by the TRIPS Agreement and acquiesced by the more powerful WTO members.[18] As a result, this group of emerging countries gradually obtained a greater share of the benefits provided by the TRIPS-based international intellectual property regime. As former WTO Director-General Roberto Azevêdo recalled:

> [I]n 1995, and earlier in the negotiations leading to the conclusion of TRIPS, the international [intellectual property] system was largely seen as a trade interest of the developed economies. Today, the picture differs dramatically. Some middle-income countries are among the major users of the global [intellectual property] system, and many other developing countries are increasingly engaged with it.[19]

Brazil, China, and India – together with Russia and South Africa making up the BRICS countries – are oft-cited examples. Other fast-growing emerging countries have also received similar benefits from the WTO and the TRIPS-based international intellectual property regime. In a book chapter written a decade ago, I identified the ten largest economies outside the Organisation for Economic Co-operation and Development (OECD) that had a gross national income per capita of less than US$15,000 yet some of the world's highest volumes of high-technology exports.[20] Referring to them as "middle intellectual property powers," that chapter highlighted the considerable economic and technological improvements in the world's fast-growing middle-income countries (see Tables 3.1 and 3.2). In addition to the BRICS countries, the ten surveyed economies included Argentina, Indonesia, Malaysia, the Philippines, and Thailand.

Based on the 2022 Global Innovation Index, five of the selected countries ranked within the world's top fifty: China (eleventh), Malaysia (thirty-sixth), India (fortieth),

[18] Sunil Mani & Richard R. Nelson, *Conclusion*, *in* TRIPS COMPLIANCE, NATIONAL PATENT REGIMES AND INNOVATION: EVIDENCE AND EXPERIENCE FROM DEVELOPING COUNTRIES 222, 223 (Sunil Mani & Richard R. Nelson eds., 2013); Wu Handong, *One Hundred Years of Progress: The Development of the Intellectual Property System in China*, 1 WIPO J. 117, 118–19 (2009); Yu, *supra* note 2, at 207–15; Peter K. Yu, *When the Chinese Intellectual Property System Hits 35*, 8 QUEEN MARY J. INTELL. PROP. 3, 12 (2018).

[19] Roberto Azevêdo, *Foreword to* THE MAKING OF THE TRIPS AGREEMENT: PERSONAL INSIGHTS FROM THE URUGUAY ROUND NEGOTIATIONS xiii, xiii (Jayashree Watal & Antony Taubman eds., 2015).

[20] Peter K. Yu, *The Middle Intellectual Property Powers*, *in* LAW AND DEVELOPMENT OF MIDDLE-INCOME COUNTRIES: AVOIDING THE MIDDLE-INCOME TRAP 84 (Randall Peerenboom & Tom Ginsburg eds., 2014).

TABLE 3.1 *Indicators on intellectual property and related developments in 2020*

Country	Patent App., Res.	Patent App., Nonres.	TM App., Res.	TM App., Nonres.	IP Payments (US$M)	IP Receipts (US$M)	Global Innovation Index
Argentina	930	2,562	64,413	14,087	1,149	210	80
Brazil	5,280	19,058	260,774	37,159	4,062	634	62
China	1.345M	152,342	9.117M	229,248	37,871	8,583	14
India	23,141	33,630	382,294	42,289	7,241	1,254	48
Indonesia	1,309	6,851	80,545	43,242	1,530	84	85
Malaysia	989	5,839	18,414	26,872	2,388	232	33
Philippines	476	3,517	30,935	25,763	519	15	50
Russia	23,759	11,225	341,414	56,826	6,809	1,164	47
South Africa	542	6,146	22,104	14,219	1,198	126	60
Thailand	863	6,662	33,165	30,322	4,504	225	44

Note: This table draws on data provided by the World Bank and WIPO in the following areas: (1) patent applications, resident; (2) patent applications, nonresident; (3) trademark applications, direct resident; (4) trademark applications, direct nonresident; (5) charges for the use of intellectual property, payments (balance of payments, current US$); (6) charges for the use of intellectual property, receipts (balance of payments, current US$); and (7) ranking in the Global Innovation Index.

TABLE 3.2 *Other science, technology, and education indicators in 2020*

Country	High-Tech Exports (%)	High-Tech Exports (US$M)	R&D Expend. (% GDP)	Researchers in R&D (M)	Technicians in R&D (M)	S&T Journal Articles	Educ. Expend. (%)	Tertiary School (%)
Argentina	7	546	0.49†	1,211†	398†	9,730	5.0	99
Brazil	11	5,945	1.16†	888††	970††	70,292	6.0*	55
China	31	757,459	2.14†	1,307†	N/A	669,744	3.6	58
India	11	21,583	0.65†	253†	73†	149,213	4.5	29
Indonesia	8	6,409	0.23†	216†	35†	32,554	3.5	36†
Malaysia	54	92,100	1.04†	2,185†	233†	21,885	3.9	43
Philippines	67	34,896	0.16**	106**	18**	3,072	3.7	33
Russia	9	6,525	0.98†	2,784†	438†	89,967	3.7	86*
South Africa	6	1,835	0.83‡	518‡	130‡	15,885	6.2	24
Thailand	28	45,838	1.00‡	1,350‡	297‡	13,963	3.1	43

* 2019 data; † 2018 data; ‡ 2017 data; ** 2015 data; †† 2014 data.

Note: This table draws on World Bank data in the following areas: (1) high-technology exports (% of manufactured exports); (2) high-technology exports (current US$); (3) research and development (R&D) expenditure (% of GDP); (4) researchers in R&D (per million people); (5) technicians in R&D (per million people); (6) scientific and technical journal articles, (7) government expenditure on education, total (% of GDP); and (8) school enrollment, tertiary (% gross).

Thailand (forty-third), and Russia (forty-seventh).[21] The rest were within the world's top seventy-five: Brazil (fifty-fourth), the Philippines (fifty-ninth), South Africa (sixty-first), Argentina (sixty-ninth), and Indonesia (seventy-fifth). Apart from these countries, Vietnam, a fast-growing lower-middle-income country with the world's fifteenth-largest population, also earned a top fifty spot in the index, placing at forty-eighth. Using the criteria outlined in my earlier chapter, one could certainly expand the list of "middle intellectual property powers" to include fast-growing emerging countries such as Vietnam.

While the intellectual property policy positions of many middle-income countries have remained close to those of other developing countries, some of these positions have begun to shift toward and align with those of their developed counterparts. Not only do the two groups of countries share similar aspirations, but some middle-income countries have also become more willing to embrace, at times reluctantly, higher intellectual property standards in international or regional negotiations.[22] Cases in point are the positions taken by Malaysia and Vietnam in the TPP negotiations and by China and the less developed members of the Association of Southeast Asian Nations (ASEAN) in the RCEP negotiations. As their economic and technological conditions continue to improve, middle-income countries will only become more active in persuading their developing country allies to support their negotiating and policy positions.

Given these rapidly changing geopolitical, economic, and policy landscapes, it is high time that we reassessed the debate on international intellectual property law and policy.[23] Although the North–South debate has been widely used in international relations and has successfully captured the tensions and conflicts between developed and developing countries in the past few decades, that debate does not fully reflect the ongoing developments in the international intellectual property regime. As middle-income countries continue to improve both economically and technologically, and as other low-income countries move up the economic ladder to become lower-middle-income countries, the gap between the Global North and the Global South will drastically reduce. Meanwhile, the challenges confronting least developed countries, which have necessitated the repeated extensions of the TRIPS transition period, will remain. In short, the debate on intellectual property,

[21] World Intellectual Property Organization, Global Innovation Index 2022: What Is the Future of Innovation-Driven Growth? 19 (Soumitra Dutta, Bruno Lanvin, Lorena Rivera León & Sacha Wunsch-Vincent eds., 2022) [hereinafter Global Innovation Index].

[22] Peter K. Yu, *TPP, RCEP and the Future of Copyright Norm-Setting in the Asian Pacific*, *in* Making Copyright Work for the Asian Pacific: Juxtaposing Harmonisation with Flexibility 19, 39–41 (Susan Corbett & Jessica C. Lai eds., 2018); Peter K. Yu, *The RCEP and Trans-Pacific Intellectual Property Norms*, 50 Vand. J. Transnat'l L. 673, 737–40 (2017).

[23] *See* Peter K. Yu, *Intellectual Property Negotiations, the BRICS Factor and the Changing North–South Debate*, *in* The BRICS-Lawyers' Guide to Global Cooperation 148, 148–49 (Rostam J. Neuwirth, Alexandr Svetlicinii & Denis De Castro Halis eds., 2017); Yu, *supra* note 2, at 216–17.

innovation, and global inequality will become more complex than a simplistic binary North–South debate.

3.2 INEQUALITY WITHIN COUNTRIES

Thus far, the debate on international intellectual property law and policy has focused primarily on global inequality. That debate has rarely gone behind territorial borders to shed light on national inequality. Since the mid-2000s, however, economists – most notably François Bourguignon, Branko Milanovic, and Thomas Piketty – have called for greater scholarly and policy attention to the ever-increasing inequalities within countries.[24] National inequality is important not only because it can be found in both the Global North and the Global South but also because it will influence how and how effectively we combat global inequality.[25]

Although inequalities within high- and low-income countries remain important and have received scholarly and policy attention, this section continues to focus on middle-income countries, for at least two reasons. First, a greater focus on inequalities within these countries will make the debate's growing complications salient. While these fast-growing middle-income countries have been slowly catching up with their developed counterparts, thereby helping to reduce global inequality, the inequalities within these countries have greatly increased. Such increase, to some extent, suggests the potential, and oft-overlooked, costs of strong intellectual property rights – the painful medicine that the Global North prescribed through the TRIPS Agreement and TRIPS-plus bilateral, regional, and plurilateral agreements.

Second, inequalities within middle-income countries will pose serious internal challenges at a point when these fast-growing countries start to align their intellectual property laws and policies more closely with those of the developed world. To respond to these challenges, policymakers may consider adjustments to strike a better domestic balance. Those adjustments not only would make the positions of these countries less coherent, but the choices and incoherences might have a significant impact on the future development of the international intellectual property regime.

For illustrative purposes, this section discusses three types of inequality within middle-income countries: geographic, sectoral, and income. While the scope and

[24] François Bourguignon, The Globalization of Inequality (Thomas Scott-Railton trans., 2017); Branko Milanovic, Global Inequality: A New Approach for the Age of Globalization (2018); Thomas Piketty, Capital and Ideology (Arthur Goldhammer trans., 2020) [hereinafter Piketty, Capital and Ideology]; Thomas Piketty, Capital in the Twenty-First Century (Arthur Goldhammer trans., 2014) [hereinafter Piketty, Capital in the Twenty-First Century]; Thomas Piketty, The Economics of Inequality (Arthur Goldhammer trans., 2015).

[25] See Chapter 11 in this volume.

length of this chapter do not allow for a greater exploration of the relationship between intellectual property protection and national inequality – and economists have yet to provide conclusive evidence on a strong causal relationship[26] – this section's observations on the three types of inequality provide useful information about the internal challenges many middle-income countries will face. Regardless of whether strong positive causality exists, those challenges will deeply affect the intellectual property policy positions taken by these countries.

3.2.1 *Geographic Inequality*

Thus far, the literature on international intellectual property law and policy has been filled with cross-country studies.[27] This nation-based focus is unsurprising, considering the need for policymakers and commentators to understand, evaluate, and appreciate the divergent policy positions adopted by the surveyed countries. Nevertheless, if policymakers and scholars are to grasp fully the internal policy challenges in each of these countries, they will have to pay greater attention to the vast subnational variations behind the countries' territorial borders.

Although subnational data remain relatively scarce, recent years have seen national intellectual property offices becoming more active in collecting these data. To highlight the deep geographical divergences within a country, there is no better dataset than the patent data collected by the China National Intellectual Property Administration (previously the State Intellectual Property Office of China).

In 2021, Guangdong, Jiangsu, and Zhejiang – the provinces with the three largest volumes of invention patent applications – had a total of 242,551, 188,241, and 129,821, respectively (see Table 3.3). Meanwhile, Yunnan, Shanxi, and Guizhou (the eighteenth to twentieth provinces) had a total of only 10,293, 10,059, and 9,869, respectively. In the same year, the total number of invention patent grants for Guangdong, Jiangsu, and Zhejiang were 102,850, 68,813, and 56,796, respectively. By contrast, the total number for Yunnan, Shanxi, and Guizhou were 3,643, 3,915, and 2,824, respectively. For both applications and grants, the figures for the more developed provinces were more than twelve times the corresponding numbers for their less developed counterparts. Had we included in the second group those provinces and autonomous regions with fewer than 5,000 patent applications and 1,200 patent

[26] See Chapter 1 in this volume.

[27] For example, Elizabeth Siew-Kuan Ng & Albert Guang-Zhou Hu, *Flexibilities in the Implementation of TRIPS: An Analysis of Their Impact on Technological Innovation and Public Health in Asia*, *in* Framing Intellectual Property Law in the 21st Century: Integrating Incentives, Trade, Development, Culture, and Human Rights 115, 118 (Rochelle Cooper Dreyfuss & Elizabeth Siew-Kuan Ng eds., 2018); U.S. Chamber of Commerce Global Innovation Policy Center, U.S. Chamber International IP Index (2018); Taylor Wessing, Global Intellectual Property Index: 5th Report (2016); Juan C. Ginarte & Walter G. Park, *Determinants of Patent Rights: A Cross-National Study*, 26 Rsch. Pol'y 283 (1997).

TABLE 3.3 *Volume of invention patent applications and grants on mainland China in 2021*

Province	Volume of Patent Applications	Volume of Patent Grants
Guangdong	242,551	102,850
Jiangsu	188,241	68,813
Zhejiang	129,821	56,796
Shandong	82,481	36,345
Anhui	64,106	23,624
Hubei	51,690	22,376
Sichuan	45,358	19,337
Shaanxi	38,643	15,516
Hunan	36,746	16,564
Henan	34,950	13,536
Fujian	31,093	12,561
Hebei	23,923	8,621
Liaoning	23,078	10,480
Jiangxi	19,171	6,741
Heilongjiang	15,018	6,337
Guangxi	13,693	4,573
Jilin	12,680	5,730
Yunnan	10,293	3,643
Shanxi	10,059	3,915
Guizhou	9,869	2,824
Gansu	6,423	2,253
Inner Mongolia	5,998	1,651
Hainan	4,497	954
Xinjiang	4,395	1,153
Ningxia	3,054	1,103
Qinghai	1,585	454
Tibet	515	184

Note: This table focuses on only mainland China and excludes Hong Kong, Macau, and Taiwan. It also does not include the four municipalities under the central government's direct administration – namely, Beijing, Chongqing, Shanghai, and Tianjin.
Sources: *Patent Applications for Invention Originated from Home by Origin*, CHINA NAT'L INTELL. PROP. ADMIN., https://english.cnipa.gov.cn/jianbao/year2021/a/a3.html (last visited May 12, 2023); *Patent Grants for Invention Originated from Home by Origin*, CHINA NAT'L INTELL. PROP. ADMIN., https://english.cnipa.gov.cn/jianbao/year2021/b/b2.html (last visited May 12, 2023).

grants, such as Hainan, Xinjiang, Ningxia, Qinghai, and Tibet, these two groups would have even starker statistical contrasts.

While the data in this section focus on China, similar geographical disparities can be found in other emerging countries. For instance, Nobel Laureate Michael Spence referred to Brazil as a "dual economy," noting the existence of "a relatively rich one whose growth is constrained by the normal forces that constrain the growth of relatively advanced economies, and a poor one where the early-stage growth dynamics … just didn't start, owing to its separation from the modern domestic economy and the global economy."[28] Fareed Zakaria also remarked that India "might have several Silicon Valleys, but it also has three Nigerias within it – that is, more than 300 million people living on less than a dollar a day."[29] Likewise, Ruchir Sharma described South Africa as "a developed market wrapped inside an emerging market."[30]

Since 2017, the Global Innovation Index report has included a top 100 ranking of the world's science and technology clusters. Among the ten middle-income countries listed in Tables 3.1 and 3.2, the 2022 rankings recognized the following subnational clusters: Shenzhen–Hong Kong–Guangzhou (second), Beijing (third), Shanghai–Suzhou (sixth), Nanjing (thirteenth), Hangzhou (fourteenth), Wuhan (sixteenth), Xi'an (twenty-second), Taipei–Hsinchu (twenty-sixth), Chengdu (twenty-ninth), Moscow (thirty-first), Qingdao (thirty-fourth), Tianjin (thirty-seventh), Changsha (forty-first), Chongqing (forty-ninth), Hefei (fifty-fifth), Harbin (fifty-sixth), Bengaluru (sixtieth), Jinan (sixty-first), Changchun (sixty-third), Delhi (sixty-fourth), Shenyang (sixty-eighth), São Paulo (seventy-first), Dalian (seventy-second), Zhengzhou (eighty-third), Mumbai (eighty-fourth), Xiamen (ninety-first), Chennai (ninety-seventh), and Lanzhou (hundredth).[31]

As shown by this list of science and technology clusters and the earlier discussion, middle-income countries experience considerable economic and technological variations at the subnational level, similar to the variations they encounter across nations in the North–South debate. To the extent that intellectual property reforms have contributed to improving the economic and technological conditions of middle-income countries, one cannot help but wonder whether such reforms have produced subnational winners and losers. Although the significant variations in many of these countries resemble those documented in the Global North,[32] the spatial concentration of innovative activities in a few middle-income countries, most notably China and India, has been much more uneven than what is found in Europe and the United States. As Riccardo Crescenzi and Andrés Rodríguez-Pose observed:

> Patent counts at the subnational level indicate that the five EU regions with the highest shares of patent applications together represent 35% of all EU patenting; for the US the corresponding figure is about 50%. By contrast, the five most innovative

[28] Michael Spence, THE NEXT CONVERGENCE: THE FUTURE OF ECONOMIC GROWTH IN A MULTISPEED WORLD 204 (2011).

[29] Fareed Zakaria, THE POST-AMERICAN WORLD 133 (2008).

[30] Ruchir Sharma, BREAKOUT NATIONS: IN PURSUIT OF THE NEXT ECONOMIC MIRACLES 173 (2012).

[31] GLOBAL INNOVATION INDEX, *supra* note 21, at 258–59. Unlike Table 3.2, which focuses on mainland China, this list covers Greater China and other parts of the world. On the concentration of innovative activities in urban hotspots and the global networks linking these hotspots, see WORLD INTELLECTUAL PROPERTY ORGANIZATION, WORLD INTELLECTUAL PROPERTY REPORT 2019: THE GEOGRAPHY OF INNOVATION: LOCAL HOTSPOTS, GLOBAL NETWORKS (2019).

[32] Annalisa Primi, *The Evolving Geography of Innovation: A Territorial Perspective*, *in* THE GLOBAL INNOVATION INDEX 2013: THE LOCAL DYNAMICS OF INNOVATION 69, 70 (2013).

Indian regions cover 75% of Indian patents; in China, the five regions with the highest patent share produce almost 80% of all patent applications.[33]

Since the adoption of the TRIPS Agreement, critics have frequently and heavily criticized it for ushering in a misguided "one size fits all" – or, more precisely, "supersize fits all" – approach to intellectual property norm-setting.[34] Although "these critiques tend to end at the national border, with the trust and expectation that a sovereign government will ultimately strike the appropriate balance for its country,"[35] policymakers and scholars should not ignore the problems a "one size fits all" approach to intellectual property norm-setting would create at the subnational level.

Just as this flawed approach fails to recognize the differing needs, interests, conditions, and priorities of over 160 WTO members, especially those in the developing world, that same approach does not sit well with the wide subnational variations found within each country, even though having uniform nationwide standards does provide some important benefits. Based on the patent statistics provided earlier in Table 3.3, it is just very difficult to imagine that a Chinese province with fewer than 10,000 patent applications and 3,000 grants per year should have the same intellectual property standards as a province that has generated more than 100,000 patent applications and 50,000 patent grants annually. Likewise, uniform nationwide standards are unlikely to work very well in India, which has little patent-based innovation "outside the … innovation hubs of Mumbai, Delhi, Bangalore, Chennai, Hyderabad or Pune."[36] Thus, policymakers should begin exploring the benefits of adopting intellectual property policies that accommodate the different economic and technological conditions at the subnational level.[37]

3.2.2 *Sectoral Inequality*

The second type of inequality that warrants scholarly and policy attention concerns the uneven sectoral developments at the subnational level. Such unevenness can be attributed to a wide variety of factors, ranging from the presence of innovation clusters to the availability of human talents and foreign investors.[38]

[33] Riccardo Crescenzi & Andrés Rodríguez-Pose, *The Geography of Innovation in China and India*, 41 Int'l J. Urb. & Reg. Rsch. 1010, 1014 (2017).

[34] Peter K. Yu, *The Global Intellectual Property Order and Its Undetermined Future*, 1 WIPO J. 1, 9 (2009).

[35] Peter K. Yu, *A Spatial Critique of Intellectual Property Law and Policy*, 74 Wash. & Lee L. Rev. 2045, 2093 (2017).

[36] Crescenzi & Rodríguez-Pose, *supra* note 33, at 1016.

[37] Outside the intellectual property field, commentators have begun to explore the advantages and challenges of place-based economic development approaches. See, for example, Andrés Rodríguez-Pose & Callum Wilkie, *Revamping Local and Regional Development through Place-Based Strategies*, 19 Cityscape 151, 153–57 (2017).

[38] Ashish Arora & Alfonso Gambardella, *Bridging the Gap: Conclusions*, *in* From Underdogs to Tigers: The Rise and Growth of the Software Industry in Brazil, China, India,

In many middle-income countries, it is not uncommon to find a few industrial sectors that are much more innovative and globally competitive than the others. For example, Embraer (Empresa Brasileira de Aeronautica) and Petrobras (Petroleo Brasileiro) have achieved notable success in Brazil.[39] Likewise, the pharmaceutical and information technology sectors have performed very well in India.[40] Similar observations can also be made about China. Based on WIPO statistics, all of the six Chinese firms that were among the world's top twenty Patent Cooperation Treaty applicants in 2022 came from the consumer electronics or information technology sector.[41]

More importantly, the uneven sectoral developments in middle-income countries can be traced back historically. When WIPO published its first *World Intellectual Property Report* in 2011, that report listed all the top R&D spenders among the middle-income countries in 2009.[42] Among the sectors in which the listed companies concentrated were aerospace, automotive, electrical, engineering and construction, Internet, machinery, mining, oil and gas, pharmaceuticals, semiconductors, and telecommunications. This list not only documented the historical developments in Brazil, China, and India – the only middle-income countries that had companies on the list – but also foreshadowed the similarly uneven sectoral developments in other newly emerging countries that seek to climb up the economic and technological ladder.

In view of the divergent sectoral developments identified in this section, one could certainly ask the same question we explored earlier in the previous section: Does it make sense to have the same intellectual property standards throughout the country? More specifically, should those standards apply equally to those industrial sectors that are globally competitive and those that are only beginning to take off?

Ireland, and Israel 275, 283–84 (Ashish Arora & Alfonso Gambardella eds., 2006) [hereinafter From Underdogs to Tigers]; Ashish Arora, Alfonso Gambardella & Steven Klepper, *Organizational Capabilities and the Rise of the Software Industry in the Emerging Economies: Lessons from the History of Some US Industries*, *in* From Underdogs to Tigers, *supra*, at 171, 172; Justin Yifu Lin, The Quest for Prosperity: How Developing Economies Can Take Off 172–75 (2012).

39 Roberto Mazzoleni & Luciano Martins Costa Póvoa, *Accumulation of Technological Capabilities and Economic Development: Did Brazil's IPR Regime Matter?*, *in* Intellectual Property Rights, Development, and Catch-up: An International Comparative Study 280, 282 (Hiroyuki Odagiri, Akira Goto, Atsushi Sunami & Richard R. Nelson eds., 2010).

40 Peter K. Yu, *Intellectual Property and Asian Values*, 16 Marq. Intell. Prop. L. Rev. 329, 358 (2012).

41 *Annex 2: Top PCT Applicants*, World Intell. Prop. Org. (Feb. 28, 2023), www.wipo.int/export/sites/www/pressroom/en/documents/pr-2023-899-annexes.pdf. These seven firms are Huawei (first), OPPO (sixth), BOE (seventh), Vivo (eleventh), ZTE (thirteenth), and DJI (twentieth).

42 World Intellectual Property Organization, 2011 World Intellectual Property Report: The Changing Face of Innovation 41 (2011). The list was drawn from the Global Innovation 1,000 database compiled by Booz & Company (now Strategy&).

To be sure, Article 27.1 of the TRIPS Agreement states that "patents shall be available for any inventions, whether products or processes, in all fields of technology."[43] Yet the Agreement refrains from requiring WTO members to offer the same level of protection across all areas of intellectual property rights. Incorporating by reference the Paris Convention for the Protection of Industrial Property (Paris Convention) and the Berne Convention for the Protection of Literary and Artistic Works (Berne Convention), the TRIPS Agreement recognizes the need for different forms or levels of protection in each distinct area of intellectual property right. Even within the same area, the Agreement anticipates that WTO members may need sectoral variations – or "differential treatment." As the WTO panel observed in *Canada – Patent Protection of Pharmaceutical Products*:

> The primary TRIPS provisions that deal with discrimination, such as the national treatment and most-favoured-nation provisions of Articles 3 and 4, do not use the term "discrimination". They speak in more precise terms. The ordinary meaning of the word "discriminate" is potentially broader than these more specific definitions. It certainly extends beyond the concept of differential treatment. It is a normative term, pejorative in connotation, referring to results of the unjustified imposition of differentially disadvantageous treatment.[44]

The recognition of the need for differentiation makes good economic sense. As Paul David reminded us, "economic efficiency would … call for great subtlety and differentiation in the nature and degree of intellectual property protection provided, based on differences among industries in technological and market circumstances."[45]

Indeed, among middle-income countries, for instance, it is common to find some countries performing much better in one intellectual property area than in others. In 2022, WIPO statistics ranked China (first), India (twelfth), Russia (twenty-third), Brazil (twenty-sixth), South Africa (thirty-fourth), Thailand (thirty-eighth), and Malaysia (thirty-ninth) within the world's top forty based on the volume of Patent Cooperation Treaty applications filed.[46] Of these countries, only China (third), Russia (fourteenth), India (twenty-second), Brazil (thirty-eighth), and Malaysia (fortieth) remained in the top forty when the rankings focused on international trademark applications under the Madrid Agreement Concerning the International

[43] TRIPS Agreement, *supra* note 4, art. 27.1.

[44] Panel Report, *Canada – Patent Protection of Pharmaceutical Products*, WTO Doc. WT/DS114/R, ¶ 7.94 (adopted Mar. 17, 2000).

[45] Paul A. David, *Intellectual Property Institutions and the Panda's Thumb: Patents, Copyrights, and Trade Secrets in Economic Theory and History*, *in* GLOBAL DIMENSIONS OF INTELLECTUAL PROPERTY RIGHTS IN SCIENCE AND TECHNOLOGY 19, 43 (Mitchel B. Wallerstein, Mary Ellen Mogee & Roberta A. Schoen eds., 1993).

[46] *Annex 1: International Patent Applications by Origin (PCT System)*, WORLD INTELL. PROP. ORG. (Feb. 10, 2022), www.wipo.int/export/sites/www/pressroom/en/documents/pr_2022_886_annexes.pdf.

Registration of Marks and its related protocol.[47] Thailand and South Africa were fifty-seventh and 127th, respectively.[48]

From a policy standpoint, the differing levels of intellectual property protection needed by the varying industrial sectors may raise an additional question concerning whether those middle-income countries with highly divergent sectoral developments could ultimately develop coherent nationwide intellectual property policies.[49] As I observed more than a decade ago, China may "prefer stronger protection of intellectual property rights in entertainment, software, semiconductors, and selected areas of biotechnology to increased protection in areas concerning pharmaceuticals, chemicals, fertilizers, seeds, and foodstuffs."[50] Although China has since moved up economically and technologically and has now opted for stronger protection in other areas, such as pharmaceutical and biological products,[51] its initial reluctance to strengthen protection in all fields of technologies underscores the challenge of formulating a coherent intellectual property policy that is responsive to the country's highly uneven economic and technological developments.

3.2.3 *Income Inequality*

The final type of inequality that warrants scholarly and policy attention pertains to the gap in income and wealth between the rich and the poor, which is often measured using Gini coefficients.[52] Drawing on World Bank statistics, Table 3.4 tracks the changes in income inequality in 1995 (the year the TRIPS Agreement entered into force), 2005 (the last year the TRIPS provisions on pharmaceutical patents were allowed to take effect in developing countries), and 2015 (twenty years after the TRIPS Agreement took effect). Considering that Gini coefficients alone may not reveal the full extent of income disparities,[53] this table also lists the

47 *Annex 5: International Trademark Applications by Origin (Madrid System)*, WORLD INTELL. PROP. ORG. (Feb. 10, 2022), www.wipo.int/export/sites/www/pressroom/en/documents/pr_2022_886_annexes.pdf.

48 *Id.*

49 Yu, *supra* note 35, at 2096.

50 Peter K. Yu, *International Enclosure, the Regime Complex, and Intellectual Property Schizophrenia*, 2007 MICH. ST. L. REV. 1, 25.

51 Peter K. Yu, *From Struggle to Surge: China's TRIPS Experience and Its Lessons for Access to Medicines*, *in* INTELLECTUAL PROPERTY LAW AND ACCESS TO MEDICINES: TRIPS AGREEMENT, HEALTH, AND PHARMACEUTICALS 172 (Srividhya Ragavan & Amaka Vanni eds., 2021); Peter K. Yu, *China's Innovative Turn and the Changing Pharmaceutical Landscape*, 51 U. PAC. L. REV. 593, 602–08 (2020) [hereinafter Yu, *China's Innovative Turn*].

52 The Gini Index provided by the World Bank "measures the extent to which the distribution of income (or, in some cases, consumption expenditure) among individuals or households within an economy deviates from a perfectly equal distribution." *Metadata Glossary*, WORLD BANK, https://databank.worldbank.org/metadataglossary/gender-statistics/series/SI.POV.GINI (last visited May 24, 2021).

53 PIKETTY, CAPITAL AND IDEOLOGY, *supra* note 24, at 26; PIKETTY, CAPITAL IN THE TWENTY-FIRST CENTURY, *supra* note 24, at 266–67.

TABLE 3.4 *Changes in income inequality from 1995 to 2015*

Country	1995 Gini	2005 Gini	2015 Gini	1995 Top 10%	2005 Top 10%	2015 Top 10%	1995 Bottom 10%	2005 Bottom 10%	2015 Bottom 10%
Argentina	48.9	47.7	41.6[*]	37.0	34.9	29.9[*]	1.1	1.3	1.8[*]
Brazil	59.6	56.3	51.9	47.5	44.6	40.9	0.8	1.0	1.2
China	35.2[**]	40.9	38.6	27.3[**]	30.9	29.4	3.1[**]	2.4	2.6
India	31.7[‡‡]	34.4[‡]	35.7[†]	26.7[‡‡]	29.2[‡]	30.1[†]	3.8[‡‡]	3.7[‡]	3.5[†]
Indonesia	32.0[‡‡]	33.0	39.7	27.0[‡‡]	27.4	32.4	3.9[‡‡]	3.6	3.0
Malaysia	48.5	46.4[§]	41.1	37.9	35.1[§]	31.3	1.8	1.8[§]	2.3
Philippines	N/A	46.6[§]	44.6	N/A	36.6[§]	34.9	N/A	2.1[§]	2.3
Russia	N/A	N/A	36.6	N/A	N/A	26.8	N/A	N/A	2.2
South Africa	59.3[‡‡]	64.8	63.0[*]	46.7[‡‡]	54.2	50.5[*]	1.3[‡‡]	1.0	0.9[*]
Thailand	43.5[††]	42.5[‡]	36.0	34.9[††]	33.8[‡]	28.4	2.5[††]	2.5[‡]	3.2

[*] 2014 data; [†] 2011 data; [‡] 2004 data; [§] 2003 data; [**] 1996 data; [††] 1994 data; [‡‡] 1993 data.
Note: This table draws on World Bank data in the following areas: (1) Gini index, (2) income share held by highest 10%, and (3) income share held by lowest 10%.

respective figures for the income share of both the top and bottom deciles in each country.

Although the Gini coefficients of countries such as China, India, and South Africa have increased from 1995 to 2005, with the top decile getting a larger share of income, similar figures for other middle-income countries have remained stagnant or fallen. The lack of conclusive evidence on correlation in this area is understandable. While stronger intellectual property protection generated by the TRIPS Agreement reduced affordable access to intellectual property–based goods and services, thereby widening the gap between the rich and the poor, the positive benefits provided by the WTO, trade liberalization, and the entry of foreign investors reduced income inequality.

A considerable increase in income inequality following the adoption of the TRIPS Agreement would certainly be alarming. Such an increase would suggest the adverse impacts of inappropriate WTO rules in intellectual property or other areas. Even a slight increase or a limited decline can still raise questions about why the change did not correspond to the more significantly reduced economic and technological gaps between the Global North and middle-income countries. Based on these developments, one may wonder whether national inequality will become a bigger issue for the latter in the near future, considering the fast-closing gap between these two groups of countries. As Branko Milanovic reminded us:

> With the increases of mean incomes in Asian countries, the gaps between countries have actually been narrowing. If this trend of economic convergence continues, not only will it lead to shrinking global inequality but it will, indirectly, also give

> relatively greater salience to inequalities within nations. In fifty years or so, we might return to the situation that existed in the early nineteenth century, when most of global inequality was due to income differences between rich and poor Britons, rich and poor Russians, or rich and poor Chinese, and not so much to the fact that mean incomes in the West were greater than mean incomes in Asia.[54]

Likewise, François Bourguignon observed:

> [A]s the rise in national inequality ... seems to coincide with the recent acceleration of globalization, we have a tendency to conclude that the latter was responsible for the former, even if, paradoxically, globalization has *also contributed* to a drop in international inequalities. However, once we have looked at it through both national and international lenses, the relationship between globalization and inequality turns out to be more complex than it first appears.[55]

In the intellectual property field, the growing attention on national inequality has raised questions about whether the imbalance in the existing international intellectual property regime could exacerbate inequality in income and wealth – the subject of fast-expanding scholarly inquiry.[56] Moreover, because an intellectual property system would inevitably affect one's ability to use new technology – which has a demonstrated impact on income inequality[57] – problems in the intellectual property system could create a vicious cycle that would further widen the gap between the rich and the poor within a country. Thus, when policymakers adjust intellectual property laws and policies – for example, to align them more closely with developed country standards – they will have to think deeper about the distributive effects of those adjustments as well as the preemptive or corrective measures that could be introduced to prevent further increasing income inequality.

3.3 RECOMMENDATIONS FOR INTERVENTIONS

Using middle-income countries as illustrations, the previous section calls for greater scholarly and policy attention to national inequality in the intellectual property

[54] MILANOVIC, *supra* note 24, at 5.

[55] BOURGUIGNON, *supra* note 24, at 2–3.

[56] Included in this fast-growing literature are Samuel Adams, *Globalization and Income Inequality: Implications for Intellectual Property Rights*, 30 J. POL'Y MODELING 725 (2008); Philippe Aghion, Ufuk Akcigit, Antonin Bergeaud, Richard Blundell & David Hemous, *Innovation and Top Income Inequality*, 86 REV. ECON. STUD. 1 (2019); Sourav Bhattacharya, Pavel Chakraborty & Chirantan Chatterjee, *Intellectual Property Regimes and Wage Inequality*, 154 J. DEV. ECON. 102709 (2022); Angus C. Chu, *Effects of Patent Policy on Income and Consumption Inequality in a R&D Growth Model*, 77 S. ECON. J. 336 (2010); Christian Kiedaisch, *Growth and Welfare Effects of Intellectual Property Rights When Consumers Differ in Income*, 72 ECON. THEORY 1121 (2021); Swati Saini & Meeta Keswani Mehra, *Impact of Strengthening Intellectual Property Rights Regime on Income Inequality: An Econometric Analysis*, 38 ECON. BULL. 1703 (2018). Thanks to Keith Maskus for suggesting these sources in Chapter 1 in this volume.

[57] BOURGUIGNON, *supra* note 24, at 85–87.

context, which has been largely underexplored when compared with global inequality. To help combat national inequality, this section recommends interventions in three areas: (1) international norm-setting, (2) national policymaking, and (3) academic and policy research. Although these interventions were developed with middle-income countries in mind, many of them will be equally relevant to high- and low-income countries.

3.3.1 *International Norm-Setting*

From the inception of the Paris and Berne Conventions, the international intellectual property regime has focused primarily on developments across nations. Although countries at that time were eager to develop international standards for protecting literary, artistic, and industrial property, the original conventions ended with a modest set of international minimum standards and a provision recognizing the principle of national treatment, which prohibits the discrimination against foreign authors and inventors.[58]

This nation-based focus on international norm-setting continues even today despite the adoption of much higher intellectual property standards, such as those enshrined in the TRIPS Agreement and TRIPS-plus bilateral, regional, and plurilateral agreements. Notwithstanding this continuous focus, the specific and detailed standards laid down in these agreements have greatly eroded the policy space that countries have traditionally retained to design intellectual property laws and policies.[59] As a result, policymakers, especially those in developing countries, have great difficulty optimizing the intellectual property system based on local conditions. Should inequalities within the country arise or grow, these policymakers will have less policy space and a tougher time harnessing the intellectual property system to combat those inequalities.

Given the significant inequalities within developing countries that have been documented in this chapter – whether at the geographic, sectoral, or income level – it is high time that policymakers explored more actively the feasibility of putting in place a system that would allow for greater subnational policy variations than what is now found in the Global North. Consider, for instance, the law and policies needed to address geographic inequality within a country. While Article 27.1 of the TRIPS Agreement states that WTO members cannot discriminate "as to the place of invention, the field of technology and whether products are imported or locally produced,"[60] the WTO panel in *Canada – Patent Protection of Pharmaceutical*

58 Berne Convention for the Protection of Literary and Artistic Works art. 5(1), Sept. 9, 1886, 1161 U.N.T.S. 3 (revised at Paris July 24, 1971); Paris Convention for the Protection of Industrial Property art. 2(1), Mar. 20, 1883, 828 U.N.T.S. 305 (revised at Stockholm July 14, 1967).

59 Peter K. Yu, *The International Enclosure Movement*, 82 IND. L.J. 827, 858–70 (2007).

60 TRIPS Agreement, *supra* note 4, art. 27.1.

Products made clear that "differentiation" does not always amount to "discrimination."[61]

Moreover, although countries tend to have nationwide intellectual property standards, a scrutiny of the actual protection on the ground shows subnational variations, which widen even more when one takes judicial enforcement into consideration. Such subnational variations are common in not only the Global South but also the Global North. In the United States, for example, appellate courts continue to disagree over the protection of intellectual property rights, generating what commentators generally refer to as "circuit splits."[62] A case in point is the protection offered by national trademark and unfair competition laws. Although the legal standards may be the same on paper – that is, based on the federal Lanham Act – they differ at times in practice, not to mention the differing levels of protection offered by state unfair competition laws.[63]

Finally, there is a growing trend for developing countries to establish "free trade zones," "customs free zones," or "export processing free zones" to attract foreign investors.[64] These free zones tend to offer "relaxed regulations, limited taxes[,] ... reduced oversight ... [and] softened Customs control" – features that differ significantly from those in other parts of the country.[65] Thus, even though subnational policy variations seem suspect under WTO rules at first glance, the question on the permissibility of these variations is not as straightforward when one goes deeper into how trade and intellectual property laws currently operate in practice. Indeed, the existence of free trade zones or their equivalents within the WTO framework strongly suggests the possibility for greater subnational policy variations or differentiation.

3.3.2 *National Policymaking*

Even if the WTO and the TRIPS-based international intellectual property regime do not prohibit subnational policy variations per se, countries may decline to adopt laws that would support such variations. For national unity, legislative convenience, practical considerations, and other reasons, countries may embrace uniform nationwide standards even when those standards do not provide benefits to every

61 Panel Report, *supra* note 44, ¶ 7.94.

62 Graeme B. Dinwoodie, *International Intellectual Property Litigation: A Vehicle for Resurgent Comparativist Thought*, 49 AM. J. COMP. L. 429, 430 (2001).

63 Peter S. Menell, *Regulating "Spyware": The Limitations of State "Laboratories" and the Case for Federal Preemption of State Unfair Competition Laws*, 20 BERKELEY TECH. L.J. 1363, 1380–95 (2005).

64 Susan Tiefenbrun, *U.S. Foreign Trade Zones, Tax-Free Trade Zones of the World, and Their Impact on the U.S. Economy*, 12 J. INT'L BUS. & L. 149, 167–80 (2013).

65 BUSINESS ACTION TO STOP COUNTERFEITING & PIRACY, INTERNATIONAL CHAMBER OF COMMERCE, CONTROLLING THE ZONE: BALANCING FACILITATION AND CONTROL TO COMBAT ILLICIT TRADE IN THE WORLD'S FREE TRADE ZONES 1 (2013).

geographic region or industrial sector. Indeed, compromises in national policymaking are both common and inevitable.

Nevertheless, policymakers pushing for higher intellectual property standards should pay greater attention to mechanisms that could help strike a more appropriate balance in the domestic intellectual property system. Among the balancing mechanisms that have received wide support in the developing world are limitations and exceptions in copyright law for educational and research purposes; limitations and exceptions in patent law for research, early working, and the development of diagnostics; restrictions on patent protection for microorganisms and diagnostic, therapeutic, and surgical methods; compulsory licensing of vaccines, pharmaceuticals, and medical technologies; support for parallel importation of copyrighted, patented, and trademarked products; limits to injunctive relief; significantly reduced penalties for noncommercial infringement; and measures to prevent abuse of intellectual property rights and other anticompetitive practices.

At the institutional level, policymakers could consider adjustments to make the intellectual property system more supportive of individual creators and inventors and small and medium-sized enterprises. In Chapter 5 in this volume, Daniel Benoliel and Rochelle Dreyfuss proposed adjustments to the patent system that would promote creation and invention in the Global South.[66] Commentators have also highlighted the pro-development potential of utility models, geographical indications, the protection of traditional knowledge and cultural expressions, and other forms of intellectual property rights.[67] As if these proposals were not enough, a growing volume of literature now showcases the positive economic and development benefits of open innovation models as well as alternative incentive frameworks, such as grants, prizes, and advance market commitments.[68] Some commentators have also advanced "new concepts such as 'frugal', 'reverse' or 'trickle-up' innovation," which are attractive to not only developing countries but also the disadvantaged populations in developed countries.[69]

While adjustments to intellectual property laws and policies often provide the first line of reform, policymakers should also consider alternative or supplemental adjustments outside the intellectual property system. For instance, they could

[66] See Chapter 5 in this volume.

[67] Geographical Indications at the Crossroads of Trade, Development, and Culture: Focus on Asia-Pacific 259–435 (Irene Calboli & Ng-Loy Wee Loon eds., 2017); Innovation without Patents: Harnessing the Creative Spirit in a Diverse World (Uma Suthersanen, Graham Dutfield & Chow Kit Boey eds., 2007); Poor People's Knowledge: Promoting Intellectual Property in Developing Countries (J. Michael Finger & Philip Schuler eds., 2004).

[68] Gene Patents and Collaborative Licensing Models: Patent Pools, Clearinghouses, Open Source Models and Liability Regimes 169–244 (Geertrui Van Overwalle ed., 2009); Amy Kapczynski, *Order without Intellectual Property Law: Open Science in Influenza*, 102 Cornell L. Rev. 1539 (2017).

[69] World Intellectual Property Organization, *supra* note 42, at 40.

develop a well-functioning transfer mechanism that would allow the anticipated winners from intellectual property reforms to share benefits with the potential losers. As Frederick Abbott reminded us about the adverse public health implications of bilateral and regional trade agreements:

> The problem with . . . using net economic gains or losses as the developing country benchmark is that gains for a developing country's textile or agricultural producers do not directly translate into higher public or private health expenditures. Salaries for part of the workforce may increase and government tax revenues may rise, and this may indirectly help to offset pharmaceutical price increases. However, in order for the health sector not to be adversely affected, there must be some type of transfer payment, whether in the form of increased public health expenditures on pharmaceuticals, by providing health insurance benefits, or other affirmative acts. In a world of economic scarcity, the prospect that governments will act to offset increases in medicines prices with increased public health expenditures is uncertain.[70]

To prevent intellectual property reforms from increasing national inequality, policymakers could undertake two general types of complementary reforms to help redistribute benefits: ex ante and ex post.[71] Ex ante redistribution could include changes in education and healthcare policies. For example, commentators have called for expanded access to education and reduced educational inequalities.[72] By transferring technology and know-how, education will help create a more level playing field for disadvantaged populations. Indeed, knowledge transfer is so important that commentators have proposed intellectual property reforms to improve the educational environment.[73]

Another ex ante mechanism for redistributing the benefits of intellectual property reforms is in the healthcare area. Healthcare reform, including efforts to make pharmaceuticals and other health products more affordable, will increase the productivity and life expectancy of disadvantaged populations and thereby enable them to amass greater wealth. In relation to China, for instance, I have advocated reform to increase public access to healthcare products and services in anticipation of the country's active push for the development of national champions in the pharmaceutical sector.[74]

70 Frederick M. Abbott, *The Cycle of Action and Reaction: Developments and Trends in Intellectual Property and Health*, *in* NEGOTIATING HEALTH: INTELLECTUAL PROPERTY AND ACCESS TO MEDICINES 27, 33 (Pedro Roffe, Geoff Tansey & David Vivas-Eugui eds., 2006).

71 BOURGUIGNON, *supra* note 24, at 167.

72 *Id.* at 167–70; MILANOVIC, *supra* note 24, at 221–22.

73 See, for example, SUSAN ISIKO STRBA, INTERNATIONAL COPYRIGHT LAW AND ACCESS TO EDUCATION IN DEVELOPING COUNTRIES: EXPLORING MULTILATERAL LEGAL AND QUASI-LEGAL SOLUTIONS (2012); Margaret Chon, *Copyright and Capability for Education: An Approach "from Below,"* *in* INTELLECTUAL PROPERTY AND HUMAN DEVELOPMENT: CURRENT TRENDS AND FUTURE SCENARIOS 218 (Wong Tzen & Graham Dutfield eds., 2010).

74 Yu, *China's Innovative Turn*, *supra* note 50, at 613–14.

Like ex ante redistribution, ex post redistribution – through tax-and-transfer mechanisms, perhaps – could be equally effective.[75] While the provision of subsidies, grants, or tax credits to local creators and inventors[76] could raise questions about national treatment under the TRIPS Agreement if those benefits would affect the availability, acquisition, or maintenance of intellectual property rights,[77] such provision would be deemed more acceptable if they were available to all creators and inventors – foreign and local alike. Because foreign creators and inventors in the developing world tend to be of a considerable size, the introduction of qualification thresholds in subsidies, grants, and tax credits could help ensure the careful tailoring of benefits to those in need, including local creators and inventors. Meanwhile, by offering identical benefits to similarly situated creators and inventors regardless of their country of origin, these incentive measures would arguably provide "effective equality of opportunities" – a criterion that WTO panels have used to evaluate treaty compliance.[78]

Thus far, economists have widely debated whether ex ante or ex post redistribution would be more efficient. The outcome of this analysis will likely depend on the specific conditions of the country involved. Given these diverging conditions, there may also be an additional question concerning what development goals the redistribution policies should prioritize. Fortunately, the U.N. General Assembly provided some helpful guidance when it adopted seventeen Sustainable Development Goals in December 2015 to replace the 2000 Millennium Development Goals. Sustainable Development Goal 10 specifically calls for reducing "inequality within and among countries" – the two types of inequality explored in this chapter. The goals' supportive plan of action, *Transforming Our World: The 2030 Agenda for Sustainable Development*, further identified "poverty eradication, health, education and food security and nutrition" as continuing development priorities.[79]

3.3.3 *Academic and Policy Research*

The last set of recommended interventions concerns academic and policy research. Emanating from this chapter's focus is a line of inquiry targeting the growing inequalities within countries and the benefits and drawbacks of greater subnational policy variations. As noted earlier, because cross-country comparisons have

75 Bourguignon, *supra* note 24, at 158–67.

76 Economic Impacts of Intellectual Property–Conditioned Government Incentives (Dan Prud'homme & Song Hefa eds., 2016).

77 TRIPS Agreement, *supra* note 4, art. 3.

78 Appellate Body Report, *United States – Section 211 Omnibus Appropriations Act of 1998*, ¶ 258, WTO Doc. WT/DS176/AB/R (adopted Jan. 2, 2002).

79 G.A. Res. 70/1, Transforming Our World: The 2030 Agenda for Sustainable Development, ¶ 17 (Oct. 21, 2015).

dominated the literature on international intellectual property law and policy, limited research has been devoted to the wide disparities within each country. Academic and policy researchers should therefore devote greater attention to inequality within countries than among countries.

A second, and related, line of inquiry pertains to the linkage between intellectual property and non–intellectual property policies, such as those relating to education, healthcare, tax, and subsidies. A greater exploration and deeper understanding of this linkage will improve our ability to use these policies to redistribute the benefits of intellectual property reforms, including the new knowledge generated from stronger intellectual property protection, from the beneficiaries in the country to the disadvantaged parts. Whether ex ante or ex post, such redistribution will help minimize national inequality.

A third line of inquiry targets specific intellectual property developments in middle-income countries. Although a fast-growing literature has covered such developments in BRICS countries,[80] with additional country-based studies conducted on Indonesia, Malaysia, Thailand, Vietnam, and other emerging countries, there remains a dearth of scholarship on intellectual property developments across middle-income countries. Academic and policy researchers should therefore undertake more extensive research in this area.

A better understanding of developments within and across middle-income countries will likely challenge our prevailing understanding of international intellectual property law and policy, especially in relation to the North–South debate. Studying these countries may also help identify new problems and challenges in the intellectual property area. For example, many middle-income countries continue to face significant piracy and counterfeiting problems even though they have become quite innovative and now experience ever-growing intellectual property activities.[81] A case in point is China, which leads the world in not only international patent applications and intellectual property litigation[82] but also in the volume of pirated and counterfeit goods. Thus far, we do not have sufficient theoretical and empirical accounts to explain how countries could cope with intellectual property developments that proceed simultaneously in two diametrically opposed directions.[83] Greater research on this topic, or other unique issues found in middle-income countries, could therefore help improve our ability to address problems in the international intellectual property regime.

80 For this literature, see sources collected in Peter K. Yu, *A Half-Century of Scholarship on the Chinese Intellectual Property System*, 67 Am. U. L. Rev. 1045, 1115 n.303 (2018).

81 Yu, *supra* note 20, at 99–100.

82 China National Intellectual Property Administration, The Status of Intellectual Property Protection in China in 2020, at 4 (2020); Peter K. Yu, *The Rise and Decline of the Intellectual Property Powers*, 34 Campbell L. Rev. 525, 544–49 (2012).

83 Peter K. Yu, *Intellectual Property, Asian Philosophy and the Yin-Yang School*, 7 WIPO J. 1, 12–13 (2015).

CONCLUSION

The arrival of middle-income countries has raised intriguing questions about intellectual property, innovation, and global inequality. The success of these countries, especially those with considerable and ever-growing strengths in the intellectual property area, has shown the oversimplification of the binary North–South debate on intellectual property law and policy and its inability to capture the ongoing developments in the intellectual property field. The wide geographic, sectoral, and income inequalities within these countries have also called for greater scholarly and policy attention to subnational developments.

Focusing on the intellectual property developments within and across a group of fast-growing middle-income countries, this chapter not only documents the considerable inequalities among and within countries but also highlights the feasibility and benefits of using subnational policy variations to combat national inequality. Specifically, this chapter recommends interventions in three areas: international norm-setting, national policymaking, and academic and policy research. It is my hope that intellectual property policymakers and scholars will start paying greater attention to inequality within countries, just as they studied inequality among countries more than two decades ago.

4

Is IPR a Facilitator of, or a Barrier to, Catch-Up by Latecomers?

Implications for Global Inequality

Keun Lee[*]

INTRODUCTION

The role of intellectual property rights (IPRs) in the economic growth of countries has long been the topic of academic research and policy debates. The classical issue of the relationship between IPRs and innovation has been whether strong or weak IPR protection stimulates innovation (Awokuse and Yin, 2010; Maskus and Penubarti, 1995; Smith, 1999). While there is some evidence of the effects of strong IPRs, particularly patent rights, on economic growth, the debate is far from settled, and the evidence is mixed. Further, even if IPR protection creates incentive effects, the linkage is valid only when innovation capability exists. Otherwise, or in the context of typical developing countries where innovation capabilities are absent, innovation would not occur even with strong IPRs (Lee, 2019). Thus, the literature has explored the possibility that IPRs could have differential effects on countries at different stages of economic development. Their importance was acknowledged in a World Bank publication (Fink and Maskus, 2005) and partly addressed in global intellectual property reforms (see Commission on Intellectual Property Rights, 2002). Indeed, a large volume of literature – albeit with mixed results – focused on this dynamic relationship between the protection of IPRs and economic growth at different stages, such as Kanwar and Evenson (2003) and Falvey et al. (2006).

More recent literature tends to shift the focus from the strength of IPR protection on economic growth at different stages to the roles of diverse forms of IPR in facilitating innovation capabilities of the lagging or latecomer economies. Kim et al. (2012) first turned to the new issue of the impacts of the different *types* of IPR, rather than the *strength* of IPR protection, that would be appropriate for countries at different stages of economic development. Given that through

[*] For two rounds of feedback and comments, the author would like to thank the reviewers and his coeditors, as well as the participants at the workshop held in Haifa, Israel.

adaptation, imitation, and incremental innovation, firms in developing economies can acquire knowledge and enjoy some learning-by-doing (Suthersanen, 2006), and the innovations they produce may not have the inventive step to merit a traditional patent, Kim et al. (2012) suggested and verified the idea that the second-tier industrial property right – namely, a utility model (or petit or petty patents) – may be relevant and useful at lower level of development, serving as a stepping stone for further technological progress.

This idea of different forms of IPR at different stages of economic development is consistent with Lee (2019), which shows that advanced economies and latecomer economies at the middle- or lower-income stages have different growth mechanisms and that a very "narrow passage" exists between these countries. Thus, one must be careful when crossing such passages to avoid falling into the middle-income trap (MIT): a situation where middle-income economies tend to face decelerated growth and consequently fail to join the ranks of high-income economies. Several studies have verified that different countries adopt varying growth mechanisms, such that economic growth at the lower-income stages is correlated with basic political institutions and human capital. In contrast, the economic growth at the higher-income stages (upper-middle- and high-income) is correlated with innovation capabilities and tertiary education.[1] The division of the world into two or three groups at different stages is consistent with the idea of an MIT.

The existence of the MIT was first mentioned by Gill and Kharas (2007) and has since gained popularity among scholars and international institutions (e.g., Eichengreen et al., 2012, 2013; Ito, 2017; Lee, 2013; World Bank, 2010). Whereas some scholars have rejected the existence of this trap, it is clear that many middle-income economies are struggling to achieve high-income status. The MIT is, therefore, a relevant issue.[2] Numerous studies have tried to investigate the key factors responsible for this trap, such as demographic conditions, institutions, industry and trade structures, diversification, physical infrastructure, and macro-financial developments (Aiyar et al., 2013). One argument, supported by an Asian Development Bank-sponsored study (Eichengreen et al., 2012, 2013) and by Lee (2013), is that innovation capabilities are the key binding constraint for the MIT. This view is also consistent with the early statement by the World Bank (2010) that middle-income economies would tend to fall under a trap because they get caught between low-wage manufacturers and high-wage innovators; their wage rates are too high to compete with low-wage exporters, and the level of their technological capability is too low to enable them to compete with advanced countries. The importance of innovation as the cause of the MIT is consistent with the experience of a very small number of East Asian economies that have successfully transitioned into

1 Lee and Kim (2009) provide some examples.

2 A study by the World Bank (2012: 12) finds that only 12 out of 101 middle-income economies have reached the status of high-income economy since 1960.

high-income economies in the past decades. Since the mid-1980s, South Korea and Taiwan transitioned from low-wage-based economies to high-end goods economies due to their growing innovation capabilities (Lee, 2013: ch. 3).

Given this linkage between innovation capability and the MIT, it is very important to explore the role of the IPR regimes in innovation and economic growth in latecomer countries. Without enhancing innovation and the growth of these countries, global inequality will not be reduced. Thus, we first discuss the roles of diverse forms of IPR in promoting innovation among latecomers. Then we turn to the issue of the impacts of strong IPR protection in Northern, or advanced, economies on the exports by Southern, or catch-up, economies to Northern markets. This issue is also related to global inequality and specifically to the Agreement on Trade-Related Aspects of Intellectual Property Rights (TRIPS).

TRIPS regulates minimum standards for domestic IPRs. Most developed economies have already surpassed the minimum TRIPS criteria (Deere, 2009; Park, 2008). However, for developing countries (or low-technology exporters), higher global minimum IPR standards may be akin to a tax in the sense that they increase research and development (R&D) expenses for net technology borrowers who incur higher royalties and licensing fees (Glass and Saggi, 2002; Siebeck, 1990). To meet higher IPR standards, developing country exporters face higher production costs to access global information and enter global markets (Helpman, 1993; Lai and Qiu, 2003). Moreover, as Auriol and Biancini (2010) and Odagiri et al. (2010) show, tighter global IPRs, particularly in developed country markets, can act as a barrier to the entry of developing country exports into developed country markets. This is particularly so if developing country products are found to be infringing or too imitative under the IPR regime of destination markets and thus cannot legally enter those markets.

Developing country exporters who enter developed country markets still face higher legal and administrative costs of procuring IPRs, such as patents, enforcing rights, and contesting IPR claims. Thus, two key burdens for developing economies exist under TRIPS. First, the domestic costs of establishing an IPR system in accordance with TRIPS have been exorbitant in the developing world (Finger, 2002; Schneider, 2005).[3] Second, if any dispute arises, the global transaction costs incurred by legal fees and litigation expenditures dampen the benefits of exporting. Thus, the overall impact of the strong IPR protection in developed countries could reduce exports from developing countries, especially those trying to promote their exports by building up innovation capabilities.

This chapter concludes by discussing the possible way to overcome IPR-related barriers to catch-up by latecomer countries – namely, the roles and potentials of leapfrogging.

[3] For example, Schneider (2005) finds this implication in her empirical results. She also argues that strong domestic IPRs may hurt innovation in developing countries, since their innovations are imitative or adaptive in nature.

4.1 FROM THE STRENGTH OF IPR PROTECTION TO DIVERSE FORMS OF IPR

4.1.1 *Regular Patents versus Utility Models for Innovation in Latecomers*

While patents are the most common form of IPR protection related to innovation, it is somewhat doubtful whether they are effective instruments for appropriating the returns to innovation in developing countries. In a well-known survey of U.S. firms, Cohen et al. (2000) found that firms patent for various purposes other than merely appropriating returns. For example, possession of patent rights plays an important role in litigation (to deter threats of infringement suits or countersuits) and in cross-licensing negotiations (where firms can better gain access to rivals' technologies if they can reciprocate with their patent rights). However, the survey found that smaller firms or inventors are less able to utilize patents for those purposes and are dissuaded from availing themselves of patent protection. Litigation costs are especially onerous for small firms since they have lower levels of output to spread the overhead costs of legal protection (e.g., legal staff).

Furthermore, smaller firms or inventors have fewer and perhaps less valuable technologies in cross-licensing negotiations. The implication for developing economies is that to the extent that a large number of their inventors are small, patents are not very effective instruments for appropriating returns or accessing technologies.[4] This may explain why developing economies do not engage as intensively in producing patentable innovations and why something like utility models may serve as a useful alternative for emerging innovation.

The classic issue of the relationship between IPRs and innovation has been whether strong or weak IPR protection stimulates innovation (Awokuse and Yin, 2010; Maskus and Penubarti, 1995; Smith, 1999). However, without innovation capability, nothing is produced even with strong IPRs (Lee, 2019). Thus, recent literature tends to shift the focus from the strength of protection on economic growth at different stages to the roles of diverse forms of IPR. This shift makes sense because innovation in many developing countries is of the adaptive, imitative type. Their innovations may not have the inventive step to merit a regular patent. Still, they may qualify for a second-tier industrial property right: a utility model. Through adaptation, imitation, and incremental innovation, firms in developing economies can acquire knowledge and enjoy some learning-by-doing (Suthersanen, 2006).

Both patents and utility models are exclusive rights granted for an invention, which allow rights holders to prevent others from commercially using the protected

4 Mazzoleni and Nelson (1998) also discuss how strong, broad patents in less-developed countries could impede the development of indigenous manufacturing capabilities by creating entry barriers. The idea that latecomers do not always have to develop high-level innovations contrasts with the argument of the vintage capital model technologies that everybody targets frontier technologies (Gilchrist and Williams, 2001).

inventions without their authorization for a limited period. However, beyond this basic definition, differences exist between invention patents and utility models, based on standards of inventiveness and legal requirements.

Patents are granted for inventions that are novel, nonobvious, and capable of industrial applicability. They are typically granted for twenty years from the date of application, cover products and processes, undergo substantive examination, and are costly to obtain (involving, where applicable, filing, attorney, and translation fees). Utility models provide second-tier protection for minor inventions, such as devices, tools, and implements, particularly in the mechanical, optical, and electronic fields. Processes or methods of production are typically excluded. The duration of protection is typically six to ten years. Utility models are generally less expensive to apply for and do not require substantive examination – for novelty, nonobviousness, and industrial applicability. The inventive step requirement is low; the invention typically must exhibit a practical or functional advantage over the prior art. Since the perceived inventive step threshold for utility models is much lower than that of patents, utility models are, in practice, sought for small, marginal innovations that may not meet the patentability criteria (Beneito, 2006).[5] Thus, utility models and patents differ in that they protect different types of innovations. Patents protect innovations of relatively high inventiveness, while utility models protect those of relatively low inventiveness.

Not all countries that grant patent rights also protect utility models; those that do not include the United States and the United Kingdom. The few developed countries that protect utility models are Germany, Japan, and some European countries. Countries that protect them are largely former or current developing economies, such as Korea, Taiwan, China, and Malaysia. In some cases, utility models are the dominant form of IPR. For example, in China, utility models accounted for nearly two-thirds of the total IPRs granted, while patents accounted for 10 percent between 1985 and 1998. The share of utility models in total IPRs has declined in China since then.

Korea is also among those developing countries where utility models have been intensively exploited. In 1961, the Korean government revised its entire system of intellectual property laws and established its first autonomous IPR system, protecting both conventional and minor innovations. Since the technological capabilities of Korean firms had been lagging during the 1960s and 1970s, firms relied heavily on imported technologies and reverse engineering and adapted them for local needs

[5] For example, utility models are granted to devices embodying a creative idea applicable to the shape, structure, or other technological aspects of a product, such as an improved device capable of reducing the amount of water used to flush a toilet, or a bottle cork remover capable of operating faster than known devices. These devices are not patentable but are inventive enough for utility model protection.

(Kim, 1997; Lee et al., 2003). This exercise enabled these firms to learn from foreign technologies. Accordingly, Korean inventors actively filed for utility model protection for their incremental innovations (Lee and Kim, 2010); until the early 1990s, the number of utility model applications in Korea exceeded that of invention patents. In the 1970s and the early 1980s, the ratio of utility models to patents was nearly two to three. This ratio peaked at more than six to one in 1984, after which it began to decline. Although the number of patent and utility model applications was still rising, the composition started to shift.

In the mid-1980s, Korea began to have as many valuable patentable assets to protect as those that foreign companies wanted to protect within Korea. Major IPR reforms were legislated in the mid-1980s, and since 1987, there has been an abrupt rise in the strength of patent protection and enlarged scope of protection. Substance patents for pharmaceutical and chemical materials and products were newly introduced, as well as for computer software and materials. The term of patent protection was also extended from twelve years to fifteen. Finally, by 1995, patent applications exceeded the number of utility model applications. These trends correspond with the transformation of Korea from a nation with limited technological resources and capabilities to one of the leading patenting nations.

In academic and policy debates, whether in the context of developed or developing countries, the focus has been on the appropriate strength of IPRs. While TRIPS does not deal with utility models, the World Intellectual Property Organization (WIPO) has recently considered the usefulness of utility model systems for lower-income countries (Commission on Intellectual Property Rights, 2002).[6] However, empirical evidence on the effects of utility models on innovation and growth is scant and is based largely on anecdotal evidence. Kumar (2002), for example, argued that in East Asia, utility models helped initiate a culture of patenting and innovation. The World Bank (2002) documented case studies in Brazil where utility models allowed domestic producers to adapt foreign innovations to local needs and conditions. More formal econometric evidence is provided by Maskus and McDaniel (1999), who studied the use of utility models in Japan and found that such protection, on balance, had a positive impact on the growth of total factor productivity in Japan.

Kim et al. (2012) first investigated the different roles of patents and utility models in the innovation and economic growth of countries at different levels of economic development. The main finding was that the relative importance of patent rights and utility model protection to innovation and growth varies by the level of technological development. Kim et al. (2012) found that patent protection contributes to innovation and economic growth in developed countries but not in developing

[6] See World Intellectual Property Organization (2022a, 2022b).

countries. Their framing is consistent with the view that patent protection matters to industrial activities only after countries have achieved a threshold level of indigenous innovative capacity and an extensive science and technology infrastructure (Kim, 1997; Lall and Albaladejo, 2001). In contrast, utility model protection weakly affects innovation and growth in developed countries but allows developing economies to build their indigenous innovative capacities.

Additionally, using data from Korean firms, Kim et al. (2012) found that when firms are technologically lagging – as in Korea before the 1990s – utility models (or minor inventions) contribute to firm growth and their capacity to produce (future) patentable inventions. Once firms become more technologically advanced – as in Korea since the 1990s – their performance has been driven less by utility model innovations and more by patentable innovations. Most importantly, the empirical analysis also shows that those firms that used to file utility model applications have evolved to file regular patents with lags of several years, providing contrast to the conventional economic model that assumes a fixed dichotomy of innovators versus imitators (Barro and Sala-i-Martin, 1997; Eeckhout and Jovanovic, 2002). This evidence also serves as a counter-argument against the concern that a country's firms could be locked into minor adaptations protected by utility models.

In sum, these results indicate that different types of IPR are more appropriate for countries at different stages of economic development. Strong or weak IPR protection is not the key issue for developing countries, and what matters to innovation and growth is the strength of IPRs and the type of protection. In developing country markets, patents raise the costs of doing business and innovation. These costs tend to be more onerous for lower-income economies. In contrast, a utility model system provides an alternative way for such economies to create incentives for innovation, albeit incremental, without affecting the costs of doing business adversely while providing the technological inputs appropriate for local needs.

The experience of Korean firms and the country-level analyses suggest that the design and strength of IPR systems should be tailored to the indigenous technological capacities of firms to best provide the appropriate incentives for innovation.

4.1.2 *Trademark-Based Path for Latecomer Innovation and Development*

The preceding subsection discussed the patent-driven path of technological development for latecomer firms, such that developing countries are advised to adopt weaker IPR protection using utility models and then switch to regular patents later. This section asks whether there is an alternative, or nonpatent-driven, path of technological development for latecomers. In answering this question, it pays attention to the role of trademarks. Recently, trademarks have been recognized as another proxy measure of innovation, complementing or substituting patents (Allegrezza and Guarda-Rauchs, 1999; Block et al., 2015; Bosworth and Rogers, 2001; Flikkema et al., 2014; Greenhalgh and Rogers, 2006a, 2006b; Malmberg,

2005; Mehrazeen et al., 2012; Mendonça et al., 2004; Sandner and Block, 2011; Schmoch, 2003). Moreover, some researchers consider trademarks a market strategy for innovative firms or ventures (Block et al., 2014; Desyllas and Sako, 2013). While patents and utility models deal with a technological or scientific invention or improvement, trademarks are more market-based than technology-based IPRs.

A trademark encourages firms not only to make good products and adhere to a consistent level of quality but to link new products and services in the market (Block et al., 2014; Helmers and Rogers, 2010). Moreover, trademarks are also used to protect and appropriate the value of innovations in sectors where patents are not a viable option (De Vries et al., 2017). Firms that regard know-how or secrecy, which is a type of tacit knowledge, as an important protection method for innovative products are less likely to apply for patents. Thus, a product made using tacit knowledge can be protected and distinguished from competitors in the market and can establish market power through trademark registration.

Using Korean data, Kang et al. (2022) discuss two different paths of technological development: patent-driven and trademark-driven. They find that in some sectors – such as food, apparel, and pharmaceuticals – trademarks have been the dominant form of IPR, with a much larger number of registrations than patents from the initial stage of development to recent times. This finding contrasts with those in other sectors, such as electronics and automobiles, where patents have provided the main form of IPR during the 1990s and 2000s. This division of sectors into one path is largely determined by the nature of sectors or sectoral systems of innovation (Malerba, 2002, 2004; Malerba and Mani, 2009).

For instance, trademarks are more important when the innovation involves tacit knowledge that cannot be filed as a patent or when firms are more oriented toward domestic markets than world markets. While trademarks may also represent innovation, they can be filed without formal R&D activities targeting technological advances. Thus, one may reason that those sectors relying on trademarks over patents may be lagging in technological advances and are therefore more oriented toward domestic markets than international markets. We also note that patents tend to reflect more codifiable or explicit knowledge than tacit knowledge. Thus, one may reason that those trademark sectors correspond to the sectors with knowledge more tacit than codifiable. Kang et al. (2022) verified such correspondence in their empirical analysis.

To analyze sectoral differences in the dominant forms of IPR across sectors, Kang et al. (2022) have constructed firm-level data from 1971 to 2010 in Korea. They find that trademarks are dominant throughout the whole period in some sectors, whereas the dominant form of the IPR in other sectors changes to patents beginning in the 1990s. These two groups – trademarks and patents – are presented, respectively, in terms of the ratio of the number of patents to the number of trademarks.

The case of the patent-dominant group is consistent with the finding of Kim et al. (2012), which analyzed and compared the firm-level patent and utility model data divided into different periods. Specifically, in the early stage (before 1987), the utility model provided the dominant form of IPR, which correlated with the financial performance of firms. In the later stage (after 1987), however, firms mainly switched to filing patents, reflecting an enhanced level of technological capabilities, which also translated into performance. However, Kim et al. (2012) did not consider the impact of sectoral heterogeneity in this relationship among the different forms of IPR and the sectors' knowledge base and performance. They failed to consider the possibility of a nonpatent-driven path of development and catch-up for latecomer firms.

Kang et al. (2022) consider both patents and trademarks, classify the sectors by registration patterns, and investigate the differences between the two groups. They examine the dynamic patterns of the patent- and trademark-dominant groups over the periods to find the following stylized facts. First, at the beginning of Korea's industrial development, trademarks were the main forms of IPR in almost all sectors, as manufacturing firms typically registered trademarks more than other IPRs until the 1980s. This is consistent with the fact that until the late 1980s, the in-house R&D of firms was very low or just starting, and thus these firms had no technological innovations to patent (Chung and Lee, 2015). Second, the division of the two groups appeared only after the mid-1990s – that is, after a certain level of technological development was achieved. Even after the mid-1990s, the firms in the trademark group continue to register more trademarks than patents. However, such registration does not necessarily mean that the firms in this group did not do any R&D. Rather, it may reflect that the R&D outcomes might not be patentable as they involve more tacit knowledge, reflecting the knowledge base of the sectors. These facts are consistent with the interpretation that the registrations of trademarks and patents are related to different sectoral knowledge base and the different levels of technological capabilities in firms in different sectors. Regressions in their study confirm that the trademark groups covered those sectors involving more tacit knowledge and domestic market orientation, which are associated with slow progress in technological capabilities. These results imply that firms facing slow technological progress in sectors driven mostly by tacit knowledge tended to rely on trademarks in their growth and focused more on domestic markets than export markets. The results are important because they imply the existence of alternative paths of economic development by latecomer firms in different sectors, aside from the patent-driven path already articulated in Kim et al. (2012).

4.2 IPR PROTECTION AS A BARRIER TO CATCH-UP BY LATECOMERS

The theoretical literature thus far has identified two opposing effects of stronger IPRs in a destination country on the exports of a source country: *a market-expansion effect* and *a market-power effect* (Maskus and Penubarti, 1995). On the one hand, the exporters perceive an expansion in their market due to a reduction in imitation by local firms. The demand curve for their exports shifts out in the destination market. On the other hand, stronger IPRs in the destination country increase the exporters' market power, reducing the elasticity of the demand they face and, thus, the volume of exports. Hence, empirical analysis is typically pursued to see which effect dominates.[7]

However, one channel not analyzed thus far in the literature is the feedback effects of foreign IPRs and the exporter's level of technology (LT) on the exportability of the source country – or, more specifically, on the profitability of the relevant exports. The existing literature implicitly assumes that a source country has a sufficiently high LT that strong (or weak) foreign IPRs mainly affect the incentives of exporters to increase (or decrease) the volume of their exports – that is, to weigh the market expansion and market power effects of stronger IPRs abroad. For countries where exporters do not have high LTs or innovative capacity, TRIPS-like standards in importing countries could dampen exports from these countries.[8]

In fact, the WTO Dispute Settlement Body has overseen numerous TRIPS-related disputes; forty-three official cases have been filed since the inception of the WTO.[9] As of 2010, most cases (twenty-six disputes) were initiated by developed countries, primarily the United States and the European Union, and developing countries were involved in sixteen disputes.[10] Outside the WTO, firm-to-firm[11] and government-to-firm disputes have also been growing rapidly. For example, as Figure 4.1 shows, the United States International Trade Commission (USITC) has overseen a quadrupling of IPR-related disputes against imports during the past two decades. Indeed, more American firms have filed complaints against IPR violations than against unfair dumping, as indicated by the falling trend in traditional trade remedies such as antidumping and countervailing duties. These developments suggest that the burden of global legal costs is quite real for exporters, especially those from developing countries.

For example, South Korea is a strong exporter, but its entry into the U.S. market has been marred by patent disputes between U.S. and Korean firms since the 1980s.

7 See Maskus and Penubarti (1995); Smith (1999); Taylor (1993).

8 The previous studies present mostly the perspective of developed countries (i.e., countries with high LT) on the adequacy of IPR protection for their exports in destination markets. For example, Maskus and Penubarti (1995) and Smith (1999) estimate the sensitivity of U.S. exports (or exports of OECD economies) to the level of IPRs across export markets using industry data. They conclude that weak IPR levels are a barrier to U.S. (or OECD) exports.

9 See World Trade Organization (2022).

10 According to Lee (2019: 46–47), unlike the cases against developed countries, all cases (ten as of 2010) targeting developing countries either were settled out of the court or ruled against developing countries. Firms in developing countries tend to prefer out-of-court settlements or summary judgments due to concerns about litigation and legal costs.

11 Within the United States, firm-to-firm IPR-related disputes have drastically increased by over 100 percent in the past two decades, and patent-related cases have increased by about 150 percent – from 1,224 cases in 1988 to 2,909 cases in 2008 (Administration Office of the U.S. Courts, 2010).

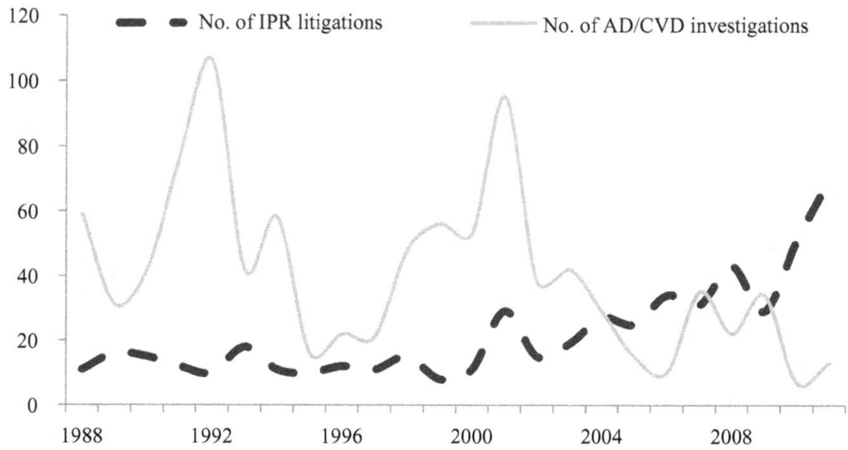

FIGURE 4.1 Trend in U.S. International Trade Commission (USITC) filings on "Unfair Imports": Increases in IPR-related litigation in the United States
Note: Year refers to September year-end (by fiscal year)
Sources: The number of antidumping and countervailing duty (AD/CVD) investigations is compiled from "AD/CVD Investigation: Federal Register History" (http://ia.ita.doc.gov/stats). The number of ITC litigations is compiled from "Section 337 Statistical Information," USITC (www.usitc.gov/press_room/337_stats.htm) (Shin et al., 2016).

A noteworthy case was the ban on Samsung's computer chip exports imposed by the USITC for violating the patent rights of Texas Instruments.[12] Thus, due to IP-induced barriers, developing countries could lose out on opportunities provided by exports to developed country markets, given that the latter markets account for the bulk of world markets and trading opportunities. Developing country exporters may find themselves confined to the technologically low end of the market, which confers relatively smaller benefits. A more interesting aspect of this observation is that the possible negative impact of this interaction between the levels of IPR protection and technology would be greater for those developing countries that are catching up rapidly – and thus command a certain level of technological capability and are active in exporting to developed country markets – than for those developing countries with very low technological capabilities and, thus, weak export performances.

While the existing literature has not touched on the interaction between IPRs and technological capabilities and its implications for exporting, this study, following Shin et al. (2016), explicitly considers the impact of IPRs on trade. It specifically examines the direct impact of IPRs and their *indirect* impact through their interaction with the exporter's LT.

To illustrate the reasoning about interaction effects, Shin et al. (2016) assume the following linear representation, allowing for some interaction between the source

[12] For details, see Lee and Kim (2010).

country's LT and the destination country's IPR level. The value of exports (E) can then be considered to take the following functional form:

$$E(IPR, LT, .) = \alpha IPR + \beta LT + \gamma IPR \times LT + \ldots \quad (4.1)$$

for which we can test whether $\gamma = 0$. It is likely that $\beta > 0$; namely, that exporting is a positive function of LT. However, a priori, α and γ are *ambiguous*, since the effect of IPRs on exports depends upon a balancing of the market power effects and market expansion effects of IPRs. Moreover, the cross effects of IPRs and LT could in principle be either negative or positive. The key advantage of having this interaction term is that the marginal impact of IPRs on exports is no longer simply α but the sum of two terms, namely $\alpha + \gamma LT$, which represents the direct impacts (α) and the interaction impacts (γLT).

There are several possible cases to consider depending on the signs of α and γ. However, the actual regressions, as will be shown later, all indicate γ to be negative or sometimes insignificant. Thus, let us focus our discussion on this interesting and dominant case of $\gamma < 0$. In this case, it is noteworthy that for some high LT ranges, the net marginal impact of IPRs on exports can be negative, such that $\partial E/\partial IPR = \alpha + \gamma LT < 0$, even if the direct impact of IPRs is positive ($\alpha > 0$).

This possibility implies that the impact of IPRs might vary according to how much a country exports IPR-sensitive products, which depends on the country's LT (i.e., patents). For a developing country with a low LT, its export items have not reached that status, as the products are less sophisticated. In contrast, a small number of "emerged or newly emerging economies" – such as Korea, Taiwan, China, India, Russia, Brazil, Mexico, and several ASEAN countries (notably Malaysia) – can produce technology-intensive products; their LTs are still low in comparison to developed countries but are highest among developing countries. For them, strong IPR enforcement in destination countries may act as a barrier to exports to rich country markets.

We can also gain a similar perspective by focusing on the impacts of changes in the exporters' LT. Raising technological capabilities is one of the most important means by which exporters can expand their exports to foreign markets. This is particularly pressing for exporters in the South. However, the net impact of an additional increase in the exporters' LT might be small when there is a substantial negative interaction effect with the level of IPR protection in the destination countries. In other words, the marginal effects of LT on exports can be expressed as $\partial E/\partial LT = \beta + \gamma IPR$, which could be negative, even with a positive direct impact (β), if γ is negative and IPR takes on a sufficiently high value. This case is a clear-cut example of the entry barrier effects of IPRs, which could frustrate the efforts of middle-income countries to try to enter developed country markets by raising the technological standard of their products through innovation. This barrier implies that one source of the so-called MIT is weak exporting by middle-income countries to developed country markets due to the latter's high IPR standards.

When countries experience the MIT, they face a slowdown in growth as they get caught between low-wage manufacturing and high-wage innovation because their wage rates are too high to compete with low-wage exporters. Meanwhile, their level of technological capability is too low to allow them to compete with advanced countries. One way out of this trap is obviously to improve their LT. However, the negative interaction between LT and IPR implies that such efforts are impeded by the IPR protection of their destination countries.

The key points of the previous discussions are that (1) the possibly negative interaction effects between LT and IPR would be more significant for exports from the South to the North than for exports from the North to the South and (2) the impact of the IPRs on exports may be negative for those developing economies (the South) whose own LT is relatively high, as strong IPRs may impede the entry of exports from countries that are catching up technologically.

Shin et al. (2016) conducted econometric estimations to verify the above. Their results confirm that the negative interaction effects between LT and IPR are significant and robust for the exports of the South to the North, compared to the exports of the North to the South. If the coefficient of the interaction term γ is negative, this means that the negative interaction effect offsets the positive effects of IPR protection alone (α). It implies that the impact of a higher level of IPR protection in the North on exports from countries in the South depends on the exporters' LT. For Southern exporters with low LTs, stronger IPRs still help promote the growth of their exports because the negative interaction effect is quantitatively too small to fully offset the positive effects of IPRs on exports. In contrast, for Southern exporters with a higher LT, the negative interaction effects are large enough to offset the positive and direct impact of IPRs.

Overall, the results confirm that IPR protection in the North may act as a barrier to the entry of Southern exports, especially those exports whose LT is relatively high. In other words, the stringent IPR protection by more advanced destination countries enables their domestic producers to exclude the products of foreign exporters whose LTs are catching up. Many cases support this empirical finding. For example, incumbent firms in the North often resort to lawsuits or WTO disputes over IPRs to edge out competitors whose technological capabilities are growing in, and threaten, their markets. As pointed out earlier, when Korea was still a developing country in the 1980s, Samsung Electronics had emerged as a rapidly growing competitor in the computer chips market. The U.S. incumbent, Texas Instruments, pursued patent infringement litigation against Samsung over ten of their patents on dynamic random access memory (DRAM). After the USITC imposed a restriction on Samsung's exports, Samsung agreed to renew a patent licensing agreement worth more than US$1 billion as part of a settlement with Texas Instruments.[13]

[13] For details, see Lee and Kim (2010) in Odagiri et al. (2010).

These results are in sharp contrast to the case of the North's exports to the South, where the coefficients of the interaction term between the North's LT and the South's IPRs are not significant. This implies that IPR protection in the South does not interfere with Northern exporting. This asymmetry also suggests that developed country exporters are possibly the major beneficiaries of a strong IPR system, as created by TRIPS in the current world trading system, and that their own IPR regimes work as a mechanism for diminishing the ability of developing countries to access their markets by enhancing the developing economies' LT. In other words, the stronger Northern IPR system appears to obstruct Southern exports with higher LTs.

Overall, the results suggest that strong IPRs have acted as a barrier to trade, discouraging exporting from the perspective of developing countries that are in the process of catching up in terms of their LT.

4.3 LEAPFROGGING AS A WAY TO OVERCOME THE IPR-RELATED BARRIER TO CATCH-UP

The preceding section discusses how IPR protection in the North can be a barrier to innovation-based catch-up by latecomers. The next question is whether there is any way to overcome this barrier. While reform of the global IPR regime is one method and has been discussed in the literature, this chapter suggests a new alternative – namely, leapfrogging. Leapfrogging makes sense to the extent that it involves latecomers moving to new areas and products ahead of incumbents, thereby avoiding direct competition against the incumbents in the same markets (Lee, 2019).

The origins of the leapfrogging thesis may be traced to Freeman and Soete (1997) and Perez and Soete (1988). Their insight is that emerging technological paradigms serve as a window of opportunity for latecomers to leapfrog: Not being locked into the old technological system, they are thus able to grab new opportunities in emerging industries. The arrival of new kinds of general-purpose technology (Helpman and Trajtenberg, 1998) can also serve as a window of opportunity when there are complementary technologies. Perez and Soete (1988) discussed latecomers' leapfrogging advantages in terms of the following three aspects: entry barrier, accessibility of knowledge, and the possibility of lock-in by the incumbents.

First, since the equipment to produce new industrial goods is not yet developed, general-purpose machines should be utilized, and production volume is small. Therefore, the entry barrier associated with the economy of scale does not exist. Second, in the initial stage of new technological paradigms, the performance of the technology is not stable and not very specific to a firm. Therefore, if only human resources can access the sources of knowledge and create new additional knowledge, entry to emerging technology can be easier than during the later stage of technological evolution. Third, catching-up countries can be said to be in a relatively advantageous position as they are not locked into old technologies.

In contrast, advanced countries tend to be locked into old technologies due to the sunk costs of their investment.

Lee and Lim (2001) fleshed out the idea of leapfrogging from the examples of the Korean industries. The concept was clarified by path-following, stage-skipping, and path-creation by latecomers in their technological development – with "path" and "stage" referring, respectively, to the trajectory of technologies and the stages in the trajectories. Lee and Lim observed that the strategies of path-creation and stage-skipping can be regarded as two variants of leapfrogging.

Thus, it can be argued that a broadly defined leapfrogging into emerging and new technologies during paradigm shifts or when new generations of innovations emerge can be a solution for overcoming the IPR-related barrier. It is so because, during the transition period, technologies and innovations tend to remain in the public domain or academia, rather than protected by patents, and there might be no dominant IPR holders. Second, leapfrogging can be a solution because it often involves the latecomers not following the same technological trajectory as the incumbents, thereby avoiding IPR disputes with the incumbents. In general, this means that the latecomer must eventually transition from imitation to innovation. In this regard, an interesting case can be Huawei, a leading information technology firm in China.

One study used patent citation data to investigate the catch-up of Huawei in China with Ericsson in Sweden and found that Huawei relied on Ericsson as a knowledge source in its early days but subsequently reduced such reliance and increased its self-citation ratio to become more independent (Joo et al., 2016). This finding is similar to the pattern between a follower – Samsung – and an incumbent – Sony – as analyzed using the method in Joo and Lee (2010). The investigation of mutual citations (direct dependence), common citations (indirect reliance), and self-citations strongly indicates that Huawei has caught up with or overtaken Ericsson by taking a different path rather than by continuing to follow Ericsson's path. Moreover, unlike Ericsson, Huawei developed its technologies by relying on recent technologies, which resulted in a patent folio with short citation lags (which means that its technologies have a short cycle). Huawei also relied heavily on scientific knowledge (so-called nonpatent literature), which is a public good that is free from IPR disputes with the incumbents. The citations to nonpatent literature and the patent folio with short citation lags imply that Huawei has extensively explored basic research and maintained up-to-date technologies to accomplish a technological catch-up, thereby avoiding another patent dispute with incumbent firms.

Overall, examining successful catch-ups (or overtaking cases) in East Asia suggests that exploring a technological path that differs from that of forerunners presents a viable catch-up strategy for latecomers and, in this sense, a "necessary" condition for overtaking. However, this strategy is not a sufficient condition (meaning that it does not always guarantee successful catching up) as it involves a higher risk (than going along a straight but jammed road) and may result in failure or accidents along the road.

REFERENCES

Administration Office of the U.S. Courts. 2010. *Annual Report of the Director: Judicial Business of the United States Courts*. Washington, DC: Administration Office of the U.S. Courts.

Aiyar, Shekar, Romain Duval, Damien Puy, Yiqan Wu, and Longmei Zhang. 2013. “Growth Slowdowns and the Middle-Income Trap.” International Monetary Fund Working Paper No. 13/71.

Allegrezza, Serge, and Alexandra Guarda-Rauchs. 1999. “The Determinants of Trademarks Deposits: An Econometric Investigation.” *Economie appliquée*, 52(2): 51–68.

Auriol, Emmanuelle, and Sara Biancini. 2010. “Intellectual Property Rights Adoption in Developing Countries.” Toulouse School of Economics Working Paper No. 09-094.

Awokuse, Titus, and Hong Yin. 2010. “Intellectual Property Rights Protection and the Surge in FDI in China.” *Journal of Comparative Economics* 38: 217–224.

Barro, Robert, and Xavier Sala-i-Martin. 1997. “Technological Diffusion, Convergence, and Growth.” *Journal of Economic Growth* 2(1): 1–26.

Beneito, Pilar. 2006. “The Innovative Performance of In-House and Contracted R&D in Terms of Patents and Utility Models.” *Research Policy* 35: 502–517.

Block, Joern H., Geertjan De Vries, Jan H. Schumann, and Phillipp Sandner. 2014. “Trademarks and Venture Capital Valuation.” *Journal of Business Venturing* 29(4): 453–484.

Block, Jörn H., Christian O. Fisch, Alexander Hahn, and Phillipp G. Sandner. 2015. “Why Do SMEs File Trademarks? Insights from Firms in Innovative Industries.” *Research Policy* 44(10): 1915–1930.

Bosworth, Derek, and Mark Rogers. 2001. “Market Value, R&D and Intellectual Property: An Empirical Analysis of Large Australian Firms.” *Economic Record* 77: 323–337.

Chung, Moon Young, and Keun Lee. 2015. “How Absorptive Capacity Is Formed in a Latecomer Economy: Different Roles of Foreign Patent and Know-How Licensing in Korea.” *World Development* 66: 678–694.

Cohen, Wesley M., Richard R. Nelson, and John P. Walsh. 2000. “Protecting Their Intellectual Assets: Appropriability Conditions and Why US Manufacturing Firms Patent (or Not).” National Bureau of Economic Research Working Paper No. 7552.

Commission on Intellectual Property Rights. 2002. *Integrating Intellectual Property Rights and Development Policy*. London: Commission on Intellectual Property Rights.

De Vries, H.J., Bert Nagtegaal, and Stijn Veenstra. 2017. “Transatlantic Harmonisation of Standards and Conformity Assessment: A Business Perspective.” In *EURAS Proceedings 2017: Digitisation: Challenge and Opportunity for Standardisation*, edited by Kai Jakobs and Knut Blind, T39–T58. Aachen: Wissenschaftsverlag Mainz.

Deere, Carolyn. 2009. *The Implementation Game: The TRIPS Agreement and the Global Politics of Intellectual Property Reform in Developing Countries*. Oxford: Oxford University Press.

Desyllas, Panos, and Mari Sako. 2013. “Profiting from Business Model Innovation: Evidence from Pay-as-You-Drive Auto Insurance.” *Research Policy* 42(1): 101–116.

Eeckhout, Jan, and Boyan Jovanovic. 2002. “Knowledge Spillovers and Inequality.” *American Economic Review* 92(5): 1290–1307.

Eichengreen, Barry, Donghyun Park, and Kwanho Shin. 2012. “When Fast Growing Economies Slow Down: International Evidence and Implications for China.” *Asian Economic Papers* 11: 42–87.

2013. "Growth Slowdown Redux: New Evidence on the Middle-Income Trap." National Bureau of Economic Research Working Paper No. 18673.

Falvey, Rodney E., Neil Foster, and David Greenaway. 2006. "Intellectual Property Rights and Economic Growth." *Review of Development Economics* 10: 700–719.

Finger, J. Michael. 2002. "The Doha Agenda and Development: A View from the Uruguay Round." Economics and Research Department Working Paper No. 21. Asian Development Bank.

Fink, Carsten, and Keith E. Maskus, eds. 2005. *Intellectual Property and Development: Lessons from Recent Economic Research*. Washington, DC and Oxford: World Bank and Oxford University Press.

Flikkema, Meindert, Ard-Peter deMan, and Carolina Castaldi. 2014. "Are Trademark Counts a Valid Indicator of Innovation? Results of an In-Depth Study of New Benelux Trademarks Filed by SMEs." *Industry and Innovation* 21: 310–331.

Freeman, Christopher, and Luc Soete. 1997. *The Economics of Industrial Innovation*. London: Routledge.

Gilchrist, Simon, and John C. Williams. 2001. "Transition Dynamics in Vintage Capital Models: Explaining the Postwar Catch-up of Germany and Japan." Federal Reserve Bank of Boston Working Paper No. 01-1.

Gill, Indermit S., and Homi J. Kharas. 2007. *An East Asian Renaissance: Ideas for Economic Growth*. Washington, DC: World Bank.

Glass, Amy J., and Kamal Saggi. 2002. "Intellectual Property Rights and Foreign Direct Investment." *Journal of International Economics* 56(2): 387–410.

Greenhalgh, Christine, and Mark Rogers. 2006a. "The Value of Innovation: The Interaction of Competition, R&D and IP." *Research Policy* 35(4): 562–580.

2006b. "Trade Marks and Market Value in UK Firms." Intellectual Property Research Institute of Australia Working Paper No. 4/06.

Helmers, Christian, and Mark Rogers. 2010. "Innovation and the Survival of New Firms in the UK." *Review of Industrial Organization* 36(3): 227–248.

Helpman, Elhanan. 1993. "Innovation, Imitation, and Intellectual Property Rights." *Econometrica* 61(6): 1247–1280.

Helpman, Elhanan, and Manuel Trajtenberg. 1998. "Diffusion of General Purpose Technologies." In *General Purpose Technologies and Economic Growth*, edited by Elhanan Helpman, 85–119. Cambridge, MA: MIT Press.

Ito, Takatoshi. 2017. "Growth Convergence and the Middle-Income Trap." *Asian Development Review* 34(1): 1–27.

Joo, Si Hyung, and Keun Lee. 2010. "Samsung's Catch-up with Sony: An Analysis Using US Patent Data." *Journal of the Asia Pacific Economy* 15(3): 271–287.

Joo, Si Hyung, Chul Oh, and Keun Lee. 2016. "Catch-up Strategy of an Emerging Firm in an Emerging Country: Analysing the Case of *Huawei vs. Ericsson* with Patent Data." *International Journal of Technology Management* 72: 19–42.

Kang, Raeyoon, Taehyun Jung, and Keun Lee. 2022. "Not Patents but Trademarks-Based Path of Technological Development of Latecomers: Evidence from the Korean Data." *Singapore Economic Review* 67(3): 923–951.

Kanwar, Sunil, and Robert Evenson. 2003. "Does Intellectual Property Protection Spur Technological Change?" *Oxford Economic Papers* 55: 235–264.

Kim, Linsu. 1997. *Imitation to Innovation*. Boston: Harvard Business Press.

Kim, Yee Kyoung, Keun Lee, Walter G. Park, and Kineung Choo. 2012. "Appropriate Intellectual Property Protection and Economic Growth in Countries at Different Levels of Development." *Research Policy* 41(2): 358–375.

Kumar, J. 2002. "Intellectual Property Rights, Technology, and Economic Development: Experiences of Asian Countries." Research and Information System for the Non-Aligned and Other Developing Countries Discussion Paper No. 25.

Lai, Edwin, and Larry D. Qiu. 2003. "The North's Intellectual Property Rights Standard for the South?" *Journal of International Economics* 59: 183–209.

Lall, Sanjaya, and Manuel Albaladejo. 2001. "Indicators of the Relative Importance of IPRs in Developing Countries." UNCTAD-ICTSD Project on IPRs and Sustainable Development Issue Paper No. 3.

Lee, Keun. 2013. *Schumpeterian Analysis of Economic Catch-Up: Knowledge, Path-Creation, and the Middle-Income Trap*. New York: Cambridge University Press.

2019. *The Art of Economic Catch-up: Barriers, Detours and Leapfrogging*. New York: Cambridge University Press.

Lee, Keun, and Byung-Yeon Kim. 2009. "Both Institutions and Policies Matter but Differently for Different Income Groups of Countries: Determinants of Long-Run Economic Growth Revisited." *World Development* 37(3): 533–549.

Lee, Keun, and Yee Kyoung Kim. 2010. "IPR and Technological Catch-Up in Korea." In *Intellectual Property Rights, Catch-Up and Development: An International Comparative Study*, edited by Hiroyuki Odagiri, Akira Goto, Atsushi Sunami, and Richard R. Nelson, 133–167. Oxford: Oxford University Press.

Lee, Keun, and Chaisung Lim. 2001. "Technological Regimes, Catching-up and Leapfrogging: Findings from the Korean Industries." *Research Policy* 30(3): 459–483.

Lee, Keun, D. Park, and C. Lim. 2003. "Industrial Property Rights and Technological Development in the Republic of Korea." *WIPO Policy Monograph*, April.

Malerba, Franco. 2002. "Sectoral Systems of Innovation and Production." *Research Policy* 31: 247–264.

2004. *Sectoral System of Innovation: Concepts, Issues and Analysis of Six Major Sections in Europe*. New York: Cambridge University Press.

Malerba, Franco, and Sunil Mani. 2009. *Sectoral Systems of Innovation and Production in Developing Countries: Actors, Structure and Evolution*. Cheltenham: Edward Elgar Publishing.

Malmberg, Claes. 2005. "Trademarks Statistics as Innovation Indicator – A Micro Study." Paper in Innovation Studies No. 2005/17. Centre for Innovation, Research and Competence in the Learning Economy (CIRCLE), Lund University.

Maskus, Keith E., and Christine McDaniel. 1999. "Impacts of the Japanese Patent System on Productivity Growth." *Japan and the World Economy* 11: 557–574.

Maskus, Keith E., and Mohan Penubarti. 1995. "How Trade Related Are Intellectual Property Rights?" *Journal of International Economics* 39: 227–248.

Mazzoleni, Roberto, and Richard Nelson. 1998. "The Benefits and Costs of Strong Patent Protection: A Contribution to the Current Debate." *Research Policy* 27(3): 273–284.

Mendonça, Sandro, Tiago S. Pereira, and Manuel Mira Godinho. 2004. "Trademarks as an Indicator of Innovation and Industrial Change." *Research Policy* 33(9): 1385–1404.

Mehrazeen, Ali Reza, Omid Froutan, and Navid Attaran. 2012. "Establishing the Relationship between Trademark Valuation and Firm Performance: Evidence from Iran." *International Journal of Economics and Finance* 4(6): 181–186.

Odagiri, Hiroyuki, Akira Goto, Atsushi Sunami, and Richard R. Nelson. 2010. *Intellectual Property Rights and Catch-Up: An International Comparative Study*. Oxford: Oxford University Press.

Park, Walter G. 2008. "International Patent Protection: 1960–2005." *Research Policy* 37: 761–766.

Perez, Carlota, and Luc Soete. 1988. "Catching-up in Technology: Entry Barriers and Windows of Opportunity." In *Technical Change and Economic Theory*, edited by Giovanni Dosi, Christopher Freeman, Richard Nelson, Gerald Silverberg, and Luc Soete, 458–479. London: Pinter Publishers.

Sandner, Philipp G., and Joern Block. 2011. "The Market Value of R&D, Patents, and Trademarks." *Research Policy* 40(7): 969–985.

Schmoch, Ulrich. 2003. "Service Marks as Novel Innovation Indicator." *Research Evaluation* 12(2): 149–156.

Schneider, Patricia H. 2005. "International Trade, Economic Growth and Intellectual Property Rights: A Panel Data Study of Developed and Developing Countries." *Journal of Development Economics* 78(2): 529–547.

Shin, Jang-Sup. 2017. "Dynamic Catch-up Strategy, Capability Expansion and Changing Windows of Opportunity in the Memory Industry." *Research Policy* 46(2): 404–416.

Shin, Wonkyu, Keun Lee, and Walter G. Park. 2016. "When an Importer's Protection of IPR Interacts with an Exporter's Level of Technology: Comparing the Impacts on the Exports of the North and South." *World Economy* 39(6): 772–802.

Siebeck, Wolfgang E. 1990. "Strengthening Protection of Intellectual Property in Developing Countries: A Survey of the Literature." World Bank Discussion Paper No. 112.

Smith, Pamela J. 1999. "Are Weak Patent Rights A Barrier to U.S. Exports?" *Journal of International Economics* 48: 151–177.

Suthersanen, Uma. 2006. "Utility Models and Innovation in Developing Countries." UNCTAD-ICTSD Project on IPRs and Sustainable Development Issue Paper No. 13.

Taylor, M. Scott. 1993. "TRIPS, Trade, and Technology Transfer." *Canadian Journal of Economics* 26: 625–638.

World Bank. 2002. *Global Economic Prospects and Developing Countries*. New York: Oxford University Press.

2010. "Escaping the Middle-Income Trap." In *World Bank East Asia and Pacific Economic Update: Robust Recovery, Rising Risks*, 27–43. Washington, DC: World Bank.

2012. *China 2030: Building a Modern, Harmonious, and Creative High-Income Society*. Washington, DC: World Bank.

World Intellectual Property Organization. 2022a. "Intellectual Property for Business." www.wipo.int/sme/en/. Accessed July 19, 2022.

2022b. "Utility Models." www.wto.org/english/tratop_e/dispu_e/dispu_agreements_index_e.htm. Accessed July 19, 2022.

World Trade Organization. 2022. "Disputes by Agreement." www.wto.org/english/tratop_e/dispu_e/dispu_agreements_index_e.htm. Accessed July 19, 2022.

5

Patents and Economic Inequality

Daniel Benoliel[*] *and Rochelle C. Dreyfuss*

INTRODUCTION

The needs of the Global South (or South) are proving to be far more complex and difficult to ameliorate than anticipated when the World Trade Organization was established amid promises of enhancing social welfare.[1] In particular, inequality among member states has persisted despite the optimistic projections made during the Uruguay Round negotiations. This is an issue of concern to intellectual property scholars because economic theory suggests that technology policy is a key contributor.[2] That is, it appears that strong patent protection and the returns on investment available to those who innovate lead to advances that increase productivity. For example, in their book *The Second Machine Age*, Erik Brynjolfsson and Andrew MacAfee found an exponential rise of digital technologies automating jobs, offering capital owners and innovators an accumulative stake of productivity.[3] With that increase, there is a concomitant growth in income for the innovators themselves, as well as both income and other benefits that accrue to the countries where these inventors reside.[4]

[*] This chapter was completed as an Oxford Intellectual Property Research Center (OIPRC) Visiting Academic, University of Oxford Faculty of Law (Hilary and Trinity Terms, 2021).

[1] Agreement on Trade-Related Aspects of Intellectual Property Rights, Apr. 15, 1994, Marrakesh Agreement Establishing the World Trade Organization, Annex 1C, 1869 U.N.T.S. 299 [hereinafter TRIPS Agreement]; Philip M. Nichols, *Trade without Values*, 90 Nw. U. L. Rev. 658 (1996).

[2] See, for example, Erik Brynjolfsson & Andrew McAfee, The Second Machine Age: Work, Progress and Prosperity in a Time of Brilliant Technologies 133 (2014) (concluding that the main driver of inequality is "exponential, digital, and combinatorial change in the technology that undergirds the economic system").

[3] *Id.* at 171–72.

[4] In the recent decade, several studies have considered the impact of innovation and patent policies on income inequality. See, for example, Philippe Aghion, Ufuk Akcigit, Antonin Bergeaud, Richard Blundell & David Hémous, *Innovation and Top Income Inequality*, 86 Rev. Econ. Stud. 1 (2019); Angus C. Chu, *Effects of Patent Policy on Income and*

Developed countries are in a superior position in this regard, not only because their technical capabilities are at the technological forefront. As economists such as Stanley Engerman and Raymond Sokoloff have demonstrated, they are also advantaged by the presence of wealthy individuals and a large middle class with a strong appetite for technological advances, which helps to spur innovation from the demand side.[5]

The situation can be very different in developing countries. Reflecting their limited market and institutional capacity to innovate, or to adapt and improve upon existing technologies,[6] many developing countries are characterized by low incomes resulting from low average productivity. There are, however, a few developing countries – such as Brazil, China, India, and Malaysia – that have achieved relatively advanced levels of technological capability.[7] Significantly, these countries have primarily relied on an explicit policy of copying foreign technologies.[8] Rather than attempting to expand the global frontier – which, as the World Bank has found, is likely beyond their past (and often present) abilities[9] – these nations advance the adoption and adaptation of preexisting technologies.[10] In short, they engage, at least partly, in what Jerome Reichman has termed "fair following."[11] In a prescient article, written as the

Consumption Inequality in a R&D Growth Model, 77 S. Econ. J. 336, 337 (2010) (finding that patent policies contributed to the recent trend of inequality in the United States). British researchers Richard Wilkinson and Kate Pickett have found higher rates and numbers of patents issued in countries and states with higher inequality. Kate E. Pickett & Richard G. Wilkinson, *Income Inequality and Health: A Causal Review*, 128 Soc. Sci. & Med. 316 (2015).

For a detailed discussion of how intellectual property inhibits innovation, see Joseph E. Stiglitz, The Price of Inequality: How Today's Divided Society Endangers Our Future 54 (2012); Joseph E. Stiglitz, Making Globalization Work (2006); Claude Henry & Joseph E. Stiglitz, *Intellectual Property, Dissemination of Innovation, and Sustainable Development*, 1 Glob. Pol'y 237 (2010). *See also* discussion in Section 5.1.

On the historical inequalities within U.S. and British patent systems, see B. Zorina Khan & Kenneth Sokoloff, *Patent Institutions, Industrial Organization and Early Technological Change: Britain and the United States, 1790–1850*, *in* Technological Revolutions in Europe (Maxine Berg & Kristine Bruland eds., 1998); B. Zorina Khan, *Intellectual Property and Economic Development: Lessons from American and European History* (Comm'n on Intell. Prop. Rts., Study Paper No. 1a, 2002); B. Zorina Khan, The Democratization of Invention: Patents and Copyrights in American Development 1790–1920 (2005).

5 Stanley L. Engerman, Stephen H. Haber & Kenneth L. Sokoloff, *Inequality, Institutions and Differential Paths of Growth among New World Economies*, *in* Institutions, Contracts and Organizations: Perspectives from New Institutional Economics 108 (Claude Ménard ed., 2000).

6 See, for example, Tilman Altenburg, *Building Inclusive Innovation Systems in Developing Countries: Challenges for IS Research*, *in* Handbook of Innovation Systems and Developing Countries 33, 35 (Bengt-Åke Lundvall, K.J. Joseph, Cristina Chaminade & Jan Vang eds., 2009).

7 *See* Jean-Eric Aubert, *Promoting Innovation in Developing Countries: A Conceptual Framework* 3 (World Bank Pol'y Rsch., Working Paper No. 3554, 2005).

8 *Id.*

9 *Id.*

10 *See id.* at 12; Altenburg, *supra* note 6, at 35.

11 Jerome H. Reichman, *From Free-Riders to Fair Followers: Global Competition under the TRIPS Agreement*, 29 N.Y.U. J. Int'l L. & Pol. 11 (1997).

Agreement on Trade-Related Aspects of Intellectual Property Rights (TRIPS Agreement) went into force, Reichman suggested that fair following creates domestic training and educational opportunities, plugs local personnel into global information networks, and gives rise to conditions conducive to growth in technological capacity.[12] Twenty-five years of experience with the TRIPS Agreement suggests that Reichman and the countries that followed his vision were right. Many lessons can be drawn from their practices, as we discuss, given the concern over economic inequality.

The first section of this chapter identifies the roles that innovation and international intellectual property protection play within the theory of economic inequality. The second section focuses on the impact of international patent law and demonstrates how the demands of the North for ever-stronger patent and patent-like protection exacerbate the problem of technological inequality. The third section suggests ways in which the patent system could be restructured to better enable local inventors to avail themselves of the global knowledge base and enhance the incentives available to innovators who fulfill the needs of the South. In our view, reducing intellectual property–based inequality in the ways we outline is a key step toward mitigating the problem of income inequality.

5.1 INEQUALITY ECONOMICS AND THE ROLE OF INTELLECTUAL PROPERTY

5.1.1 *The Kuznets Theorem and Its Demise*

Much of the intellectual framework that led to the present-day economic inequality critique emerged as the backdrop of postwar theories put forth by economists Simon Kuznets and John Maynard Keynes.[13] Kuznets used twentieth-century U.S. tax returns to correlate income as measured by GDP per capita with income inequality. The resulting inverted U-shaped curve demonstrated that as per capita income increases, inequality at first increases as well but eventually declines.[14] Kuznets viewed the shape of the curve optimistically and hypothesized that as economic development increases per capita income, more people are put in a position to take advantage of the opportunities presented. As a result, Kuznets theorized, inequality would decline over time and stabilize at a tolerable level.[15] The Kuznets curve

[12] *Id.* at 80–81.

[13] For discussion of the two economists, see THOMAS PIKETTY, CAPITAL IN THE TWENTY-FIRST CENTURY 13–15 (2014); David Singh Grewal & Jedediah Purdy, *Inequality Rediscovered*, 18 THEORETICAL INQUIRIES L. 61, 64–66 (2017).

[14] Simon Kuznets, *Economic Growth and Income Inequality*, 45 AM. ECON. REV. 1 (1955); *see also* Emmanuel Saez & Gabriel Zucman, *Wealth Inequality in the United States since 1913: Evidence from Capitalized Income Tax Data*, 131 Q.J. ECON. 519 (2016).

[15] As Piketty explains, the share of total income accruing to the top 1 percent declined remarkably from about 24 percent in the mid-1920s to a low of about 9 percent in the early 1970s. PIKETTY, *supra* note 13, at 300.

became macroeconomic shorthand for confidence about the social value of economic growth and led to numerous theoretical ramifications. Most notable was Grossman and Krueger's "environmental Kuznets curve," which suggests a comparable relationship between income and environmental degradation.[16]

Keynes presented the second theory, which is that the "economic problem" of scarcity was solvable.[17] In his view, the state had gained the capability, authority, and legitimacy to improve economic well-being. While Keynes's main contribution was that business cycles could be managed by inducing demand through the use of public spending or low interest rates,[18] the application of his findings had broader social and political ramifications. Taken together, the optimistic views of Kuznets and Keynes implied that economic inequality would not increase. Moreover, if inequality did grow, there was no reason that a democratic political order would not be able to correct the problem.

Nonetheless, since the early 1970s, economic inequality has risen steadily.[19] During the 1990s, Klaus Deininger and Lyn Squire collected data on changes in the Gini index of income distribution in numerous countries and developed an intertemporal correlation between growth and inequality.[20] They concluded that the correlation Kuznets found between economic growth and inequality is more often disproved than confirmed. Sudhir Anand and R.S.M. Kanbur,[21] as well as others,[22] including notably Joseph Stiglitz[23] and Thomas Piketty,[24] offered comparable critiques that systematically refuted Kuznets' findings. Concern about the optimistic view of inequality spread from economics to political philosophy, law,

[16] Gene M. Grossman & Alan B. Krueger, *Economic Growth and the Environment*, 110 Q.J. Econ. 353 (1995) (arguing that pollution rises early in the development process and then falls as wealthy societies adopt environmental regulations).

[17] John M. Keynes, *Economic Possibilities for Our Grandchildren*, *in* Essays in Persuasion 358 (W.W. Norton & Co. 1963) (1931).

[18] *Id.*

[19] Piketty, *supra* note 13, at 300.

[20] Klaus Deininger & Lyn Squire, *A New Data Set Measuring Income Inequality*, 10 World Bank Econ. Rev. 565 (1996); *see also* Klaus Deininger & Lyn Squire, *New Ways of Looking at Old Issues: Inequality and Growth*, 57 J. Dev. Econ. 259 (1998).

[21] Sudhir Anand & S.M.R. Kanbur, *The Kuznets Process and the Inequality-Development Relationship*, 40 J. Dev. Econ. 25 (1993).

[22] Robert Barro, *Inequality and Growth in a Panel of Countries*, 5 J. Econ. Growth 5 (2000); Matthew Higgins & Jeffrey G. Williamson, *Explaining Inequality the World Round: Cohort Size, Kuznets Curves and Openness* (Nat'l Bureau of Econ. Rsch., Working Paper No. 7224, 1999); Andreas Savvides & Thanasis Stengos, *Income Inequality and Economic Development: Evidence from the Threshold Regression Model*, 69 Econ. Letters 207 (2000); *see also* Anthony B. Atkinson, *The Changing Distribution of Income: Evidence and Explanations*, 1 German Econ. Rev. 3 (2000); Anthony B. Atkinson, *Income Inequality in OECD Countries: Data and Explanations*, 49 CESifo Econ. Stud. 479 (2003).

[23] Joseph E. Stiglitz, The Great Divide: Unequal Societies and What We Can Do about Them 88 (2015) (providing a comparison of the wealth controlled by the top 1 percent over time).

[24] Piketty, *supra* note 13.

and public policy.[25] It began to engage thinking within the international intellectual property community, as this volume demonstrates.

5.1.2 *Economic Inequality, Capital, and Innovation*

To date, economic inequality in the United States is still largely explained by unequal income effects. Thus, the perception is that stagnancy within the middle- and lower-income classes – their lack of consumption relative to the rich – hampers sustainable economic growth.[26] The presence of wealth does not help, as the rich, under this view, are thought to have reached the point of saturation.

This conception of the problem has had a substantial influence on the literature of the economics of intellectual property. Thus, Angus Chu,[27] alone and with Shin-Kun Peng,[28] and Christian Kiedaisch[29] examined the causal effect of patent policy on inequality. Similarly, Philippe Aghion and his coauthors found that "the top 1% income share in a given U.S. state in a given year, was positively and significantly correlated with the state's degree of innovativeness,"[30] and that there is a "causal effect of innovation-led growth on top incomes."[31] In recent work, researchers demonstrated that intellectual property–based capital accounts entirely for the observed decline of the U.S. labor share measured by wages paid to employees. Wages are otherwise constant for traditional capital. This decline in the labor share arguably reflects the transition that the United States is undergoing to a more knowledge-based economy.[32]

The effects of intellectual property protection have also been noted. Joseph Stiglitz argued that one effect of monopoly rent regimes is that they impede access to healthcare, which creates inequality and hampers growth more generally.[33] Keith Maskus added that an effective intellectual property regime has an impact not only

[25] Grewal & Purdy, *supra* note 13, at 64.

[26] Federico Cingano, *Trends in Income Inequality and Its Impact on Economic Growth* 18 (Org. for Econ. Co-operation & Dev., Soc., Emp. & Migration Working Paper No. 163, 2014); GANESH SITARAMAN, THE CRISIS OF THE MIDDLE-CLASS CONSTITUTION: WHY ECONOMIC INEQUALITY THREATENS OUR REPUBLIC 17 (2017).

[27] Chu, *supra* note 4.

[28] *See* Angus C. Chu & Shin-Kun Peng, *Effect of TRIPS on Growth, Welfare and Income-Inequality in an R&D Growth Model*, 33 J. MACROECONOMICS 276 (2011) (finding that strengthening intellectual property protection increases growth rates, which raises disparities in wealth distribution and ultimately leads to an increase in income inequality).

[29] Christian Kiedaisch, *Growth and Welfare Effects of Intellectual Property Rights When Consumers Differ in Income* (Univ. of Zurich, Dep't of Econ., Working Paper No. 221, 2016).

[30] Aghion et al., *supra* note 4, at 3.

[31] *Id.*

[32] Dongya Koh, Raül Santaeulàlia-Llopis & Yu Zheng, *Labor Share Decline and Intellectual Property Products Capital* (Barcelona Graduate Sch. of Econ., Working Paper No. 927, 2016).

[33] Joseph E. Stiglitz, *How Intellectual Property Reinforces Inequality*, N.Y. TIMES (July 14, 2013), https://opinionator.blogs.nytimes.com/2013/07/14/how-intellectual-property-reinforces-inequality/.

on the incentive to create new knowledge and disseminate it but also on the structure of markets, prices, and distributional equity.[34] In a vast panel regression analysis, Samuel Adams found that strengthening intellectual property protection has a positive and statistically significant effect on income inequality.[35]

Some scholars further elucidated the connection between inequality and intellectual property. One core observation related to the unique contribution of capital. As Piketty showed, capital is distributed less evenly than labor income, and this factor has a significant impact on overall household income.[36] Significantly, he defined capital to include land, real estate, equipment, financial capital, and also intellectual property.[37] According to Piketty, Kuznets's predictions were wrong because he failed to take into account capital – tangible and intangible – as a central variable. To correct the problem, Piketty developed an updated Kuznets curve for a 100-year period, from 1910 to 2010. According to this curve, until 1955, the share of the top income decile in the United States changed in the same manner as shown in Kuznets's paper. This share declined from the 1920s to the end of World War II and then leveled out until the early 1980s. However, starting in the 1980s, when deregulation and privatization policies were launched, the share of inequality increased dramatically.[38] Changes in the strategies for privatizing innovation, primarily through the aggregation of thousands of patents, shifted the sole focus from the value of one patent to the size and diversity of a portfolio. These strategies regularly posed a new and more substantial threat to entry because they forced the targets of litigation to face multiple simultaneous infringement allegations, which raised the cost and difficulty of mounting a successful defense.[39]

[34] Keith E. Maskus, *Intellectual Property Rights and Economic Development*, 32 CASE W. RSRV. J. INT'L L. 471 (2000).

[35] Adams examines the relationship between intellectual property rights and income inequality for a cross-section of sixty-two developing countries over the period 1985–2001. *See* Samuel Adams, *Globalization and Income Inequality: Implications for Intellectual Property Rights*, 30 J. POL'Y MODELING 725 (2008).

[36] PIKETTY, *supra* note 13, at 266–69. For earlier findings, see Deborah Reed & Maria Cancian, *Sources of Inequality: Measuring the Contributions of Income Sources to Rising Family Income Inequality*, 47 REV. INCOME & WEALTH 321 (2001) (showing that asset income causes about one-fourth of the increase in income inequality in the 1990s, compared to one-tenth of the rise in income inequality in the 1970s).

[37] PIKETTY, *supra* note 13, at 61.

[38] *Id.* at 172.

[39] *See* Tom Ewing & Robin Feldman, *The Giants among Us*, 1 STAN. TECH. L. REV. 1 (2012); Colleen V. Chien, *From Arms Race to Marketplace: The Complex Patent Ecosystem and Its Implications for the Patent System*, 62 HASTINGS L.J. 297, 299 (2010); Julien Pénin, *Strategic Uses of Patents in Markets for Technology: A Story of Fabless Firms, Brokers and Trolls*, 84 J. ECON. BEHAV. & ORG. 633 (2012); James E. Bessen & Michael J. Meurer, *The Private Costs of Patent Litigation*, 9 J.L. ECON. & POL'Y 59, 80 (2012) (discussing the deterring effect of costly patent litigation); Rosemarie Ham Ziedonis, *Don't Fence Me In: Fragmented Markets for Technology and the Patent Acquisition Strategies of Firms*, 50 MGMT. SCI. 804, 817 (2004) (using transaction cost theory to predict that firms with many patents will be inclined to patent more aggressively).

Another strand of literature examined the global dimension of inequality as it interrelates with economic development in the South. During the 1980s and 1990s, there was a sharp increase in wage inequality matched by a sharp decrease in the relative demand for less skilled workers. Elias Dinopoulos and Paul Segerstrom provided the common North–North trade explanation for these results, which presumably also applies to income inequality in the South.[40] In this view, income inequality results from trade liberalization, which enhances the benefits of upgrading skills and engaging in research and development (R&D).[41] The relationship between skilled employment and R&D activity, as well as between trade liberalization and R&D, received renewed attention during the 1990s. Studies by Alberto Alesina and Dani Rodrik, among others, found a negative correlation between inequality and economic development across the North–South divide.[42] Alesina and others suggest that the effect is largely caused by patterns of foreign investment. After the TRIPS Agreement came into force, developing countries were required to amend their intellectual property laws to conform to its requirements.[43] This led to a proliferation of intellectual property rights, followed by an upsurge in income inequality in the South. TRIPS conformity had, in short, further increased skilled labor wages and created a wage bias in favor of skilled, relative to unskilled, labor. In this way, compliance with the TRIPS Agreement aggravated income inequality across the development divide.[44] Because higher levels of inequality tend to generate political instability and result in policies that favor income redistribution, inequality also discouraged investment, and, in turn, further slowed economic growth.

[40] Elias Dinopoulos & Paul Segerstrom, *A Schumpeterian Model of Protection and Relative Wages*, 89 AM. ECON. REV. 450 (1999).

[41] *Id.*

[42] Alberto Alesina & Dani Rodrik, *Distributive Politics and Economic Growth*, 109 Q.J. ECON. 465 (1994); Roberto Perotti, *Income Distribution and Development*, 38 EUR. ECON. REV. 129 (1994); Alberto Alesina & Roberto Perotti, *Income Distribution, Political Instability, and Investment*, 40 EUR. ECON. REV. 1203 (1996). See Lawrence Khoo & Benjamin Dennis, *Income Inequality, Fertility Choice, and Economic Growth: Theory and Evidence* (Harv. Inst. for Int'l Dev., Discussion Paper No. 687, 1999) for a cross-national study of seventy-nine to ninety-one countries between 1960 and 1985 witnessing the negative effect of income inequality on economic growth. For earlier findings, see also Torsten Persson & Guido Tabellini, *Is Inequality Harmful for Growth? Theory and Evidence*, 84 AM. ECON. REV. 600 (1996); Perotti, *supra*.

[43] Swati Saini and Meeta Mehra argue that intellectual property rights increased within-country income inequality for a cross-section of sixty-five developed and developing countries between 1995 and 2009. *See* Swati Saini & Meeta K. Mehra, *Impact of Strengthening Intellectual Property Rights Regime on Income Inequality: An Econometric Analysis*, 38 ECON. BULL. 1703 (2018). For economic literature concluding that developing countries have been losing in terms of economic growth due to stringent TRIPS standards, see also Edwin L.C. Lai, *International Intellectual Property Rights Protection and the Rate of Product Innovation*, 55 J. DEV. ECON. 133 (1998); Gene Grossman & Edwin L.C. Lai, *International Protection of Intellectual Property*, 94 AM. ECON. REV. 1635 (2004).

[44] *See* Saini & Mehra, *supra* note 43, at 4.

Observations that are valid for intellectual property generally can be especially acute for the international patent system, where there are several dimensions to the inequality problem. First, there is a gap in patent ownership between developed and developing countries. Although data gathered by the World Intellectual Property Organization (WIPO) suggest that the divide in the distribution of ownership is gradually narrowing, it is doing so only for the more technologically sophisticated developing countries. Another problem relates to patent commercialization.[45] With regard to the volume of licensing and royalty revenues, most developing countries appear to be drastically marginalized.[46] An additional, and perhaps most important, issue is social surplus. As a general matter, patent owners cannot capture the full value of their advances; some benefit is enjoyed by consumers who acquire the product at a price below that which they would be willing to pay. Furthermore, innovations often have spillover R&D effects: They can prompt collateral developments and lead to follow-on inventions that do not fall within the scope of the original patents.[47] When patents are not granted and inventions are not commercialized in a particular country, the citizens of that country cannot experience these positive externalities. Thus, the divide in patent activity also depresses the social surplus available to the South.[48]

[45] *See* Eugene Mattes, Michael C. Stacey & Dora Marinova, *Surveying Inventors Listed on Patents to Investigate Determinants of Innovation*, 69 SCIENTOMETRICS 476, 483 (2006) (reviewing studies on patent commercialization concluding that approximately 43–54 percent of patents get commercialized); *see also* PatVal EU Project, *The Value of European Patents: Evidence from a Survey of European Inventors* 41 fig.6.3 (2005), www.ipeg.com/wp-content/uploads/2015/02/PatVal-EU-study-2005.pdf (providing a European Commission-funded survey that focused on "important" patents, upholding that 38 percent of the patents were never commercialized); STAFF OF SUBCOMM. OF PAT., TRADEMARKS & COPYRIGHTS, COMM. ON THE JUDICIARY, 85TH CONG., AN ECONOMIC REVIEW OF THE PATENT SYSTEM 12 (Comm. Print 1958) (Fritz Machlup). For the scope of developing countries, see Roya Ghafele & Benjamin Gibert, *IP Commercialization Tactics in Developing Country Contexts*, 5 J. MGMT. & STRATEGY 2 (2014).
For a discussion on the various costs of patent commercialization, see Ted Sichelman, *Commercializing Patents*, 62 STAN. L. REV. 341, 362–81 (2010) and sources therein (further proposing to create an entirely new form of patents labelled as "commercialization patents," to reduce the risks associated with commercializing inventions).

[46] *See* Ghafele & Gibert, *supra* note 45, at 3–4, 6, tbls. 1, 2 (suggesting that licensing revenues remain unequally distributed across nations, with high-income countries receiving \$237,309,868,237 in royalties from licensing in 2012, middle-income countries receiving \$4,473,163,968 (1.18 percent of high-income countries), and low-income countries receiving \$63,957,821 and noting further that the gap cannot be explained by the gap in patent ownership).

[47] *See* Michael Kremer, *Patent Buy-Outs: A Mechanism for Encouraging Innovation* 1 (Nat'l Bureau of Econ. Rsch., Working Paper No. 6304, 1997); Steven Shavell & Tanguy V. Ypersele, *Rewards versus Intellectual Property Rights* 5–6 (Nat'l Bureau of Econ. Rsch., Working Paper No. 6956, 1999).

[48] The social surplus loss due to patents that are commercialized is measured in the short term. *See* Jeffrey L. Bran, *Turning Intellectual Assets into Business Assets*, *in* FROM IDEAS TO ASSETS: INVESTING WISELY IN INTELLECTUAL PROPERTY 65, 78 (Bruce Berman ed., 2002) (finding that market adoption occurs between three and five years); Christoph Palmberg, *The Sources of*

5.2 PATENTED LAW AS A SOURCE OF ECONOMIC INEQUALITY

It is not only the availability of patented technology that plays a role in inequality. Patent law itself contains features that contribute to the loss of social welfare predominantly in the South. Two factors stand out. First, patent rights wall off segments of the world's knowledge base. Exclusivity can prevent others from making incremental improvements or adaptations, including advances that meet the needs of the poor but which the patent holder refuses to fulfill. Second, the patent system fails to deliver incentives to invest in inventions of interest to the South because the knowledge base – whether accessible or not – nonetheless constitutes prior art. As a result of this so-called novelty trap, the developer of advances that fulfill the demands of the South is unlikely to acquire the protection that would allow it to earn a return on investment.[49]

5.2.1 *Access*

The access problem is well recognized in the context of patented products and public health, where the ability of the South to enjoy the benefits of progress in the life sciences is limited by the TRIPS Agreement, TRIPS-plus provisions found in subsequent free trade agreements (FTAs) and various side agreements, as well as procedures certifying implementation.[50] The effect of giving right holders more control over the availability of their advances is illustrated by Ellen 't Hoen's work documenting the problem of distributing medicines to those stricken with HIV/AIDS[51] and by Amy Kapczynski's and Ana Santos Rutschman's studies of the delivery of vaccines.[52] Carlos Correa has more generally explored the impact of intellectual property on health in developing countries.[53]

Success of Innovations – Determinants of Commercialization and Break-Even Times, 26 TECHNOVATION 1253, 1259 tbl. 4 (2006) (finding that commercialization times ranged from 2.5 to 4.1 years in the chemical sector).

49 Rochelle C. Dreyfuss & Daniel Benoliel, *Technological Self-Sufficiency and the Role of Novelty Traps*, 24 VAND. J. ENT. & TECH. L. 441 (2022).

50 See, for example, Dominican Republic–Central America–United States Free Trade Agreement Implementation Act, § 101(b), Pub. L. 109-53, 19 Stat. 462 (2005) (providing provisions similar to those used in connection with the FTAs with Chile, Oman, Singapore, and Bahrain); Carlos M. Correa, *Mitigating the Regulatory Constraints Imposed by Intellectual Property Rules under Free Trade Agreements* 14–16, 27 (S. Ctr., Rsch. Paper No. 74, 2017); UNAIDS, *The Potential Impact of Free Trade Agreements on Public Health* (2012), www.unaids.org/sites/default/files/media_asset/JC2349_Issue_Brief_Free-Trade-Agreements_en_0.pdf.

51 Ellen 't Hoen, *TRIPS, Pharmaceutical Patents, and Access to Essential Medicines: A Long Way from Seattle to Doha*, 3 CHI. J. INT'L L. 27 (2002).

52 *See* Amy Kapczynski, *Order without Intellectual Property Law: Open Science in Influenza*, 102 CORNELL L. REV. 1539 (2017); Ana S. Rutschman, *IP Preparedness for Outbreak Diseases*, 65 UCLA L. REV. 1200 (2018).

53 Carlos M. Correa, *Public Health and Patent Legislation in Developing Countries*, 3 TUL. J. TECH. & INTELL. PROP. 1 (2001).

To a considerable extent, changes have been made to deal with this dimension of the access problem. As initially drafted, the TRIPS Agreement provided for transition periods,[54] recognized the right of member states to enact exceptions and limitations and to issue compulsory licenses,[55] and permitted parallel importation.[56] When these provisions proved inadequate, World Trade Organization (WTO) members issued ministerial declarations emphasizing the right to protect health and added (or extended) transition periods several times. The WTO also supplemented the TRIPS Agreement with a provision allowing for the use of compulsory licensing to manufacture pharmaceuticals on behalf of a country that cannot produce sufficient supply for itself.[57] Newer bilateral investment agreements and FTAs are now similarly negotiated to take account of access issues, especially in the health sphere.[58]

Less appreciated is the connection between access and innovation capacity – that is, the ways in which patent protection limits the ability of inventors to engage in follow-on innovation, including advances that deal with the technological needs of the South. Thus, while the problem of patents impeding R&D in the North has been addressed, particularly regarding patents on fundamental science and abstract ideas,[59] scant attention has been paid to the ways in which patents inhibit research aimed at producing "good enough" technologies, by the poor for the poor.[60] Such

[54] TRIPS Agreement, *supra* note 1, art. 66.1.

[55] *Id.* arts. 27, 30, 31.

[56] *Id.* art. 6.

[57] Council for TRIPS, *Extension of the Transition Period under Article 66.1 for Least Developed Country Members: Decision of the Council for TRIPS of 29 June 2021*, WTO Doc. IP/C/88 (June 29, 2021); World Trade Org., *Declaration on the TRIPS Agreement and Public Health of 14 November 2001*, WTO Doc. WT/MIN(01)/DEC/2, 41 I.L.M. 746 (2002); TRIPS Agreement, *supra* note 1, art. 31 *bis*.

[58] Rochelle C. Dreyfuss, *ISDS and Intellectual Property in 2019: The Case of the Dog That Didn't Bark*, *in* Yearbook on International Investment Law & Policy 2019, at 249 (Lisa Sachs, Lise Johnson & Jesse Coleman eds., 2021); Correa, *supra* note 50. A vast literature has addressed the "flexibilities" available under the TRIPS Agreement and the negative impact of FTAs on access to medicines. See, for example, German Velasquez, Carlos Correa & Xavier Seuba, *IPR, R&D, Human Rights and Access to Medicines – An Annotated and Selected Bibliography* (2012), www.southcentre.int/wp-content/uploads/2016/05/Bk_2012_IPR-RD-HRs-Access-to-medicine_EN.pdf.

[59] Michael A. Heller & Rebecca S. Eisenberg, *Can Patents Deter Innovation? The Anti-Commons in Biomedical Research*, 280 Science 698 (1998); *see also* Lab. Corp. of Am. Holdings v. Metabolite Labs., Inc., 548 U.S. 124, 126 (2006), in which Justice Breyer, dissenting from the denial of certiorari, opined that too much protection can "impede rather than promote ... progress." Recent cases limiting patents on abstract ideas and fundamental science are seen as a solution to this problem. *See* Rochelle C. Dreyfuss, Jane Nielsen & Dianne Nicol, *Patenting Nature – A Comparative Perspective*, 5 J.L. & Biosciences 550 (2018).

[60] *See* Richard Heeks, Christopher Foster & Yanuar Nugroho, *New Models of Inclusive Innovation for Development*, 4 J. Innovation & Dev. 175–85 (2014) (discussing inclusive innovation as a policy lever for development); *Beijing Forum Promotes Inclusive Innovation for Sustainable Growth*, World Bank (June 21, 2012), www.worldbank.org/en/news/feature/2012/06/21/beijing-forum-promotes-inclusive-innovation-for-sustainable-growth (discussing the spread of inclusive innovation in emerging markets).

technologies include appliances that work without a steady supply of electricity, farm machinery that operates in challenging environments, and food that meets local taste and nutritional needs and grows under local conditions.[61]

Experience with seed patenting illustrates the point. At one time, protection for seeds was highly limited; farmers were free not only to save seeds for replanting but also to experiment and develop new plant varieties. Indeed, much of this work took place at public institutions, including land-grant colleges and the U.S. Department of Agriculture, which freely disseminated their inventions.[62] The advent of patent and patent-like protection for seeds may well have spurred new agricultural developments.[63] However, the availability of exclusive rights has also led to higher prices for farmers (and presumably consumers) and concentrated the industry. Furthermore, because these rights are largely held by patent holders in the North, the availability of protection has exacerbated the general problem of inequality.[64] Significantly here, these rights have also imposed obstacles to breeding plants that grow well under conditions unique to developing countries or that meet their special needs.[65] These are generally not markets rich enough to appeal to patent holders. Nonetheless, the patents can block needed development.

An example is the effort to deal with vitamin A deficiency, which caused morbidity and blindness in much of the South, through the development of a rice rich in this nutrient. Scientists interested in breeding so-called Golden Rice were, however, confronted with multiple patents that complicated their research and potentially barred commercialization.[66] While the Golden Rice problem was solved through public–private partnerships, similar problems have been experienced in achieving other advances, such as farm machinery addressing the climate and soil conditions in poor countries; not all of these problems have proved amenable to the

[61] *See* Heeks et al., *supra* note 60.

[62] Daniel J. Kevles, *Patents, Protections, and Privileges: The Establishment of Intellectual Property in Animals and Plants*, 98 ISIS 323 (2007).

[63] See, for example, Plant Patent Act, 35 U.S.C. § 161; Plant Variety Protection Act, 7 U.S.C. § 2402; J.E.M. Ag Supply, Inc. v. Pioneer Hi-Bred Int'l, Inc., 534 U.S. 124 (2001).

[64] See, for example, Keith Aoki, *Weeds, Seeds & Deeds: Recent Skirmishes in the Seed Wars*, 11 CARDOZO J. INT'L & COMPAR. L. 247 (2003); Jane Payumo, Howard Grimes, Antonio Alfonso, Stanley P. Kowalski, Keith Jones, Karim Maredia & Rodolfo Estigoy, *Intellectual Property and Opportunities for Food Security in the Philippines*, 21 MICH. ST. INT'L. L. REV. 125 (2013).

[65] See, for example, Debra M. Strauss, *The Application of TRIPS to GMOs: International Intellectual Property Rights and Biotechnology*, 45 STAN. J. INT'L L. 287 (2009); THE INTELLECTUAL PROPERTY-REGULATORY COMPLEX OVERCOMING BARRIERS TO INNOVATION IN AGRICULTURAL GENOMICS (Emily Marden, R. Nelson Godfrey & Rachael Manion eds. 2016).

[66] Payumo et al., *supra* note 64, at 138–42.

Golden Rice solution.[67] In addition, in many countries that could benefit from Golden Rice, there were no patents to block dissemination. However, as patenting spreads even to small markets through mechanisms such as the Patent Cooperation Treaty and regional agreements such as the European Patent Convention, and as FTAs require the enactment of stronger protection than required by the TRIPS Agreement, R&D and commercialization are likely to encounter more obstacles in the future.[68] We may be seeing such problems at the time of this writing, in connection with developing cures and vaccines for the COVID-19 pandemic.[69]

5.2.2 *Incentives*

The incentives problem is no less worrisome. The number of patents is increasing, as are technical publications and Internet disclosures.[70] Especially as the world moves to an absolute standard of novelty,[71] these disclosures function as prior art. They can render an invention nonnovel or obvious (noninventive) even when they are not, as a practical matter, available in the South. Moreover, because the standards for disclosure and obviousness depend on the person of ordinary skill in the art, these materials can block patents despite being insufficient to teach those with little absorptive capacity how to benefit from the invention or improve upon it. While local working requirements might remedy the absorption problem by providing opportunities for locals to learn by doing, international agreements have, over time, diminished their availability.[72] Indeed, the TRIPS Agreement arguably abolished their use.[73]

[67] *Id.* at 142–46.

[68] Graeme B. Dinwoodie & Rochelle C. Dreyfuss, A Neofederalist Vision of TRIPS: The Resilience of the International Intellectual Property Regime (2012); Jerome H. Reichman, *Universal Minimum Standards of Intellectual Property Protection under the TRIPS Component of the WTO Agreement*, 29 Int'l Law. 345 (1995); Jerome H. Reichman & David Lange, *Bargaining around the TRIPS Agreement: The Case for Ongoing Public-Private Initiatives to Facilitate Worldwide Intellectual Property Transactions*, 9 Duke J. Compar. & Int'l L. 11 (1998).

[69] Enrico Bonadio & Andrea Baldini, *COVID-19, Patents and the Never-Ending Tension between Proprietary Rights and the Protection of Public Health*, 11 Eur. J. Risk Regul. 390 (2020).

[70] World Intell. Prop. Org., World Intellectual Property Indicators 12 (2019); Jeffrey L. Furman, Markus Nagler & Martin Watzinger, *Disclosure and Subsequent Innovation: Evidence from the Patent Depository Library Program* 2 (Nat'l Bureau of Econ. Rsch., Working Paper No. 24660, 2018) (examining the expansion of the U.S. Patent and Trademark Office's Patent and Trademark Depository Library system from 1975 to 1997).

[71] In 2001, WIPO conducted the most thorough survey on prior art policies, reviewing forty-nine countries which have confirmed this finding. *See* World Intell. Prop. Org., *Information Provided by the Members of the Standing Committee on the Law of Patents (SCP) Concerning the Definition of Prior Art Brief Summary*, WIPO Doc. SCP/6/INF/2 (Nov. 2, 2001).

[72] See, for example, TRIPS Agreement, *supra* note 1, art. 27(1) (barring discrimination as to "whether products are imported or locally produced").

[73] Rochelle Dreyfuss & Susy Frankel, *From Incentive to Commodity to Asset: How International Law Is Reconceptualizing Intellectual Property*, 36 Mich. J. Int'l L. 557 (2015).

Another problem was noted earlier: Developed countries have an important advantage on the demand side. Because the wealthy are willing to pay for technologically advanced products, the patent system offers rich opportunities for returns on "high tech" investment. A strong middle class is likewise beneficial, for its combined purchasing power similarly creates the potential for significant rewards from inventing even standardized products. Developing countries lack these advantages. Thus, the potential reward is likely to be too small to encourage patent holders in the North to exploit their patents and build on or adapt them for use in the South, or even to undertake the cost of negotiating licenses to allow others to do so.[74]

To make matters worse, solutions to the access problem work at cross-purposes with solutions to the incentives problem. For example, the TRIPS Agreement and subsequent Ministerial Declarations or Decisions dealt with access by creating a series of defenses to infringement. Recently, guarantees provided by international investment agreements have also been relaxed.[75] NGOs, intergovernmental organizations, and activists have supplemented these responses with advice on how to meet TRIPS obligations with minimal levels of protection,[76] as well as through the propagation of counter-norms that emphasize the right of everyone to, for example, "share in scientific advancement and its benefits."[77] While that effort may go a long way to solving the first problem, it exacerbates the second one in that these measures further reduce the potential rewards available under the patent system.

74 *See* UNCTAD, World Investment Report 2015: Reforming International Investment Governance 119–20 & tbl.III.1 (2005); *see also* Keith E. Maskus, *The Role of Intellectual Property Rights in Encouraging Foreign Direct Investment and Technology Transfer*, 9 Duke J. Compar. & Int'l L. 109, 128 (1998) (identifying the various factors involved in improving a nation's foreign direct investment (FDI), adding that the multinational enterprises are primarily concerned with the likelihood that FDI will raise expected profits); Carlos A. Primo Braga & Carsten Fink, *The Relationship between Intellectual Property Rights and Foreign Direct Investment*, 9 Duke J. Compar. & Int'l L. 163 (1998) (describing the influence of strong intellectual property protection on the levels of FDI); Peter Nunnenkamp & Julius Spatz, *Intellectual Property Rights and Foreign Direct Investment: The Role of Industry and Host-Country Characteristics* 2 (Kiel Inst. for World Econ., Working Paper No. 1167, 2003) (providing evidence that FDI responds to intellectual property protection only in host countries that have reached a minimum threshold of development and have a capacity to imitate inventions); José L. Groizard, *Technology Trade*, 45 J. Dev. Stu. 1526 (2009) (finding, based on panel data for eighty countries for the year 1970, that FDI is higher for countries with stronger intellectual property rights).

75 *See supra* notes 54–58.

76 See, for example, Max Planck Inst. for Innovation & Competition, Declaration on Patent Protection: Regulatory Sovereignty under TRIPS (2014), www.mpg.de/8132986/Patent-Declaration.pdf. *See also* Farida Shaheed (Special Rapporteur in the Field of Cultural Rights), *Cultural Rights*, U.N. Doc. A/70/279 (Aug. 4, 2015) (examining the relationship between human rights and patent rights); Correa, *supra* note 53.

77 Universal Declaration of Human Rights art. 27, G.A. Res. 217 A (III), U.N. Doc. A/RES/3/217 A (Dec. 10, 1948); Dinwoodie & Dreyfuss, *supra* note 68.

5.3 REFORMING THE PATENT SYSTEM

In our view, a more fruitful approach to remedying economic inequality is to directly attack the systematic ways in which the international regime throws obstacles in the road toward technological self-sufficiency. We offer a menu of approaches that a country should consider (individually or in the aggregate) in revising its laws to promote innovation geared to local capabilities and domestic conditions. These include choosing an exclusivity regime appropriate to its technological and legal situation, structuring the landscape of prior art to facilitate access to the world's knowledge base, and choosing the right beneficiaries for protection. We discuss the choices available in each category as well as their compliance with international obligations.

5.3.1 *Nature of the Exclusivity*

While patent law is the primary regime for protecting technical innovations, it is not the only mechanism. Plants, for example, can be protected by the International Union for the Protection of New Varieties of Plants (UPOV) system;[78] many countries have, among other approaches, long recognized petit patents, patents of importation, patents of improvement, certificates of addition, and utility models.[79] Even today, countries are considering or experimenting with new forms of protection, including commercialization patents,[80] supplementary protection certificates (SPCs),[81] and data and market exclusivities.[82]

A nation interested in encouraging technological development with exclusive rights should consider each of these alternatives. As described in more detail later in the chapter, modifying the patent system is one approach. It could be altered by changing the landscape for determining novelty and nonobviousness; it could also be designed to recalibrate incentives automatically as domestic inventors increase in technological sophistication. The patent alternative offers a potentially substantial benefit. It has the advantage of socializing actors within the regime to the

[78] International Convention for the Protection of New Varieties of Plants, Mar. 19, 1991, 815 U.N.T.S. 89.

[79] Jerome H. Reichman, *The TRIPs Component of the GATT's Uruguay Round: Competitive Prospects for Intellectual Property Owners in an Integrated World Market*, 4 FORDHAM INTELL. PROP. MEDIA & ENT. L.J. 171, 249 (1993) (describing historical models that many industrialized countries favored at earlier stages of development). Reichman also mentions Japan. *See* Reichman, *supra* note 11, at 67.

[80] Sichelman, *supra* note 45.

[81] Council Regulation 1768/92, 1992 O.J. (L 182) 1 (EC).

[82] *See generally* Reichman, *supra* note 79, at 252–53; Alberto Bercovitz-Rodriguez, *Historical Trends in Protection of Technology in Developed Countries and Their Relevance for Developing Countries* 2–3, U.N. Doc. UNCTAD/ITP/TEC/18 (Dec. 26, 1990); STEPHEN P. LADAS, PATENTS, TRADEMARKS, AND RELATED RIGHTS: NATIONAL AND INTERNATIONAL PROTECTION 1898–99 (1975).

predominant form of protection internationally. Thus, in addition to incentivizing innovation, it would help create a class of local investors, examiners, and patent lawyers, as well as new jobs and training opportunities. However, patent regimes require a country to devote resources and personnel to an examination system, and they require innovators to expend efforts on patent prosecution. Other types of exclusivity require less of the system and its participants because they can be based on mere registration. Although rights under these regimes typically last fewer years and include more exceptions and thus return less of a reward, they may nonetheless be sufficient to spur local innovation.

A close study of the behavior of "Tiger" countries and their Asian predecessor, Japan, suggests that reliance on subpatent exclusivities is more prevalent than might be imagined and that it has proved to be a critical factor in moving countries to the technological frontier. As Nagesh Kumar's work showed, strong intellectual property rights adversely affect the absorption of knowledge spillovers; countries that started with "soft" regimes that favored local inventors prospered.[83] For example, prior to the TRIPS Agreement, Japan explicitly designed its patent policy to favor domestic inventors and encourage the absorption of spillovers from foreign activities. It, along with Korea and Taiwan, encouraged a patenting culture with a utility model and industrial design system that allowed and motivated local inventors to modify inventions made elsewhere. Until Japan developed technological capacities on par with those of developed economies, it used longer pendency periods for foreign inventors coupled with efforts to narrow foreign claims. It also adopted other techniques to cut down on foreign patenting in favor of domestic applicants. Korea tolerated lax enforcement (and multiple complaints from the United States) to facilitate duplicative imitation that eventually led to a strong technological sector. In sum, Kumar stated:

> [T]he east Asian countries, viz. Japan, Korea and Taiwan have absorbed substantial amount of technological learning under weak IPR [intellectual property right] protection regime during the early phases. These patent regimes facilitated the absorption of innovation and knowledge generated abroad by their indigenous firms. They have also encouraged incremental innovations on the foreign inventions by domestic enterprises and developed a patent culture through utility models and design patents. As the local technological capabilities matured and the domestic industry sought stronger protection for guarding their own inventions, the IPR regime was strengthened ...[84]

[83] Nagesh Kumar, *Intellectual Property Rights, Technology and Economic Development: Experiences of Asian Countries*, 38 Econ. & Pol. Wkly. 209 (2003) (based on a report submitted to the UK Commission on Intellectual Property Rights); *see also* Khan, *supra* note 4 (documenting the many ways that the United States and European countries once favored particular classes of inventors).

[84] Kumar, *supra* note 83, at 217.

Systems such as these not only provide a better match between protection and technological capacity, but they are also fully consistent with the TRIPS Agreement. That Agreement requires patent protection only for advances that meet the standards of novelty and nonobviousness. And as can be seen by its incorporation of the Paris Convention's reference to "patents of importation, patents of improvement and certificates of addition, etc.,"[85] the TRIPS Agreement envisions other forms of protection as well.

5.3.2 *Landscape of Prior Art*

Countries that wish to focus exclusively on patenting could make changes to that system in order to increase their technological capacity. As suggested earlier, one problem developing countries face is that the move to an absolute standard of novelty for patent protection allows the North to shower its art (patented or not) on the South and undermine patent incentives to engage in follow-on innovation. The TRIPS Agreement does not define novelty; instead, it gives members a degree of flexibility to interpret the term for themselves.[86] Thus, members could break the novelty trap by defining novelty relatively and consider as prior art only that which is accessible locally. Thus, a country could include in prior art only inventions that are practiced locally or protected by domestic patents (or published in a locally accessible publication). Those who import (or reinvent) knowledge that is only accessible abroad, or adapt that knowledge to the local market, could then take advantage of the domestic patent system and earn returns on their efforts. At the same time, the fear of local patenting might encourage foreign originators to engage in activities that qualify their advances as prior art. Either way, more inventions would be available locally, presumably at a price set by local demand (or by the collective demand of all the countries that altered the landscape in this way).[87] Indeed, a country could go further and limit the landscape of prior art to inventions actually practiced locally.

To create even more space for local inventors to operate, the bar of the inventive step could also be lowered. Instead of measuring the knowledge of a person of ordinary skill by global standards, the inquiry could be limited to the inventive capacity of domestic scientists. That would permit a local inventor to acquire protection for adaptations of foreign inventions even when the changes are ones that the North might consider too modest to merit protection. In fact, this is the approach taken to the diversity of technological sophistication among technological

[85] TRIPS Agreement, *supra* note 1, art. 1.1; Paris Convention for the Protection of Industrial Property art. 1(4), Mar. 20, 1883, 21 U.S.T. 1583, 828 U.N.T.S. 305.

[86] Dinwoodie & Dreyfuss, *supra* note 68.

[87] *Cf.* Venetian Patent Law of 1474, *reprinted in* Graeme B. Dinwoodie, William Hennessey, Shira Perlmutter & Graeme Austin, International Intellectual Property Law and Policy 413 (2d ed. 2008); 35 U.S.C. § 102(a).

sectors. As Dan Burk and Mark Lemley noted, when a new technology emerges, the knowledge in the area is low, and it is easier to acquire protection. The ease with which patents can be obtained encourages more innovators to enter the field; as the sector matures, more is required to obtain protection.[88] In the same way, measuring technological capacity locally would encourage more inventive activity and ultimately lead to an increasingly sophisticated pool of domestic innovators.

5.3.3 *Beneficiaries*

Under the TRIPS Agreement, a member state is required to offer to the nationals of other member states "treatment no less favorable than that it accords its own nationals with regard to the protection of intellectual property."[89] It must also give most-favored-nation status to the nationals of other members of the Agreement.[90] Accordingly, a nation that restructures its system of TRIPS-protected rights must provide the same rights to the nationals of other WTO member states.

Countries that comply with this obligation by offering the same protection to foreigners and locals might benefit from encouraging innovation in ways that meet local needs.[91] That would improve the domestic availability of the fruits of technological advancement. But if foreigners are more technically adept than locals, they could crowd out domestic innovators. Accordingly, the system would not significantly improve the country's own technological capacity. Locals would pay higher prices for protected innovations without enjoying the benefit of encouraging domestic technological growth. Countries may therefore wish to limit these new (or newly configured) rights to their own innovators. Such an effort is not entirely unprecedented: As noted earlier, Japan slowed examination for foreign inventors, thus improving the chances for domestic innovators to obtain patent rights.

One approach for dealing with the incompatibility of this approach with the TRIPS Agreement's bar on discrimination may be to limit the exclusivities available under the new regime to nationals from any country that is categorized as developing – for example, to those with a GDP below a certain level. This would avoid a complaint of de jure discrimination because nationals of any country that fits the

88 Dan L. Burk & Mark A. Lemley, *Policy Levers in Patent Law* 1651, 89 VA. L. REV. 1575 (2003).

89 TRIPS Agreement, *supra* note 1, art. 3.1.

90 *Id.* art. 4.

91 Coined by Vijay Govindarajan and Chris Trimble in their seminal 2012 book, the term "reverse innovation" explains how in certain cases Northern countries adopt Southern innovative products developed in Southern nations. *See* VIJAY GOVINDARAJAN & CHRIS TRIMBLE, REVERSE INNOVATION: CREATE FAR FROM HOME, WIN EVERYWHERE (2012) (providing numerous case studies of production by reverse innovation); Vijay Govindarajan, *The Case for "Reverse Innovation" Now*, BLOOMBERG (Oct. 26, 2009), www.bloomberg.com/news/articles/2009-10-26/the-case-for-reverse-innovation-nowbusinessweek-business-news-stock-market-and-financial-advice#xj4y7vzkg (discussing the historical path leading to reverse innovation).

category would qualify for protection. However, a de facto claim is another matter: A WTO panel found that when the qualification for protection is too tightly associated with nationality, it can constitute discrimination.[92] Yet the observed persistence of technological inequality suggests that the concept of nondiscrimination requires reconceptualization. As the U.N. Conference on Trade and Development (UNCTAD) once cautioned, "equality of treatment only makes sense when the parties involved are in a general way equal; when they are not, equality of treatment simply gives the stronger party unlimited freedom to utilize his power at the expense of the weaker party."[93] The nondiscrimination provision of the General Agreement on Tariffs and Trade applies to goods only when they are alike.[94] We join Henning Grosse Ruse-Khan in urging that under the TRIPS Agreement, the same analysis should apply to nationality. Thus, a member state should be permitted to differentiate among nationals when they are from countries that are different along a significant axis, such as wealth or technological capacity.[95]

CONCLUSION

Economic research has demonstrated an intimate connection between technological capacity, income, and inequality. As a result, reducing economic inequality requires an examination of the factors that lead to technological disparities among nations. While these differences have multiple causes, patent law is an important explanatory factor. As the experience of emerging economies shows, greater use of exclusivities that are less technologically demanding than patent rights may ameliorate these problems. However, restructuring the patent system to alter the landscape of prior art and calibrate the inventive step to domestic capabilities is also worthy of consideration. This chapter suggests the use of a relative novelty standard that includes in the prior art only locally available technology and a standard of inventiveness that takes into account the capacity of domestic innovators.

[92] *See* Panel Report, *European Communities – Protection of Trademarks and Geographical Indications for Agricultural Products and Foodstuffs*, WTO Doc. WT/DS174/R (Mar. 15, 2005).

[93] UNCTAD, *The Role of the Patent System in the Transfer of Technology to Developing Countries*, ¶ 320, U.N. Doc. TD/B/AC.11/19/Rev.1 (1975), https://digitallibrary.un.org/record/526090?ln=en.

[94] General Agreement on Tariffs and Trade, art. III, Oct. 30, 1947, 61 Stat. A11, 55 U.N.T.S. 194.

[95] Henning Grosse Ruse-Khan, The Protection of Intellectual Property in International Law § 5.43 (2016); *see also* Graeme B. Dinwoodie & Rochelle C. Dreyfuss, *Diversifying without Discriminating: Complying with the Mandates of the TRIPS Agreement*, 13 Mich. Telecomm. & Tech. L. Rev. 445, 450 (2007).

PART II

Intellectual Property and National Inequalities

6

Are Men and Women Creating Equal?

Contextualizing Copyright and Gender in the United States

Dotan Oliar and Marliese Dalton

INTRODUCTION

In 1790, Mercy Otis Warren registered her collection of patriotic poems with the District Court for the District of Massachusetts, becoming one of the first women to register a copyright in the United States.[1] When copyright functions were centralized in the Library of Congress in 1870, several women songwriters were among the first to protect their original works by registering their music compositions.[2] Decades later, in 1905, Clare Kummer became the first woman to solely author and register a musical work with the United States Copyright Office ("USCO").[3] Despite these early milestones in women's authorship, women today remain underrepresented as copyright authors. An analysis of copyright registration data between 1978 and 2012 reveals that two-thirds of registered authors are men.[4] The gap between authorship by men and women varies by type of work, but the existence of a gap in every work category raises questions about who is benefiting from our copyright system and why women create and register works at lower rates than men do.

Although copyright registration became voluntary in 1978, the USCO has generally continued to process more than 300,000, and often 400,000, registrations each year. Registration is not required for copyright protection, but it entails several advantages. It is a necessary prerequisite for bringing an infringement action for a

1 FEDERAL COPYRIGHT RECORDS 1790–1800, at 74 (James Gilreath ed., 1987).

2 *See* Alison Hall, *Celebrating Women's History Month: Female Songwriters*, U.S. COPYRIGHT OFF. (Mar. 2018), www.copyright.gov/history/lore/pdfs/201803%20CLore_March2018.pdf.

3 *See* Alison Hall, *Early Female Musical Writers Discovered through Copyright Records*, U.S. COPYRIGHT OFF. (Nov. 2018), www.copyright.gov/history/lore/pdfs/201811%20CLore_November2018.pdf.

4 *See* Robert Brauneis & Dotan Oliar, *An Empirical Study of the Race, Ethnicity, Gender, and Age of Copyright Registrants*, 86 GEO. WASH. L. REV. 46, 73 (2018).

U.S. work and for receiving statutory damages and attorney's fees.[5] It makes it easier for copyright owners to prevent the importation of infringing copies and, if the work is registered within five years of publication, the registration constitutes prima facie evidence of copyright validity and authorship in litigation.[6] In addition, registration reduces transaction costs and makes it easier for copyright holders to financially benefit from selling or licensing their works.[7] This is particularly helpful for entrepreneurs seeking legitimacy or an increase in their young company's selling potential.[8] These benefits are intended to encourage registration and reward creativity.[9] But if women are not registering copyrights as frequently as men, do the benefits of registration appeal less to women? Or are there structural, systemic, industry-specific, or other barriers to women's participation in the copyright system?

These questions are difficult to answer fully, but it is possible that rather than women failing to appreciate the benefits of registration, the gender gap in copyright registrations is in part reflective of more general social realities, including inequitable patterns of property ownership by women as well as persistent inequality within creative industries. Notably, women are underrepresented in ownership of copyrights, trademarks, and patents compared to their share of the U.S. workforce. In 2010, women made up 46.7 percent of the U.S. workforce but received only 33.31 percent of granted trademarks.[10] Likewise, in 2015, women represented 28 percent of the STEM (science, technology, engineering, and mathematics) workforce, but only 12 percent of the inventors listed on granted patents.[11] Some creative fields, such as the music industry, have been plagued by allegations of gender bias and accompanying low levels of women participation, underscoring the finding that women registered only 24.02 percent of music copyrights between 1978 and 2012.[12]

5 17 U.S.C. §§ 411(a), 412.

6 17 U.S.C. § 410(c); 19 C.F.R. §§ 133.31–.37 (2020).

7 *See* Dotan Oliar, Nathaniel Pattinson & K. Ross Powell, *Copyright Registrations: Who, What, When, Where, and Why*, 92 Tex. L. Rev. 2211, 2217 (2012).

8 *See* Jessica Milli, Emma Williams-Baron, Meika Berlan, Jenny Xia & Barbara Gault, Inst. for Women's Pol'y Rsch., Equity in Innovation: Women Inventors and Patents 15–16 (2016) (discussing the impact of women-held patents on the economy and how intellectual property rights increase the value of businesses).

9 Oliar et al., *supra* note 7, at 2212–13.

10 *See* U.S. Dep't of Lab., Women in the Labor Force, www.dol.gov/agencies/wb/data/facts-over-time/women-in-the-labor-force#civilian-labor-force-by-sex (last visited May 20, 2020) (providing data on the gender composition of the labor force by job category); Delixus & Nat'l Women's Bus. Council, Intellectual Property and Women Entrepreneurs: Quantitative Analysis 83 tbl.A.5, 84 tbl.A.6, 93 tbl.A.16 (2012) (providing data concerning the rate of granted trademark applications by gender and year).

11 *See* U.S. Pat. & Trademark Off., Progress and Potential: A Profile of Women Inventors on U.S. Patents 3 (2019), www.uspto.gov/ip-policy/economic-research/publications/reports/progress-potential [hereinafter Progress and Potential]; U.S. Dep't of Lab., *supra* note 10.

12 Brauneis & Oliar, *supra* note 4, at 76. See, for example, Becky Prior, Erin Barra & Sharon Kramer, Women in the U.S. Music Industry: Obstacles and Opportunities 7 (2019)

One may think that the disparity in intellectual property rights ownership only affects a limited number of artists, entrepreneurs, and scientists. However, intellectual property–intensive industries – industries whose growth is fueled by effective protection of intellectual property rights – accounted for 27.9 million U.S. jobs in 2014 and 38.2 percent of U.S. GDP.[13] A great deal of economic value is added by effectively protecting intellectual property rights and by promoting creativity and innovation among as many people as possible.

The USCO does not ask registration applicants for their demographic information. While this does not necessarily mean that gender bias could not sometimes play a role when applications are reviewed, it is at least consistent with its mission to promote creativity "for the benefit of all."[14] It should be uncontroversial to point out that the quality and breadth of works produced would be better with a diverse and more inclusive set of authors and when barriers to entry are removed.[15] However, it is clear that either women do not respond to the current copyright system's set of incentives or, more likely, that the incentives operate in conjunction with social and psychological factors[16] to motivate women to create and register certain types of work but not others, and at rates that generally fall below those at which men create and register works.[17] If the USCO is to properly carry out Congress' constitutional charge to "promote the Progress of Science and useful Arts,"[18] then we must understand what is underlying lower rates of creative authorship and subsequent registration by women.

We will seek to address some of these factors by considering the extent to which the gender disparity is or is not merely reflective of gender dynamics in other types of intellectual property holdings. Through a further discussion of patterns of inequality in other forms of property ownership, it will be possible to contextualize gender

(reporting that three-quarters of surveyed women experienced gender bias while working in the music industry).

13 Econ. & Stat. Admin. & U.S. Pat. & Trademark Off., Intellectual Property and the U.S. Economy: 2016 Update, at ii (2016) (reporting on the economic impact of intellectual property rights and companies that frequently rely on them on the U.S. economy).

14 *See* Overview of the Copyright Office, U.S. Copyright Off., www.copyright.gov/about/ (last visited May 29, 2020).

15 *See* Brauneis & Oliar, *supra* note 4, at 91–92 (discussing in greater detail some of the benefits of diverse authorship).

16 *Id.* at 90.

17 One study has found that women publish academic papers in STEM at similar rates as men despite being much less likely to apply for patents. Papers written by women in this study were also cited more frequently than papers written by men, suggesting that the gap in women's ownership of intellectual property rights is not due to a lack of creativity or capability compared with men. See, for example, Waverly W. Ding, Fiona Murray & Toby E. Stuart, *Gender Differences in Patenting in the American Life Sciences*, 313 Science 665, 666 (2006).

18 U.S. Const. art. I, § 8, cl. 8; Dotan Oliar, *Making Sense of the Intellectual Property Clause: Promotion of Progress as a Limitation on Congress's Power*, 94 Geo. L.J. 1771 (2006) (suggesting that "Promot[ion of] Progress" is not only part of the constitutional grant of power to Congress but also an independently enforceable limitation on it).

inequality in intellectual property. This will be further supplemented by a discussion of gender dynamics across different types of creative professions in the hopes of understanding some of the reasons why women may be less likely to author and register creative works in certain industries.[19]

The first section reviews recent data and demonstrates patterns of copyright authorship by men and women that vary over time by work type. The second section reviews recent studies on gendered trends in patent and trademark ownership. Available data suggest that women are underrepresented in every category of intellectual property rights ownership. The third section discusses similar gender-linked differences in other forms of property, such as home and corporate ownership. These data suggest that the gender-based trends in copyright ownership reflect some more general trends of property ownership. The fourth section considers the extent to which copyright registration gender differences by type-of-work category are reflective of gender inequality within creative professions. The fifth section identifies explanations and factors that may contribute to lower rates of authorship by women. We ultimately conclude that it is impossible to rule out, based on available data, the possibility that our copyright system, in conjunction with its related industries, may have a discriminatory effect on women's incentives to create.

6.1 THE COPYRIGHT GENDER GAP

Drawing on data from the USCO Electronic Catalog ("Catalog"), a study coauthored by one of us ("Study") was the first to identify demographic patterns of copyright authors.[20] It reveals a striking degree of imbalance between population demographics and rates of authorship, particularly concerning rates of authorship among men and women. In the surveyed data, men authored an estimated two-thirds of registered works. The degree and nature of the differences between men and women went beyond mere rates of authorship, and have varied over time and across work types, showing that what seems like a gender-neutral system may produce a disparate incentive effect on men and women.[21]

6.1.1 *The Data Set and Methodology*

The Study analyzed the over 14 million copyrighted works registered with the USCO between 1978 and 2012.[22] Registration records contain information about

[19] While this chapter will focus on dynamics between men and women, that is not to say that the relationships described later apply uniformly across different racial or ethnic groups or to LGBTQ individuals. These and other distinctions warrant further study. *See also infra* note 27.

[20] Brauneis & Oliar, *supra* note 4.

[21] *Id.* at 73.

[22] *Id.* at 51. The study focused on original and valid registrations. "Original" means that supplementary and renewal registrations were excluded from the data set because they were primarily

the work, such as its title, date of application, publication status, and creative category.[23] Usefully, the Study converted all work types into six basic categories: text, music, art, movies, drama, and software.[24]

In analyzing gender demographics, the Study focused on works by known, named individual authors.[25] Registrants are not asked to self-report demographic information in their copyright registration applications. Using gender-related data extracted from the 1990 Census, the Study could assign to authors a probabilistic gender based on their first names.[26] First names are highly indicative of gender: 82 percent of the authors had a 99 percent or higher likelihood of being either a man or a woman.[27] Works created by business associations and anonymous and pseudonymous works were excluded from the gender statistics because the author's gender could not be determined probabilistically.[28]

6.1.2 *Key Findings*

This study revealed a wide variation in gender parity across time, type of work, and publication rates, among other aspects. Strikingly, in 2012, 64 percent of authors were men.[29] While this was a decrease from 1978, when 70 percent of the authors were men, it was still well above their labor market share in 2012.[30] The percentage

used to extend the length or scope of copyright protection and were not practically useful for measuring trends in authorship. "Valid" means that the registrations have not been canceled by the USCO and can thus form the basis for a legal claim. The data set did not include "serials," that is, works that are published in a series with multiple authors, because it was often difficult to determine authorship and properly classify the "work" within a certain work type category. *Id.* at 53.

23 Out of the isolated 14,598,621 registrations, 7,863,069 (or roughly 54 percent) were published at the time of registration. *Id.* at 56 n.31. *See generally* Oliar et al., *supra* note 7, at 2224 (stating that a work is considered "published" if it has been "distributed to the public by sale, transfer, lease, rental, loan, or has been offered to be distributed").

24 Brauneis & Oliar, *supra* note 4, at 56.

25 *See id.* at 52–54.

26 In this study, 982,234 registrations reported at least one author whose first name was not included in the 1990 U.S. Census list of first names and these names were excluded from the study. *Id.* at 72–73; *see also* Shervin Malmasi & Mark Dras, *A Data-Driven Approach to Studying Given Names and Their Gender and Ethnicity Associations*, *in* Proceedings of Australasian Language Technology Association Workshop 145, 146 (2014) (discussing the connection between first names and predicting likely gender).

27 While there are multiple categories of gender expression, the statistics linking gender to first names reflect the 1990 U.S. Census Office's decision to allow only these two options and on respondents' self-selection into these categories.

28 An estimated 28 percent of registrations did not have any authors who were identified individuals and were thus excluded from the data set for gender analytics. This excluded, for example, authors of works made for hire, as assigning gender to employers or corporate authors was impossible. *See* Brauneis & Oliar, *supra* note 4, at 73 n.76, 74.

29 The gender of registrations was determined by averaging the gender of its individual authors. *Id.* at 73 n.76.

30 In 2012, men made up 53.1 percent of the labor force. *Id.* at 73.

of women in the labor market increased from 41.7 percent in 1978 to 46.9 percent in 2012, while the share of women authors has only increased from 30 percent in 1978 to 36 percent in 2012.[31]

6.1.2.1 Gender Variation across Work Types

The disparity between authorship rates among men and women has varied across type-of-work categories. Between 1978 and 2012, men registered 88.22 percent of software copyrights and 78.16 percent of movie copyrights.[32] Both categories have experienced a relative increase in authorship by women over time, but when combined, these categories represent only 2.5 percent of registrations by individuals.[33] The most significant gains toward gender parity have been made in the text category, which makes up over a third of the individual registrations.[34] While men were listed as authors for 57.45 percent of all text registrations, the share of women authors increased from 33.98 percent to 45.83 percent between 1978 and 2012. The drama and music categories, which account for 5 percent and 44 percent of individual registrations, respectively, did not experience a significant change in gender parity between 1978 and 2012. Overall, men authored 66.99 percent of all drama registrations and 75.98 percent of all music registrations.[35] The art category experienced the greatest fluidity between 1978 and 2012, with the percentage of authorship by men decreasing between 1978 and 1984 and rising again by 2012. Art represents 11 percent of individual registrations, with men authoring 54.34 percent of total art registrations and 59.1 percent of art registrations in 2012.[36]

6.1.2.2 Gender Variation in Publication Status

The data suggest that women are more likely to create and register copyrights in categories of work where the work has typically already been published at the time of registration.[37] In the study, 39 percent of registrations authored by men were published at the time of registration, compared with 44 percent of works authored by women.[38] However, these statistics are affected partly by the different types of work men and women tend to register. For example, half of all registrations authored by women were in the text category, and within that category, 61 percent of women had published their work by the time it was registered. While men

[31] *Id.*
[32] *Id.* at 76.
[33] In 2012, the percentage of authors who were women was 10.49 percent for movies and 11.85 percent for software. *Id.*
[34] *Id.* at 76.
[35] *Id.*
[36] *Id.*
[37] *Id.* at 77.
[38] *Id.* at 76.

demonstrated a similar propensity to publish textual work before registering it for copyright, text registrations represented only 33 percent of registrations authored by men.[39] On the other hand, music registrations represented half of the registrations authored by men, and this category only had a 22 percent prior-publication rate for men. Women, in contrast, had a 15 percent prior-publication rate for music registrations, but music registrations only made up 29 percent of women-authored registrations.[40] In the software and art categories, women were more likely to publish their work before registration than men, but in the drama category, men and women had equal publication rates.[41]

6.1.2.3 Gender Variation in Age and Coauthorship

The Study concluded by examining coauthorship patterns and author age differences by gender and work type. First, in comparing registrations with more than one author listed, the Study found that authors generally worked with coauthors of the same gender. Conditional on one of the authors being a man, there was about an 80 percent chance that the other author was also a man. Conditional on one of the authors being a woman, there was about a 50 percent chance that the other author was also a woman. If authors had picked their coauthors randomly and neutrally, we would expect these statistics to have been about 71 percent and 29 percent.[42] Men and women, therefore, show a clear tendency to collaborate with same-gendered coauthors.

While there was some variation in age demographics between men and women, the difference in size was dependent on the type of work registered.[43] For example, women authors of registered works were on average one year older than men in the movie category, two years older in the music category, and three years older in the software category. On the other hand, women were generally a year or less younger than men in the text, drama, and art categories.[44]

6.2 PATENT AND TRADEMARK OWNERSHIP

The gender disparity in copyright registration is mirrored in both patent and trademark ownership. The degree of disparity varies for patents and trademarks,

39 Sixty-six percent of registrations for textual work written by men were published at the time of registration. *Id.* at 77.

40 *Id.*

41 *Id.*

42 The sample size for this analysis was 1,708,442 data points and the percentage of authors who were women was 29 percent. *Id.* at 75.

43 *Id.* at 77.

44 *Id.*

but in both cases, women are underrepresented compared with men. Women submit fewer applications than men and have fewer patents granted.[45] Focusing strictly on metrics drawn from the intellectual property system obscures the factors and events that precede a patent or trademark application. Rather than indicating a lack of ability, creativity, or interest, lower numbers of applications and grants are likely indicative of barriers to full access to and participation in the system by women. The existence of such barriers, particularly among women applying for patents, has been confirmed by researchers seeking to understand the behavior of women prior to and after securing intellectual property rights. Considered in conjunction with copyright registration, there may be systemic barriers within the intellectual property system hindering women.

Similar to copyright registration data, studies have indicated that gender disparity in patent and trademark ownership varies widely by the subcategory, or class, into which the particular patent or trademark falls. Some of these distinctions can be justified by gendered patterns of educational attainment, but additional factors suggest something other than education is disincentivizing or preventing women from seeking intellectual property rights ownership within their fields. As with copyrights, some studies on patent ownership have also indicated that women have different collaboration patterns than men and are very unlikely to patent an invention as a sole inventor.

Like the USCO, the U.S. Patent and Trademark Office (USPTO) does not record demographic information for its applicants. Therefore, the data provided later in the chapter is based on studies that used a similar procedure of matching the first names of listed owners with their likely gender using U.S. Census data.

6.2.1 *The Patent Gender Gap*

In 1977, only 2.6 percent of granted U.S. patents listed at least one woman as an inventor.[46] More recently, in 2016, women were listed on 21 percent of granted patents.[47] However, this remains below women's share of the STEM labor force.[48] Furthermore, the total inventor rate – that is, the percentage of all inventors listed on

45 *See* Delixus & Nat'l Women's Bus. Council, *supra* note 10, at 83 tbl.A.5, 84 tbl.A.6 (showing the number of patent applications filed by men and women by year from 1975 to 2010); *id.* at 89 tbl.A.11, 90 tbl.A.12 (showing the number of trademark applications filed by men and women by year from 1980 to 2010); *see also* Kyle Jensen, Balázs Kovács & Olav Sorenson, *Gender Differences in Obtaining and Maintaining Patent Rights*, 36 Nature Biotechnology 307, 309 (2018) (finding that applications submitted by all-women teams are rejected at higher rates than applications submitted by all-men teams).

46 U.S. Dep't of Com., Buttons to Biotech: 1996 Update Report with Supplemental Data through 1998, at 8 (1999) (reporting on the inclusion of women in U.S. patent applications and granted patents).

47 Progress and Potential, *supra* note 11, at 4 (containing data about the women inventor rate for patents over time).

48 The share of women in STEM has increased from 25 percent in 2000 to 28 percent in 2015. This measure combines the percentage of women in life and physical sciences, engineering,

granted patents who are women – has only increased from 10 percent in 2000 to 12 percent in 2015.[49] If we disaggregate some of these patent statistics, we find that the degree of gender disparity varies widely over time and by scientific field. For example, while some fields, such as life sciences, have achieved near gender parity, other fields, such as engineering, have remained vastly disproportionate.[50] This trend is reflected in STEM educational data, labor force makeup, and patent statistics.

Unlike trademarks and copyrights, the expertise required to invent something patentable would often necessitate some formal education or expertise in STEM, a high level of education, or at least a background in STEM.[51] As a result, gender disparities in a degree program at both the undergraduate and graduate levels may explain part of the gender disparity in patent rates.[52] For example, one study has argued that individuals with mechanical and electrical engineering degrees produce more patents than most other STEM degrees, but women have historically received less than 10 percent of the mechanical and electrical engineering degrees awarded to men. Because individuals with these STEM degrees have a high likelihood of patenting compared to other degree programs, a lack of women in the degree program could affect the disparity in overall patent rates between men and women.[53]

and computer occupations. *See id.* at 5 (showing the women inventor rate and gender composition of STEM fields).

49 *Id.*

50 The share of women in life and physical sciences has grown consistently since 1970. By 2010, women were 39 percent of this workforce, and by 2018, the number had risen to 45 percent. In contrast, the share of women in engineering has experienced minimal and largely stagnant growth. By 1990, women made up 12 percent of the engineering workforce, which increased to only 14 percent by 2010. In 2018, women made up 16 percent of the engineering workforce. These broad categories can be further subdivided by job type and industry. *See* U.S. DEP'T OF LAB., *supra* note 10 (providing information about the share of women in the labor force); W. DuBow & J.J. Gonzalez, Nat'l Ctr. for Women & Info. Tech., *NCWIT Scorecard: The Status of Women in Technology* (2020), www.ncwit.org/bythenumbers (providing data on the gender composition of STEM industries and educational programs).

51 *See* MILLI ET AL., *supra* note 8, at 8 (discussing how an increase in STEM degrees awarded to women corresponds with an increase in patenting activity among women).

52 Jennifer Hunt, Jean-Philippe Garant, Hannah Herman & David J. Munroe, *Why Are Women Underrepresented amongst Patentees?* 42 RSCH. POL'Y 831, 834 (2013) (explaining how disparity in STEM degree programs by gender explains part of the disparity between men and women patent rates).

53 The educational statistics are reflected in the percentage of women employed as electrical and mechanical engineers. In 2018, 9.4 percent of electrical engineers and 10.9 percent of mechanical engineers were women. BUREAU OF LAB. STAT., WOMEN IN THE LABOR FORCE: A DATABOOK 49 tbl.11 (2019); Hunt et al., *supra* note 52, at 832, 834–35 (finding that electrical and mechanical engineering are two of the most patent-heavy fields of study in STEM, and the scarcity of women in electrical and mechanical engineering, as well as their lack of representation in design or development roles within those fields, explains an estimated 40 percent of the gap in men and women patent rates); NAT'L SCI. FOUND., EMPLOYED SCIENTISTS AND ENGINEERS, BY OCCUPATION, HIGHEST DEGREE LEVEL, AND SEX: 2006 tbl.9-5 (2006) (containing degree information by gender and occupation in STEM fields).

On the other hand, women have been more proportionally represented in biological and physical science degree programs, and in 2015, women represented 48 percent of biological and life scientists. These STEM degrees are much less likely than mechanical and electrical engineering to lead to patent activity, but while men and women are nearly equally employed as biological and life scientists, in 2015, only 25 percent of the inventors for biotechnology patents and 23 percent of inventors for pharmaceutical patents were women, suggesting educational attainment alone does not determine patent rates.[54]

6.2.1.1 Level of Gender Equality Varies by Workplace Type

Granted patents are often assigned to an employer, and by looking at assignment data, it is possible to draw conclusions about the types of work environments that either attract more women or perhaps place greater emphasis on gender equality. Between 2007 and 2016, nearly 20 percent of the inventors listed on patents assigned to universities or hospitals were women. This was followed closely by public research organizations, where 15 percent of listed patent inventors were women. These two sectors have shown the largest and most continued improvement in the share of female inventors. Between 2007 and 2016, among individual-owned patents, just under 15 percent of inventors were women.[55] Only 12 percent of the inventors listed on patents assigned to private companies were women.[56]

These data support a couple of propositions. First, these statistics suggest that women are much less likely than men to individually develop and patent a new invention.[57] Second, these data support studies that concluded that women might be more likely to patent while working for academic institutions or public companies than for private companies.[58] This could be tied to the organizational

[54] *See* Progress and Potential, *supra* note 11, at 5–6 (containing data for the percentage of women in STEM by field as well as inventor rate for biotechnology and pharmaceutical patents); Hunt et al., *supra* note 52, at 835 (finding that women are in the majority of life science degree holders but that individuals with a life sciences degree have a relatively low likelihood of patenting compared with other STEM fields).

[55] *Id.* at 9.

[56] *Id.*

[57] Women are also less likely to have the same financial resources and connections to the patent industry as men do. Delixus & Nat'l Women's Bus. Council, *supra* note 10, 15 (discussing the findings of a study that involved interviews with women entrepreneurs who reported a lack of connections to the patent industry as well as the high cost of patenting as two reasons why they have not pursued patents in the past); Emma Williams-Baron, Jessica Milli & Barbara Gault, Inst. for Women's Pol'y Rsch., Innovation and Intellectual Property among Women Entrepreneurs 12 (2018), https://iwpr.org/publications/innovation-intellectual-property-women-entrepreneurs/ (containing data on the likelihood of women entrepreneurs to own intellectual property rights compared with men).

[58] See, for example, Cassidy R. Sugimoto, Chaoqun Ni, Jevin D. West & Vincent Larivière, *The Academic Advantage: Gender Disparities in Patenting*, 10 PLoS One 1, 6 (2015), https://journals

structure of most private companies[59] or could be reflective of the private sector's difficulties in retaining women in STEM roles.[60]

6.2.1.2 Patterns of Coauthorship

Several studies have found that women are more likely to work with coinventors than to apply for patents by themselves. Most often, patent teams with women have two to five total inventors. While larger teams are becoming more common overall, teams with women on them are much more likely to include four or more inventors than teams of only men.[61]

While women are more likely than men to collaborate with coinventors, they are unlikely to work as part of an all-women team. Between 2007 and 2016, only 4 percent of patents had only women listed as inventors.[62] Furthermore, patents with only women listed as inventors are cited less frequently than mixed-gender and men-only patent inventor teams.[63] However, mixed-gender teams are cited more frequently in later patent applications than men-only and women-only teams, which may be indicative of either the relative value of average patents produced by diverse, mixed-gender teams or the added value of large teams of inventors.[64]

6.2.1.3 Gender-Linked Behavioral Differences in Patent Applications

There are several differences between men and women during and immediately after the patent application process. First, all-women teams may be subject to gender

.plos.org/plosone/article/file?id=10.1371/journal.pone.0128000&type=printable (finding that women around the world are most likely to patent within academic institutions).

59 *See* Kjersten Bunker Whittington & Laurel Smith-Doerr, *Women Inventors in Context: Disparities in Patenting across Academia and Industry*, 22 GENDER & SOC'Y 194, 197–99 (2008) (discussing differences in women's participation in STEM fields, as well as patenting activity, on the basis of different fields relying on different organizational dynamics with some fields attracting more women by being more collaborative and flexible).

60 About one-fifth of women with STEM degrees end up leaving the workforce, and around half end up leaving the private sector for a start-up, public-sector, or self-employed role. SYLVIA ANN HEWLETT, CAROLYN BUCK LUCE, LISA J. SERVON, LAURA SHERBIN, PEGGY SHILLER, EYTAN SOSNOVICH & KAREN SUMBERG, THE ATHENA FACTOR: REVERSING THE BRAIN DRAIN IN SCIENCE, ENGINEERING, AND TECHNOLOGY 50 (2008).

61 PROGRESS AND POTENTIAL, *supra* note 11, at 11 (containing information about the percentage of women who work with coinventors by the number of coinventors).

62 *Id.* at 12.

63 JESSICA MILLI, BARBARA GAULT, EMMA WILLIAMS-BARON & MEIKA BERLAN, INST. FOR WOMEN'S POL'Y RSCH., THE GENDER PATENTING GAP 6 (2016), https://iwpr.org/publications/the-gender-patenting-gap/ (discussing the number of citations women-only invented patents receive).

64 *Id.*; CATHERINE ASHCRAFT & ANTHONY BREITZMAN, NAT'L CTR. FOR WOMEN & INFO. TECH., WHO INVENTS IT?: WOMEN'S PARTICIPATION IN INFORMATION TECHNOLOGY PATENTING 4 (2012) (suggesting that mixed-gender teams receive more citations due to the size of the inventor team or its value).

bias or discrimination by patent examiners. One study found that for all-women teams of inventors that submitted patent applications, inventors with "common" names for women were 8.2 percent less likely to have their patent applications approved than all-men teams.[65] The magnitude of this effect decreased when women inventors had "rare" names that might not be socially connected to either gender.[66] All-women teams are also less likely to appeal rejected patent applications and less likely to have their patents maintained by their assignee than mixed-gender or all-men teams.[67] Second, women are less likely to commercialize their patents, resulting in less monetary gain from their patenting activity.[68] This is a reflection of both having women as inventors and some of the fields they specialize in. For example, while women are well-represented in life sciences, only 39 percent of life sciences patents are commercialized.[69]

6.2.1.4 Explanations

Ultimately, only part of the patent gap is likely linked to the absence of women in STEM.[70] The lack of gender equality in patent-intensive fields such as engineering may disproportionately affect the patent gender gap.[71] However, even in areas of STEM where women are well-represented, they still do not patent at the same rates as men. This is particularly clear in academia, where men and women have been shown to publish similar-quality papers at similar rates. Still, men remain much more likely to patent than women.[72]

Another potential problem could be the cost and complexity of the patent application process. Applying for and maintaining a patent could cost upwards of tens of thousands of dollars, and due to historical exclusion from STEM, women may not have the connections to the patent industry that men have.[73] These connections both with the patent industry and within STEM fields may be

65 Jensen et al., *supra* note 45, at 309.

66 All-women teams with "rare" names were 2.8 percent less likely to have their applications approved than teams of men. *Id.*

67 *Id.* at 308.

68 Milli et al., *supra* note 8, at 20 (discussing differences in patenting activity by men and women including commercialization).

69 Hunt et al., *supra* note 52, at 834 (discussing the connection between STEM fields where women are prominent and the likelihood of patent commercialization in those fields).

70 *Id.* at 832 (arguing that other factors must contribute to lower patent rates among women because women with STEM degrees do not patent at significantly higher rates than women without STEM degrees).

71 *Id.* at 840 (suggesting that women are less likely than men to work in design or development roles that lend themselves to patent activity).

72 *See* Ding et al., *supra* note 17, at 665–66 (discussing patenting rates by men and women in academia compared with paper publication rates and the average number of citations for papers published by men and women).

73 Milli et al., *supra* note 8, at 18–19 (discussing possible explanations why fewer women than men apply for patents); Delixus & Nat'l Women's Bus. Council, *supra* note 10, at 15, 19–20

important resources for individuals to gain valuable expertise and insight into whether or not they should apply for a patent and what that process entails.[74]

There are also several ways in which women applying for a patent may face some degree of discrimination. While progress has been made in recent decades, some women still report encountering either implicit bias or sexist behavior in STEM workplaces. While it is unclear how widespread these kinds of experiences may be, they may lead women to leave their jobs in STEM more frequently than men and steer women away from patent activity.[75] Even in academia, researchers have found that some science faculty may be implicitly biased against women. In a study where researchers submitted identical resumés for a lab manager position, both men and women STEM faculty members rated the resumé with a common name for a man as more qualified and offered a higher starting salary than the resumé with a common name for a woman.[76] In addition, data suggest that examiners at the USPTO show gender bias in processing applications.[77]

(containing information from interviews with women entrepreneurs who cited the high cost of patenting and a lack of connections as two reasons why they have not applied for patents).

[74] See, for example, Ding et al., *supra* note 17, at 666–67 (suggesting that women are less likely than men to have connections, or prior experience, with commercial science, which are particularly important in the early stages of patent development but that this gendered difference is not as pronounced among younger scientists); MILLI ET AL., *supra* note 8, at 22–23, 26 (discussing the importance of networks for women who patent and discussing the role of socialization, particularly in academia, as an important source of incentives or disincentives for women who patent based on the messages that they receive from their peers); HEWLETT ET AL., *supra* note 60, at 14–15 (arguing that women in some private companies in STEM face a lack of mentors and "sponsors" and that this resulting isolation leads women to leave STEM jobs at higher rates than men); Yu Meng, *Collaboration Patterns and Patenting: Exploring Gender Distinctions*, 45 RSCH. POL'Y 56, 64 (2016) (finding that women in academia are more likely to patent if they have ties to other academics ["collaboration ties"] and that a lack of knowledge of the patent industry and a lack of connections to patenting make women less likely to patent than men).

[75] See, for example, Hunt et al., *supra* note 52, at 834 (finding that women are more likely than men to work in fields unrelated to their STEM degrees, thereby lowering their likelihood of patenting); MILLI ET AL., *supra* note 8, at 27 (discussing some examples of women being deterred or discouraged from patenting after not being taken seriously as inventors as a result of their gender); HEWLETT ET AL., *supra* note 60, at 7–11 (describing "macho" and at-times predatory behavior in some private sector STEM workplaces); Cary Funk & Kim Parker, *Women and Men in STEM Often at Odds over Workplace Equity*, PEW RSCH. CTR. (Jan. 9, 2018), www.pewsocialtrends.org/2018/01/09/women-and-men-in-stem-often-at-odds-over-workplace-equity/ (discussing the results of a survey among men and women in STEM that found that 44 percent of women in gender-balanced STEM workplaces had experienced gender discrimination and 78 percent of women in majority-men private sector STEM workplaces had experienced gender discrimination).

[76] Corinne A. Moss-Racusin, John F. Dovidio, Victoria L. Brescoll, Mark J. Graham & Jo Handelsman, *Science Faculty's Subtle Gender Biases Favor Male Students*, 109 PROCS. NAT'L. ACAD. SCI. U.S. 16474, 16475–76 (2012) (finding that all else being equal, STEM faculty members have an implicit or explicit bias in favor of students who are men).

[77] Jensen et al., *supra* note 45, at 309 (suggesting that patent applications submitted by women with names commonly associated with women are rejected at higher rates than women with uncommon names due to patent examiner gender bias); *see also* Dan L. Burk, *Do Patents Have*

6.2.2 *The Trademark Gender Gap*

Unlike patents, there has been relatively little research done on women's trademark ownership. Still, available data suggest a similar gap exists between the number of men and women who own trademarks, although there are signs of greater equality over time. In 1980, women received 16.7 percent of trademarks granted, and by 2010 they still received only 33.31 percent.[78] Unlike patents, no set of educational indicators is associated with people who will apply for a trademark. Trademarks have occasionally been connected to entrepreneurial activity, but a 2015 survey conducted by the U.S. Census Bureau found only a marginal difference in the share of women-owned businesses with a trademark compared with men-owned businesses.[79] That being said, women as a whole are less likely to become entrepreneurs, and in that study, only 20.8 percent of the surveyed businesses were women-owned.[80]

Like copyright and patent rates, women appear to specialize in different areas than men. In 2010, women were granted the most trademarks in the following classes: advertising and business, clothing, education and entertainment, and paper goods and printed matter.[81] While these categories were among the most frequently used trademark classes between 2004 and 2013, notably missing are the electrical and scientific apparatus and computer and scientific classes, the first and fourth most-used classes in that period.[82]

Gender?, 19 Am. U. J. Gender Soc. Pol'y & L. 881, 886 (2011) (discussing how gender-based effects and differences can make the patent system "gendered" despite the system lacking intentional and explicit gender preferences).

78 This figure represents the share of trademarks granted to women as individuals. Trademarks granted to businesses were excluded from the data set, but in 2010, only an estimated 4.8 percent of granted trademarks were awarded to businesses. Delixus & Nat'l Women's Bus. Council, *supra* note 10, at 83 tbl.A.5, 84 tbl.A.6, 93 tbl.A.16 (containing data for the number of trademark applications submitted by men and women and the percentage of applications that were approved for both genders).

79 *See* U.S. Census Bureau, Annual Survey of Entrepreneurs, www.census.gov/data/developers/data-sets/ase.html?# (last visited May 20, 2020) (containing surveys for the years 2014–16, and showing that in 2015, 6.1 percent of women-owned businesses had at least one trademark compared with 7.0 percent of men-owned businesses); Williams-Baron et al., *supra* note 57, at 12 (summarizing and providing a visual representation of the results of the 2015 Annual Survey of Entrepreneurs).

80 *See* Williams-Baron et al., *supra* note 57, at 3 (containing data reflecting the number of women-owned, men-owned, and equally owned firms between 1997 and 2015); *see also* Candida G. Brush, Patricia G. Greene, Lakshmi Balachandra & Amy E. Davis, Diana Project, Women Entrepreneurs 2014: Bridging the Gender Gap in Venture Capital 5–6 (2014) (linking the lower number of women-owned and operated businesses to lower amounts of venture capital available to women).

81 Delixus & Nat'l Women's Bus. Council, *supra* note 10, at 45 (containing data on the most frequently used trademark classes for trademark applications submitted by women).

82 Econ. & Stat. Admin. & U.S. Pat. & Trademark Off., *supra* note 13, at 59 tbl.A-8 (containing information about the most frequently used trademark classes in the United States).

Interestingly, women's trademark applications were accepted more frequently than applications by men between 1988 and 2000. However, the ratio of successful trademark applications made by women and men has been nearly equal since 2000.[83] Therefore, women are likely underrepresented as trademark owners due to a lack of applications compared with men. There has not been much research done on why women file fewer applications than men. But one study has suggested that women may be hesitant to apply for trademarks due to a lack of knowledge about how they work and uncertainty about the financial value of obtaining a trademark.[84]

6.3 GENDER TRENDS ACROSS PROPERTY OWNERSHIP

While some factors and explanations are specific to intellectual property rights ownership, the disparity between men and women in the intellectual property rights context is consistent with more general inequities in other forms of property ownership and corporate power. Therefore, to fully understand lower rates of intellectual property rights ownership by women, it is necessary to contextualize our findings within the broader scheme of property ownership and wealth accumulation. In their lifetimes, women are more likely to experience poverty,[85] receive social welfare benefits,[86] and retire with few if any retirement savings compared with men.[87] Women on average make less than men for the same job, even in industries where women predominate, perpetuating both a wage and a wealth gap between men and women.[88] Despite making up half of the U.S. labor force, women

83 While the ratio of acceptance rates for men and women has remained roughly equal, the overall acceptance rate for trademark applications filed by women has decreased over time from 88.28 percent in 1985 to 49.6 percent in 2010. DELIXUS & NAT'L WOMEN'S BUS. COUNCIL, *supra* note 10, at 40–41 (containing data reflecting the ratio of successful trademark applications made by men and women over time).

84 *Id.* at 14–15 (summarizing the findings of a series of interviews with women entrepreneurs who were asked why they did not apply for trademarks or patents).

85 *See* JESSICA SEMEGA, MELISSA KOLLAR, JOHN CREAMER & ABINASH MOHANTY, U.S. CENSUS BUREAU, INCOME AND POVERTY IN THE UNITED STATES: 2018, at 15 (2019) (reporting that women have a higher likelihood of experiencing poverty in their lifetime than men – 12.9 percent compared with 10.6 percent).

86 *See* SHELLEY K. IRVING & TRACY A. LOVELESS, U.S. CENSUS BUREAU, DYNAMICS OF ECONOMIC WELL-BEING PARTICIPATION IN GOVERNMENT PROGRAMS, 2009–2012: WHO GETS ASSISTANCE? 16 tbl.1 (2015) (discussing the demographics of individuals who receive government program assistance).

87 *See* CATHERINE COLLINSON, TRANSAMERICA CTR. FOR RETIREMENT STUD., HERE AND NOW: HOW WOMEN CAN TAKE CONTROL OF THEIR RETIREMENT 9–10 (2018), www.transamericacenter.org/docs/default-source/women-and-retirement/tcrs2018_sr_women_take_control_of_retirement.pdf (explaining that women are much more likely than men to have low, if any, retirement savings).

88 *See* INST. FOR WOMEN'S POL'Y RSCH., THE GENDER WAGE GAP BY OCCUPATION AND BY RACE AND ETHNICITY 3 tbl.1, 4 tbl.2 (2019), https://iwpr.org/publications/the-gender-wage-gap-by-occupation-2019/ (containing data for the average wages for men and women in the most common occupations for men and women, respectively).

represent only 5.8 percent of its CEOs.[89] A thorough exploration of gender inequality is beyond the scope of this chapter, but understanding some of the forms of inequality that affect property ownership and wealth accumulation will allow us to contextualize and explain some of the gender differences in the copyright registration data.

6.3.1 *Gender Disparity in Property Ownership and Wealth Accumulation*

6.3.1.1 Wage Gap and Wealth Gap

Women across the country are compensated less than men for their labor, and this disparity ultimately contributes to a lifetime wealth gap. In 2019, women on average earned 81.5 cents for every dollar earned by a man with the same job.[90] This gap has been more pronounced in occupations commonly held by men. For example, several professions with men in the majority have paid women only 70–75 percent of what they pay men for the same job.[91] In addition to varying across professions, the wage gap has also varied by geography, with women in 2013 earning between 67.3 percent and 87.6 percent of what men made based on their state.[92] One estimate suggests that the gender wage gap will not be closed in some states until after 2100.[93]

The perpetuation of this wage gap contributes to women experiencing higher levels of poverty than men and is one large contributor to the wealth gap between men and women. In addition to base wage differences, women are twice as likely to be part-time workers, constitute the majority of minimum-wage and low-wage workers, and typically have more caregiving responsibilities than men, all of which can limit their ability to save for the future and accumulate wealth at the same rate as men.[94] Some studies have also found that women are more risk-averse in terms of

[89] *List: Women CEOs of the S&P 500*, CATALYST (May 1, 2020), www.catalyst.org/research/women-ceos-of-the-sp-500/ (containing a list of women CEOs of S&P 500 companies as of May 1, 2020).

[90] *See* INST. FOR WOMEN'S POL'Y RSCH., *supra* note 88, at 3 tbl.1 (containing information about the overall wage gap between men and women); CYNTHIA HESS, JESSICA MILLI, JEFF HAYES & ARIANE HEGEWISCH, INST. FOR WOMEN'S POL'Y RSCH., THE STATUS OF WOMEN IN THE STATES: 2015, at 48 tbl.2.2 (2015) (finding that women earn less than men within racial groups as well, but when compared with white men, women in some racial/ethnic groups earn only a little more than 50 percent of what white men are paid for the same job).

[91] *See* INST. FOR WOMEN'S POL'Y RSCH., *supra* note 88, at 4 tbl.2 (containing average wage information for the twenty most common occupations for men in 2019).

[92] *See* HESS ET AL., *supra* note 90, at 39 tbl.2.1 (containing data for the ratio of men to women's salaries by state).

[93] *See id.* at 45 tbl.2 (containing estimates of the year every state will close the gender wage gap if wage disparity continues to decrease at the same rate).

[94] *See* HEATHER MCCULLOCH, CLOSING THE WOMEN'S WEALTH GAP, CLOSING THE WOMEN'S WEALTH GAP WHAT IT IS, WHY IT MATTERS, AND WHAT CAN BE DONE ABOUT IT 7 (2017), https://womenswealthgap.org/report/ (suggesting that women often have more caregiving

taking financial risks, which may contribute to lower rates of wealth accumulation.[95] As a result of all of these factors, women are disproportionately unprepared for retirement compared with men.[96]

6.3.1.2 Welfare Benefits

Correlated with the wage and wealth gap, women are more likely to receive welfare benefits than men. In 2018, women were more likely to experience poverty than men in every age category after turning eighteen.[97] In 2012, 23.3 percent of women in the United States received some form of welfare benefits compared with 19.3 percent of men. The statistics were starker for single mothers. In 2012, 58 percent of "female-householder families" received welfare benefits compared with 37.2 percent of "male-householder families" and 19.9 percent of married couples.[98] These statistics have varied by education level and geography, but women in the South and parts of the Western United States with less than a college-level education as a whole have had a high likelihood of experiencing poverty.[99] A variety of factors contribute to these bleak statistics the wage gap, and increased likelihood for women to be in low-paying or part-time jobs compared with men are among the most prominent.[100]

6.3.1.3 Home Ownership

Home equity is the largest source of wealth for U.S. households, followed by business ownership, and this is one of the few areas in which women outperform men by some measures.[101] Since the 1990s, single women have owned more homes than single men.[102] In 2017, single women owned 22 percent of available homes in the United States, while single men owned only 13 percent.[103] However, most

burdens than men, are more often part-time or lower-wage workers, and are more financially risk averse than men, all of which may add to the wealth gap).

95 *Id.* at 8.

96 *See* Collinson, *supra* note 87, at 9–10 (reporting differences in retirement savings between men and women).

97 Semega et al., *supra* note 85, at 15 (containing data about poverty rates among men and women by age).

98 A "female-householder family" ("male-householder family") is a family that is led by a woman (man) with no spouse reported. Irving & Loveless, *supra* note 86, at 10 (discussing the demographics of individuals who receive government program assistance).

99 *Id.* at 13 (containing data about poverty rates by gender and educational attainment); Hess et al., *supra* note 90, at 125 tbl.4.1 (containing data about poverty rates among women by state).

100 *See* Hess et al., *supra* note 90, at 137, 143 (suggesting that if the wage gap were eliminated, the poverty rate for working women would be half of what it currently is).

101 *See* McCulloch, *supra* note 94, at 9 (discussing the role of home ownership among women as a tool for wealth-building).

102 *Id.*

103 Tendayi Kapfidze, LendingTree a Different Kind of Gender Gap: Homeownership Is More Common among Single Women than Single Men (2019), www.lendingtree.com/

homes are still owned by married couples, and as soon as additional family members are added to the household, home-ownership rates by single women rapidly decrease compared with men.[104] Furthermore, despite owning more homes as a group, a recent study has suggested that women can still end up worse off than men because, on average, they buy their home for 2 percent more and sell it for 2 percent less than similarly positioned men.[105] As the dominant form of savings for many households, the disparity in purchasing and selling prices over time likely contributes to the wealth gap between men and women.[106]

6.3.2 *Entrepreneurial Success and Corporate Power*

6.3.2.1 Women's Entrepreneurship

Entrepreneurial activity among women and various forms of corporate ownership are related, contributing factors to property ownership and wealth accumulation. In 2012, women-owned businesses accounted for only 36 percent of U.S. businesses and earned, on average, only 22.5 percent of what men-owned businesses made.[107] Revenue differences varied widely by sector. In some industries such as arts/entertainment and scientific services, women-owned businesses made under 40 percent of the revenue of men-owned businesses. Notably, 93.7 percent of women-owned businesses were in either a service or retail industry. But the combined revenue of women-owned businesses in retail made only 13.5 percent of the revenue earned by men-owned retail businesses.[108]

Part of the financial disparity between entrepreneurship by men and women is tied to a lack of funding for women-owned businesses. Men are much more likely to

home/mortgage/homeownership-gender-gap-study/ (containing rates of home ownership for single men and women around the United States).

[104] Woman-headed household (no spouse of live-in partner reported) with two or more people living in the house have lower rates of home ownership than male-headed households of two or more people. *Id.*; U.S. Census Bureau, Household Estimates for the United States, by Age of Householder, by Family Status: 2000 to Present (2019), www.census.gov/housing/hvs/data/histtabs.html.

[105] *See* Paul Goldsmith-Pinkham & Kelly Shue, *The Gender Gap in Housing Returns* 16–18 (Nat'l Bureau of Econ. Rsch., Working Paper No. 26914, 2020) (discussing the results of a study that looked at returns on real estate investments by gender).

[106] *Id.* at 24–25 (suggesting that this gap in housing returns could explain 30 percent of the gender gap in wealth accumulation by the time women reach retirement).

[107] In 2012, women-owned businesses, on average, made US$144,000, compared with US$638,000 for businesses owned by men. Inst. for Women's Pol'y Rsch., Women-Owned Businesses Have Increased in Number, but Still Face Obstacles to Growth 4 (2020), https://iwpr.org/wp-content/uploads/2020/02/Kauffman-Fact-Sheet-for-layout-2-7-2020-1.pdf (containing data about the proportion of businesses in the United States owned by men and women and average profits of both).

[108] *Id.* at 5 (containing data about the revenue ratio between men- and women-owned businesses and the share of women-owned businesses in the service and retail industries).

receive venture capital than women, and even when women receive venture capital, they receive smaller investments than men.[109] Some studies have found that this may be caused at least in part by investors evaluating women-proposed projects differently than projects proposed by men. In a study of a top venture capital pitching competition, researchers found that women were more likely to be asked how they would avoid business failure while men were more likely to be asked how they expected to maximize profits.[110] While this may seem just a difference in semantics, this type of failure-avoidance questioning was associated with projects receiving less or no funding compared with comparably positioned companies that were asked about profit maximization.[111] Another part of the funding problem is a lack of women in top venture capital firms, as only 8 percent of global venture capital partners are women. Venture capital firms with women partners have been shown to be more likely to invest in women-owned companies than firms without women partners.[112] Still, to a lesser extent, the gap in venture capital funding may also be connected to women being less likely to own intellectual property rights than men, as some studies have found that new companies with a patent receive venture capital much more quickly than others.[113]

Women, however, may be less inclined than men to start their own businesses. One study found that in 2013, 11 percent of working women were running or starting their own business compared with 16 percent of men, but it is difficult to say whether this is indicative of a preference among women or a consequence of other barriers to women's entrepreneurship.[114] For example, in a survey of successful men and women entrepreneurs, women were much more likely to believe that having a robust professional network and prior experience as an entrepreneur is crucial for entrepreneurial success and securing outside funding.[115]

[109] See, for example, U.S. Senate Comm. on Small Bus. & Entrepreneurship, Tackling the Gender Gap What Women Entrepreneurs Need to Thrive 31 (2017), www.sbc.senate.gov/public/_cache/files/2/5/25bd7ee9-a37b-4d2b-a91a-8b1ad6f5bd58/536DC6E705BBAD3B555BFA4B60DEA025.sbc-tackling-the-gender-gap.december-2017-final.pdf (reporting that in 2016, women received only around 2 percent of venture capital funding; women as a whole apply for loans at lower rates and for less funding than men).

[110] *See* Dana Kanza, Laura Huang, Mark A. Conley & E. Tory Higgins, *We Ask Men to Win and Women Not to Lose: Closing the Gender Gap in Start-Up Funding*, 61 Acad. Mgmt. J. 586, 603–04 (2018) (reporting the results of a study on the success and patterns of men and women in a venture capital pitch competition).

[111] *Id.* at 601–02.

[112] *See* U.S. Senate Comm. on Small Bus. & Entrepreneurship, *supra* note 109, at 32–33 (linking the gender composition of venture capital firms to their support of women-owned businesses).

[113] *See* Milli et al., *supra* note 8, at 15–16 (suggesting that patents are useful for securing venture capital as well as other sources of funding such as commercial banks and investment banks).

[114] Brush et al., *supra* note 80, at 5 (containing data for the percentage of women compared with men starting their own businesses).

[115] *See* J. McGrath Cohoon, Vivek Wadhwa & Lesla Mitchell, Kauffman, Are Successful Women Entrepreneurs Different from Men? 5–6 (2010), www.kauffman

6.3.2.2 Corporate Ownership and Positions of Power

In December 2019, out of the S&P 500 companies, only twenty-nine (5.8 percent) company CEOs were women.[116] In a study of equity ownership in companies and C-suite executives, women on average owned forty-nine cents in equity for every dollar owned by a man.[117] While these dynamics are often reflective of individuals at the very top percentiles of income and success, they reinforce the conclusion that gendered wealth disparity permeates every income bracket. At a high level, of the companies surveyed, women represented 34 percent of the employees but held only 20 percent of the companies' combined equity value. Part of the problem is that there are not as many women involved in the early stages of start-ups when it is more likely for the company to grow immensely and for early employees to be awarded considerable equity.[118]

Another problem is the lack of women in C-suite positions. As people are promoted, firms that start with relatively equal numbers of men and women shift to become majority men. By the time people are promoted to a C-suite position, men predominate.[119] These dynamics are also reflected in company board demographics. Among Fortune 500 companies, only 22.5 percent of board positions were filled by women in 2018,[120] representing an improvement from 2004 when it was only 15.7 percent.[121]

6.4 GENDER DISPARITY IN CREATIVE PROFESSIONS

While professional participation in a creative industry is not a prerequisite for creating or registering copyrightable material, gender-based inequities and discrimination within creative industries may contribute to lower rates of creation and registration of works by women. As a general rule, creating a copyrighted work of

.org/wp-content/uploads/2009/07/successful_women_entrepreneurs_510.pdf (containing findings from interviews with successful men and women entrepreneurs that found in part that women are more likely to believe that prior experience "is crucial" and that professional networks are incredibly important as well).

116 *List: Women CEOs of the S&P 500*, *supra* note 89 (containing a list of women CEOs as of May 1, 2020).

117 *See* Emily Kramer, Carta, Table Stakes Study Analyzing the Gender Equity Gap (2019), https://tablestakes.com/study/ (summarizing findings from a study of equity holdings and C-suite positions among women).

118 *Id.*

119 *Id.*

120 *See* Deloitte, Missing Pieces Report: The 2018 Board Diversity Census of Women and Minorities on Fortune 500 Boards 17 (2019), https://www2.deloitte.com/us/en/pages/center-for-board-effectiveness/articles/missing-pieces-fortune-500-board-diversity-study-2018.html (containing data for the gender and racial composition of boards and additionally finding that only 4.6 percent of board positions in surveyed companies were held by minority women).

121 *Id.* at 18.

authorship does not necessitate a formal, educational, technical, or professional skill or training at the level that creating a patented invention often does. With a lower barrier to entry than STEM fields, one may expect creative industries to be more equally representative of both men and women, and in some ways, they are. However, many creative industries still struggle with a lack of women in positions of leadership, as well as allegations of implicit gender bias or outright gender-based discrimination. If these conditions create additional professional and social barriers to entry for women, then that may explain some of the gender disparity in the rates of copyright registration.

Available studies are overly dependent on understanding gender by looking at finished work products, such as released movies, top-played songs, and plays selected for performance. Therefore, it is difficult to gauge gender disparities at levels below the tip of the success iceberg or at supporting roles – such as editors in the book publishing industry or artists who are not yet prominent enough to be featured in a museum. That being said, broadly discussing gender dynamics within creative professions provides useful perspectives for understanding why some women may be disinclined or unable to create in certain fields.

6.4.1 *Book Industry*

Women have traditionally been in the majority at every stage of book publishing.[122] In 2012, roughly 55.6 percent of self-reported writers or authors were women.[123] That same year, 52.3 percent of periodical, book, and directory publishers were women as well.[124] Nevertheless, despite authors being majority women, the majority of authors (54.17 percent) of registered textual works in 2012 were men.[125]

While women for all purposes appear to be in the majority representation-wise, there are a set of gendered patterns that may discourage women authors or otherwise act to decrease the representation of women within the industry. First, although women are overrepresented in the publishing industry, some of the largest

[122] *See* Laura M. Jimenz & Betsy Beckert, *Where Is the Diversity in Publishing? The 2019 Diversity Baseline Survey Results*, Lee & Low Books (Jan. 28, 2020), https://blog.leeandlow.com/2020/01/28/2019diversitybaselinesurvey/ (finding that the publishing industry is 75 percent female and 60 percent of book publishing executives are women).

[123] There was also a category for news analysts/reporters/correspondents, but it is unclear whether journalists or writers for a "serial" publication would label themselves as writers and authors. Bureau of Lab. Stat., Women in the Labor Force: A Databook 36 tbl.11 (2014) (containing data for the percentage of women in each field for 2012).

[124] *Id.* at 52 tbl.14.

[125] While a degree is not necessary to become an author, women have received more creative writing MFA degrees than men since the 1990s. Rosie Cina, *Bias, She Wrote: The Gender Balance of The* New York Times *Best Seller List*, Pudding (June 2017), https://pudding.cool/2017/06/best-sellers/ (containing data on gender representation by genre over time on *The New York Times* best seller list).

publishing houses do not publish books written by women at the same rate as they publish books written by men.[126] One study found that out of thirteen publishing houses, only two had more than 30 percent of their published books authored by women.[127] With over 50 percent of self-reported authors being women, it is difficult to argue that this unequal representation in publishing houses is due to women's lack of interest or ability.

Even when women's books are published, on average, they sell for less, and their publishers invest less in their promotion compared with books written by men.[128] As a result, women profit less from their textual creativity than men. Furthermore, books written by women are comparatively less likely to be reviewed in magazines.[129] Men also have historically had a greater likelihood of having their books appear on *The New York Times*' bestseller list.[130] While these statistics could be tied to lower numbers of books written by women being published in the first place, book reviewers have also predominantly been men.[131] With this background, it is perhaps unsurprising that women may not be encouraged to write and register their work as much as men.

6.4.2 *Music Industry*

The music industry has long struggled with a lack of women both as performers and in music production. In 2018, 35 percent of self-reported musicians and singers and only 12.4 percent of broadcast and sound engineers were women.[132] This represented an improvement for the industry from 2010 when only 31.9 percent of musicians and singers and 9.9 percent of broadcast and sound engineers were women.[133] However,

[126] *See* Jimenz & Beckert, *supra* note 122; Ruth Franklin, *A Literary Glass Ceiling?*, NEW REPUBLIC (Feb. 6, 2011), https://newrepublic.com/article/82930/vida-women-writers-magazines-book-reviews (containing data from the 2010 catalogs of thirteen publishing houses to determine what percentage of books published by major publishers are women).

[127] The two publishers who had better representation said 45 percent and 37 percent of their published authors were women. Franklin, *supra* note 126.

[128] *See* Dana B. Weinberg & Adam Kapelner, *Comparing Gender Discrimination and Inequality in Indie and Traditional Publishing*, 13 PLoS ONE 1, 13–15 (2018) (arguing that books written by women are sold for less in both traditional publishing and self-publishing, but that the difference between average prices for books written by men and women is lower when authors self-publish).

[129] See, for example, AMY KING, VIDA, THE 2010 VIDA COUNT (2010), www.vidaweb.org/vida-count/the-count-2010/ (reporting that in some newspapers, books written by women were only 15–25 percent of the books reviewed that year).

[130] Cina, *supra* note 125 (containing data on gender representation on *The New York Times Best Seller List*).

[131] *See* Franklin, *supra* note 126 (discussing the demographics of book reviewers and the gender composition of authors published by thirteen major book publishers).

[132] BUREAU OF LAB. STAT., *supra* note 53, at 51 tbl.11 (reporting gender composition statistics for industries in the United States in 2018).

[133] BUREAU OF LAB. STAT., WOMEN IN THE LABOR FORCE: A DATABOOK 31 tbl.11 (2011) (reporting gender composition statistics for industries in the United States in 2010).

despite these improvements, women remain underrepresented as musical artists and in music production. In a study of representation on the Billboard Hot 100 Year-End Charts between 2012 and 2019, only 21.7 percent of artists, 12.5 percent of songwriters, and 2.6 percent of producers were women.[134] This disparity varies by genre, with women in pop representing 32.6 percent of artists but only 11 percent of artists in alternative music.[135] This lack of representation is reinforced in awards show nominations. Between 2013 and 2020, 88.3 percent of Grammy Award nominees were men, though the number of women nominees has been trending upward over time.[136]

While it is unclear whether this is a cause or an effect, the music industry has been plagued by allegations of gender-based discrimination.[137] In one study that surveyed women in different parts of the music industry, 78 percent of respondents reported that they had been treated differently due to their gender.[138] In another study, women reported that their colleagues did not take them seriously and that their contributions both as producers and performers were not seen by their colleagues as important or valuable.[139] While these barriers would not necessarily prevent a self-recording artist from creating and registering new work, they may be part of why men authored 75.98 percent of copyright registrations in the music category.[140]

[134] *See* Stacy L. Smith, Katherine Pieper, Marc Choueiti, Karla Hernandez & Kevin Yao, USC Annenberg Inclusion Initiative, Inclusion in the Recording Studio? Gender and Race/Ethnicity of Artists, Songwriters & Producers across 800 Popular Songs from 2012–2019, at 2 (2020) (containing data on the race and gender composition of the songwriters, producers, and artists of the Billboard Top 100 songs for the year between 2012 and 2019).

[135] *Id.* at 11.

[136] *Id.* at 3.

[137] In recent years, the #MeToo movement has highlighted some examples of gender-based violence and harassment in the music industry. See, for example, Hanif Abdurraqib, *Year in Music: The Slow Road to Music's #MeToo Moment*, Billboard (Dec. 13, 2018), www.billboard.com/articles/events/year-in-music-2018/8489958/metoo-movement-music-industry-year-in-music-2018 (discussing some of the early moments in the #MeToo movement in the music industry); Shanon Lee, *When Will the Music Industry Have Its #MeToo Moment?*, Forbes (Jan. 22, 2020), www.forbes.com/sites/shanonlee/2020/01/22/when-will-the-music-industry-have-its-metoo-moment/#748ee6107803 (discussing recent allegations of sexual harassment and assault within the music industry and arguing that the music industry should receive more attention for these allegations); Associated Press, *When Music Producers Are Accused of Being Predators* (Mar. 1, 2019), www.billboard.com/articles/news/8500693/music-producers-accused-predators (discussing some of the #MeToo allegations against pop music producers and describes how pervasive similar behavior has been in the music industry).

[138] *See* Prior et al., *supra* note 12, at 16 (containing data from a survey among women in the music industry about whether they have experienced gender bias and organizes the results by age, employment type, and specific occupation).

[139] These observations and others like them have suggested the music industry has particularly high barriers to women in the form of gender stereotypes and biases. *Id.* at 16–17.

[140] This statistic includes music copyright registrations between 1978 and 2012. *See* Brauneis & Oliar, *supra* note 4, at 76.

6.4.3 *Film Industry*

Men hold the vast majority of roles in the film industry. In 2010, women represented only 7 percent of directors, 2 percent of cinematographers, and 15 percent of executive producers for the top 250 grossing films of the year.[141] By 2019, these numbers have improved, though there is still a way to go. Of the top 250 grossing films of 2019, women represented 13 percent of directors, 5 percent of cinematographers, and 23 percent of executive producers.[142] This inequality is mirrored among film actors and actresses as well. In 2010, only 30 of the top 100 movies for the year featured a woman as a lead or colead. By 2019, this had increased to 43 out of the top 100 movies.[143] However, for actresses, this inequality does not appear to be tied to a lack of interest. One of the most popular college majors for professional actors and actresses is visual and performing arts, and in 2017, women received 60.1 percent of visual and performing arts bachelor's degrees.[144] The lack of gender representation goes all the way up to the top of movie studio leadership, with one study finding that 82 percent of chief executives for some of the country's largest movie studios are men.[145]

While it is unclear whether some women choose to steer clear of the film industry or whether the industry as a whole creates additional barriers to entry for women, the film industry has faced allegations of gender-based discrimination for years.[146]

[141] *See* Martha M. Lauzen, The Celluloid Ceiling: Behind-the-Scenes Employment of Women on the Top 250 Films of 2010, at 1–2 (2011), https://womenintvfilm.sdsu.edu/files/2010_Celluloid_Ceiling.pdf (containing data on the percentage of women in behind-the-scenes roles in the top 250 films of 2010).

[142] *See* Martha M. Lauzen, The Celluloid Ceiling: Behind-the-Scenes Employment of Women on the Top 250 Films of 2019, at 3 (2020), https://womenintvfilm.sdsu.edu/wp-content/uploads/2020/01/2019_Celluloid_Ceiling_Report.pdf (containing data on the percentage of women in behind-the-scenes roles in the top 250 films of 2010).

[143] *See* Stacy L. Smith, Annenberg Inclusion Initiative, Inequality across 1,300 Popular Films: Examining Gender and Race/Ethnicity of Leads/Co Leads from 2007 to 2019, at 1 (2020), http://assets.uscannenberg.org/docs/aii-inequality-leads-co-leads-20200103.pdf (containing data on the percentage of women in behind-the-scenes roles in top movies in 2019).

[144] Data USA: Actors, https://datausa.io/profile/soc/actors#education (last visited June 28, 2020) (containing data on the diversity, average salary, and popular majors among actors in the United States); Data USA: Visual & Performing Arts, https://datausa.io/profile/cip/50#demographics (last visited June 28, 2020) (detailing the gender composition among visual and performing arts majors).

[145] *See* Elizabeth A. Harris, *How #MeToo Is Smashing the Casting Couch*, N.Y. Times (Jan. 30, 2020), www.nytimes.com/2020/01/30/arts/metoo-hollywood.html (discussing changes that have occurred in the film industry connected with the #MeToo movement as well as modern gender dynamics).

[146] See, for example, *id.*; Tom Teodorczuk, *How the #MeToo Movement Is Changing Hollywood*, MarketWatch (June 28, 2018), www.marketwatch.com/story/how-the-metoo-movement-economically-and-culturally-transformed-hollywood-2018-06-27 (discussing the ways in which the #MeToo movement has shed a light on gender dynamics within the film industry); Derek Thompson, *The Brutal Math of Gender Inequality in Hollywood*, Atlantic (Jan. 11, 2018), www.theatlantic.com/business/archive/2018/01/the-brutal-math-of-gender-inequality-in-hollywood/

Actresses have often been paid less for their creative labor than their costars, underscoring the finding that in a list of the top ten highest-paid actors and actresses for 2019, only two out of the top ten were women.[147] In addition, stories about men refusing to work with women directors and women's contributions behind the scenes being challenged by their coworkers suggest that there may be social barriers that could discourage women from entering or remaining in the film industry.[148]

6.4.4 *Theatre Industry*

Like the film industry, men predominate in almost every role, both on stage and behind the scenes for theatrical works. In a study of theatrical productions on Broadway between 2018 and 2019, 13 percent of directors, 24 percent of choreographers, 13 percent of writers, and 32 percent of named characters were women.[149] However, women are in the majority or close to the majority as costume designers (52 percent), stage managers (47 percent), and company managers (57 percent).[150] These trends have been mirrored in Off-Broadway productions as well. In 2010, 25 percent of directors and 31 percent of playwrights were women.[151] Notably, some theaters have had years where they did not feature a single play written by a woman, and in the 2013–14 season, women wrote only 29 percent of the plays produced in Off-Broadway theaters.[152]

5 (commenting on the results of the Celluloid Ceiling report and highlighting the need for greater representation of women in the industry).

147 *See* Farah Andrews, *Forbes Reveals the World's Highest Paid Actors and Actresses*, NATIONAL (Feb. 13, 2020), www.thenational.ae/arts-culture/film/forbes-reveals-the-world-s-highest-paid-actors-and-actresses-1.978476 (commenting on the list of the highest paid actors and actresses in 2019 and pointing out that women in film are paid much less than men); *see also* Madeline Berg, *Everything You Need to Know about the Hollywood Pay Gap*, FORBES (Nov. 12, 2015), www.forbes.com/sites/maddieberg/2015/11/12/everything-you-need-to-know-about-the-hollywood-pay-gap/#3e4b02dc5cf1 (discussing the various facets of pay inequality in the film industry, including some actors receiving back-end pay while actresses do not, and some actresses receiving as little as 10 percent of what their costars are paid if their costars are men).

148 See, for example, Elizabeth Day, Liz Hoggard & Kathryn Bromwich, *99% of Women Working in the Film and TV Industries Have Experienced Sexism*, GUARDIAN (Sept. 27, 2015), www.theguardian.com/film/2015/sep/27/sexism-film-industry-stories (reporting results from interviews with women in the film industry with some women reporting experiences where men refused to work with them and did not take their feedback seriously, among other expressions of biases).

149 *See* BROADWAY BY THE NUMBERS 2019, https://production.pro/broadway-by-the-numbers (last visited June 29, 2020) (containing data about the gender composition of Broadway plays by role type).

150 *Id.*

151 *See* MARTHA WADE STEKETEE, LEAGUE OF PRO. THEATRE WOMEN, WOMEN COUNT: WOMEN HIRED OFF-BROADWAY 2010–2017, at 5 tbl.3 (2018), http://theatrewomen.org/women-count/ (containing data about the gender composition of directors and playwrights of Off-Broadway plays).

152 *Id.* at 6 tbl.4.

Women playwrights may be particularly discouraged from writing because their lack of exposure and access to theaters is a nationwide problem.[153] Between 2011 and 2014, a study of 153 theaters across the United States found that women wrote only 22 percent of the plays produced despite making up around two-thirds of theater audiences.[154] While some of this disparity may be tied to theaters relying on a certain number of revived productions year to year, men also hold an estimated 80 percent of artistic director positions in regional theater companies, and these individuals often have the greatest influence on the plays that are selected.[155] The data may however suggest a relative female inclination toward originality: While men wrote 84 percent of the revivals produced in 2016–17, women wrote 35 percent of the "new" plays produced that year.[156]

6.4.5 *Other Copyright-Related Industries: Art, Dance, and Architecture*

Despite making up roughly 46 percent of artists in the United States between 2012 and 2016, women in the arts are not given the same opportunities as men and are compensated less for their work.[157] While this statistic suggests that men and women have a roughly equal interest in the arts, works produced by men constituted 87 percent of U.S. museum collections in 2018.[158] While 51 percent of visual artists in recent years have been women, women have received only 27 percent of solo exhibitions between 2013 and 2020.[159] This lack of exposure in museums is effected partly by women being underrepresented in art markets and fairs around the world, as well as by potential bias within museum leadership.[160]

[153] *See* JULIA JORDAN, DRAMATISTS GUILD, THE COUNT 2.0 WHO'S GETTING PRODUCED IN THE US? 8–9 (2017), www.dramatistsguild.com/advocacy/the-count (containing data about the percentage of women playwrights produced in 153 theaters around the country).

[154] *See* Karen McConarty & Heidi Rose, *Beyond the 22%: Gender Inequity in Regional Theatres' Show Selections*, 40 WOMEN'S STUD. COMMC'N 212, 212 (2017) (proposing some explanations for why women playwrights are underrepresented in regional theaters including the need to appeal to audiences and an unwillingness to take risks on new playwrights).

[155] *Id.* at 215.

[156] *See* JORDAN, *supra* note 153, at 6 (containing data about the percentage of new plays and revivals selected by regional theaters that were written by women).

[157] *See* NAT'L ENDOWMENT FOR THE ARTS, ARTISTS AND OTHER CULTURAL WORKERS: A STATISTICAL PORTRAIT 8 (2018), www.arts.gov/publications/artists-and-other-cultural-workers-statistical-portrait (discussing in part the demographics of artists).

[158] Rebecca Wilson, *How the $760 Billion Art Industry Could Change If Women Were Given Equal Exposure*, OBSERVER (Feb. 10, 2020), https://observer.com/2020/02/women-artists-market-art-industry-worth/ (containing data about the representation of women in the arts in galleries and arguing that this exclusion results in lost economic value in the international art market).

[159] *Id.*

[160] *See* Julia Halperin & Charlotte Burns, *Female Artists Represent Just 2 Percent of the Market. Here's Why – and How That Can Change*, ARTNET (Sept. 19, 2019), https://news.artnet.com/womens-place-in-the-art-world/female-artists-represent-just-2-percent-market-heres-can-change-1654954 (containing data about the percentage of women featured in international art galleries

Part of the earnings gap may be tied to differences in occupation selection. For example, between 2012 and 2016, women represented 81.4 percent of dancers and choreographers but only 25 percent of architects.[161] While architects in this period made, on average, US$76,680 per year, dancers and choreographers made only US$31,150.[162] Even within the same field, women are still paid less than men. One study found that women across art professions make around US$20,000 less per year than men in the same field.[163] In addition to their undercompensated labor, women's art is not valued as highly as art produced by men. In the fine art industry, one study found that, on average, women's artwork sells at auction for 47.6 percent less than artwork created by men.[164] To put this into perspective, between 2008 and the first half of 2019, US$196.6 billion was spent at international art auctions, and only 2 percent of this figure, US$4 billion, was spent on works created by women.[165] Works by just five women accounted for US$1.6 billion of the total US$4 billion spent on women artists.[166] Part of the problem with women's art valuation is that rather than comparing works by women with art produced by both men and women, it may be common in the industry to compare art prices only to works created by other women artists, which may lead to lower price growth and valuation over time.[167]

6.5 TAKING STOCK

Gender inequality is pervasive across different sectors and industries, but while some explanations for inequality are fact-, sector-, or industry-specific, there are several takeaways from inequality in intellectual property, property, and creative professions that may inform our understanding of why more men than women register copyrights. These explanations, in turn, can form the basis for a broader examination of

and auctions and arguing that the lack of representation may be tied in part to lower valuation of their work, as well as to prejudice among men and women in the industry).

161 NAT'L ENDOWMENT FOR THE ARTS, *supra* note 157, at 11 tbl.2b (containing data about the gender composition and average salary for various art professions between 2012 and 2016).

162 *Id.* at 25 tbl.4a.

163 Isaac Kaplan, *Nearly $20,000 Wage Gap between Men and Women Working in the Arts, Study Finds*, ARTSY (Nov. 21, 2016), www.artsy.net/article/artsy-editorial-new-study-finds-women-in-arts-make-almost-20-000-less-than-men (reporting on the results of a study looking at average wages for artists by gender).

164 *See* Anny Shaw, *Female Artists Really Do Earn Less than Men, Survey Finds*, ART NEWSPAPER (Dec. 14, 2017), www.theartnewspaper.com/news/female-artists-really-do-earn-less-than-men-survey-finds (reporting the difference in auction prices for men and women artists and reports that men buyers may find artwork created by women inferior compared with artwork created by men).

165 Halperin & Burns, *supra* note 160 (containing data for the amount spent at international art auctions for women-created artwork).

166 *Id.*

167 *Id.* (containing data for the amount spent at international art auctions for women-created artwork and proposing possible explanations for the disparity).

the U.S. copyright system and ultimately support a conclusion that the copyright system and related industries might be associated with a discriminatory effect on women.

As a wealth of intellectual property scholarship demonstrates, women are underrepresented across patent, trademark, and copyright ownership. This disparity may be due partly to a lack of institutional support, and higher barriers to entry for women.[168] While trademark ownership remains under-researched, researchers have found that the concentration of women in STEM fields is correlated in part with the number of patents granted to women inventors.[169] This suggests that a lack of women in a given field impacts the percentage of intellectual property rights awarded to women. Furthermore, while patentable material may sometimes necessitate larger team sizes than copyrightable material, research has suggested that women are much more likely to work with coinventors than men and often work with one to four coinventors.[170] Finally, some studies have indicated that patent examiners may be biased against women applicants if the applicant has a name that is socially construed as a woman's name.[171]

On a broader level, women are less likely than men to engage in entrepreneurial activity, which may affect the likelihood of women investing the time and resources necessary to secure intellectual property rights.[172] This trend is partly driven by women generally having less access than men to venture capital funding.[173] It may also be partially explained by either risk aversion among women or higher perceived barriers to entry, such as lacking prior experience or robust professional networks.[174]

[168] See, for example, Moss-Racusin et al., *supra* note 76 (finding that all else being equal, STEM faculty members have an implicit or explicit bias in favor of students who are men); Jensen et al., *supra* note 45, at 309 (arguing in part that women are more likely to have their patent applications denied due to bias from patent examiners).

[169] *See* Hunt et al., *supra* note 52, at 834 (arguing in part that the gap in STEM representation between men and women accounts for part of the gap in patenting rates between men and women).

[170] *See* Progress and Potential, *supra* note 11, at 11 (containing data on average numbers of coinventors for women and for both men and women to find, in part, that women are more likely to work with coinventors than are men).

[171] *See* Jensen et al., *supra* note 45, at 309 (reporting that all-women inventor teams are less likely to have their patent applications approved in part due to bias from patent examiners).

[172] *See* Inst. for Women's Pol'y Rsch., *supra* note 107, at 4 (containing data about the gender composition of entrepreneurs in the United States).

[173] *See* U.S. Senate Comm. on Small Bus. & Entrepreneurship, *supra* note 109, at 32–33 (reporting that in 2016, women received only around 2 percent of venture capital funding).

[174] *See* McGrath Cohoon et al., *supra* note 115, at 5–6 (reporting findings from interviews with successful men and women entrepreneurs that found, in part, that women are more likely to believe that prior experience "is crucial" and that professional networks are incredibly important as well before undertaking an entrepreneurial venture); McCulloch, *supra* note 94, at 8 (suggesting that women often have more caregiving burdens than men, are more often part-time or lower-wage workers, and are more financially risk-averse than men).

In addition, with women on average experiencing higher poverty rates than men[175] and earning less for their labor, women are likely rewarded less for their creative labor than men if they are working as full-time artists or creatives.[176] Furthermore, as studies on the gender makeup of venture capital firms have indicated, when there are women in leadership positions, firms are more likely to support women-owned start-ups.[177] This may indicate that a lack of women in positions of power in creative industries could, in some cases, lead to fewer opportunities for women within those industries.

Finally, our exploration of gender dynamics within several creative industries revealed widespread inequality between men and women as well as potential gender-based discrimination. While copyright registrants may not all work professionally in a creative field, the extent to which their creativity is encouraged by the larger industry may affect how much a registrant can expect to profit from their work and whether they continue to create new works.

6.5.1 *Inequality or Discrimination?*

Given the undeniable disparity between authorship rates among men and women, the question remains whether this difference is tied to existing forms of inequality between men and women or whether women register works at lower rates than men due to gender-based discrimination.

6.5.1.1 Inequality

As suggested in the preceding sections, gender inequality is pervasive and touches almost every component of participation in creative industries. With a wealth gap between men and women and higher poverty rates among women, the gap in women's ownership of copyright registrations is consistent with more general social patterns of inequality in property ownership by women. While registering a copyright is not as large of a financial burden as applying for a patent, some women may lack networks that promote knowledge or encourage or promote the value of obtaining copyrights, which studies have found to be important for trademarks and patents as well.[178] Part of the gap in registration rates is also likely a reflection of existing inequality within creative professions, which would be consistent with

[175] *See* SEMEGA ET AL., *supra* note 85, at 15 (containing data about the demographic information of individuals receiving federal program assistance).

[176] *See* INST. FOR WOMEN'S POL'Y RSCH., *supra* note 88, at 3 tbl.1 (reporting salary differences between men and women by state).

[177] *See* U.S. SENATE COMM. ON SMALL BUS. & ENTREPRENEURSHIP, *supra* note 109, at 32–33 (reporting the gender composition of leadership of top venture capital firms and arguing that firms with women in positions of leadership are more likely to support women entrepreneurs).

[178] DELIXUS & NAT'L WOMEN'S BUS. COUNCIL, *supra* note 10, at 14 (reporting the results of interviews with women entrepreneurs who did not pursue trademarks and patents).

studies on patent frequency that have suggested that the number of women inventors increases as the proportion of women in STEM fields increases.[179] Even though several creative industries are achieving greater levels of gender parity, in some cases, women still have to overcome past inequality that may continue to discourage their creativity.[180]

Women also may be disinclined to create and register their works because they continue to be compensated less for their work than men. This may even deter some women from pursuing a creative profession, knowing they have a smaller likelihood of success in some industries. And even if they become successful, they may not be compensated as much as similarly positioned men.[181]

6.5.1.2 Discrimination

While an unknown portion of the disparity in registration rates between men and women is likely tied to existing forms of inequality, women face additional barriers to full participation in the copyright system both within their fields as well as within the copyright system itself. Some portion of the gender imbalance in creative professions may be tied to women self-selecting certain fields in greater numbers than men. However, when women do not have the same opportunities to be published authors,[182] have their plays produced,[183] or have their artwork shown in a gallery,[184] it is difficult to argue that creative professions are free from some degree of gender-based discrimination that may discourage some women from creative authorship.

179 Hunt et al., *supra* note 52, at 832 (arguing in part that the gap in STEM representation between men and women accounts for part of the gap in patenting rates between men and women).

180 For example, while women are featured more frequently when new plays are selected, men have authored the vast majority of "revivals" selected by theater companies, which may be due in part to lower numbers of women playwrights in the past. JORDAN, *supra* note 153, at 6.

181 For example, in the fine art industry, works by five women constituted nearly 40 percent of the total amount of money spent on artwork created by women, and works by women represented only 13 percent of artwork in museum collections in the United States in 2018. *See* Wilson, *supra* note 158 (containing data about the representation of women in the arts in galleries and arguing that this exclusion results in lost economic value in the international art market); Halperin & Burns, *supra* note 160 (containing data about the percentage of women featured in international art galleries and auctions and arguing that the lack of representation may be tied in part to lower valuation of their work as well as prejudice among men and women in the industry).

182 *See* Franklin, *supra* note 126 (reporting women are less likely to be selected for publications by publishers than men).

183 See, for example, McConarty & Rose, *supra* note 154, at 212 (reporting that women are less likely to have their plays produced than men in regional theaters and offering some possible explanations as to why that may be).

184 Wilson, *supra* note 158 (containing data about the representation of women in the arts in galleries around the world).

Despite purporting to incentivize original works of authorship by all, regardless of gender, the current copyright system does not protect forms of creative expression that have traditionally been associated with women. For example, recipes, fashion designs, and sewing and knitting patterns have traditionally received little or no copyright protection.[185] Women traditionally dominated these industries, and many had a communal aspect whereby multiple women would collaborate and build off of each other's creativity.[186] Their exclusion may suggest that women's creative expression is not valued as highly as men's in terms of being perceived as a form of creativity that needs, and is worth, incentivizing. At the same time, including these fields and forms of creativity may either change the communal aspect of these industries by enforcing individual claims of authorship or entail substantial changes to the law of copyright, such as a revision of the nature of the originality requirement.[187]

The copyright system may have a discriminatory effect on women due to its requirement that to become a coauthor, one must make an independently copyrightable contribution to the joint work. This standard is reflected in case law,[188] as well as in the USCO's definition of coauthorship.[189] This requirement for coauthorship may have a disparate impact on women who prefer to work collaboratively or operate in fields that involve communal creativity because multiple individuals may make important contributions that are nevertheless not independently copyrightable. Creative expression does "not occur in splendid isolation," yet the creative contributions of individuals go unrewarded when their contributions do not qualify them as "authors."[190] Between 1976 and 2012, only 14.2 percent of copyright registrations had multiple authors.[191] Yet, from research on patent behavior among

[185] *See* Ann Bartow, *Fair Use and the Fairer Sex: Gender, Feminism, and Copyright Law*, 14 AM. U. J. GENDER SOC. POL'Y & L. 551, 557 (2006) (arguing in part that clothing and cooking are traditional forms of creativity for women and that neither are protected by copyright law); Kara W. Swanson, *Cat Ladies, Quilters, and Creativity*, 10 LANDSLIDE 47, 48 (2018) (pointing out that sewing and knitting patterns, among others, are forms of creativity for women that are not protected under copyright law).

[186] *See* Debora Halbert, *Feminist Interpretations of Intellectual Property*, 14 AM. U. J. GENDER SOC. POL'Y & L. 431, 442 (2006) (arguing in part that for some women, creativity is a communal experience that is different from the creativity protected by the copyright system).

[187] *See* Bartow, *supra* note 185, at 557–58 (arguing that the U.S. copyright system protects creativity by men because men have defined what "authorship" entails and what forms of creative expression warrant protection and that this may impede creativity by women).

[188] See, for example, Aalmuhammed v. Lee, 202 F.3d 1227 (9th Cir. 2000).

[189] 17 U.S.C. § 101.

[190] *See* Dan L. Burk, *Feminism and Dualism in Intellectual Property*, 15 AM. U. J. GENDER SOC. POL'Y & L. 183, 193–94 (2007) (arguing that sole authorship is not often an accurate reflection of creative production and that unrecognized contributors are more likely to be women than men).

[191] Brauneis & Oliar, *supra* note 4, at 74.

women[192] as well as an understanding of traditional forms of creativity among women, we know that some women may be inclined toward collaborative creative expression.[193] While the "independently copyrightable contribution" standard emerged from Professor Paul Goldstein and was subsequently adopted by case law, it is possible that Professor David Nimmer's alternative standard for coauthorship – one that merely requires each coauthor's contribution to be more than de-minimis – would better incentivize women's creativity.[194] Finally, at least one study has indicated that officers within the patent system may be biased against applicants with names commonly associated with women; it might not be unfounded to surmise that there could be a similar effect within the copyright system.[195]

CONCLUSION

When women make up roughly 50 percent of the U.S. population but only one-third of the authors of registered works, it is necessary to understand why women do not create and register works at the same rates as men. Unfortunately, this gender disparity is not unique to copyright registrants. Women are less likely to own trademarks and are less likely to apply for patents than men. This is consistent with larger and more general trends in property ownership. Women as a whole are much less likely to achieve the same level of financial success as men due in part to persistent wealth and wage gaps. This disparity in the financial payoff is just one aspect of existing forms of gender-based inequality in many creative industries.

It is likely not feasible for the copyright system to fully mitigate the impact of gender disparity within creative professions. However, understanding some of the factors that may discourage creativity, participation, and copyright registration among women is a crucial first step for determining how to encourage creativity moving forward. Despite encountering additional barriers inside and outside the copyright system, women have persisted as successful authors, playwrights, musicians, and artists. But if all or even some of the additional barriers were removed, the increased creative output among women could be even more remarkable and work to society's benefit.

[192] *See* PROGRESS AND POTENTIAL, *supra* note 11, at 11 (containing data on average number of coinventors for women and for both men and women to find in part that women are more likely to work with coinventors than men).

[193] *See* Halbert, *supra* note 186, at 441 (arguing that women's creativity has long been communally centered).

[194] For a discussion of Nimmer's "de-minimis" standard for coauthorship, and its comparison to Goldstein's "independently copyrightable contribution" standard, see Erickson v. Trinity Theatre 13 F.3d 1061, 1069–70 (7th Cir. 1994).

[195] *See* Jensen et al., *supra* note 45, at 309 (discussing the possibility of gender bias among patent examiners after a study found that all-women inventor teams with common names for women had their patent applications rejected at higher rates than all-women inventor teams with less-common names).

7

Building Innovation Skills to Overcome Gender Inequality

Mexico, India, and Brazil

Alenka Guzmán and Flor Brown

INTRODUCTION

"Without women, life is pure prose," wrote Nicaraguan poet Rubén Darío. Not only have women inspired male poetic creativity, but they have also contributed to progress in the world, and evidence of female artistic and intellectual attributes has been left behind throughout history. During prehistoric times, women must have been anonymous inventors, creating a number of objects and activities needed for everyday survival while the men were off hunting. The creative potential of the "fairer sex" has been marginalized, limited, and unacknowledged due to unequal gender treatment at different periods in human history.

This chapter attempts to shed light on the efforts that women inventors from three emerging countries – Brazil, India, and Mexico – have undertaken to overcome the obstacles of inequality and how relevant these challenges can be for economic development and society. In particular, it seeks to (1) analyze gender differentiation in creativity, innovation, and science; (2) define the nature and dynamics of female inventive activity by using data provided by the U.S. Patent and Trademark Office (USPTO) on patents granted in Brazil, India, and Mexico; (3) determine which factors influencing the growing propensity of women to invent help reduce gender inequality in knowledge economies; and (4) contribute policy proposals that target greater female participation in inventive activities.

The key questions for this research are thus: What are the characteristics and dynamics of female inventive activity in emerging countries with different economic development paths? What factors influence women's propensity to invent? Do female inventive skills complement those of men?

We consider that women possess potential abilities for invention-innovation and that their propensity to be inventors, by themselves or in co-participation with men, will depend on their scientific background and variables related to inventive activity.

The findings of this research suggest that factors influence, to varying degrees, the propensity of women to invent in Brazil, India, and Mexico. Each case offers different strands of analysis according to the innovation trajectories of each country and the incorporation of women into scientific and technological (S&T) research. For instance, the fact that the stock of prior knowledge is significant only in the size of inventor teams has a positive influence on women inventors in Brazil and Mexico. Concerning patents, patents by firms positively affect women inventors in Mexico and India, while patents by institutions and individuals only affect Mexico and Brazil, respectively. Regarding the technological field, mechanical is significant in Mexico, while pharmaceutical, medical, electrical and electronics, and "others" are important in Brazil. In contrast, in India, no particular field is influential on the propensity of women to invent. The presence of foreign researchers increases this propensity in Mexico. The outcomes suggest specific policies that will promote the incorporation of women and the development of their inventive potential in the different technological fields. To that extent, gender inequalities in inventive activity can be overcome, and this will be expressed through improved economic growth and social welfare.

The following section provides a short, specialized literature review on the factors influencing women's ability to display their inventive capabilities. The second section deals with whether policies geared toward reducing gender inequalities in education, science, and technological knowledge have been implemented in Brazil, India, and Mexico. The third section focuses on analyzing the dynamics of female inventive activity in these emerging countries, specifying the empirical model used to test the hypotheses, analyze the results, and formulate policy proposals. The last section presents conclusions and advances some policy recommendations.

7.1 REVIEW OF LITERATURE ON WOMEN INVENTORS

Despite women's enormous potential to contribute to economic growth through scientific, technological, inventive, management, and business activities, they have historically been marginalized in education, particularly in S&T fields of study (Asgeirsdottir, 2006). The growing incorporation of women into S&T careers and their professional performance in these fields is seen as a potential source of economic growth and well-being in society (Hunt et al., 2012; Huyer, 2015; Kahler, 2012; UKIPO, 2016). As more women develop new scientific knowledge and technological innovations, a positive impact on countries' productivity, economic growth, and social well-being is expected (European Commission, 2008). Especially when women are involved in science, technology, engineering, and mathematics (STEM) fields, they acquire the skills to develop new S&T ideas that have innovative potential and foster entrepreneurship (Kuschel et al., 2020).

Some authors maintain that women have participated in the development of science since the beginning. Yet, their involvement and contributions have been mainly ignored by historians or deliberately concealed behind male figures (van den Eynde, 1994). Today, the deficiencies in women's participation in science and technology are more visible (UNESCO, 2018).[1]

Historic gender discrimination notwithstanding, some women have succeeded in standing out for their scientific work. For example, Marie Curie received two Nobel Prizes: in 1903 for physics, shared with her husband Pierre and Henri Becquerel, and in 1911 for chemistry, all by herself. Rosalind Franklin's X-ray diffraction photographs were crucial for the double helix model of DNA, for which James Watson and Francis Crick were awarded the Nobel Prize in Physiology or Medicine in 1962.

In the realm of technology, women have also developed inventions that have significantly impacted industrially and successful businesses at different times in history. Women's inventions have moved from household utensils, clothing, and other fields to inventions of greater technological complexity (Table 7A.1). Women inventors in developed countries stand out. As developing nations have made efforts in science and technology, women involved in these fields – albeit in a much smaller proportion than men – have been publishing scientific findings in journals, patenting inventions, and receiving awards – including "Women in Science" Awards from UNESCO–L'Oréal–ABC (Agência Brasil, 2018). Concerning the emerging countries selected in this study, India reports significant scientific achievements from women in various fields (Ramesh, 2020). Brazilian women scientists have been critical players in life sciences and health, and women in Mexico have made essential contributions in the same area (Table 7A.1).

The interest in studying the contributions of women inventors is recent. Several studies offer a historical focus, giving an account of the social impact of inventions made by women in different periods and industrialized countries (Blashfield, 1996; Braun, 2007; Currie, 2001; Karnes and Bean, 1995; Whittington and Smith-Doerr, 2008, among others). Others have made remarkable efforts to identify women inventors across countries, regions, technological fields, and sectors, using data on Patent Cooperation Treaty (PCT) applications from the World Intellectual Property Organization between 1995 and 2015 (Martínez et al., 2016). Another effort to identify women inventors was made by the UK Intellectual Property Office (2016), which analyzed ninety million documents compiled from the European Patent Office (EPO) and its Worldwide Patent Statistical Database (PATSTAT). Additionally, the USPTO (2020) has analyzed patent data from 1976 to 2019 to identify women inventors compared to men. The findings of these studies coincided, identifying that a vital gender gap still exists, but there is a growing trend in

[1] UNESCO (2018: 13) reports that 28.8 percent of researchers and 35 percent of students in STEM-related fields are women. Two regions studied (Central Asia and Latin America) have increased gender parity among researchers (48.1 percent and 45.4 percent, respectively), while almost a third of all countries worldwide had done so since 2016.

the incorporation of women in inventor teams. There are also differences between countries in the technological fields in which women are involved (Martínez et al., 2016; UKIPO, 2016; USPTO, 2020).

Some studies centered on analyzing patented inventions with female inventors' participation in information technology (Ashcraft and Breitzman, 2012; Kahler, 2012). Still, other studies have spotlighted the problem of the significant gap in female participation as inventors, as patent owners, and in the commercialization of inventions (Frietsch et al., 2009; Giuri et al., 2020; Hunt et al., 2012; Jung and Ejermo, 2014; Kahler, 2012; Milli et al., 2016; Whittington and Smith-Doerr, 2008) (Table 7A.2). Considering that women have gradually increased their participation in academia over the past sixty years, some studies have focused on women's working conditions, seeking to identify reasons that inhibit greater female involvement in S&T research projects. Some authors point out that family/career tradeoffs disadvantage women's academic positions and, therefore, women in science may value authorship of scientific articles more than inventorship reflected by patents (Lissoni et al., 2013). In the view of these authors, women are less likely to patent than men (Whittington and Smith-Doerr, 2008), even if they have a similar history of publications (Azoulay et al., 2007; Breschi et al., 2005; Stephan et al., 2007, cited by Lissoni et al., 2013).

Either way, gender-differentiated academic performance is seen across scientific fields and countries in terms of the number of women and men authors and their productivity, citations, recognition, and salary. This seems related to diverse publishing, career longevity, and dropout rates, particularly in academic careers across STEM fields (Huang et al., 2020). The fact that women graduate with STEM degrees in a lower proportion than men means that they have fewer opportunities to operate in business and commercialization circuits, even if they are inventors (Giuri et al., 2020; Kuschel et al., 2020; Lissoni et al., 2013). However, in some fields, such as biotechnology, women scientists are more likely to become inventors in patents by firms, especially when those firms are more flexible and less hierarchical in their organizational management and favor collaboration with academia and other companies.

Other reasons explaining the persistent academic gender productivity gap include "differences in family responsibilities, ... career absences, resource allocation, the role of peer review, collaboration, role stereotypes, academic rank, specialization, and work climate." Insofar as the case studies are limited, the analysis of this phenomenon needs to be deepened, covering the whole longitudinal, disciplinary, and geographical landscape (Huang et al., 2020: 4609).

As for emerging and developing countries, studies of Mexico (Guzmán, 2012) and comparative studies of Latin American countries (Sifontes Fernandez and Morales Valera, 2014) have been conducted. These studies show the huge gap in female participation in inventive activities, identify the technological sectors in which women participate, and explain the rate of female involvement in an innovative activity associated with external collaboration and the patenting of universities and institutions (Sifontes and Morales, 2020).

The literature on women inventors[2] and, in particular, on factors affecting women's propensity to invent remains limited. However, once the barriers faced by women in accessing patenting and commercializing innovations have been identified, the authors put forward interesting suggestions to overcome these barriers (Hunt et al., 2012; Meng, 2018; Milli et al., 2016). The relevance of this research resides in the fact that it identifies factors influencing the propensity of women to be inventors, in addition to characterizing the activity and dynamics of inventive activity involving at least one woman in three emerging countries. This analysis allows us to corroborate the extent to which the U.N. Sustainable Development Goals are met, which will contribute positively to their economic and social development (Table 7A.2).

7.2 HAVE THERE BEEN POLICIES IN BRAZIL, INDIA, OR MEXICO FOR REDUCING GENDER INEQUALITIES IN EDUCATION, SCIENCE, AND TECHNOLOGICAL KNOWLEDGE?

A crucial aspect of sizing gender inequalities in the knowledge economy is highlighting the stylized facts,[3] of the gaps in the Gender Development Index (GDI)[4] and in human capital specialization by gender. This paves the way for the empirical analysis of women inventors in the emerging countries selected. Therefore, the next section deals with whether policies geared toward reducing gender inequalities in education, science, and technological knowledge have been implemented.

7.2.1 *Gender Inequality Index: Brazil, India, and Mexico in the Global Context*

According to the Gender Inequality Index (GII),[5] Brazil and Mexico stand out for nearly converging in the 2014 GDI (with index scores of 0.997 and 0.943, respectively), whereas India has a lower index score of 0.795 (Figure 7A.1). India, however,

2 "Women inventors" are defined as women who take part in the invention of a patented product or process. Although not all inventions are patented, patent-classified documents provide consistent (in the statistical sense), long-term information identifying inventors, and therefore also women inventors – of course, after a lot of hard work by the researchers.

3 Stylized facts refer to empirical evidence – that is, observable data over time that lead to theoretical analysis. See Oxford Reference (n.d.).

4 "GDI measures gender inequalities in achievement in three basic dimensions of human development: health, measured by female and male life expectancy at birth; education, measured by female and male expected years of schooling for children and female and male mean years of schooling for adults ages 25 years and older; and command over economic resources, measured by female and male estimated earned income" (UNDP, n.d.-a).

5 "GII is a composite metric of gender inequality using three dimensions: reproductive health, empowerment and the labour market. A low GII value indicates low inequality between women and men, and vice-versa" (UNDP, n.d.-b). The GII, produced by the U.N. Development Programme, includes 166 countries, divided into four categories of human development: very high, high, medium, and low. Despite unavailable data for previous years, we are able to see the gender gaps, which appeared four to eight years after the launch of the U.N. Millennium Development Goals in 2000.

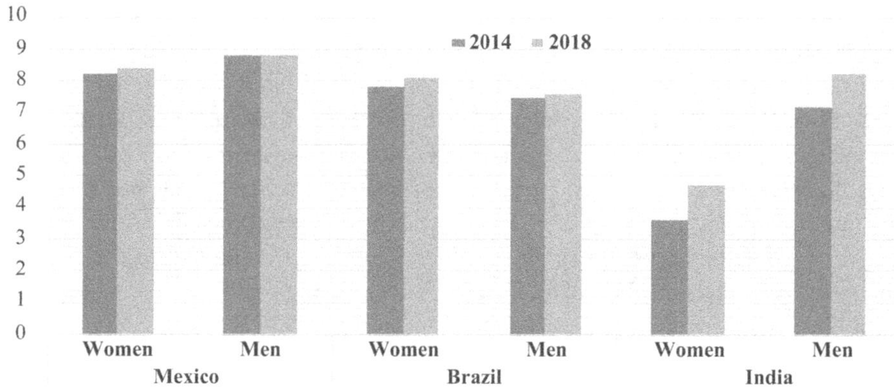

FIGURE 7.1 Average years of schooling by gender, 2014 and 2018: Mexico, Brazil, and India.
Source: U.N. Development Programme (n.d.-c).

rose in the GDI in 2018; Mexico and Brazil had marginal improvements. The Latin American countries' GII scores rank between very high human development (VHHD) and high human development (HHD), while India ranks in the low human development category.

In terms of average years of schooling, gender advances were observed between 2014 and 2018 in the three emerging countries studied (Figure 7.1). Compared with VHHD and HHD countries, the average years of schooling in Brazil, India, and Mexico were lower for both sexes, especially in India. In Mexico, there was a marginal increase in average years of schooling from 8.2 to 8.4, while the corresponding figure remained 8.8 years for men. In Brazil, women exceeded the average years of schooling for men: 8.1 versus 7.6 average years, respectively, in 2018. Finally, there were more significant differentials in India, with only 4.7 average years of schooling for women and 8.2 for men.

7.2.2 *Human Capital Specialization by Gender: Toward Which Scientific Disciplines Are Women in Higher Education Oriented?*

The graduate gender gap in the scientific field has different dimensions across countries. Having gender gaps in engineering, manufacturing, and construction, as well as in STEM, is a fact for all three countries (Figure 7.2). There has been very little improvement from 2014 to 2017 – with none, in fact, in Mexico in the STEM field. More men than women in Brazil and Mexico graduate in information and communication technologies, and the same is true for India's agriculture, forestry, fisheries, and veterinary sciences. These gaps have even increased from 2014 to 2017. However, across all three emerging countries, graduation percentages for women are higher in natural sciences, mathematics, and statistics and are robust in health and welfare. Only minor changes have occurred (UNESCO, 2016, 2018).

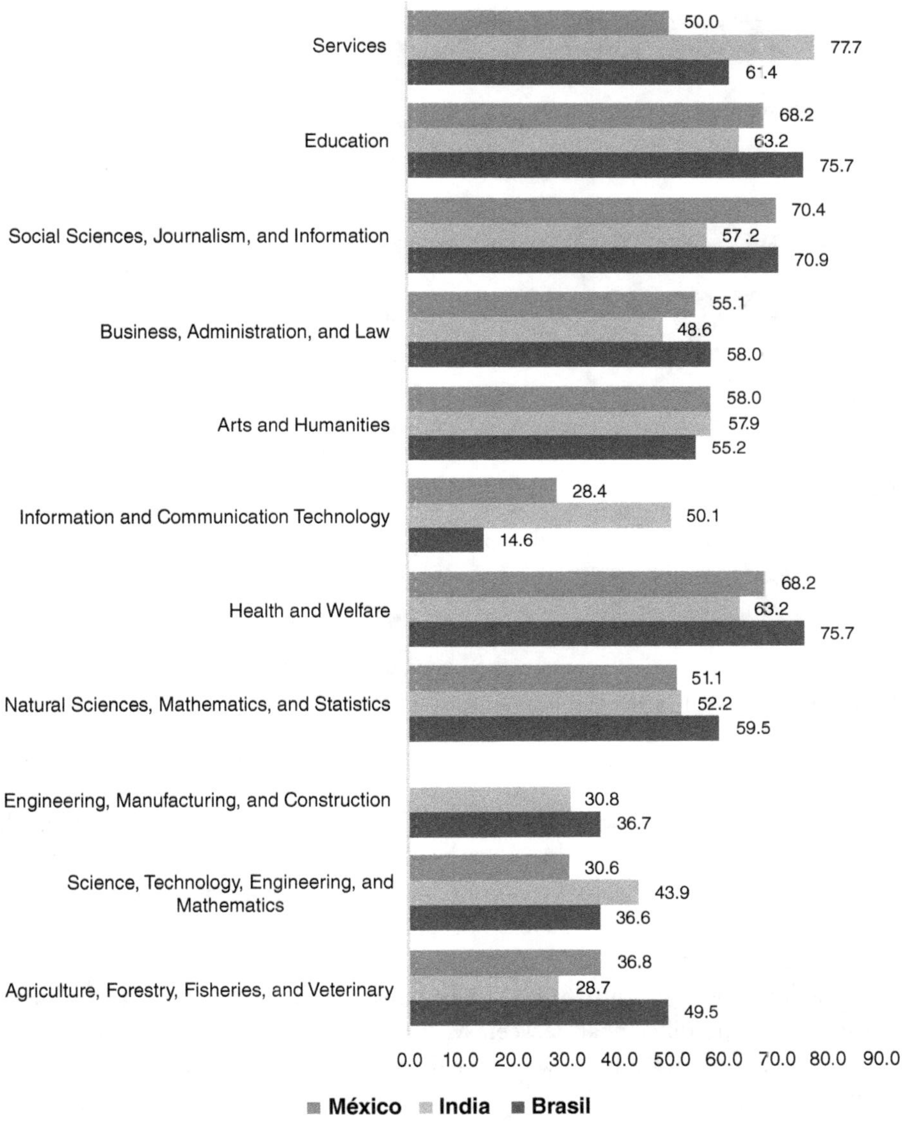

FIGURE 7.2 Percentage of female graduates by STEM career categories, 2017.
Sources: UNESCO (n.d.); UNESCO, UIS Statistics. Distribution of tertiary graduates by field of study Years selected. http://data.uis.unesco.org/index.aspx?queryid=3830

Participation of female graduates in STEM careers in 2017 registered significant and differentiated progress across countries. In India, female graduates reached parity in information and communication technologies. In health and welfare, women surpassed men in all three countries, especially in Brazil (75 percent women). Women

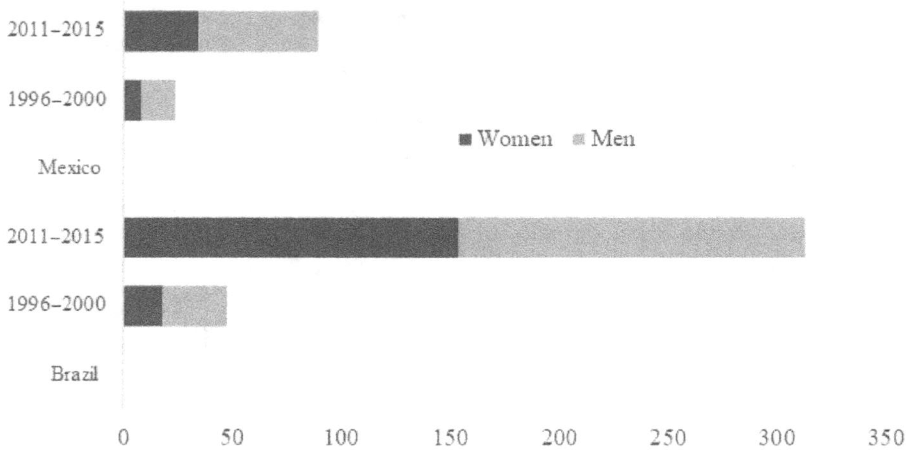

FIGURE 7.3 Number of researchers by gender* in Mexico and Brazil, 1996–2000 and 2011–2015 (thousands of researchers).
* Among named and gendered author profiles.
Source: Elsevier Research Intelligence (2017).

reached parity in natural sciences, mathematics, and statistics, especially in Brazil (59.5 percent). However, women still lagged behind men in traditional fields (Figure 7.2).

7.2.3 *Inclusion of Women in S&T Research*

The participation of women within the total group of researchers in Brazil and Mexico[6] improved between 2011 and 2015, when compared with the period between 1996 and 2000 (Figure 7.3). In general, the number of researchers in Mexico increased more for men (an increase of 39,000) than for women, from 8,100 to 34,400 researchers (an increase of 26,300). As for Brazil, the increase was noteworthy and even higher for women (136,000 women researchers compared with 129,000 men researchers).[7] The differential between Mexico and Brazil (89,500 compared with 312,800 researchers) is most likely associated with the fact that Mexico has had little GDP expenditure on research and development (R&D) (an average of 0.4 percent). In contrast, Brazil intensified its efforts in this area (1 percent) (Table 7A.3).[8]

When identifying researchers by scientific areas in the two Latin American countries between 2011 and 2015, diversification and greater integration of women

6 Information was not available for India.

7 In the United States, the increase in women researchers was slightly higher than the increase in men. As a whole, the increase for the twenty-eight European Union countries slightly favored men (Elsevier Research Intelligence, 2017).

8 In Mexico, military defense spending is 1 percent of the GDP (National Institute of Statistics and Geography, INEGI).

in the various scientific fields are observed. Although Brazil and Mexico, respectively, have 25 percent and 22 percent of women in medicine, the differential between the two countries in the number of women researchers in this field was substantial (see Figure 7.3). The count for Brazil was 80,600 during 2011–2015, an increase of 9.4 times from 1996 to 2000, and the corresponding figure for Mexico was 17,300 researchers during 2011–2015, an increase of 4.6 times. Other areas of importance are agriculture and biological sciences, biochemistry, genetics, and molecular biology (an average of 10 percent each) and, to a lesser degree, immunology, and microbiology (5 percent), with only marginal percentages in other fields.

7.2.4 *Launch of Knowledge Empowerment Policies*

We find STEM and Gender Advancement (SAGA) among the international projects. Efforts have focused on pushing for reforms to close gender gaps in STEM at the education and research levels – and also drawing lessons from evidence and the policy mix to improve national science, technology, and innovation (STI) policies. These efforts encourage the incorporation of women into the knowledge economy. In addition, they develop a better understanding of women and girls in science. Finally, they provide estimates and help build sex-disaggregated data, and design and implement the STI policy instruments that affect gender equality in STEM (UNESCO, 2016).

As noted in the UNESCO study, there are several important facts about women researchers: (1) Women are slightly less likely than men to collaborate across academic and corporate sectors on research papers; (2) there is a relatively slight variation between comparator countries and regions in the percentage of cross-sector collaboration between academia and industry; (3) the proportion of scholarly output resulting from the academic–corporate collaboration is slightly lower for women researchers than for men researchers; (4) women tend to have a slightly higher share of the top 10 percent of interdisciplinary scholarly output relative to their total scholarly output than men; (5) among researchers, women are generally less internationally mobile than men; and (6) the highest citation impact is associated with transitory researchers (those who move internationally for periods of less than two years) (Elsevier Research Intelligence, 2017: 7).

7.3 EMPIRICAL STUDY: FACTORS AFFECTING THE PROPENSITY OF WOMEN TO INVENT

This section analyzes the nature and dynamics of female inventive activity in Mexico, Brazil, and India and then tests a hypothesis. First, we characterize the inventive activity of USPTO patents granted to those emerging countries where at least one woman participates. Second, we state the hypothesis and specify the econometric model seeking to identify the factors that contribute to increasing the propensity of women to invent. Third, we verify the validity of the hypothesis and analyze the results.

7.3.1 *Nature and Dynamics of Female Inventive Activity: Data*

Our analysis of emerging female inventors focuses on three countries in the study: India, Brazil, and Mexico. We have used the USPTO database of patents granted to the holders in three countries. The period for each country is different: Mexico, 1980–2015; Brazil, 1997–2013; and India, 1997–2010. We identified those patents with at least one woman inventor and then organized the list of women inventors, associating with them the information on the patent(s).

We observe different growth dynamic paths for USPTO patents granted to the three countries. On the one hand, India was favored by a ten-year transition period following the adoption of the Agreement on Trade-Related Aspects of Intellectual Property Rights (TRIPS Agreement), showing an increasing dynamic in the case of pharmaceuticals. From 1997 to 2010, 2,685 patents were granted to Indian holders, of which 1,219 involved at least one woman inventor and 1,416 involved only men inventors (see Figure 7.4). India registered an annual average growth rate (AAGR) of 20.9 percent, which was higher for those patents with at least one woman inventor (24.7 percent). Two subperiods stand out in the evolution of patents granted to Indian holders. The first, 1997–2003, showed an AAGR of 40 percent on total patents, and patents with female collaboration were notably higher (54.2 percent). The second subperiod, 2004–2010, had a lower AAGR of 8.34 percent, particularly for patents with women inventors (6.7 percent) (Figure 7.4). Perhaps in the following years, patent expansion grew and was equaled by that of at least one woman.

On the other hand, we have Mexico with lower growth. Indeed, 1,193 USPTO patents were granted to Mexican assignees from 1986 to 2015, with an AAGR of 8.4 percent. Although female participation in total patents is characterized by a large gap, the 108 patents identified with at least one woman inventor were slightly higher (AAGR of 8.7 percent). Women's collaboration increased in 2007, with seven patents, and reached seventeen in 2014 (Figure 7.5). Innovative activity in Mexico remains low because of a lack of entrepreneurial and institutional investment in R&D activities that target innovation and patenting.

Concerning Brazil, of the 1,434 patents granted to Brazilians between 1997 and 2013, 388 (27 percent) had at least one woman inventor on the team of researchers. The growth path was very similar to that for all patents. The country has a small and volatile trajectory, but this trajectory is growing as the R&D/GDP percentage increases (Figure 7.6). Although the most significant proportion of patents with female involvement in Brazil is individual, teams with two or more inventors have become the practice since the end of the 1990s.

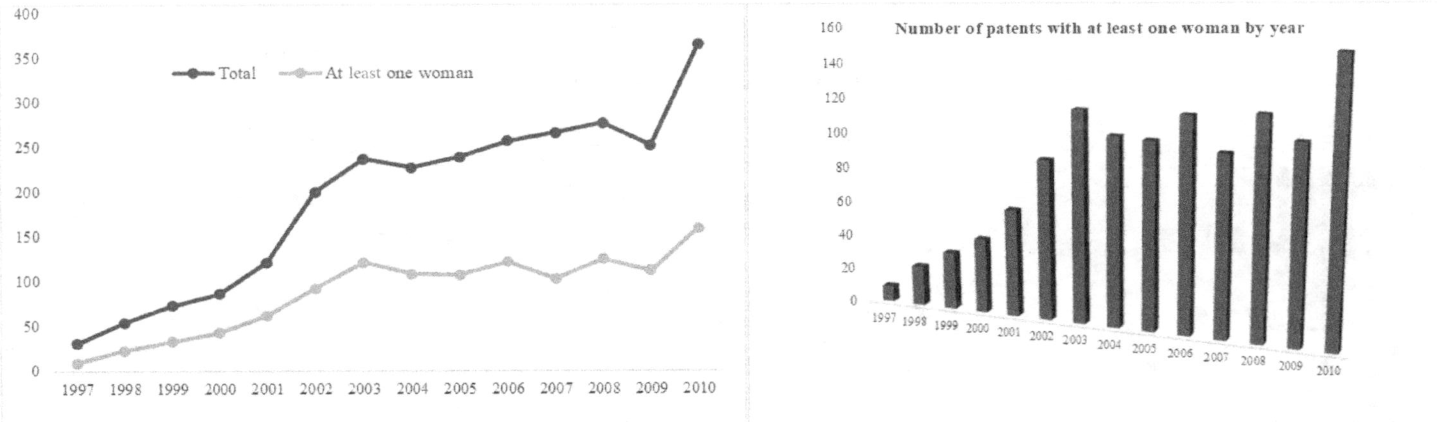

FIGURE 7.4 India: Evolution of USPTO patents granted (total and those having at least one woman inventor), 1997–2010.
Source: Authors' own elaboration, based on USPTO data.

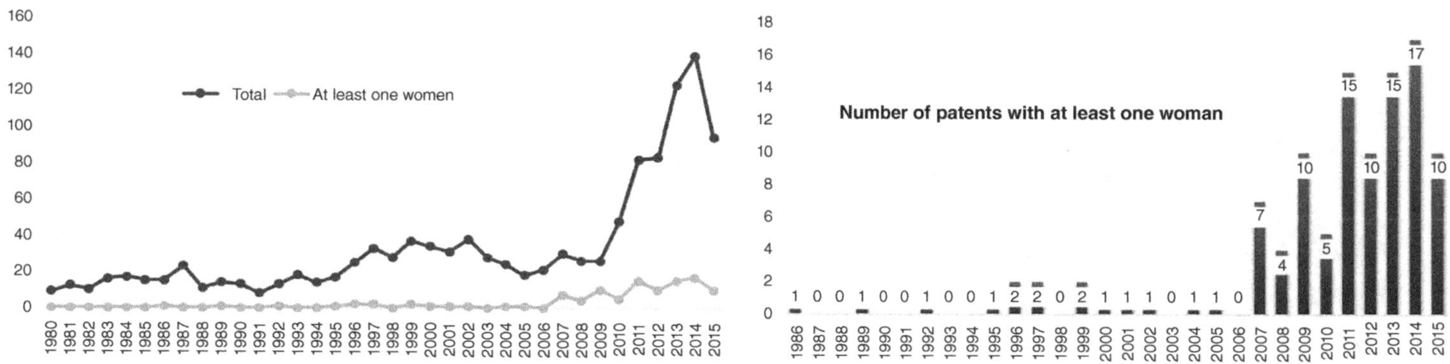

FIGURE 7.5 Mexico: Evolution of USPTO patents granted (total and those having at least one woman inventor), 1980–2015.
Source: Authors' own elaboration, based on USPTO data.

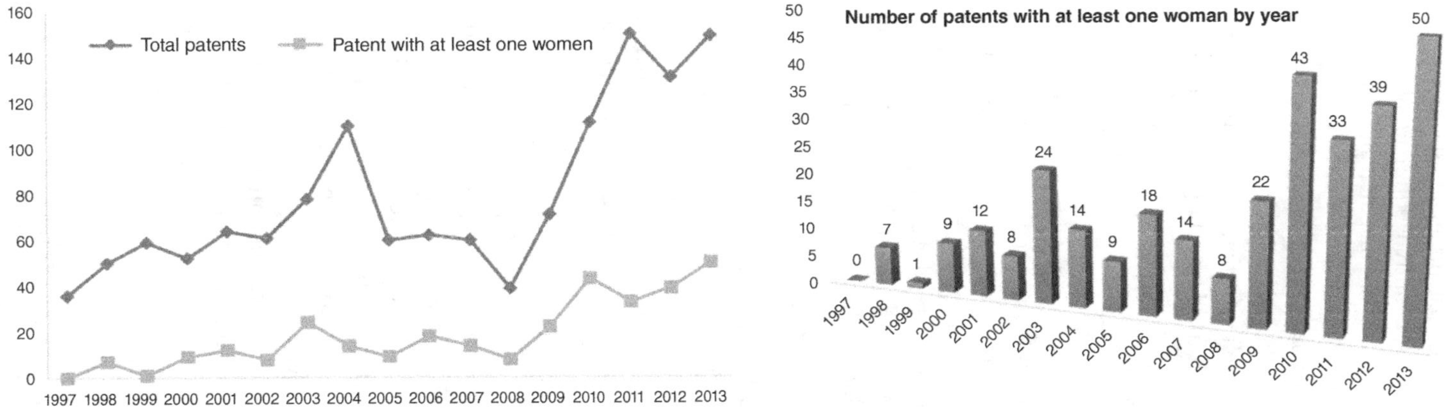

FIGURE 7.6 Brazil: Evolution of USPTO patents granted (total and those having at least one woman inventor), 1997–2013.
Source: Authors' own elaboration, based on USPTO data.

In short, the evolution of granted patents analyzed shows that even if the participation of women inventors in each country is still marginal, it has been increasing, especially in India. It is worth pointing out that men are also on those inventor teams with at least one woman inventor. The differentiated abilities across genders seem to strengthen the scope of innovation.[9] We assume that the increase of women in inventor teams is associated with the increasing incorporation of female inventors in STEM careers and related research activities. This phenomenon is more evident in India and Brazil. There is growth in Mexico but at a lower level.

7.3.2 *Nature of Innovation*

We proceed to identify the features of patents involving women inventors. It is interesting to compare the patent number by team size in the three emerging countries in this study. In general, the teams are mixed, except in patents with only one inventor. India leads with 45 percent of patents with groups including women, followed by Brazil with 24 percent and Mexico with just 21 percent. During the total period analyzed, the whole patents with teams of two to five inventors predominate in all three countries: two-thirds in India and just over 70 percent in Mexico and Brazil.

Regarding teams with more than six researchers, India stands out, with almost one-third of the patents, and the two Latin American countries have around 10 percent. Individual women's participation in patenting is relatively marginal. This is especially the case for India, where 3.4 percent of patents are characterized as individual patents. Mexico and Brazil slightly exceed 15 percent. In contrast, for patents in which only men participate, individual participation is significant in Brazil and Mexico, but the figure is lower in India (see Table 7.1).

Regarding patent assignees, institution holders are prominent in India (65 percent) and Mexico (54 percent). In contrast, firms have greater weight in Brazil (73 percent), although there has been less participation in patents with women inventors in Mexico (44 percent) and India (34 percent) (Figure 7.7).

During 1997–2013 in Brazil, 401 female inventors were identified, representing 18.5 percent of all inventors. In 2003, the Natura companies and the Johnson & Johnson subsidiary in Brazil had the greatest participation, in many cases with inventor teams composed of several researchers. In 2006, a similar situation was seen with the Foundation for Research Support in the State of São Paulo. There is a clear growing trend, which has been most noteworthy in the past few years and seems to be associated with a higher incidence of larger inventor teams.

9 Taking into account studies on neuronal differences, men and women also have differentiated abilities. Therefore, by combining the abilities of both sexes, the creation of new ideas is enhanced, and the breadth of innovation strengthened (Morales Otal et al., 2009).

TABLE 7.1 *Patents by size and gender of team in Mexico, Brazil, and India*

Country	Team size	Total number of patents	Number of patents with at least one female inventor by team size	Number of patents with only male inventors by team size
Mexico	One inventor	227	20	207
	Two to five	324	87	237
	Six or more inventors	36	16	20
Brazil	One inventor	631	62	569
	Two to five	688	256	432
	Six or more inventors	115	31	84
India	One inventor	348	41	307
	Two to five	1,801	796	1,005
	Six or more inventors	537	371	166

Source: Authors' own estimation, based on USPTO data.

During 1980–2015 in Mexico, sixty-one female inventors were identified, representing 5.3 percent of the total number of inventors. Outstanding for their participation are Sabritas (six of the sixty-one), Mabe (three), El Instituto Mexicano del Petróleo (nine), and the Universidad Nacional Autónoma de México (seven). As in Brazil, the trend is for working in relatively large teams. The average number of researchers per patent is three, but as many as five in the chemical, pharmaceutical, and medical sectors. Individual patents are registered only in the electrical and electronic sectors.

From 1997 to 2010 in India, 219 female and 659 male inventors were identified in the 1,208 patents with at least one woman. Over half (53 percent) of the patents had the Council of Scientific and Industrial Research as the patent assignee. Companies that had more than seven patents were Aurobind–Pharma (seven), Dr. Reddy's Laboratories (nineteen), Hetero Drugs (twelve), Indian Oil Corporation (twelve), Ittiam Systems (fourteen), and Reliance Life Sciences (forty-one). A trend toward working in increasingly larger teams of inventors has been recorded in India, as it is the country with the most effective teams – in fact, with ten inventors in the "others" category and nine inventors in chemical. In Brazil, the largest teams of inventors are in pharmaceutical and medical (nine inventors), chemical (seven inventors), and "others" (seven inventors).

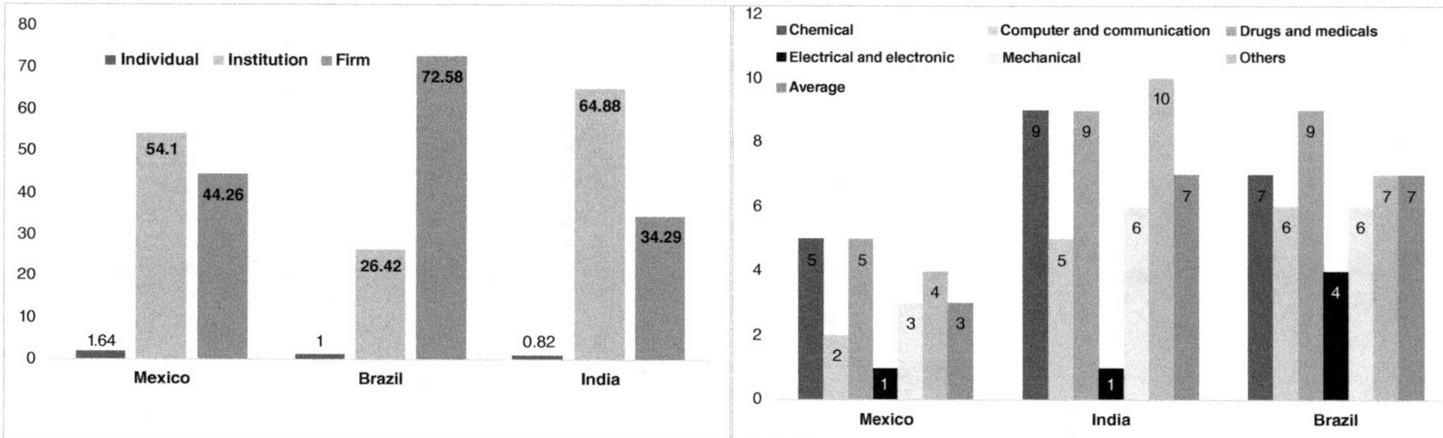

FIGURE 7.7 Distribution of women in patent assignee type and by technological field in Mexico, Brazil, and India (by percent).
Source: Authors' own estimation, based on USPTO data.

For the field of technology, where patents are classified, we underscore the following evidence. In all three countries, women's participation stands out in pharmaceutical, medical, and chemical patents. Specifically, nearly two-fifths of India's women inventors are in the pharmaceutical and medical sector, and 42 percent are in the chemical sector, according to the higher percentage of women graduates in these sectors and their integration as researchers (Table 7A.3). Studies have found a positive correlation between the increasing number of women graduates in STEM careers and research activities and a higher number of female inventors (Giuri et al., 2020; Kuschel et al., 2020; Lissoni et al., 2013). However, this study did not explore such correlations due to a lack of information on each woman.

The distribution of women inventors in Brazil and Mexico is similar in the pharmaceutical and medical sectors – 37 percent and 29 percent, respectively. In the chemical sector, the distribution is 31 percent and 26 percent, respectively. Few women inventors, however, are found in mechanical, electrical, and electronic sectors, with percentages ranging between 2 percent and 4 percent. In the "others" category, differentials are observed among the three countries, with Mexico – where women inventors collaborate on a third of the patents – standing out.

In every patent document, previously consulted patents are recorded as Backward Patent Citations (*BwPatCit*) to show that the work done by the researchers is state of the art in their technological field. We consider this variable the stock of previous technological knowledge. We estimate this indicator based on the average of *BwPatCit* per patent where a woman is present. Mexico has the highest average (forty-seven citations per patent), whereas India and Brazil have averages of fifteen and sixteen citations, respectively.

Regarding patent value, we use the number of forward patent citations (*FwPatCit*) per patent as a proxy variable. We observe that, in all three countries, the importance is still relatively low, especially in India.

India has a notably higher percentage of claims in the pharmaceutical and medical sector and the chemical sector (a combined 83 percent). Both sectors are essential for the other two countries, but with a lower proportion: 66 percent for Mexico and 68 percent for Brazil. The percentages for the "others" category are 29 percent and 19 percent, respectively. There is marginal diversification in the other technology categories.

Table 7.2 shows the distribution of patents with at least one woman inventor by variable, which we consider the nature of innovation, and by technological field. It summarizes what was previously said.

7.3.3 *Hypothesis Research and Model Specification*

Considering the historical marginalization of women in S&T activities, we expect that women possess potential abilities for invention-innovation and that their inclusion in the sphere, in co-participation with men, will positively affect the

TABLE 7.2 *Women's participation according to innovation nature variables*

		Mexico	Brazil	India
TechField		%	%	%
	Chemical	26	29	42
	Computer and communication	3	4	8
	Drugs and medicals	31	37	40
	Electrical and electronic	3	2	2
	Mechanical	2	4	3
	Others	34	24	6
	Total	100	100	100
Ȧ		%	%	%
	Chemical	51	28	4
	Computer and communication	1	2	9
	Drugs and medicals	8	46	75
	Electrical and electronic	2	2	2
	Mechanical	0	5	2
	Others	38	17	8
		100	100	100
ValuePat		%	%	%
	Chemical	34	29	28
	Computer and communication	0	5	3
	Drugs and medicals	18	45	57
	Electrical and electronic	1	0	2
	Mechanical	0	2	3
	Others	47	18	7
		100	100	100
TechInnScope		%	%	%
	Chemical	38	29	42
	Computer and communication	3	4	7
	Drugs and medicals	28	39	41
	Electrical and electronic	2	3	1
	Mechanical	0	6	3
	Others	29	19	5
	Total	100	100	100
AssigPat		%	%	%
	Individual	2	1	1
	Institution	54	26	65
	Firm	44	73	34
	Total	100	100	100
MobInv		%	%	%
	1	93	90	99
	More than 1	7	10	1
	Total	100	100	100

		Mexico	*Brazil*	*India*
SizeRT		Average	Average	Average
	Chemical	5	7	9
	Computer and communication	2	6	5
	Drugs and medicals	5	9	9
	Electrical and electronic	1	4	1
	Mechanical	3	6	6
	Others	4	7	10
	Total average	3	7	7
Women by team participation		%	%	%
	Chemical	50	45	35
	Computer and communication	75	43	47
	Drugs and medicals	67	50	40
	Electrical and electronic	100	59	56
	Mechanical	66	49	37
	Others	60	64	36
	Total average	70	52	42

Source: Authors' own estimation, based on USPTO data.

creation of new processes and technological products. The factors associated with innovation that especially affect this propensity are (1) the stock of previous knowledge, (2) the type of patent assignee, (3) the technological field of the patent, (4) the invention scope of each patent, (5) international inventor mobility, and (6) patent value. Therefore, we propose a regression model, which is estimated for each woman inventor in Mexico, Brazil, and India and is specified in the following equation:

$$Wm_jPropInv_{ij} = \dot{A}, SizeRT, AssigPat, TechField, TechInnScope, ScTech\_links, MobInv, ValuePat$$

Where the dependent variable:

$$Wm_jPropInv_{ij} = \text{women's propensity to invent. It has been estimated as follows:}$$

$$Wm_jPropInv_{ij} = \text{number of women inventor patents/number of patents where there is at least one woman/total of patents granted by the USPTO to Mexican, Brazilian, or Indian holders.}$$

According to this estimate, a reduced $Wm_jPropInv_{ij}$ is shown in the three countries (Table 7.3). Compared with Mexico, India and Brazil are relatively higher.

TABLE 7.3 *Women's propensity to invent, by country*

		Mexico	Brazil	India
$Wm_jPropInv_{ij}$		Average	Average	Average
	Chemical	0.19	0.26	0.21
	Computer and communication	0.08	0.22	0.23
	Drugs and medicals	0.22	0.4	0.26
	Electrical and electronic	0.08	0.23	0.12
	Mechanical	0.16	0.24	0.21
	Others	0.14	0.24	0.21
	Total average	0.15	0.27	0.21

Source: Authors' own estimation, based on USPTO data.

They are similar in all technological fields – except that India is higher in the electrical and electronics sector while Brazil is higher in the pharmaceutical and medical sectors. Mexico is notably lower in almost all sectors, although less so in the pharmaceutical, medical, and chemical sectors.

The independent variables are taken from USPTO patent information. They characterize the inventions. Based on the literature reviewed, these variables allow us to assume how each invention influences $Wm_jPropInv_{ij}$ (Table 7.4).

7.3.4 *Analysis of Outcomes*

According to the results of each model, we have partially verified our hypothesis, with a different pattern in each of the three countries. The independent variables – the stock of prior knowledge, the size of inventor teams, the type of patent holder, technological field, and presence of foreign influence – impact positively on women's propensity to invent ($Wm_jPropInv_{ij}$) in a differentiated manner in each country. In some cases, they did not. These results are detailed subsequently and shown in Table 7.5.

Concerning the stock of previous knowledge, $\dot{A}$ has been statistically significant only in Mexico. According to our elasticity estimation (0.012), if the number of *BwPatCit* increases by 10 percent, the propensity for women to invent grows by 0.12 percent. In the tradition of Griliches (1990), several authors have used *BwPatCit* to study knowledge flows and *FwPatCit* to analyze the invention value (Gay et al., 2008; Lerner and Seru, 2017, among others). An essential aspect to consider, however, is when it is used as a proxy value for knowledge links among inventors to explore the nature of knowledge flows and the factors affecting these flows (Jaffe and Rassenfosse, 2017). In this research, we consider *BwPatCit* as the stock of previous knowledge upon which inventors develop their new ideas. As references to prior technology that has been used or on which current patents build (Hall, 2005), *BwPatCit* involves an R&D effort, which, when increased, makes it possible to include women in inventive activities. The fact that it has positively impacted

TABLE 7.4 *Independent variables and hypothesis*

Variable	Variable proxy	It is expected that
$\dot{A}$	Stock of previous knowledge. Number of *BwPatCit* as a proxy variable	. . . the higher the *BwPatCit*, which reflects increased R&D expenditure, the higher is the propensity of women to become inventors (Aldieri et al., 2019; Duguet and MacGarvie, 2005; Guzmán et al., 2020; Hall, 2005; Jaffe et al., 1993)
SizeRT	Size of research teams. Number of inventors involved in the generation of the patent	. . . a larger research team, by incorporating women, increases the diversity of new technological ideas and therefore the propensity of women to become inventors (Bianco and Venezia, 2019; Breitzman and Thomas, 2015)
AssigPat	Patent assignee. 1 = Firm; 2 = Institution; 3 = Individual; 4 = Co-patent firms; 5 = Co-patent firm-institution	. . . the higher number of firms patents a greater probability to scale at the industrial level, to eventually commercialize, and for government and university innovation efforts to crystallize in patents, and therefore contributed to a higher propensity of women to become inventors (Chatterjee and Ramu, 2017; Giuri et al., 2020; Meng, 2018; Murray, 2004; Whittington and Smith-Doerr, 2008; Woolley, 2019)
TechField	Technological field of the patent. 1 = Chemical; 2 = Computer and communication; 3 = Drugs and medical; 4 = Electrical and electronic; 5 = Mechanical and 6 = Others	. . . the higher distribution of women inventors by technological fields will be differentiated among countries according to the importance of those fields and the advances in science and technology in each case (Cook and Kongcharoen, 2010; Hunt et al., 2012; Kahler, 2012; Maldonado Carbajal et al., 2015; Martínez et al., 2016)
TechInnScope	Invention scope of each patent. Number of claims as the proxy variable	. . . the higher the number of claims, the higher is the propensity of women to become inventors (Jensen et al., 2018)

(*continued*)

TABLE 7.4 (*continued*)

Variable	Variable proxy	It is expected that
MobIn	International inventor mobility. Dummy variable, where 0 = inventors of the same nationality; 1 = foreign inventors	. . . the higher mobility favors the spillover of codified and tacit knowledge, and therefore contributes to as higher propensity of women to become inventors (Bianco and Venezia, 2019)
ValuePat	Value of the patent. This variable specifies the number of patent citations made in successive patents. A proxy variable is the number of *FwPatCit* obtained	. . . the larger the *FwPatCit*, which suggests a wider diffusion of new patents and increased importance of new knowledge, the higher is the propensity of women to become inventors (Bransteter, 2003; Branstetter and Ogura, 2005; Breschi et al., 2005)

Source: Authors' own elaboration, based on USPTO data.

TABLE 7.5 *Empirical model outcomes: Factors affecting the propensity of women to invent*

Variable	Mexico	Brazil	India
$\dot{A}$	0.0004**	0	
SizeRT	0.020***	0.051***	0
AssigPat			
Institution	0.020***		
Firm	0.081***	0.006	0.0442***
Individual		0.104**	
TechField			
Computer and communication;	-0.004	-0.023	0.03
Drugs and medicals	-0.007	0.055**	0.024
Electrical and electronic	-0.035	0.157***	0.008
Mechanical	0.039**	0.017	-0.023
Others	-0.031	0.130***	0.019
TechInnScope		0	0.0002***
MobInv	0.140***	-0.083	0.017
ValuePat	0	0	0.045
_cons	0.046	-0.073	-0.05
	0.236	0.163	0.477
N	61	299	728
R^2	0.67	0.76	0.68
F	6.89	9.14	3.06

Note: $p < 0.01^{***}$ $p < 0.05^{**}$ $p < 0.010^{*}$

Source: Authors' own estimation based on model proposed.

$WmjPropInv_{ij}$ is a reminder of the need to disclose patents, just as they are meant to be.

Relative to *SizeRT*, there is a positive influence in Mexico and Brazil. When the research team is 10 percent bigger, $Wm_jPropInv_{ij}$ increases 4.9 percent (Mexico) and 10.9 percent (Brazil). Bianco and Venezia (2019: 14) state that "the presence of more members on a team certainly brings more diverse and variegated knowledge and can therefore produce better results."

Contrary to the importance of institution holders in Mexico and India, firms have a positive influence on $Wm_jPropInv_{ij}$ in both countries (0.08 and 0.04, respectively). Institutions have been positively significant for Mexico as well, but only individual assignees are positively significant in Brazil. The reason for a positive effect is understandable considering the importance of public R&D expenditure in Mexico and India, even though such expenditure remains marginal in Mexico. Women academic inventors are key to understanding their involvement in scientific research – and eventually the discovery of new products and processes that could make it to the productive sphere, depending on the degree of links between firms and institutions. According to Murray (2004: 643), "The first element that the firm may leverage is the academic's local laboratory network – a network to current and former students and advisors established by the inventor through his laboratory life."

Although Martínez et al. (2016), in their study of women inventors from 182 countries with PCT patents, do not analyze the causal effects of ownership on $Wm_jPropInv_{ij}$, they have identified that an average of 48 percent of women participate in the academic sector, while only 28 percent are in the business sector. Their findings coincide with previous studies (Whittington and Smith-Doerr, 2008). It is pointed out that China, Brazil, and Spain have higher percentages of PCT patent applications with women inventors in the academic sector (around two-thirds). In particular, Mexico has 69 percent participation in the academic sector and 26 percent in firms (Martínez et al., 2016). Unlike India, Mexico has few entrepreneurial businesspeople, and technological dependence dominates every sector. Women in India have increased their presence in business activities, and they discuss the challenges that they have to face to reduce inequalities (Chatterjee and Ramu, 2017). In Brazil, however, the increase in R&D efforts surpasses the inventive activity of institutions toward companies (Maldonado Carbajal et al., 2015).

Regarding the technological field, the mechanical sector is statistically significant for Mexico, while the fields of pharmaceutical and medical, electrical and electronic, and others are statistically significant for Brazil. In India, however, not a single field has an impact on $Wm_jPropInv_{ij}$. We have confirmed the results of previous research on the positive influence of the pharmaceutical and medical sector in Mexico and Brazil, but we are now modeling each woman inventor and not each patent (Guzmán and Orozco, 2011; Maldonado Carbajal et al., 2015). The current study is also connected to the importance achieved by female graduates and researchers in medicine and related disciplines. Our findings coincide with the study by Cook and Kongcharoen (2010), where advancement by women in life sciences places them in the realms of innovation and marketing. The involvement of women inventors in different technological fields is one of the topics that have been addressed more in studies, especially with a focus on identification. Some of these studies find that technological fields differ across countries (Martínez et al., 2016) and are probably associated with the country's technological specialization, as in certain Latin American countries where chemistry and metallurgy are the main sectors (Sifontes Fernandez and Morales Valera, 2014). Few studies have thus far analyzed the impact of factors relating to the nature of innovation on the propensity of women to invent, let alone provide analysis based on a micro-level model that considers each woman inventor. Hunt et al. (2012) find that to close the gender gaps in patenting, it is essential for the participation of women in physics and engineering to grow. That could increase the GDP by 2.7 percent if we keep in mind GDP growth among countries in the long run and that patents are found among explanatory variables of the country.

In economic literature, mobility has been detected as a factor favorably affecting innovation. In Mexico, we find that the presence of foreign inventors has a positive influence on research teams; when there is a 10 percent increase in foreign inventors, $Wm_jPropInv_{ij}$ grows by 0.5 percent. The results reinforce the finding of Bianco and Venezia (2019: 14) that "the presence of external inventors broadens the scope of the patent, [and] longer working experience of inventors affects technological and market value, whereas inventors who have already patented in the past develop new product architectures, with broader scope and higher scientific value." The results also confirm consistency with contributions by previous authors, underscoring that openness and experience positively influence the innovative capabilities of teams. In India, female researcher mobility tends to occur outwardly, and knowledge spillovers take place in research centers with other colleagues. The need for such mobility finally finds channels of communication in India.

We cannot, however, confirm the influence of patent value for any country. The fact that the countries studied are emerging may mean their innovations are essentially incremental as they follow leading countries, so they are not as well recognized as industrialized countries yet. Patent value is still low, but it might be interesting to study Indian, Brazilian, and Mexican inventors collaborating on patents in developed countries and identify the contributions of women therein. New technology patented by mixed teams is often cited in the following patents. This suggests that diversity of ideas could lead to the development of patents that are more useful and consequently more successful (Hunt et al., 2012).

CONCLUSION AND RECOMMENDED POLICIES

Some countries have achieved gender parity in scientific training or are close to doing so. For others, the gap remains wide. Among emerging countries, Brazil, India, and Mexico have made progress in overcoming gender disparities in education, with differences in specializations. Brazil and India stood out for striving to increase R&D spending, thereby helping to incorporate more researchers – among them women – while expanding innovative domestic capacities. Such development is especially notable in India, whose patents are in high technology (Mani, 2015).

Analyzing each country separately, we observed different patterns for women inventors in the three countries. We also found that some policies could be furthered through our model's estimations.

The evidence of factors in Mexico that positively affect $Wm_jPropInv_{ij}$ indicates that policies must be oriented toward fostering diffusion of the technological knowledge codified in patent documents. As team inventors increase the number of *BwPatCit*, the stock of previous knowledge ($\dot{A}$) and the propensity of women to join as inventors could go up.[10] Another recommendation is to increase inventor team size and include more women inventors. Indeed, an increase in innovation in firms and institutions favors $Wm_jPropInv_{ij}$. As Mexico has specialized in the mechanical sector, one recommendation is to support development and innovation in this area, incorporating more women inventors and thus diminishing gender inequalities. That, nevertheless, does not eliminate the importance of other fields, especially those with greater knowledge intensity. Finally, the presence of foreign researchers in the inventor teams could be suggested as a way of having positive effects on increasing $Wm_jPropInv_{ij}$.

In Brazil, the results suggest a focus on the following policies: (1) increasing the number of researchers on teams, encouraging women to join; (2) further stimulating individual innovation (surprisingly for this Latin American country); and (3) coinciding with Brazil's specialization, strengthening patented innovation in the pharmaceutical and medical, electrical and electronic, and sectors in the "others" category.

Finally, in India, the right policies could be directed to improve innovative firms, and therefore patents, and incorporate more women in R&D activities – especially in the pharmaceutical and medical sector, the electrical and electronic sector, and sectors in the "others" category. Encouraging an increase in claims per patent (*TechInnScope*), which is apparently associated with seeking a broader range of claims, requires not only the talents of men but also women. This requirement differs from the idea that each sex has different creative abilities neurologically. While India is the most backward country in terms of the various aspects of the GII, the country has registered steps forward that make greater inventive activity possible for women and are thus reflected in the dynamism of patent growth, especially those

[10] The fact that $\dot{A}$ positively impacts the propensity to innovate leaves the lesson about the externalities of technological knowledge. In this sense, patent disclosure should be leveraged with increasing R&D efforts. That is, deepening the frontier of patent knowledge in the required scientific field, incorporating more female researchers, and investing in fully equipped research laboratories will contribute to the propensity of women to become inventors.

that are more technologically intense. The potential growth and well-being of nations in the world will have to be supported by the merging of cognitive skills and innovation of women and men.

This empirical study focused on a model where independent variables correspond to patent data that characterize innovation in each USPTO patent. However, the results could be strengthened by incorporating individual information from women inventors on their level of education and age, among other characteristics. In future research, we can go deeper with new model proposals.

ANNEX

Multicollinearity, Reset, and Normal Test

	VIF	Reset	Normal
Mexico	6.73	0.00	0.00
Brazil	1.25	0.00	0.00
India	1.09	0.00	0.00

REFERENCES

Agência Brasil. 2018. "Brazilian Female Scientists Awarded by UNESCO." *Agência Brasil*, August 14. https://agenciabrasil.ebc.com.br/en/geral/noticia/2018–08/brazilian-female-scientists-awarded-unesco.

Aldieri, Luigi, Fabio Carlucci, Concetto Paolo Vinci, and Tan Yigitcanlar. 2019. "Environmental Innovation, Knowledge Spillovers and Policy Implications: A Systematic Review of the Economic Effects Literature." *Journal of Cleaner Production* 239: 118051.

Asgeirsdottir, Berglind. 2006. "Women in Scientific Careers: Unleashing the Potential." OECD–French Research Ministry Workshop, Paris.

Ashcraft, Catherine, and Anthony Breitzman. 2012. "Who Invents IT? Women's Participation in Information Technology Patenting." National Center for Women and Information Technology. www.researchgate.net/publication/297918434.

Azoulay, Pierre, Waverly Ding, and Toby Stuart. 2007. "The Determinants of Faculty Patenting Behavior: Demographics or Opportunities?" *Journal of Economic Behavior and Organization* 63(4): 599–623.

Bianco, Federica, and Marica Venezia. 2019. "Features of R&D Teams and Innovation Performances of Sustainable Firms: Evidence from the 'Sustainability Pioneers' in the IT Hardware Industry." *Sustainable* 11(17): 1–19.

Blashfield, Jean F. 1996. *Women Inventors*. Minneapolis, MN: Capstone Press.

Branstetter, Lee. 2003. "Exploring the Link between Academic Science and Industrial Innovation." Columbia Business School Discussion Paper No. 29.

Branstetter, Lee, and Yoshiaki Ogura. 2005. "Is Academic Science Driving a Surge in Industrial Innovation? Evidence from Patent Citations." National Bureau of Economic Research Working Paper No. 11561.

Braun, Sandra. 2007. *Incredible Women Inventors*. Toronto: Second Story Press.

Breitzman, Anthony, and Patrick Thomas. 2015. "The Emerging Clusters Model: A Tool for Identifying Emerging Technologies across Multiple Patent Systems." *Research Policy* 44 (1): 192–205.

Breschi, Stefano, Francesco Lissoni, and Fabio Montobbio. 2005. "From Publishing to Patenting: Do Productive Scientists Turn into Academic Inventors?" *Revue d'Economie Industrielle* 110: 75–102.

Chatterjee, Chirantan, and Swapnika Ramu. 2017. "Gender and Its Rising Role in Modern Indian Innovation and Entrepreneurship." *IIMB Management Review* 30(1): 62–72.

Cook, Lisa D., and Chaleampong Kongcharoen. 2010. "The Idea Gap in Pink and Black." National Bureau of Economic Research Working Paper No. 16331.

Currie, Stephen. 2001. *Women Inventors*. San Diego, CA: Lucent Books.

Elsevier Research Intelligence. 2017. Gender in the Global Research Landscape: Analysis of Research Performance through a Gender Lens across 20 Years, 12 Geographies, and 27 Subject Areas. www.elsevier.com/connect/elseviers-reports-on-gender-in-research.

European Commission. 2008. *Evaluation on Policy: Promotion of Women Innovators and Entrepreneurship*. Directorate-General for Enterprise and Industry. https://op.europa.eu/en/publication-detail/-/publication/ec383efd-99d5-4652-964b-8919b7459c89.

van den Eynde, Ángeles. 1994. "Género y ciencia, ¿términos contradictorios? Un análisis sobre la contribución de las mujeres al desarrollo científico." *Revista Iberoamericana de Educación* 6: 79–101.

Duguet, Emmanuel, and Megan MacGarvie. 2005. "How Well Do Patent Citations Measure Flows of Technology? Evidence from French Innovation Surveys." *Economics of Innovation and New Technology* 14(5): 375–393.

Frietsch, Ranier, Inna Haller, Melanie Funken-Vrohlings, and Hariolf Grupp. 2009. "Gender-Specific Patterns in Patenting and Publishing." *Research Policy* 38(4): 590–599.

Gay, Claudine, William Latham, and Christian Le Bas. 2008. "Collective Knowledge, Prolific Inventors and the Value of Inventions: An Empirical Study of French, German and British Patents in the US, 1975–1999." *Economics of Innovation and New Technology* 17(1–2): 5–22.

Giuri, Paola, Rosa Grimaldi, Anna Kochenkova, Federico Munari, and Laura Toschi. 2020. "The Effects of University-Level Policies on Women's Participation in Academic Patenting in Italy." *Journal of Technology Transfer* 45: 122–150.

Green, Josie. 2019. "Who Invented the Dishwasher, Windshield Wiper, Caller ID? Women Created These 50 Inventions." *USA Today*, March 16, 2019. www.usatoday.com/story/money/2019/03/16/inventions-you-have-women-inventors-thank-these-50-things/39158677/.

Griliches, Zvi. 1990. "Patent Statistics as Economic Indicators: A Survey." *Journal of Economic Literature* 28(4): 1661–1707.

Guzmán, Alenka, Flor Brown, and Edgar Acatitla. 2020. "Innovative Factors Affecting Diffusion of the New Nanotechnology Paradigm, 1983–2013." *Seoul Journal of Economics* 34(3): 329–364.

Guzmán, Alenka, and M.R. Orozco. 2011. "Dinámica y naturaleza de la actividad inventiva de las mujeres en México, 1980–2010. Un estudio de patentes." In *Crecimiento y Desarrollo Económico*, edited by Ignacio Perrotini-Hernández, 127–153. Puebla: Benemérita Universidad de Puebla.

Hall, Bronwyn H. 2005. "Innovation and Diffusion." In *The Oxford Handbook of Innovation*, edited by Jan Fagerberg and David C. Mowery, 459–484. Oxford: Oxford University Press.

Huang, Junming, Alexander J. Gates, Roberta Sinatra, and Albert-László Barabási. 2020. "Historical Comparison of Gender Inequality in Scientific Careers across Countries and Disciplines." *PNAS* 117(9): 4609–4616.

Hunt, Jennifer, Jean-Philippe Garant, Hannah Herman, and David J. Munroe. 2012. "Why Don't Women Patent?" National Bureau of Economic Research Working Paper No. 17888. www.nber.org/papers/w17888.

Huyer, Sophia. 2015. "Is the Gender Gap Narrowing in Science and Engineering?" In *UNESCO Science Report: Towards 2030*, 85–103. Paris: UNESCO Publishing. https://unesdoc.unesco.org/ark:/48223/pf0000235406.

Jaffe, Adam B., and Gaétan de Rassenfosse. 2017. "Patent Citation Data in Social Science Research: Overview and Best Practices." *Journal of the Association for Information Science and Technology* 68(6): 1360–1374.

Jaffe, Adam, Manuel Trajtenberg, and Rebecca Henderson. 1993. "Geographic Localization of Knowledge Spillovers as Evidenced by Patent Citations." *Quarterly Journal of Economics* 79(3): 577–598.

Jensen, Kyle, Balázs Kovács, and Olav Sorenson. 2018. "Gender Differences in Obtaining and Maintaining Patent Rights." *Nature Biotechnology* 36(4): 307–309.

Jung, Taehyun, and Olof Ejermo. 2014. "Demographic Patterns and Trends in Patenting: Gender, Age, and Education of Inventors." *Technological Forecasting and Social Change* 86: 110–124.

Kahler, Annette I. 2012. "Examining Exclusion in Woman Inventor Patenting: A Comparison of Educational Trends and Patent Data in the Era of Computer Engineer Barbie." *American University Journal of Gender, Social Policy and the Law* 19(3): 773–798.

Karnes, Frances A., and Suzanne M. Bean. 1995. *Girls & Young Women Inventing: Twenty True Stories about Inventors Plus How You Can Be One Yourself.* Minneapolis, MN: Free Spirit Publishers.

Krishna, Swapna. 2022. "These Trailblazing Indian Women Are Shaking Up Science and Technology." *Now*, February 16. https://now.northropgrumman.com/these-trailblazing-indian-women-are-shaking-up-science-and-technology/.

Kuschel, Katherina, Kerstin Ettl, Cristina Díaz-Garcia, and Gry Agnete Alsos. 2020. "Stemming the Gender Gap in STEM Entrepreneurship – Insights into Women's Entrepreneurship in Science, Technology, Engineering and Mathematics." *International Entrepreneurship and Management Journal* 16: 1–15.

Lax-Martínez, Gema, Julio Raffo, and Kaori Saito. 2016. "Identifying the Gender of PCT Inventors." World Intellectual Property Organization Economic Research Working Paper No. 33. www.wipo.int/publications/en/details.jsp?id=4125.

Lerner, Josh, and Amit Seru. 2017. "The Use and Misuse of Patent Data: Issues for Corporate Finance and Beyond." National Bureau of Economic Research Working Paper No. 24053.

Lissoni, Francesco, Fabio Montobbio, and Lorenzo Zirulia. 2013. "Inventorship and Authorship as Attribution Rights: An Enquiry into the Economics of Scientific Credit." *Journal of Economic Behavior and Organization* 95: 49–69.

Maldonado Carbajal, Karina, Alenka Guzmán Chávez, and Felipe de Jesús Peredo. 2015. "La actividad inventiva de las mujeres en Brasil, 1997–2013." *Economía: teoría y práctica, Especial* 3: 53–81. https://doi.org/10.24275/ETYPUAM/NE/E032015/Maldonado.

Mani, Sunil. 2015. "India." In *UNESCO Science Report: Towards 2030*, 598–619. Paris: UNESCO Publishing.

Meng, Yu. 2018. "Gender Distinctions in Patenting: Does Nanotechnology Make a Difference?" *Scientometrics* 114(3): 971–992.

Milli, Jessica, Barbara Gault, Emma Williams-Baron, Jenny Xia, and Meika Berlan. 2016. "The Gender Patenting Gap." Institute for Women's Policy Research Briefing Paper No. C441.

Morales Otal, Adriana, Olayo Lortia Jesús, Velázquez Moctezuma Javier, and Ferreira Nuño Armando. 2009. "Brain Sexual Differentiation and the Biological Basis of the Sexual Orientation." In *Advances in Selected Topics in Endocrinology*, edited by Ignacio Camacho Arroyo, 73–92. Iztapalapa: Universidad Autónoma Metropolitana.

Murray, Fiona. 2004. "The Role of Academic Inventors in Entrepreneurial Firms: Sharing the Laboratory Life." *Research Policy* 33(4): 643–659.

Oxford Reference. n.d. "Stylized Facts." www.oxfordreference.com/view/10.1093/oi/authority.20110810105949304.

Ramesh, Sandhya. 2020. "These Are the 11 Indian Women Scientists the New STEM Chairs Are Named After." *The Print*, March 2. https://theprint.in/science/these-are-the-11-indian-women-scientists-the-new-stem-chairs-are-named-after/374077/.

Sifontes, Domingo, and Rosa Morales. 2020. "Gender Differences and Patenting in Latin America: Understanding Female Participation in Commercial Science." *Scientometrics* 124: 2009–2036.

Sifontes Fernandez, Domingo, and Rosa Maria Morales Valera. 2014. "La Actividad Innovadora por Género en América Latina: Un Estudio de Patentes." *Revista Brasiliera de Inovação* 13(1): 163–186.

Stephan, Paula E., Shiferaw Gurmu, Albert J. Sumell, and Grant Black. 2007. "Who's Patenting in the University? Evidence from the Survey of Doctorate Recipients." *Economics of Innovation and New Technology* 16(2): 71–99.

UK Intellectual Property Office (UKIPO). 2016. *Gender Profiles in Worldwide Patenting: An Analysis of Female Inventorship*. www.gov.uk/government/publications/gender-profiles-in-worldwide-patenting-an-analysis-of-female-inventorship.

U.N. Development Programme (UNDP). n.d.-a. "Gender Development Index (GDI)." https://hdr.undp.org/gender-development-index#/indicies/GDI.

n.d.-b. "Gender Inequality Index (GII)." https://hdr.undp.org/data-center/thematic-composite-indices/gender-inequality-index#/indicies/GII.

n.d.-c. "Human Development Reports." https://hdr.undp.org/data-center/specific-country-data.

UNESCO. 2016. "Measuring Gender Equality in Science and Engineering: The SAGA Science, Technology and Innovation Gender Objectives List (STI GOL)." UNESCO SAGA Working Paper No. 1. http://uis.unesco.org/sites/default/files/documents/saga-sti-objectives-list-wp1–2016-en.pdf.

2018. "Telling SAGA: Improving Measurement and Policies for Gender Equality in Science, Technology and Innovation." UNESCO SAGA Working Paper No. 5. https://unesdoc.unesco.org/ark:/48223/pf0000266102.

n.d. "Distribution of Tertiary Graduates by Field of Study Years Selected." http://data.uis.unesco.org/index.aspx?queryid=3830.

U.S. Patent and Trademark Office (USPTO). 2020. *Progress and Potential 2020 Update on U.S. Women Inventor-Patentees*. Washington, DC: U.S. Patent and Trademark Office.

Whittington, Kjersten Bunker, and Laurel Smith-Doerr. 2008. "Women Inventors in Context: Disparities in Patenting across Academia and Industry." *Gender and Society* 22(2): 194–218.

Woolley, Jennifer L. 2019. "Gender, Education, and Occupation: How Founder Experiences Influence Firm Outcomes." *Academy of Management Discoveries* 5(3): 266–290.

APPENDIX A

TABLE 7A.1 *Women inventors from developed countries and scientific women in Brazil, India, and Mexico*

Woman inventor from developed countries	Invention	Year	Acknowledged scientific woman and woman inventor from . . .	Scientific field of contribution
Tabitha Babbitt	Circular saw	1812	**Brazil**	
Jeanne Villepreux-Power	Glass aquarium	1832		
Nancy Johnson	Ice cream maker	1843	Ethel Wilheim, Angélica Viera	Therapies for the treatment of respiratory conditions
Ada Lovelace	Computer algorithm	1843		
Sarah Mather	Submarine lamp and telescope	1845	Fernanda Cruz	Therapies for the treatment of respiratory conditions
Margaret Knight	Paper-bag-making machine	1871		
Josephine Cochran	Dishwasher	1872	Sabrina Lisboa	Posttrauma stress disorder and how it affects the brain
Ellen Fitz	Globes	1875		
Mary Walton	Locomotive chimney	1879	Nathalia Bezerra	Method to increase the durability of cement
Adeline D. T. Whitney	Alphabet blocks (to reduce train noise)	1882	Chu Ming Silveira	Designs for telephone booths
Maria Beasley	Life raft	1882	**India**	
Josephine Cochran	Mechanical dishwasher	1886		
Anna Connelly	Fire escape	1887	Asima Chatterjee	Chemistry
Sarah Boone	Ironing board	1892	Darsha Ranganathan	Biochemistry
Margaret A. Wilcox	Car heater	1893	Kamal Ranadive	Pathology
Letitia Geer	Medical syringe	1899	Kadambini Ganguly	Physics
Florence Parpart	Street sweeper	1900	Rajeshwari Chatterjee	Physics
Mary Anderson	Windshield wiper	1903	Raman Parimala	Mathematics
Hedy Lamarr	Wireless transmission technology	1941	Anna Mani	Meteorology
Maria Telkes	Thermoelectric power generator	1947	Muthayya Vanitha	Mission Chandrayaan-2
Maria Telkes	Solar heating system; thermoelectric refrigerator	1953	Gagandeep Kang	Medicine (rotavirus and COVID-19 vaccines)
			Kamakshi Sivaramakrishnan	Communication chip used on board the NASA's New Horizons spacecraft
Grace Murray Hopper	Computer software	1952		
Erna Schneider	Automated telephone switching system	1954	Pratibha Gai	Atomic-resolution environmental transmission electron microscope

Edith Flanigen	Oil refining	1956	Sylvia Ratsanamy	Distributed hash table
Rachel Fuller Brown and Elizabeth Lee Hazen	Antifungal antibiotics	1957	**Mexico**	
Gertrude Belle Elion	Immunosuppressive drug	1957	Esther Orozco	Biologist, specialized in amoebas and genetics
Evelyn Berezin	Word processor	1971	Alejandra Bravo	Bacterial toxin that acts as a potent insecticide
Olga Gonzalez-Sanabria	Space station batteries	1980	Victoria Chagoya	Biochemistry, cirrhosis and liver remodeling, structural and functional remodeling of the heart after experimental infarction or heart failure
Patricia Bath	Laser cataract surgery	1986		
Ann Tsukamoto	Stem cell isolation	1991		
			Isaura Meza	Biologist, structure and characterization of cytoskeleton protein genes in eukaryotic models
			Tessy López	Chemistry, catalytic nanomedicine treatment of cancer, epilepsy, and chronic lesions

Sources: Green (2019); Krishna (2022).

TABLE 7A.2 *Review of women inventors*

Authors	Data	Aim	Findings
Ashcraft and Breitzman (2012)	USPTO patents granted in information and communication technologies (ICT), 1985–2010	To examine the growth rate of women's patent applications in the ICT field	Thirteen percent of the patents during 1985–2005 have at least 1 woman inventor. The women's growth rate has increased (1980s: 2 percent; 2005: 6 percent, and 2010: 8 percent). It is more dynamic than in total patents.
Bianco and Venezia (2019)	Patents filed in IT hardware companies, 2000–2005 (PATSAT)	To characterize the R&D teams of sustainable firms (SF) and analyze how they perform in terms of patent quality	SF R&D teams feature a higher degree of mobility but less experience than those from non-SF. A less receptive attitude toward open innovation is observed. Even if SF develop fewer patents, the quality is higher, and the R&D size is associated with inventors who have published on Scopus.
Cook and Kongcharoen (2010)	USPTO patents, 1975–2008. U.S. Census Bureau's list common names by race and commercial technology	To identify ethnically heterogeneous women inventors; to analyze patenting and marketing patterns among women; to analyze recent African American patenting and patent-related marketing behavior	Gender and racial differences in commercial activity related to invention are less than previously thought. Advanced training in engineering is correlated with better marketing outputs for African American women than for U.S. inventors as a whole, for whom advancing in life sciences is more important.
Jung and Ejermo (2014)	Patent EPO 1993–1997; surveys from Japanese and U.S. studies (RIETI and Georgia Tech)	To examine gender, age, and education of Swedish inventors	The gender gap is closing but at a slower pace than in other areas of society. Level of education shows different patterns across different technologies. Inventor age has decreased since the late 1990s. There are three mechanisms for improving equality: (i) dynamic knowledge renewal, (ii) new technological opportunities, and (iii) a generally increased propensity to patent.

Giuri et al. (2020)	2,538 patents EPO application, 1996–2007, with Italian academic inventors. Own identification of the inventors' gender	To analyze if university patent transfer linkages with science and technology parks are positively associated with women's involvement in academic patenting	University policies play a positive role in addressing the gender gap in technology transfer activities.
Guzmán and Orozco (2011)	USPTO patents granted to Mexican assignees, 1980–2010	To analyze the evolution and nature of Mexican patents with at least one woman inventor; to analyze the association between gender variable and innovation-related variables	Women participation is still low, but growth tendency is increasing. Inventor teams are small. There is more woman inventor participation in drugs and medical products and chemical. Firm patent assignees with women inventors are higher. Women's involvement in patented inventions is associated with technological field and inventor team size.
Hunt et al. (2012)	U.S. patents commercialized survey with license from National University Graduates in 2003	To find how many women holders commercialize their patents	Commercialized patent holders account for only 5.5 percent. Only 7 percent of the gender gap is explained by a lower probability of women having a degree in science or engineering. In order to close gender gaps, the incorporation of women in STEM should be promoted at all levels of schooling.
Jensen et al. (2018)	2.7 million USPTO utility patent applications from 2001 to 2014	To find out, through the examination of individual U.S. utility patent applications prosecution process, how women are less favorable than men, in terms of patents granted, claims, and citations	Women inventors are belittled in this system, and they have fewer opportunities than men in the process of obtaining and maintaining patents and also to be cited. So, changes are needed to diminish the inequalities in the patent system.
Kahler (2012)	U.S. Statistics, Science and Engineering Degrees, 1996–2006 (National Science Foundation). USPTO patents assigned in electrical, mechanical, and chemical classifications	To set the stage for more meaningful and empirically based participation of women in IP and invention	Women are catching up in S&T fields and have a tendency toward becoming part of the inventor community. Patents with women inventors decrease in chemical, sharply rise in electrical, and have modest growth in engineering and computer science.

(*continued*)

TABLE 7A.2 (*continued*)

Authors	Data	Aim	Findings
Kuschel et al. (2020)	Research about (i) women's entrepreneurship and (ii) the gender aspect of STEM fields review	To propose addressing institutional, organizational, and individual factors influencing women's entrepreneurship in STEM, based on contributions of authors; to discuss implications and highlight areas for future research needed in order to close the gender gap in STEM fields	Proposals for future research are needed in the following directions: (i) define and explore the characteristics of women's entrepreneurship within the STEM fields; (ii) examine women in STEM who more often explore entrepreneurship as an option for STEM graduates; (iii) analyze beyond the early recruitment of women to STEM entrepreneurship the correlation between the nature of inventive activities and the (lack of) involvement in STEM entrepreneurship; and (iv) interrogate the gendered nature of entrepreneurial ecosystems, especially on technology entrepreneurial ecosystems.
Maldonado et al. (2015)	USPTO patents granted to Brazilian assignees, 1997–2013	To analyze the evolution and nature of inventive activities of Brazilian women inventors; to estimate, using a multifactorial model, the propensity of women to innovate and the explanatory factors	Dynamic growth of patents with at least one woman is higher than that of all patents. Collaboration of women and men inventors is mainly in chemical, drugs and medical products, and others. The propensity of women to become inventors is associated with R&D expenditure, holder firms, larger inventor team size, and technological and academic link in the patented inventions.
Martínez et al. (2016)	PCT applications, 1995–2015. 6.2 million inventor names for 182 countries to identify the gender	To analyze inventor gender in international patent applications, considering countries, technological fields, and sectors	There is a lack of gender equality in PCT applications; proportion of women inventors is improving over time. Involvement of women inventors differs substantially across countries, technological fields, and sectors.
Meng (2018)	USPTO domestic patents granted in nanotechnology classes 1990–2005	To analyze gender differences in technological productivity in nanotechnology, showing the relationship between gender and time, collaboration, research	The gap to women's disadvantage was smaller in nanotechnology than in all technology fields combined. While the patenting in more than 90 percent of patents across an industry is least likely to be collaborative, nano-patents have more diverse origins (9 percent industry; 21 percent universities, government, public institutions, and cross-sectoral collaboration) and are more likely to be collaborative outcomes (including industry). In nanotech

		preference, and workforce sector	environments, women are more able to get collaborative opportunities and engage in patenting. In order to close gender gaps, the incorporation of women in STEM should be promoted at all levels of schooling. It is also important to promote the participation of women in networks and value their efforts in performance evaluations.
Milli et al. (2016)	USPTO patents and trademarks granted to women entrepreneurs, 1977–2010	To study patents quantitatively and qualitatively with focal groups concerning patent benefits and barriers	Leadership in patents and trademarks increases in the period studied. Patents granted to women rapidly increase. Women have much greater participation in trademark activity than patents. The success of applications by women and men differs by a minimum of 73.4 percent in 1986 and a maximum of 93.6 percent in 2002. To overcome barriers to women inventors and potentially entrepreneurial activities, there should be support for patenting costs, access to start-up capital, or venture capital funding. These findings coincide with the proposals of Hunt et al. (2012).
Sifontes Fernandez and Morales Valera (2014)	USPTO patent applications from Argentina, Brazil, Mexico, Colombia, Cuba, Peru, Chile, and Venezuela, 1990–2006	To classify patents by gender; to analyze gender participation, contribution, and novelty impact across countries, agents, and technological fields	A fifth of inventions involve female contribution. There is greater gender inequality in Peru, Argentina, and Mexico. Chemistry and Metallurgy are the main fields of women inventors' participation.
Sifontes and Morales (2020)	USPTO patents granted to Argentina, Brazil, Costa Rica, Chile, Cuba, Colombia, Mexico, Panama, Peru, Uruguay, and Venezuela, 1976–2011	To explain the rate of female participation in patenting activity	The average involvement of women is 22 percent. External and internal collaboration, the institutional sector of the grantee, and innovations related to life sciences have impacts on the probability of having female participation in patenting in selected Latin American countries. There is likewise influence on women's fertility rate and human development.
USPTO (2020)	USPTO, patent data, 1976–2019	To identify and characterize the nature of female inventive	Patents with at least one woman inventor increased from 7 percent in the 1980s to 20.7 percent in 2016 and 21 percent in 2019. But only

(continued)

TABLE 7A.2 (*continued*)

Authors	Data	Aim	Findings
		activity vis-à-vis that of men inventors	12.1 percent and 12.8 percent of all inventors-patentees who take part in 2016 and 2019, respectively, are women. There is still a gender gap in science and engineering patents, even though women have increased their labor activities in the field. Among the top assignees, higher average women inventor rate is in healthcare products and pharmaceuticals, in a lesser degree in the ICT field, and still lower in electrical and mechanical engineering technologies. Women are increasingly likely to patent on large, gender-mixed inventor teams.
Whittington and Smith-Doerr (2008)	USPTO granted resident patents and data from a sample of academic and industrial life scientists working in United States, 1983–1995	To examine how variation in organizational logic affects sex differences in scientists' commercial productivity, measured by patenting	Women are less likely to patent than men. However, in biotechnology firms – industrial settings characterized by flatter, more flexible, network-based organizational structures – women scientists are more likely to become patent-holding inventors than in more hierarchical organizational settings in industry or academia.

TABLE 7A.3 *Number of researchers by gender and scientific field, 1996–2000 vis-à-vis 2011–2015*

		Brazil				México			
Scientific field	Period	Women	Men	Total	% Women	Women	Men	Total	% Women
Agriculture and Biological Sciences	1996–2000	4,429	6,253	10,682	41.5	1,652	3,014	4,666.00	35.4
	2011–2015	40,433	42,251	82,684	48.9	8,578	13,067	21,645.00	39.6
Arts and Humanities	1996–2000	61	91	152	40.1	50	70	120.00	41.7
	2011–2015	3,195	3,452	6,647	48.1	1,010	1,406	2,416.00	41.8
Biochemistry, Genetics and Molecular Biology	1996–2000	4,696	4,716	9,412	49.9	1,877	2,287	4,164.00	45.1
	2011–2015	34,620	28,462	63,082	54.9	8,690	11,305	19,995.00	43.5
Business, Management and Accounting	1996–2000	30	108	138	21.7	15	60	75.00	20.0
	2011–2015	2,334	4,317	6,651	35.1	413	869	1,282.00	32.2
Chemistry	1996–2000	1,977	2,838	4,815	41.1	328	962	1,290.00	25.4
	2011–2015	14,998	15,972	30,970	48.4	2,451	4,454	6,905.00	35.5
Chemical Engineering	1996–2000	896	1,802	2,698	33.2	821	1,497	2,318.00	35.4
	2011–2015	8,040	9,550	17,590	45.7	4,111	6,690	10,801.00	38.1
Computer Science	1996–2000	509	2,107	2,616	19.5	146	800	946.00	15.4
	2011–2015	5,985	19,896	25,881	23.1	2,333	7,833	10,166.00	22.9
Decision Sciences	1996–2000	51	193	244	20.9	10	78	88.00	11.4
	2011–2015	1,660	4,892	6,552	25.3	168	557	725.00	23.2
Dentistry	1996–2000	307	401	708	43.4	34	76	110.00	30.9
	2011–2015	7,073	5,682	12,755	55.5	199	272	471.00	42.3
Earth and Planetary Sciences	1996–2000	548	1,819	2,367	23.2	4,468	8,763	13,231.00	33.8
	2011–2015	444	1,480	1,924	23.1	1,722	3,902	5,624.00	30.6

(continued)

TABLE 7A.3 (*continued*)

Scientific field	Period	Brazil Women	Brazil Men	Brazil Total	Brazil % Women	México Women	México Men	México Total	México % Women
Economic, Econometrics and Finance	1996–2000	36	125	161	22.4	36	119	155.00	23.2
	2011–2015	800	2,027	2,827	28.3	306	771	1,077.00	28.4
Energy	1996–2000	194	911	1,105	17.6	145	1,037	1,182.00	12.3
	2011–2015	2,684	7,539	10,223	26.3	423	2,453	2,876.00	14.7
Engineering	1996–2001	993	5,176	6,169	16.1	423	2,453	2,876.00	14.7
	2011–2015	11,549	27,783	39,332	29.4	3,638	11,806	15,444.00	23.6
Environmental Science	1996–2000	1,091	2,056	3,147	34.7	819	1,495	2,314.00	35.4
	2011–2015	13,248	17,725	30,973	42.8	4,247	7,550	11,797.00	36.0
Health Professions	1996–2000	135	319	454	29.7	61	135	196.00	31.1
	2011–2015	13,248	17,725	30,973	42.8	301	453	754.00	39.9
Immunology and Microbiology	1996–2000	2,944	2,629	5,573	52.8	996	1,347	2,343.00	42.5
	2011–2015	17,190	12,411	29,601	58.1	3,766	4,552	8,318.00	45.3
Mathematics	1996–2000	437	1,876	2,313	18.9	151	967	1,118.00	13.5
	2011–2015	3,657	11,058	14,715	24.9	1,384	5,614	6,998.00	19.8
Materials Science	1996–2000	924	2,629	3,553	26.0	483	1,603	2,086.00	23.2
	2011–2015	8,291	14,108	22,399	37.0	2,723	6,745	9,468.00	28.8
Medicine	1996–2000	8,617	11,194	19,811	43.5	3,721	5,784	9,505.00	39.1
	2011–2015	80,635	64,902	145,537	55.4	17,282	21,205	38,487.00	44.9
Multidisciplinarity	1996–2000	285	473	758	37.6	61	179	240.00	25.4
	2011–2015	2,681	3,347	6,028	44.5	520	1,039	1,559.00	33.4
Neuroscience	1996–2000	1,171	1,377	2,548	46.0	434	602	1,036.00	41.9
	2011–2015	8,860	7,008	15,868	55.8	1,790	1,376	3,166.00	56.5

Nursing	1996–2000	386	146	532	72.6	60	82	142.00	42.3
	2011–2015	10,556	3,916	14,472	72.9	1,524	1,027	2,551.00	59.7
Pharmacology, Toxicology and Pharmaceuticals	1996–2000	1,751	1,377	3,128	56.0	828	1,037	1,865.00	44.4
	2011–2015	8,860	7,008	15,868	55.8	2,930	3,175	6,105.00	48.0
Physics and Astronomy	1996–2000	1,144	4,171	5,315	21.5	506	2,383	2,889.00	17.5
	2011–2015	8,415	16,942	25,357	33.2	2,727	8,259	10,986.00	24.8
Psychology	1996–2000	221	242	463	47.7	254	236	490.00	51.8
	2011–2015	5,343	2,931	8,274	64.6	1,512	1,424	2,936.00	51.5
Social Sciences	1996–2000	450	658	1,108	40.6	282	468	750.00	37.6
	2011–2015	11,743	12,014	23,757	49.4	2,904	4,077	6,981.00	41.6
Veterinary	1996–2000	768	1,484	2,252	34.1	153	309	462.00	33.1
	2011–2015	11,385	10,908	22,293	51.1	1,072	2,178	3,250.00	33.0

Source: U.N. Development Programme (n.d.-c).

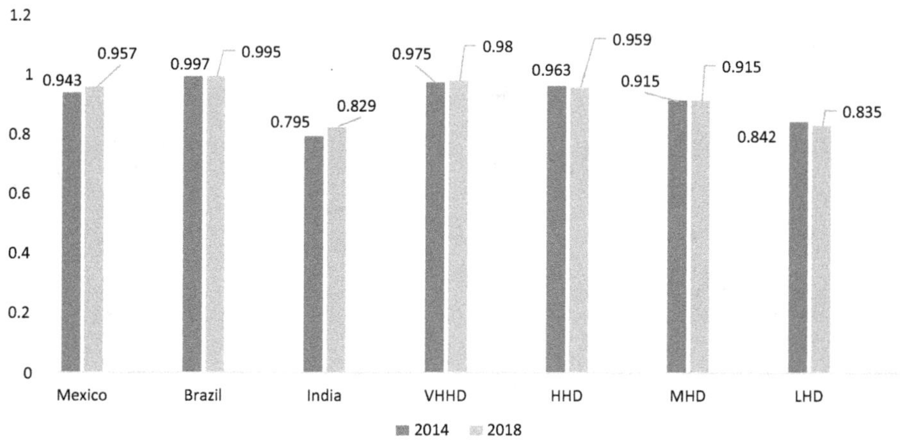

FIGURE 7A.1 GDI of Mexico, Brazil, and China vis-à-vis different country groups*.
*For the four groups of countries, it is GII average years.
Source: U.N. Development Programme (n.d.-c).

8

Unregistered Patents and Gender Equality

A Global Perspective

Miriam Marcowitz-Bitton, Yotam Kaplan, and Emily Michiko Morris[*]

INTRODUCTION

Women are currently underrepresented among patent holders. Studies show that female inventors, in both industry and academia, hold fewer patents, file fewer patent applications, and have their applications more often rejected by the patent office than men do.[1] As a result, female inventors are less likely to receive patent protection for their innovative efforts or to attract the investment necessary to commercialize their inventions, hindering their success in highly technological fields.[2]

Although a variety of measures are needed fully to resolve the patent gender gap, one possible measure that could help women access protections for their innovations is allowing unregistered patent rights in addition to the existing regime of registered patent rights.[3] The proposed unregistered rights would extend only to

* The authors wish to thank Daniel Benoliel, Thomas Cottier, Estelle Derclaye, Rochelle Dreyfuss, John Duffy, Graham Dutfield, Janet Freilich, Ruth Okediji, Dotan Oliar, Julio Raffo, Shlomit Yanisky-Ravid, Peter Yu, and Lior Zemer.

1 *See* Waverly W. Ding, Fiona Murray & Toby E. Stuart, *Gender Differences in Patenting in the Academic Life Sciences*, 313 SCIENCE 665, 665 (2006); Kjersten B. Whittington, *Mothers of Invention? Gender, Motherhood, and New Dimensions of Productivity in the Science Profession*, 38 WORK & OCCUPATIONS 417, 418–20 (2011); Kjersten B. Whittington & Laurel Smith-Doerr, *Women Inventors in Context: Disparities in Patenting across Academia and Industry*, 22 GENDER & SOC'Y 194 (2008); Miriam Marcowitz-Bitton, Yotam Kaplan & Emily Michiko Morris, *Unregistered Patents & Gender Equality*, 43 HARV. J.L. & GENDER 47 (2020).

2 As noted by several scholars, including two of the authors here, gaps in patenting may exist according to race as well as gender. See Miriam Marcowitz-Bitton & Emily Michiko Morris, *The Distributive Effects of IP Registration*, 23 STAN. TECH. L. REV. 306, 333–35 (2020), and sources cited therein. As acknowledged throughout this chapter, the unregistered rights system proposed here may benefit such other disadvantaged inventors as well. *See id.* at 363–69.

3 "Registered rights" refers to systems that grant patent rights on only a registration-only basis as well as those that require both registration and substantive examination. *See also* text accompanying notes 82–91 (discussing registration-only patent systems).

inventions that meet the standard substantive requirements for patentability but would do so without requiring inventors to go through the expensive, complicated, and time-consuming patent examination process. Such unregistered patents would grant exclusive rights to inventions for a limited period of time and only against direct and knowing copying. They nonetheless would provide much-needed protections for female innovators, who face many obstacles in obtaining registered patent rights for their innovative efforts.

8.1 INEQUALITY IN PATENT PROTECTION WORLDWIDE

Although the numbers vary substantially by country, technology, and sector, the overall percentage of women among patentees and patent applicants remains low worldwide.[4] The comprehensive study of Patent Cooperation Treaty applications from 151 countries conducted by the World Intellectual Property Organization (WIPO) highlights the significant gender gap in patent protection.[5] The study found that less than 30 percent of all patent applications listed female inventors, with less than 5 percent listing women as sole inventors.[6] This gender gap persisted even in fields that otherwise exhibited near-gender parity.[7] For example, biotechnology and academia generally offer women better opportunities[8] than electrical and mechanical engineering and industry,[9] but even in bioscience, women are still underrepresented among patent holders.[10]

Similarly, a study the UK Intellectual Property Office conducted using the Worldwide Patent Statistical Database (PATSTAT) and PatBase found that women have constituted less than 2 percent of inventors for most of the twentieth century, rising only to just over 10 percent by 2015.[11] Importantly, although patents listing female inventors are increasing, this trend has been slow.[12] Variation between

4 Gema L. Martinez, Julio Raffo & Kaori Saito, *Identifying the Gender of PCT Inventors* 8 (World Intell. Prop. Org., Working Paper No. 33, 2016).

5 *Id.* at 6–8. The study analyzed all patent applications filed from 1995 through 2015, containing the names of 8,788,617 individual inventors.

6 *Id.* at 8.

7 Ding et al., *supra* note 1, at 665.

8 Susan Eaton, *Surprising Opportunities: Gender and the Structure of Work in Biotechnology Firms*, 869 ANNALS N.Y. ACAD. SCI. 175, 179–82 (1999).

9 Jennifer Hunt, Jean-Philippe Garant, Hannah Herman & David J. Munroe, *Why Don't Women Patent?* 3 (Nat'l Bureau of Econ. Rsch., Working Paper No. 17888, 2012).

10 Ding et al., *supra* note 1, at 665.

11 *Id.*

12 See, for example, *id.* at 666; Rainer Frietsch, Inna Haller, Melanie Funken-Vrohlings & Hariolf Grupp, *Gender-Specific Patterns in Patenting and Publishing*, 38 RSCH. POL'Y 590, 597 (2009); Taehyun Jung & Olof Ejermo, *Demographic Patterns and Trends in Patenting: Gender, Age, and Education of Inventors*, 86 TECH. FORECASTING & SOC. CHANGE 110, 110 (2014).

countries in the percentage of female inventors did not correlate with socio-economic indicators such as GDP or the number of women in the labor market.[13]

Organizational context matters as well. Women in hierarchical firms are less likely to patent, for example.[14] Women are also less likely to work as sole inventors[15] and more likely to work in large research groups,[16] where they often cede their patent rights to colleagues.[17] Patenting patterns among academics reveal similar trends, with women holding fewer patents than men.[18] Women in academia instead seem to focus their efforts more on teaching and publishing[19] and are less likely to pursue commercial opportunities.[20] When female academics do patent their inventions, on the other hand, it is their male coauthors who often drive the patenting process.[21]

The much lower rate at which women file for patents stems mainly from the cost, complexity, and frequently discriminatory nature of the patent registration and examination process. The overall cost for a twenty-year patent term of protection averages tens of thousands of dollars.[22] Investing in a patent is also risky, as the sizable costs of application, examination, and maintenance may never be recouped. The value of a patent depends on its successful commercialization, which in turn depends on highly uncertain economic and technological factors. The resulting financial barriers to patenting are especially daunting for women.[23] Although

[13] Informatics Team, U.K. Intell. Prop. Off., Gender Profiles in Worldwide Patenting: An Analysis of Female Inventorship 16–18 (2016), https://assets.publishing.service.gov.uk/government/uploads/system/uploads/attachment_data/file/567518/Gender-profiles-in-worldwide-patenting.pdf; Frietsch et al., *supra* note 12, at 594–95; Fulvio Naldi, Daniela Luzi, Adriana Valente & Ilaria Vannini Parenti, *Scientific and Technological Performance by Gender*, *in* Handbook of Quantitative Science and Technology Research 299, 307 (Henk F. Moed, Wolfgang Glänzel & Ulrich Schmoch eds., 2004).

[14] Whittington & Smith-Doerr, *supra* note 1, at 196.

[15] Naldi et al., *supra* note 13, at 307–08; Jung & Ejermo, *supra* note 12, at 110.

[16] Kordula Kugele, *European Studies on Gender Aspects of Inventions – Statistical Survey and Analysis of Gender Impact on Inventions* 2 (Eur. Stud. on Gender Aspects of Inventions, Work Report No. 1, 2008), www.esgi.de/uploads/media/071112_WorkReport1.pdf; James Moody, *The Structure of a Social Science Collaboration Network: Disciplinary Cohesion from 1963 to 1999*, 69 Am. Soc. Rev. 213, 219, 226 (2004) (analyzing women participation in sociological studies); Naldi et al., *supra* note 13, at 307; Hunt et al., *supra* note 9, at 17–19.

[17] Francesco Lissoni, Fabio Montobbio & Lorenzo Zirulia, *Inventorship and Authorship as Attribution Rights: An Enquiry into the Economics of Scientific Credit*, 95 J. Econ. Behav. & Org. 49, 50 (2013).

[18] Ding et al., *supra* note 1, at 665.

[19] Frietsch et al., *supra* note 12, at 595.

[20] Ding et al., *supra* note 1, at 666.

[21] *Id.*

[22] *See USPTO Fee Schedule*, U.S. Pat. & Trademark Off. (last revised July 1, 2022). www.uspto.gov/learning-and-resources/fees-and-payment/uspto-fee-schedule.

[23] Jessica Milli, Emma Williams-Baron, Meika Berlan, Jenny Xia & Barbara Gault, Inst. for Women's Pol'y Rsch., Equity in Innovation: Women Inventors and Patents 7, 18–19 (2016), https://iwpr.org/wpcontent/uploads/wpallimport/files/iwprexport/publications/C448%20Equity%20in%20Innovation.pdf.

venture capitalists often fund patent filings, men are much more likely to secure such outside investment.[24] This perhaps is due partly to biases among venture capitalists[25] and partly to the fact that men are more likely to apply for patents and, therefore, to attract investors.[26]

Moreover, patenting requires access to expertise on how best to negotiate the complexity of the application and prosecution process.[27] Connections with experts and experienced inventors can prove instrumental in both navigating the process and evaluating its risk and potential profitability.[28] Women typically have fewer of these kinds of social and professional network connections and support.[29]

Furthermore, women are less likely not only to apply for patent protection but also to obtain a patent once they do apply.[30] Some studies have found that patent applications by women are up to 21 percent less likely to be granted than those by men.[31] This stems partly from the fact that women tend to file applications in fields in which patents are generally harder to obtain.[32] Even when controlling for scientific field, however, patent applications by women are still 7 percent less likely to be granted.[33] In the life sciences, for example, all-female inventive teams are 11 percent less likely to have their applications granted than are all-male teams, despite the prominence of women in the field.[34] Even when women are granted patents, they typically have more independent claims disallowed and are more likely

[24] Alicia Robb, *Access to Capital among Young Firms, Minority-Owned Firms, Women-Owned Firms, and High-Tech Firms* 19 (2013), www.sba.gov/sites/default/files/files/rs403tot(2).pdf.

[25] Paula E. Stephan & Asmaa El-Ganainy, *The Entrepreneurial Puzzle: Explaining the Gender Gap*, 32 J. Tech. Transfer 475, 481–84 (2006).

[26] Carolin Häussler, Dietmar Harhoff & Elisabeth Mueller, *To Be Financed or Not . . . – The Role of Patents for Venture Capital-Financing* 2 (ZEW – Centre for Eur. Econ. Rsch., Discussion Paper No. 09-003, 2012), http://ssrn.com/abstract=1393725.

[27] Nat'l Women's Bus. Council, Intellectual Property and Women Entrepreneurs: Qualitative Analysis 15 (2012).

[28] Wenpin Tsai & Sumantra Ghoshal, *Social Capital and Value Creation: The Role of Intrafirm Networks*, 41 Acad. Mgmt. J. 464, 473 (1998); *see also* Atul Nerkar & Srikanth Paruchuri, *Evolution of R&D Capabilities: The Role of Knowledge Networks within a Firm*, 51 Mgmt. Sci. 771, 771 (2005).

[29] Nat'l Women's Bus. Council, *supra* note 27, at 15; Tsai & Ghoshal, *supra* note 28, at 470, 473; Nerkar & Paruchuri, *supra* note 28, at 771.

[30] Dana Kanze, Laura Huang, Mark A. Conley & E. Tory Higgins, *We Ask Men to Win and Women Not to Lose: Closing the Gender Gap in Startup Funding*, 61 Acad. Mgmt. J. 586, 587–88 (2018); Milli et al., *supra* note 23; Martinez et al., *supra* note 4, at 8 (focusing on trends in the industry); Kyle Jensen, Balázs Kovács & Olav Sorenson, *Gender Differences in Obtaining and Maintaining Patent Rights*, 36 Nature Biotech. 307, 308 (2018).

[31] Jensen et al., *supra* note 30, at 308.

[32] *Id.*

[33] *Id.*

[34] *Id.* at 308–09.

to have their remaining claims narrowed.[35] Patent examiners also cite patents granted to women less often.[36]

The lower patent issuance rates among women arise to some extent from the often male-oriented interpretation of patentability doctrines such as the notoriously nebulous PHOSITA (person having ordinary skill in the art) standard, used to measure the equally ambiguous utility and nonobviousness requirements for patentability, among other things.[37] These disparities likewise stem from biases among patent examiners, who have been shown to grant patents at lower rates when applicants had easily recognizable feminine names.[38]

The costs of the gender gap in patenting are significant. Patent protection can be essential in commercialization, and investors are typically reluctant to invest in inventions that are not patent protected.[39] Thus, as a consequence of their lesser patent protections, women are less likely to see their inventions developed and commercialized and to recoup their investments in inventing. This patent gender gap can have implications for economic growth and social equality.

8.2 UNREGISTERED PATENTS

As the previous discussion suggests, truly leveling the playing field for women in technology would necessitate many changes, including changes to the patent system. More consciously, nongendered patentability doctrines and an anonymous application system could help women achieve greater parity and better outcomes. One possible measure that has been overlooked, however, is expanding opportunities for patent protection.

Patent protection is currently unavailable absent registration and examination with a national patent office.[40] In this way, patents differ from most other intellectual property rights, many of which offer protection to both registered and unregistered

35 *Id.*; *see* Robert P. Merges & John F. Duffy, Patent Law and Policy 31–32, 58 (7th ed. 2017) (stating that "prosecutions" are patent office examinations for patentability and "claims" establish patents' exclusive boundaries).

36 Jensen et al., *supra* note 30, at 308.

37 Dan L. Burk, *Diversity Levers*, 23 Duke J. Gender L. & Pol'y 25, 42 (2015); Dan L. Burk, *Do Patents Have Gender?*, 19 Am. U. J. Gender Soc. Pol'y & L. 881, 904 (2011); Kara W. Swanson, *Intellectual Property and Gender: Reflections on Accomplishments and Methodology*, 24 Am. U. J. Gender, Soc. Pol'y & L. 175, 185 (2015).

38 Jensen et al., *supra* note 30, at 309.

39 Stuart J.H. Graham, Robert P. Merges, Pam Samuelson & Ted Sichelman, *High Technology Entrepreneurs and the Patent System: Results of the 2008 Berkeley Patent Survey*, 24 Berkeley Tech. L. J. 1255, 1287–1309 (2009); Häussler et al., *supra* note 26, at 2; Milli et al., *supra* note 23, at 3–8; Ted Sichelman & Stuart J.H. Graham, *Patenting by Entrepreneurs: An Empirical Study*, 17 Mich. Telecomm. & Tech. L. Rev. 111, 111–12 (2010).

40 See, for example, 35 U.S.C. § 111. *See also* Dan L. Burk & Mark A. Lemley, The Patent Crisis and How the Courts Can Solve It 9 (2009) (describing formal requirements for patent registration).

creations. Trademarks and design rights, for example, often feature a two-tier structure that offers some minimal protection absent registration but also offers stronger protections for right holders who register their creations.[41] Similarly, copyright protections often employ a two-tier structure to protect both registered and unregistered works, although many countries do not have a registration system for copyrighted works.[42]

In the case of copyright, protection typically is available from the moment a copyrightable work is created, whether or not it has been registered.[43] Registration is available in some countries such as the United States, where it creates a presumption of "constructive notice" that a work is copyrighted, thereby assisting in proving infringement.[44] Trademarks likewise can be protected without registration, albeit only in the geographic area where the mark actually is used in commerce.[45] To gain nationwide protection and additional remedies, however, owners have to register their marks.[46] Likewise, both EU and UK law protect unregistered designs against direct copying for a limited duration but are subject to the defense of independent creation;[47] only registered designs are protected against independent creation.[48] Registration also gives designs a longer term of protection.[49]

Our proposal for the patent system follows this general structure of a two-tier intellectual property right, offering narrow protections of limited duration for unregistered inventions while retaining the option of the standard twenty-year term of protection for those who submit their inventions for registration and examination. This proposal also can be applied globally through an existing international agreement such as the Agreement on Trade-Related Aspects of Intellectual Property Rights and used to address the global gender gap in patenting.

8.2.1 *The Proposed Model*

The proposed model would offer inventors a novel form of protection with no need for registration. Inventors who wish to secure full patent protection would still have to register their inventions and undergo an examination process, just as they do

41 See, for example, 15 U.S.C. § 1127 (trademark rights in the United States); Charles-Henry Massa & Alain Strowel, *Community Design: Cinderella Revamped*, 2003 Eur. Intell. Prop. Rev. 68, 74 (2003) (industrial design rights in the European Union).

42 Marcowitz-Bitton & Morris, *supra* note 2, at 32.

43 H.R. Rep. No. 94-1476, at 52–53 (1976); 35 U.S.C. § 102(a); 17 U.S.C. § 401(a).

44 17 U.S.C. § 410(c).

45 15 U.S.C. § 1127.

46 *Id.* § 1126; Eastman Kodak Co. v. Bell & Howell Document Mgmt. Prods. Co., 994 F.2d 1569 (Fed. Cir. 1993); Commodore Elecs. Ltd. v. Cbm Kabushiki Kaisha, 26 U.S.P.Q.2d 1503 (T.T.A.B. 1993); 15 U.S.C. §§ 1072, 1507(c).

47 Copyright, Designs and Patents Act 1988, c. 48 § 213 (U.K.); Council Regulation 6/2002, art. 11, 2002 O.J. (L 3) 1; Massa & Strowel, *supra* note 41.

48 Council Regulation 6/2002, art. 19(2), 2002 O.J. (L 3) 1.

49 Massa & Strowel, *supra* note 41.

today. The central difference between the existing form of registered rights and the proposed form of unregistered rights is the scope and duration of protection afforded under each. The proposed unregistered patents would protect subject inventions for only three years and against only knowing and direct copying. Thus, unlike registered patent rights, these unregistered rights would provide relatively short protections and no protection against independent creation.

Note that the distinction in rights between unregistered and registered patents follows naturally from the rationale behind the registration and examination of traditional patents. Registration has long been seen as providing the public with notice of *in rem* rights.[50] Because the proposed unregistered patent system by definition would not make registration and description of patent rights public, it would be inefficient and arguably unfair for potential infringers to be held unknowingly liable for infringement. Those who directly copy an invention, by contrast, obviously would know that it is another's creation and, therefore, would notice that another person could hold unregistered rights in the invention, despite the lack of registration of those rights.

Moreover, inventions eligible for our proposed unregistered rights still would need to meet the existing patentability requirements of subject matter eligibility,[51] novelty,[52] utility,[53] and nonobviousness.[54] Only for inventions meeting these traditional substantive standards would unregistered protections become available. Those protections would then automatically arise as soon as the invention becomes available to the public. Public availability would be measured under the same standards used for novelty under current U.S. patent law, including public availability of a description of the invention, public use of the invention, or the invention becoming otherwise available to the public.[55]

Unlike the twenty-year term for a registered patent, however, the duration of an unregistered patent under our proposal would run for only three years from the date the subject invention first became publicly available. Inventors who wish to extend their rights for more than three years would have the option to do so but would have to undergo the usual registration and examination with the applicable patent office, even if their unregistered patent rights had already been successfully enforced in

[50] *See* Douglas G. Baird & Thomas H. Jackson, *Information, Uncertainty, and the Transfer of Property*, 13 J. LEGAL STUD. 299, 303–04 (1984) (discussing a "filing system of title claims").

[51] 35 U.S.C. § 101 (stating that subject-matter eligibility means the patent falls under one of the standard categories of utility patent, design patent, or plant patent).

[52] 35 U.S.C. § 102(a); BURK & LEMLEY, *supra* note 40, at 9.

[53] 35 U.S.C. § 101; BURK & LEMLEY, *supra* note 40, at 9.

[54] 35 U.S.C. § 103; BURK & LEMLEY, *supra* note 40, at 9.

[55] 35 U.S.C. § 102(a). Our proposal adopts this standard of public availability rather than an actual-reduction-to-practice or other standard for the same reason the current registered patent system does – to prevent patentees from taking from the public inventions that already have become part of the prior art. See, for example, Atlas Powder Co. v. Ireco, Inc., 190 F.3d 1342, 1356 (Fed. Cir. 1999).

court. Inventors would have to file for such registered rights no more than a year after their unregistered rights attach; inventors who do not file applications for registered rights within a year of acquiring unregistered rights would forfeit registered patent protection altogether, leaving them with only the remaining two years of their unregistered patent rights.

In this way, the proposed unregistered rights regime would comport with what many patent systems already do under their novelty (or statutory bar) provisions. Almost all countries allow inventors to disclose their inventions publicly up to a year before filing their patent applications without anticipating themselves or otherwise being barred from patent eligibility.[56] The law in the United States, for example, establishes a one-year grace period that allows inventors to disclose their invention publicly before filing, in effect measuring novelty and nonobviousness as of the disclosure date rather than the filing dates.[57] Our proposal applies this "first to file or to publicly disclose" approach to both registered and unregistered rights holders.[58] Granted, even under U.S. patent law, patentees cannot sue others for infringement occurring in that first prefiling year the way they would be able to under our proposal. Nonetheless, the effect is that under both systems, an inventor who applies for registered patent rights within a year of publicly disclosing her invention can exclude others until the twenty-first year after that initial prefiling disclosure.

Finally, our proposal would allow inventors only a limited presumption of validity of their unregistered patent rights. In bringing an enforcement action, inventors initially would not need to prove that their inventions meet the standard patentability requirements; instead, the inventors would have to establish only the date their invention became public. They would, however, at all times bear the burden of proving direct copying by the defendant. Once the inventors establish these basic elements of their claim, the defendant would have the right to challenge the validity of the inventors' unregistered rights by showing that their invention fails to meet one or more of the patentability requirements. Importantly, the defendant would need to rebut the presumed validity of an unregistered patent by mere preponderance of the evidence, unlike the clear and convincing evidence required under U.S. law to invalidate a registered patent.[59] The lower preponderance of the evidence standard would reflect the fact that no patent office had yet vetted the invention's patentability and that a court would thus have no need to defer to the patent office's

[56] World Intell. Prop. Org., Certain Aspects of National Regional Patent Laws (2019), www.wipo.int/export/sites/www/scp/en/national_laws/grace_period.pdf.

[57] 35 U.S.C. § 102(b) (allowing inventors who publicly disclose their inventions up to twelve months before filing to avoid use of any other, later disclosed technological references for the purpose of establishing unpatentability).

[58] *See* Merges & Duffy, *supra* note 35, at 390–91 (describing "first to file or first to publicly disclose" under U.S. patent law). A minority of jurisdictions provide grace periods of only six months and apply them to only some types of public disclosures. However, these jurisdictions might have to modify their grace period policies accordingly.

[59] 35 U.S.C. § 282.

expertise.[60] If the proposed unregistered patent rights were found to be valid as well as infringed, the remedies for infringement would include both injunctions and damages.

However, it may seem odd to grant unregistered patents any presumption of validity, given that neither unregistered trademarks nor copyrights enjoy such a presumption. In both trademark and copyright law, owners of unregistered rights bear the burden of proving the validity of their rights.[61] Shifting the burden to alleged infringers may be more efficient in the patent context, however. The exceedingly rigorous standards for patentability make it relatively easy for defendants to identify prior art references that prove unpatentability, even with regard to registered patents previously examined by a patent office.[62] Allowing a defendant to proceed immediately to its invalidity argument may thus lead to faster and less costly disposition of infringement proceedings.

8.2.2 *The Costs and Benefits of Unregistered Patents for Gender Equality*

Two critical questions our proposal presents are whether unregistered patent rights would in fact help female inventors and, if so, whether the benefits would outweigh the costs of creating such a system. As noted earlier, simply decreasing the barriers women face in obtaining patent protections would go far in helping them to capitalize on their innovations and to participate in technological industries generally. While our proposal would increase the number of patent rights overall, the proposed unregistered rights would be carefully cabined to avoid creating excessive drag on future innovation. Our proposal is thus tailored to ease many of the disadvantages women face in protecting their inventions while avoiding undue burdens on technological progress overall.

First, an unregistered patent regime would enable inventors to obtain patent protection without the oft-prohibitive costs of registration, examination, and maintenance. Women would thus have easier access to the patent system despite frequent difficulty in securing funding. Similarly, unregistered patent rights under the

[60] *See id.*; Microsoft Corp. v. I4I Ltd. P'ship, 564 U.S. 91, 97–98 (2011) (confirming clear and convincing evidence to rebut presumption of validity under § 282).

[61] 17 U.S.C. § 411 (allowing enforcement of unregistered works of non-U.S. origin or whose registration application has been refused); 87 C.J.S. Trademarks, Etc. § 309 (2020) (stating that an owner of an unregistered trademark has burden of proving validity).

[62] Shine Tu, *Invalidated Patents and Associated Patent Examiners*, 18 Vand. J. Ent. & Tech. L. 135, 151–52 (2015) (surveying litigated patents); Michael Tierney & William Saindon, *Boardside Chat: New Developments*, U.S. Pat. & Trademark Off. (June 11, 2020), www.uspto.gov/sites/default/files/documents/PTAB_boardside_chat_new_trial_stats_sas_and_operational_faqs_06_11_2020.pdf (surveying administrative adjudications under the Leahy-Smith America Invents Act). In the vast majority of cases, issued patents were invalidated based on defendant-identified prior art previously unseen by the U.S. Patent and Trademark Office. Stephen Yelderman, *Prior Art in the District Court*, 95 Notre Dame L. Rev. 837, 883–84 (2019); Tu, *supra*, at 61, 160–61.

proposed regime would be automatic and therefore would not favor those who have access to a network and other support for guidance on the patenting process. This also will help women and others who lack such connections.

Of course, inventors would have to bear the costs of enforcing their patents, including any litigation costs. The policing costs for infringement of unregistered patents would be lower than those for registered patents, however, as monitoring for only purposeful copying is presumably cheaper than monitoring for both knowing and "innocent" infringement, such as independent design. More importantly, enforcement costs would have to be born only *ex post*, after direct copying has been detected, and the value of the invention thereby demonstrated. That value – along with the protection the invention would automatically enjoy under unregistered patent rights – could in turn help attract investors. As with any other invention, venture capital and other investment funds can be used for defending rights in the invention through litigation or other means, filing for registered rights and paying for subsequent maintenance fees, and commercialization and licensing generally.

All the same, investors may be hesitant to invest even in innovations valuable enough to have been copied if they lack registered patent rights. The proposed unregistered rights would not enjoy the cachet of vetting by a patent office or the presumption of validity rebuttable only by clear and convincing evidence that comes with such vetting. The proposed rights also would last for only three years. As a result, unregistered patents might not have the same signaling effect in attracting investment.

Investing in unregistered patents may not be significantly riskier than investing in registered patents, however. Investing in technological innovation is always risky, as even registered patents have only speculative economic value and probabilistic legal validity.[63] Under our proposal, outside investors also would know that even unregistered inventions would have at least some protection, compared to their current lack of protection. Such protection could be converted to registered protection if still within the one-year grace period. Moreover, many technologies do not need the full twenty years of registered protection. The three years of protection under our proposed unregistered rights could be more than enough to recoup investments in industries such as computer software and electronics.[64]

A second and equally important benefit is that automatic, unregistered patent rights would allow women to bypass many of the biases inherent in the patent system. The most obvious are patent examiner biases against patent applicants with recognizably feminine names. Less obvious are workplace biases leading to less

[63] Mark A. Lemley & Carl Shapiro, *Probabilistic Patents*, 19 J. ECON. PERSPECTIVES 75, 75 (2005).

[64] Verne A. Luckow & Steven C. Balsarotti, *Statistical Analysis of Federal District Court Cases Seeking Longer Patent Term Adjustments in the Wake of Wyeth v. Kappos*, 10 J. MARSHALL REV. INTELL. PROP. L. 1, 3 (2010).

support for women in filing for patent rights. Automatic rights would make these biases less important in barring access to patent protection.

That being said, unregistered rights holders seeking to enforce their rights may need to rely on the court system, which itself is subject to bias. Allowing courts to recognize unregistered intellectual property rights nonetheless could be more equitable than forcing inventors to go through the patent registration and examination process or forgo their rights altogether. Like investors, courts may be more apt to recognize the value of an invention once others have affirmatively copied it and therefore be more inclined to protect the invention against appropriation. Courts also may be more inclined to look to broader economic and social values to evaluate patent rights with more focus on equity than a patent office would.[65] Administrative agencies such as patent offices, by contrast, lack many of the procedural justice and due process constraints to which courts are subject.[66] Members of the judiciary may be less subject to the biases affecting the science, technology, engineering, and mathematics (STEM) fields from which patent offices typically draw their examiners.[67] While administrative agency decisions are subject to judicial review, this review often tends to be somewhat deferential.[68] Thus, using courts to recognize unregistered intellectual property rights would at least provide an alternative venue for women and other inventors to protect their interests.[69]

What are the costs and pitfalls of the proposed new regime of unregistered patent rights, however? The fact that no jurisdiction has ever provided unregistered, automatic patent rights reflects a discomfort with the idea. Many have argued that excessive patent rights would impose much greater burdens on future innovation and creation than would similarly excessive grants of copyright, trademark, design, and trade secret rights. The breadth and robustness of patent rights mean that granting patents too lavishly or easily could lead to hold-outs, patent thickets,[70]

65 *See* Richard J. Pierce, Jr., *Political Control versus Impermissible Bias in Agency Decisionmaking: Lessons from* Chevron *and* Mistretta, 57 U. Chi. L. Rev. 481, 516 (1990).

66 Ronald J. Krotoszynski, Jr., *Taming the Tail That Wags the Dog: Ex Post and Ex Ante Constraints on Informal Adjudication*, 56 Admin. L. Rev. 1057, 1058 (2004).

67 Martin H. Redish & Kristin McCall, *Due Process, Free Expression, and the Administrative State*, 94 Notre Dame L. Rev. 297, 298 (2018). *But see* Adrian Vermeule, *Deference and Due Process*, 129 Harv. L. Rev. 1890, 1928–29 (2016) (arguing that agency motivation seldom affects decision-making).

68 See, for example, Dickinson v. Zurko, 527 U.S. 150, 152 (1999) (holding that the Administrative Procedures Act generally requires judicial deference to agency findings of fact).

69 Provisions on postgrant proceedings recently enacted in the United States could also be changed to allow review of unregistered patent rights. *See* 35 U.S.C. §§ 301–307 (ex parte reexamination); *id.* §§ 311–319 (*inter partes* review); *id.* §§ 321–329 (postgrant review). While less expensive and time-consuming than litigation, *see* Merges & Duffy, *supra* note 35, at 19, the administrative judges in these proceedings may suffer from the same biases as patent examiners.

70 Carl Shapiro, *Navigating the Patent Thicket: Cross Licenses, Patent Pools, and Standard Setting*, 1 Innovation Pol'y & Econ. 119, 121–22 (2000); Miriam Marcowitz-Bitton & Yotam Kaplan, *Recalibrating Patent Protection for COVID-19 Vaccines: A Path to Affordable Access*

patent "trolling,"[71] and other phenomena that wastefully deter other inventors from valuable research. Technologies in which development and commercialization are inherently cumulative and complementary are particularly prone to these issues.[72]

In contrast to other forms of intellectual property right, patent law also has very few safety valves to protect inventors from opportunistic claims of infringement that might over-deter them from building on existing technologies.[73] Unlike copyright and trade secrecy,[74] patent law has no independent creation defense to infringement liability,[75] nor does patent law have the fair use defense seen in copyright and trademark law.[76] Even the experimental use exception available in the patent systems in many countries applies only in limited circumstances, such as regulatory approval of pharmaceuticals or use of medical treatment methods.[77] Although prior user rights also are common in many countries, they are limited to only those using an invention commercially before the patentee filed its patent application.[78]

and Equitable Distribution, 12 U.C. IRVINE L. REV. 423 (2022) (discussing patent thickets in the pharmaceutical industry as a bar to innovation).

71 John F. Duffy, *Reviving the Paper Patent Doctrine*, 98 CORNELL L. REV. 1359 (2013); Mark A. Lemley & A. Douglas Melamed, *Missing the Forest for the Trolls*, 113 COLUM. L. REV. 2117, 2117 (2013); Miriam Marcowitz-Bitton, Yotam Kaplan & Maayan Perel, *Recoupment Patent*, 98 N.C. L. REV. 481, 485 (2020) (discussing patent trolls and the costs they impose).

72 Dan L. Burk & Mark A. Lemley, *Policy Levers in Patent Law*, 89 VA. L. REV. 1575, 1612–13 (2003); Richard R. Nelson, *The Market Economy, and the Scientific Commons*, 33 RSCH. POL'Y 455, 464 (2004).

73 Some scholars doubt the effectiveness of such safety valves in buffering against the negative effects of intellectual property rights on others. See, for example, Christopher Sprigman, *Reform(aliz)ing Copyright*, 57 STAN. L. REV. 485, 487 (2004).

74 See, for example, Feist Publications, Inc. v. Rural Tel. Serv. Co., 499 U.S. 340, 345 (1991); Procter & Gamble Co. v. Colgate-Palmolive Co., 199 F.3d 74, 77–78 (2d Cir. 1999). Trademark law does not allow an independent creation defense, however. See, for example, Blendco, Inc. v. Conagra Foods, Inc., 132 Fed. App'x 520, 523 (5th Cir. 2005).

75 Commil USA, LLC v. Cisco Sys., Inc., 135 S. Ct. 1920, 1926 (2015); Kewanee Oil Co. v. Bicron Corp., 416 U.S. 470, 490 (1974).

76 Gideon Parchomovsky & Alex Stein, *Intellectual Property Defenses*, 113 COLUM. L. REV. 1483, 1505 (2013) (fair use allows descriptive use of another's trademark); Elizabeth L. Rosenblatt, *Intellectual Property's Negative Space: Beyond the Utilitarian*, 40 FLA. ST. U. L. REV. 441, 452 (2013) (fair use as "use-based carve-out areas" from copyright infringement liability). Copyright law in the United States also contains a number of compulsory licenses, and other countries avail themselves of compulsory licensing of patents as well, as allowed under the TRIPS Agreement. In the United States, rights holders have thus far successfully resisted compulsory licensing of trade secrets, trademarks, and patents.

77 *See* Hans-Rainer Jaenichen & Johann Pitz, *Research Exemption/Experimental Use in the European Union: Patents Do Not Block the Progress of Science*, 5 COLD SPRING HARBOR PERSP. MED. a020941 (2015) (experimental-use exception in EU member states); 35 U.S.C. § 287(c); *see also* Cynthia M. Ho, *Patents, Patients, and Public Policy: An Incomplete Intersection at 35 U.S.C. § 287(c)*, 33 U.C. DAVIS L. REV. 601, 641–45 (2000) (§ 287(c) immunity for some patented medical procedures).

78 U.S. PAT. & TRADEMARK OFF., REPORT ON PRIOR USER RIGHTS 2–3, www.uspto.gov/sites/default/files/ip/global/prior_user_rights.pdf (last visited Mar. 31, 2024).

Instead, the patent system relies on its comparatively stringent limitations to reduce both the number of patents and breadth of patent rights.[79] Patent law has far more limited terms than copyright, trademark, design, or trade secret law,[80] as well as novelty and statutory bar provisions that force inventors to file their patent applications or lose their eligibility to patent.[81] These limitations serve to release inventions into the public domain as soon as possible. Unconditional patent rights granted without examination or even registration appear at first glance to completely dismantle patent law's carefully calculated system for cabining patent law's otherwise robust rights of exclusivity.[82]

The unregistered rights proposed here would be very closely limited to avoid unduly burdening overall innovation, however. Unlike registered patent rights, the proposed unregistered rights would be subject to a number of safety valves to protect downstream innovation. In addition to applying all of the standard patentability requirements, the proposed unregistered patent regime would protect only against copying, not independent creation, and for only three years from the date the subject invention first became publicly available. These constraints establish significant safeguards against placing undue burdens on others.

Some might argue that unregistered patent rights would exacerbate the innovation bottlenecks created by "bad" or "weak" patents – that is, patents of suspect validity.[83] As with registered patents, however, the proposed unregistered rights would be subject to judicial review for validity. Our proposal in this way invokes the same efficiencies of various proposed "soft-look" registration approaches. Under these latter proposals, patent applications would undergo only minimal administrative examination prior to issuance, and only those that were important enough to give rise later to litigation would then face more substantive judicial examination.[84] Such judicial review *ex post*, only when needed, is more resource-efficient than the current system of administratively examining all patent applications *ex ante*. In addition, judicial review *ex post* would have the benefit of not only the defendants' field-related expertise and motivation to invalidate patents but also a

[79] William M. Landes & Richard A. Posner, The Economic Structure of Intellectual Property Law 302–08 (2003); Burk & Lemley, *supra* note 72, at 1575–76, 1612–13.

[80] Landes & Posner, *supra* note 79, at 295; Gregory N. Mandel, *The Public Perception of Intellectual Property*, 66 Fla. L. Rev. 261, 267 (2014).

[81] *See* Merges & Duffy, *supra* note 35, at 509–10.

[82] *Cf.* Burk & Lemley, *supra* note 72, at 1575–76, 1612–13 (describing checks and balances in registered patent system).

[83] See, for example, Christopher A. Cotropia, *The Folly of Early Filing in Patent Law*, 61 Hastings L.J. 65, 69–71 (2009); David Fagundes & Jonathan S. Masur, *Costly Intellectual Property*, 65 Vand. L. Rev. 677, 679, 726–28 (2012).

[84] For example, F. Scott Kieff, *The Case for Registering Patents and the Law and Economics of Present Patent-Obtaining Rules*, 45 B.C. L. Rev. 55 (2003) (proposing that these registration-only patents also enjoy a presumption of validity rebuttable by preponderance of the evidence); *see also* Mark A. Lemley, *Rational Ignorance at the Patent Office*, 95 Nw. U. L. Rev. 1495, 1526–27 (2001) (discussing such proposals).

presumption of validity rebuttable by a mere preponderance of the evidence.[85] Registration-only patents rest on the idea that the high costs of eliminating bad patents administratively *ex ante* outweigh the social costs of waiting to eliminate those patents judicially *ex post*.[86] Similarly, the unregistered patent regime proposed here rests on the idea that the cost of patent registration and examination and how it sidelines women and other inventors outweighs the cost of potentially bad unregistered patents.[87]

Regardless of whether patents are "good" or "bad," simply adding to the overall volume of patent rights still could impose a drag on innovation. Technology may be more incremental, cumulative, or complementary than expressive works, trademarks, or trade secrets,[88] and inventive concepts are often more difficult to design around.[89] The fear of litigation and the uncertainty of proving invalidity therefore often causes competitors to fear innovating in heavily patented technologies.[90] This *in terrorem* effect can over-deter competitors from innovating near or around others' patents, particularly given the patent system's lack of independent creation, fair use, and other defenses available in other forms of intellectual property right.[91] In this way excessive patent rights may be more likely than other intellectual property rights to over-deter future innovation.

The proposed unregistered patent regime would provide a number of safe harbors to address this problem, the most obvious of which would be for independent creation. Cumulative or complementary innovation might still be unduly deterred from copying needed components, however. So unlike the current patent regime in the United States, the proposed regime would therefore not impose treble damages for knowing infringement, especially if only for experimental use. Perhaps most importantly, the proposed unregistered rights would be very limited in duration; other innovators could thus just wait three years to copy an invention with impunity.

85 Kieff, *supra* note 84, at 73–76.

86 Lemley, *supra* note 84, at 1508–11.

87 Allowing patent protections on a registration-only basis resembles the utility model or "petty" patents that many countries issue to protect technological improvements. Utility model patents vary a great deal but typically require less technological merit, provide less protection, and expire more quickly than "regular" patents. *See* J.H. Reichman, *Legal Hybrids between the Patent and Copyright Paradigms*, 94 Colum. L. Rev. 2432, 2456–59 (1994); Richard H. Stern, *A Sui Generis Utility Model Law as an Alternative Legal Model for Protecting Software*, 1 U. Balt. Intell. Prop. L.J. 108, 112–13 (1993). While a registration-only or utility model patent system could be much less expensive and therefore more accessible for women and other similarly disadvantaged inventors, an automatic, unregistered patent system would be even more accessible, particularly for inventors who lack the networks and other support necessary to know how to navigate such patent systems.

88 John Shepard Wiley Jr., *Copyright at the School of Patent*, 58 U. Chi. L. Rev. 119, 146, 167, 182 (1991).

89 *See* Fagundes & Masur, *supra* note 83, at 712–14.

90 Christopher R. Leslie, *The Anticompetitive Effects of Unenforced Invalid Patents*, 91 Minn. L. Rev. 101, 117–18 (2006).

91 *See* Fagundes & Masur, *supra* note 83, at 713–15.

The limited duration and scope of these unregistered rights would greatly lower the risk of patent trolling, nuisance suits, patent thickets, and holdouts. The proposed unregistered rights would thus broaden access to patent protection without either increasing or prolonging them.

As an unregistered regime, our proposed patent rights could undermine the public-notice function of patent registration, however, thereby increasing the informational costs of establishing freedom to operate within a particular technological space. The breadth of patent rights and the relatively limited defenses to patent infringement call for clear public notice of what constitutes such infringement. Indeed, this is one of the foremost values of registering patent rights and perhaps the primary reason that, in contrast to copyright, trademark, and trade secret law, unregistered rights in patent law never emerged. The patent registration system already falls short of this public-notice ideal, as the clearance costs of identifying and interpreting all the patents potentially relevant to one's project are often astronomical.[92] Injecting unregistered, unrecorded rights into the existing system could exacerbate these costs exponentially. Under the proposed unregistered rights system, by contrast, infringers would have demonstrated actual notice of the protected invention by virtue of copying it. Public notice, therefore, would not be an issue. Downstream inventors would have to determine the date the invention became publicly available, of course, which could be costly, but this cost is already part of the existing registered rights system.[93]

One final objection could be that the proposed unregistered regime would undermine the peripheral-claiming system.[94] In the United States, peripheral-claiming mandates that registered patents include claims "particularly pointing out and distinctly claiming" the subject invention.[95] Peripheral claiming is designed to delineate a patent's boundaries as precisely as possible to give the public detailed notice. An unregistered patent system, by contrast, would give the public only the inventions themselves as indicators of their patent boundaries in a way resembling the now-obsolete central-claiming system. Under the central-claiming system in the United States, courts could only compare an allegedly infringing device with the patented invention, without the benefit of claims or other express boundaries, often leading to surprise and uncertainty.[96] Reversion to a central-claiming-like system may thus seem inefficient,[97] but in practice the modern-day peripheral-claiming

[92] *See generally* Christina Mulligan & Timothy B. Lee, *Scaling the Patent System*, 68 N.Y.U. Ann. Surv. Am. L. 289 (2012).

[93] *See supra* text accompanying note 55 (discussing public availability and novelty and statutory bar requirements).

[94] 35 U.S.C. § 112(b).

[95] *Id.*

[96] *See* Merges & Duffy, *supra* note 35, at 651, 711; Martin J. Adelman, *Patent Claiming in the United States: Central, Peripheral, or Mongrel?*, 1 IP Theory 71, 72–75 (2010).

[97] Dan L. Burk & Mark A. Lemley, *Fence Posts or Sign Posts? Rethinking Patent Claim Construction*, 157 U. Pa. L. Rev. 1743, 1747 (2009).

system introduces its own inefficiencies.[98] Peripheral claiming has led to the notoriously difficult problems of construing patent claims and widespread complaints about the uncertainty to which they lead.[99] Indeed, some commentators have even called for a return to the central-claiming system as a more equitable and flexible approach to patenting.[100]

Lastly, none of what is proposed here should be taken as urging the abolition of existing registered patent systems. Without a doubt, registration and examination of patents yield many benefits, including greater public notice and independently vetted patentability. Registration and examination come at a high cost for inventors, but for many inventors – and their employers or investors – this cost will not pose an obstacle to patenting inventions perceived to be worthwhile.[101]

For all its benefits, however, the high cost of the patent application and examination process falls disparately on women and other disadvantaged inventors. Predicting the commercial value of an invention is immensely difficult, and deciding whether to invest in the process of applying for patent protection, even if only provisionally, is a gamble.[102] To assume that investors and employers evaluate inventions from a purely rational, rent-maximizing perspective is undoubtedly inaccurate, especially for inventions by female inventors. As a result, a disproportionately large number of female inventors are disenfranchised by the costs and complexities of patent registration and examination and their inherent biases.[103] Adding an unregistered regime such as the one proposed here would help ameliorate the gender gap in patent rights without creating undue burdens on innovation.[104] The benefits of unregistered patent protection, even if for a relatively brief period, could be quite significant and thus outweigh the potential risks of such a regime.

CONCLUSION

The stark gender gap in patenting is unlikely to disappear in the near future due partly to the *ex ante* registration currently required for patent protection. The patent registration and examination process is risky, expensive, time-consuming, and

98 *Id.* at 1751–61.

99 Janet Freilich, *Patent Clutter*, 103 Iowa L. Rev. 925, 925 (2018) (describing the different issues that make patents difficult to read and understand).

100 Burk & Lemley, *supra* note 97, at 1747; Jeanne C. Fromer, *Claiming Intellectual Property*, 76 U. Chi. L. Rev. 719 (2009).

101 Fagundes & Masur, *supra* note 83, at 701.

102 Provisional patent applications are typically less expensive to file because they do not undergo examination and simply preserve the applicants' filing date. 35 U.S.C. § 111(b)(4). These applications, however, must be converted to nonprovisional status within a year, so applicants must eventually assume the full cost of prosecuting their applications. 35 U.S.C. § 111(b)(5).

103 Kanze et al., *supra* note 30, at 588; Milli et al., *supra* note 23; Martinez et al., *supra* note 4, at 6–8.

104 *See* 17 U.S.C. at § 302(a); H.R. Rep. No. 94-1476, *supra* note 43, at 133–36; Zechariah Chafee, *Reflections on the Law of Copyright*, 45 Colum. L. Rev. 503, 719–21, 725–27, 729–30 (1945).

complex and poses significant barriers for many inventors, particularly women. Excluding women and other similarly disadvantaged inventors from patent protections is detrimental to both equality and economic growth and stifles overall innovation.

A novel regime offering inventors automatic, unregistered patent rights for even a limited period of time could help make the patent system more inclusive and egalitarian by avoiding the cost and risk of the patent registration and examination process. The version of unregistered patent rights proposed here would be carefully narrowed to allow protection only against knowing and direct copying to maintain the appropriate balance between inventors and the public and between the need to protect existing inventions and the need to allow future innovation. Naturally, this proposal cannot achieve perfect gender equality on its own but would be a meaningful step in the right direction.

9

Can Decentralization Encourage Equality in the Patent System?

Lital Helman

INTRODUCTION

In principle, the patent system is equally accessible to all inventors.[1] Big corporations, small start-ups, and individuals all have their patent applications scrutinized by the same patent office. If granted, their patents receive the same protection, duration, and remedies.[2] This equality principle serves an important purpose. It guarantees a neutral position of patent law and pledges equal opportunity to all inventions to win in the marketplace.[3] Theoretically, equality serves another vital objective: to ensure diversity of inventions.[4] It does so by giving new and small inventors the same treatment as experienced and well-known inventors and not granting an advantage to inventors who may be perceived as having a higher chance of success.

However, the patent system is not equally accessible to all. Some actors are more likely than others to file for patents and have their patents granted.[5] Thus, patents are

1 *See generally* Wendy J. Gordon, *A Property Right in Self-Expression: Equality and Individualism in the Natural Law of Intellectual Property*, 102 YALE L.J. 1533 (1993) (discussing equality in intellectual property under Lockean principles).

2 *See* 35 U.S.C. § 154(a)(1) ("Every patent shall contain . . . a grant to the patentee, his heirs or assigns, of the right to exclude others from making, using, offering for sale, or selling the invention . . . ."); *see also* Abraham Bell & Gideon Parchomovsky, *Reinventing Copyright and Patent*, 113 MICH. L. REV. 232, 234 (2014) ("Whatever the patent, the law offers a monopoly consisting of a specified set of rights over the invention for a fixed period of time."). An obvious exception to this rule is the availability of patent term extension for certain products that require regulatory approval. *See* Drug Price Competition and Patent Term Restoration Act of 1984, Pub. L. No. 98-417, 98 Stat. 1585 (codified as amended at 21 U.S.C. § 355 and 35 U.S.C. §§ 156, 271, 282).

3 *See infra* Section 9.1.

4 *See* Peter Lee, *Toward a Distributive Agenda for U.S. Patent Law*, 55 HOUS. L. REV. 321, 366–67 (2017) ("It seems likely that minority, women, and low-income inventors would be well situated to develop technologies sensitive to the needs of such communities.").

5 See, for example, Alex Bell, Raj Chetty, Xavier Jaravel, Neviana Petkova & John Van Reenen, *Who Becomes an Inventor in America? The Importance of Exposure to Innovation* (Nat'l Bureau

more handily granted to men over women, whites over minorities, and big companies over start-up firms.[6] Granted, this reality is largely a product of the broader phenomenon of inequality in other spaces, such as academia and entrepreneurship, rather than a feature of the patent system per se.[7] Yet, in this chapter, I propose that a decentralized design of the patent system, particularly the patent record, can mitigate this inequality. Although this chapter focuses on the patent system in the United States, much of the analysis can apply to patent systems worldwide.

The extant patent system in the United States is centralized almost from end to end. The U.S. Patent and Trademark Office (PTO) is responsible for examining patent applications, publishing the granted patents, and increasingly managing postexamination proceedings.[8] For a number of reasons, the centralization of all of these functions within the PTO has adverse effects on equality. First, the current system involves high entry costs and requires particular know-how that benefits repeat players and highly capitalized inventors. Second, centralization requires a single agency to examine the entire pool of patent applications. The immense quantity of patent applications compels examiners to use decision shortcuts and proxies. It should come as no surprise that these shortcuts work in favor of big and repeat players and to the disadvantage of traditionally underrepresented groups in the patent system. Third, the current system grants many unmerited patents, mainly to big corporations.[9] These patents create barriers to entry for newcomers. Finally, the current system features a limited patent record – a static registry that holds only

of Econ. Rsch., Working Paper No. 24062, 2017) (finding inventorship disparities based on parental income, gender, race, and ethnicity); Kjersten Bunker Whittington & Laurel Smith-Doerr, *Women Inventors in Context: Disparities in Patenting across Academia and Industry*, 22 GENDER & SOC'Y 194 (2008) (discussing gender disparities in inventorships); SCOTT A. SHANE, THE ILLUSIONS OF ENTREPRENEURSHIP: THE COSTLY MYTHS THAT ENTREPRENEURS, INVESTORS, AND POLICY MAKERS LIVE BY 134 (2008) (same); Michael W. Schuster, R. Evan Davis, Kourtenay Schley & Julie Ravenscraft, *An Empirical Study of Patent Grant Rates as a Function of Race and Gender*, 57 AM. BUS. L.J. 281 (2020) (examining the rate at which patent applications are granted as a function of the inventor's race and gender). *See also infra* note 51 and accompanying text.

6 *See infra* Section 9.1.

7 See, for example, Paul A. Gompers & Sophie Q. Wang, *Diversity in Innovation* 14 (Harv. Bus. Sch., Working Paper No. 17-067, 2017) (discussing the low share of women entrepreneurs); Dana Kanze, Laura Huang, Mark A. Conley & E. Tory Higgins, *We Ask Men to Win and Women Not to Lose: Closing the Gender Gap in Startup Funding*, 61 ACAD. MGMT. J. 586 (2018) (discussing gender gaps in venture funding); JESSICA MILLI, EMMA WILLIAMS-BARON, MEIKA BERLAN, JENNY XIA & BARBARA GAULT, EQUITY IN INNOVATION: WOMEN INVENTORS AND PATENTS 20–21 (2016), https://iwpr.org/wpcontent/uploads/wpallimport/files/iwprexport/publications/C448%20Equity%20in%20Innovation.pdf (discussing entrepreneurial effects of gender stereotypes); Maya A. Beasley & Mary J. Fischer, *Why They Leave: The Impact of Stereotype Threat on the Attrition of Women and Minorities from Science, Math and Engineering Majors*, 15 SOC. PSYCH. EDUC. 427 (2012) (discussing attrition of minorities and other groups from STEM studies).

8 *See infra* note 32 and accompanying text.

9 *See infra* notes 25–26 and accompanying text.

basic information about inventions. Acquiring updated and relevant information regarding the technological, legal, or commercial status of inventions is costly. The cost barrier places underfunded inventors at a disadvantage and at risk of falling victim to patent trolls.[10]

In a recent work, I considered an idea to decentralize the patent system.[11] In particular, I proposed to open the public record to input by market and state actors during the examination process and throughout the lifetime of the patent, using blockchain or other technology. During the examination period, third parties could submit prior art and weigh in on obviousness. Following the patent issuance, patentees would be able to register updates to the patent, the underlying invention, or products that rely on it. They will also be able to offer licenses via smart contracts or otherwise. The court system would add to the record cases that pertain to the patent. That article argued that decentralization could improve the productivity and effectiveness of the patent system and accelerate the introduction of inventions to the market.[12]

In this chapter, I explore the possibility that decentralization could boost equality in the system by removing access barriers and turning the patent record into an effective platform to learn about inventions and commercialize them affordably. The first part of this chapter discusses the principle of equality in patent law in theory and practice. The second part explores the distributive problems that the current system entails and the future improvements for equality with the shift to a decentralized architecture. A short conclusion ensues.

9.1 EQUAL ACCESS TO THE PATENT SYSTEM

In theory, equal access is a key feature of the patent system.[13] With few exceptions, patent law abides by a strict nondiscrimination principle.[14] Neither the examination

[10] *See infra* Section 9.1.

[11] Lital Helman, *Decentralized Patent System*, 20 Nev. L.J. 68 (2019).

[12] *Id.*

[13] *See* Agreement on Trade-Related Aspects of Intellectual Property Rights art. 21.1, Apr. 15, 1994, Marrakesh Agreement Establishing the World Trade Organization, Annex 1C, 1869 U.N.T.S. 299 ("[P]atents shall be available and patent rights enjoyable without discrimination as to . . . the field of technology."); Lowell v. Lewis, 15 F. Cas. 1018, 1019 (Cir. Ct. D. Mass. 1817) (stating that inventions need to compete in the marketplace); Madhavi Sunder, *IP³*, 59 Stan. L. Rev. 257, 259 (2006) (noting that "intellectual property utilitarianism does not ask who makes the goods"); Lee, *supra* note 4, at 328–29 ("In theory, the patent system creates a neutral market for technology that enables the invisible hand of supply and demand to allocate resources for technological development.").

[14] A notable exception is set forth in the Leahy-Smith America Invents Act, Pub. L. No. 112-29, § 25, 125 Stat. 284 (2011) (allowing for "prioritization of examination of applications for products, processes, or technologies that are important to the national economy or national competitiveness"). Notably, the exception advances applications in the queue but grants no superior rights. Other exceptions include specific arrangements for specific contexts, such as patent term extension. *See supra* note 2. Courts also offer differential treatment de facto in different

criteria nor the rights attached to patents grant favorable treatment to inventors based on their experience, size, financial status, or the likelihood that the invention would be valid as a patent, manufactured or sold.[15]

Nondiscrimination is a crucial principle. It ensures that all inventors, including small entities and members of marginalized communities, have an equal chance to protect their inventions. Consequently, under the assumption that patents incentivize invention, the equality principle augments everyone's incentives to invent.[16] Beyond its distributive value, the equality promise is designed to increase innovation gains by diversifying the inventive base.[17] A broad pool of inventors can yield a diversity of products, markets, and processes because different founders see different innovation needs.[18] In particular, inventors from underrepresented groups can tackle issues that sit in the blind spots of others or address well-known problems with more inclusive solutions.[19] Access of small technology companies to the patent system bears particular importance.[20] Small entities are both disproportionately innovative and crucially dependent on patents to secure funding and market entry.[21] Yet small

industries. See, for example, JAMES BESSEN & MICHAEL J. MEURER, PATENT FAILURE HOW JUDGES, BUREAUCRATS, AND LAWYERS PUT INNOVATORS AT RISK (2009).

15 *See supra* note 2.

16 *See supra* note 13.

17 *See* Lee, *supra* note 4, at 366 ("[D]isproportionately low participation by other groups represents a missed opportunity."); Jennifer Hunt, Jean-Philippe Garant, Hannah Herman & David J. Munroe, *Why Don't Women Patent?* 2 (Nat'l Bureau of Econ. Rsch., Working Paper No. 17888, 2012) (estimating that a gender-inclusive entrepreneurship can increase GDP per capita by 2.7 percent); W. Keith Robinson, *Protecting American Innovators by Combating the Decline of Patents Granted to Small Entities*, 88 ST. JOHN'S L. REV. 379, 385 (2014) (suggesting that increasing small-entity patenting would boost innovation); Jay Mattappally, *Goliath Beats David: Undoing the Leahy-Smith America Invents Act's Harmful Effects on Small Businesses*, 58 LOY. L. REV. 981, 985 (2012) (arguing that small businesses' patenting can create jobs).

18 *See* Ingrid Verheul, André Van Stel & Roy Thurik, *Explaining Female and Male Entrepreneurship at the Country Level*, 18 ENTREPRENEURSHIP & REG'L DEV. 151 (2006) (discussing differences between male and female entrepreneurship).

19 *Id.*

20 *See* Richard J. Rosen, *Research and Development with Asymmetric Firm Sizes*, 22 RAND J. ECON. 411 (1991) (showing small firms disproportionately patent major inventions); Anthony Breitzman & Patrick Thomas, Small Bus. Admin., Office of Advocacy, *Analysis of Small Business Innovation in Green Technologies* 11 (2011), www.sba.gov/sites/default/files/rs389tot.pdf (showing that small firms obtain more patents per employee than large firms); C.J. Isom & David R. Jarczyk, Small Bus. Admin., Office of Advocacy, *Innovation in Small Businesses: Drivers of Change and Value Use* (2009), www.sba.gov/sites/default/files/rs342tot_0.pdf (showing that small businesses' patents are substantially more likely to be among the top 1 percent of cited patents).

21 *See* Ashish Arora & Robert P. Merges, *Specialized Supply Firms, Property Rights and Firm Boundaries*, 13 INDUS. & CORP. CHANGE 451, 454 (2004) (arguing that patents facilitate investments); Mark Lemley, *The Surprising Resilience of the Patent System*, 95 TEX. L. REV. 1, 53 (2016) (same); Jonathan M. Barnett, *Intellectual Property as a Law of Organization*, 84 S. CAL. L. REV. 787 (2011) (same); Lee, *supra* note 4, at 36–65 (explaining that small firms' patenting facilitates market entry); EUR. UNION INTELL. PROP. OFF., HIGH-GROWTH FIRMS AND

entities are less likely to make use of the patent system.[22] Guaranteeing the access of small entities to the patent system thus best furthers the objective of the patent system to promote innovation.[23]

Despite the significance of the equality principle, equal access to the patent system remains largely theoretical. As Peter Lee put it, on the ground, "the U.S. patent system has become highly corporatized and concentrated."[24] Indeed, most patents are issued to large corporations,[25] with some industries featuring extreme concentration.[26] Inequality overwhelmingly persists among individual inventors as well. Women are issued around 20 percent of patents, and only 8 percent of patents feature women as the primary inventor.[27] The rate of minority inventorship is somewhat under-researched,[28] but indications are that this rate is very low, particularly among Blacks.[29] Generally, as Dan Burk and Mark Lemley observe, "even those [patents] granted to individuals and small corporations are often incubated in large research universities."[30]

Intellectual Property Rights: IPR Profile of High-Potential SMEs in Europe (2019) (showing that patents boost the likelihood of European start-up growth).

[22] *See* Stuart J.H. Graham, Robert P. Merges, Pam Samuelson & Ted Sichelman, *High Technology Entrepreneurs and the Patent System: Results of the 2008 Berkeley Patent Survey*, 24 Berkeley Tech. L.J. 1255 (2009).

[23] U.S. Const. art. I, § 8, cl. 8.

[24] Lee, *supra* note 4, at 347.

[25] See, for example, Dan L. Burk & Mark A. Lemley, The Patent Crisis and How the Courts Can Solve It 41 (2009) ("The overwhelming majority of patents today are granted to large corporations, and even those granted to individuals and small corporations are often incubated in large research universities.").

[26] See, for example, Joel Reidenberg, *Small Participants in Smartphones*, 18 Stan. Tech. L. Rev. 375, 393 (2015) (showing that 90.4 percent of smartphone-related patents belong to large companies).

[27] *See* World Intell. Prop. Org., The Global Gender Gap in Innovation and Creativity: An International Comparison of the Gender Gap in Global Patenting over Two Decades 2, 33 (2023) (finding that between 1999–2020, women were involved in 23 precent of all Patent Cooperation Treaty (PCT) applications, representing 13 percent of all inventors listed, and pointing to 31 percent of women's share in PCT filings in 2020); *see also* U.S. Pat. & Trademark Off., Where Are U.S. Women Patentees? Assessing Three Decades of Growth 1 (2022) (finding that women comprised 13 percent of U.S. patent holders by 2019); Saurabh Vishnubhakat, *Gender Diversity in the Patent Bar*, 14 J. Marshall Rev. Intell. Prop. L. 67 (2014); Jennifer Hunt, Jean-Philippe Garant, Hannah Herman & David J. Munroe, *Why Are Women Underrepresented amongst Patentees?*, 42 Rsch. Pol'y 831, 831 (2013).

[28] Data deficiency on racial participation in patenting may be decreasing, as the America Invents Act directs the PTO to "establish methods for studying the diversity of patent applicants, including those applicants who are minorities, women, or veterans." Pub. L. No. 112-29, § 29, 125 Stat. 284, 339 (2011).

[29] See, for example, Adams Nager, David Hart, Stephen Ezell & Robert D. Atkinson, Info. Tech. & Innovation Found., *The Demographics of Innovation in the United States* 10 (2016), http://www2.itif.org/2016-demographics-of-innovation.pdf (noting that minorities comprise 8 percent of innovators, with Blacks comprising about 0.5 percent); Schuster et al., *supra* note 5; 157 Cong. Rec. H4484 (daily ed. June 23, 2011) (statement of Rep. Moore) (stating that minority-owned companies hold fewer patents than other companies).

[30] *See supra* note 25.

Several reasons for the unequal distribution of patents have nothing to do with the patent system per se. Social, economic, and other pressures force some groups out of the innovation economy and other inventive spaces.[31] Yet part of the problem, and perhaps partial solutions, may lie in issues pertaining to the patent system. The next part discusses such issues and explores the possibility that decentralizing the patent system can improve equality.

9.2 A DECENTRALIZED PATENT SYSTEM

Currently, the patent system features a rigorously centralized structure. The PTO examines patent applications, publishes the granted patents to the public, and increasingly manages postexamination proceedings.[32] While surely unintended, the centralized structure of the patent system jeopardizes equality in three main ways. First, a central examination entity involves high entry costs and requires particular know-how, including institutional knowledge. High entry costs work to the detriment of new and under-resourced inventors.[33] Second, centralization congests the system and induces patent examiners to use decision shortcuts and proxies that favor strong and repeat players. Third, the current system over-grants patents, mainly to big corporations, and these patents form barriers to entry for newcomers. Finally, the current system features an inadequate patent record that lacks vital information about inventions and frustrates the use of that record as a source for consultation in the invention ecosystem. Acquiring such information elsewhere is cost-prohibitive for small inventors, but operating without it exposes them to market and legal risks. The thesis advanced in this chapter is that decentralizing some of the PTO's functions can effectively address these concerns and boost equality.

9.2.1 *The Problems in a Centralized Patent Regime*

The most apparent distributive concern in the patent system involves high entry costs.[34] Patent prosecution has become increasingly expensive, partially due to the

[31] *See supra* note 7; *see also* Christian Kiedaisch, *Growth and Welfare Effects of Intellectual Property Rights When Consumers Differ in Income* (Univ. of Zurich, Dep't of Econ., Working Paper No. 221, 2017), www.econ.uzh.ch/static/wp/econwp221.pdf. (discussing a differential effect of another intellectual property policy – the length of intellectual property protection for rich and poor households).

[32] *See* 35 U.S.C. § 153. For scholarship regarding the administrative review of patent examination, see Sarah Tran, *Patent Powers*, 25 HARV. J.L. & TECH. 595, 599 (2012); Brian J. Love & Shawn Ambwani, *Inter Partes Review: An Early Look at the Numbers*, 81 U. CHI. L. REV. DIALOGUE 93, 94–97 (2014); Saurabh Vishnubhakat, *The Youngest Patent Validity Proceeding: Evaluating Post-Grant Review*, 24 TEX. INTELL. PROP. L.J. 333, 340 (2016); Mark Consilvio & Jonathan R.K. Stroud, *Unraveling the USPTO's Tangled Web: An Empirical Analysis of the Complex World of Post-Issuance Patent Proceedings*, 21 J. INTELL. PROP. L. 33 (2013); Paul R. Gugliuzza, *(In)Valid Patents*, 92 NOTRE DAME L. REV. 292 (2016).

[33] *See infra* Section 9.2.1.

[34] *See* Graham et al., *supra* note 22, at 1311 (reporting findings that patent acquisition costs over US$38,000).

prolonged processes at the PTO, which compound legal and other expenses, and partly because the complexity of these processes requires expensive professionals to navigate them.[35] Patent prosecution may be even *costlier* for small inventors, who, among other things, do not have in-house patent attorneys.[36]

The financial barrier to the patent system prompted Congress to lower the filing fees for small firms and micro-entities through the Leahy-Smith America Invents Act.[37] This statute also entitles small entities and independent and unrepresented inventors to technical, pro bono, and pro se assistance.[38] Despite such measures, inequality seems to worsen with time.[39] The reduced fees have not moved the needle, most likely because these fees are negligible in the overall expenses of patent prosecution. Also, the rate of abandoned applications is more than twofold for pro se applicants than for represented applicants.[40]

High entry costs confine small companies and individuals more than well-resourced corporations. The most obvious result of costly patent prosecution is that small inventors give up on patents. While avoiding patenting may be rational for small entities,[41] it exposes their inventions to copying and may yield an inferior position in the marketplace.[42] Indeed, the rise of trade secrets protection provides alternative, cheaper protection that often suits better the financial capabilities, focus, and business of small entities and individual inventors.[43] Yet, if patents exist as a tool to generate an incentive to create, then the exclusion of certain groups from

[35] *Id.*; *see also* Gene Quinn, *Patent Search 101: Why US Patent Searches Are Critically Important*, IPWATCHDOG (Jan. 13, 2018), https://ipwatchdog.com/2018/01/13/patent-search-101-patent-searches. ("[B]efore spending thousands of dollars to obtain a patent you should obtain a professional patent search and patentability opinion.").

[36] Graham et al., *supra* note 22, at 1311–12 (quoting a technology executive).

[37] 35 U.S.C. § 41(h)(1) (2012); 37 C.F.R. § 1.16.

[38] *See* Pub. L. No. 112-29, § 28, 125 Stat. 339 (2011); Jennifer M. McDowell & Saurabh Vishnubhakat, *The USPTO Patent Pro Bono Program*, 7 CYBARIS INTELL. PROP. L. REV. 1 (2015); Lee, *supra* note 4, at 350–51 (describing the development of the assistance programs).

[39] Lee, *supra* note 4, at 347 n.161 (showing trends); Dennis Crouch, *Small Entity Status*, PATENTLY-O (Feb. 12, 2013), https://patentlyo.com/patent/2013/02/small-entity-status.html (showing that patent filings by small entities declined from approximately 30 percent in 1990 to approximately 18 percent in 2010).

[40] *See* Kate S. Gaudry, *The Lone Inventor: Low Success Rates and Common Errors Associated with Pro-Se Patent Applications*, 7 PLOS ONE e33141, at 3 (2012).

[41] *See* Susan C. Morse, *Entrepreneurship Incentives for Resource-Constrained Firms*, *in* THE CAMBRIDGE HANDBOOK OF LAW AND ENTREPRENEURSHIP IN THE UNITED STATES 197, 199–200 (D. Gordon Smith, Brian Broughman & Christine Hurt eds., 2022) ("[C]apital is often available to a resource-constrained firm in discrete portions, and not continuously. Therefore, a resource-constrained startup often faces a zero-sum tradeoff between making a legal incentive investment and spending on its business."); Lital Helman, Innovation Policy and the Valley of Death (2022) (unpublished manuscript) (on file with author).

[42] *See* Ted Sichelman & Stuart J.H. Graham, *Patenting by Entrepreneurs: An Empirical Study*, 17 MICH. TELECOMM. & TECH. L. REV. 111, 115 (2010) (reporting surveys that show that cost is the main reason start-ups avoid patenting).

[43] *See* Lital Helman, *Trade Secrets and Personal Secrets*, 55 U. RICH. L. REV. 447, 453–56 (2020); David S. Levine & Ted Sichelman, *Why Do Startups Use Trade Secrets?*, 94 NOTRE DAME

patenting adversely affects their incentives to invent.[44] But high costs can be even more devastating; small inventors depend on investments, but investors are reluctant to fund patent prosecution and often delay investments until patents are secured.[45] Consequently, inventors may be forced to relinquish their ventures altogether or settle for lower valuations than their invention is worth.[46]

Consider now the backlog of the patent system. Currently, the PTO examines all patent applications alone, generating severe delays.[47] A high pendency rate has a differential effect on the market. For small players, pendency shrinks the duration and thus the value of patent protection.[48] Big players, in contrast, can make lemonade out of the long application process lemon. Such players can file numerous broad patents, including for embryonic ideas that did not go through full development or feasibility testing. They can then strategically use the "patent pending" status of their applications to persuade others to back away from their asserted territory during the long examination period, even if the application would eventually be denied or reduced in scope.[49]

The backlog at the PTO potentially affects the incentives of examiners as well.[50] While probably unintended, proxies for validity – such as inventors' names, former

L. REV. 751, 758–60 (2019) (showing that trade secrets are better tailored to software start-ups and the like).

44 *See* U.S. CONST. art. I, § 8, cl. 8. Doubts that patents actually promote innovation abound. See, for example, BESSEN & MEURER, *supra* note 14, at 14, 16 (arguing that patents promote innovation only in some industries); Lemley, *supra* note 21, at 52 ("[P]ersuasive evidence that the patent system drives innovation is surprisingly hard to come by."); Petra Moser, *How Do Patent Laws Influence Innovation? Evidence from Nineteenth-Century World's Fairs*, 95 AM. ECON. REV. 1214, 1221 (2005) (finding that patents promote innovation when copying or reverse engineering are easy in a particular industry).

45 *See supra* note 21.

46 *See* ARTI RAI, STUART GRAHAM & MARK DOMS, PATENT REFORM: UNLEASHING INNOVATION, PROMOTING ECONOMIC GROWTH & PRODUCING HIGH-PAYING JOBS: A WHITE PAPER FROM THE U.S. DEPARTMENT OF COMMERCE 1 (2010), www.commerce.gov/sites/default/files/documents/migrated/Patent_Reform-paper.pdf (noting that problems in the patent system could lead to "foregone innovation").

47 *See* U.S. PAT. & TRADEMARK OFF., THE FUTURE PERFORMANCE & ACCOUNTABILITY REPORT 15 (2017), www.uspto.gov/sites/default/files/documents/USPTOFY17PAR.pdf (noting a two-year pendency); Ron A. Katznelson, *My 2010 Wishes for the U.S. Patent Examiner* 85 (2010), http://j.mp/RDK-2010-wishes (criticizing the nontransparent measures by which the PTO measures pendency); Mark A. Lemley & Bhaven Sampat, *Examining Patent Examinations*, 2010 STAN. TECH. L. REV. 2, 3 (2009) (discussing patent pendency).

48 35 U.S.C. § 154(a)(2) (providing that patents shall last for a "term beginning on the date on which the patent issues and ending 20 years from the date on which the application for the patent was filed in the United States").

49 *Cf.* Lemley, *supra* note 21, at 53–54 (noting that patent applications may be filed for reasons unconnected to their validity).

50 *See* Michael D. Frakes & Melissa F. Wasserman, *Is the Time Allocated to Review Patent Applications Inducing Examiners to Grant Invalid Patents?: Evidence from Micro-Level Application Data*, 99 REV. ECON. & STAT. 550 (2017) (hereinafter Frakes & Wasserman, *Is the Time Allocated*); Michael D. Frakes & Melissa F. Wasserman, *Empirical Scholarship on the Prosecution Process at the PTO*, *in* 2 RESEARCH HANDBOOK ON THE LAW & ECONOMICS OF

acquaintance with the representing agent, and institutional affiliation – are almost inevitable considering the severe examination backlog at the PTO and the time constraints imposed on examiners.[51] These biases are compounded by the notorious public choice problems at the PTO that further the interests of large corporate patent filers and other repeat players at the expense of smaller inventors.[52] Institutional capture easily penetrates into the individual level of examiners, who may be contemplating their next career step as patent prosecutors or major patent holders.[53]

The third challenge that the extant regime poses to equality concerns the prevalence of low-quality patents. The issue of patent quality has long troubled patent scholars.[54] From the equality prism, the concern is that the PTO is biased

Intellectual Property 77 (Peter S. Menell, David L. Schwartz & Ben Deporter eds., 2019) (hereinafter Frakes & Wasserman, *Empirical Scholarship*) ("[A]n examiner, on average, spends only 19 hours reviewing a patent application, including reading the patent application, searching for prior art, comparing the prior art with the patent application, writing a rejection, responding to the patent applicant's arguments, and often conducting an interview with the applicant's attorney."); Gene Quinn, *High Value Patents – Where Strength Meets Quality*, IPWatchdog (Dec. 11, 2014), www.ipwatchdog.com/2014/12/11/high-value-patents-where-strengthmeets-quality/id=52569/ ("It is unrealistic to expect an examiner to thoroughly review an average of nearly 50 references per patent in the 16 to 17 hours an examiner can spend per patent while processing the necessary number of patent applications." (quoting Stephen Kunin, former Deputy Commissioner for Patent Examination Policy)).

51 See, for example, Kyle Jensen, Balázs Kovács & Olav Sorenson, *Gender Differences in Obtaining and Maintaining Patent Rights*, 36 Nature Biotech. 307, 308 (2018) (finding more rejections of patents filed by inventors with female names); Gaétan de Rassenfosse, Paul Jensen, T'Mir Julius, Alfons Palangkaraya & Elizabeth Webster, *Who Monitors TRIPS?* (Swinburne Ctr. for Transformative Innovation, Working Paper No. 4/18, 2018), www.swinburne.edu.au/media/swinburneeduau/research/research-centres/cti/working-papers/CTI-Working-Paper_4-18_Who_Monitors_TRIPS.pdf (finding bias against foreign patent applicants); *Lost Einsteins: Lack of Diversity in Patent Inventorship and the Impact on America's Innovation Economy: Hearing before the Subcomm. on Courts, Intell. Prop., and the Internet of the H. Comm. on the Judiciary*, 116th Cong. 84–85 (2019) (statement of Lisa D. Cook, Department of Economics, Michigan State University) (proposing blind patent review).

52 *See* Shobita Parthasarathy, Patent Politics: Life Forms, Markets, and the Public Interest in the United States and Europe 27–28 (2017) (discussing the influence of patent professionals, big corporations, and PTO personnel on the design of the patent system); Burk & Lemley, *supra* note 25, at 107 ("It is little wonder . . . that the USPTO in the 1990s stated its mission as 'to help our customers get patents.' That's capture."); John M. Golden, *Patentable Subject Matter and Institutional Choice*, 89 Tex. L. Rev. 1055, 1098 (2011) ("USPTO examiners primarily interact with parties seeking to obtain patent rights. There is therefore natural cause for concern that USPTO personnel will become subject to a form of intellectual or informational capture and tend to view the world through patent applicants' lenses.").

53 *See* Golden, *supra* note 52, 1100–01 (speculating that patent attorneys "might exert a strong gravitational pull on an administrative agency that works nearly exclusively with such lawyers and agents in adjudicative contexts, and many of whose personnel might contemplate a later career in patent prosecution"); Corinne Langinier & Philippe Marcoul, *Monetary and Implicit Incentives of Patent Examiners* (Univ. of Alberta, Dep't of Econ., Working Paper No. 2009-22, 2009) (discussing career considerations of PTO examiners).

54 See, for example, Frakes & Wasserman, *Empirical Scholarship*, *supra* note 50, at 77 ("There is widespread agreement that the [PTO] allows too many invalid patents"). For discussions of

toward granting patents, de facto disadvantaging small inventors who file fewer patents and must penetrate a dense screen of patents to function. Remarkably, Alberto Galasso and Mark Schankerman find that innovation by small firms is often triggered by invalidating large firms' patents, suggesting that those patents thwart innovative efforts.[55]

A key reason for the over-grant bias is that the PTO has limited access to the information and proficiency required to disqualify patents and insufficient time to acquire such information and proficiency.[56] Indeed, patent applications must be granted absent reasons to deny them.[57] But assessing applications' novelty and nonobviousness typically requires highly contextual, fact-intensive, industry-specific information (to disqualify patents based on a lack of novelty) and very specific expertise (to deny patents based on their obviousness).[58] Such knowledge is naturally dispersed in society rather than concentrated in one agency.[59]

What is more, the incentives of the PTO are set up to make it an ineffective gatekeeper for patent quality. The PTO is largely self-funded by patentees' fees, generating an institutional disincentive to reject patents.[60] Studies even indicate that the PTO grants more patents in areas where fees are higher.[61] To avoid time-

costs that low-quality patents generate, see, for example, FED. TRADE COMM'N, TO PROMOTE INNOVATION: THE PROPER BALANCE OF COMPETITION AND PATENT LAW AND POLICY 5–7 (2003); BESSEN & MEURER, *supra* note 14, at 3; ADAM B. JAFFE & JOSH LERNER, INNOVATION AND ITS DISCONTENTS: HOW OUR PATENT SYSTEM IS ENDANGERING INNOVATION AND PROGRESS, AND WHAT TO DO ABOUT IT 11–13 (2004); Shubha Ghosh & Jay Kesan, *What Do Patents Purchase? In Search of Optimal Ignorance in the Patent Office*, 40 HOUS. L. REV. 1219, 1227–35 (2004); Roger Allen Ford, *The Patent Spiral*, 164 U. PA. L. REV. 827 (2016); T.R. Beard, George S. Ford, Thomas M. Koutsky & Lawrence J. Spiwak, *Quantifying the Cost of Substandard Patents: Some Preliminary Evidence*, 12 YALE J.L. & TECH. 240 (2010).

55 *See* Alberto Galasso & Mark Schankerman, *Patents and Cumulative Innovation: Causal Evidence from the Courts*, 130 Q.J. ECON. 317, 322 (2015).

56 *See* Gregory Mandel, *The Non-Obvious Problem: How the Indeterminate Nonobviousness Standard Produces Excessive Patent Grants*, 42 U.C. DAVIS L. REV. 57 (2008); Rebecca S. Eisenberg, *Obvious to Whom – Evaluating Inventions from the Perspective of PHOSITA*, 19 BERKELEY TECH. L.J., 885, 887 (2004) ("An invention that seems obvious to a person having ordinary skill in the field might nonetheless seem patentworthy to a person who lacks such skill, even after reading the prior art record."); *see also supra* note 50.

57 *See* Frakes & Wasserman, *Is the Time Allocated*, *supra* note 50, at 552 (discussing the "presumption of validity").

58 See, for example, JOHN R. THOMAS, TAILORING THE PATENT SYSTEM FOR SPECIFIC INDUSTRIES 3–4 (2015), https://fas.org/sgp/crs/misc/R43264.pdf (discussing the diversity of inventions and patents).

59 *See* Craig Allen Nard & John F. Duffy, *Rethinking Patent Law's Uniformity Principle*, 101 NW. U. L. REV. 1619, 1631 (2007) ("Within economics there exists the basic assumption that having multiple information gathering points – multiple private actors operating in markets – allows for the generation of more complete and reliable data.").

60 *See* Omnibus Reconciliation Act of 1990, Pub. L. No. 101-508, § 10101, 104 Stat. 1388, 1388–91 (explaining examination fee, issuance fee, and annual maintenance fee).

61 *See* Michael Frakes & Melissa Wasserman, *Does Agency Funding Affect Decision Making?: An Empirical Assessment of the PTO's Granting Patterns*, 66 VAND. L. REV. 67 (2014) (finding support for the hypothesis that the PTO's fee structure incentivizes over-granting patents).

consuming disputes, a swamped PTO is also better off granting borderline patents, particularly to applicants who will likely challenge rejections.[62]

Finally, another way that a centralized patent system contributes to inequality concerns information problems in the patent record. Naturally, a PTO-operated patent record can only include information that the PTO possesses at the time of publication.[63] But such a record is gravely deficient. The current record lacks information about the background science of the invention and any developments since it was filed. Neither does it include information relating to litigations or transactions, such as available licenses and prices.[64] However, its immense value, including robust information in the patent record, is unrealistic under a centralized model. The PTO has no access to the information that is most relevant to make the record useful for the inventive community. Much of this information is also dynamic and is changing over time. A central agency cannot realistically be responsible for collecting and registering updates to the record.

An inhibited record has distributive effects. Highly capitalized inventors can overcome information deficiencies by investing in other methods to acquire information, which is cost-prohibitive for small players.[65] But running an underinformed business involves market and legal risks. The main risk concerns exposure to "patent trolls" – nonpracticing entities who accumulate vast portfolios of dubious patents and use them for strike suits against innocent infringers.[66]

[62] *See* Joseph Scott Miller, *Building a Better Bounty: Litigation-Stage Rewards for Defeating Patents*, 19 Berkeley Tech. L.J. 667, 687–88 (2004) (showing that challenging unmerited grants is rare); Roger Allen Ford, *Patent Invalidity versus Noninfringement*, 99 Cornell L. Rev. 71, 110 (2013) (same); John R. Thomas, *Collusion and Collective Action in the Patent System: A Proposal for Patent Bounties*, 2001 U. Ill. L. Rev. 305, 333 (2001) (same); Lemley, *supra* note 21, at 44 (same).

[63] *See* 35 U.S.C. § 122(b)(1); 37 C.F.R. § 1.211 (2018).

[64] *See* 35 U.S.C. § 112(a); 313 *Recording of Licenses, Security Interests, and Documents Other than Assignments [R-07.2015]*, U.S. Pat. & Trademark Off., www.uspto.gov/web/offices/pac/mpep/s313.html (last visited Oct. 5, 2019); *Search for Patents*, U.S. Pat. & Trademark Off., www.uspto.gov/patents-application-process/search-patents (last visited Nov. 13, 2019) (detailing the items the record entails).

[65] Large companies typically run a mergers-and-acquisitions department to actively look for companies with complementary technology, often to identify acquisition opportunities. Market analysis providers are also providing such services. See, for example, *Find Investments*, Crunchbase, www.crunchbase.com (last visited Oct. 8, 2019); *About Our Company*, Dun & Bradstreet, www.dnb.com/about-us/company.html (last visited Oct. 8, 2019). Free patent search tools exist, but they are limited and may also be tracking searches for the benefit of their operators. See, for example, Google Patent Search (www.google.com/patents) and Free Patents Online (www.freepatentsonline.com/). Free tools to obtain transactional and other patent-related information are not readily available.

[66] See, for example, Mark A. Lemley & Doug Lichtman, *Rethinking Patent Law's Presumption of Validity*, 60 Stan. L. Rev. 45, 48 (2007) ("Sadly, a large and growing number of 'patent trolls' today play this exact strategy, using patents on obvious inventions quite literally to tax legitimate business activity.").

These problems did not go unnoticed, and Congress, courts, and the PTO have attempted to tackle some of them.[67] Yet, high costs, congestion, information problems, and capture are inherent to a centralized PTO and will render any solution that maintains the current structure partial at best. Next, I explore whether decentralizing some PTO functions can provide a better way forward.

9.2.2 *Can Decentralization Provide a Solution?*

Imagine that the power to write information into the record was not exclusive to the PTO but distributed among state and market actors. The patent record would be built on a blockchain or another platform that enables the autonomous sharing of information by authorized parties.[68] Such parties would be able, and in some cases obliged, to update the record with relevant information during the examination process and throughout the duration of the patent. Under a decentralized model, third parties and scientists could submit prior art and weigh in on obviousness for the use of examiners during the examination period. After patents are issued, patentees could include in the record commercial information, such as licensing and pricing information, and even plug-in smart contracts. Courts would list decisions and outstanding cases that pertain to the patents. These updates would inform the patent community whether patent claims are in question, whether the patent holder is prone to litigation, and other useful information that is costly to obtain under the extant regime. The PTO would be responsible for reviewing the patent record and fixing errors.

In my previous work, I tackled the practical aspects of this proposal and the related concerns.[69] The main concern revolves around whether there are adequate incentives for market players to contribute to a decentralized record. This is a critical point. After all, a functioning patent record is a public good. Without private incentives to participate in it, the record would be unable to achieve its goals.

The first answer to that concern is that some contributions to the decentralized record would be automatic or mandatory and would be independent of the

67 *See* Helman, *supra* note 11, at 83–84 (describing measures taken to fix the system).

68 Blockchains are a type of distributed data containers that enable recording transactions without central management or intermediaries. *See* Jean Bacon, Johan David Michels, Christopher Millard & Jatinder Singh, *Blockchain Demystified: A Technical and Legal Introduction to Distributed and Centralised Ledgers*, 25 Rich. J.L. & Tech., no. 1, 2018; Arvind Narayanan, Joseph Bonneau, Edward Felten, Andrew Miller & Steven Goldfeder, Bitcoin and Cryptocurrency Technologies: A Comprehensive Introduction (2016); Primavera De Filippi & Aaron Wright, Blockchain and the Law: The Rule of Code (2018); Don Tapscott & Alex Tapscott, Blockchain Revolution: How the Technology Behind Bitcoin Is Changing Money, Business, and the World (2016). Blockchain is a good candidate for a patent registry due to its distributed nature, which can enable time-stamped registration of patents, sharing robust information about them, and commercializing them autonomously. Yet, this chapter explicitly shuns proposing a particular technology. New technologies can be developed in the future that would be at least as fitting for this task.

69 *See* Helman, *supra* note 11, at 104–11.

participants' goodwill. For example, patent applications would be fully published, with automatic references to similar materials on the record;[70] information about litigations would be added by courts as created, and patentees would be obliged to maintain the accuracy of the information on available licenses. This information would already be a substantial improvement over the current regime.

Consider now the incentives for market players to participate in the system voluntarily. It is relatively easy to see the incentives for patentees to add licensing information to the record. Adding such information would enable patentees to commercialize their inventions without much effort. Some patentees, such as big pharmaceutical companies, may prefer to continue licensing their patents individually.[71] Yet, this functionality can be extremely valuable for small companies or individual patentees that do not have resources to negotiate each license individually, as well as for owners of vast patent portfolios who can build a cost-effective licensing model.

How about the interests of third parties to contribute information to the record? During the examination process, firms would be incentivized to question the validity of patents that would curb their free operations. From their point of view, this mechanism would be a cheaper, easier way to battle a patent than postreview examination, let alone litigation.[72] The concern may be that such parties would be *too* eager to provide invalidating information in a way that would jeopardize the efficiency of the system. My previous work addressed this concern.[73]

Other contributors, such as academics or scientists, may be motivated to participate by other considerations, such as reputation or exposure to new information in their field. Volunteer reviewers are the regular case in many academic frameworks, such as reviews of submissions to scientific journals and grants. It would thus not be surprising to see scientists weigh in on an invention in their field.[74] At the postexamination stage, technology firms and scientists would be incentivized to update and consult the record as an affordable mechanism to avoid infringements, as well as to learn of new inventions and form collaborations.

[70] See, for example, Richard J. Gilbert & Michael L. Katz, *Should Good Patents Come in Small Packages? A Welfare Analysis of Intellectual Property Bundling*, 24 Int'l J. Indus. Org. 931, 931 (2006) (discussing how some patents are connected).

[71] See, for example, Helsinn Healthcare v. Teva Pharm. USA, Inc., 855 F.3d 1356, 1364, 1367–68 (Fed. Cir. 2017) (noting that individual licensing enables patentees to enter differential contracts and to keep licensing terms confidential).

[72] For discussion and comparison between the PTO and court postreview and appeal procedures, see, for example, Consilvio & Stroud, *supra* note 32, at 41–42; Gugliuzza, *supra* note 32, at 272–73 (criticizing the inconsistencies resulting from parallel jurisdiction of the PTO and courts); Saurabh Vishnubhakat, Arti K. Rai & Jay P. Kesan, *Strategic Decision Making in Dual PTAB and District Court Proceedings*, 31 Berkeley Tech. L.J. 45, 69–70 (2016) (comparing litigants' use of Patent Trial and Appeal Board procedures and Article III litigation).

[73] *See* Helman, *supra* note 11.

[74] *See* Daryl E. Chubin & Edward J. Hackett, Peerless Science: Peer Review and U.S. Science Policy 91–95 (1990).

Decentralizing the patent record could transform the record from a static database that includes basic filing information that is barely used in the industry into an up-to-date platform that forms a central tool in the innovation economy. This strategy can potentially improve equality in the patent system in three main ways. First, it would tackle distributive concerns in the patent examination process. Second, it would protect small inventors from information problems. Third, it would boost the commercialization of patents, particularly for small inventors.

Consider first how decentralization can cure distributive harms in the examination process. As discussed, the patent prosecution process is done ex parte under the current regime. However, market actors hold superior information, such as knowledge of instances where the invention was offered for sale or disclosed publicly.[75] The PTO alone is entrusted with raising arguments to reject the patent or narrow down its claims.[76] It performs this task in a suboptimal manner, under time and knowledge constraints.[77] Decentralization would make invalidating information handily available to examiners and reduce the rate of low-quality patents, which form entry barriers for small players. A broader information basis would also save examiners search time and attenuate their need to rely on proxies, which have discriminatory effects.

Even greater equality can be found in the postexamination period. An updated patent record would provide a cost-effective means to gain useful technological, transactional, and legal information throughout the duration of the patents. Making robust information available to small players levels the playing field between them and big players, rendering it less likely that entrenched firms could learn about patents and new players in their field more than start-up ventures.[78] Tackling information problems would also enable innovators to avoid infringements, thus battling patent strike suits, which can devastate small entities.

Finally, decentralization of the record would introduce a platform to commercialize inventions globally. Patentees could list licensing options, potential use cases, and prices on the patent record. Once the record contains such robust transactional information, cooperation with commercial bodies to bring the invention to the

[75] *See Helsinn Healthcare*, 855 F.3d at 1371 (holding that secret agreements can also preclude novelty).

[76] Timothy B. Lee, *Why the Roots of Patent Trolling May Be in the Patent Office*, ARS TECHNICA (Mar. 5, 2018), https://arstechnica.com/tech-policy/2018/03/why-the-roots-of-patent-trolling-may-be-in-the-patent-office/ ("Patent examiners do not just decide whether or not to approve a patent. They're also supposed to narrow a patent's claims to make sure it only covers what the inventor actually invented."); *cf.* 35 U.S.C. 122(e) (sets forth the third-party preissuance submissions).

[77] *See supra* Section 9.1.

[78] *See supra* note 65.

market is much more likely.[79] A distributed registry could also enable functionality not existing today, such as plugging in smart contracts and allowing third parties to act on available licenses automatically.[80] This functionality can be extremely valuable for small companies or individual patentees that do not have resources to negotiate each license individually.

The benefit of this policy is twofold. First and foremost, the dynamic record can further the goal of the patent system – to accelerate the path of innovation to the market.[81] Second, improved commercialization would have a dynamic effect. It could spur innovation and patenting because patents would become an effective reward for inventors.[82]

CONCLUSION

The technological ability to decentralize the power to write into the patent record presents intriguing opportunities to generate a patent system that is more inclusive and diverse and to address the pressing issues of equality in the patent system.

An intriguing question can arise in this context: Considering the pledged efficiency of a blockchain-based database for inventions, why has the market not stepped in to create such a registration itself? The answer to this question is that some trading platforms between inventors and licensees exist worldwide.[83] Yet, without regulation, these platforms are underdeveloped. The first reason is that the market does not internalize the distributive concerns discussed in this chapter, and therefore market-based registries may not develop as efficiently as they should. In this vein, a second issue with market initiatives concerns information and collective action problems. Too many actors from various industries and jurisdictions need to join together to generate an effective patent record on the free market.

Yet the most fundamental reason is that it is simply more efficient to decentralize the state-run patent registry than to create a new registry, especially when distributive concerns are considered. The patent registry is a legal creature. It is set by the law and operates under the controlling statutes in each country. Thus, market initiatives

79 *See* Mark A. Lemley, *Faith-Based Intellectual Property*, 62 UCLA L. REV. 1328, 1334 (2015) (noting that the lion's share of patents today is never commercialized, licensed, or used).

80 *See* Pierluigi Cuccuru, *Beyond Bitcoin: An Early Overview on Smart Contracts*, 25 INT'L J.L. & INFO. TECH. 179 (2017).

81 *See* Gaia Bernstein, *In the Shadow of Innovation*, 31 CARDOZO L. REV. 2257, 2259 (2010) ("Attaining the progress objective . . . requires not just innovation but also an adoption process. Progress can be attained only if people adopt and use the new technology.").

82 Mark A. Lemley, *Property, Intellectual Property, and Free Riding*, 83 TEX. L. REV. 1031, 1031 (2005) ("Intellectual property protection in the United States has always been about generating incentives to create.").

83 See, for example, *Who We Are*, BERNSTEIN, www.bernstein.com (last visited Oct. 8, 2019).

cannot *replace* the existing record, but they can rather duplicate the platform and add to it. This reality harms efficiency and generates distributive harm by adding another registry and multiplying registration costs. At the end of the day, while a market-based scheme has its advantages, it would be more efficient to channel the resources and efforts that are already being made for patent registration to a registry that is valuable to the market.

10

Inequality and Asymmetry in the Making of Intellectual Property a Constitutional Right

Lior Zemer[*]

INTRODUCTION

As the "highest normative act of the state,"[1] a constitution is a unique national product that defines a set of commitments relating to preserving a country's "shared collective existence."[2] Constitutions serve as the basic scripts that enable countries and their citizens to be bound by values and principles that define their social and political construction. The recent "rise of world constitutionalism"[3] resulted in fundamental changes to the unique constitutional culture of many countries, irrespective of their ability to enforce these changes. The inclusion of intellectual property as a socio-economic right in the formal constitutions of many countries of the world provides a striking example of these changes and questions the role of

[*] The ideas developed in this chapter benefited from comments provided on earlier drafts. For this I am grateful to Aharon Barak, Daniel Benoliel, Ben Berger, Margaret Chon, Graeme Dinwoodie, Rochelle Dreyfuss, Susy Frankel, Amir Khoury, Roberta Rosenthal Kwall, David Law, Sonia Lawrence, Amnon Lehavi, Mark Lemely, Miriam Marcowitz-Bitton, Robert Merges, Suzie Navot, Ruth Okediji, Gideon Parchamovsky, Jerome Reichman, Yaniv Roznai, David Vaver, Mila Versteeg, and Peter Yu. Reut Dahan, Amit Elazari, and Yehonatan Hezroni have provided invaluable research assistance. Earlier versions were presented at numerous conferences, including as a keynote speaker at the IP Osgoode Speakers Series at Osgoode Hall Law School in Toronto and at the Third International Intellectual Property Scholars Roundtable at DePaul University College of Law.

[1] Benedikt Goderis & Mila Versteeg, *Transnational Constitutions*, *in* Social and Political Foundations of Constitutions 103, 120 (Denis J. Galligan & Mila Versteeg eds., 2013); Ran Hirschl, *The Political Economy of Constitutionalism in a Non-Secularist World*, *in* Comparative Constitutional Design 164, 174 (Tom Ginsburg ed., 2012); Zachary Elkins, Tom Ginsburg & James Melton, The Endurance of National Constitutions 85 (2009); Mila Versteeg, *Unpopular Constitutionalism*, 89 Ind. L.J. 1133, 1136 (2014).

[2] Beau Breslin, From Words to Worlds: Exploring Constitutional Functionality 5 (2009).

[3] Bruce Ackerman, *The Rise of World Constitutionalism*, 83 Va. L. Rev. 771 (1997).

constitutions as "uniquely national products."[4] Similar to other "legal norms that are exported and imported across borders,"[5] intellectual property laws have been transplanted into the systems of many countries without making necessary changes to align them with the local culture and legal environment. This includes constitutionalizing intellectual property as a basic socio-economic right as early as 1801, as well as ordinary intellectual property legislation.

The process of constitutionalizing intellectual property rights highlights absurdities associated with unequal and asymmetrical power relations within the politics of intellectual property. The findings in this chapter expose the inherent conflicts between international legal harmonization and unbalanced trade powers in intellectual property constitutionalism and how these conflicts affect the most defining document of a nation – the constitution. These findings confirm the "naïve assumption that ideological adherence in constitutions has automatic and immediate effects,"[6] and introduce a new layer to contemporary discourses on the design processes of effective intellectual property regimes. Various ideological motivations explain the reasons behind constitutionalizing intellectual property as a fundamental socio-economic right. These motivations impact conceptions of constitutional autonomy and the preservation of global cultural diversity and question the intuitive assumption that the constitutional protection of a particular right will secure protection on the ground. Recent empirical research has dealt with this proposition and finds that "the poorer a country's human rights record, the greater the number of rights that its constitution tends to contain."[7] This research also finds that there is a negative correlation between constitutionally recognized rights and the level of actual rights protection.[8]

The first section demonstrates the gap between the mere existence of a constitutional equality provision and its application on the ground and presents the three core objectives of the chapter. The second section focuses on intellectual property and examines how inequality is a defining concept in intellectual property that can be articulated in many forms. The third section takes intellectual property and inequality one step further, discussing intellectual property constitutionalism and highlighting the lack of scholarly attention to intellectual property in formal constitutions and the implications. The fourth section demonstrates the incorrect

4 Benedikt Goderis & Mila Versteeg, *The Diffusion of Constitutional Rights*, 39 Int'l Rev. L. & Econ. 1 (2014).

5 Gregory Shaffer, *Transnational Legal Ordering and State Change*, *in* Transnational Legal Ordering and State Change 1, 5 (Gregory Shaffer ed., 2013).

6 John Boli-Bennett & John W. Meyer, *Constitutions as Ideology*, 45 Am. Sociol. Rev. 525, 526 (1980).

7 David S. Law & Mila Versteeg, *The Evolution and Ideology of Global Constitutionalism*, 99 Calif. L. Rev 1163, 1169 (2011).

8 *Id.* at 1248; *see also* Adi Leibovitch, Alexander Stremitzer & Mila Versteeg, *Aspirational Rules* 15 (2019), http://micro.econ.kit.edu/downloads/Stremitzer,%20Leibovitch,%20Versteeg%20-%20Aspirational%20Rules.pdf.

assumption that adding intellectual property rights to a constitution will provide better protection for these rights and highlights how this assumption is predominantly a result of global political inequality and asymmetrical power relations. This section first evaluates the ideological motivations of countries to adopt intellectual property as a socio-economic right in their formal constitutions. It then introduces and empirically analyzes the results of the data collected. This chapter concludes by discussing the inequality-related consequences of unbalanced intellectual property constitutional commitments.

10.1 THREE OBJECTIVES

Catharine MacKinnon applied the claim that a country's inclusion of a particular fundamental right in its formal constitution does not project its enforceability. Her article examined the inclusion of the concept of gender equality in formal constitutions and compared measures of "sex equality" in constitutions.[9] Of the two countries with the highest international ranking for equality of the sexes, Norway has no equality provision in its constitution, while Australia has no formal written bill of rights. In contrast, many countries with the lowest equality rankings in the world have strongly worded provisions guaranteeing equality in general and gender equality in particular. Malawi has one of the most detailed constitutional provisions for equality of the sexes in the world, guaranteeing equal protection for women, invalidating laws that discriminate based on gender, and requiring legislation to be passed to eliminate discriminatory customs and practices, including "sexual abuse, harassment, and violence"[10] as well as "discrimination at work and in property."[11] Malawi sits at 153rd in sex equality among the 169 nations ranked.[12] Indeed, many states have anchored the term "equality" in their formal constitutions. In 2020, Jody Heymann, Aleta Sprague, and Amy Ruab mapped equality clauses in world constitutions.[13] The study examined 193 U.N. member states and found that 20 percent of the constitutions generally protect equality without explicitly mentioning inequality concerning a particular category.[14] Irrespective of the frequent appearance of

[9] Catharine A. MacKinnon, *Gender in Constitutions*, *in* THE OXFORD HANDBOOK OF COMPARATIVE CONSTITUTIONAL LAW 398 (Michel Rosenfeld & András Sajó eds., 2012).

[10] *Id.* at 401.

[11] *See id.*

[12] *See id.*

[13] JODY HEYMANN, ALETA SPRAGUE & AMY RAUB, ADVANCING EQUALITY: HOW CONSTITUTIONAL RIGHTS CAN MAKE A DIFFERENCE WORLDWIDE 22 (2020).

[14] *Id.* The study further found that 76 percent of the constitutions explicitly refer to equality in the context of race or ethnicity and 44 percent of constitutions explicitly prohibit inequality based on language. *Id.* at 25. The study also found that the number of constitutions protecting equality has increased over the years and that constitutions tend to protect equality and nondiscrimination based on religion or belief. *Id.* at 29, 106.

"equality" in constitutions, the authors reminded us how far we still have to go in order to practically and adequately protect equality.

Another example demonstrating the gap between the mere existence of a constitutional equality provision and its application on the ground is the constitution of South Africa. That constitution begins with a commitment that "[t]he Republic of South Africa is one, sovereign, democratic state founded on the following values: . . . Human dignity, the achievement of equality and the advancement of human rights and freedoms."[15] Despite the explicit and detailed defense of equality in the South African Constitution, it appears that, in practice, there exist significant wage gaps based on both race[16] and gender.[17] South Africa is ranked 149 out of 150 in the Gini World Index[18] and is rated 92 out of 153 in economic participation and opportunity in the *Global Gender Gap Report 2020*.[19]

The same conflict was recently examined in relation to the freedoms of expression, movement, association and assembly, religion,[20] private property,[21] torture,[22] and health.[23] An example of the right to health is the constitution of Afghanistan, which commits the State to "provide free preventive health care and treatment of diseases as well as medical facilities to all citizens in accordance with the law."[24] And yet, despite this commitment, Afghanistan has one of the lowest life expectancies in the world.[25] These examples raise complex questions that are critical in the constitutional context, such as the following: Why would countries adopt constitutional

15 S. Afr. Const., 1996, art. 1(a).

16 Haroon Bhorat & Sumayya Goga, *The Gender Wage Gap in Post-Apartheid South Africa: A Re-examination*, 22 J. Afr. Econ. 827 (2013).

17 Debra Shepherd, *Post-Apartheid Trends in Gender Discrimination in South Africa: Analysis through Decomposition Techniques* (Univ. of Stellenbosch, Dep't of Econ., Stellenbosch Economic Working Paper No. 06/08, 2008); Rulof Burger & Rachel Jafta, *Returns to Race: Labour Market Discrimination in Post-Apartheid South Africa* (Univ. of Stellenbosch, Dep't of Econ., Stellenbosch Economic Working Paper No. 04/06, 2006).

18 *GINI Index (World Bank Estimate): South Africa*, World Bank, https://data.worldbank.org/indicator/SI.POV.GINI (last visited July 21, 2022).

19 World Econ. F., Global Gender Gap Report 2020, at 12 (2020), http://www3.weforum.org/docs/WEF_GGGR_2020.pdf. This report measures gender-based inequalities in terms of key outcome variables relating to access to resources such as economic opportunities, education, health, and political empowerment. It is important to note that the overall result of South Africa is good compared with other countries, but inequalities still exist in terms of incorporating women into senior positions in the business sector. *See also* Catherine Ndinda, *Present but Absent: Women in Business Leadership in South Africa*, 13 J. Int'l Women's Stud. 127 (2012).

20 Linda Camp Keith, *Constitutional Provisions for Individual Human Rights (1977–1996): Are They More than Mere "Window Dressing?"* 51 Pol. Rsch. Q. 111 (2002); Adam S. Chilton & Mila Versteeg, *Do Constitutional Rights Make a Difference?*, 60 Am. J. Pol. Sci. 575 (2016).

21 Mila Versteeg, *The Politics of Takings Clauses*, 109 Nw. U. L. Rev. 695, 695–746 (2015).

22 David S. Law, *Constitutions*, *in* The Oxford Handbook of Empirical Legal Research 376, 382 (Peter Cane & Herbert M. Kritzer eds., 2010).

23 *See* Chilton & Versteeg, *supra* note 20.

24 Constitution Jan. 26, 2004, art. 52 (Afghanistan).

25 *See* Law & Versteeg, *supra* note 7, at 869.

commitments that cannot be enforced? What are the ideological motivations for countries to adopt socio-economic rights that conflict with and are unsuitable to their political and social realities? This chapter addresses these questions.

Intellectual property displays a similarly misleading assumption and raises the same questions. This chapter examines this assumption and provides theoretical and empirical support to this claim. It has three main objectives. First, the chapter shows how asymmetrical power relations dictate which countries will include intellectual property as a constitutional guarantee. Second, it discusses how these unequal power relations nurture a wrongful assumption according to which intellectual property as a constitutional guarantee secures better protection in practice. For example, Venezuela, which has one of the most detailed intellectual property provisions in its constitution, was ranked last among 128 nations in the 2016 International Property Rights Index.[26] The text from the Constitution of Venezuela reads as follows:

> Cultural creation is free. This freedom includes the right to invest in, produce and disseminate the creative, scientific, technical and humanistic work, as well as legal protection of the author's rights in his works. The State recognizes and protects intellectual property rights in scientific, literary and artistic works, inventions, innovations, trade names, patents, trademarks and slogans, in accordance with the conditions and exceptions established by law and the international treaties executed and ratified by the Republic in this field.[27]

Haiti has the oldest provision situating intellectual property as a fundamental human right in the world, which dates back to 1801.[28] Despite redrafting its working constitution in 2012,[29] Haiti is ranked three places before last.[30] To quote MacKinnon, "often the reasons for the gap between guarantee and reality lie elsewhere than in constitutions."[31]

Third, this chapter invites the constitutional aspect into scholarship that heavily criticizes the lack of balance between countries in global intellectual property affairs, where weaker countries are coerced into accepting the standards of dominant countries. One of the main expressions of this criticism revolves around the unilateral acts that certain countries inflict upon other countries and the suitability of international intellectual property standards and their enforcement in certain parts

[26] Sary Levy-Carciente, 2016 International Property Rights Index: Executive Summary4 (2016), www.indiapropertyrights.org/2016-International-Property-Rights-Index.pdf.

[27] Constitution Mar. 24, 2000, No. 5.453 Ext, art. 98 (Venez.).

[28] Constitution de Saint-Domingue de 1801 [Haitian Constitution of 1801], July 8, 1801, art. 13 (Haiti).

[29] The new version of the intellectual property clause provides: "Scientific, literary and artistic property is protected by law." Loi Constitutionnelle de 2012 Portant Amendement de la Constitution de 1987 [Haiti's Constitution of 1987 with Amendments through 2012], June 20, 2012, art. 38 (Haiti).

[30] *See* Levy-Carciente, *supra* note 26, at 4.

[31] *See* MacKinnon, *supra* note 9, at 402.

of the world. As this chapter shows, coercing countries to constitutionalizing intellectual property rights drives many adopting countries into severe violation of these rights and to consequently appear on lists of countries that do not adequately protect intellectual property. This chapter aims to add a layer to this discourse by examining how asymmetrical power relations do not leave constitutions unaffected.

10.2 INTELLECTUAL PROPERTY AND INEQUALITY

Intellectual property systems increase the benefits and reward the owners or investors of an idea, product, or process gained from their activity.[32] Inequality is a concept embedded within contemporary intellectual property discourses and explains many of the system's deficiencies. The following three examples highlight this claim. First, inequality in intellectual property explains limits on access to knowledge and their effect on income equality and local stability.[33] Because these systems have been transformed into a "hegemonic battleground,"[34] rather than preserving their role as "an indispensable tool of modern economic management,"[35] they feed power asymmetries that dictate who owns and controls products of knowledge. In this regard, Rebecca Eisenberg and Richard Nelson claim:

> Patent rights motivate private firms to invest in research, but they also introduce significant inefficiencies that may inhibit future research. Patents permit innovators to restrict access to, and thus raise prices for, their inventions. Although sometimes necessary to allow firms to recover R&D [research and development] costs and thus profit from innovation, such pricing is inefficient, because it excludes users who would be willing to pay enough to cover marginal production costs but not the additional patent premium.[36]

Another empirical study found that increasing patent breadth leads to economic growth by increasing R&D but also simultaneously increases income inequality by increasing the rate of return on assets. The researchers also examined the macroeconomic effects of international intellectual property rights. They found that strengthening patent protection in any given country increases global economic

[32] The U.S. Constitution demonstrates this purpose in section 8, which lists the powers of Congress and states that one of these powers is "[t]o promote the Progress of Science and useful Arts, by securing for limited Times to Authors and Inventors the exclusive Right to their respective Writings and Discoveries." U.S. CONST. art. I, § 8, cl. 8.

[33] Amy Kapczynski, *The Access to Knowledge Mobilization and the New Politics of Intellectual Property*, 117 YALE L.J. 804 (2008).

[34] JOHN TEHRANIAN, INFRINGEMENT NATION: COPYRIGHT 2.0 AND YOU 170 (2011).

[35] Peter Drahos, *Thinking Strategically about Intellectual Property Rights*, 21 TELECOMM. POL'Y 201, 207 (1997).

[36] Rebecca S. Eisenberg & Richard R. Nelson, *Public vs. Proprietary Science: A Fruitful Tension?*, 131 DAEDALUS 89, 92 (2002). See, for example, SIVA VAIDHYANATHAN, COPYRIGHTS AND COPYWRONGS: THE RISE OF INTELLECTUAL PROPERTY AND HOW IT THREATENS CREATIVITY 50–52 (2001).

growth but also worsens income inequality in both developed and developing countries.[37] Similarly, the *World Social Report 2020*, which addresses complex issues of inequality,[38] states that technological changes are driving wage and income inequality upward and most highly skilled workers away. The report further refers to intellectual property, saying that it must become one of the main focal points of the international community, alongside transnational crimes and international trade, to reduce inequalities in an interconnected world.[39] States must agree on "a more flexible approach to intellectual property rights that can provide adequate patent protection, while enabling and facilitating access to technological enhancements within and among countries."[40]

Second, inequality in intellectual property results in social exclusion and explains the rapid growth in counterfeit goods. This is another way to demonstrate unequal power relations between weak and strong private members of society. Intellectual property laws act as laws of social exclusion, building cultural fences around goods of high social symbolism. Consumers react to this exclusion by massively using counterfeit goods, thereby creating and financially feeding a market where violations of intellectual property rights flourish. The consumption of these goods is a "strategic response to the general cultural struggle of acceptance and recognition in the context of class divided property relations."[41] In other words, using these counterfeit goods is a "social reaction to inequality and marginalization ... the counterfeit trade thrives in the context of organized, historically rooted, structural inequality."[42]

Third, on the international level, inequality persists and defines differences between weak and strong countries – for example, in access to medicine.[43] In this area, inequalities are magnified by intellectual property regulations.[44] The third example is best explained using the explanatory narratives Peter Yu provides for the developing countries' accession to the Agreement on Trade-Related Aspects of Intellectual Property Rights (TRIPS Agreement). The bargain narrative provides that this agreement is a product of a compromise between developing and developed countries. While developed countries received stronger protection for intellectual property rights and a reduction in restrictions against foreign direct

[37] Angus C. Chu & Shin-Kun Peng, *International Intellectual Property Rights: Effects on Growth, Welfare and Income Inequality*, 33 J. MACROECONOMICS 276, 277, 284 (2011).

[38] *See* UNITED NATIONS DEP'T OF ECON. & SOC. AFFS., WORLD SOCIAL REPORT 2020: INEQUALITY IN A RAPIDLY CHANGING WORLD (2020) [hereinafter WORLD SOCIAL REPORT 2020].

[39] *Id.* at 15.

[40] *Id.* at 79.

[41] Chris Rojek, *Counterfeit Commerce: The Illegal Accumulation and Distribution of Intellectual Property*, *in* THE SAGE HANDBOOK OF INTELLECTUAL PROPERTY 189, 200 (Matthew David & Debora Halbert eds., 2015).

[42] *Id.*

[43] *See generally* INTELLECTUAL PROPERTY, PHARMACEUTICALS AND PUBLIC HEALTH: ACCESS TO DRUGS IN DEVELOPING COUNTRIES (Kenneth C. Shadlen, Samira Guennif, Alenka Guzmán & N. Lalitha eds., 2011).

[44] MIKAYLA NOVAK, INEQUALITY: AN ENTANGLED POLITICAL ECONOMY PERSPECTIVE 139 (2018).

investment, developing countries obtained lower tariffs on textiles and agriculture as well as protection against unilateral sanctions imposed by the United States and other developed countries via the mandatory dispute settlement process.[45] This narrative, however, does not give enough weight to the fact that power relations between developed and developing countries at the time of the negotiations were far from equal. The coercion narrative declares that "the TRIPs Agreement is considered an unfair trade document that developed countries imposed on their less developed counterparts. The Agreement is 'coercive,' 'imperialistic,' and does not take into consideration the goals and interests of less developed countries."[46] An additional narrative suggests that developing countries did not fully understand the importance and implications of intellectual property protection, which has led to an agreement that does not reflect their interests.[47]

These narratives highlight how unequal power relations impact the development of international and national intellectual property laws in developing and politically weaker countries.[48] In times of health crisis, highlighted since the COVID-19 pandemic began to control the life of people in every corner of the world, inequality in access to medicine will have a devastating effect on these countries. According to the U.N. Development Programme, the crisis threatens to devastate developing country economies and ramp up inequality disproportionately.[49] Interestingly, the constitution of only one country in the world explicitly mentions access to medicine as part of its clause protecting intellectual property as a fundamental socio-economic right.[50] Article 41 of the Bolivian Constitution of 2009 provides:

> I. The State shall guarantee the access of the population to medicines.
> II. The State shall prioritize generic medicines through the promotion of their domestic production and, if need be, shall decide to import them.
> III. The right to access medicine shall not be restricted by intellectual property rights and commercial rights, and it contemplates quality standards and first generation medicines.

Access to medicine is not the only area of conflict between developed and developing countries. Yu notes that both domestic and international digital

[45] Peter K. Yu, *TRIPs and Its Discontents*, 10 Marq. Intell. Prop. L. Rev. 369, 371 (2006).

[46] *Id.* at 373.

[47] *Id.* at 375; *see also* Graeme B. Dinwoodie & Rochelle Cooper Dreyfuss, *Designing a Global Intellectual Property System Responsive to Change: The WTO, WIPO and Beyond*, 46 Hous. L. Rev. 1187 (2009).

[48] World Social Report 2020, *supra* note 38, at 166.

[49] *COVID-19: Looming Crisis in Developing Countries Threatens to Devastate Economies and Ramp Up Inequality*, United Nations Dev. Programme (Mar. 30, 2020), www.undp.org/content/undp/en/home/news-centre/news/2020/COVID19_Crisis_in_developing_countries_threatens_devastate_economies.html.

[50] For constitutional guarantees of access to medicines in general, see S. Katrina Perehudoff, Brigit Toebes & Hans Hogerzeil, *Essential Medicines in National Constitutions: Progress since 2008*, 18 Health & Hum. Rights J. 141 (2016).

copyright enforcement measures pose threats to human rights such as free speech and free press.[51] He explains how favoring rights holders over the public in copyright feeds inequality:

> [I]n an age where digital literacy is highly important, users who cannot exercise their right to freedom of opinion and expression are unlikely to be able to function effectively in the digital environment. It is therefore no surprise that UN bodies and developing country governments have expressed grave concern that the growing global digital divide could cause many individuals and developing countries to lose out on the unprecedented opportunities generated by the information revolution. Such impeded access would make it difficult for individuals to fully realize themselves and to develop ... human capabilities.[52]

What needs to be done, in the words of Laurence Helfer, is to "reorient a legal discourse that privileged the private (and often corporate) ownership of IP [intellectual property] over human rights and other societal values."[53] Inequality and power asymmetries, as defining defects of global intellectual property developments, have brought many scholars, such as Graeme Dinwoodie and Rochelle Dreyfuss, to declare that "the North had the South over a barrel."[54] Daniel Benoliel, in his recent inquiry into patents and economic growth, further explains the North–South dichotomy. His approach raises concerns relating to asymmetrical power relations within global intellectual property clubs of states:

> Growing evidence reveals differences between developing countries in their ability to make use of [intellectual property rights] as a tool for fostering domestic innovation. All these pieces of evidence are startling when placed against the backdrop of a traditional World Bank-led and rather inflexible North/South country-group dichotomy, or some variant thereof. Such an innovation policy setting continually highlights the asymmetries between Northern countries, which are deemed to generate innovative products and technologies, and Southern countries, which are generally thought to consume them.[55]

In sum, inequality in intellectual property can be demonstrated in many forms. It can be demonstrated through the restriction on access to knowledge, through social exclusion that fosters gaps between weak and strong private members of society – and, of course, through fostering such gaps between the countries of the

[51] Peter K. Yu, *Digital Copyright Enforcement Measures and Their Human Rights Threats*, *in* Research Handbook on Human Rights and Intellectual Property 455 (Christophe Geiger ed., 2015).

[52] *Id.* at 458.

[53] Laurence R. Helfer, *Human Rights and Intellectual Property: Mapping an Evolving and Contested Relationship*, *in* The Oxford Handbook of Intellectual Property Law 117, 127–28 (Rochelle Dreyfuss & Justine Pila eds., 2018).

[54] Graeme B. Dinwoodie & Rochelle C. Dreyfuss, A Neofederalist Vision of TRIPS 33 (2012).

[55] Daniel Benoliel, Patent Intensity and Economic Growth 49 (2017).

world at the international level. As mentioned at the beginning, this chapter takes the discussion further and shows how inequality permeates formal constitutions through intellectual property protection clauses. The next section, therefore, lays down the fundamental discussion on intellectual property and constitution and highlights the absence of scholarly debate on intellectual property in formal constitutions.

10.3 INTELLECTUAL PROPERTY CONSTITUTIONALISM

Contemporary scholarship on the relationship between intellectual property and constitutionalism has focused on the way scholars have addressed intellectual property–related constitutional clauses, such as the U.S. constitutional clause that empowers Congress "[t]o promote the Progress of Science and useful Arts, by securing for limited Times to Authors and Inventors the exclusive Right to their respective Writings and Discoveries."[56] This focus has left outside the discourse a two-century phenomenon, in which countries protect intellectual property as a socio-economic constitutional right alongside the rights to health, work, education, housing, and private property.[57] The presence of intellectual property in bills of rights has much to tell about the nature of the right, its constitutional status in different countries and geographical regions, and the constitutional and cultural ideologies underlying the decision to adopt the right.[58] Such presence further highlights the benefits of learning from other systems and allows a better viewpoint on the image of intellectual property as a system of rules that protects cultural diversity and the universality of human rights.

The first time a constitution included intellectual property as a basic right, as opposed to an empowerment clause, was the 1801 Constitution of Haiti declaring the right to benefit from inventions in rural machinery.[59] According to Article 70 of that constitution, "The law provides for awards to inventors of rural machines, or for the preservation of the exclusive ownership of their discoveries." Two of the youngest countries in the world, South Sudan and Kosovo, have made intellectual property part of their constitutions. The 2011 constitution of the former includes

[56] U.S. CONST. art. I, § 8, cl. 8. See, for example, Thomas B. Nachbar, *Intellectual Property and Constitutional Norms*, 104 COLUM. L. REV. 272 (2004); David Lange, *Sensing the Constitution in* Feist, 17 U. DAYTON L. REV. 367 (1992); Edward C. Walterscheid, *Conforming the General Welfare Clause and the Intellectual Property Clause*, 13 HARV. J.L. & TECH. 87 (1999); Dotan Oliar, *Making Sense of the Intellectual Property Clause: Promotion of Progress as a Limitation on Congress's Intellectual Property Power*, 94 GEO. L.J. 1771, 1845 (2006). *See also* Eldred v. Ashcroft, 537 U.S. 186, 223 (2003); Golan v. Holder, 565 U.S. 302 (2012); Lawrence Lessig, *Copyright's First Amendment*, 48 UCLA L. REV. 1057, 1065 (2001).

[57] Goderis & Versteeg, *supra* note 4, at 7.

[58] See, for example, Fabrício Bertini Pasquot Polido & Mônica Steffen Guise Rosina, *The Emergence and Development of Intellectual Property Law in South America, in* THE OXFORD HANDBOOK OF INTELLECTUAL PROPERTY LAW, *supra* note 53, at 431, 444–47.

[59] HAITIAN CONSTITUTION OF 1801, *supra* note 28.

"intellectual property rights" in the list of "national powers."[60] Article 46 deals with the right to own property and its limits while stating that "intellectual property is protected by law."[61] Only a handful of scholars in the field of intellectual property or comparative constitutionalism referred to this phenomenon – intellectual property as part of a list of fundamental socio-economic rights in a formal constitution. These inquiries only briefly mentioned intellectual property.[62]

The wisdom behind adopting intellectual property rights in formal constitutional documents is embedded in the presumptions that constitutional laws "send a message about the priority of particular policies"[63] and that "constitutional commitments are potentially credible ones and send a strong signal to potential buyers and investors."[64] Although the idea of written constitutions has spread to virtually every corner of the world, scholars are divided over the strength of constitutional text as a source for learning about constitutional practice. On the one hand, "constitutions are gaining recognition as enforceable legal documents, rather than mere declarations."[65] On the other hand, the gap between constitutional text and its applicability raises questions about the role and impact of the text. Horowitz defines this gap as one between "law in books" and "law in action," explaining as follows: "[T]he gap between a formal constitution and the practice under its aegis is perhaps greater than with ordinary law. Because constitutions often perform symbolic or aspirational functions that have little relationship to the ways in which constitutional law actually operates."[66] Moreover, some constitutions are just "sham."[67] For example, they could bear "no relationship to reality."[68]

David Law and Mila Versteeg explain this tension by drawing a distinction between de jure, written, codified, or formal constitutions ("large-C"

60 Constitution (2011), sched. (A)24 (S. Sudan).

61 Kushtetuta e Republikës Së Kosovës [Constitution of the Republic of Kosovo], art. 46.

62 See, for example, Goderis & Versteeg, *supra* note 4; Zachary Elkins, Tom Ginsburg & Beth Simmons, *Getting to Rights: Treaty Ratification, Constitutional Convergence, and Human Rights Practice*, 54 Harv. Int'l L.J. 61, 72 (2013). *See also* Tom Ginsburg, Terence C. Halliday & Gregory Shaffer, *Constitution-Making as Transnational Legal Ordering, in* Constitution-Making and Transnational Legal Order 10 (Tom Ginsburg, Terence C. Halliday & Gregory Shaffer eds., 2019); Christophe Geiger, *"Constitutionalizing" Intellectual Property Law? The Influence of Fundamental Rights on Intellectual Property in the European Union*, 37 Int'l Rev. Intell. Prop. & Competition L. 371 (2006).

63 Elkins, Ginsburg & Simmons, *supra* note 62, at 81.

64 Goderis & Versteeg, *supra* note 1, at 114; Daniel A. Farber, *Rights as Signals*, 31 J. Legal Stud. 83, 85–94, 98 (2002).

65 Vlad Perju, *Constitutional Transplants, Borrowing, and Migrations, in* The Oxford Handbook of Comparative Constitutional Law, *supra* note 9, at 1313, 1314–15.

66 Morton J. Horowitz, *Constitutional Transplants*, 10 Theoretical Inq. L. 535, 536 (2009); *see also* Henc van Maarseveen & Gen van der Tang, Written Constitutions: A Computerized Comparative Study 11 (Oceana Publications 1978) (1943).

67 David S. Law & Mila Versteeg, *Sham Constitutions*, 101 Calif. L. Rev. 863 (2013).

68 *Id.* at 879.

Constitutions) on the one hand and de facto, unwritten, uncodified, or informal constitutions ("small-c" constitutions) on the other.[69] The latter attracted much scholarly debate, while the former has much less debate even though it represents an "act of making reasoned, explicit, commitments in written form."[70] A focus on formal constitutions has its limits. Certainly, "not all that is constitutional is written, and not all that is written is constitutional."[71] However, "the text pays extraordinary dividends both in terms of analytic leverage and in understanding change in the broader constitutional order."[72] For certain countries, the choice to constitutionally codify intellectual property as a basic right projects their commitment toward certain goals in pursuing the common good and highlights their will to become members of the international community. As this chapter will show, this choice sometimes violates norms of equality and enforces cultural hegemony.

10.4 INEQUALITY AND INTELLECTUAL PROPERTY CONSTITUTIONALISM

After discussing and illustrating inequality in intellectual property and how it is articulated in formal constitutions, this chapter shows the asymmetrical motivations of countries in adopting intellectual property rights in their constitutions. This section shows that, in reality, adding intellectual property rights to a constitution does not necessarily provide better protection to these rights, in contrast to the intuitive assumption that the constitutional protection of a particular right will secure protection on the ground. This section further highlights how this assumption is predominantly a result of global political inequality and asymmetrical power relations. It also shows that this assumption often stimulates constitutional templates unsuitable for the local culture or the countries' ability to apply these templates locally. This section is divided into two subsections. The first subsection evaluates the ideological motivations of countries to adopt intellectual property as a socio-economic right in their formal constitutions, and the second subsection introduces and empirically analyzes the results of the data collected that support the main claim of this chapter. The findings undoubtedly show that when countries adopt intellectual property rights in their constitutions, sometimes due to asymmetrical power relations, it does not assure protection on the ground.

10.4.1 *Asymmetrical Motivations*

Constitutional ideas diffuse across borders, systems, and contexts.[73] David Strang defines diffusion as "the process by which the prior adoption of a trait or practice in a

[69] Law & Versteeg, *supra* note 7, at 1188; *see also supra* Section 10.2.

[70] Perju, *supra* note 65.

[71] ELKINS, GINSBURG & MELTON, *supra* note 1, at 36.

[72] *Id.*

[73] See further inquiry in THE MIGRATION OF CONSTITUTIONAL IDEAS (Sujit Choudhry ed., 2009).

population alters the probability of adoption for the remaining non-adopters."[74] In their study of the diffusion of 108 rights across 188 countries in sixty-one years, Benedikt Goderis and Mila Versteeg found evidence of diffusion to particular groups of countries. For example, countries with a common aid donor or a common colonizer suggest that constitutions are affected by coercive pressures from aid donors and former colonizers.[75] Diffusion can also be found among countries that compete for foreign capital[76] or aim to be acculturated into the constitutional norms of world culture.[77] In these situations, unequal power relations dictate the content and structure of many norms that found their way into constitutions, regardless of ideological preferences that aim to protect cultural diversity and local legal history. When intellectual property is at stake, these diffusion channels exhibit how unequal power relations result in countries adding to their formal constitutions rights and duties that they cannot protect.

Various pathways define foreign influences and mechanisms of rights diffusion in constitutional design. The common mechanisms employed are coercion, learning, competition, and acculturation.[78] The logic behind competition suggests that states strategically imitate foreign constitutions in order to attract foreign capital. Competition is the rivalry between two or more states for material benefits.[79] Thus, countries act strategically in order to attract foreign capital, design a set of rules, and establish institutions that signal to investors and buyers that the local market can accommodate their interests, limit economic risks, and provide stability. Constitutional documents and lists of fundamental rights provide one of the ultimate sources of good signals to alleviate foreign investors' concerns. Contemporaneous observers have found that a high level of protection of basic human rights renders countries more attractive to foreign investment.[80] Investors believe that "regimes with strong human rights records are typically stable ones"[81] and that public reception will be better if their company gains a reputation that promotes fair trade, does not engage child labor, or builds where basic income is unavailable. Thus, when governments offer a strong and detailed list of rights in a constitution, they believe it "may attract economic benefits."[82] Property and

[74] David Strang, *Adding Social Structure to Diffusion Models: An Event History Framework*, 19 Sociol. Methods & Rsch. 324, 324 (1991).

[75] Goderis & Versteeg, *supra* note 1, at 124.

[76] *Id.* at 112–14.

[77] *Id.* at 124–26.

[78] See, for example, Roderic O'Gorman, *Environmental Constitutionalism: A Comparative Study*, 6 Transnat'l Envtl. L. 435, 446–47 (2017); Hanna Lerner & Amir Lupovici, *Constitution-Making and International Relations Theories*, 20 Int'l Stud. Persp. 412, 420–21 (2019).

[79] David S. Law, *Globalization and the Future of Constitutional Rights*, 102 Nw. U. L. Rev. 1277, 1307–11 (2008).

[80] Matthias Busse & Carsten Hefeker, *Political Risk, Institutions and Foreign Direct Investment*, 23 Eur. J. Pol. Econ. 397 (2007).

[81] Goderis & Versteeg, *supra* note 1; Leibovitch, Stremitzer & Versteeg, *supra* note 8, at 113.

[82] Goderis & Versteeg, *supra* note 1, at 114.

intellectual property as constitutional human rights are important to foreign investors. In other words, when a state constitutionalizes intellectual property rights in its highest formal legal script, it invites investors to view its commitment to their rights.

Another example of how constitutional ideas diffuse across the border is the "learning" process. Learning means that "countries borrow each other's constitutional provisions because the constitutional choices of others have altered their preexisting beliefs: they adopt certain arrangements only when they are convinced that these will be beneficial."[83] Learning raises interesting issues with regard to intellectual property laws. Countries are open to learning from foreign sources, mainly because "the new global obligations from the treatment of intellectual property are transmitted from the international to the national level."[84] Intellectual property rights

> have gained increased prominence on the international economic agenda, rich and poor countries alike have responded by reforming their copyright, patent and trademark regimes, introducing new legislation, and creating new administrative and judicial institutions to facilitate the enforcement of these rights. In so doing, most countries have brought their [intellectual property right] systems into conformity with – and at times exceeded – the standards required by TRIPs.[85]

Ruth Okediji further reminded us how these processes affect weaker countries:

> Progressive harmonization of international IP law has continued in various fora, exacerbating historical and continuing burdens on the economic prospects of developing and least-developed countries. In particular, multilateral, regional, and bilateral trade agreements have assumed a crucial role in the creation of new international IP norms, with even stronger requirements and fewer safeguards for public welfare interests.[86]

The above reflects how "states respond to cultural forces"[87] and how, in doing so, they often emulate foreign constitutional templates irrespective of their content, unsuitable dialectics to the local culture, or even their ability to apply them locally. This diffusion mechanism is defined as acculturation – denoting, as Ryan Goodman and Derek Jinks explain, "the general process of adopting the beliefs and behavioral patterns of the surrounding culture."[88] Acculturation is different from coercion or

[83] *Id.* at 115; *see also* Tom Ginsburg, Svitlana Chernykh & Zachary Elkins, *Commitment and Diffusion: How and Why National Constitutions Incorporate International Law*, 2008 U. Ill. L. Rev. 201, 229.

[84] Kenneth C. Shadlen, Andrew Schrank & Marcus J. Kurtz, *The Political Economy of Intellectual Property Protection: The Case of Software*, 49 Int'l Stud. Q. 45, 46 (2005).

[85] *Id.*

[86] Ruth L. Okediji, *Does Intellectual Property Need Human Rights?*, 51 N.Y.U. J. Int'l L. & Pol. 1, 15 (2018).

[87] Ryan Goodman & Derek Jinks, *How to Influence States: Socialization and International Human Rights Law*, 54 Duke L.J. 621, 654 (2004).

[88] *Id.* at 638.

competition because it explains how states act in order to reap social benefits. The logic behind acculturation is premised on organizational sociology, implying that organizations adopt models "not because of their functional utility but because of their legitimacy and the social relationships they represent."[89] Acculturation brings states to sign international human rights agreements and adopt environmental policies and other trade treaties without intending to comply with their requirements.[90] For example, as discussed earlier, the number of constitutions that include provisions on gender equality is increasing. However, as MacKinnon has found, the existence of such a provision is disconnected from its practical applicability.[91] What states achieve through acculturation is an option to signal to domestic and international audiences that they value integration in world society and comply with cultural norms. Acculturation has been a defining component in contemporary discourse on intellectual property protection for indigenous cultures and native communities[92] and on the tension between preserving ancient languages and cultural assimilation.[93] Acculturation in these ways has impacted biodiversity, cultural diversity,[94] as well as individual acceptance of the effects of acculturation.[95]

Many countries, rather than engaging in deliberate processes of adopting foreign constitutional norms and textual choices, are coerced into applying values alien to their national identity. Coercion sets aside the constitutional autonomy of a country and its cultural and legal histories.[96] Under this logic, "weaker states will converge upon the models provided by stronger states."[97] Powerful countries often pursue coercion unilaterally to overcome resistance to international treaties,[98] respect international norms, and join multilateral institutions. However, coercion can also be used as a mechanism to assist countries in nation-building.[99]

89 *Id.*

90 *Id.* at 648.

91 MacKinnon, *supra* note 9, at 402.

92 Julie Hollowell, *Intellectual Property Protection and the Market for Alaska Native Arts and Crafts*, *in* Indigenous Intellectual Property Rights: Legal Obstacles and Innovative Solutions 55, 71 (Mary Riley ed., 2004).

93 Esther Almeida, *Traditional Knowledge: An Analysis of the Current International Debate Applied to the Ecuadorian Amazon Context*, *in* Human Rights and Intellectual Property Rights: Tensions and Convergences 209, 215 (Mpazi Sinjela ed., 2007).

94 Josephine R. Axt, M. Margaret Lee & David M. Ackerman, Biotechnology, Indigenous Peoples, and Intellectual Property Rights 20 (1993).

95 Ngulube Patrick, Handbook of Research on Theoretical Perspectives on Indigenous Knowledge Systems in Developing Countries 403 (2017).

96 See, for example, David S. Law, *Imposed Constitutions and Romantic Constitutions*, *in* The Law and Legitimacy of Imposed Constitutions 34, 37 (Richard Albert, Xenophon Contiades & Alkmene Fotiadou eds., 2018).

97 Goderis & Versteeg, *supra* note 1, at 123.

98 See, for example, Jed Rubenfeld, *Unilateralism and Constitutionalism*, 79 N.Y.U. L. Rev. 1971, 1978 (2004).

99 Constance Grewe & Michael Riegner, *Internationalized Constitutionalism in Ethnically Divided Societies: Bosnia-Herzegovina and Kosovo Compared*, 15 Max Planck Yb. United Nations L. Online 1 (2011); *see also* Richard Albert, *Constitutions Imposed with Consent?*, *in*

Coercion is not an alien concept in contemporary intellectual property discourse. From a multilateral perspective, the TRIPS Agreement has been at the forefront of critiques. The primary complaint is that "there were elements of coercion and questionable trade-offs may have been made between market access for commodities and intellectual property protection."[100] The aggressive imposition of intellectual property norms on developing countries has become associated with concepts such as "recolonization"[101] and economic imperialism.[102] From a unilateral perspective, coercion has become a matter of trade policy in intellectual property. Lack of intellectual property protection risks economic isolation and unilateral acts such as economic sanctions and placement on lists of counterfeiting countries. The U.S. Trade Representative's *Special 301 Report*[103] is an example where a government empowers trade representatives to unilaterally test the level of intellectual property protection in other countries. Another example is the European Union's annual *Report on the Protection and Enforcement of Intellectual Property Rights in Third Countries*. In its 2020 Report, the European Commission has remarked that one of the main objectives of the report is to "inform right holders, in particular small and medium-sized enterprises, about potential risks to their [intellectual property rights] when engaging in business activities in certain third countries and thus to allow them to design business strategies and operations to protect the value of their intangibles."[104]

The motivations of countries to include intellectual property in their constitutional bills of rights affect the structure of intellectual property constitutional clauses. Such clauses are sometimes shaped as a result of external interests or the influence of strong elites, as these clauses may "bear the imprint of the powerful."[105] These imprints, as discussed earlier, disturb constitutional cultures that countries aim to preserve. These imprints project a desired and unequal cultural hegemony that

THE LAW AND LEGITIMACY OF IMPOSED CONSTITUTIONS (Richard Albert, Xenophon Contiades & Alkmene Fotiadou eds., 2018).

100 DINWOODIE & DREYFUSS, *supra* note 54, at 41.

101 Peter Drahos, *Global Property Rights in Information*, 13 PROMETHEUS 6, 9 (1995).

102 SAM F. HALABI, INTELLECTUAL PROPERTY AND THE NEW INTERNATIONAL ECONOMIC ORDER: OLIGOPOLY, REGULATION, AND WEALTH REDISTRIBUTION IN THE GLOBAL KNOWLEDGE ECONOMY 53 (2018).

103 The *Special 301 Reports* from 1989 to 2015 are available at https://ustr.gov/issue-areas/intellectual-property/Special-301.

104 EUR. COMM'N, REPORT ON THE PROTECTION AND ENFORCEMENT OF INTELLECTUAL PROPERTY RIGHTS IN THIRD COUNTRIES 3 (2020), https://trade.ec.europa.eu/doclib/docs/2021/april/tradoc_159553.pdf.

105 David S. Law, *Constitutional Dialects: The Language of Transnational Legal Orders*, *in* CONSTITUTION-MAKING AND TRANSNATIONAL LEGAL ORDER, *supra* note 62, at 110, 124; *see also* O. Kahn-Freund, *On Uses and Misuses of Comparative Law*, 37 MOD. L. REV. 1, 12–13 (1974) (discussing the transplantation of legal norms and arguing that there are different degrees of transplantation, which are dependent, inter alia, on "sociological factors," such as the role of strong social groups in the law-making process).

conflicts with the legal history and political autonomy of constitutional regimes and affects the actual protection these constitutions can afford to adopt on the ground.

10.4.2 *Empirical Results*

A comprehensive and original dataset was created to provide modest empirical support to the main claim of this chapter. The findings show how asymmetrical power relations may bring countries to constitutionalize intellectual property protection. In reality, however, constitutionalization cannot guarantee protection on the ground – and, in the case of developing countries, this guarantees the opposite. The dataset covers all constitutional provisions since 1801 that protect intellectual property as a fundamental right. Compiling the dataset involved a range of methodological choices. A choice has been made to focus on formal, written constitutions.[106] A search has been conducted in numerous databases using keywords pertaining to intellectual property rights.[107] The findings were cross-referenced with the WIPO Lex database constructed by the World Intellectual Property Organization (WIPO),[108] the Comparative Constitutions Project,[109] Constitution Finder,[110] Oxford Constitutions of the World,[111] HeinOnline, and Constitutions of Nations.[112] The data includes information gathered from sources such as the U.S. Trade Representative, which publishes an annual report on intellectual property protection in designated countries.[113] Two indices were used for the purpose of evaluating the level of de facto intellectual property protection given by the relevant country: the Intellectual Property Rights Index constructed by the Property Rights Alliance (IPR)[114] and the U.S. Chamber International Intellectual Property Index (GIPC).[115] It is important to mention again that the data collected for this chapter

[106] The dataset refers to documents explicitly labeled as constitutions and does not include "laws that are not explicitly labeled 'constitutional' but which govern functionally constitutional matters." Law & Versteeg, *supra* note 7, at 1188.

[107] These keywords include intellectual, patent, invention, authors, copyright, trademarks, science, and culture.

[108] Available per country at WIPO LEX, www.wipo.int/wipolex/en/.

[109] COMPAR. CONSTS. PROJECT, http://comparativeconstitutionsproject.org/about-constitute/. This database is commonly used as well. See, for example, Zachary Elkins, Tom Ginsburg & James Melton, *The Content of Authoritarian Constitutions*, *in* CONSTITUTIONS IN AUTHORITARIAN REGIMES 141–42 (Tom Ginsburg & Alberto Simpser eds., 2013).

[110] CONSTITUTE, www.constituteproject.org/search?lang=en. This is a database constructed by the University of Richmond School of Law.

[111] OXFORD CONST. L.: OXFORD CONSTS. WORLD, https://oxcon.ouplaw.com/home/OCW.

[112] 1–3 AMOS J. PEASLEE, CONSTITUTIONS OF NATIONS (1950). This is the first compilation in English of the texts of the constitutions of nations throughout the world.

[113] *See supra* text accompanying note 105.

[114] INT'L PROP. RTS. INDEX 2018, www.internationalpropertyrightsindex.org/about.

[115] The GIPC Index maps the level of intellectual property protection in thirty-eight countries which collectively account for nearly 85 percent of GDP. U.S. CHAMBER INT'L IP INDEX, www.uschamber.com/report/us-chamber-international-ip-index.

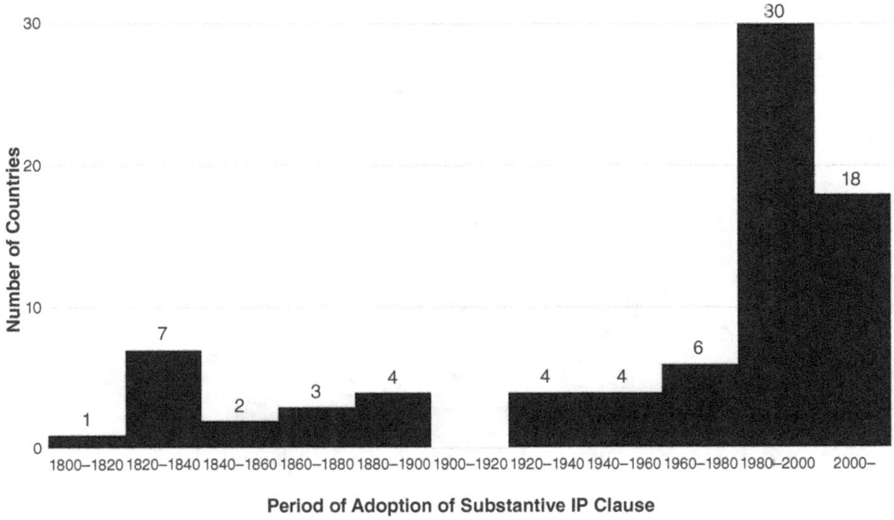

FIGURE 10.1 Period of adoption of intellectual property as a fundamental constitutional right

deals with intellectual property as a fundamental right in constitutional provisions; it does not thoroughly evaluate provisions referring to intellectual property as a legislative empowerment clause. The dataset is updated to January 2017.

As Figure 10.1 shows, the number of countries adopting intellectual property as a fundamental constitutional right has risen. Rapid growth can be seen since 1974 when Sweden adopted intellectual property rights in its formal constitution. Since then, fifty-one countries have followed suit. Haiti was the first country to adopt intellectual property as a fundamental constitutional right in 1801,[116] and Nepal is the most recent country to have adopted such a provision in 2015. Between 1895 and 1973, only nine countries adopted an intellectual property clause. Colonial histories determined the structure of the constitutional design, and states in Central and South America were the first to adopt an intellectual property clause as a fundamental right in the nineteenth century after Portugal's adoption of such a clause in 1826. Since the early twentieth century, including intellectual property in bills of rights has become more common among countries. As presented later, the major growth occurred during the last two decades of the twentieth century, shortly after Sweden adopted such a provision in its formal constitution in 1974. Another interesting insight is that many countries that adopted intellectual property as a fundamental constitutional right during that period were developing countries.

[116] Haiti has also been found to be the first to include the right to free public education. Mila Versteeg & Emily Zackin, *American Constitutional Exceptionalism Revisited*, 81 U. CHI. L. REV. 1641, 1673 (2014).

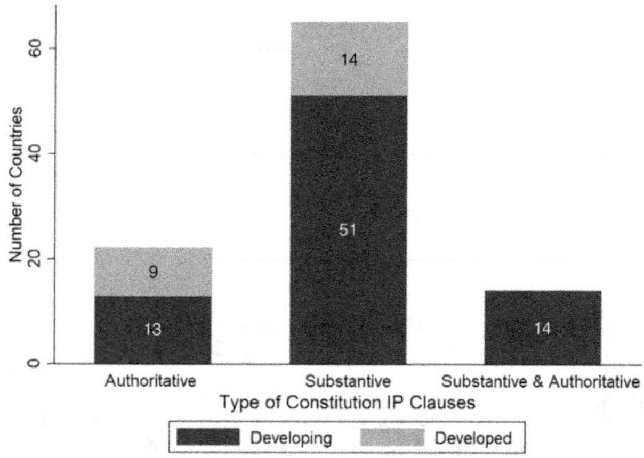

FIGURE 10.2 Types of constitutional intellectual property clauses

There are currently seventy-eight countries with a clause protecting intellectual property as a fundamental constitutional right.

Countries refer to intellectual property in their constitution in two ways. First, they adopt an authoritative/empowerment clause – namely, a commitment vested in the state to legislate and regulate in the field. An example of such a clause is the U.S. Constitution, which empowers Congress "[t]o promote the Progress of Science and useful Arts," as discussed at the beginning of the third section. Second, and more substantively, countries treat the right to own and protect intellectual property as a fundamental socio-economic right and make it part of a given bill of rights.

Some countries refer to intellectual property in both ways. As illustrated in Figure 10.2, twenty-two countries (thirteen of which are developing countries) adopted only an authoritative/empowerment clause;[117] sixty-five countries (fifty-one of which are developing countries) adopted a substantive clause;[118] and fourteen (all of which are developing countries) adopted an authoritative *as well as* a substantive clause.[119] It can be assumed that the status of a country as developed or developing will impact the way the country adopts such a clause.

[117] These countries were Australia, Austria, Belize, Canada, Germany, Hungary, India, Italy, Malaysia, Mexico, Micronesia, Nigeria, Pakistan, Palau, Papua New Guinea, South Sudan, Spain, Sri Lanka, Sudan, Thailand, Uganda, United Arab Emirates, and the United States.

[118] These countries included Afghanistan, Albania, Chad, Chile, Estonia, Fiji, Guatemala, Guinea-Bissau, Haiti, Korea, Kosovo, Kyrgyzstan, Lao, Latvia, Lesotho, Libya, Liechtenstein, Lithuania, Macedonia, Madagascar, Moldova, Mongolia, Montenegro, Mozambique, Nicaragua, Panama, Paraguay, Peru, the Philippines, Portugal, Romania, Sao Tome and Principe, Serbia, the Slovak Republic, Slovenia, Sweden, the Syrian Arab Republic, Taiwan, Tunisia, Turkey, Turkmenistan, Ukraine, Uruguay, Vietnam, and Yemen.

[119] These countries included Argentina, Azerbaijan, Bolivia, Colombia, the Democratic Republic of Congo, Costa Rica, Ethiopia, Georgia, Honduras, Kenya, Myanmar (Burma), the Russian Federation, and Venezuela.

TABLE 10.1 *Textual ranking index*

Where the constitutional clause	Score
Explicitly provides "IP shall be protected" and specifically mentions all three main IP branches/elements (author/copyright, inventor/patent/invention, trademark) as well as additional principles such as moral rights	9
Explicitly provides "IP shall be protected" and specifically mentions all three main IP branches/elements (author/copyright, inventor/patent/invention, trademark) (including when the clause's text provides "and other rights")	8
Explicitly provides "IP shall be protected" and specifically mentions two of the three main IP branches/elements (author/copyright, inventor/patent/invention, trademark)	7
Explicitly provides "IP shall be protected" and specifically mentions one of the three main IP branches/elements (author/copyright, inventor/patent/invention, trademark)	6
Explicitly provides "IP shall be protected"	5
Does not explicitly mention IP but refers to three additional branches/elements (author/copyright, inventor/patent/invention, trademark)	4
Does not explicitly mention IP but refers to two of the three additional branches/elements (author/copyright, inventor/patent/invention, trademark)	3
Does not explicitly mention IP but refers to one of the three additional branches/elements (author/copyright, inventor/patent/invention, trademark)	2
Provides weak reference to intellectual property	1

Including intellectual property protection in constitutional bills of rights does not guarantee enforcement of these rights on the ground. That is, the mere existence of the right in a constitution can sometimes amount to a false signal: "False can be detected by a conspicuous absence of real enforcement mechanisms."[120] Applied to the present argument, the adoption of intellectual property clauses sends a false signal if it lacks the possibility of enforcement. This section offers a modest empirical answer to this assumption. It explores the relations between the scope of protection given in a constitution (as measured by the textual ranking index created for this chapter)[121] and the level of protection given de facto to intellectual property in the applicable country (as measured by two available comparative data indices commonly used in the literature).[122] Table 10.1 provides the score of intellectual property clauses received, which were then applied to the data gathered from the indices:

[120] Versteeg, *supra* note 21, at 707.

[121] *See* Table 10.1.

[122] For an application of the indices in literature, see, for example, Benjamin Balsmeiera & Julie Delanote, *Employment Growth Heterogeneity under Varying Intellectual Property Rights Regimes in European Transition Economies: Young vs. Mature Innovators*, 43 J. COMPAR. ECON. 1069, 1072 (2015); Antonio Della Malva & Enrico Santarelli, *Intellectual Property Rights, Distance to the Frontier, and R&D: Evidence from Microdata*, 6 EURASIAN BUS. REV. 1, 8–9 (2016).

Analysis of the textual ranking, alongside the ranking of the state in the two indices examined, reveals a paradoxical reality: The more a constitution expands the scope of the protection by explicitly specifying the main branches of intellectual property rights (e.g., copyright, patents, and trademarks) in the text of the constitution and makes efforts to encompass different intellectual property doctrines and principles (e.g., moral rights) and rights holders (e.g., indigenous people), *the less* intellectual property protection is given de facto (in the manner the indices capture the latter). For example, Venezuela, a country with a broad constitutional language for de jure protection of intellectual property rights,[123] was given a maximum textual ranking of 9. Venezuela is also the country with the minimal overall GIPC score, at 6.88 out of 35. Similarly, Azerbaijan, which specifically includes in its constitutional language protection for "copyright, patent rights and other rights for intellectual property" as well as safeguarding "the right for intellectual property,"[124] achieved almost the maximum textual ranking score (8), but minimal de facto overall IPR score at 2.8 out of 10. Egypt, a country that provides constitutional protection to "all types of intellectual property rights in all fields,"[125] scored a similar textual ranking of 8 and low de facto intellectual property indices scores (overall IPR score of 4.4 and overall GIPC score of 9.4 out of 35). In contrast, the textual ranking score of Sweden, a leading nation in intellectual property de facto protection, is only 2 even though it has a GIPC overall score of 30.99 and overall IPR score of 8.2.

These findings uncover the apparent paradox concerning the constitutional protection of intellectual property rights, where countries with strong de facto protection of intellectual property rights do not offer broad explicit protection of those rights in their formal constitutions. The majority of the IPR and GIPC scores – Singapore, Switzerland, France, Belgium, Denmark, the Netherlands, Finland, Japan, Germany, the United Kingdom, and the United States (except Sweden) – do not refer to intellectual property as a fundamental socio-economic right in their constitutions. The geographical spread of textual ranking worldwide, illustrated in Figure 10.3, explains the almost inevitable pattern: Many countries with the highest score in the Textual Ranking Index are developing countries.

As Figure 10.4 illustrates, the textual ranking of developing countries (4.431) is, on average, higher than those of developed countries (2.929). This is, of course, not surprising, given that most countries that adopted a substantive clause in their constitutions are developing countries, as Figure 10.2 shows. Figure 10.4, therefore, emphasizes this through a more detailed explanation. These findings lend credence to the conflicting motivations of countries to adopt intellectual property as a fundamental constitutional right. Figure 10.4 confirms that regimes pay lip service or send false signals to appease the international community, certain powerful states,

[123] CONSTITUCIÓN (1999), título 3, capitulo 6, art. 98 (Venez.); *id.* título 3, capítulo 8, art. 124.
[124] CONSTITUTION (1995), art. 30 (Azer.).
[125] CONSTITUTION Jan. 18, 2014, art. 69 (Egypt).

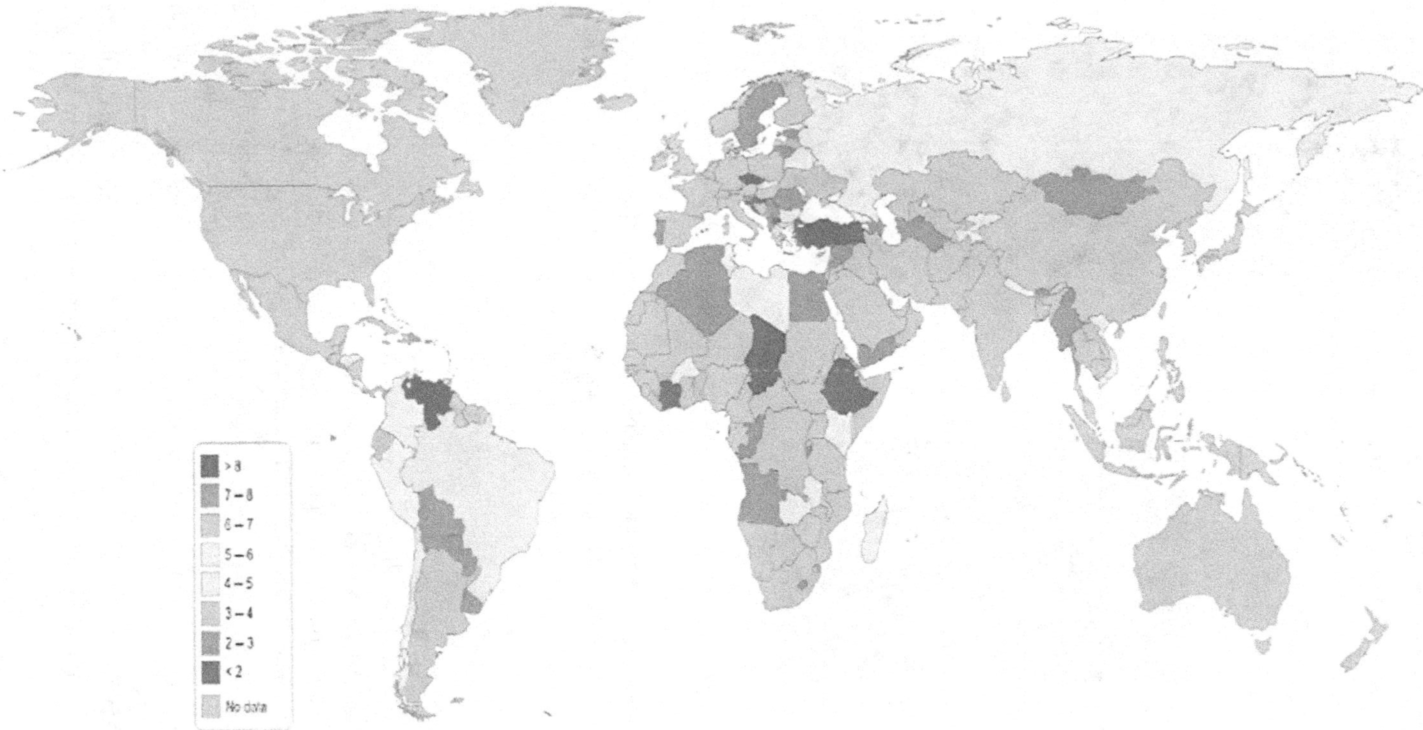

FIGURE 10.3 Textual ranking of constitutions with intellectual property as a fundamental right

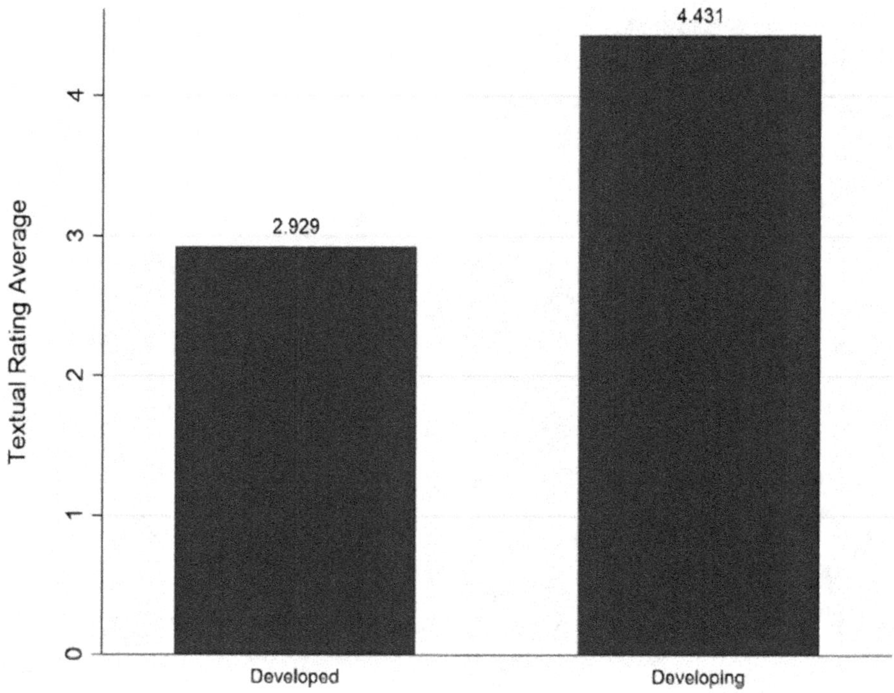

FIGURE 10.4 Average of textual ranking for developing and developed countries

and potential foreign investors without an ability to honor these rights or the ability to enforce them due to various reasons such as political unrest and economic instability.

CONCLUSION

Constitutions have protected intellectual property as a socio-economic right for over two centuries. To date, this phenomenon has been absent from the scholarly discourse. This chapter provided theoretical and empirical support to the conflicting motivations of countries to adopt such a right and challenges the claim that protecting intellectual property in a constitution guarantees better protection on the ground. The case of intellectual property rights constitutionalism provides evidence for the argument that the "poorest nations by definition lack the resources to honor the kinds of positive socio-economic rights that have grown increasingly popular in recent years."[126] This chapter highlights how global political inequality dictates what rights appear in the constitutions of certain countries and demonstrates the neglected value of constitutional intellectual property rights as an exemplar of

[126] Law & Versteeg, *supra* note 67, at 867–68.

the paradoxical consequences introduced by processes of global constitutionalism. Imposing a duty on countries to protect intellectual property rights in their constitution ignores, in many cases, the cultural history and social needs of these countries, leaving them unable to meet their constitutional commitments. One of the main consequences of this process is widening the distance between de jure and de facto protection of constitutional rights.[127]

[127] Goderis & Versteeg, *supra* note 1, at 126.

PART III

Intellectual Property and Global Inequality

11

Inequality and Intellectual Property

Equity, Innovation, and Creative Imitation

Thomas Cottier[*]

INTRODUCTION

Justice in the distribution of income and wealth among nations has been at the heart of the development debate since decolonization began after World War II. The right to development and recourse to global equity has been informed by massive gaps in the distribution of wealth and income. International economic law and the World Trade Organization (WTO) have been strongly criticized for producing adverse effects.[1] In contrast, supporters of the system have drawn attention to the fact that the WTO has contributed to reducing such gaps.[2] Statistically, much of it is owed to the impressive growth of China due to global value chains. But all emerging economies and developing countries benefited from the multilateral system, except for the numerous least-developed countries. They amount to 2 percent of the world economy, and their share in world trade has not exceeded 1 percent since 2008.[3] Overall, however, it is recognized that the multilateral trading system, due to its principles of

[*] The author is indebted to the anonymous reviewer for valuable comments and suggestions.

[1] See, for example, Thomas Pogge, *The Role of International Law in Reproducing Massive Poverty*, *in* THE PHILOSOPHY OF INTERNATIONAL LAW 417 (Samantha Besson & John Tasioulias eds., 2010), and the nuanced reply by Robert Howse & Ruth Teitel, *Global Justice, Poverty, and the International Economic Order*, *in* THE PHILOSOPHY OF INTERNATIONAL LAW, *supra*, at 437. For a recent history and account of developing countries in the multilateral trading system, see AMRITA NARLIKAR, POWER PARADOXES IN INTERNATIONAL TRADE NEGOTIATIONS (2020).

[2] Thomas Cottier, *The Legitimacy of WTO Law*, *in* THE LAW AND ECONOMICS OF GLOBALISATION: NEW CHALLENGES FOR A WORLD IN FLUX 11 (Linda Yueh ed., 2009). Oisin Suttle develops why we need a theory of distributive justice in international economic law, yet without addressing intellectual property. OISIN SUTTLE, DISTRIBUTIVE JUSTICE AND WORLD TRADE LAW: A POLITICAL THEORY OF INTERNATIONAL TRADE REGULATION (2018).

[3] UNCTAD, THE LEAST DEVELOPED COUNTRIES REPORT 2018, at 59 (2018).

nondiscrimination and market access, contributes significantly to more equal conditions of competition in the world economy.[4] Trade shares of developing countries in world trade in goods and services in 2018 amounted to 44 and 34 percent, respectively.[5]

Today, the debate has shifted to the problem of intergenerational equity, given environmental challenges of climate change and exhaustion of natural resources – in particular, the loss of biodiversity caused by unprecedented growth and agricultural soil exploitation.[6] While still shaped in terms of North–South relations, these issues amount to common concerns of humankind.[7] They affect all countries but expose poorer and more vulnerable ones, further increasing inequalities. The COVID-19 pandemic is likely to improve them further. These issues call for enhanced international cooperation beyond existing levels.

After the financial crisis and the Great Recession of 2007–2012, preoccupation and focus shifted to inequality within states, impairing much-needed international cooperation. The process of globalization, the increase of global value chains, and the relocation of industries away from industrialized countries fueled populist political movements. They resulted in an isolationist U.S. government in 2018 and the United Kingdom leaving the European Union in 2020. In both cases, the onslaught on multilateral institutions was caused by increasing domestic inequality and dissatisfaction with national government policies. The European Union (in the case of Britain) and the WTO (in the case of the United States) were blamed for inherently domestic failures to secure social coherence and distributive justice. Previous governments largely ignored that free markets require adequate safety nets in social policy. For too long and tragically, free traders have often combated social policy, and adherents to the welfare state tended to support protectionism and mercantilism for ideological reasons.[8] Countries adequately combining the two areas were able to avoid populists taking power. As an overall result, international cooperation within multilateral organizations has suffered. The setback today delays effective cooperation in addressing common concerns of humankind, including inequality among nations.

4 World Bank, World Development Report 2020: Trading for Development in the Age of Global Value Chains 2020 (2020); Richard Baldwin, The Great Convergence: Information Technology and the New Globalization (2016).

5 World Trade Org., World Trade Statistical Review 2019, at 15 (2019).

6 Edith Brown Weiss, In Fairness to Future Generations: International Law, Common Patrimony and Intergenerational Equity (1989); Intergenerational Equity: Environmental and Cultural Concerns (Thomas Cottier, Shaheeza Lalani & Clarence Siziba eds., 2019) [hereinafter Intergenerational Equity].

7 The Prospects of Common Concern of Humankind in International Law (Thomas Cottier & Zaker Ahmad eds., 2021) [hereinafter Common Concern].

8 *See* Thomas Cottier, *Poverty, Redistribution, and International Trade Regulation*, *in* Poverty and the International Economic Legal System: Duties to the World's Poor 48 (Krista Nadakavukaren Schefer ed., 2013).

Increasing income and wealth distribution gaps set in with neoliberal policies in the 1980s.[9] Income from capital increasingly exceeded income from labor. Property today again plays a significant role in increasing gaps and inequality of wealth in income.[10] The 2018 *World Inequality Report* documents that income inequality has increased globally since 1980 – rapidly in North America, China, and Russia, but only moderately in Europe, ending postwar egalitarian regimes.[11] Statistics consistently show that inequalities were much less prominent after World War II with the advent of the welfare state.[12] Historians show that mass mobilization warfare, transformative revolution, state collapse, and plague – the four horsemen – have been the great levelers of income and wealth allocation. They tend to decline upon overcoming a major crisis.[13] Importantly, it was shown that massive income and wealth inequality throughout history triggered international conflict and civil strife. It may do so in the future. It is a threat to international peace and security, and it is argued elsewhere that gross domestic inequalities amount to a common concern of humankind.[14] Likewise, Goal 10 of the 2030 Sustainable Development Goals seeks to

[9] For a detailed analysis, see ALEXANDER BEYLEVELD, TAKING A COMMON CONCERN APPROACH TO ECONOMIC INEQUALITY: IMPLICATIONS FOR (COOPERATIVE) SOVEREIGNTY OVER CORPORATE TAXATION (2022); Alexander Beyleveld, *Exploring the Recognition of New Common Concerns of Humankind: The Example of the Distribution of Income and Wealth within States, in* COMMON CONCERN, *supra* note 7 [hereinafter Beyleveld, *Exploring Recognition*].

[10] THOMAS PIKETTY, CAPITAL IN THE TWENTY-FIRST CENTURY (Arthur Goldhammer trans., 2014). This seminal study induced increased attention to history as a driving force, rather than sociology, in understanding inequalities. *See* MIKE SAVAGE, THE RETURN OF INEQUALITY: SOCIAL CHANGE AND THE WEIGHT OF THE PAST (2021).

[11] FACUNDO ALVAREDO, LUCAS CHANCEL, THOMAS PIKETTY, EMMANUEL SAEZ & GABRIEL ZUCMAN, WORLD INEQUALITY REPORT 2018, at 7 (2018) [hereinafter WORLD INEQUALITY REPORT]:

> The poorest half of the global population has seen its income grow significantly thanks to high growth in Asia (particularly in China and India). However, because of high and rising inequality within countries, the top 1% richest individuals in the world captured twice as much growth as the bottom 50% individuals since 1980. Income growth has been sluggish or even zero for individuals with incomes between the global bottom 50% and top 1% groups. This includes all North American and European lower- and middle-income groups.
>
> The rise of global inequality has not been steady. While the global top 1% income share increased from 16% in 1980 to 22% in 2000, it declined slightly thereafter to 20%. The income share of the global bottom 50% has oscillated around 9% since 1980. The trend break after 2000 is due to a reduction in between-country average income inequality, as within-country inequality has continued to increase.

For a digest of figures, see Beyleveld, *Exploring Recognition*, *supra* note 9.

[12] THOMAS PIKETTY, THE ECONOMICS OF INEQUALITY (Arthur Goldhammer trans., 2015).

[13] WALTER SCHEIDEL, THE GREAT LEVELER: VIOLENCE AND THE HISTORY OF INEQUALITY FROM THE STONE AGE TO THE TWENTY-FIRST CENTURY (2017).

[14] Beyleveld, *Exploring Recognition*, *supra* note 9.

reduce inequalities, addressing all policy and regulatory areas.[15] The matter, therefore, is also of importance for intellectual property. It forms part of capital and wealth and thus potentially contributes to inequality.[16]

The advent of the Agreement on Trade-Related Aspects of Intellectual Property Rights (TRIPS Agreement) in 1995 coincided with the heydays of trade liberalization in the wake of dominating neoliberal policies. While not an agenda of deregulation but rather a reinforcement of worldwide disciplines for the protection of intellectual property, we are confronted with the issue of to what extent higher standards of protection and commitments to enforcing such rights have contributed to wealth and income inequality. To what extent have monopoly rights contributed to or reduced equal conditions of competition and opportunities?

Property and property rights are major factors in income and wealth distribution. Most of it traditionally relates to movable capital (shares, assets, and savings) and real estate. Between 1970 and 2016, the share of private capital significantly increased in industrialized countries at the expense of publicly owned capital.[17] The role of intellectual property is more difficult to assess. In the same period, the value of intangible property surpassed that of tangible property and became essential for global value chains.[18] The number of registered titles constantly increased.[19] While numbers are not conclusive for the value of such titles and thus wealth, the importance and impact of intellectual property increased in the process of globalization. In political and ideological debates, it is generally assumed that higher levels of protection increase income and wealth inequality. The view has fueled long-standing resistance to effective protection prior to the TRIPS Agreement. It informs much of the debate on TRIPS-plus standards in bilateral and plurilateral

[15] *Goal 10: Reduce Inequality within and among Countries*, United Nations, https://sustainabledevelopment.un.org/sdg10 (lasts visited Apr. 3, 2020).

[16] Piketty includes intellectual property but does not deal with it in *Capital*. Piketty, *supra* note 10, at 49.

[17] World Inequality Report, *supra* note 11, at 14 fig.E6.

[18] World Intell. Prop. Org., World Intellectual Property Report 2017, at 11 (2017).

[19] World Intell. Prop. Org., WIPO IP Facts and Figures 2019, at 7–9 (2019):

> Innovators around the world filed 3.3 million patent applications in 2018, up 5.2% for a ninth straight yearly increase. Trademark filing activity amounted to 14.3 million, up 15.5% and representing a fourth consecutive year of double-digit growth. Worldwide industrial design filing activity reached 1.3 million, while applications for utility models exceeded 2 million for the first time. ...
>
> There were around 14 million patents in force worldwide in 2018. The largest numbers in force were recorded in the United States of America (U.S.) (3.1 million), China (2.4 million) and Japan (2.1 million). Of the 49.3 million trademark registrations active worldwide, the greatest number in force were in China (19.6 million), followed by the U.S. (2.4 million), India (1.9 million) and Japan (1.9 million). Likewise, the greatest numbers of industrial design registrations in force were in China, which accounted for 40.4% of the world total. In addition, China accounted for 93% of the total utility models in force.

cooperation agreements.[20] Upon expounding in detail recent developments in international intellectual property treaty-making, Carlos Correa assumes that they contribute to inequality: "[intellectual property] provisions contained in [free trade agreements] are likely to aggravate current inequalities among and within countries, particularly low- and middle-income countries."[21] This argument is supported by the general importance of property for income and wealth allocation. The more it is concentrated, the greater is the inequality between different percentiles of society. Yet no econometric studies or models are available showing conclusively that intellectual property protection causes or contributes to international and domestic income and wealth inequality.[22] Capital shares increased due to increased investment in intangible assets in corporate expenditure.[23] According to Carsten Fink, one possible explanation is the effect of reduced competition due to concentration, which may be caused, among other things, by intellectual property rights generating economic rents.[24] Causality is difficult to demonstrate, and a counterfactual under nonexistent intellectual property protection does not exist. Even the impact of increased levels of protection is difficult to assess. Conclusions may be drawn from findings of increased concentration in intellectual property–related industries and their push for high levels of protection, but there are many factors contributing to this effect. It is difficult to isolate the impact of intellectual property rights.

Given the empirical uncertainty of the impact of intellectual property on increasing income and wealth inequality internationally and domestically, this chapter addresses the issue from the angle of law and legal methodology. Thomas Piketty, while an economist, stresses in his recent work the important impact of

[20] *Cf.* Thomas Cottier, *Intellectual Property and Mega-Regionals Trade Agreements: Progress and Opportunities Missed, in* MEGA-REGIONAL TRADE AGREEMENTS: CETA, TTIP AND TISA 151 (Stefan Griller, Walter Obwexer & Erich Vranes eds., 2017).

[21] Carlos M. Correa, *Intellectual Property: A Regulatory Constraint to Redress Inequalities, in* INTERNATIONAL POLICY RULES AND INEQUALITY: IMPLICATIONS FOR GLOBAL ECONOMIC GOVERNANCE 179, 202 (José Antonio Acampo ed., 2019).

[22] Correspondence of the author with Keith Maskus and Carsten Fink (Mar. 25–26, 2020) (on file with author).

[23] WORLD INTELL. PROP. ORG., *supra* note 18, at 11.

[24] Carsten Fink writes:

> One possibly IP [intellectual property]-related explanation is weakening competition, which leads successful companies to generate higher profits (which empirically shows up as returns to intangible asset investments). There are numerous economists who have made this argument for the US economy (most prominently, see Thomas Philippon, The Great Reversal: How America gave up on Free Markets (The Belknap Press of Harvard University 2019)). Even then, most advocates of this hypothesis probably would not focus on IP policy as the explanation for reduced competition, but look at other factors (superstar effects, natural monopolies/network effects, captured regulators). That said, within that space, I think there is scope to think through the role of IP ownership and IP policy, as IP exclusivity ultimately is a way of generating rents.

Correspondence of the author with Keith Maskus and Carsten Fink, *supra* note 22 (quoted with permission).

constitutionalism and the importance of property notions and of law for the allocation of income and wealth. Much depends upon the shape of the legal order and its directions.[25] The scope of intellectual property rights is critical, so is the importance of competition and the avoidance of undeserved economic rents. Government policy and thus the law cannot possibly support such rents, as they are not in the public interest and do not foster general welfare. This chapter examines the potential of taking into account considerations of income and wealth distribution in the process of interpreting existing rules (see Section 11.2). It turns to the overall balance of rights and obligations from an angle of fostering investment in innovation and creative imitation. It also suggests recalibrating rules on the duration of patents, copyright, trademarks, and trade secret protection. The latter is not subject to limitation and time and may thus contribute to unjustified economic rents detrimental to human investment (see Section 11.3). The following section first turns to setting the scene and background of international intellectual property protection.

11.1 THE IMPACT OF INTELLECTUAL PROPERTY PROTECTION

At the outset of the TRIPS negotiations, developing countries believed that enhanced levels of intellectual property protection undermine import substitution policies and should therefore be avoided. Efforts at reinforcing the Paris Convention for the Protection of Industrial Property (Paris Convention) and the Berne Convention for the Protection of Literary and Artistic Works (Berne Convention) had failed for such reasons, and industrialized countries tabled the matter at the General Agreement on Tariffs and Trade (GATT) during the Uruguay Round.[26] These countries were increasingly dependent upon high levels of protection due to the increasing division of labor and global value chains in globalization. Attitudes of developing countries altered after the fall of the Soviet Union and the shift to market economies and dependence upon foreign direct investment. China joined the WTO in 2001 and was committed to the TRIPS standards and their implementation. Upon completion of the Uruguay Round, negotiation fora shifted to bilateral and regional free trade agreements on comprehensive economic cooperation, adding TRIPS-plus protection subject to most-favored-nation (MFN) obligations under the TRIPS Agreement and increasingly lifting international minimum standards of protection across the board.[27] Developing countries were willing to accept such

[25] Thomas Piketty, Capitalism and Ideology (Arthur Goldhammer trans., 2020).

[26] *Cf.* The Making of the TRIPS Agreement: Personal Insights from the Uruguay Round Negotiations (Anthony Taubman & Jayashree Watal eds., 2015). For an account of motives driving higher levels of protection and enforcement of intellectual property rights in the 1980s, informing the TRIPS negotiating process, see Kenneth W. Dam, *The Growing Importance of International Intellectual Property Protection*, 21 Int'l Law. 627 (1987).

[27] *Cf.* Susan K. Sell, *Cat and Mouse: Industries', States' and NGOs' Forum-Shifting in the Battle over Intellectual Property Enforcement* (Sept. 2009), https://ssrn.com/abstract=1466156; Correa, *supra* note 21; Cottier, *supra* note 20.

obligations in return for enhanced market access rights, particularly on the part of the United States and the European Union. In the long run, such concessions will inform the reform of the TRIPS Agreement and other multilateral treaties.[28] The main focus of reform under the TRIPS Agreement was the effort to improve access to essential drugs under the Doha Declaration on TRIPS and Public Health. It eventually led to the only revision of the TRIPS Agreement so far.[29]

There is no need to discuss the strategic value of enhanced levels of protection for industrialized countries. Substantial differences showed in detail, and most disputes in the WTO concerned relations among industrialized countries with high trading volumes and strong interests.[30] Except for Brazil, India, and China, developing countries were spared and benefited from what can be called a philosophy of benign neglect because insufficient levels of protection and enforcement did not substantially harm international trade flows and foreign direct investment. It is interesting to observe that recent WTO TRIPS-related disputes also brought challenges to developing countries, albeit driven by the interests of multinational corporations.[31]

For developing countries, the TRIPS Agreement brought about short-term costs but long-term advantages and investment in the rule of law. The transition to higher standards has been costly – and mainly benefited foreign companies at first. The obligation to protect property rights, however, substantially reinforces the rule of law and prospects of domestic and foreign direct investment, with collateral benefits to other regulatory sectors. Property protection was found to be one of the pillars of successful development, and intellectual property protection is part of it.[32] Recent

[28] Thomas Cottier, Charlotte Sieber-Gasser & Gabriela Wermelinger, *The Dialectical Relationship of Preferential and Multilateral Trade Agreements*, *in* Trade Cooperation: The Purpose, Design and Effects of Preferential Trade Agreements 465 (Andreas Dür & Manfred Elsig eds., 2015).

[29] Protocol Amending the TRIPS Agreement, WTO Doc. WT/L/641 (Dec. 8, 2005); Agreement on Trade-Related Aspects of Intellectual Property Rights art. 31*bis*, Apr. 15, 1994, Marrakesh Agreement Establishing the World Trade Organization, Annex 1C, 1869 U.N.T.S. 299 [hereinafter TRIPS Agreement] (entered into force Jan. 23, 2017).

[30] *Cf.* Matthew Kennedy, WTO Dispute Settlement and the TRIPS Agreement: Applying Intellectual Property Standards in a Trade Law Framework 226 (2016). Strong interests are involved in these disputes. Compliance failed in the United States. Panel Report, *United States – Section 110(5) of the US Copyright Act*, WTO Doc. WT/DS160/R (adopted June 15, 2000). Instead of amending its laws, the United States, exceptionally, offered one-time financial compensation to Irish collecting societies.

[31] In particular, Panel Report, *Australia – Certain Measures Concerning Trademarks, Geographical Indications and Other Plain Packaging Requirements Applicable to Tobacco Products and Packaging*, WTO Docs. WT/DS 435/R, WT/DS441/R, WT/DS458/R, WT/DS467/R (adopted June 28, 2018), with findings affirmed by Appellate Body Report, *Australia – Certain Measures Concerning Trademarks, Geographical Indications and Other Plain Packaging Requirements Applicable to Tobacco Products and Packaging*, WTO Docs. WT/DS435/AB/R, WT/DS441/AB/R (adopted June 9, 2020).

[32] *See* Daron Acemoglu & James A. Robinson, The Origins of Power, Prosperity and Poverty 77 (2013) ("The process of innovation is made possible by economic institutions that encourage private property, uphold contracts, create a level playing field, and encourage and

studies indicate that higher levels of patent protection enhance exports of high-tech products and components to developing countries.[33] Keith Maskus and Lei Yang show that there is evidence, based on trade data, that higher levels of patent protection introduced by the TRIPS Agreement have stimulated the production and export of high-value products from developed countries and developing and emerging economies, albeit to a lesser extent for the latter group.[34] Enhanced levels of protection sought by industrialized countries thus are not merely benefiting the domestic industry. Still, they may contribute to dislocations of jobs abroad in the process of globalization to benefit emerging and developing economies.

The problem is no longer whether there should be protection or not, but how much and at what levels. The devil is in the details in defining appropriate levels of commitment in international law and appropriate space for policies that may be affected by intellectual property protection and enforcement, such as health, education, or culture. Articles 7 and 8 of the TRIPS Agreement are of basic importance in expressing an appropriate balance. The commitment to transfer of technology and benefits to rights holders and users and the reservation of essential policy interests, including competition policy, informs the interpretation of intellectual property

allow the entry of new business that can bring new technologies to life."); DAVID LANDES, THE WEALTH AND POVERTY OF NATIONS (1998) (stressing the importance of the rule of law and ownership of property for democracy and prosperity throughout the comprehensive comparative and historical study); Theo S. Eicher & Monique Newiak, *Intellectual Property Rights as Development Determinants*, 46 CAN. J. ECON. 4 (2013).

33 Jenny X. Lin & William Lincoln, *Pirate's Treasure*, 109 J. INT'L ECON. 235 (2017):

> [The study] suggests that intellectual property rights protections affect the distribution of goods available to both consumers and producers in foreign countries. This is likely to have impacts on both groups due to love of variety effects and access to a wider range of intermediate inputs. It is particularly important in the developing country context, where firms are often reliant on imports of intermediate capital goods that embody the latest technologies.

I am grateful to Keith Maskus for drawing attention to this and his paper in the following note.

34 Keith E. Maskus & Lei Yang, *Domestic Patent Rights, Access to Technologies and the Structure of Exports*, 51 CAN. J. ECON. 483, 509 (2018):

> The empirical results conform broadly with the underlying hypothesis that stronger [patent rights] can boost export performance in sectors that are relatively more R&D [research and development] intensive. Moreover, we find that the effects of stronger [patent rights] on exports are strongest in countries with high R&D shares and developed countries. However, the positive effects persist, albeit at lower levels of sensitivity, for countries with lower R&D investment ratios and developing and emerging economies. In addition, there is some evidence that the relationship grew stronger between 2000 and 2005, a period in which many emerging and developing economies implemented their TRIPS obligations. Finally, we find that countries with relatively more inward sectoral patent applications and industry-level intra-firm imports from U.S. multinational enterprises have a higher sensitivity of R&D-intensive exports to changes in patent protection. This is a novel result that should invite more analysis going forward.

rights and their scope, albeit these commitments are subject to the detailed provisions of the agreement and thus of limited practical effect.

Since the TRIPS Agreement was adopted, there has been a basic consensus that intellectual property is a necessary component of domestic and international trade. All countries are interested in protecting trademarks and related forms of protection. All countries share an interest in protecting copyright and patents but vary on the proper scope of protection. Voices arguing that the TRIPS Agreement does not belong to the WTO since the Agreement juxtaposes free trade by creating monopoly rights are largely a matter of the past.[35] Both the absence of protection and the excessive protection of intellectual property rights cause restrictions and distortions to trade. Today's debate is much more about the adequacy of TRIPS-plus standards in bilateral and plurilateral agreements. While some of these provisions necessarily fill lacunae of the TRIPS Agreement (such as test data), others reflect predominant economic interests undermining the overall balance and putting the authority of intellectual property protection and enforcement of standards at risk. Foremost, these additional standards mainly reflect the interests of industrialized countries and fail to consider the interest of developing countries with much larger rural areas and thus an interest in protecting traditional knowledge, grassroots innovation, and geographical indications (GIs). Overall, we assume the following effects.

An enhanced level of intellectual property protection certainly secures income in operating global value chains. Such chains, and decentralized production, have benefited millions of workers, albeit often under dire conditions. These developments, in return, triggered efforts to improve corporate social responsibility and transparency while increasing liability of multinational corporations. Trade volume increased, and income inequality on national levels reduced in the process of globalization between nations. Much of these effects are due to the rise of China, while other countries benefited much less or even lost trading shares and income. Moreover, these results do not discuss domestic distributive effects, which strongly depend upon constitutional and political arrangements and power relations.

In a domestic context, property protection raises fundamental income and wealth distribution questions. Private property rights were the main target of communism,

[35] In particular, Jagdish Bhagwati, an astute free trade economist, wrote in a 2001 letter to the *Financial Times*:

> As early as 1990, in my Harry Johnson Lecture at London, I argued – and now world-class economists such as Professors Srinivasan and Panagariya have also written in this vein – that such protection does not belong in the WTO. That institution must be about mutually gainful trade. Intellectual property protection, on the other hand, is for most poor countries a simple tax on their use of such knowledge, constituting therefore an unrequited transfer to the rich, producing countries. We were turning the WTO, thanks to powerful lobbies, into a royalty-collection agency, by pretending through continuous propaganda, that our media bought into, that somehow the question was "trade-related."

Letter from Professor Jagdish Bhagwati to Editor, FINANCIAL TIMES (Feb. 14, 2001), www.columbia.edu/~jb38/papers/pdf/FT_Letter_on_IPP.pdf.

which led to expropriation, state capitalism, and power concentration, which is predominant today in China. Intellectual property was a nonissue in these systems and only became relevant with the turn to allowing and developing product markets under state capitalism. In the West and market economies, it would seem that intellectual property offers an important foundation for competing industries, many of which are comprised of small- and medium-sized companies. The same holds for the cultural and communications sectors. They depend upon the patent, copyright, and trademark protection under price competition. Intellectual property thus is an instrument of horizontal balancing and power-sharing. This does not exclude strong differences among sectors and depends upon the size of the corporations. Many of the richest companies in the world depend upon intellectual property protection.

While intellectual property partly provides the foundation of the legal protection of such wealth, income distribution would seem to be equally, if not predominantly, determined by competition, fiscal, and monetary policies. Taxation of intellectual property rights and licenses forms an important part of corporate tax, and the recent introduction of patent boxes significantly reduces tax burdens in a competitive environment. Exchange rates deploy an important effect on trade flows of intellectual property–protected goods and services. Much, therefore, depends upon the interaction with other policy areas and the ability to harness excessive accumulation of wealth due to intellectual property protection. It is a matter of achieving an overall fair balance between property rights and the interests of information users. In doing so, it is important to consider intellectual property not in isolation but in combination with other parts of international law – in particular, trade rules, human rights, and competition policy.[36] If properly embedded in international and domestic law, excessive imbalances in wealth and income distribution can be avoided and properly harnessed by recourse to such policies and related rules. But this does not exempt us from revisiting existing intellectual property protection. The question is to what extent potential effects of unequal distribution can be potentially mitigated within the intellectual property system itself. We see an enhanced role for equity here.

11.2 THE POTENTIAL ROLE OF EQUITY IN CASE LAW

Equity in international law emerged as a topical methodology that requires taking all facts, considerations, and interests into account in a balancing process.[37] This could

[36] Thomas Cottier, *Embedding Intellectual Property in International Law*, *in* CURRENT ALLIANCES IN INTERNATIONAL INTELLECTUAL PROPERTY LAW-MAKING 15 (Pedro Roffe & Xavier Seuba eds., 2017).

[37] THOMAS COTTIER, EQUITABLE PRINCIPLES OF MARITIME BOUNDARY DELIMITATION: THE QUEST FOR DISTRIBUTIVE JUSTICE IN INTERNATIONAL LAW (2015) [hereinafter COTTIER, EQUITABLE PRINCIPLES] (setting out the fact-intensive methodology of equity in international law); Thomas Cottier, *Equity in International Law*, *in* INTERGENERATIONAL EQUITY, *supra* note

also entail considerations of wealth and income distribution under the specific facts of a particular problem and case.

By its classical functions, equity in international law always addresses particular cases and configurations; it does not amount to abstract rules that may, in reality, need adjustment to serve justice and fairness. Equity may influence the interpretation, complete the law, or even rule against existing norms – particularly in the case of an abuse of rights or unjust enrichment, as discussed later. Apart from specific rules developed in English law,[38] equity allows taking the particular facts of a case into account, avoiding rigid applications of the law that produce *summa jus summa injuria*.[39] Equity entails a balancing process and dialogue with existing rules, employing judicial discretion while respecting, at the same time, the need for legal security.

In intellectual property, equity has not played much of an explicit role. This is certainly true for international law. Implicitly, it informs the scope of rights and exceptions such as fair use. Yet, in international law, the pursuit of legitimate public policies remains subject to specific rules of the TRIPS Agreement.[40] The field is largely dominated by positive technical rules, leaving ample room to maneuver in their application. Human rights partly assumed the role of equity, such as the rights to health and life, in shaping the rules on access to essential drugs. It will likely play an important role in the equitable distribution of vaccines against COVID-19, but fairness and equitable principles can only be explicitly found in general rules relating to enforcement in the TRIPS Agreement.[41]

Potential doors of entry for equitable considerations in TRIPS interpretation were elaborated elsewhere, so they are not repeated here in detail.[42] The point is that equity can also be invoked in the interpretation and application of rules when equality or inequality is at stake in reading a particular provision. For example, provisions relating to patenting pharmaceuticals may be assessed in light of potential effects on distributive justice and income inequality and wealth. Considerations of

6, at 11; Thomas Cottier, *The Prospects of Equity in International Economic Law, in* RESTORING TRUST IN TRADE: LIBER AMICORUM IN HONOUR OF PETER VAN DEN BOSSCHE 119 (Denise Prévost, Iveta Alexovicova & Jens Hillebrand Pohl eds., 2019); CATHARINE TITI, THE FUNCTION OF EQUITY IN INTERNATIONAL LAW (2021), CHRISTOPHER R. ROSSI, EQUITY AND INTERNATIONAL LAW: A LEGAL REALIST APPROACH TO INTERNATIONAL DECISION-MAKING (1993), WILFRED C. JENKS, THE PROSPECTS OF INTERNATIONAL ADJUDICATION 316–427 (1966).

38 *See* Jill E. Martin, HANBURY & MARTIN: MODERN EQUITY (15th ed. 1997).

39 *See generally* EQUITY IN THE WORLD'S LEGAL SYSTEMS: A COMPARATIVE STUDY (Ralph A. Newman ed., 1972).

40 TRIPS Agreement, *supra* note 29, art. 8(1) (including the language "provided that such measures are consistent with the provisions of this Agreement").

41 Article 42 of the TRIPS Agreement is entitled "Fair and Equitable Procedures."

42 Thomas Cottier, *The Protection of Intellectual Property and Foreign Direct Investment: The Impact of Equity*, in HANDBOOK ON INVESTMENT AND INTELLECTUAL PROPERTY 433, 445–49 (Christophe Geiger ed., 2020).

income and wealth distribution can thus be considered under equity when assessing fair use exemptions. It may, for instance, lead to a new assessment of stockpiling in assessing the point when generic products can be produced, taking into account a cost–benefit analysis for the health system, patients, and health insurance.[43] The advantage of recourse to equity is that under the facts of particular configurations, all pertinent interests are taken into account beyond the wording of a specific provision. The same holds in defining the scope of rights, fair use exemptions, and compulsory licensing. Last, explicit reference to equity even mandates taking these interests into account when enforcing intellectual property rights.

A related issue here is the problem of parallel importations. Article 6 of the TRIPS Agreement is an agreement to disagree, and it leaves the matter to WTO member states. Conventional wisdom allows countries to apply the principle of national exhaustion, resulting in market segmentation, price differentiation, and potentially rent-seeking. This is particularly widespread in pharmaceuticals and, therefore, directly relevant to the issue of inequality, particularly in countries not operating price controls. A detailed examination of the WTO questions such findings. The ban on parallel importation of original products marketed abroad is contrary to Articles III(4) and XI of GATT.[44] It cannot be generally justified under Article XX, which requires meeting a necessity test. This test balances the different interests at stake and calls for well-calibrated solutions. Again, considerations of income inequality and wealth distribution in healthcare may be entertained here, implicitly engaging the topical methodology of WTO law. In this respect, this is very similar to the functions of equity in domestic and international law.[45] Equity supports the view that parallel importation is primarily dealt with by GATT rules and trumps the policy space under Article 6 of the TRIPS Agreement, where national exhaustion contributes to income inequality due to market segmentation and price differentiation, to the detriment of consumer welfare.

Equity is confined here to the existing regulatory system and a particular case. Global equity has been elusive and without much impact in reshaping the rules in the first place.[46] To assess from the point of view of inequality, we need to reconsider basic components of the overall intellectual property system.

[43] *Cf.* Panel Report, *Canada – Patent Protection of Pharmaceutical Products*, WTO Doc. WT/DS114/R ¶¶ 7.17–7.38 (adopted Mar. 17, 2000). While the panel considered Articles 7 and 8 of the TRIPS Agreement, it did not take into account the balance of all economic interests at stake in interpreting the notion of "making" in Article 28 of the TRIPS Agreement.

[44] General Agreement on Tariffs and Trade, Oct. 30, 1947, 61 Stat. A-11, 55 U.N.T.S. 194.

[45] Thomas Cottier, *Parallel Trade and Exhaustion of Intellectual Property in WTO Law Revisited*, *in* Intellectual Property Ordering beyond Borders 198–235 (Henning Grosse Ruse-Khan & Axel Metzger eds., 2022).

[46] The invocation of equity for global justice is discussed in Cottier, Equitable Principles, *supra* note 37, at 21.

11.3 INNOVATION AND CREATIVE IMITATION

Perhaps the most important issue in the present context is a discussion of innovation and imitation in shaping intellectual property law. It is key to achieving an overall fair balance within the legal system and thus potentially contributes to lessening income and wealth inequality.

11.3.1 *The Conceptual Neglect of Creative Imitation*

The focus and *raison d'être* of intellectual property has been innovation and its promotion and protection. In conventional thought, innovation is at the heart and center of the field, particularly in patent and copyright. Although other functions are served – particularly product identification, consumer protection in trademarks and GIs, or the protection of existing information in trade secrets or data collection protection – innovation amounts to the main motivation and justification for granting exclusive monopoly rights.[47]

On the other hand, imitation is not equally recognized as a part of the equation. It is prohibited as counterfeiting and piracy and may amount to unfair competition. The scope of creative and lawful imitation indirectly enters through the door of the scope and duration of rights to define exceptions and finds expression in the goal of disseminating technology to the benefit of rights holders and users, as expressed in Article 7 of the TRIPS Agreement. However, there is no formal place in the legal system for imitation driving economic evolution. Creative imitation is tolerated because legal provisions allow freedom to reproduce and imitate. The scope of creative imitation is defined by what is left to the information market, by what government intervention to correct market failures does not assign to exclusivity or no longer does so. Imitation lawfully takes place to the extent that information is in the public domain and has become a public good. Imitation, in other words, takes place by default to the extent that information is not protected by private intellectual property rights. Creative imitation is not a recognized goal or feature of the intellectual property system itself. It does not have a place of its own in the canon of values but is a gray area looked upon with suspicion. We do not know a natural right to creative imitation. Developing countries have taken the matter up indirectly, first by refusing to renegotiate the Paris and Berne Conventions and, after the TRIPS Agreement, by stressing the need for domestic policy space. TRIPS-plus developments discussed earlier further reduce such policy space and, thus, the potential for creative imitation.[48] This may contribute to income inequality and wealth

[47] Innovation is also the starting point of a critical theory. *See* JOSEPH H. STIGLITZ & BRUCE E. GREENWALD, CREATING A LEARNING SOCIETY: A NEW APPROACH TO GROWTH, DEVELOPMENT AND SOCIAL PROGRESS 254 (2015).

[48] Correa, *supra* note 21; Sell, *supra* note 27; Cottier, *supra* note 20. *But see also infra* text accompanying note 58.

distribution by further reinforcing private property rights and concentration of economic power.

Upon reflection, the conceptual lack of recognition of creative imitation and the reduction of tolerance within the overall system is somewhat astonishing. Much of our life is based upon imitation, from which new ideas, features, and things evolve. Education and schooling of children and students are built upon it. We mainly learn by imitating. The acquisition of social skills and interaction is learned from looking at the behavior and conduct of others. Societies require a large amount of imitation, repetition, and reproduction in daily life to work and function properly. It is, in many respects, a prerequisite of innovation. Without imitation, innovation cannot occur.

These facts are also indirectly reflected in the evolution of nations in terms of social and economic development. The Netherlands and Switzerland, today's champions of strong intellectual property protection, heavily depended upon imitation in the nineteenth century and were reluctant to adopt protection of mainly imported products.[49] The evolution of the Paris Convention of 1883 and the Berne Convention of 1886 was based upon national legislation and a set of bilateral agreements imposed by then-dominant economies, France and Germany in particular, with a view to include neighboring jurisdictions on equal terms of protection and conditions of competition.[50] Japan strongly depended upon imitation after World War II and increased its higher-quality reproductions of Western inventions such as cameras, TV sets, and recording equipment.[51] China followed suit, and much of the present trade war with the United States is rooted in this social and economic development stage. The claim of insufficient enforcement and even of "theft" of intellectual property within and by companies controlled by the state is mainly related to the phasing of economic and social development at a juncture where Chinese technology competes with Western technology. Much of this "theft" is based upon agreed contractual arrangements of value chains and is lawful, while

[49] Eric Schiff, Industrialization without National Patents: The Netherlands 1869–1912, Switzerland 1850–1907 (1971). The hostility to patents in Europe and the battle for patent protection is famously recalled by Fritz Machlup & Edith T. Penrose, *The Patent Controversy in the Nineteenth Century*, 10 J. Econ. Hist. 1 (1950); *see also* Christopher May & Susan K. Sell, Intellectual Property Rights: A Critical History (2006). We note that much of the evolution of intellectual property protection occurred by means of domestic case law and enforcement, also in the twentieth century. *See* Beatrice Nybert, The Evolution of Patent Protection: A Comparative and Historical Analysis of Patent Litigation and Enforcement in Germany, Sweden, Switzerland, the United Kingdom and the United States in the Twentieth Century (2020) (Ph.D. dissertation, University of Bern).

[50] Edith T. Penrose, The Economics of the International Patent System (1951).

[51] Landes, *supra* note 32, at 471–72 ("Some know-how came to them because producers in other countries hired Japanese firms to make objects (watches, auto parts) that the more advanced countries could label and sell as their own. Much they copied by reverse engineering, taking Western models apart and learning to make them better.").

only espionage of trade secrets held by unrelated companies is illegal. The same holds for developing countries in general, albeit the impact of imitation has been felt less in international markets and thus allows for benign neglect, as discussed earlier.

The same holds domestically. Start-ups and new ventures depend upon ample space for creative imitation, which existing monopoly rights may curb. Many tensions arise because the relationship between creative innovation and creative imitation has not been properly addressed in intellectual property law and the legal order at large. It is submitted that both innovation and creative imitation should be recognized, and the case for exclusive rights fostering innovation needs particular attention and justification. It is submitted that focusing on incentives for investment plays a crucial role in balancing the two.

11.3.2 *Focusing on Investment*

One way to approach and reconsider the equation is to put less emphasis on innovation and focus on stimulating and rewarding investment. The very reason to grant monopolies on and exclusive rights to information is to foster and honor investment in creating such information, even though it may not always be original and new. The latter holds true for the fields of intellectual property, which rely on product distinction (trademarks and GIs), the protection of existing information (undisclosed information and data collections, big data in particular), and the protection of traditional knowledge. From an economic point of view, the protection of trademarks and GIs does not focus only on product distinction. It also entails protection of massive investment, advertisement, and the promotion of such products. Protection of data collections, particularly big data and traditional knowledge, primarily protects the investment made in collecting, cultivating, arranging, and using preexisting information. So far, investment and investment protection have provided the foundation of *sui generis* data protection beyond copyright in EU law.[52] It has not yet been recognized in law as a general underpinning and justification for traditional intellectual property rights.

If we look at investment and what is needed to stimulate new information, creative imitation can be recognized next to innovation on equal footing. We recognize a right to creative imitation and leave a concept behind that treats creative imitation merely as an exception to innovation, balancing the two in regard to the scope of protection, legal and compulsory licensing, and duration of rights. It remains necessary to draw a line between lawful and unlawful imitation for reasons of legal and business security. However, the overall equation may change upon recognizing creative imitation as a proper goal of the overall system of fostering investment in creating new information and applications. It offers a check on monopoly rights. Conceptually, it will put an end to pressing for ever-increasing

[52] Directive 96/9, art. 7, *amended by* 2019 O.J. (L 130) 92.

levels of protection of innovation without due regard to the implications for creative imitation in the process of social and economic development, both domestically and internationally. We argue later that creating exclusive rights warrants special justification and reasoning that market conditions and government funding supporting innovation are insufficient and intellectual property rights are necessary.

11.3.2.1 Investment in Information as a Public Good

Human investment in capital, natural resources, time, and human resources serves the production of goods and services. It also serves the needs of society at large by shaping general framework conditions, including statehood and the legal order, the economy, culture, and other fields of human life. The investment is based upon existing information and knowledge. We reiterate that people build upon experience. Much of it is dedicated to reproducing existing goods and services essential in daily life. Out of this, incremental innovation and change result in new ideas and information contributing to evolution. New information falls into the public domain and is treated as a public good. Everybody can use it, and such use does not diminish the information.[53] It is submitted that reproduction and incremental creation of information is the normal state of play in human investment. It takes place under the umbrella of the general legal order and policies of open-source access. In market economies, the framework is defined by the laws of contracts, torts, and unfair competition and is bounded by penal law prohibitions. It is supported by government policies, education, and research funding. The risks involved in such investments are reasonable, as they deal with known information and experience. They take place in corresponding information markets.

11.3.2.2 Investment in Information as a Private Good and Property

Beyond the normal acts of reproduction, imitation, and incremental innovation in society, deliberate efforts at innovation are made in the process of human investment. They venture into new territory based on existing information. These efforts are financially risky as they cannot rely upon existing patterns and needs. Research and development beyond incremental change thus call for a particular legal framework. For the private sector, this is where intellectual property protection enters the stage. Exclusive rights are necessary to incentivize the production of products and ideas and to secure a fair return on the investment, without which private operators would not make an effort in the first place. In the public sector, basic research funded by taxpayers or charities, and by applied research and development, parallels

[53] Paul A. Samuelson, *The Pure Theory of Public Expenditure*, 36 Rev. Econ. & Stat. 387, 387–89 (1954).

the intellectual property system. Sometimes the two are combined by means of private–public partnerships.

Intellectual property protection thus amounts to a *lex specialis* for promoting and protecting financially risky investments in innovation. Exclusive rights, deviating from open access and use of information otherwise in the public domain, call for a particular justification in terms of state intervention and restrictions of freedom of commerce, whatever the form of law is. It is not a given, and rules should respect the principle of proportionality. Generally speaking, measures need to be suitable, necessary (not in excess of what is necessary to achieve a policy goal), and appropriate, taking into account all the interests at stake.[54] That also informs the shaping of intellectual property law. Throughout history, there has been a debate on using intellectual property as an expression of utilitarian philosophy. Some elevated it to the status of human rights. The European Convention on Human Rights includes intellectual property as a right to property in Protocol I.[55] There is no need to question the fundamentals here. The principles of intellectual property are deeply enshrined in legal orders and the world economy. However, attention is drawn to the scope of protection of rights, and the relationship to public information requires particular and constant attention. The equation changes with changing technologies. Yet, additional standards, pressed for by vested interests, are not necessarily in the public interest. Ceilings on standards need to be considered in domestic and international law to establish a proper balance between investment in public goods and investment in private goods to foster general welfare and the reduction of overall inequality in income and wealth, both influenced by property rights.[56] The conventional approach of setting minimum standards in international law and the federalist approach focusing on national policy space do not sufficiently reflect the need to harness domestic law.[57] It is not simply a matter of granting policy space to domestic legislation but equally containing it on the international level, commensurate with the doctrine of multilevel governance and vertical checks and balances.[58]

54 Thomas Cottier, Roberto Echandi, Rachel Liechti-McKee, Tetyana Payosova & Charlotte Sieber, *The Principle of Proportionality in International Law: Foundations and Variations*, 18 J. World Inv. & Trade 628 (2017).

55 For a detailed account, see Thomas Cottier, *Copyright and the Human Right to Property: A European and International Law Approach*, *in* Intellectual Property and the Judiciary 116 (Christophe Geiger, Craig Allan Nord & Xavier Seuba eds., 2018); Research Handbook on Human Rights and Intellectual Property (Christophe Geiger ed., 2015).

56 Annette Kur & Henning Grosse Ruse-Khan, *Enough Is Enough: The Notion of Binding Ceilings in International Intellectual Property Protection*, *in* Intellectual Property Rights in a Fair World Trade System: Proposals for Reform of TRIPS 359 (Anne Kur with Marianne Levin ed., 2011).

57 *Cf.* Graeme B. Dinwoodie & Rochelle C. Dreyfuss, A Neofederalist Vision of TRIPS: The Resilience of the International Intellectual Property Regime 138 (2012).

58 *See* Thomas Cottier, *Towards a Five Storey House*, *in* Constitutionalism, Multilevel Trade Governance and International Economic Law 495 (Christian Joerges & Ernst-Ulrich Petersmann eds., 2011).

Intellectual property as a matter of nontariff barriers is not different from other policy fields, such as the promotion and facilitation of renewable energy or effective human rights protection.[59]

It would be wrong to assume that human investment in imitation, reproduction, and innovation can be neatly separated. Problems delineating protection and public domain exist through all forms of existing intellectual property protections. Disputes on the patentability of inventions make the point. One may flow out of the other, as penicillin was discovered from a reproduction process. It was not designed and intended as such in the first place. Yet, as investment turns to new territory and thus risks, the net of intellectual property rights offers adequate prospects of return if and only if the effort is successful. A substantial risk remains uncovered in case of failure and leaves little else than costs. It entails the option of bankruptcy under both public and private information models.

11.3.3 *Appropriate Return of Capital and Reasonable Profits*

The fundamental question is how far society, government, and the law should enable return on capital in intellectual property protection beyond market rules and freedom of commerce – and to what extent and for how long this includes profits. In the present context of increasing inequality of wealth and income, this is a crucial issue. From the point of view of the public interest and thus intellectual property policy, it follows from the purpose of having exclusive rights in the first place that the investment made should be recovered with a fair share of profits to shareholders and stakeholders alike. It also follows that the privilege of exclusivity should not include excessive profits to the detriment of ordinary investment in reproduction and incremental innovation. Of course, defining reasonable, nonexcessive profits remain a matter of debate and uncertainty. But in principle, there is no justification for granting exclusive rights to information beyond this point from the point of view of the public interest. The scope of rights and the duration of exclusive rights are crucial.

11.3.3.1 The Scope of Rights

In defining the scope of intellectual property rights, the importance of creative imitation in and through the public domain must be considered. History shows a long record of gradually building levels of protection and exemptions thereof. These levels are outcomes of fierce political battles of different vested interests, prospects of

[59] Thomas Cottier, *Renewable Energy and WTO Law: More Policy Space or Enhanced Disciplines?*, 5 Renewable Energy L. & Pol'y Rev. 40 (2014); Thomas Cottier, *International Trade, Human Rights and Policy Space*, *in* Local Engagement with International Economic Law 3 (Lilyana Biukovic & Pittman B. Potter eds., 2017).

private profits often prevailing over public welfare concerns. The international intellectual property law protection today does not offer an effective balance. As indicated, it is essentially limited to minimal standards that countries can exceed, either unilaterally or using international agreements. Due to MFN obligations, higher standards are applied across the board and not limited to the parties of a preferential agreement. They lift all yachts with the tide. This open-ended approach raises problems of flexibility, and limitations, on the scope of protection.

The proper balance of creative imitation and innovation, however, depends much upon the state and process of social and economic development of a particular country. The need for intellectual property protection varies, and uniform minimum standards are not always suitable. While the TRIPS Agreement allows for flexibilities and is far from harmonized, there is a need for more variable geometry on essential regulations. It could be realized by the graduation approach as it can be found more recently in the WTO Agreement on Trade Facilitation.[60] While international law defines standards of protection, the phasing-in of such standards over time is made dependent upon the attainment of economic factors and indicators to be negotiated in advance. The approach, replacing traditional and rigid special and differential treatment, offers predictability as to when a country, due to its share in world trade in a particular sector, will be obliged to assume specific additional obligations of intellectual property protection.[61]

Except for rules on enforcement and a few areas, the TRIPS Agreement and TRIPS-plus obligations in preferential trade agreements do not know ceilings of protection. Such ceilings are essentially left to domestic law, including competition law, which is absent in international law.

The focus on promotion and protection of investment asks to what extent ceilings on levels of protection are required to protect creative imitation and to what extent investment necessarily depends upon sui generis intellectual property protection. A case needs to be made that protection is required to recuperate investment and to make a reasonable profit. The burden of persuasion lies with those seeking intellectual property protection. Answers vary and depend upon technological advances. For example, the legal treatment of big data and artificial intelligence depends on

60 Trade Facilitation Agreement, Feb. 22. 2017, www.wto.org/english/docs_e/legal_e/tfa-nov14_e.htm.

61 Javier Lopez-Gonzalez, Maximilio Mendez Parra, Peter Holmes & Anirudh Shingal, *TRIPS and Special and Differential Treatment – Revisiting the Case for Derogations in Applying Patent Protection for Pharmaceuticals in Developing Countries* (Nat'l Ctr. of Competence in Rsch., Working Paper No. 2011/37, 2011); MONIRUL AZAM, INTELLECTUAL PROPERTY AND PUBLIC HEALTH IN THE DEVELOPING WORLD (2016); Thomas Cottier, *From Progressive Liberalization to Progressive Regulation in WTO Law*, 9 J. INT'L ECON. L. 779 (2006); Thomas Cottier, *Sovereign Equality and Graduation in International Economic Law*, *in* REFLECTIONS ON THE CONSTITUTIONALISATION OF INTERNATIONAL ECONOMIC LAW: LIBER AMICORUM FOR ERNST-ULRICH PETERSMANN 215 (Marisa Cremona, Peter Hilpold, Nikos Lavranos, Stefan Schneider & Andreas Ziegler eds., 2014).

whether sufficient incentives exist to develop and collect data and write algorithms under market conditions and using open-source information. Appropriation of information should only be made if incentives for investment, adequate returns, and reasonable profits otherwise cannot sufficiently materialize. The same holds, for example, in assessing the exclusivity of test data for pharmaceutical products or qualification of essential interconnection standards.[62] The law should consider the investment made and define reasonable profits up to which protection exists and elapses after that. The topical method of equity described earlier can be put to use by taking into account all relevant economic and financial factors in assessing such prospects. It can build upon the general principle of unjust enrichment, which is based on equity and recognized in domestic and international law.[63] Ceilings in law should thus be formulated to the effect that the main purpose of protection is the promotion and recovery of investment, including the generation of a reasonable, nonexcessive profit. The law should not exceed such bounds in formulating and applying for intellectual property protection.

11.3.3.2 The Duration of Rights

An important and often neglected issue in the present context relates to the duration of rights, particularly rights unlimited in time and thus a foundation of long-term income and wealth allocation.

The current duration of patent protection of at least twenty years as of filing (set out in Article 31 of the TRIPS Agreement), plus supplementary protection for regulated sectors, and at least ten years for industrial designs (Article 26(3)), contrasts with a much longer period in copyright law of at least fifty years postmortem (Article 12). The latter period has been further extended to seventy years postmortem in domestic law – in particular, in the European Union and the United States.[64] While the law provides for minimal standards – which domestic law or other agreements can extend – there is an implied understanding that in domestic law, the duration of these rights is conceptually limited in time. Information should, at some point, fall into the public domain as a public good. In patent law, limitations in time were the

[62] *See* Simon Brinsmead, Access to Interoperability Standards and Standards-Essential Intellectual Property: International Approaches (2020).

[63] *See* Christina Binder & Christoph Scheuer, *Unjust Enrichment, in* 10 Max Planck Encyclopedia of Public International Law 588, 588 (Rüdiger Wolfram ed., 2012) ("The concept of unjust or unjustified enrichment has been defined as 'adjusting shifts of assets from one person to another which are at variance with the final allocation of assets envisaged by the law.'").

[64] The European Union extended copyright protection to seventy years postmortem in Council Directive 93/98/EEC in 1993, followed by the extension in the United States in 1998 through the Copyright Term Extension Act, Pub. L. No. 105-298, 112 Stat. 2827 (1998). This extension was challenged before the U.S. Supreme Court but affirmed. Eldred v. Ashcroft, 537 U.S. 186 (2003).

great bargain. Next to transparency, fair use, and compulsory licensing, a major compromise was reached between advocates and opponents of patent law in the nineteenth century.[65]

The proper duration of rights limited in time is controversial, and the determination thereof, to some extent, necessarily arbitrary. This is particularly apparent in the identical treatment of all inventions and fields of technology, irrespective of complexity and investment required.[66] Countries can unilaterally or by agreement further extend the duration of protection, fostering monopoly rights and curbing competition, or extend unending entitlement to royalty payments.[67] Theoretically, all rights could be extended without time limits under international law. Competing interests in competition law may counterbalance such efforts but not prevent them, depending upon the political clout of vested interests. Excessive periods bear the potential of economic rents and distortion of competition. They foster patent trolls and rents. They may unreasonably contribute to income inequality and wealth. The duration of rights, therefore, should be addressed by ceilings in international law. Domestic policy space should be limited by international economic law. From the point of view of investment, the multilateral agreements should limit the extension of such rights and define a range within which members may settle patent and copyright terms. These ranges should be informed by considerations of recovery of investment, balancing reasonable profits against the competition, and the public interest in fostering information as a public good.

The even more striking contrast is with trademarks (Article 18 of the TRIPS Agreement: renewable protection), GIs, and undisclosed information, which are not subject to the limitation in time. While criticism today mainly and perhaps unjustifiably focuses on patent law and research-based pharmaceutical companies, a major problem lies with the rights of unlimited duration as these rights bear the potential of substantial rents enhancing inequality without the support of the public interest. Insufficient attention has been paid to this angle. Conventional wisdom considers the absence of time limitation in trademarks and GIs to be logical due to

[65] *Cf.* Machlup & Penrose, *supra* note 49.

[66] The literature on duration of rights, apart from copyright extension, seems to be quite scarce. *Cf.* David S. Abrams, *Did TRIPS Spur Innovation? An Analysis of Patent Duration and Incentives to Innovate*, 157 U. PA. L. REV. 1616 (2009) (examining the implications of the patent term extension from seventeen to twenty years in the United States).

[67] Thus, the singular Peter Pan exception in UK law, extending unending royalties, is not inconsistent with the TRIPS Agreement. *See* Copyright, Designs and Patents Act 1988 c. 48, § 301:

> The provisions of Schedule 6 [CDPA 1988] have effect for conferring on GOSH Children's Charity for the benefit of Great Ormond Street Hospital for Children a right to a royalty in respect of the public performance, commercial publication or communication to the public of the play *Peter Pan* by Sir James Matthew Barry or of any adaption of that work, notwithstanding that copyright in the work expired on 31st December 1987.

the distinctions of products. And the protection of undisclosed information is timeless due to its very nature as a secret outside the public domain.

Again, from the perception of intellectual property as part of investment law, rights subject to unlimited time bore the potential of return on investment and continued profits turning into rents, which may contribute to income inequality and wealth in the long run. They exclude information from entering the public domain. Such rights, therefore, need a particular justification, which can be found as long as the product that they denominate exists on the market and needs to be distinguished from other products. However, trademarks are sold or licensed as a financial asset for good money and independently of a particular product. Independent and famous trademarks claim protection independently of a product to be distinguished. Internet domain names are registered and may be sold and traded for unwarranted windfall profits. None of this is limited in time. The requirement to use a trademark does not protect from such activities but instead supports them. The law treats trademarks as independent private assets, separate from the original function to promote and protect investment and distinguish products on the market for the benefit of consumers. Licensing or selling such trademarks amounts to a rent that cannot be justified by the investment made in the first place. A trademark no longer used in relation to a particular product (whether goods or services) should fall back into the public domain, open for creative imitation. The monopoly granted by the government should not lend itself to realizing unwarranted rents and thus increasing inequalities. Again, international law should set ceilings on trademark and GI protection based upon the principle of unjust enrichment, avoiding such effects that cannot be justified by the very function of these rights.

The same holds for protecting undisclosed information, which is unlimited in time. It is not a coincidence that trade secret protection is increasingly important under current rules, substituting for patent protection. This may also share the responsibility for increasing concentrations and inequality of income and wealth. Trade secrets should be protected in law only to the extent they relate to a particular product or process. At what point should they lapse and fall into the public domain from the point of view of the public interest in fostering reproduction and competition among products? It seems that trade secret protection can be justified only by an investment made. Once a reasonable profit has been generated, it should no longer be protected by law. Under this standard, for example, Coca-Cola's undisclosed information would no longer be protected. Of course, the company can make continued efforts to keep its trade secrets. Yet, if leaked to competitors at this stage, it would not give rise to tort or penal sanctions beyond employees' contractual obligations but would be considered a contribution to enhanced competition to the benefit of consumers. Otherwise, the restrictions in time imposed on patent law are being undermined. International economic law should set ceilings accordingly.

11.3.3.3 The Defense of Unjust Enrichment

Beyond temporal limitations, it is conceivable to contemplate a defense and objection to alleged violations of intellectual property rights and exclusivity on the ground of excessive profits due to the dominant position granted. We recall the principle that lawful recourse to existing information and reliance upon it in the process of creative imitation would depend upon whether or not the costs of investment incurred to produce the information in the first place have been appropriately recovered. This entails an appropriate and reasonable margin of profit on return, which would be limited. Intellectual property protection, however, should stop here and not give rise to economic rents for which a public interest does not exist. Foundations to this effect can be found in the principle of unjust enrichment.[68] The application of the principle is generally subject to positive law and thus of limited use unless negotiators and legislators take it into account in shaping the scope of intellectual property protection.

Based on equity and topical jurisprudence discussed earlier, the principle of unjust enrichment would grant objections and defenses to exclusivity, on a case-by-case basis, during the term of protection. The law would need to state the principle of preventing economic rents and the prohibitions of abuse of rights and unjust enrichment. Again, the burden of persuasion and proof lies with the rights holder claiming monopoly rights, demonstrating that investment has not yet been recovered and reasonable profits have not yet been made. Alternatively, those profits could be made subject to stringent discovery rules. Examples are the protection of a successful and highly profitable high-priced blockbuster patent – that of a famous trademark generating income and wealth independently of the products for which it is used, and the protection of a trade secret sold or licensed depending on the issue of whether the initial investment and effort made has been sufficiently recovered and thus no longer requires exclusive marketing rights. The intellectual asset, therefore, may subsequently be open to imitation and generic production in ordinary channels of the market economy even during the term of protection. Noneconomic aspects of intellectual property rights – in particular, moral rights or the protection of personality under human rights standards – would not be affected. Authors and successors in title would remain entitled to defend the integrity of a work.

11.3.4 *Fostering Competition*

This kind of thinking – based upon investment, appropriate return, and reasonable profit – entails a fundamental shift in conceptualizing patent and copyright law, particularly the unending extension of trademark and trade secret protection.

[68] Binder & Scheuer, *supra* note 63.

It would require rights holders to make new efforts at innovation as existing information falls into the public domain once the costs of creating the information and an appropriate profit (allowing the development of new information in research and development) are fully recuperated. Particular functions of intellectual property rights in product differentiation and securing safe products remain in place. As long as products are produced, trademarks must be attached, and consumers protected from false and dangerous imitations. The regime, however, may at some point limit the sale and exclusive licensing of independent rights used to make profits into the intellectual property portfolio. Information falls into the public domain and thus can be used for ordinary processes of creative imitation. International economic law should set appropriate parameters for this effect.

These effects foster competition, stimulate innovation, and reduce dominant positions and concentration. They likely could contribute to even more distributions of income and wealth. Defenses to intellectual property protection will mainly affect large corporations that are able to substantially profit from existing rights beyond an appropriate return on investment and profits. Problems caused by excessive power, wealth, and income based on intellectual property rights would no longer need to be remedied ex post by means of often ineffective competition policy, combating the abuse of dominant positions.[69] Intellectual property law would contribute to curbing such positions in the first place.

Many objections will be raised. The approach allegedly violates the minimum standards of the TRIPS Agreement and TRIPS-plus obligations. It lacks sufficient legal security and may entail excessive litigation in assessing the existence of exclusive rights. More importantly, rights holders can no longer make unlimited profits, and a fundamental principle of capitalism and entrepreneurship is thus at stake. Furthermore, the approach will require full financial transparency of companies beyond listed companies and impair the confidentiality of business relations. Finally, the approach entails strong state intervention in potentially curtailing existing rights.

In reply, it may be argued that the law would define the parameters of return on investment and appropriate profit, which would be served by granting a monopoly right. Ideally, these parameters are introduced when revising international agreements, as such revision offers new foundations. But the approach may also be adopted unilaterally, challenging international law in the process of claims and response. Whether the approach is compatible with the current TRIPS Agreement depends on the detailed drafting of instruments, considering the goals of Article 7 of

[69] Except for merger control, competition law does not deploy preventive effects and often remains ineffective to curb the abuse of intellectual property rights. *See* Eleanor M. Fox, *Can Anti-Trust Policy Protect the Global Commons from the Excesses of IPRs?*, *in* International Public Goods and Transfer of Technology under a Globalized Intellectual Property Regime 758 (Keith E. Maskus & Jerome H. Reichman eds., 2005).

the Agreement. If framed in terms of competition law, it falls under Article 40 of the TRIPS Agreement and currently cannot be challenged by recourse to nonviolation complaints.[70]

CONCLUSION

Squaring inequality and intellectual property rights is a difficult topic. There is a lack of empirical data demonstrating the relationship. It forms part of the larger debate on distributive justice among and within nations. It is at the heart of international economic law. This topic thus includes intellectual property protection, which has substantially increased contrary to the general trend of deregulation and trade liberalization under WTO rules.

We know that enhanced property rights support the concentration process, which favors economic rents at the expense of competition. In line with general property theory, it can be assumed that enhanced property rights contribute at least indirectly to increasing income inequality and wealth. Recourse to equity, as developed in international law as a topical methodology, allows taking into account wealth and income distribution aspects in applying and interpreting existing intellectual property rights. Equity informs the interpretation of existing rules and may even deny applications to do justice in a particular case. Moreover, it is important to apply intellectual property in the context of all international economic law, in particular GATT rules. This is particularly important in assessing bans on parallel importation and thus price discrimination.

The topic, however, encourages reconsidering the relationship between innovation and imitation. An attempt is made to approach the issue by conceptualizing human investment in capital, natural resources, time, and human resources in terms of imitation, reproduction, and innovation, all three based upon existing information. The legal order seeks to allow for appropriate returns on investment and fair profits for all activities. In areas of innovation, public funding or intellectual property rights absorb particular risks to create incentives to invest in human capital. Exclusive rights are justified only as long as, and to the extent that, they secure such returns and reasonable profits. International economic law should thus set ceilings

70 Nonviolation complaints under GATT art. XXIII and Dispute Settlement Understanding art. 26 are currently under a moratorium and do not apply to the TRIPS Agreement. The moratorium was extended in June 2022. World Trade Organization, *TRIPS Non-Violation and Situation Complaints: Ministerial Decision*, WTO Doc. WT/MIN(22)/26 (June 22, 2022). Even if applied, it is unlikely that new legislation and measures could be challenged. This is because they must be nonforeseeable at the conclusion of the TRIPS Agreement, which is not the case for disciplines related to fostering competition or price controls supported by Articles 7 and 8 of the Agreement. *See generally* Thomas Cottier & Krista Nadavukaren Schefer, *Non-Violation Complaints in WTO/GATT Dispute Settlement: Past, Present and Future*, *in* International Trade Law and the GATT/WTO Dispute Settlement System 145 (Ernst-Ulrich Petersmann ed., 1997).

and adopt a timeframe, including maximum periods of duration of patents, industrial designs, and copyright. Rights unlimited in time, particularly trademarks and GIs, should only be protected as long as they serve the purpose of distinguishing products and until an investment is recuperated with a reasonable profit. The latter should also apply to trade secret protection. Recourse to unjust enrichment should be encouraged. The law must prevent exclusivity from being used for rent-seeking, which contributes to wealth and income inequality and does not respond to the public interest in fostering human investment in reproduction, creative imitation, and innovation.

12

Managed Trade and Technology Protectionism

A Formula for Perpetuating Inequality?

Frederick M. Abbott[*]

12.1 DEVELOPING ECONOMIES AND TECHNOLOGY CAPACITY

12.1.1 *Technology and Disparity*

There are a variety of factors that perpetuate economic disparity. Among these is a disparity in levels of technological development. Successful industrial policy is not only a matter of access to technology. Access to capital, infrastructure development, education and training, design of social welfare systems, and other factors are important to economic development and welfare. Whether a particular form of government is a strong determinant of successful economic development is an open question. In recent years, some autocratically governed countries employing substantial state intervention in economic activity have performed well in economic development metrics. The Western liberal idea that democracy and economic progress are necessarily linked has been challenged.

While technology is not the sole determinant of economic development, it is an important determinant because the efficiency of national industry and the international competitiveness of economies are dependent on the capacity to develop and implement technical solutions. The question addressed in this chapter is how the recent trend toward "economic nationalism" that employs managed trade relations to pursue strategic interests may affect the ability of low- and middle-income countries (LMICs) to develop and implement new technologies, potentially resulting in a deterioration of the relative economic performance of LMICs vis-à-vis the dominant national or regional economies. If deterioration is a realistic prospect, are there policy measures LMICs may take to protect against that?

[*] The author gratefully acknowledges comments on an earlier version of this work from Pedro Roffe, as well as comments and suggestions from editors and reviewers of this volume, Daniel Benoliel, Padmashree Gehl Sampath, and Peter Yu.

In some areas, the possibility is present for LMICs to keep pace with the leading economic powers in terms of innovation. For example, the barriers to entry in software development and digital platform creation are relatively low. India has exploited this opening in the development of its digital sector. But in areas such as the development of new microprocessors, electric and autonomous vehicles, biotechnology, and aerospace, the barriers to entry remain high. Innovation expenditures in these fields are typically in the billions of U.S. dollars. To compete in these areas, LMICs likely need technology policies that attract foreign investment and cooperation.

Patent databases show that the vast preponderance of new technologies is being developed in a relative handful of countries.[1] The list has a new major entrant – China – but China is the exception, not the rule. Otherwise, the United States, Japan, the European Union, South Korea, and Taiwan dominate.[2] The United States continues to lead in the number of patents filed abroad.[3]

12.1.2 *The Continuing Vulnerability of Developing Economies*

The past decade has seen a narrowing of the gap in GDP per capita between developed and developing economies. However, much of that narrowing has been accounted for by GDP growth in China and other countries of East Asia.[4] Yet there remains a wide disparity in average income levels among countries.

In its *2019 Handbook of Statistics*, the U.N. Conference on Trade and Development (UNCTAD) summarizes:

[1] See Daniel Benoliel & Michael Gishboliner, *The Effect of Economic Crises on Patenting Activity across Countries*, 14 Chi.-Kent J. Intell. Prop. 316 (2015), and sources therein.

[2] Stephanie Nebehay, *In a First, China Knocks U.S. from Top Spot in Global Patent Race*, Reuters Tech. News (Apr. 7, 2020), www.reuters.com/article/us-usa-china-patents/in-a-first-china-knocks-us-from-top-spot-in-global-patent-race-idUSKBN21P1P9:

> The World Intellectual Property Organization, which oversees a system for countries to share recognition of patents, said 58,990 applications were filed from China last year, beating out the United States which filed 57,840.
>
> China's figure was a 200-fold increase in just 20 years, it said. The United States had filed the most applications in the world every year since the Patent Cooperation Treaty system was set up in 1978.
>
> More than half of patent applications – 52.4% – now come from Asia, with Japan ranking third, followed by Germany and South Korea.

India has made some progress as a source of relative patent filings.

[3] World Intell. Prop. Org., World Intellectual Property Indicators 2021, at 14–16 (2021).

[4] Countries cannot be neatly divided into developed and developing. There is a range of levels of economic development. It is conventional today to refer to high-income countries, middle-income countries (MICs), and low-income countries (LICs), as well as to combine reference to MICs and LICs as LMICs. This chapter adopts that convention.

Over the last 10 years, the global distribution of nominal GDP per capita between economies has become more equal. For example, in 2008, the poorest economies, accounting for 80 per cent of the world's population, contributed 23 per cent to world GDP. By 2018, their share in GDP rose to 33 per cent. Between 2013 and 2018, however, inequalities in GDP per capita reduced mainly among economies with moderately high income. The relative distance between the richest and poorest economies in the world remained almost unchanged.[5]

Recognizing this progress, it nonetheless remains that LMICs are far more vulnerable to economic shock than developed economies.[6] One of the principal reasons for this is the buffer of financial capital available to these economies. As the manager of the world's reserve currency, the United States maintains extensive power to "print money" in times of crisis.[7] The European Union, through the European Central Bank and the euro, has a similar, even if less extensive, capacity to create capital.[8] Such observations can also be made about the Bank of Japan and, to a lesser extent, the People's Bank of China.[9] In addition, with well-functioning securities markets, the United States and the European Union tend to be less vulnerable to equity shocks.

While developing country central banks can undertake operations in the same way as the U.S. Federal Reserve, they face significant challenges in printing money to meet obligations because they must pay their external debts in one of the major reserve currencies (such as U.S. dollars).[10] Moreover, as evidenced throughout the

[5] UNCTAD, 2019 HANDBOOK OF STATISTICS 45 (2019). UNCTAD adds: "Not all regions of the world recorded equal economic growth in 2018. Growth remained high, at 5.3 per cent, in developing Asia and Oceania, whereas in the developing economies of America GDP increased by only 0.7 per cent. The growth rate of transition and developed economies stood at 2.8 and 2.2 per cent, respectively." *Id.*

[6] The ability of the U.S. Federal Reserve to mitigate a near-catastrophic financial shock by acting as the monetary mechanism of last resort was illustrated during the 2008 mortgage-backed security–related meltdown. See, for example, FIN. CRISIS INQUIRY COMM'N, THE FINANCIAL CRISIS INQUIRY REPORT: FINAL REPORT OF THE NATIONAL COMMISSION ON THE CAUSES OF THE FINANCIAL AND ECONOMIC CRISIS IN THE UNITED STATES 6 (2011).

[7] The Federal Reserve Bank creates credits and purchases Treasury securities, funding the federal government and maintaining low rates of interest for borrowers. Although the Treasury Department is obligated to pay principal and interest to non-Federal Reserve purchasers of Treasury securities (e.g., foreign government buyers), the Federal Reserve can simply "cancel out" obligations otherwise owed and payable to it by the Treasury.

[8] See European Central Bank (www.ecb.europa.eu/ecb/tasks/stability/tasks/html/index.en.html).

[9] With respect to China, this is mainly because the renminbi is not generally accepted as a reserve currency because of the control by the political branches of the Chinese government over its reserve bank. However, as an alternative means for maintaining economic stability in times of stress, China has built up very substantial foreign currency reserves, including through purchase of U.S. treasury securities that can all be liquidated or otherwise deployed as circumstances warrant. *See* Qiao Yu, *Relocating China's Foreign Reserves*, BROOKINGS REP. (Nov. 21, 2013), www.brookings.edu/research/relocating-chinas-foreign-reserves/.

[10] Increasing the domestic money supply within a country means that a greater amount of currency in circulation is available to purchase an equivalent quantity of goods and services. All things being equal, this reduces the value of the currency and has an inflationary impact.

COVID-19 pandemic, the policies of LMIC central banks and treasuries depend on policies determined by the U.S. Federal Reserve that place U.S. interests first while taking into account the impact on the broader global economy.

The International Monetary Fund and other major international financial institutions recognized that the COVID-19 pandemic would have a more significant impact from a relative standpoint on developing economies than developed ones, acknowledging that the impact on developed economies was severe.[11]

12.2 THE MOVE TO MANAGED TRADE

12.2.1 *The Resurgence of Economic Nationalism and "Reshoring"*

Recent global developments do not portend an economic shift in favor of LMICs. Beginning in 2016, the United States led a sharp turn away from multilateral cooperation under the umbrella of the "Make America Great Again" agenda pursued by then-president Trump. The United States withdrew from the Paris Agreement on climate change, imposed trade barriers inconsistent with World Trade Organization (WTO) norms while blocking the appointment of WTO Appellate Body members, threatened withdrawal from the World Health Organization, and so on.[12] With the election of President Biden, U.S. policy began shifting back toward cooperation (including rejoining the Paris Agreement). Still, the return to its traditional multilateralist approach has been gradual and incomplete (such as in relation to the WTO), reflecting continued wariness regarding the strategic interests of other countries. The United States is not alone. The United Kingdom has withdrawn from the European Union. India is pursuing a "Make in India" agenda. Before the most recent deterioration, China adopted its Made in China 2025 program, which focused on making China the world leader in important technologies, including biotechnology, electric vehicles, robotics, and aerospace.[13] High-income countries (HICs) and more economically advanced middle-

Foreign purchasers of the currency need a larger amount to secure the same goods or services, depreciating its relative value. This may (or may not) stimulate domestic economic activity and growth, but it typically makes repayment of reserve currency (e.g., dollar-denominated) debt more costly. In addition, it is not as easy for LMIC companies to obtain new funding by issuing equity securities as it is for U.S. and European companies.

[11] Staff of Int'l Monetary Fund, *COVID-19 – Impact and Policy Considerations* (Int'l Monetary Fund, G-20 Surveillance Note, 2020), www.imf.org/external/np/g20/pdf/2020/041520.pdf.

[12] See, for example, Frederick M. Abbott, *Confronting COVID-19 in a World without WHO – Seriously?*, Health Pol'y Watch (Apr. 14, 2020), https://healthpolicy-watch.org/confronting-covid-19-in-a-world-without-who-seriously/.

[13] *See* Off. of the U.S. Trade Representative, Findings of the Investigation into China's Acts, Policies, and Practices Related to Technology Transfer, Intellectual Property, and Innovation under Section 301 of the Trade Act of 1974 (2018).

income countries (MICs) are turning inward with policies intended to redirect capital to domestic investment, including by boosting the role of automated production processes to reduce reliance on lower-cost foreign sources of labor.

The COVID-19 pandemic has exacerbated deterioration in international relations as the United States accused China of aggravating the impact of the virus. It has also, perhaps more important for present purposes, strengthened the resolve of governments to assure self-sufficiency in the production of important products, especially in the pharmaceutical and health arena. The United States encourages "reshoring" manufacturing, particularly from China.[14] In a similar vein, the Japanese government is encouraging reshoring from China. The European Union has been looking for regional industrial champions to counter the scale of Chinese penetration of its markets and to better compete with China in external markets.[15]

Many countries historically emphasized the importance of "food security." Concern for food security played an important role in the special situation of agriculture (including agricultural subsidies) in international trade relations. It will not be surprising if the concept enjoys a rebirth in the aftermath of the pandemic.[16]

12.2.2 *Diversification*

Countervailing the reshoring trend is a diversity trend, in which multinational corporations (MNCs) seek to diversify sources of supply for their supply chains. While this interest in supply-chain diversification may appear inherently contradictory with interest in reshoring, it reflects a practical recognition by the MNC business community that reshoring to the United States (and *pari passu* in the cases of the European Union and Japan)[17] is structurally limited. The U.S. labor force, for example, will resist the transition to repetitive assembly jobs (e.g., sewing jeans or assembling computer monitors) and would demand substantially higher wages than those paid in East Asia. Moreover, the pool of technically skilled labor "sitting on the sidelines" in the United States, Europe, and Japan is limited. Even considering that

[14] See, for example, Russell J. Greenberg, *Reshoring, Tariffs Brighten US Manufacturing Outlook*, IndustryWeek (Mar. 3, 2020), www.industryweek.com/the-economy/article/21125312/reshoring-tariffs-brighten-us-manufacturing-outlook; Rick Sobey, *Coronavirus Fallout: Reshoring Manufacturing Is Key for Economy and National Security, Experts Say*, Bos. Herald (Apr. 19, 2020), www.bostonherald.com/2020/04/19/coronavirus-fallout-reshoring-manufacturing-is-key-for-economy-and-national-security-experts-say/.

[15] See, for example, Jorge Valero, *Europe Looks for Its "Formula" to Create Industrial Champions*, Euractiv (July 23, 2019), www.euractiv.com/section/economy-jobs/news/europe-looks-for-its-formula-to-create-industrial-champions/.

[16] See, for example, Samuel Mehmet, *Brazilian Officials Warn of "Agriculture Nationalism" amid Pandemic*, New Food Mag. (May 5, 2020), www.newfoodmagazine.com/news/109871/brazilian-officials-warn-of-agriculture-nationalism-amid-pandemic/.

[17] See, for example, Mercy Kuo, *Japan Prods Firms to Leave China, Affecting Ties with Beijing and Washington*, Japan Times (May 8, 2020), www.japantimes.co.jp/news/2020/05/08/national/politics-diplomacy/tokyo-china-us-relations-business/.

MNCs are deploying automated production processes as part of reshoring efforts, diversification creates opportunities for LMICs outside China to attract relocating foreign direct investment (FDI). So far, major beneficiaries of that diversification trend have been countries of East Asia, such as Vietnam, Malaysia, and Thailand.[18]

The possibilities for individuals and businesses to use technologically advanced products have expanded dramatically, mainly due to the Internet, electronic commerce, and other digital technologies. However, while access to products embodying new technologies improves the quality of life, that may not translate into enhancing the domestic innovation infrastructure in LMICs. Suppose South Korea and China offer low-price cellular telephones that individuals in LMICs can afford. In that case, the possibilities for LMIC local industries to develop handsets that compete with those offerings – given the capital intensity of the R&D – are quite limited. The incentives for undertaking such efforts are not so clear. Though there are openings in some higher value-added points of the global supply chain, LMICs may find it difficult to escape from the trap of serving as low-labor-cost assembly platforms. Even that position could be threatened as robotics manufacturing technologies advance.

12.2.3 *De-Legalization*

We are moving away from the "legalized" international trading structure embodied in the WTO.[19] One reason for this move to "de-legalization" is frustration among U.S. trade officials with what is perceived as an abuse of the rule-based system by China. The U.S. frustration is not without some cause, even though China's policies, from a developmental standpoint, have helped it transform its economy and transition many millions of individuals into the middle-income class. The United States has spent decades negotiating bilateral agreements with China intended to improve the protection of U.S.-origin intellectual property[20] and to address matters such as cyberpiracy (including state-sponsored cyberpiracy).[21]

[18] See, for example, Michael Ryan, *Pivot to Vietnam: Reorienting America's Supply Chain*, INDUSTRY WEEK (Feb. 11, 2020), www.industryweek.com/the-economy/trade/article/21122771/pivot-to-vietnam-reorienting-americas-supply-chain.

[19] *See* Frederick M. Abbott, *Technology Governance in a Devolved Global Legal Order: Lessons from the China-USA Strategic Conflict*, *in* A NEW GLOBAL ECONOMIC ORDER (Cheng Chia-Jui ed., 2021).

[20] See, for example, China–U.S. bilateral agreements of 1992 and 1995 requiring modifications of Chinese intellectual property laws and enforcement procedures, *reprinted in* 2 FREDERICK ABBOTT, THOMAS COTTIER & FRANCIS GURRY, THE INTERNATIONAL INTELLECTUAL PROPERTY SYSTEM: COMMENTARY AND MATERIALS 1592–1608 (1999).

[21] The WTO has not been particularly helpful as a way for the United States to address its concerns with respect to China's intellectual property and transfer of technology practices. The United States attempted to redress what it perceived as deficiencies in China's intellectual property enforcement rules in *China – Measures Affecting the Protection and Enforcement of*

Following the imposition of WTO-inconsistent trade sanctions on China, the United States negotiated the Economic and Trade Agreement between the Government of the United States of America and the Government of the People's Republic of China, which incorporated the U.S. negotiating objectives of precluding so-called "forced technology transfer," whether express or tacit and strengthening rules regarding electronic intrusion (i.e., cyberpiracy).[22] There is no more assurance that China will change its behavior through effective implementation of this Agreement as compared with any other of the arrangements China has made with the United States previously, particularly as China accepted the terms of this arrangement "under duress" in the form of WTO-inconsistent tariff sanctions. Perhaps the most interesting element of the agreement is the complete eschewing of legalized dispute settlement, which has been replaced with the judgment and "untethered" discretion of diplomats. If either side is dissatisfied with the judgments and discretion, they walk away from the Agreement. There is no attempt to disguise this Agreement as anything other than implementing a balance-of-power diplomacy.

12.3 FOREIGN DIRECT INVESTMENT AND ITS LIMITS

12.3.1 *TRIPS Constraints*

The point of the WTO Agreement on Trade-Related Aspects of Intellectual Property Rights (TRIPS Agreement) was to foreclose developing countries from "appropriating" developed countries' technology.[23] For MICs, the obligation to provide patents across all subject matters that became fully operational in 2005 should prevent locally based companies from using foreign-owned, patented technology without the consent of the patent owners. As is well known, this foreclosure is subject to some exceptions or "flexibilities," but those flexibilities are not like an innovation pathway. (For least developed countries (LDCs), the obligation to provide patent protection generally can be avoided until 2034,[24] yet many LDCs have not indicated an intention to take advantage of this flexibility and continue to grant and enforce patents.)

The question of whether LMICs have the flexibility to make use of foreign-owned technology is only important if the other elements necessary to create successful

Intellectual Property Rights (2009) and was fatally hampered by the unwillingness of its U.S.-based companies to provide identifiable evidence to support the case.

22 This Phase One trade deal was signed on January 15, 2020. See discussion of relevant provisions in U.S. trade and investment agreements (TIAs) in Section 12.3.3.

23 *See* Frederick M. Abbott, *Protecting First World Assets in the Third World: Intellectual Property Negotiations in the GATT Multilateral Framework*, 22 Vand. J. Transnat'l L. 689 (1989).

24 Council for Trade-Related Aspects of Intellectual Property, Extension of the Transition Period under Article 66.1 for Least Developed Country Members: Decision of the Council for TRIPS of 29 June 2021, WTO Doc. IP/C/88 (June 29, 2021).

business enterprises are present. These include adequate capital, infrastructure, and technically trained staff to successfully implement innovative technologies.[25]

Because of limitations concerning these elements, the path for moving up the innovation curve has been encouraging FDI. Although large privately owned MNCs may prefer to invest in geographic areas with adequate infrastructure, if the opportunity is substantial enough, even electricity generation can be addressed through small power generation stations. Of course, the MNC brings with it capital and trained personnel.[26]

In this regard, there is a well-worn path – hosting FDI – for LMICs to develop manufacturing industries that use more advanced technologies. The question is whether this well-worn path leads to indigenous capacity for innovation and the creation of locally owned advanced technology industries or merely creates a perpetual situation of inequality between the technology "haves" and "have-nots." Can LMICs influence the arc of technological progress through policy options?

12.3.2 *Technology Transfer Obligations*

Through legislation and/or regulatory measures, governments can improve the terms of trade for local businesses by setting ground rules that improve the capacity, that is, bargaining power, of local enterprises in negotiating the terms of FDI.[27] One mechanism for accomplishing this objective is to establish requirements that foreign direct investors enter into joint venture arrangements with local enterprises to pursue their objectives and share technology with those joint venture partners as part of such arrangements.

There are myriad potential configurations for joint venture arrangements and other technology-sharing arrangements. The business and legal questions that must be addressed include the relative percentages of ownership and control over the business, the composition of management, how the capital of the business will be contributed and/or raised, how funds will be repatriated, and so forth. The technology-sharing questions include the defined subject matter of the relevant technology (including such matters as identification of relevant patent portfolios), potential geographic limitations on the sale of products incorporating the

[25] *Cf.* World Health Org., Indian Policies to Promote Local Production of Pharmaceutical Products and Protect Public Health (2017); World Health Org., China Policies to Promote Local Production of Pharmaceutical Products and Protect Public Health (2017). This author prepared both studies.

[26] Using its own model, China is today well-known for creating largely self-sustaining manufacturing operations in developing countries, including with Chinese national staff.

[27] The use by a developing country of the requirement that a foreign direct investor engage with a local partner in order for an investment to be approved may constitute a technology transfer requirement, notwithstanding the absence of a specific reference in legislation or regulations to technology *as such*. Virtually by definition, a foreign direct investor from a high-technology country engaging with a local partner will be bringing technology into the arrangement.

technology, ownership and control of technologies newly developed by the joint venture, contributions of trade secrets and other information, residual interests in technology upon dissolution or sale of the joint venture or party interest, and so forth.

Just as there are myriad potential configurations for joint venture and technology sharing, there are many ways that host governments may go about creating and implementing the requirements that may be established. Principally, this would involve choices between macro- and micro-management. The government might establish macro-benchmarks such as requirements regarding percentages of ownership and control and largely leave to the parties the negotiation of the specific terms and conditions of the arrangement, including for technology transfer. Alternatively, the government might more precisely establish expected terms and conditions – for example, concerning technology licensing conditions. There is also a question of whether the government would seek to maintain a review and approval mechanism before the commencement of business operations. Alternatively, it might be left to the parties to assure compliance with the preestablished rules, with the possibility of ex post facto regulatory intervention.

A substantive objection by the United States to China's policies and practices concerning joint ventures and technology sharing was, and still is, that demands by Chinese authorities were conveyed informally and "off the record" as a condition to FDI approval. The maintenance of nontransparent regulatory requirements creates a risk of discriminatory treatment of investors that could be based on various factors (e.g., national origin) and should not be recommended. This is of particular concern if public securities markets and investors are involved in a venture, as the investors will not have an adequate basis to evaluate the business without transparency.

Recent economic research strongly supports the conclusion that China's joint venture requirements for foreign investors have resulted in more robust technology transfer to Chinese enterprises (including downstream enterprises) than wholly foreign-owned investments.[28] In the case of China, the available evidence suggests that "forced technology transfer" in the context of investment approvals has exerted a positive internal impact.

12.3.3 *Limitations in Preferential Trade and Investment Agreements*

12.3.3.1 Transfer of Technology

There is a trend of incorporating provisions precluding technology transfer conditions in preferential trade and investment agreements (TIAs). This is not a new

[28] Kun Jiang, Wolfgang Keller, Larry D. Qiu & William Ridley, *International Joint Ventures and Internal vs. External Technology Transfer: Evidence from China* (Nat'l Bureau of Econ. Rsch., Working Paper No. 24455, 2019).

phenomenon. The United States secured commitments from developing countries, at least as early as its bilateral free trade agreement (FTA) with Chile in 2004, that approval of investments would not be conditioned on a performance requirement: "to transfer a particular technology, a production process, or other proprietary knowledge to a person in its territory."[29] This provision, in a substantially similar format, has become a "staple" of U.S.-negotiated TIAs and is found in the text of the Trans-Pacific Partnership Agreement (TPP),[30] preserved in the Comprehensive and Progressive Agreement for Trans-Pacific Partnership (CPTPP).

The United States is not alone in demanding restrictions on technology transfer obligations. The recently concluded Comprehensive Economic and Trade Agreement (CETA) between Canada and the European Union includes a restriction on technology transfer requirements.[31]

The Regional Comprehensive Economic Partnership Agreement (RCEP) includes a performance requirement similar to that in the TPP regarding technology transfer.[32] Of some interest, the RCEP has a carveout in its investment chapter of the prohibition on technology transfer requirements in favor of Cambodia, Lao PDR, and Myanmar. India pushed back against including such a provision during the RCEP negotiations, and its unwillingness to accept a provision of that type may have partly been why India did not join the RCEP.[33]

12.3.3.2 Competition

Transfer of technology, and economic growth more generally, may be stymied by anticompetitive practices engaged in by market actors. Commercial arrangements that might otherwise improve the position of locally based businesses and entrepreneurs may be frustrated through licensing and other conditions that make it difficult

[29] Chile–United States Free Trade Agreement, Chile–U.S., June 6, 2003, art. 10.5.1(f).

[30] Article 9.9.1 of Trans-Pacific Partnership Agreement provides:

> No Party shall, in connection with the establishment, acquisition, expansion, management, conduct, operation, or sale or other disposition of an investment of an investor of a Party or of a non-Party in its territory, impose or enforce any requirement, or enforce any commitment or undertaking . . . to transfer a particular technology, a production process or other proprietary knowledge to a person in its territory . . . .

[31] Article 8.5.1 of CETA provides:

> A Party shall not impose, or enforce the following requirements, or enforce a commitment or undertaking, in connection with the establishment, acquisition, expansion, conduct, operation, and management of any investments in its territory to . . . transfer technology, a production process or other proprietary knowledge to a natural person or enterprise in its territory . . . .

[32] Regional Comprehensive Economic Partnership Agreement, Nov. 15, 2020, art. 10.1(f).

[33] See, for example, V.S. Seshadri, *Regional Comprehensive Economic Partnership Agreement: Need for a Strategy* (Rsch. & Info. Sys. for Developing Countries, Discussion Paper No. 209, 2017), www.ris.org.in/regional-comprehensive-economic-partnership-agreement-need-strategy-0.

for technology transferees to employ the relevant technologies or that impose oppressive conditions otherwise. In addition, assuming that locally based businesses emerge to compete with more established foreign-owned enterprises, their evolution into effective competitors may be hampered by anticompetitive practices of dominant actors.

In recent years, competition authorities in LMICs have begun to assert themselves more vigorously and are actively prosecuting cases involving anticompetitive behaviors, including those concerning licensing agreements.[34] One potential risk that LMICs face is the trend toward incorporating competition chapters in TIAs that establish rules for conducting competition investigations. Most of these chapters are directed toward procedural protections, though some involve substantive rules.

While, in principle, the assurance of fair process in governmental investigations, including competition law investigations, is important, the historical assertion of TIA rules by HICs has a blemished record. Seemingly benign procedural rules regarding the conduct of competition investigations may provide the basis for threats of trade sanctions that, in turn, may have a chilling effect on the willingness of competition authorities to pursue such actions. LMICs should very cautiously approach the negotiation of competition chapters in TIAs. Competition authorities worldwide may enter into cooperative arrangements for conducting investigations, sharing information, and so forth without codifying these rules in TIAs. Though it is important to assure fairness in investigation processes, this can be accomplished under national law in LMICs without embedding the possibility that the investigation targets will have recourse to threats from their home governments to obstruct those investigations.

12.3.3.3 Investor–State Dispute Settlement

Until recently, there was a distinct trend in TIAs to incorporate an investor–state dispute settlement (ISDS) mechanism for disputes between nationals of the parties and the host country of investment.[35] Typically, recourse might be had by the private investor to third-party arbitration under the auspices of the International Centre for the Settlement of Investment Disputes (ICSID) and/or pursuant to United Nations Commission on International Trade Law (UNCITRAL) rules. However, ISDS has fallen out of favor for several reasons. First, defining limitations on the types of disputes that could be initiated proved challenging. Private investors

[34] *See generally* Frederick M. Abbott, *Let International Competition Negotiations Sleep a While Longer: Focus on Tools and Capacity*, 49 Int'l Rev. Intell. Prop. & Compar. L. 259 (2018).

[35] Private investors tend to prefer ISDS because they control the process from the standpoint of their own interests and do not need to rely on their government to pursue (i.e., espouse) and resolve a claim. Private investors are concerned that their interest may be compromised by their own government for political or other reasons that are outside the private investor's immediate economic interest.

brought claims concerning alleged regulatory or judicial takings that went well beyond traditional concepts of nationalization or expropriation. These included claims regarding government regulation of tobacco advertisement and ordinary judicial patent invalidation processes.[36] Second, the establishment of ISDS implies a lack of sovereign capacity to fairly administer judicial proceedings within a host state. More recent TIAs have made efforts to limit the scope of the claims that may be brought and/or the characteristics of the arbitral tribunal that will decide ISDS disputes.[37] The United States–Mexico–Canada Agreement (USMCA) nearly eliminates ISDS. Several countries have announced their intention to move away from including ISDS provisions in their TIAs.[38] Innovation in the area of ISDS is taking place to limit efforts to redress abuse to the traditional concepts of expropriation and nationalization.

From the standpoint of LMICs, ISDS presents special difficulties. Such proceedings are very costly to defend and are likely to absorb significant government legal and financial resources that could be better deployed elsewhere.[39] Because claims will arise under customary international law, there is no need to specially incorporate a state-to-state investment dispute settlement mechanism in a TIA. It is within the customary international legal practice for a state that obtains compensation on behalf of a private investor to return that compensation to the investor.[40]

12.3.3.4 Tread Cautiously with TIAs

LMICs need to be on guard in the negotiation of TIAs to avoid the surrender of important policy options with respect to technology transfer and economic development. There is no good reason from an LMIC perspective to accept a provision precluding governmental measures requiring joint venturing and/or technology

[36] Regarding tobacco packaging regulation, see Philip Morris Asia Ltd. v. The Commonwealth of Austl., PCA Case No. 2012-12, Award on Jurisdiction and Admissibility (Dec. 17, 2015); Philip Morris Brands Sàrl v. Oriental Republic of Uru., ICSID Case No. ARB/10/7, Award (July 8, 2016). Regarding patent invalidation proceedings, see Eli Lilly v. Government of Can., ICSID Case No. UNCT/14/2, Final Award (Mar. 16, 2017).

[37] See, for example, the Comprehensive and Economic Trade Agreement (CETA) between Canada and the European Union, which establishes a standing Arbitral Tribunal and an associated Appellate Tribunal. Comprehensive Economic and Trade Agreement between Canada and the European Union and Its Member States, Can.-EU, ch. 8, § F, Oct. 30, 2016.

[38] *See* UNCTAD, *Reforming Investment Dispute Settlement: A Stock-Taking* 1 (UNCTAD, IIA Issues Note, 2019), https://unctad.org/en/PublicationsLibrary/diaepcbinf2019d3_en.pdf.

[39] Incorporation of a state-to-state espousal mechanism is recognized as an alternative. *Id.* Traditionally, when a foreign private investor (i.e., an alien) considered that a host state had undertaken a wrongful act, such as expropriating an investment without paying adequate compensation, the private investor sought "espousal" of its claim by its home state against the host state alleged to have acted wrongfully. The claim became the subject of state-to-state dispute settlement.

[40] In principle, the private investor does as well under a state-to-state dispute settlement procedure as through ISDS.

transfer obligations in the context of FDI. Nor is there a good reason to include a competition chapter in a TIA that can be used as the basis for HIC threats to withdraw trade concessions as a reaction to competition enforcement actions. Whether LMICs have the bargaining power to avoid these types of obligations is a different question. It is worth bearing in mind that ISDS obligations seemed to be an inevitability only a few years ago, and public perceptions about ISDS obligations shifted.

12.4 OPTIONS FOR LMICS

12.4.1 *Revitalizing Multilateralism?*

The idea that LMICs will climb the technology curve through some voluntary technology transfer programs adopted by HICs does not appear to be a particularly viable development solution. The multilateral system is largely broken down; even when it was "working," there was very little in the nature of HIC government support for technology transfer. This is at least substantially explainable by the fact that technology is predominantly owned and controlled by private enterprises. Even if the will was present, HIC governments would face substantial obstacles in mandating that businesses make their technology available through some type of institutional program.

With the world economy shifting to a "beggar thy neighbor" approach in which the major technology powers seek to undermine each other's progress, LMICs need to fend for themselves. We may be reverting to a late nineteenth-century model, where preferential alliances replace the mid-twentieth-century most-favored-nation model. In this devolved scenario, LMICs may find themselves with some technology acquisition bargaining power if they can successfully trade access to their markets for better terms of trade. It is hard to have confidence in such a model, given the disparities in economic strength. But it may be where we are headed.

12.4.2 *Leapfrog Technologies*

As noted earlier, there may be some subject-matter areas where the barriers to entry for advanced technology industries are lower than others. Some of these are areas that countries such as India have exploited. The Internet has made available vast libraries of technical know-how at negligible cost.[41] When there are gaps in knowledge and skills, there are consultants to help LMICs fill those gaps and train local

[41] Just as the average homeowner may today choose to repair his or her own washing machine by watching a YouTube video on disassembly, identification of faulty parts, and reassembly, along with purchasing the necessary parts from eBay or Alibaba, so may technologists in LMICs use access to the Internet for know-how regarding matters such as planning and executing infrastructure development. See, for example, Jose Luis Blanco, Andrew Mullin, Kaustubh Pandya & Mukund Sridhar, *The New Age of Engineering and Construction Technology*, McKinsey & Co. (July 2017), www.mckinsey.com/industries/capital-projects-and-infrastructure/our-insights/the-new-age-of-engineering-and-construction-technology.

individuals.[42] Information, including patent databases, is far more readily available worldwide than at any time in human history.

It is not only the possibility for creating new, locally developed technical solutions that may be enhanced through bypassing steps in the technology chain but also for deploying infrastructure that previously required large-scale investments of capital but which now can be accomplished with much more modest investment. The build-out of telecommunications infrastructure relying on satellite relays in contrast to wires and cables is one illustration.

Given the expansion of available information, building capacity for technology absorption may be the priority task for most developing countries. The benefits that can be obtained by piggybacking on externally created innovation will depend on the level of expertise within the recipient country. This depends on education – which historically required the physical presence of trained educators and hard-copy instructional materials. Access to online educational resources that were previously the province of a few select educational institutions mainly located in HICs represents another change that opens up new possibilities for LMICs.[43]

Developments in smartphone technology and associated financial payment systems have made it possible for countries to upgrade their transaction processing

[42] The extent of the global transformation in the availability of technical resources is difficult to overstate. As recently as the conclusion of the GATT Uruguay Round, the Internet was an emerging technology, and the WTO TRIPS Agreement barely accounted for the digitization of information. Access to patent data typically involved subscriptions to hard-copy patent office journals. Particularly for LMICs, access to scientific publications was a costly and limited means for keeping abreast of developments. Demands for assistance with technology transfer took account of the barriers that needed to be overcome to move scientific and technical information from Point A to Point B. Today databases at the major patent offices (including through WIPO) are largely open to anyone with an Internet connection. Except for constraints imposed by intellectual property laws, including patents and trade secrets, most barriers are gone. This is not to suggest that advancing technologically is easy, but that access to technology resources is a much different matter than the 1970s debates on a New International Economic Order.

Self-evidently, the open Internet is proving to represent both very positive and very negative attributes. Access to technology is counterbalanced by cybersecurity breaches and misappropriation of valuable commercial and personal information. As governments grapple with the downsides of the open Internet, it is not clear that today's access to technology will persist indefinitely. But the long run defies prediction.

[43] See, for example, *UNESCO Launch for Massive Open Online Courses Guide for Developing Countries*, UNESCO (June 24, 2016), www.unesco.org/new/en/media-services/single-view/news/unesco_launch_for_massive_open_online_courses_guide_for_deve/; Coursera (www.coursera.org/); edX (www.edx.org/); World Bank, Open Learning Campus, olc.worldbank.org/. Using these educational resources entails some expenses, such as purchasing computers, providing Internet access (e.g., through satellite dish), and engaging supervisory personnel to assist students. But, with a modest expenditure of resources, an LMIC government can put together schools from early learning through advanced degrees, notwithstanding a limited number of locally trained specialist teachers. The obstacles to distance learning are not to be underestimated. But there is a good deal of charitable or foundation support for this endeavor, and companies are willing to contribute to these efforts.

in ways that enable low-income individuals to transact business without the build-out of expensive technological infrastructure.[44] The major beneficiaries of mobile payment system innovation may be the micro-scale operators – proprietors of street stalls and so forth. In addition, the evolution of payment systems is dramatically lowering the costs of repatriating foreign-earned income for expatriate workers, all to the potential benefit of LMICs. Mobile Internet technology has facilitated possibilities for efficient communication, planning, and execution in business.

Small-scale solar energy generation stations and other sustainable energy generation technologies have created opportunities for more remote areas to electrify without large infrastructure expenditure.[45] This is perhaps a more challenging area than education or payment systems in the sense that sustainable energy systems require building physical energy storage capacity for continuous use.[46] Similarly, much work is being done to reduce the costs of water purification systems, including developing small-scale water purification units. This type of technology is extremely important to many LMIC environments.

The foregoing references are just a few of the areas where recent advances in technology are creating new possibilities for LMICs.[47] It is not simply that it may be cheaper and easier to improve quality of life, such as through improved telecommunications and electronic payments, but that as technical solutions increase connectivity to a larger innovative community, local innovators are likely to adapt and advance that technology. This is not intended to suggest an over-optimistic portrayal of current conditions or the future, but some building blocks are present for advancing an economy by leapfrogging stages of technological development.

12.4.3 *Attracting Capital Investment*

The scarce resource for LMICs is the investment capital necessary to implement concepts. This perhaps states an obvious, if not a circular, proposition. That is,

[44] Aaron Klein, *Is China's New Payment System the Future?*, Brookings Inst. (June 2019), www.brookings.edu/wp-content/uploads/2019/05/ES_20190617_Klein_ChinaPayments.pdf.

[45] See, for example, *Small-Scale Renewable Energy in Developing Countries*, Energy Cent. (Feb. 24, 2012), www.energycentral.com/c/ec/small-scale-renewable-energy-developing-countries; Int'l Energy Agency, Renewable Energy Services for Developing Countries: In Support of the Millennium Development Goals: Recommended Practice & Key Lessons (2008); *A 750 Ultra-Mega Solar Plant Will Help Power Delhi's Metro Rail System in India*, Solar (World Bank) (Nov. 29, 2017), www.worldbank.org/en/results/2017/11/29/solar.

[46] Nonetheless, even if only daytime solar energy generation is possible for areas previously without access to electricity, this is a major step forward.

[47] *See also* Keun Lee, The Art of Economic Catch-Up: Barriers, Detours and Leapfrogging in Innovation Systems (2019).

LMIC economies would do better with more money.[48] From a global perspective, ample capital is available for investment, and that investment is seeking returns.[49] The question for LMICs is how to "package" their national economies to attract that investment capital.[50]

12.4.3.1 Sound Governance

One approach to attracting investment involves establishing a reputation for "sound governance," which refers to a sound legal system[51] and the absence of corruption in regulatory institutions.[52] For the investor, the enforceability of contractual arrangements and consistency in implementing regulatory norms is important to executing

48 Though it is not clear that objective evidence supports the criticism, there have been concerns regarding whether Chinese investments in Africa, including associated loans, are overburdening the recipients with debt. See, for example, *"No Strings Attached" to Africa Investment, Says China's Xi*, FRANCE 24 (Sept. 3, 2018), www.france24.com/en/20180903-africa-china-summit-beijing-investment-infrastructure-debt-xi-jinping; Joseph Goldstein, *Kenyans Say Chinese Investment Brings Racism and Discrimination*, N.Y. TIMES (Oct. 15, 2018), www.nytimes.com/2018/10/15/world/africa/kenya-china-racism.html. There have also been concerns regarding the construction of communities of Chinese nationals within certain East Asian countries, and such construction has begun to face pushback. See, for example, Andy Mukherjee, *No Chinese Belt, Road or Bedrooms for Mahathir's Malaysia: The Prime Minister Is Throwing Up Hurdles to China's Influence in the Country*, BLOOMBERG (Aug. 28, 2018), www.bloomberg.com/opinion/articles/2018-08-28/malaysia-shuts-out-chinese-infrastructure-property-projects.

49 See, for example, Ewa Skormas & Elisabeth Bautista Suarez, *2022 Global Private Equity Outlook, S&P Global Market Intelligence*, S&P GLOB. MKT. INTEL. (Apr. 20, 2022), www.spglobal.com/marketintelligence/en/news-insights/research/2022-global-private-equity-outlook; FREDERICK M. ABBOTT, RYAN B. ABBOTT, JOSEPH FORTUNAK, PADMASHREE GEHL SAMPATH & DAVID WALWYN, OPPORTUNITIES, CONSTRAINTS AND CRITICAL SUPPORTS FOR ACHIEVING SUSTAINABLE LOCAL PHARMACEUTICAL MANUFACTURING IN AFRICA: WITH A FOCUS ON THE ROLE OF FINANCE 33–48 (2021), https://nova-worldwide.com/OSF-PHP_report.

50 There is an inherent relationship between "risk" and "reward." Some investors may be willing to accept a high level of risk by investing in an LMIC environment, where there is insecurity and/or limits on the capacity to repatriate investments. Still, on the whole, such investments appeal to a limited segment of potential investors.

51 One of the hallmarks of a well-functioning market economy is the presence of a robust legal framework in which private and government contracts are enforceable. Payments should be made when goods and services are delivered unless there are legally justified grounds for nonpayment. Traditional mechanisms can be used as substitutes for legally enforceable contracts, such as letters of credit assuring payment upon delivery of goods and appropriate documentation. Increasingly, blockchain solutions will be offered as substitutes for contract enforcement. With that said, a well-functioning legal system is a relatively efficient mechanism for assuring the secure flow of goods and services.

52 Government corruption is a heavy tax on businesses and the consumer. It is a serious obstacle to economic development in LMICs, and government corruption has adversely impacted areas such as public health in significant ways. There is no obvious "easy solution" to addressing corruption. Particularly in low-income environments, the temptations presented by financial mismanagement are considerable. Ultimately it is up to the public to demand accountability from government officials. In countries where the government is not responsive to the public, it is difficult for the public to achieve this objective.

business plans. The absence of sound governance is a risk factor that necessarily increases the cost of capital and creates a drag on the economy. Achieving sound governance is a long-term project for any country, especially for LMICs.[53]

12.4.3.2 Autonomous Investor Agreements

In addition to trying to assure the neutrality of courts and regulators, an LMIC and its private-sector enterprises may also support and negotiate contractual arrangements that entail defining with some specificity the terms of investment, including the potential for third-party arbitration. Given that LMICs have arguably faced difficulties with some existing international arbitration institutions, carefully defined self-standing agreements might be an alternative.[54]

The subject of international commercial arbitration is dealt with in detailed literature in which the potential issues have been laid out.[55] Alternative dispute settlement arrangements may be important to establish a secure environment for investors in LMICs.[56] At the same time, it is important that LMICs can negotiate third-party arbitration mechanisms that do not tilt against their interests.

In recent years, international donors have stressed financial management oversight as part of their activities, and this may be of some help. Investors of private capital in local projects can, of course, attempt to put in place strict financial controls. It is easier for private companies to demand accountability from their employees and joint venture partners because future contributions of capital and other investments can be withheld in the event of a breach of trust. However, a reputation for dishonest private dealings within a particular country will also have the effect of raising risk and limiting investment.

53 This is not to suggest that HIC governments do not face problems of corruption and misuse of political power.

54 An issue from the standpoint of LMIC private business operators is that subjecting disputes to arbitration by one of the prominent dispute settlement providers, such as the International Chamber of Commerce, will result in the appointment of an arbitrator or arbitrators more likely to favor the interests of a foreign investor or contract party and may entail a high level of expense that makes participation problematic.

55 On international commercial arbitration generally, see GARY B. BORN, INTERNATIONAL COMMERCIAL ARBITRATION (2d ed. 2014). To be more specific, private parties based in different national legal jurisdictions entering into commercial arrangements are ordinarily subject to litigation in the place where a contract is carried out (i.e., the place of performance). However, there are alternative bases that might subject the parties to jurisdiction in other places (e.g., the place of contract negotiation and execution, or the place where an injury occurs). Absent an alternative arrangement, the parties are typically subject to the jurisdiction of the local courts where there is a sufficient jurisdictional nexus. The concern of prospective private-party investors in an LMIC is that business disputes involving contracts, including joint venture arrangements, will be subject to the jurisdiction of the local courts. For one or more reasons, the private investor believes that the local courts will not treat its claims (or defenses) fairly. Putting aside the concerns about corruption, there may be potential delays due to insufficient legal infrastructure and/or multiple layers of appeal that make dispute settlement by the local courts appear problematic.

56 A few elements that might be considered in such agreements include (1) selection of an arbitrator or arbitrators during the contracting phase and (2) agreement that the award of the

12.4.3.3 Support for Private-Sector Initiative

Because many small- and medium-sized enterprises (SMEs) in LMICs do not have the experience and expertise to negotiate sophisticated investment and licensing agreements with foreign investors, it is important that governments try to make available consulting resources for assisting SMEs with their transactions.

12.4.4 *Balancing Protective Measures*

A key question for any developing or emerging market government is how much of the national economy to "protect" through tariff, trade, or tax measures to provide local development space. Consumers bear the cost of protectionism, which can and should be tolerated at a certain level, but blanket protectionism simply makes the functioning economy too expensive.

As the United States has moved away from a low-tariff approach to international trade relations toward strategic targeting of its trading partners, the idea that growth can be promoted by granting preferences to local companies is likely to gain traction. The net effect will be a reduction in global output, but this does not mean that the strategic use of tariffs will not benefit a particular country in individual cases. For an LMIC, it may be necessary to provide at least transitory tariff and/or quota protection for an "infant industry." But it is important to limit the use of tariffs and quotas because they otherwise have the effect of raising prices for consumers and may harm general welfare.[57]

12.5 PERPETUATING INEQUALITY?

LMICs are confronted with a new world order in which the major economic powers that promoted multilateralism have moved toward nationalism, localization of

arbitrator is automatically enforceable and, if necessary, through a compulsory process in the appropriate jurisdictions (e.g., where the parties have assets).

The selection of an arbitrator in advance of the dispute is not a foolproof mechanism in the sense that events, such as those affecting the health of the arbitrator, may intervene, but such contingencies may be addressed. Perhaps ideally, the contracting parties may, in advance, identify a single person with whom both parties would be willing to repose confidence in resolving a prospective dispute. This would likely reduce the costs and complexity of an eventual arbitration.

[57] Intellectual property is a two-edged sword in the development context. On the one hand, it provides the mechanism for private parties to securitize technology and engage in out-licensing and other technology transfer components, such as training. It is also important to allow local businesses to protect investments in branding, expression, and innovation. On the other hand, it provides a mechanism by which foreign investors and intellectual property owners protect monopolies within the local market, restricting access to local entrepreneurs and solidifying their potential market dominance. Patents and other forms of exclusivity covering new technologies may inhibit LMIC adoption of specific solutions or approaches. Still, much use can be made of technologies that are a generation back, and licensing may be a reasonable approach in other cases.

production, and de-legalization of dispute settlement in favor of balance of power diplomacy. A counterpart to this trend is declining interest in developmental assistance, whether actual or rhetorical.

There is a military overlay, so this new world may also be dangerous. It remains to be determined how countries that are not part of the new great power dynamic will acclimate to this new world. During the Cold War that lasted from 1946 to 1989, a bit more than four decades, countries of the so-called Third World sought to play the First and Second World countries off against each other, seeking economic and military alliances with one side or another. It may be that we are moving into a new technological world order in which the less powerful countries must choose to ally themselves in a technological sense with one or another of the dominant technology powers. This should not be taken as a proposal but rather an identification of one potential new reality.

Regrettably, as part of the "exercise of power" equation, there is a trend among the capital-exporting countries to negotiate bilateral and plurilateral agreements with LMICs that preclude regulatory measures requiring a transfer of technology as a condition of FDI, including within joint venture arrangements. Because individual private investors within LMICs may lack substantial bargaining power, this diminishes the capacity of LMICs to secure favorable terms for the transfer of technology. There is no obvious solution to this problem other than seeking to avoid commitments of this nature.

At the same time, based largely on the evolution of digital technologies, LMICs have the opportunity to leapfrog in the current technological environment. There remains the requirement of securing adequate capital investment, including through the private sector. Attracting that capital entails creating conditions in which investors are reasonably secure.

Sound governance and transparency may be important elements. National self-interest should move a country in that direction, regardless of its effect on the perception of prospective investors. Developing mechanisms for fair third-party arbitration of private commercial disputes may help foster an attractive investment climate.

LMICs have seen their relative economic circumstances deteriorate vis-à-vis the HICs due to the COVID-19 pandemic.[58] All economies were hit hard, but the HICs had more capacity to absorb the shock and are recovering reasonably well. LMICs confront terms of trade that favor the HICs, including provisions in TIAs that preclude requirements for the transfer of technology, as well as the ascendance more broadly of managed trade policy among economically powerful states. These factors portend the perpetuation of the marked disparity in the distribution of global income and wealth. There are no "magic bullet" solutions on the horizon.

58 See, for example, Venkat Gopalakrishnan, Divyanshi Wadhwa, Sara Haddad & Paul Blake, *2021 Year in Review in 11 Charts: The Inequality Pandemic*, World Bank (Dec. 21, 2021), www.worldbank.org/en/news/feature/2021/12/20/year-2021-in-review-the-inequality-pandemic.

13

Sharing Pathogen Sequence Data for Global Scientific Research under the Nagoya Protocol to the Convention on Biological Diversity

Jerome H. Reichman, Carolina dos S. Ribeiro, George B. Haringhuizen, and Paul F. Uhlir

13.1 TENSIONS CONCERNING THE COVERAGE OF GENETIC SEQUENCE DATA UNDER THE CONVENTION ON BIOLOGICAL DIVERSITY

The Convention on Biological Diversity (CBD)[1] may be characterized as a response by low- and middle-income countries (LMICs) to a preexisting state of inequality with regard to the development and commercialization of products deriving from the access to and use of biological diversity in nation states. Historically, scientists from the more economically developed countries, while exploring the genetic resources in LMICs, would help themselves both to physical specimens from plants, animals, and microbiological materials and to traditional knowledge (TK) of indigenous populations about how to make economical use of such resources and knowledge. One needs to recognize that the CBD was a concerted effort to invalidate such practices and, instead, to assert sovereign ownership over both local genetic resources and TK as well as a fair share of any economic benefits arising from their commercial applications. The adopted Nagoya Protocol[2] to the CBD then supplied strong enforcement measures to implement new remedies to the old inequalities that the CBD sought to rectify.

[1] The CBD is a multilateral treaty adopted under the United Nations on June 5, 1992, and entered into force on December 29, 1993. Its objective is to develop national strategies for the conservation and sustainable use of biological diversity. It is generally seen as the key document regarding sustainable development.

[2] The Nagoya Protocol to the Convention on Biological Diversity on Access to Genetic Resources and the Fair and Equitable Sharing of Benefits Arising from Their Utilization is a supplementary agreement to the CBD that aims to implement one of the three objectives: the fair and equitable sharing of benefits arising out of the utilization of genetic resources. The protocol was adopted on October 29, 2010, and entered into force on October 12, 2014.

This chapter does not question the policy decisions embodied in the CBD and its Nagoya Protocol to eliminate practices rooted in the preexisting state of inequality. By the same token, we emphasize the importance of scientific research and TK as a potential source of major benefits to all humanity. In this context, the current debate about access to genetic sequence data (GSD) must be considered. There is no going back on the foundational obligations of the CBD concerning negotiated access to genetic resources and the data resulting from their study and applications, including the relevant TK of indigenous populations. Nevertheless, it must be made clear that neither the CBD nor the Nagoya Protocol will be allowed to interfere with basic scientific research so long as the relevant genetic resources were obtained in the first instance by modalities sanctioned under the treaties in question. These modalities, in turn, support basic scientific research without undermining the rights of provider countries to a fair share of any benefits resulting from commercial applications of such scientific research based on specific genetic resources and TK obtained from those countries. The rest of this chapter explains how to reconcile these tensions in the specific case of GSD, using pathogen research data as an example.

Preserving the Earth's biodiversity is essential to human survival and a major factor in global economic development (Kolbert, 2014). Research on the components of biodiversity, especially genetic resources, not only enables scientists to discover and understand their characteristics and promote needed conservation but also contributes to the development of innovative products and applications while bolstering efforts to strengthen public health, among other goals (Halewood et al., 2012; Ribeiro et al., 2018b).

Conservation and management of the Earth's biodiversity include manifold stakeholders that range from LMICs to the most developed countries, along with not-for-profit organizations, industries, scientists, and local indigenous communities (Access and Benefit-Sharing Clearing-House, n.d.; Aoki, 2008; Jeffery, 2004). The divergent views of these stakeholders with respect to the proper treatment of genetic resources and GSD – now designated as "digital sequence information" (DSI) for purposes of current negotiations (Morgera et al., 2019) – typically depend on whether they regard themselves primarily as potential providers or users of genetic resources (AHTEG, 2019).

These views reflect different approaches to rights and obligations concerning the management of such resources. More economically developed nations, the primary users and exploiters of resources for for-profit and nonprofit goals, mostly promote open exchanges of data, materials, and knowledge to achieve public benefits. LMICs, which often possess the most diverse and rich biodiversity resources, position themselves as provider countries seeking to restrict access in order to effectively claim a fair share of revenues and overall commercial benefits (Morgera et al., 2019). It is important, however, to point out that in accessing and using genetic resources, today's providers might, and in many cases will, become users in time, just as some users may eventually become providers (Rohden and Scholz, 2021).[3]

To support sustainability and fairness in the management of biodiversity, the CBD expresses the following objectives: (1) the conservation of biological diversity, (2) the sustainable use of its important components, and (3) the fair and equitable sharing of benefits arising from the utilization of genetic resources (preamble, arts. 2, 8, 15–16). The Conference of the Parties to the CBD (COP) later developed the Nagoya Protocol in 2010 to further regulate access to genetic resources regarding the sharing of benefits. This legal framework subjects all users of plant, microbial, and animal genetic resources to national legal requirements of prior informed consent (PIC), mutually agreed terms (MAT), and access and benefit-sharing (ABS) agreements. A primary objective of the Nagoya Protocol is to enable member states as providers of genetic resources to share monetary and nonmonetary benefits derived from using such resources (arts. 3–5; Curci, 2010).

What seems clear in recent years is that the CBD, as bolstered by its Protocol on enforcement measures, can undermine scientific research on planetary biodiversity. A clear impediment to science that merits particular attention is the growing difficulty of complying with varying national ABS measures for conducting both *in situ* and *ex situ* not-for-profit research that requires access to, or some uses of, genetic resources (Sett et al., 2022). This impediment can affect ethically conducted bioprospecting as well as the collection of fundamental research data that serve primary societal needs, including critical health interventions, whether focused on human, animal, or plant life that require scientifically valid evidence to determine the best course of action (Bhatti et al., 2009; Scutchfield and Lamberth, 2010).

In the specific domain of public health, restrictions on access to and use of GSD can have serious adverse effects on not only upstream public health measures but also follow-on research for innovation and applications, such as the development of diagnostics, therapeutics, and vaccines, which are essential for the containment of cross-border epidemics and the spread of disease generally (National Research Council, 2009; WHO, 2005).[4] The role of GSD in public health surveillance and response continues to grow in importance (WHO, 2019), yet the willingness of countries to share such resources and, especially, related data has palpably diminished, despite the emphasis on the equitable sharing of benefits under the Nagoya Protocol. Epidemics – such as MERS, Ebola, ZIKA, and most recently COVID-19 – have emerged since the Protocol was adopted, during which countries refused to

[3] This study showed that (1) the main users of the public databases of the International Nucleotide Sequence Database Collaboration – the United States and China – are also the main providers, (2) every country around the world has database users, and (3) users typically sample and use GSD from their own country much more than from abroad.

[4] There are very substantial research and health aspects of regulating planetary biodiversity and maintaining open access to genetic materials and related data that need to be preserved.

rapidly share pathogen materials or sequences owing to countervailing concerns about the need to defend ownership and the sovereign rights of provider states (Halabi, 2019; Peeling et al., 2020; Pisani et al., 2018; Sett et al., 2022).

The CBD and its Nagoya Protocol have further contributed to this tension. PIC, MAT, and ABS conditions can conflict with international guidelines or other sharing obligations, such as those of the International Health Regulations of the World Health Organization (WHO), the International Covenant on Economic, Social and Cultural Rights (Aarestrup and Koopmans, 2016),[5] or even the Declaration on the TRIPS Agreement and Public Health (Abbott and Reichman, 2007). For example, the impetus given to parties to the CBD under Article 8(b) of the Nagoya Protocol with respect to the rapid sharing of genetic resources in health emergencies insufficiently recognizes the constraints on related ABS obligations otherwise imposed from two directions. First, other treaties, such as the International Health Regulations, demand that each country promptly share critical information, including scientific data – and arguably GSD – which is now crucial in determining public health risks and possible countermeasures to address infectious disease outbreaks. Second, global efforts to address serious health threats will, in many cases, entail research on the nature of pathogens and on the collective international sharing of critical data derived from pathogen genetic resources that domestic ABS laws may now regulate.

It thus seems a complex task to develop a one-size-fits-all solution to this problem of conflicting interests that would address the concerns and needs of all stakeholders, all subject matter fields, and all disciplines involved. The complexity of managing tangible or intangible assets, such as GSD, constitutes additional challenges to the evolving task of reconciling the legal obligations under the CBD with the needs of global public health (Buck and Hamilton, 2011). Nonetheless, the COP needs a coherent approach to scientific information in general and GSD in particular to avoid potential barriers to research and burdensome (re)negotiation of legal texts to cover major new scientific tools, discoveries, and their implications.

Public health interventions during outbreaks and epidemics are time-sensitive, and delays in access to pathogenic materials and GSD can conflict with the moral imperative to save lives through the prevention of and response to public health threats (Ribeiro et al., 2018a; WHO, 2019).[6] Because pathogens and, to a still unknown extent, related data are considered genetic resources within the CBD, they are potentially subject to the Nagoya Protocol's robust enforcement measures and the resulting legal problems (Bagley, 2016).

5 See Articles 12 and 27 of the International Covenant on Economic, Social and Cultural Rights for collaboration to recognize the right of everyone to the highest standard of prevention, treatment and control of epidemic, endemic, occupational, and other diseases.

6 The authors recognize that both plants and animals are also covered by the CBD, although they are often less data-intensive than the field of microbiology.

Although the CBD and the Nagoya Protocol have as one of their core goals to enhance fairness in the sharing of benefits arising from the use of genetic resources, their negative impact on public health research and response can reinforce inequalities in outbreak preparedness and response capacity. Epidemics commonly emerge in many LMICs through zoonotic spillovers due to the proximity of humans, livestock, and wildlife. Because of weaker public health systems and a lack of sufficient response capacity, these countries are usually the ones most affected and take longer to recover from the devastating impact of epidemics (WHO, 2018b). The global and rapid sharing of pathogen materials and data and international collaboration for developing pharmaceutical and nonpharmaceutical countermeasures help affected countries to control and mitigate disease within their borders and the rest of the world to prevent and control the spread of the epidemic. As the world faces increasing infectious disease threats with global impacts, solidarity and collaboration are more important than ever to address critical policy, operational, and capacity barriers ahead of an emergency.

Accordingly, this chapter focuses on how to conform ABS practices to pathogens and related GSD, independently of how coverage is ultimately defined under the CBD. In so doing, the authors draw attention to the obstacles that compliance with the CBD might otherwise have on biodiversity research in general and on pathogens and infectious diseases in particular. The authors further examine the real-world consequences of their proposal for global public health initiatives, with particular attention to sharing practices already adopted in the public health field that enable the free exchange of genetic materials and, increasingly, of related data for research purposes.[7]

13.2 THE DISRUPTIVE COMPLEXITY OF GENETIC SEQUENCE DATA

The COP must recognize and suitably resolve the rapidly evolving tensions that scientific research and technologies continue to generate for implementing the Nagoya Protocol's legal framework. Complex legal problems also arise from the growing importance of GSD in scientific research generally and public health in particular, and especially from mounting pressures on originators to make such data freely available for follow-on research and development (Morgera et al., 2019; National Academies of Sciences, Engineering, and Medicine, 2021; Reichman and Uhlir, 2003).

On the one hand, when GSD are traceable to specific genetic resources and their providers, a case for coverage by the CBD can more readily be made. On the other hand, to the extent that open access to GSD enables scientists to recreate, say,

[7] National Research Council (2009) stressed the potential impact on public health, research, and applications of maintaining open access to genetic materials and related data generally within the context of regulating planetary biodiversity.

viruses and enhance their functions, it could make the need to access and use biological samples (physical materials) less acute or eventually even obsolete, to the detriment of those otherwise entitled to benefit-sharing obligations under the Nagoya Protocol.[8]

Article 2 of the CBD expressly applies to genetic resources and "other elements of heredity" (Schei and Tvedt, 2010). The question of whether this clause implicitly covers GSD or not depends, in the first instance, on how the term is defined, as well as on the scope of the textual language adopted by the Nagoya Protocol. There is, however, no agreed definition of GSD for this purpose, nor was there any agreement on the status of the current replacement descriptor, that is, DSI, apart from thornier questions about the extent to which the CBD covers GSD at all (COP, 2016: preamble; Houssen et al., 2020).

By the time of the fourteenth CBD-COP meeting in 2018, the term DSI had been adopted as a placeholder for GSD, and a study on the concept and scope of DSI, including its then-current usage, was formally requested in the absence of any consensus.[9] Against this background, major decisions were made in March 2020, when the Ad Hoc Technical Expert Group on Digital Sequence Information on Genetic Resources (AHTEG) adopted a surprisingly broad and coherent set of definitions in its report (AHTEG, 2020b). The experts successfully classified relevant "genetic and biochemical information" into three broad categories that are conceptually cumulative – namely (1) Group 1, covering "DNA and RNA"; (2) Group 2, covering "proteins and epigenetic modifications" plus the contents of Group 1; and Group 3, covering "metabolites and other macromolecules" plus the combined contents of Groups 1 and 2 (AHTEG, 2020b: annex 1, 9 tbl.1).

The avowed object of this report was to advise the Open-Ended Working Group on the Post-2020 Global Biodiversity Framework.[10] The AHTEG accordingly concluded with the recognition that measures governing ABS in compliance with the CBD might need to vary within the three main groupings of DSI. In so doing, AHTEG deliberately avoids recommendations about how DSI should ultimately be

8 Third World Network (2019) described the case of the pharmaceutical company Regeneron that used GSD of a Guinean Ebola virus collected in 2014 to create a treatment. To make the drug, Regeneron downloaded the Guinean GSD from GenBank, which was made available by the German Nocht Institute. By downloading the GSD from GenBank and then synthesizing it, rather than requesting a virus sample from Nocht, Regeneron did not sign an MTA requiring negotiation of a benefit-sharing agreement. Therefore, the company is arguably manufacturing a product without complying with the binding obligations for benefit sharing with Africa and Guinea.

9 For the decision of the COP serving as the meeting of the Parties to the Protocol (COP-MOP) in 2018 to establish an Ad Hoc Technical Expert Group on Digital Sequence Information on Genetic Resources and an invitation to parties and stakeholders to submit views and information about how the CBD should cover DSI, see AHTEG (2021). Altogether four peer-reviewed studies on DSI were commissioned during the 2019–21 inter-sessional period, with the first focused on the concept and scope of DSI itself (AHTEG, 2020a).

10 Established by the COP under Decision 14.34.

governed for purposes of compliance with the CBD, which was not its mission.[11] What it has clarified is the definitional confusion surrounding DSI/GSD in previous discussions so that the COP should better understand what it is dealing with.

Meanwhile, the term DSI is perceived as comprising a broad range of matter subject to interpretation (i.e., DNA sequences and derivatives, but not subsidiary information). In contrast, GSD had acquired a narrower scope in CBD discussions, typically limited to nucleotide sequence data (DNA and RNA) in closer proximity to material genetic resources (Houssen et al., 2020; WHO, 2011).[12] That proximity, in turn, makes it easier to accurately identify or infer the genetic resource from which the relevant data in question were derived for purposes of ABS applications. Because the term GSD thus lends itself to a narrower, more workable subject matter concept for legal interpretation, GSD throughout this chapter is used as a counterweight to the possibly broader notion of DSI.

Enforcing ABS obligations under the CBD, however, depends largely on the ability or inability to monitor the uses of any specific genetic resources and on maintaining control over the chain of custody. Because the authors assume that GSD/DSI will likely become reachable under the CBD in many, if not most, cases, the deeper substantive issues will depend on the consequences of such coverage.

Meanwhile, context and comparison give GSD their actual value through comparing sequences on a large scale combined with the application of knowledge gained from scientific research in an iterative fashion (Rohden and Scholz, 2021). This process is made possible through comprehensive virtual libraries, such as the open-access databases of the International Nucleotide Sequence Database Collaboration (INSDC).[13] At the same time, the huge volume and constant growth of publicly available genetic sequences constitute a clear obstacle to any attempt to monitor all transactions involved in accessing and using any given set of GSD. Once GSD are shared in open-access repositories, it is not always clear – and therefore very hard – to monitor how they will be used in the future (Laird and Wynberg, 2018).

For example, genetic sequences accessed for academic research purposes that are subsequently uploaded onto public databases may eventually be used commercially

[11] The AHTEG report nonetheless notes possible approaches, including “flat-fee access with benefit-sharing triggered by utilization or commercialization and/or a possible multilateral approach.”

[12] WHO’s view on “the order of nucleotides found in a molecule of DNA or RNA” is that they contain the genetic information that determines the biological characteristics of an organism or a virus. This definition clarifies the extent of what is included as only DNA/RNA, thus excluding proteins, metabolites, and metadata associated with the genetic resource.

[13] The INSDC (www.insdc.org) consists of a longstanding foundational joint effort to collect and disseminate databases containing DNA and RNA sequences. It involves the following computerized databases: the National Institute of Genetics’s DNA Data Bank of Japan, the National Center for Biotechnology Information’s GenBank in the United States, and the European Molecular Biology Laboratory–European Bioinformatics Institute’s European Nucleotide Archive. All of the data in INSDC is available for free and have unrestricted access, for any purpose, with no restrictions on analysis, redistribution, or re-publication of the data.

by many different actors without the original providers becoming even aware of or involved in the process. Other potential loopholes in the ABS framework could arise when commercial firms only use specified GSD for full product development, whether by bioengineering or for testing products. While even legitimate bioprospecting could trigger some ABS obligations under the CBD, the firms in question might partner with academic institutes or laboratories to test the resulting products under a "noncommercial" umbrella, thus delaying if not concealing legal liability.[14] Moreover, once private-sector entities acquire GSD from open-access repositories, they might have little incentive to disclose potential benefits to distant providers (Gostin et al., 2017).

While further work on tracking and tracing genetic sequences may help engender trust, another complicating factor is that GSD acquires an intermediate scientific status over time, in the sense that component sequences may be used in an ever-expanding variety of scientific research projects. As a result, questions of ownership and property rights – if not unknown or unknowable – may inhibit further basic research projects and commercial innovations (Flach et al., 2019; Rohden and Scholz, 2021).[15]

Consider, for example, that networks of researchers from diverse institutional or sectoral affiliations – industry, government, academia, and the laboratories of all sectors – may span the globe in the process of collaborative innovation. In such cases, users may add incremental value by providing data and knowledge along a chain that involves "swift compilation, comparison and reanalysis of genetic information from a variety of sources, across multiple databases and gene sequences."[16] Genetic materials from diverse organisms originating from different habitats around the world are thus often combined in developing new products, processes, and technologies. The result may well depend on a derivative sequence that reflects an "average" of all the various input sequences, thus making it virtually impossible to determine the relative value of each component sequence as part of the ultimate ensemble (Laird and Wynberg, 2018).

Synthetic or modified GSD may also be created from long-standing, publicly available sequences, many of which may not have recorded links to the original

[14] WHO (2018a: annex 3) discussed ABS under the Pandemic Influenza Preparedness Framework.

[15] Given large-scale meta-analysis projects involving big data analysis, the information from many studies and experiments may be collected and analyzed together. Moreover, many new bioinformatics tools and biological databases are built by developing new algorithms and scientific approaches and subsequently mining public databases for existing knowledge, as well as performing new bioinformatic analysis.

[16] Laird and Wynberg (2018) provide an example, mentioned by the International Chamber of Commerce, on the development of a new consensus phytase to improve the nutritional value of animal feed: "[I]n state-of-the-art bioinformatics projects, hundreds of thousands of (amino acid or nucleic acid) sequences may be used to develop a particular commercial product. The final product has a sequence that represents an 'average' of all input sequences; as a result, it is virtually impossible to determine the relative value of each individual input sequence."

genetic resource or country of origin. This factor complicates how benefit-sharing should attach to GSD/DSI over time under the CBD. One study asks "whether there is ever a point where the original genetic material has passed through so many stages of transformation that ABS requirements attached to the original material no longer apply?" (Reichman et al., 2015).

Commercial applications of GSD are thus so varied and so rapidly evolving that it becomes extremely difficult, if not impossible, to characterize with any certainty the utilization of specific sequences or estimate their commercial value. Even when GSD contribute to developing a given commercial product, they may also be used to develop other industrial processes, research tools, or improved technologies that are not sold and may be freely shared (Laird and Wynberg, 2018; Rohden and Scholz, 2021). These complex arrangements cast further doubt on the ability to attribute shared benefits to any single country or provider, especially when relevant data are easily accessed or processed for further utilization irrespective of the territorial boundaries where genetic resources may have originated.

Given the added value of open-access databases and the fact that there is no way to predict whether any specific genetic sequence components may prove useful in research and product development, broader availability ought to be favored whenever feasible, especially in view of their widening use to support many important societal needs (Ribeiro et al., 2018a). Impeding the flow and use of such information would significantly undermine research projects in diverse fields, including those that contribute to the specific objectives of the CBD and the Nagoya Protocol. The importance of GSD for global public health as an essential tool for disease surveillance, investigation, source-tracing, and the development of medical countermeasures further supports the case for the free availability of such a socially beneficial resource.

13.3 CODIFYING MULTILATERAL COMPLIANCE MEASURES FOR UPSTREAM GSD

This chapter contends that a relatively acceptable solution is attainable once the parties shift the focus of attention away from the "coverage" issues and directly address the consequences of potential ABS coverage of GSD. If a satisfactory compromise concerning the scope of protection and the modality of implementation can thus be found, it would help diffuse the pressure hitherto concentrated on definitions and eligibility.

13.3.1 *The Basic Proposal*

The freedom to access and use genetic resources for global public health purposes, once confirmed by the COP, must accordingly be coupled with a corresponding duty to share proceeds from the results with the country or countries providing genetic materials – in this case, any pathogens at issue. An obligation to this effect must thus be embodied in any waiver for research purposes adopted by the parties to the CBD. Such a waiver should free scientific researchers from negotiating access and usage at the upstream, noncommercial research stage but not from the duty to report and share proceeds from all downstream commercial applications.

Ideally, any solution to the problems of conforming potential uses of pathogen GSD to the CBD requirements would ultimately be embodied in a multilateral agreement applicable to all the member states. Such a regime should incorporate a waiver of PIC and MAT for noncommercial scientific access and uses. Benefit-sharing terms would nonetheless be triggered when, and only if commercial applications are envisioned using a "change of intent" clause that expressly guarantees compliance with the CBD's benefit-sharing obligations.

From a purely legal perspective, the legitimacy of such an initiative would follow from Articles 4 and 8 of the Nagoya Protocol. Article 4 validates multilateral arrangements for facilitated access to genetic resources for research and applications, which would override the need to bargain directly with national governments in every case, as otherwise required under Article 8 (Reichman et al., 2015). A multilateral framework adopted to facilitate scientific research would thus be necessary to bring any given project within the scope of Article 4. Once codified by the COP, any standard-form waiver favoring pathogen research that covered specific projects should thereafter suffice (Reichman, 2018).

To implement such a waiver, Standard Material Transfer Agreements (SMTAs) authorizing noncommercial research under the CBD should likewise embody a "change of intent" clause and define how that clause should apply to specific collaborative ventures (Reichman, 2018; Ribeiro et al., 2018a). In principle, parties to these SMTAs would not need to expressly prohibit commercial use of public-research results, whether by private-sector or public-research entities. Instead, when applicable, drafters of both bioprospecting contracts and SMTAs to be covered by the proposed waiver should consider expressly allowing eventual commercial applications with some built-in equitable sharing of revenues if and when they are generated. Correctly devised and implemented "change of intent" clauses could thus help to stimulate both research and commercial applications.

Compliance measures of this kind could thus be validated a priori under either an amendment to the CBD or a waiver embodied in a multilateral Memorandum of Understanding (MoU) to be devised expressly for pathogen genetic resources with the collaboration and endorsement of relevant international organizations. If the global public health community were to take the lead, the proposed waiver for GSD would logically be developed by the WHO, with inputs from the microbiological community as represented by the World Federation of Culture Collections (WFCC).[17] Such an MoU would necessarily impose its waiver for noncommercial research purposes

[17] See Microbial Resource Research Infrastructure (MIRRI), www.mirri.org/about/. The WFCC has already developed an SMTA for nonprofit research on genetic materials.

allowing unrestricted access to both pathogen materials and related data, including GSD. By the same token, the WFCC and the INSDC could conform to their standard sharing practices (Rohden and Scholz, 2021), through SMTAs, notification of terms and conditions, or other access agreements. Additionally, they could provide links between the available resources and the legal (ABS) conditions of use for commercial applications, thereby acknowledging the proposed waiver for noncommercial research purposes.

In the long run, however, an MoU regulating pathogen sharing should serve as a steppingstone to a broader, more comprehensive waiver favoring noncommercial research access and use of all GSD and potentially other genetic resources – plant, animal, and microbial – under the CBD as a whole. Such a general waiver would have to be adopted by the COP. Once adopted, the resulting "change of intent" clauses to be embodied in SMTAs should enable local researchers to freely engage in international collaborations, as long as they are covered by the terms and conditions in the standard agreements.

The efficacy of such a regime would depend in part on the successful development of the tracking system under consideration at the World Intellectual Property Organization (WIPO), the WFCC, and INSDC (Bagley, 2016).[18] It is worth noticing, moreover, that microbes already cannot legally be exchanged for any research purposes without bearing unique identifiers that must be cited in all relevant publications (Reichman et al., 2015). The eventual ability of researchers to file SMTAs with the ABS Clearing House to be established under Article 14 of the Nagoya Protocol could then make it unnecessary for researchers engaged in international collaborations to notify their respective governments, so long as binding standard PIC, MAT, and ABS terms were embodied in the relevant SMTAs.

If the CBD's COP or the WHO eventually decided to establish a consortium for purposes of exploiting pathogens and GSD on a globally regulated basis, they could also adopt a liability rule – that is, a "take and pay" rule – for commercial applications of GSD taken from the commons (or semi-commons, as the case may be) (Calabresi and Melamed, 2018; Reichman and Lewis, 2005). In assessing payment options, moreover, it seems worthwhile to consider the methods already adopted for such a purpose by the multilateral regime governing the Crop Commons, as established under the International Treaty on Plant Genetic Resources for Food and Agriculture (ITPGRFA) in 2001 (Reichman et al., 2015). This approach entails a built-in "take and pay" rule for plant cultivars taken from the Crop Commons by commercial plant breeders. Suppose a similar scheme were to be adopted by the proposed multilateral regime to cover GSD under the CBD. In such a case, a liability rule could then require payment of a small percentage of any future

[18] Whether WIPO will succeed in developing a tracking system for some or all genetic resources and related data remains to be seen.

commercial revenues back to the CBD's commons to support the costs of the sharing enterprise.

Under this approach, a percentage of any commercial revenues stipulated ex ante must be paid either to the provider country when known or to the General Fund of the CBD under Article 10 of the Nagoya Protocol, if undetermined. Smaller access charges could also be required to support the costs of any global public repositories to be devised for GSD under pending proposals. As matters stand, the CBD already requires firms undertaking commercial applications to engage in prior benefit-sharing negotiations (bilaterally) with countries that provide relevant genetic resources or with other designated authorities covered by the treaty in certain cases. Under the aforementioned proposal, the obligation to share benefits with provider countries would instead be expressly incorporated into the waiver to be adopted by the multilateral regime for this purpose.

13.3.2 *Further Implications of the Proposed Waiver*

One persuasive argument for a codified waiver allowing research access and uses of pathogen GSD is that the concomitant obligation to share any proceeds from commercial applications would likely yield more monetary benefits for CBD countries that possess relevant genetic resources over time than any policy that otherwise restricted upstream scientific research. That realization should, in turn, make provider countries more willing to allow bioprospecting under the proposed waiver for research uses than at present. A case can also be made that such a waiver should lead to more nonmonetary societal benefits for all CBD member states in the form of better public health outcomes and more innovation. So, in the spirit of the CBD enhancing fairness in the utilization of genetic resources, such a multilateral system can also raise more funds to address inequalities in research capacity and strengthen public health response efforts.

Transnational collaborations to support responses to outbreaks also illustrate how the timely sharing of pathogen genetic resources benefits society, irrespective of whether they originated from provider or user countries. Experience with regard to the 2013–16 Ebola outbreak in West Africa supports this thesis. During that crisis, gaps in the sharing of viral samples and (meta)data, coupled with delays in the public release of GSD, led to speculation about the sources of infection, the possibilities of diagnosing the infection with available assays, and possible mutations over time that increased transmissibility (Dudas et al., 2017; Ribeiro et al., 2018b). Although at later stages of that outbreak, the near real-time sequencing of strains did finally provide essential information directly to public health officials, the suboptimal sharing of data throughout the outbreak eventually allowed the virus to spread to other countries in the region and evolve into a global health crisis.

It is also worth noting that the measures proposed in this chapter would not necessarily exclude other ancillary approaches. For example, even if global repositories for sharing pathogen GSD were eventually established, the contractual waiver proposed earlier in this chapter would remain viable and important in keeping with the goals of the CBD. Consider, for example, that the mere existence of publicly available repositories would not ensure that all relevant data would end up in such repositories (apart from the definitional issues concerning the scope of GSD/DSI discussed earlier) (Ribeiro et al., 2018a). A globally adopted waiver under the auspices of the CBD would, instead, apply to all relevant uses of pathogen data and materials, whether or not stored in public repositories, and the implementing instrument should expressly prohibit SMTAs from overriding the proposed waiver by contract.

In other words, once embodied within the CBD and its Nagoya Protocol, the waiver would become useful in every case. At the same time, any pooling of relevant repositories under the CBD, if successful, would further enhance the global scientific infrastructure. However, the willingness of biodiversity-rich countries to accept such a built-in waiver cannot be taken for granted. Besides concerns about enforceability, their participation may depend on estimates of the nonmonetary benefits likely to flow from open-data sharing and on the misconception that all genetic resources are likely to generate revenues for benefit-sharing purposes (Reichman et al., 2015).

In this context, the prospect of greater access to public databases (and possibly related technology) may seem to be an insufficient incentive to potential providers, especially if biodiversity-rich countries lack adequate molecular research capacity or biotechnology infrastructure to make domestic use of any resulting global repositories. The prospect of shipping samples abroad for sequencing is also an enduring concern for local governments that fear losing control over genetic resources whose data could easily be loaded into public databases. There have been cases, for instance, where samples initially shared for purposes of analysis were later presented at international meetings without advance notification or attribution to providers as authors (Sedyaningsih et al., 2008).

To address these remaining inequalities, rather than restricting access based on bilateral benefit sharing, a situation that is likely to be technically and logistically infeasible and would only benefit a few, a multilateral system for GSD would generate more access, use, and therefore benefits. These monetary and nonmonetary benefits could be directed to capacity-building initiatives in developing countries, such as bioinformatics training, building data infrastructures, and developing and providing data-analytical tools.

Still, it remains true that big companies and well-endowed research institutions may sometimes profit more from open-access policies and an expanding public domain than smaller competitors. For example, big players may find it easier to file patent applications on genetic markers, targets, specific genotypes, and the like (disregarding variations by country in what qualifies as patentable subject matter) (Bagley, 2016). Meanwhile, smaller enterprises that lack such capacity may be locked out.[19] Nevertheless, since such unequal opportunities are built into any competitive economic system, they constitute a fact of life that the COP cannot fully resolve.

One way around this problem is through the formation of a patent-holding consortium, whereby each contributor to the knowledge valorization process, including providers of genetic resources, researchers, and both large and small enterprises, are rewarded with a share of any funds arising from the resulting property rights (Simon et al., 2005). Such a de facto patent pool could become a recognized component of ABS obligations under the CBD as a form of monetary benefit sharing. Moreover, properly devised "change of intent" clauses would further enable provider countries to benefit from foreign patents by means of built-in sharing conditions applicable to patents, patent pools, or other monetary sources.

To date, very few examples exist of patent pools during epidemics (Simon et al., 2005). In May 2020, the WHO launched the COVID-19 Technology Access Pool (C-TAP) for developers of COVID-19 therapeutics, diagnostics, vaccines, and other health products to share their intellectual property through nonexclusive licenses in a patent pool. Nevertheless, the C-TAP failed to engage the major vaccine developers, which resulted in inequality in access to vaccines in developing countries (Van de Pas et al., 2022). This means that for such mechanisms to work during a crisis, they need to be embedded in a structured, democratic, multilateral governance framework and not dependent on political willingness and pressure during a crisis, guided mainly by narrow national interests.

In any event, steps should be taken to ensure that commercial entities identifiable by their Internet URLs are not excluded a priori from accessing and using pathogen GSD covered by the proposed waiver. A treaty-based waiver for pathogen genetic resources, including GSD, must recognize that "noncommercial" refers to the nature of the use and not the users. Commercial entities, not-for-profit organizations, and academic institutes should be allowed to use GSD for noncommercial research purposes. In contrast, their actual undertaking of commercial applications should always trigger the duty to pay reasonable royalties under the GSD waiver and the corresponding "change of intent" clause.

As regards the modality of implementing monetary obligations for both the commercial use of pathogen resources and funding for the multilateral system, as noted earlier, we endorse a built-in "take and pay" rule (i.e., "liability rule") under which a small percentage of any commercial revenues stipulated ex ante must be paid either to the provider country or to a General Fund when that country remains unknown. In so doing, the COP might well consider that a simple set of standardized royalty obligations, like those of the ITPGRFA, would engender more upstream

[19] See The Cambia Bios Initiative – Supporting Rationale, https://cambia.org/bios-landing/the-cambia-bios-initiative/.

uses of GSD, which in the long run might create more likelihood for commercial revenues to be shared under the CBD.

One must recognize that some stakeholders may still cling to the notion that all uses of GSD should require prior negotiation on ABS. The fallacy of such a position is that neither side can accurately predict which products or revenues, if any, would ever result from upstream scientific research (Reichman et al., 2015). Moreover, an *ex ante* liability rule would significantly lower transaction costs for all relevant parties and clarify potential risks and costs for commercial entities when engaging in product development.

Will the CBD countries insist on some advance payment even for noncommercial or potentially commercial research using pathogenic resources? As previously noted, a relatively small "user's fee" might become tenable when pathogen GSD are taken from a global commons or semi-commons, as the case may be, because such fees would help defray the costs of upkeep for the repositories in question (Reichman et al., 2015). Absent such an approach, the idea of charging substantial amounts for upstream research would almost certainly foster a needless barrier to both science and global public health, one that scientists will resist, disregarding any difficulties of implementation and enforcement.

As matters stand, any researcher wishing to publish internationally must lodge data with the open-access system, including researchers from biodiversity-rich countries working on domestic species (Rohden and Scholz, 2021). However, if governments restrict this practice over time, it will become hard for local researchers to collaborate and publish internationally. Ironically, if publication or GSD use becomes restricted by governments, or if the industry cannot acquire legal certainty to use these resources, research may shift (and already has in some cases) to countries that do not have ABS measures or to nonparties to the Nagoya Protocol. This can not only limit the understanding of Earth's biodiversity but also bias global scientific and public health research and development, such as in the case of the annual development of globally comprehensive seasonal influenza vaccines.[20]

Although many scientific journals still impose restricted (paid) access on their publications, after the genomic revolution – with the Human Genome Project and the adoption of the Bermuda Principles (Collins et al., 2003)[21] – there has been a strong trend toward the Open Science movement, with free sharing of GSD and

[20] WHO (2016) noted that the Nagoya Protocol has challenged the development of comprehensive and effective seasonal influenza vaccines, with the difficulty of including influenza strains from countries that have in place strict ABS regulations and time-consuming compliance processes.

[21] The Bermuda Principles set out rules for the rapid and public release of GSD. The Human Genome Project, a multinational effort to sequence the human genome, generated vast quantities of data, but even more remarkable than that was the speed at which that data has been released to the public, under the umbrella of the Bermuda Principles.

related scientific data. Restricting this previously achieved freedom in data access, use, and sharing would constitute a regrettable step backward.

13.4 OTHER FACTORS BEARING ON COLLABORATIVE RESEARCH UNDER THE CBD

Assuming that the prior proposal merits serious attention, there is a further need to consider how existing policies governing the production, storage, and distribution of pathogens and related GSD would need to be adapted in conformity with such a global multilateral arrangement. In what follows, the authors describe some current and innovative practices already being adopted for the management of both genetic resources and GSD. Also assessed are some remaining challenges to conforming the sharing of pathogen GSD to the overall ABS infrastructure.

13.4.1 *The Key Role of Open and Semi-Open Repositories for GSD*

The use of sequencing technologies revolutionized the scientific community's understanding and management of plant, animal, environmental, and human health. However, their optimal use has been dependent on the willingness and ability of countries to share relevant GSD. In this context, GSD function as inputs and outputs of the research process that should be made widely available for further research and public health purposes. This dual functionality has, in turn, elicited growing demands to place GSD in public repositories (WHO, 2017). Such repositories can be open to all legitimate users in the form of what is often labeled as a "commons" (Ostrom, 1990). In appropriate cases, access and use may be limited to specified communities that have collectively contributed to and managed the repositories in question, as would occur under a "semi-commons" (Reichman et al., 2015).

The most prominent open-access approach to sharing pathogen GSD is the INSDC in which 95 percent (705 out of 743 at the time of writing) of all relevant databases directly link to or download their sequence data (Rohden and Scholz, 2021).[22] The INSDC has adopted a policy that rejects conditions that impose any restrictions on accessing its stored data, thereby enabling every person and institution, regardless of their background and intended use, to access these resources (Brunak et al., 2002). This data-access model is the most prominent example of an existing repository completely compatible with the Open Science movement. At this time, however, its very openness also poses the biggest challenges for monitoring ABS compliance. Efforts to make the INSDC open-access policies consistent with

[22] This analysis was based on more than 1,600 biological databases listed in the annual publication of the *Nucleic Acids Research Database Issue*, which promotes understanding of the GSD database landscape and structure.

the multilateral approach proposed in this chapter could facilitate ABS implementation for pathogen resources generally. This follows because the GSD could be freely shared for noncommercial uses in keeping with the recognition of the nonmonetary benefits of Open Science. By the same token, a "change of intent" clause with regard to monetary benefit sharing could later be imposed through binding SMTAs as needed.

In contrast, a good example of a semi-commons model for sharing pathogen GSD was established by the Global Initiative on Sharing All Influenza Data (GISAID EpiFlu) (n.d.) as the global database for sharing influenza gene sequences and related metadata. GISAID plays an essential role in sharing influenza sequences among the WHO Collaborating Centers and National Influenza Centers under the WHO's Pandemic Influenza Preparedness Framework for biannual influenza vaccine virus recommendations (WHO, 2014). The GISAID (2011) data-access policy is based on a legally binding agreement that every user must sign before being granted access. Users are not allowed to share GISAID's sequence data with other nonsignatories to the agreement. GISAID thus provides an alternative to public domain databases in which data providers and users are not identified. Through its access agreement, GISAID could likewise provide a basis for monitoring and enforcing compliance with ABS obligations under the CBD. The GISAID model also addresses some of the inequality issues in open-access systems through the binding conditions in its data-access agreement, which stipulate that users acknowledge data providers in future publications and, when possible, engage them in research efforts.

Another recent initiative of interest was the Collaborative Management Platform for Detection and Analyses of (Re-)Emerging, and Foodborne Outbreaks in Europe (COMPARE) (2015), a major European Commission research project to which some of the authors of this chapter were external advisors and others were Consortium members. This project addressed the need to make sequence data broadly available to support rapid containment, identification, and mitigation of emerging infectious diseases and foodborne outbreaks. To accomplish this goal, COMPARE developed a database and sharing platform for GSD from diverse pathogens, enabling stakeholders in the human health, animal health, and food safety domains to readily access and use these same resources under a One Health approach (Gibbs, 2014).[23] To address inequalities in bioinformatics and data-analytics capacity, COMPARE (2015) also offered free online analytical tools that could help scientists and other users from ill-equipped institutions and countries to analyze and interpret the available data without having to mobilize large amounts of resources in computer memory and data storage.

Within its broad investigation of barriers to data sharing, the COMPARE project identified specific stakeholder groups with different interests to be taken into

[23] The One Health approach is defined as the collaboration of professionals from different fields to support human health, animal health, and environmental resilience.

account when devising their roles as potential users of the COMPARE platform (Ribeiro et al., 2018b). The project nonetheless recognized that even these legitimate concerns should not block the timely and open sharing of data, which would compromise the project's primary objectives. In addressing this quandary, COMPARE established separate data hubs in which sensitive data could be shared only among an agreed group of stakeholders under confidentiality terms, on the condition that after a reasonable period (six to twelve months, in general), that same data could ultimately be placed in the public domain. By means of this temporary embargo, which could be deemed a semi-commons arrangement, a delay in public sharing became acceptable when necessary. This model also addressed other key barriers to data sharing, including the need to allow a priority of use for analyzing the data by local researchers in provider countries while also enabling long-term access and use of the same data for legal research purposes. The model thus established a trusted environment for the prepublication of data with relevant stakeholders who might otherwise have been reluctant to deposit the data directly in the open-access site.

13.4.2 *Further Policy Considerations*

Looking beyond the question of access to pathogen GSD via either public or more restricted repositories, the sharing process under the CBD still requires attention to other important policy issues. First, the nature of the benefits at stake has evolved, with research collaborations, capacity building, and technology transfer modalities taking on new forms through the sharing of software, analytical tools, and other technologies, as well as increased sharing of GSD (and components thereof). As previously discussed, promising new research arrangements in the form of "global commons" or "semi-commons" (Reichman and Okediji, 2012, Reichman et al., 2015) both retain attribution and coauthorship as benefits and, in some cases, authorize more complex research collaborations in lieu of monetary rewards. These approaches are especially useful in precompetitive phases, when commercial applications for the resources or knowledge at issue are not yet, or may never be, established.

In addition, distinctions between "commercial" and "noncommercial" research should yield different implications for benefit sharing under the CBD. Yet, the lines between these two categories have become blurred in recent decades, as academic and government researchers increasingly partner with industry or otherwise act commercially (Overmann and Scholz, 2017), and as the industry itself also contributes noncommercial findings and research to upstream research projects. In the public health field, this distinction becomes even more complex, given that the development of pharmaceutical products to respond to epidemics and other disease outbreaks sometimes generate low-profit margins (if any) and are increasingly subsidized by governments and health agencies in public–private partnerships (Van de Burgwal et al., 2018).

Although a multilateral system could authorize noncommercial research under SMTAs, while a "change of intent" clause would still cover subsequent decisions to use research results in commercial applications (art. 8(a) of the Nagoya Protocol), the practical distinctions concerning when and in which specific cases commercial use is to be triggered would need to be defined. In practice, the authors acknowledge that there are limits to the technical legal device of "change of intent" clauses, especially in cases where GSD are shared in the public domain. Because such sequences move fluidly between commercial and noncommercial institutions, once uploaded to open-access databases, they become available for all to use, regardless of the distinction between the two types of use.

Tracking and tracing GSD to monitor their access, use, and sharing are also essential steps to the enforcement of ABS compliance and, at the same time, constitute a major challenge for the inclusion of GSD within the scope of the Nagoya Protocol. From a purely technical perspective, these issues depend on the implementation of technologies that enable the tracking, tracing, and monitoring of genetic resources (Rohden and Scholz, 2021). But even when tracking becomes technically more reliable, it may not fully resolve some managerial problems. For example, with or without tracking, questions could remain as to who did the work that led to commercialization; what GSD they employed; who the owners of the sequences in question are; and what rights they should have, if any, against those who solved the problem that produced a commercial application (Butler, 2013).[24] Moreover, monetary benefits flowing from the use of GSD remain inherently speculative due to challenges in identifying both the provenance and value of any given sequence or its components in complex applications.

Another fundamental issue to be addressed under a multilateral framework is ensuring that benefits are shared with legitimate providers and that they otherwise contribute to the original objectives of the CBD and its Nagoya Protocol. Grantors that fund research projects likely to involve pathogens and other related sequence data should expressly require grantees to comply with the CBD and Nagoya Protocol and, in particular, their ABS obligations. This approach would thus resemble the typical requirements of grantees to respect intellectual property rights under the Agreement on Trade-Related Aspects of Intellectual Property Rights (TRIPS Agreement). In appropriate cases, funders could also require that GSD resulting from a grantee's project be deposited in designated and certified repositories.

[24] In the case of MERS, there were endless discussions on the patenting of the virus coming from a Saudi patient by a Dutch lab. Under strong criticism from the international community (in the 2012 World Health Assembly), the Dutch scientists claimed that the reason for patenting the virus was to be able to rapidly develop diagnostic tests and make them available to affected countries, which could be a different situation if a commercial company had owned the patent.

CONCLUDING OBSERVATIONS

A primary goal in writing this chapter was to help avoid the risk that intellectual property treaties and related administrative initiatives might disrupt the use of pathogens for public health research purposes. Consistent with the CBD and the Nagoya Protocol's legal framework, we propose a narrow but workable approach that aims to remove the "coverage" issue as the focus of attention from discussions of the COP, specifically concerning pathogen material and including GSD, however ultimately defined. Under this approach, those who legally access pathogen resources covered in an MoU should officially be granted a legal right of use under the CBD for noncommercial purposes in lieu of bilateral access and benefit-sharing agreements.

All such uses would, however, become subject to a built-in "change of intent" clause recognizing the respective users' liability for specified benefit-sharing royalties from any eventual commercial applications of the initially exempted materials or data. The codified multilateral solution for pathogens in this chapter could alleviate the need for agreement on more complex issues. It could also provide a flexible means of facilitating scientific research on pathogen GSD without compromising the interests of diverse stakeholders under the CBD while rebuilding trust among the parties.

The history of the Nagoya Protocol is marked by polarization between provider and user countries (Muzaka and Serrano, 2020). Because these groups perceive their interests as conflicting, they tend to focus their arguments on the protection of national interests rather than on the achievement of a common goal. Discussions concerning proper access to and use of genetic resources were already somewhat compromised by the adoption of the TRIPS Agreement in 1994, when international intellectual property law began to limit access to and the availability of such resources generally, with a resulting deficit in trust (Reichman, 2018; Six et al., 2015). From this perspective, the CBD itself may be perceived as a developing-country response to the TRIPS Agreement negotiations, one that protects inputs to innovations from developing countries and not just outputs from developed countries (Dreyfuss and Ng, 2018).

Meanwhile, the variety of stakeholders involved in managing genetic resources, with their diverse and often conflicting interests, tends to engender growing mistrust. The politicized nature of the decision-making environment within the CBD may sometimes prevent stakeholders from fully evaluating the practical implications of the enforcement measures embodied in the Nagoya Protocol. It also seems advisable that contributors to scientific research and public health should be better represented within the governing apparatus of the CBD itself.

To rebuild trust in the process of sharing genetic resources, including GSD, the concerns of all stakeholders should be taken into consideration and translated into common goals. To this end, realistic expectations must be built into an improved governance system that will not hamper the freedom to access, use, and share essential inputs for research and public health that generate societal benefits. The objective should be to support fair and equitable collaborations and the sharing of benefits in innovative ways that conform to the needs of technological and infrastructural developments and resulting applications.

Instead of expecting stakeholders to surrender secrecy, control, and exclusivity due to extrinsic monetary incentives, a trustworthy system of collective action should focus on alternative values rendering the discussion more practical and fruitful. These additional values would reflect both common informal norms and codes of conduct arising from the exploration of biodiversity and from scientific and public health practices that embrace principles of reciprocity, openness, and collaboration (Six et al., 2015).

As discussed throughout this chapter, inequalities exist in terms of public health capacity, bioinformatics, and data-analytics capacity. A bilateral ABS mechanism, however, is unlikely to address these inequalities, as there are no guarantees that the funds will be invested in capacity-building initiatives. The countries with more data collection and sequencing capacity will share more GSD and therefore receive most of the benefits, reinforcing the existing gaps. In a truly multilateral system, benefit-sharing funds can instead be invested in countries with the biggest needs – for example, in data-analytics capacity building or epidemic response during a public health crisis. This represents a more sustainable approach to ABS when, in the future, developing countries can more equally profit from open science and open-data structures and policies.

A number of collective networks and sharing platforms are already experimenting with innovative governance arrangements, and their lessons and experiences should constitute valuable inputs for future CBD discussions. Any proposal for a feasible and sustainable solution should move away from burdensome, costly, and time-consuming bilateral negotiations to ensure globally harmonized governance rules covering the rights and obligations of all the parties that are unambiguous and universally applicable.

The ultimate goal should be to ensure that research on pathogens proceeds under fair precepts of global cooperation while enforcing ABS obligations under the CBD in the least intrusive manner possible. The proposals set out in this chapter strive to promote these objectives. The authors thus urge the COP to simplify their negotiations in this respect, with a view to better promoting both science and the larger social welfare interests at stake while updating the objectives of the CBD to better reflect the evolution of scientific research methods, technological developments, and global health over time.

REFERENCES

Aarestrup, Frank M., and Marion G. Koopmans. 2016. "Sharing Data for Global Infectious Disease Surveillance and Outbreak Detection." *Trends in Microbiology* 24(4): 241–245.

Abbott, Frederick M., and Jerome H. Reichman. 2007. "The Doha Round's Public Health Legacy: Strategies for the Production and Diffusion of Patented Medicines under the Amended TRIPS Provisions." *Journal of International Economic Law* 10(4): 921–987.

Access and Benefit-Sharing Clearing-House. n.d. *Getting Started Using the ABS Clearing-House for Stakeholders*. https://absch.cbd.int/en/about/gettingStartedOthers.

Ad Hoc Technical Expert Group on Digital Sequence Information on Genetic Resources (AHTEG). 2019. "Intersessional Period 2017–2018" (Submissions from Parties, Other Governments, Relevant Organizations and Stakeholders). www.cbd.int/abs/dsi-gr/ahteg .shtml#submissions.

2020a. "Digital Sequence Information on Genetic Resources: Concept, Scope and Current Use." CBD/DSI/AHTEG/2020/1/3.

2020b. "Report of the Ad Hoc Technical Expert Group on Digital Sequence Information on Genetic Resources." CBD/DSI/AHTEG/2020/1/7.

2021. "What Has Been Done on Digital Sequence Information on Genetic Resources." www.cbd.int/abs/dsi-gr-whatdone.shtml.

Aoki, Keith. 2008. *Seed Wars: Controversies and Cases on Plant Genetic Resources and Intellectual Property*. Chapel Hill, NC: Carolina Academic Press.

Bagley, Margo A. 2016. "Digital DNA: The Nagoya Protocol, Intellectual Property Treaties, and Synthetic Biology." Virginia Public Law and Legal Theory Research Paper No. 11.

Bhatti, Shakeel, Santiago Carrizosa, Patrick McGuire, and Tomme Young, eds. 2009. "Contracting for ABS: The Legal and Scientific Implications of Bioprospecting Contracts." International Union for Conservation of Nature Environmental Policy and Law Paper No. 67/4.

Brunak, Soren, Antoine Danchin, Masahira Hattori, Haruki Nakamura, Kazuo Shinozaki, Tara Matise, and Daphne Preuss. 2002. "Nucleotide Sequence Database Policies." *Science* 298(5597): 1333–1334.

Buck, Matthias, and Clare Hamilton. 2011. "The Nagoya Protocol on Access to Genetic Resources and the Fair and Equitable Sharing of Benefits Arising from Their Utilization to the Convention on Biological Diversity." *Review of European Community and International Environmental Law* 20(1): 47–61.

Butler, Declan. 2013. "Tensions Linger over Discovery of Coronavirus." *Nature News*, January 14.

Calabresi, Guido, and A. Douglas Melamed. 2018. "Property Rules, Liability Rules, and Inalienability: One View of the Cathedral." In *Economics and Liability for Environmental Problems*, edited by Kathleen Segerson, 5–44. London: Routledge.

Collins, Francis S., Michael Morgan, and Aristides Patrinos. 2003. "The Human Genome Project: Lessons from Large-Scale Biology." *Science* 300(5617): 286–290.

COMPARE. 2015. "About COMPARE." www.compare-europe.eu/about.

Conference of the Parties to the Convention on Biological Diversity. 2016. "Digital Sequence Information on Genetic Resources (2016) (DSI)." CBD/COP/DEC/XIII/16.

Curci, Jonathan. 2010. *The Protection of Biodiversity and Traditional Knowledge in International Law of Intellectual Property*. Cambridge: Cambridge University Press.

Dreyfuss, Rochelle Cooper, and Elizabeth Siew-Kuan Ng, eds. 2018. *Framing Intellectual Property Law in the 21st Century: Integrating Incentives, Trade, Development, Culture, and Human Rights*. Cambridge: Cambridge University Press.

Dudas, G. et al. 2017. "Virus Genomes Reveal Factors That Spread and Sustained the Ebola Epidemic." *Nature* 544: 309–315.

Flach, Joost, Carolina dos S. Ribeiro, Mark B. van der Waal, Raymond X. van der Waal, Eric Claassen, and Linda H.M. van de Burgwal. 2019. "The Nagoya Protocol on Access to Genetic Resources and Benefit Sharing: Best Practices for Users of Lactic Acid Bacteria." *PharmaNutrition* 9: 100158.

Gibbs, E. Paul J. 2014. "The Evolution of One Health: A Decade of Progress and Challenges for the Future." *The Veterinary Record* 174(4): 85–91.

Global Initiative on Sharing All Influenza Data (GISAID). n.d. "About Us: Mission." www.gisaid.org/about-us/mission/.

2011. "GISAID EpiFlu™ Database Access Agreement." www.gisaid.org/registration/terms-of-use/.

Gostin, Lawrence O., Mary Clare DeBartolo, and Rebecca Katz. 2017. "The Global Health Law Trilogy: Towards a Safer, Healthier, and Fairer World." *The Lancet* 390(10105): 1918–1926.

Halabi, Sam F. 2019. "Viral Sovereignty, Intellectual Property, and the Changing Global System for Sharing Pathogens for Infectious Disease Research." *Annals of Health Law* 28: 101.

Halewood, Michael, Isabel López Noriega, and Sélim Louafi, eds. 2012. *Crop Genetic Resources as a Global Commons: Challenges in International Law and Governance*. Abingdon: Routledge.

Houssen, Wael, Rodrigo Sara, and Marcel Jaspars. 2020. "Digital Sequence Information on Genetic Resources: Concept, Scope and Current Use." Meeting of the AHTEG, March 17–20.

Jeffery, Michael I. 2004. "Intellectual Property Rights and Biodiversity Conservation: Reconciling the Incompatibilities of the TRIPS Agreement and the Convention on Biological Diversity." In *Intellectual Property and Biological Resources*, edited by Burton Ong, 185–225. Singapore: Marshall Cavendish Academic.

Kolbert, Elizabeth. 2014. *The Sixth Extinction: An Unnatural History*. London: Bloomsbury.

Laird, Sarah, and Rachel Wynberg. 2018. "A Fact-Finding and Scoping Study on Digital Sequence Information on Genetic Resources in the Context of the Convention on Biological Diversity and the Nagoya Protocol." Meeting of the AHTEG, February 13–16.

Morgera, Elisa, Stephanie Switzer, and Miranda Geelhoed. 2019. "Study for the European Commission on 'Possible Ways to Address Digital Sequence Information – Legal and Policy Aspects.'" Consultancy project conducted for the European Commission, ENV. F. 3/SER/2019/6175145.

Muzaka, Valbona, and Omar Ramon Serrano. 2020. "Teaming up? China, India and Brazil and the Issue of Benefit-Sharing from Genetic Resource Use." *New Political Economy* 25(5): 734–754.

National Academies of Sciences, Engineering, and Medicine. 2021. "Advancing Commercialization of Digital Products from Federal Laboratories." Consensus Science Report.

National Research Council. 2009. *A New Biology for the 21st Century*. Washington, DC: National Academies Press.

Ostrom, Elinor. 1990. *Governing the Commons: The Evolution of Institutions for Collective Action*. Cambridge: Cambridge University Press.

Overmann, Jörg, and Amber Hartman Scholz. 2017. "Microbiological Research under the Nagoya Protocol: Facts and Fiction." *Trends in Microbiology* 25(2): 85–88.

Peeling, Rosanna W., Debrah Boeras, Annelies Wilder-Smith, Amadou Sall, and John Nkengasong. 2020. "Need for Sustainable Biobanking Networks for COVID-19 and Other Diseases of Epidemic Potential." *The Lancet Infectious Diseases* 20(10): e268–e273.

Pisani, Elizabeth, Amrita Ghataure, and Laura Merson. 2018. "Data Sharing in Public Health Emergencies: A Study of Current Policies, Practices and Infrastructure Supporting the Sharing of Data to Prevent and Respond to Epidemic and Pandemic Threats." Wellcome Trust.

Reichman, Jerome H. 2018. "Why the Nagoya Protocol to the CBD Matters to Science and Industry in Canada and the United States." Centre for International Governance Innovation Paper No. 158.

Reichman, Jerome H., and Tracy Lewis. 2005. "Using Liability Rules to Stimulate Local Innovation in Developing Countries: Application to Traditional Knowledge." In *International Public Goods and Transfer of Technology under a Globalized Intellectual Property Regime*, edited by Keith E. Maskus and Jerome H. Reichman, 337–366. Cambridge: Cambridge University Press.

Reichman, Jerome H., and Ruth L. Okediji. 2012. "When Copyright Law and Science Collide: Empowering Digitally Integrated Research Methods on a Global Scale." *Minnesota Law Review* 96(4): 1362–1480.

Reichman, Jerome H., and Paul F. Uhlir. 2003. "A Contractually Reconstructed Research Commons for Scientific Data in a Highly Protectionist Intellectual Property Environment." *Law and Contemporary Problems* 66(1/2): 315–462.

Reichman, Jerome H., Paul F. Uhlir, and Tom Dedeurwaerdere. 2015. *Governing Digitally Integrated Genetic Resources, Data, and Literature: Global Intellectual Property Strategies for a Redesigned Microbial Research Commons*. Cambridge: Cambridge University Press.

Ribeiro, Carolina dos S., Marion P. Koopmans, and George B. Haringhuizen. 2018a. "Threats to Timely Sharing of Pathogen Sequence Data." *Science* 362(6413): 404–406.

Ribeiro, Carolina dos S., Martine Y. van Roode, George B. Haringhuizen, Marion P. Koopmans, Eric Claassen, and Linda H.M. van de Burgwal. 2018b. "How Ownership Rights over Microorganisms Affect Infectious Disease Control and Innovation: A Root-Cause Analysis of Barriers to Data Sharing as Experienced by Key Stakeholders." *PLOS One* 13(5): e0195885.

Rohden, Fabian, and Amber Hartman Scholz. 2021. "The International Political Process around Digital Sequence Information under the Convention on Biological Diversity and the 2018–2020 Intersessional Period." *Plants, People, Planet* 4(1): 51–60.

Schei, Pete Johan, and Morten Walløe Tvedt. 2010. "Genetic Resources in the CBD: The Wording, the Past, the Present and the Future." *Genetics* 6: 533–543.

Scutchfield, F. Douglas, and Cynthia D. Lamberth. 2010. "Public Health Systems and Services Research: Bridging the Practice-Research Gap." *Public Health Reports* 125(5): 628–633.

Sedyaningsih, Endang R., Siti Isfandari, Triono Soendoro, and Siti Fadilah Supari. 2008. "Towards Mutual Trust, Transparency and Equity in Virus Sharing Mechanism: The Avian Influenza Case of Indonesia." *Annals Academy of Medicine Singapore* 37(6): 482.

Sett, Scarlett, Carolina dos Santos Ribeiro, Christine Prat, George Haringhuizen, European Virus Archive Principal Investigators, and Amber Hartman Scholz. 2022. "Access and Benefit-Sharing by the European Virus Archive in Response to COVID-19." *The Lancet Microbe* 3(4): E316–E323.

Simon, James H.M., Eric Claassen, Carmen E. Correa, and Albert D.M.E. Osterhaus. 2005. "Managing Severe Acute Respiratory Syndrome (SARS) Intellectual Property Rights: The Possible Role of Patent Pooling." *Bulletin of the World Health Organization* 83(9): 707–710.

Six, Benjamin, Esther Van Zimmeren, Florin Popa, and Christine Frison. 2015. "Trust and Social Capital in the Design and Evolution of Institutions for Collective Action." *International Journal of the Commons* 9(1): 151–176.

Third World Network. 2019. "Comments of Third World Network on Digital Sequence Information." www.cbd.int/abs/DSI-views/2019/TWN-DSI.pdf.

Van de Burgwal, Linda H.M., Carolina dos S. Ribeiro, Mark B. Van der Waal, and Eric Claassen. 2018. "Towards Improved Process Efficiency in Vaccine Innovation: The Vaccine Innovation Cycle as a Validated, Conceptual Stage-Gate Model." *Vaccine* 36(49): 7496–7508.

Van De Pas, Remco, Marc-Alain Widdowson, Raffaella Ravinetto, Prasanth N. Srinivas, Theresa J. Ochoa, Thierno Oumar Fofana, and Wim Van Damme. 2022. "COVID-19 Vaccine Equity: A Health Systems and Policy Perspective." *Expert Review of Vaccines* 21 (1): 25–36.

World Health Organization (WHO). 2011. *Pandemic Influenza Preparedness Framework for the Sharing of Influenza Viruses and Access to Vaccines and Other Benefits*. Geneva: WHO Press.

2014. "Global Influenza Surveillance and Response System (GISRS)." www.who.int/initiatives/global-influenza-surveillance-and-response-system.

2016. "Implementation of the Nagoya Protocol and Pathogen Sharing: Public Health Implications." www.who.int/docs/default-source/documents/nagoya-protocol/nagoya-full-study-english.

2017. "WHO R&D Blueprint Meeting on Pathogen Genetic Sequence Data (GSD) Sharing in the Context of Public Health Emergencies, 28–29 September 2017." https://indico.un.org/event/24764/material/slides/5.pdf.

2018a. "Approaches to Seasonal Influenza and Genetic Sequence Data under the PIP Framework: Analysis." https://cdn.who.int/media/docs/default-source/pip-framework/governance/analysis-of-seasonal-influenza-gsd-under-the-pip-framework/analysis-document/wha70108b_analysis.pdf?sfvrsn=156f1357_5.

2018b. *Managing Epidemics: Key Facts about Major Deadly Diseases*. Geneva: WHO Press.

2019. "WHO's Code of Conduct for Open and Timely Sharing of Pathogen Genetic Sequence Data during Outbreaks of Infectious Diseases." https://moodle2.units.it/pluginfile.php/393844/mod_resource/content/1/WHO_pathogen_sequencing_data_release.pdf.

14

Distributive Justice beyond Intellectual Property Laws

An International Perspective

Shlomit Yanisky-Ravid[*]

INTRODUCTION

The United Nations recently adopted seventeen global Sustainable Development Goals (SDGs) to ensure that by 2030 all people enjoy peace and prosperity, with no one left behind. Among the SDGs that countries have committed to are the following: no poverty, zero hunger, good health and well-being, quality education, gender equality, affordable and clean energy, decent work, peace and justice, industry, innovation, and infrastructure.[1] The SDGs are more powerful tools than U.N. declarations since they target specific goals within time limits, have quantifiable outcomes, and involve the responsibility and commitments of countries around the globe, especially developed countries.[2] However, in the digital era, where rapid

[*] I would like to thank the prominent coeditors of this book: Dr. Francis Gurry, Professor Daniel Benoliel, Professor Peter Yu, and Professor Keun Lee. I would also like to thank Michal Svantner, Director of the WIPO Department for Transition and Developed Countries, for wonderful collaboration over the years. My deepest gratitude to Professor Matthew Diller, Dean of the Fordham Law School, and Professor Hugh Hansen, founder and director of the Fordham IP Institute and the Annual Intellectual Property Law & Policy Conference, for their precious and endless support. I am also thankful to the students in the Intellectual Property and Advanced Technology and artificial intelligence and blockchain courses at Fordham Law School and the participants in the Yale Law School Information Society Project Writing Workshops for their excellent comments. Last but not least, I would like to thank Ms. Elizabeth Levin, Yale Law 2020, Mr. Nimrod Ravid, Harvard University 2025, Mr. Adam Guttentag, Fordham Law 2023, and Ms. Judy Arad, Ono Academic College, for their outstanding contribution as research assistants. The chapter is dedicated to the blessed memory of Professor Joel Reidenberg, Founder of the Center on Law and Information Policy at Fordham Law School.

1 *See Sustainable Development Goals*, United Nations Dev. Programme, www.undp.org/sustainable-development-goals (last visited July 21, 2022); *see also* Sakiko Fukuda-Parr, Millennium Development Goals: Ideas, Interests, Influence (2017); Sakiko Fukuda-Parr, *Millennium Development Goals: Why They Matter*, 10 Glob. Governance 395–402 (2004) [hereinafter Fukuda-Parr, *Millennium Development Goals*].

2 Fukuda-Parr, *Millennium Development Goals, supra* note 1, at 395–99.

technological development captures the spheres we live in, intellectual property (IP) assets have become essential for progress and sustainability and may contribute to achieving other SDGs.[3] Although the SDGs mention innovation, they focus on tangible rather than intangible needs and IP goals.[4] The SDGs also missed the major role played by international professional organizations, such as the World Intellectual Property Organization (WIPO), one of the main international players in this arena. Nonetheless, SDGs reveal the interrelation between the different goals and, hence, raise the need to rethink and redefine the concept of IP – that is, beyond the current IP laws and their traditional viewpoint to include new global values and goals, including equality, accessibility, and fairness between developing and developed countries. To reach a new understanding of the IP regime, it is crucial to develop and adopt necessary support mechanisms for IP as well as new theoretical justifications.[5]

For example, when artificial intelligence (AI) systems create works of art or when blockchain-based nonfungible tokens (NFTs) provide global peer-to-peer distribution of IP assets, we have to ask ourselves: Should we rethink how we look at IP assets in general? Are they accessible? Can all creators and inventors in developing countries access these developments, and are they in a competitive position within the IP arena to access their outcomes?[6]

3 *See* Daniel Benoliel, Patent Intensity and Economy Growth (2017). *See generally* Intellectual Property at the Edge: The Contested Contours of IP (Rochelle Cooper Dreyfuss & Jane C. Ginsburg eds., 2014) [hereinafter Intellectual Property at the Edge] (describing the edge of intellectual property laws in the digital era); Carol M. Rose, *A Real Property Lawyer Cautiously Inspects the Edges of Intellectual Property*, *in* Intellectual Property at the Edge, *supra*; Megan Boler, Digital Media and Democracy 303 (2010) (describing the implications of the massive amount of users that free services attract); Jonathan Taplin, Move Fast and Break Things: How Facebook, Google, and Amazon Cornered Culture and Undermined Democracy (2017) ("Google, Amazon and Facebook are all monopolies."); *The Case for Reforming the Rules of Copyright*, Fin. Times (July 6, 2018), www.ft.com/content/20a8d1e0-810a-11e8-bc55-50daf11b720d:

> Silicon valley companies – now the largest, richest corporate entities in the world … which amount in effect to billions of dollars in subsidies. That is a key reason why the European Parliament … voted to reject a draft reform of EU copyright laws that would have forced internet groups, such as Facebook and Google, the owner of YouTube, to use content filters to avoid breaching copyright, or to pay publishers for the right to use their content.

4 Fukuda-Parr, *Millennium Development Goals*, *supra* note 1, at 399 (stating that some academics, social activists, and government officials have focused on many objectives such as employment, reproductive health, human rights, and many other issues).

5 *Id.*

6 Kishore Vasan, Milan Janosov & Albert-Laszlo Barabási, *Quantifying NFT-Driven Networks in Crypto Art*, 12 Sci. Rep. 2769 (2022) ("NFTs offer a mechanism for artists to create digital works of art and validate their work as unique, eternal, and worth collecting, and offers collectors the ability to showcase their collections on digital platforms. Driven by this technological innovation, digital art experienced $2.5 Billion in sales just within the first two quarters of 2021."); Katya Fisher, *Once upon a Time in NFT: Blockchain, Copyright, and the Right of First Sale*

In the face of the current "digital 3A" era of automated, autonomous, and advanced technologies,[7] this chapter issues a call to rethink IP norms to ensure that all players and stakeholders – from creators and inventors to end-users worldwide – can access and make the most of existing IP. Broader opportunities should be extended to industries being disrupted by advanced technologies.[8] Without access to IP, inequality may occur, creating destructive effects on social stability, the economy, and democracy. It is therefore worthwhile to ask who is excluded from access to IP through both the vertical and horizontal perspectives.[9]

As "rapid technological developments continue to transform the way works and other IP subject matter are created, produced, distributed and exploited,"[10] this chapter calls for a new and broader understanding of the scope of IP rights, particularly in light of the SDGs that enhance more equality and equal access within an international perspective. IP shall be redefined to address legal and practical uncertainties for both rights holders and users of works.

Furthermore, living in the digital era, we cannot refer to IP regimes without considering an international perspective. Seeing the current global society through this lens illuminates the need to shift from traditional theoretical perspectives –

Doctrine, 37 CARDOZO ARTS & ENT. L.J. 629 (2019); Shlomit Yanisky-Ravid, *Generating Rembrandt: Artificial Intelligence, Copyright, and Accountability in the 3A Era – The Human-Like Workers Are Already Here – A New Model*, 2017 MICH. ST. L. REV. 659, 707–17 (discussing the question of ownership when AI systems generate artworks); Shlomit Yanisky-Ravid & Edward Kim, *Patenting Blockchain: Mitigating the Patent Infringement War*, 83 ALB. L. REV. 603 (2019) (discussing ownership on blockchain); Shlomit Yanisky-Ravid & Grace Monroy, *The Promised Land: Blockchain and the Fashion Industry*, 87 BROOK. L. REV. 609 (2022) (arguing that blockchain technology can cure the lack of IP protection in regard to fashion design).

7 Dr. Shlomit Yanisky-Ravid & Xiaoqiong (Jackie) Liu, *When Artificial Intelligence Systems Produce Inventions: An Alternative Model for Patent Law at the 3A Era*, 39 CARDOZO L. REV. 2215 (2018) (coining the term "3A era" to describe advanced, automated, and autonomous AI systems and arguing that patents laws are outdated, irrelevant, and inapplicable in situations where AI systems produce inventions, and that new tools, external to the legal regime, should therefore replace patent laws).

8 JACQUES BUGHIN, ERIC HAZAN, SREE RAMASWAMY, MICHAEL CHUI, TERA ALLAS, PETER DAHLSTROM, NICOLAUS HENKE & MONICA TRENCH, ARTIFICIAL INTELLIGENCE: THE NEXT DIGITAL FRONTIER? 5, 15, 19, 71 (2017) (demonstrating that one major example of a first taker is the entertainment industry, which heavily relies on advanced technologies); *IFPI Global Music Report 2018*, IFPI (Apr. 24, 2018), www.ifpi.org/ifpi-global-music-report-2018/ (stating that "[s]-treaming revenues grow 41.1% to become largest revenue source, driven by 176 million users of paid subscription accounts," "[t]hird consecutive year of growth following 15 years of revenue decline," and "[c]ampaign to achieve full and fair value for music in digital marketplace continues"); *IFPI Global Music Report 2019*, IFPI (Apr. 2, 2019), www.ifpi.org/ifpi-global-music-report-2019/ (stating that "[t]otal streaming revenues grew 34.0% to nearly half of all revenue, driven by paid streaming").

9 Sakiko Fukuda-Parr, *Keeping Out Extreme Inequality from the SDG Agenda – The Politics of Indicators*, 10 GLOB. POL'Y 61 (2019) [hereinafter Fukuda-Parr, *Keeping Out Extreme Inequality*] (discussing vertical versus horizontal inequality).

10 Council Directive 2019/790, art. 3 (entering into force June 7, 2019) (targeting "a well-functioning marketplace for copyright").

namely, law and economics, personality, and Lockean labor theory – to a more open and equal global approach, such as the distributive justice approach that will be discussed in this chapter. The latter approach is crucial when focusing globally. International procedures should occur through an independent, objective entity recognized and trusted by the nations. This chapter suggests that international professional organizations, such as WIPO in the IP field, are the best players to administer these challenges.

The challenges that IP regimes face when the discourse on IP is altered beyond its traditional boundaries are the focus of this chapter.

14.1 TRADITIONAL JUSTIFICATIONS OF INTELLECTUAL PROPERTY LAWS

Intellectual property laws were created to achieve ideals that policymakers believed were important for society.[11] However, since the IP arena is constantly evolving and facing new challenges, such as the Internet and digital developments (e.g., AI systems, blockchain, and NFTs), policymakers must consider how IP regimes might adequately address these ideals and any other new goals.

Traditionally, the discourse concerning the theoretical justifications of IP has been focused on three main substantive theories: law and economics, personality theory, and Lockean labor theory.

The law-and-economics theory aims to maximize the total socio-economic welfare of the public.[12] It examines IP products and processes according to their efficiency and their contribution to promoting science and useful arts.[13] The law-and-economics approach to IP focuses on the incentives of players and stakeholders within the industry to develop and distribute IP goods. By granting exclusive rights that exclude others from using the legally protected goods, the invention is

[11] Elizabeth L. Rosenblatt, *Intellectual Property's Negative Space: Beyond the Utilitarian*, 40 FLA. ST. U. L. REV. 441, 446 (2013) ("[B]y pinpointing the theoretical justification we can understand to what extent the laws achieve or fail to achieve these aims and how the laws should evolve to reflect those goals."); *see* William Fisher, *Theories of Intellectual Property*, *in* NEW ESSAYS IN THE LEGAL AND POLITICAL THEORY OF PROPERTY 168, 194–99 (Stephen R. Munzer ed., 2001) (discussing the importance of theoretical discussion).

[12] DONALD S. CHISUM & MICHAEL A. JACOBS, UNDERSTANDING INTELLECTUAL PROPERTY LAW § 1C (1992); Margot E. Kaminski & Shlomit Yanisky-Ravid, *The Marrakesh Treaty for Visually Impaired Persons: Why a Treaty Was Preferable to Soft Law*, 75 U. PITT. L. REV 255, 259, 265 (2014); *see* U.S. CONST. art. I, § 8, cl. 8; Fisher, *supra* note 11, at 169–70 (discussing incentive theory); Amy Kapczynski, *The Cost of Price: Why and How to Get beyond Intellectual Property Internalism*, 59 UCLA L. REV. 970, 970, 977–79 (2012) ("Giving full scope to distributive justice and other values thus requires us to telescope out from the internalism that characterizes the field, and to countenance a broader role for commons-based production and government procurement.").

[13] U.S. CONST. art. I, § 8, cl. 8; 17 U.S.C. § 107.

economically incentivized.[14] Preventing free riders and ensuring an economic return for the most efficient stakeholders are just a few goals this approach targets. Once the exclusivity period expires, the goods become part of the public domain.[15]

Although the law-and-economics approach to IP is dominant, especially in the United States, some scholars have found its prevailing influence troublesome.[16] Further, there has been much criticism regarding developing countries.[17]

Personality theory and Lockean labor theory focus on creators and inventors as humans. Based on the philosophy of Hegel, the personality justification focuses on representing the creators' personalities in their works.[18] An individual's right to control his property relates to his personhood; property developed by an individual is seen as an extension of his personality, justifying his ownership.[19] An IP regime premised on this view would protect personal assets more vigorously than fungible assets and would incorporate strict restrictions on transfer.[20]

Under Lockean labor theory, one's interest in her property is justified because the property is the fruit of her labor.[21] Intellectual property ownership of her creations is based on the same entitlements as one's rights over her own body and soul. In other words, the outcomes of people's efforts must become their possessions.[22]

14 CHISUM & JACOBS, *supra* note 12, § 1C.

15 Yochai Benkler, *Free as the Air to Common Use: First Amendment Constraints on Enclosure of the Public Domain*, 74 N.Y.U. L. REV. 354, 360–62 (1999).

16 Andreas Rahmatian, *A Fundamental Critique of the Law-and-Economics Analysis of Intellectual Property Rights*, 17 MARQ. INTELL. PROP. L. REV. 191, 192–97 (2013).

17 *See also* Hannibal Travis, *Injury, Inequality, and Remedies: Developments in Injunctive Relief and Damages in Intellectual Property Cases*, 21 J. HIGH TECH. L. 34 (2021) (discussing copyright and patent systems as framed to exclude others to be followed by trademarks and trade secrets, which borrowed its remedial structure from federal statutes, focusing on remedies, such as injunctions and royalties, and inequality); Peter Yu's Chapter 3 in this volume ("[I]n developing countries, the Global South lamented the unfair distribution of benefits within the international intellectual property regime.").

18 *See also* G.W.F. HEGEL, PHILOSOPHY OF RIGHT 40–45 (T.M. Knox trans., Oxford University Press 1952) (1821); Fisher, *supra* note 11, at 171 (summarizing the main points of the connection between personality theory and intellectual property); Justin Hughes, *The Philosophy of Intellectual Property*, 77 GEO. L.J. 287, 331 (1988) (discussing the personality approach).

19 Fisher, *supra* note 11, at 169; Hughes, *supra* note 18, at 330.

20 Margaret Jane Radin, *Property and Personhood*, 34 STAN. L. REV. 957, 986 (1982) (claiming the more expensive *personal* property is, the more nonfungible and nontransferable it becomes); *see also* Fisher, *supra* note 11, at 169; Hughes, *supra* note 18, at 336–37.

21 *See* Fisher, *supra* note 11, at 169–75 (describing various theories underlying intellectual property); Hughes, *supra* note 18, at 288–89 (same).

22 JOHN LOCKE, TWO TREATIES OF GOVERNMENT 287–88 (Peter Laslett ed., Cambridge University Press 1988) (1690) (describing Lockean labor theory as based in part on Locke's argument that an acquirer of property must leave sufficient materials or "building blocks" for others); *see also* SHLOMIT YANISKY-RAVID, INTELLECTUAL PROPERTY IN THE WORKPLACE: THEORETICAL AND COMPARATIVE PERSPECTIVES (2013); Fisher, *supra* note 11, at 170 (discussing labor theory); ROBERT P. MERGES, JUSTIFYING INTELLECTUAL PROPERTY 32–33 (2011) (discussing the Lockean labor approach as the preferred approach to understanding intellectual property); Hughes, *supra* note 18, at 297–99 (seeing instrumentalist and normative bases in the Lockean labor approach); Frank I. Michelman, *Property, Utility, and Fairness: Comments*

In sum, the traditional approaches to IP define, interpret, create, and recreate IP laws according to these three theoretical justifications. However, this chapter argues that, when addressing the digital 3A era, personality and labor theories are less applicable than law and economics. When sophisticated systems, such as AI, are involved in the creative process, and when the involvement of users in creating and disseminating IP assets is significant, concepts such as "incentive," "personality," and "labor" may lose their meaning. Furthermore, law and economics addresses a broader range of players and stakeholders in the IP industry, including investors and users. At the same time, the personality and labor theories focus solely on flesh-and-blood creators. By looking at economic justifications beyond IP, we can discover different international institutional approaches to scientific and cultural production that are no less efficient. These prevailing approaches conflict with the values of distributive justice, discussed in more detail in the next section, because reliance upon one feature (incentive, labor, or personality) may yield the unjust distribution of existing information and other resources and the unjust production of future information and resources.[23] These theories fail to explain the collective feature of IP assets.

The traditional justifications for IP almost entirely mishandle IP in the digital 3A era and the supportive and necessary tools that have become crucial to fulfilling the goals of the IP regime. The following section will present and address the approach that this chapter suggests as more germane to our era: the distributive justice approach.

14.2 DISTRIBUTIVE JUSTICE

14.2.1 *The Principles of Distributive Justice*

The principles of distributive justice are not necessarily consistent with economic-utilitarian considerations,[24] personhood considerations, or possession of assets (as the

on the Ethical Foundations of "Just Compensation" Law, 80 HARV. L. REV. 1165, 1203–04 (1967) (arguing that labor theory is an ethical foundation of property ownership).

[23] Kapczynski, *supra* note 12, at 972–80 (2012) (giving full scope to distributive justice and other values thus requires us to go beyond the internalism that characterizes the field and to countenance a broader role for commons-based production and government procurement).

[24] *See also* RICHARD POSNER, ECONOMIC ANALYSIS OF LAW 32–39, 40 (6th ed. 2003) (explaining that the law-and-economics approach establishes rules of distribution by type according to the principles of justice aimed at maximizing welfare); Duncan Kennedy, *Distributive and Paternalist Motives in Contract and Tort Law, with Special References to Compulsory Terms and Unequal Bargaining Power*, 41 MD. L. REV. 563, 571–73 (1982) (discussing reasons for preferring the theory of efficiency over distributive justice and noting that the two theories bring contradictory results: The efficiency approach aims to improve both groups whereas the distributive approach prefers one group (the weak) over another in distributing resources).

fruits of someone's work).[25] Instead, distributive justice is concerned with the allocation and reallocation of social resources, including capital and other goods and tools as well as power and rights, in their broadest sense.[26] Although discussed by some scholars, distributive justice is considered neither a substance nor a major justification of IP; it is seen as an exception or postscript to the mainstream theoretical justifications.[27]

This chapter contends that the theory of distributive justice is an integral and essential part of understanding the IP regime and the need for international IP supportive tools.[28]

"Distributive justice" is a general title coined by Homans in 1961.[29] The term is broad and varies according to the different moral perspectives of what is the desired "fairness."[30] The theory determines the appropriate principles of resource allocation by which distribution will be made.[31]

Karen Cook and Karen Hegtvedt offered one of the best overarching descriptions: "All social systems evolve mechanisms for distributing valued resources and for allocating rights, responsibilities, costs, and burdens. Theories of distributive justice specify the conditions under which particular distributions (and, more recently, distributional procedures) are perceived to be 'just' or 'fair'."[32]

[25] Stewart E. Sterk, *Rhetoric and Reality in Copyright Law*, 94 MICH. L. REV. 1197, 1234–39 (1996) (stating that copyright laws contradict theories about distribution of justice).

[26] G.A. Cohen, *Where the Action Is: On the Site of Distributive Justice*, 26 PHIL. & PUB. AFFS. 3, 3 (1997) (referring to distributive justice "as just distribution of benefits and burden on society").

[27] On distributive justice and intellectual property, see ERIC RAKOWSKI, EQUAL JUSTICE 85–87 (1991) (discussing rules for distributing benefits); J.W. Harris, *Who Owns My Body*, 16 OXFORD J. LEGAL STUD. 55, 66 (1996); William M. Landes, *Copyright Protection of Letters, Diaries and Other Unpublished Works: An Economic Approach*, 21 J. LEGAL STUD. 79 (1992) (implementing Rawls's theory on the veil of ignorance and the entitlement of authors to rights in unpublished works).

[28] MERGES, *supra* note 22, at 151–53 (stating that efficiency "is not capable of serving as a stand-alone foundation" for explaining intellectual property laws).

[29] *See also* GEORGE C. HOMANS, SOCIAL BEHAVIOR: ITS ELEMENTARY FORMS (1961); TORSTEIN ECKHOFF, JUSTICE: ITS DETERMINANTS IN SOCIAL INTERACTION (1974); Karen S. Cook & Karen A. Hegtvedt, *Distributive Justice, Equity, and Equality*, 9 ANN. REV. SOCIO. 217, 218 (1983) ("[T]he terms denote distinct types of justice. In concluding this section, we use Eckhoff's . . . five principles of equality to indicate how most existing conceptions of justice fit within a more general theoretical framework."); JERALD GREENBERG & RONALD L. COHEN, EQUALITY AND JUSTICE IN SOCIAL BEHAVIOR (1982); MELVIN J. LERNER & SALLY C. LERNER, THE JUSTICE MOTIVE IN SOCIAL BEHAVIOR ADOPTING TO TIMES OF SCARCITY AND CHANGE (1981).

[30] *See also* Fisher, *supra* note 11, at 175 (describing a "Social Planning Theory" of intellectual property based on political philosophy theorists, including Jefferson, Marx, and the legal realists); Rosenblatt, *supra* note 11, at 458 (citing Fisher *supra* note 11, at 192) (discussing those values in relation to the incentive to create).

[31] Robert P. Merges, *Foundations and Principles Redux: A Reply to Professor Blankfein-Tabachnick*, 101 CAL. L. REV. 1361, 1379–81 (2013); *see also* MERGES, *supra* note 22, at 102 (describing distributive justice in the context of intellectual property as built mainly on the insights of Locke, Kant, and Rawls).

[32] Cook & Hegtvedt, *supra* note 29, at 218.

Allocation occurs when an allocator distributes valued rewards, resources, rights, or obligations to an array of recipients.[33] In his books, Gerald Allen Cohen argues that equality, freedom, and accessibility are major features of the distributive justice approach.[34]

Using norms of justice to regulate exchange and allocation processes has important social structural consequences.[35] This analysis of distributive justice provides a general framework in relation to commercial transactions, the emergence of markets, and the evolution of agreements regulating exchange and allocation activity in various social systems, among participants of varying degree of interdependence.[36] Whereas libertarians' concerns focus on the government misusing its power, distributive justice advocates are more concerned about the concentration of resources and power in the hands of a small number of groups or individuals.[37]

One of the most desirable concepts underlying the establishment of distributive justice rules is the principle of equality.[38] Products and services, including IP assets in the current digital era, would be distributed in ways that provide individuals a share based on merit. Distribution may be based on rights, power, goods, capital, benefits, needs, efforts, and achievements. From a legal standpoint, a decision regarding which of these criteria is most important has not been made.[39] Under a

[33] *Id.* at 219 ("Whether the recipients are involved in a direct exchange relation with the distributor or indirectly with each other is a secondary analytical distinction. Furthermore, in many situations exchange and allocation processes combine.").

[34] *See also* GERALD ALLEN COHEN, RESCUING JUSTICE AND EQUALITY (2008); GERALD ALLEN COHEN, DISTRIBUTIVE JUSTICE AND ACCESS TO ADVANTAGE (2015); GERALD ALLEN COHEN, ON THE CURRENCY OF EGALITARIAN JUSTICE AND OTHER ESSAYS ON POLITICAL PHILOSOPHY (2011).

[35] Cook & Hegtvedt, *supra* note 29, at 234.

[36] *Id.* at 234–35.

[37] *See also* CHARLES E. LINDBLOM, POLITICS AND MARKETS 170–88 (1977); ROBERT NOZICK, ANARCHY, STATE, AND UTOPIA 150–53, 160, 175–82 (1974); C. Edwin Baker, *Property and Its Relation to Constitutionally Protected Liberty*, 134 U. PA. L. REV. 741, 748–51, 753 (1986); Daphna Lewinsohn-Zamir, *In Defense of Redistribution through Private Law*, 91 MINN. L. REV. 326, 335–36 (2006); Frank Michelman, *Tutelary Jurisprudence and Constitutional Property*, *in* LIBERTY, PROPERTY, AND THE FUTURE OF CONSTITUTIONAL DEVELOPMENT 127, 139, 149–57 (Ellen Frankel Paul & Howard Dickman eds., 1990); Carol M. Rose, *Property as the Keystone Right?*, 71 NOTRE DAME L. REV. 329, 342–44 (1996).

[38] *See* THOMAS NAGEL, EQUALITY AND PARTIALITY 12, 68–69 (1991); JOSEPH RAZ, THE MORALITY OF FREEDOM 193, 198, 206 (1989); Frank I. Michelman, *Possession vs. Distribution in the Constitutional Idea of Property*, 72 IOWA L. REV. 1319, 1319–20, 1329 (1987); *see also* ARISTOTLE, THE NICHOMACHEAN ETHICS OF ARISTOTLE 145 (F.H. Peters trans., 15th ed., Kegan Paul, Trench, Trübner & Co. 1893) ("For in distribution all men allow that what is just must be according to merit or worth of some kind, but they do not all adopt the same standard of worth.").

[39] See, for example, W. Air Lines, Inc. v. Criswell, 472 U.S. 400, 404, 413–15 (1985); Geduldig v. Aiello, 417 U.S. 484, 495–96 (1974). EEOC v. Mo. State Highway Patrol, 748 F.2d 447, 455 (8th Cir. 1984); Wendy W. Williams, *The Equality Crisis: Some Reflections on Culture, Courts, and Feminism*, 7 WOMEN'S RTS. L. REP. 175, 175 (1982).

distributive justice approach, all would be considered, and an asset would be shared if "fair" under all these factors.

Distributive justice principles are strongly affiliated with John Rawls's theory of justice.[40] These principles can be applied to IP tools, primarily and most effectively within an international environment. Under Rawls's theory of justice, distribution rules serve as the basis for allocating rights to promote social justice.[41] Rawls sought to establish the principles of justice used by policymakers. When setting rules, especially about property and possession, policymakers should ensure equality and fairness for all, rather than favoring and promoting their interests or the interests of the stronger party.[42]

Rawls proposed an imaginary assembly of people acting under a "veil of ignorance" to ensure that decision-makers have no actual knowledge regarding their interests, guaranteeing equality, freedom, and fairness in their decisions.[43] Rawls suggested two principles of justice: The first principle is that all people have an equal right to a broad range of basic freedoms; the second principle espouses equal opportunity for all. These principles support the weaker parties and result in a more egalitarian and fair distribution of goods (including IP assets in the broadest sense).[44]

IP regimes are traditionally applied firstly within a single territorial state. This national approach seems to limit the sharing of advanced technologies arbitrarily. This hurdle is particularly stark in the distributive justice of IP assets. Local governments tend to prefer local IP industries. This traditional perception of IP needs to change, particularly in the digital era. Building on the author's other work, this chapter calls for abandoning the focus on national IP and adopting an international vision of distributive justice.[45] As one commentator observed:

> Global development goals are important because they create consensus norms. They define priority objectives and ethical standards that are considered legitimate and influence the behavior of diverse stakeholders. Though global goals are international agreements without enforcement mechanisms, they exert influence in

[40] Shlomit Yanisky-Ravid, *The Hidden Though Flourishing Justification of Intellectual Property Laws: Distributive Justice; National versus International Approach*, 21 Lewis & Clark L. Rev. 1, 7–8, 14–17 (2017) (arguing for the distributive justice approach as an internal basis for national and international intellectual property regimes). For a more general concept, *see* Michael Blake, *Distributive Justice, State Coercion, and Autonomy*, 30 Phil. & Publ. Affs. 257, 257–96 (2001) (endorsing the idea that we can defend principles of sufficiency abroad and principles of distributive equality at home, because these principles can be understood as distinct implications of impartial principles in distinct institutional contexts).

[41] John Rawls, A Theory of Justice 6–7 (rev. ed. 1999); Merges, *supra* note 22, at 102–03 (discussing Rawls's theory as one which resembles distributive justice in regard to intellectual property); *see also* John Rawls, Justice as Fairness – A Restatement 7, 25 (Erin Kelly ed., 2001).

[42] Yanisky-Ravid, *supra* note 40, at 14–17.

[43] Rawls, *supra* note 41; Yanisky-Ravid, *supra* note 40, at 14–17.

[44] Rawls, *supra* note 41; Yanisky-Ravid, *supra* note 40, at 14–17.

[45] Yanisky-Ravid, *supra* note 40.

large part by creating narratives and framing debates about how development challenges should be conceptualized. At face value, the 2030 Agenda would appear to contain a strong norm for reducing inequality.[46]

14.2.2 *Intellectual Property Regime through a Distributive Justice Lens*

This chapter contends that the distributive justice approach is relevant to the IP regime. Although scholars differ from one another in their approaches to this question, this chapter argues that distributive justice is crucial to understanding IP laws, especially in the digital era, when it is difficult to imagine the process of creation and invention without significantly relying on input from many sources, including technological systems.[47]

Scholars tend to fall under two prevailing theories, the "externalist" and the "internalist" perspectives, as was described in other works of the author. Some "externalist" scholars see law and economics as the sole or the main approach to IP,[48] with the IP regime being detached from any distributive justice goals.[49] Under this perspective, IP focuses on entities that develop and distribute their assets and ignore values such as inequality and accessibility.[50] The second approach, dubbed by the author as the "internalist approach," sees distributive justice as a source only of potential exceptions and limitations to IP, incorporated through concepts such as "fair use."[51]

In contrast to the approaches described earlier, this chapter proposes a third concept that ties distributive justice to a broader assessment of IP laws recognizing the digital era. This approach claims that IP laws reflected distributive justice principles from the beginning, as both were "born" together and can "get along" in harmony and synergy.[52] The now-prevalent understanding of IP, which

46 Fukuda-Parr, *Keeping Out Extreme Inequality*, *supra* note 9.

47 Yanisky-Ravid, *supra* note 40, at 17–19.

48 *Id.*

49 Kapczynski, *supra* note 12, at 973–74, 978–79. Areas such as science, Internet entertainment, Wikipedia, and free software are generated by a "common based approach" or with governmental funding to develop public domain products, both of which are totally different from the exclusive approach of intellectual property. Intellectual property is not just a problematic way to distribute scientific and cultural goods but is also a problematic way to produce them. A system based on price will probably prioritize the wealthy and leave out the poor. *Id.*; *see also* Rosenblatt, *supra* note 11, at 447–52 (discussing "negative spaces," which are areas that are not controlled by intellectual property rules). Both Kapczynski and Rosenblatt challenge the conclusion usually taken for granted that intellectual property protection is necessary to encourage authors and inventors to invest in the creative process.

50 Yanisky-Ravid, *supra* note 40, at 17–19.

51 Molly Shaffer Van Houweling, *Distributive Values in Copyright*, 83 Tex. L. Rev. 1535, 1537–39, 1567 (2005) (stating that poor artists who do not profit from their works should more easily benefit from the fair use doctrine); Kapczynski, *supra* note 12, at 975.

52 Yanisky-Ravid, *supra* note 40, at 17–19.

essentially adopts the law-and-economics interpretation of IP laws, emerged only later, influenced by certain groups with specific interests.[53]

In his article, Lior Zemer supports this third approach, which can be coined the collective approach.[54] He claims that generations of scholars have struggled to redefine copyright to afford users public comprehensive access rights and privileges. Zemer suggests a new theoretical justification for copyright features in translating inter-human relations into the language of creative properties and defining copyright as a dialogue between authors and others, especially in the digital environment.[55] This approach interprets IP assets as being created through the contribution of many personas, entities, and institutions, as well as the general public, rather than focusing on the author as the sole creator. Consequently, authorship may be distributed among all contributors.

This chapter expands this argument and states that the IP arena has experienced major changes in light of the digital revolution and that the traditional theories that explained the regime in the past should be reconsidered to justify collective intellectual assets – currently and, most probably, also in the near future. Adopting a new approach to IP is crucial, especially in the digital era; otherwise, we may end up limiting the scope of the IP regime by expanding its exceptions and limitations or even invalidating IP laws when technological tools, such as AI systems, dominate the creative process. In other words, as more and more IP assets are being created by using digital tools, and as the volume of creative art that can be generated with one click becomes almost unlimited, the value of IP laws may first be challenged. Then, when digital tools capture the market, IP laws may become incapable of coping with the digital creation of IP assets and of being enforced – and, therefore, invalid.

This concern has already come true in the wake of *Naruto v. Slater* (the monkey selfie case),[56] when the U.S. Copyright Office declared that the copyright regime does not include nonhuman creations.[57]

IP laws have changed over the years.[58] Thus, embracing distributive justice as a dominant approach to the IP regime may be integral to its natural evolution. This chapter states that the international arena may play a major role in pursuing the distributive justice approach to IP. The next section discusses the important role of

[53] *Id.*

[54] Lior Zemer, *Dialogical Transactions*, 95 Or. L. Rev. 141 (2016).

[55] *Id.* at 214 ("Information networks, as opposed to traditional creative industries, offer an unprecedented wealth of information and opportunities to dialogically transact with others.").

[56] 888 F.3d 418 (9th Cir. 2018).

[57] The United States Copyright Office, citing Burrow-Giles Lithographic Co. v. Sarony, 111 U.S. 53 (1884), stated: "To qualify as a work of 'authorship' a work must be created by a human being . . . . Works that do not satisfy this requirement are not copyrightable." U.S. Copyright Off., Compendium of Copyright Office Practices § 313.2 (3rd ed. 2017). The Copyright Office also states that it "will not register works produced by a machine or mere mechanical process that operates randomly or automatically without any creative input or intervention from a human author." *Id.* § 313.2.

[58] Kapczynski, *supra* note 12.

international organizations, while also focusing on WIPO and its tools to exemplify this approach.

14.3 DISTRIBUTIVE JUSTICE IN INTERNATIONAL TOOLS FOR ALL

14.3.1 *The Benefits of International Distribute Justice: Harmony, Certainty, and Trust*

The modern digital era has elevated tension between collective and individualistic interests, as well as between national and international interests. Companies will inevitably make choices in favor of their interests, maximizing income and avoiding the sharing of information regarding their business to maintain their advantage over competitors. This incentive for companies to focus on their individualistic interests is driven by financial rewards, which have further bolstered IP laws. In contrast, the global society may profit from strategies incorporating worldwide collective efforts, distributing information and assets, including IP, to achieve progress in the fastest and most efficient ways. An effective distribution system of shared data can be achieved by cross-country exchange systems that allow everyone who wants to share valuable information with others to do so. Collaboration benefits societies worldwide, and many companies can provide important information and intellectual resources in return for their participation.[59] To gain the trust (and participation) of dominant players, such systems should be universal, transparent, reliable, and impartial.

Companies can protect their assets and interests by using self-help tools. Some examples of self-help are calling out copycats and advocating openly against copying.[60] However, these self-help measures are limited in providing reasonable means of protection and their ability to follow the IP regime worldwide. They also serve a company's specific interest, rather than the public's.[61]

Distributive justice enhances two sets of value-distribution activities: (1) sharing and distributing knowledge, and (2) helping humanity promote human rights values or preserve cultural artifacts and historical data. Under this view, open access to books, art, music, and even medicine has become a fundamental right in our world. International tools can enhance accessibility and better distribution of tangible and intangible assets to millions of users around the globe, especially in developing countries.[62]

59 Devi Gnyawali & Byung-Jin Park, *Co-opetition between Giants*, 40 Rsch. Pol'y 650–63 (2011) (describing study demonstrating the challenge of coopetition and yet being very helpful for firms to address major technological challenges, to create benefits for partnering firms and to advance technological innovation; it also shows that coopetition between giants causes subsequent coopetition among other firms and results in advanced technological development).

60 *Id.*

61 *Id.*

62 Margaret Chon, *Intellectual Property and the Development Divide*, 27 Cardozo L. Rev. 2821, 2907–08 (2006) (favoring exceptions and limitations in intellectual property treaties).

One of the goals international organizations target while adopting global distributive justice approaches is to achieve a better balance between developed and developing countries in the flow of capital, access to knowledge, economic growth, workforce quality, and many other important factors.[63] These goals can be achieved through international tools that grant exemptions and limitations in favor of developing countries according to their special needs. Important treaties have been designed to serve as a means to achieve these goals. Examples include the Agreement on Trade-Related Aspects of Intellectual Property Rights, the Marrakesh Treaty to Facilitate Access to Published Works for Persons who are Blind, Visually Impaired or Otherwise Print Disabled (regarding exceptions and limitations to traditional IP laws aimed at assisting visually impaired persons and supporting higher percentages of these individuals in developing countries), and the Kyoto Protocol to the United Nations Framework Convention on Climate Change (regarding the reduction of gas emissions). These all impose lower levels of obligations on developing countries. The Anti-Counterfeiting Trade Agreement and the Doha Declaration on the TRIPS Agreement and Public Health further take a flexible stance concerning balancing private IP rights and public interests to promote access to essential medicines for all.[64]

The international view reveals a different reality. Interestingly and surprisingly, WIPO has changed its policy in recent years by adopting a new approach that considers distributive justice as part of its agenda. Contemporary international IP tools being developed by the organization adopt distributive justice as their main goal, even though their implementation at the international level may require further adjustments for developing countries.[65]

Research analyzing patent provisions in bilateral, regional, and plurilateral agreements, compared to international tools, reveals that the latter are more efficient in attaining their IP goals.[66] This conclusion is especially true when we address WIPO's involvement. First, the involvement of an international entity such as

[63] Ali Imam, *How Patent Protection Helps Developing Countries*, 33 AIPLA Q. J. 377, 379 (2005). *See generally* Nora Maija Tocups, *The Development of Special Provisions in International Copyright Law for the Benefit of Developing Countries*, 29 Bull. Copyright Soc'y U.S.A. 402 (1981).

[64] *See also* Rochelle Dreyfuss & Susy Frankel, *From Incentive to Commodity to Asset: How International Law Is Reconceptualizing Intellectual Property*, 36 Mich. J. Int'l L. 557, 557–60 (2015); Ilan Benshalom, *Rethinking International Distributive Justice: Fairness as Insurance*, 31 B.U. Int'l L.J. 267, 285–86 (2013); Kaminski & Yanisky-Ravid, *supra* note 12; Miriam Bitton, *Rethinking the Anti-Counterfeiting Trade Agreement's Criminal Copyright Enforcement Measures*, 102 J. Crim. L. & Criminology 67 (2012); Margot E. Kaminski, *An Overview and the Evolution of the Anti-Counterfeiting Trade Agreement (ACTA)*, 21 Alb. L.J. Sci. & Tech. 385, 387–88 (2011).

[65] Ofer Tur Sinai, *The Trans-Pacific Partnership: Experimental Use of Patents on the International Agenda*, 16 N.C. J.L. & Tech. 16 (2014).

[66] *Id.* at 64 (criticizing the Trans-Pacific Partnership on experimental use of patents and concluding that international tools are more efficient).

WIPO, unlike local and even bilateral or regional treaties, may have a greater impact on the laws of member states. Second, WIPO can not only provide impactful tools but also create an objective and professional dispute resolution mechanism.[67] Finally, national legislation may be too narrow or may fail to address the important feature of IP tools as still evolving.

The next section maintains that distributive justice principles should not only govern an international IP regime but should also extend to affiliated tools that have become essential to executing IP laws globally. This chapter focuses on three such tools: (1) WIPO Proof, (2) WIPO Match, and (3) WIPO Re:Search.

14.4 WIPO'S INTERNATIONAL IP TOOLS

WIPO has recently launched several services exemplifying a distributive justice approach to IP, expanding its frontiers to new digital services and making them accessible to all. Provided by the leading international organization in the field, these services demonstrate a transition to a new understanding of the industry, incorporating distributive justice values and international perspectives as an integral part of IP. The next subsections are based on information provided by WIPO.

14.4.1 *New Business Service Providing Evidence of the Existence of an Intellectual Asset: WIPO Proof*

Intellectual property regimes consistently struggle to reduce the number of counterfeits at both the national and international levels. Despite the efforts and the capital invested in the war against counterfeits, it is indisputable that counterfeit rates have continuously grown.[68] "As exemplified by the statistics, counterfeiting in today's globalized environment is a global problem that can only be combated on an international scale."[69] Fighting counterfeits in the digital era has also been a

[67] *WIPO Alternative Dispute Resolution (ADR)*, WORLD INTELL. PROP. ORG., www.wipo.int/amc/en/ (last visited July 21, 2022):

> The WIPO Arbitration and Mediation Center offers time- and cost-efficient alternative dispute resolution ... options, such as mediation, arbitration, expedited arbitration, and expert determination to enable private parties to settle their domestic or cross-border commercial disputes. The WIPO Center is international and specialized in IP and technology disputes. The WIPO Center is also the global leader in the provision of domain name dispute resolution services under the WIPO-designed [Uniform Domain Name Dispute Resolution Policy].

[68] WIPO Proof has been discontinued as of January 31, 2022, but the principles behind the service mirror the ideas in this chapter. *Discontinuation of the WIPO Proof Token Generation Service*, WORLD INTELL. PROP. ORG., www.wipo.int/wipoproof/en/news/2021/news_0003.html (Oct. 11, 2021); Bitton, *supra* note 64, at 68 (suggesting that the criminal enforcement systems in place have not significantly deterred or affected people's behavior in this field).

[69] Bitton, *supra* note 64, at 113–15 (discussing different aspects of ACTA and concluding that the international treaty follows the U.S. model for criminal enforcement of copyright law).

significant legal challenge.[70] The current era is confronted with a growing array of data files containing valuable and often IP-protected information. This data can easily fall prey to misuse or misappropriation. Endangered digital files vary from musical scores, research results, large data sets, and business information to highly sophisticated software. Moreover, digital files are common in creative works and design, such as audio-visual works, textile designs, software, industrial design sketches, books, and scripts.[71]

A few solutions to address these challenges have been suggested and tested. Fingerprint digital stamps are available on the market. The use of blockchain technology and smart contracts, including NFTs, exemplifies digital tools that try to certify original authors and make IP regimes more accessible and open to all. Blockchain features such as distributed, shared, and encrypted databases that serve as irreversible and incorruptible public repositories of information[72] can be especially attractive to IP industries that suffer in the digital era from a lack of protection, face hurdles in proof of originality and proof of copying, experience rampant counterfeiting, have to rely on third parties as distributors with high cuts of sales, and have trouble collecting fees.[73] Because blockchain is decentralized, it may be an attractive platform to smaller creators with fewer resources. By eliminating the third party, the platform promotes efficiency created in a peer-to-peer economy. Notwithstanding all of their benefits, these tools have been criticized on several grounds, including the economic interest of their distributors.[74]

This section argues that for IP validation services to be trustworthy, they should rely on the existing agreed-upon and accepted concepts of global IP law. In addition, for the authentication process to be effective, it should be equally available and accessible to anyone worldwide.

70 Kaminski, *supra* note 64, at 413–14 (criticizing ACTA efforts to fight counterfeits "as new products or programs that have not yet found a market will be prohibited under this language so long as it can be shown that they circumvent technological measures").

71 *WIPO Proof – Trusted Digital Evidence*, WORLD INTELL. PROP. ORG., www.wipo.int/wipoproof/en/index.html (last visited July 21, 2022) [hereinafter *WIPO Proof*]; *WIPO Proof – Trusted Digital Evidence to Your Intellectual Assets*, WORLD INTELL. PROP. ORG., https://wipoproof.wipo.int/wdts/ (last visited July 21, 2022).

72 Yanisky-Ravid & Kim, *supra* note 6, at 607–10 (describing ten salient features of blockchain platforms).

73 *See also* Alan Cohn, Travis West & Chelsea Parker, *Smart after All: Blockchain, Smart Contracts, Parametric Insurance, and Smart Energy Grids*, 1 GEO. L. TECH. REV. 273 (2017); Ioannis Karamitsos, Maria Papadaki & Nedaa Baker Al Barghuthi, *Design of the Blockchain Smart Contract: A Use Case for Real Estate*, 9 J. INFO SEC. 177 (2018); John Ream, Yang Chu & David Schatsky, *Upgrading Blockchains: Smart Contract Use Cases in Industry*, DELOITTE INSIGHTS (June 8, 2016), https://www2.deloitte.com/us/en/insights/focus/signals-for-strategists/using-blockchain-for-smart-contracts.html; John Zarocostas, *The Role of IP Rights in the Fashion Business: A US Perspective*, WIPO MAG. (Aug. 2018), www.wipo.int/wipo_magazine/en/2018/04/article_0006.html; Yanisky-Ravid & Monroy, *supra* note 6.

74 Yanisky Ravid & Kim, *supra* note 6; Yanisky-Ravid & Monroy, *supra* note 6.

Consistent with distributive justice and the rising need for international tools, WIPO suggested a new online business service called WIPO Proof. This service provided proof of the existence of a digital file at any point in time.[75] WIPO Proof provided an easy-to-use global online service that rapidly generated tamper-proof evidence proving that a digital file existed at a specific time and had not been altered since. In other words, it produced a unique fingerprint of your digital file, dated and timestamped the second it is created.[76]

Proof of originality includes the date of creation, which has become particularly difficult to validate in digital works. The goal of this tool was to create verifiable actions to guard the different digital outputs of creators and innovators in their work. It can also be useful to prove counterfeits and prevent future misuse. Social networks can also rely on a system like this to avoid liability when displaying online copyrightable content. The fact that WIPO Proof was an efficient tool for creating evidence of an asset's digital files at each point in time allowed it to solve and prevent potential future legal disputes. It laid a foundation for the registration of a formal IP right. The service was open to everyone and could have efficiently helped young or emerging creators and innovators.[77] WIPO Proof tokens were purchased for a small fee. After a token had been purchased, one individual received a copy with the other being stored securely on WIPO's servers.[78]

Distributive justice principles are reflected in the open access of the tool. Anyone could access WIPO Proof's secure online website to request a token for a digital file.[79] It was available online to *every user in the world.*[80] WIPO used industry-

[75] *WIPO Proof, supra* note 71.

[76] *Id.*

[77] Shlomit Yanisky-Ravid & Sean Hallisey, *"Equality and Privacy by Design": A New Model of Artificial Intelligence Data Transparency Certification as Safe Harbor*, 46 FORDHAM URB. L.J. 428 (2019); *see also WIPO Proof, supra* note 71.

[78] *WIPO Proof, supra* note 71.

[79] *Id.* WIPO Proof provides innovators and creators worldwide with secure evidence that a creation existed at a given point in time and can be verified by anyone. For creative works, the ability to prove their existence at the time of creation is fundamental to safeguarding them from potential misappropriation or infringement. By creating a date and time-stamped fingerprint of a digital file, WIPO Proof provides a sort of digital notary service, offering a trusted, cost-effective, and efficient service worldwide. WIPO does not read the file's contents nor store a copy of it. Moreover, WIPO Proof's secure, one-way algorithm interacts locally with the requestor's browser to create a unique digital fingerprint of the file. WIPO Proof tokens deliver the highest level of certainty that the date and time on the token is exact and has not been tampered with.

[80] Creating and innovating is often a long, iterative process that generates many valuable outputs along the way. Proving that an idea, lyric, sketch, or other original creation existed before someone else's can add substantially to its value. Furthermore, WIPO claims that the token system is reliable and is backed by WIPO's 130 years of experience providing secure, trustworthy IP services worldwide.

leading security technology to generate a globally recognized digital fingerprint of each habitant's intellectual asset.[81]

This service, along with other services discussed later, included complimentary tools to WIPO's existing IP systems that provided another way for the strategic global management of intellectual assets necessary to maintain IP laws.

14.4.2 *The New International Digital IP Match-Maker: WIPO Match*

A company's ability to develop IP assets depends on many variables. One critical variable is the company's ability to obtain and use financial and human resources. Many small businesses face difficulties getting investments; government assistance may be limited by local interests such as tax reduction, a desire to employ residents, locating a business in rural areas, and preventing a business from moving to other countries. Finding funding is a challenge that small and medium enterprises struggle with. It is even more challenging for businesses positioned for the international arena.

Surprisingly, despite the global nature of the current investment market, due to "home country bias," a significant percentage of people and companies still prefer to invest in familiar surroundings – in their home or regional markets or in familiar markets they believe they can trust.[82] Businesses in developing countries face major hurdles in attracting huge investments. Possibly, and regretfully, a lack of stable legal systems, or even the difference in language and culture, may create mistrust among potential international investors. Further, local investors face fewer tax hurdles when buying domestic shares and lower foreign currency risks.[83] The governmental policy also tends to encourage local investment.[84] The average American with a stock portfolio invests 79 percent of it in U.S.-listed stocks. Similarly, investors in Australia have an average of two-thirds of their portfolio in local shares.[85]

Establishing a reliable, unbiased system for international investment can help overcome these hurdles, encourage investments worldwide, and consequently stimulate global progress and equality.[86] Such an approach would enhance collaboration between investors and developers and help businesses in developing countries attract funding despite the hurdles described earlier, especially in the digital era.

[81] WIPO Proof uses public key infrastructure (PKI) technology to generate the tokens. The technology is considered one of the most internationally accepted and recognized digital certification methods.

[82] Kim Iskyan, *Investing Solely in Your Home Country Is Like Juggling Live Dynamite*, BUS. INSIDER (Aug. 9, 2016), www.businessinsider.com/investing-in-home-country-like-juggling-dynamite-2016-8.

[83] Investors often "trust" companies and stocks outside their borders less than they do in their own country.

[84] Iskyan, *supra* note 82.

[85] *Id.*

[86] Many open questions can be raised. What is the significance of the tendency toward local investment? Is it that specific global market incentives are needed? Must solutions counter these tendencies? How might a global IP protection regime specifically induce investment?

Using its international role to globally amplify principles of distributive justice and equality, WIPO has recently launched a new service supporting developing countries with IP developments. It aims to overcome the challenge that companies in developing countries face in attracting financial investments to enhance their economic growth. WIPO Match is a free online tool to match seekers of specific IP-related developmental needs with potential providers of resources.[87] WIPO acts as an international facilitator and publicizes successful matches. The service amplifies WIPO's resources and multiplies existing partnerships within the international IP arena. WIPO Match aims to harness the power of industry and the private sector to promote economic, social, and cultural development in developing countries and countries in transition. WIPO tries to empower the innovation and creativity of smaller IP stakeholders.[88] WIPO Match invites seekers and providers to engage in this project. Seekers must come from developing countries, countries in transition, or least developed countries.[89] While WIPO provides a clear definition of potential seekers, it does not limit potential providers.[90] WIPO's goal is to allow small businesses with limited resources to access IP-protected information, turning IP into a tool for collaboration, rather than an obstacle to growth.

14.4.3 *Global Collaboration with Bio Venture for Global Health: WIPO Re: Search Project*

The traditional IP regime, particularly in the United States and other developed countries, is based on granting exclusive rights – which allows, for instance, the pharmaceutical industry to dictate its licensing terms and conditions. This leads to high prices for patented drugs. These costs result in many people, particularly in developing countries, unable to afford these drugs. As a practical matter, this represents an oft-insurmountable hurdle, depriving millions of people from full access to necessary medications and better health.[91] WIPO identified this hurdle and launched WIPO Re:Search. This project aims to improve the collaboration

[87] *WIPO Match: Leveraging Intellectual Property for Development*, World Intell. Prop. Org., www.wipo.int/wipo-match/en/ (last visited July 21, 2022).

[88] *Id.*

[89] *Id.* WIPO's definition of seekers includes nongovernmental organizations from developed countries working with projects in developing countries and/or countries in transition, IP offices, IP-related government bodies, public research institutions, universities, foundations, inter-governmental organizations, and companies.

[90] *Id.* The open-ended provider list includes governments, nongovernmental organizations, intergovernmental organizations, foundations, companies, and universities.

[91] See, for example, Krista L. Cox, *The Medicines Patent Pool: Promoting Access and Innovation for Life-Saving Medicines through Voluntary Licenses*, 4 Hastings Sci. & Tech. L.J. 291, 293–94 (2012); Amir H. Khoury, *The "Public Health" of the Conventional International Patent Régime and the Ethics of "Ethicals": Access to Patented Medicines*, 26 Cardozo Arts & Ent. L.J. 25, 32–33 (2008); Peter K. Yu, *Access to Medicines, BRICS Alliances, and Collective Action*, 34 Am. J.L. & Med. 345, 358 (2008); Dean Baker, *Current Drug-Patent System Is Bad*

between pharmaceutical firms and large corporations by harnessing the power of public and private partnerships to help make IP available to the scientists who need it. Re:Search specifically targets the fight against neglected tropical diseases such as malaria and tuberculosis.[92]

Historically, WIPO has taken a stance in supporting traditional IP policy and encouraging developed countries to adopt an IP regime.[93] However, there has been an interesting shift in WIPO policy, reflected in a broader definition of the goals of IP systems and global distributive justice concepts, as previously discussed in this chapter. WIPO's Re:Search project emphasizes data sharing and access to health.[94] WIPO established this project to address the essential need for new and better drugs, diagnostics and vaccines.[95] Through WIPO Re:Search, organizations share without royalty IP, compounds, expertise, know-how, and facilities. The open environment promotes cooperation and collaboration among researchers from leading pharmaceutical firms.[96] It enables them to develop medical solutions for diseases that will affect developing countries.[97] The collaborative and open-access policy exemplifies several basic distributive justice values, such as enabling open access, promoting

Medicine, ALJAZEERA AM. (Nov. 24, 2014), http://america.aljazeera.com/opinions/2014/11/drug-patents-pharmaceuticalindustrygenericsindia.html.

92 *WIPO Re:Search*, WORLD INTELL. PROP. ORG., www.wipo.int/research/en/ (last visited July 21, 2022).

93 *See* Sisule F. Musungu & Graham Dutfield, *Multilateral Agreements and a TRIPS-Plus World: The World Intellectual Property Organization (WIPO)* (Quaker United Nations Off., TRIPS Issues Paper No. 3, 2003).

94 *WIPO Re:Search*, *supra* note 92. WIPO Re:Search was established in 2011 by WIPO in collaboration with BIO Ventures for Global Health and with the active participation of leading pharmaceutical companies and other private- and public-sector research organizations. *About WIPO Re:Search*, WORLD INTELL. PROP. ORG., www.wipo.int/research/en/about/ (last visited July 21, 2022); *see also* WORLD HEALTH ORG., WORLD INTELL. PROP. ORG. & WORLD TRADE ORG., PROMOTING ACCESS TO MEDICAL TECHNOLOGIES AND INNOVATION: INTERSECTIONS BETWEEN PUBLIC HEALTH, INTELLECTUAL PROPERTY AND TRADE (2d ed. 2020); Catherine Jewell, *Catalyzing Research into Neglected Tropical Diseases*, WIPO MAG. (Feb. 2013), at 15, www.wipo.int/wipo_magazine/en/2013/01/article_0004.html.

95 Anatole Krattiger, *Promoting Access to Medical Innovation*, WIPO MAG. (Oct. 2013), at 5, www.wipo.int/wipo_magazine/en/2013/05/article_0002.html; *see also Neglected Tropical Diseases*, WORLD HEALTH ORG., www.who.int/neglected_diseases/diseases/en/ (last visited July 21, 2022) ("Neglected tropical diseases (NTDs) – a diverse group of communicable diseases that prevail in tropical and subtropical conditions in 149 countries – affect more than one billion people and cost developing economies billions of dollars every year.").

96 *Id.* According to WIPO, NTDs such as "malaria and tuberculosis affect more than one billion people across the globe. Although recent years have seen the arrival of new [research-and-development] models and extra resources, there remains a pressing need to bridge research gaps and bring together knowledge, skills and infrastructure from the private, non-profit, and academic sectors." *Sharing Innovation in the Fight against Neglected Tropical Diseases*, WORLD INTELL. PROP. ORG. (Aug. 2014), www.wipo.int/export/sites/www/research/docs/flyer_wiporesearch_2014.pdf.

97 *WIPO Re:Search*, *supra* note 92.

equality by supporting developing countries, and sharing data rather than prioritizing exclusive rights.[98]

CONCLUSION

The example of WIPO Re:Search is one of many that reflect distributive justice principles; the tools benefit developing countries by providing certain favorable conditions, such as improving access to medicines to the benefit of the poor and needy, enhancing access to knowledge and technology for developing countries, and encouraging developed countries to share knowledge and technology. According to WIPO, more than a hundred countries have agreed to the model, and leading pharmaceutical firms, such as Novartis, and leading universities have joined the project.[99]

The phenomenon of giving IP laws a new and different meaning by adopting the distributive justice approach, which enhances access to IP assets, stands in contrast to the traditional perspective on the IP regime. WIPO Re:Search provides the necessary incentive for research and development by providing exclusive rights for a limited time to owners that solely control their IP products and processes.

This chapter contends that, in the face of the digital era, this one-sided, narrow, local, and traditional perspective should and can be expanded beyond IP by adopting new tools and distributive justice from an international perspective.[100]

98 *Id.*

99 *See Collaboration Agreements*, WORLD INTELL. PROP. ORG. (Aug. 24, 2016), www.wipo.int/export/sites/www/research/docs/collaboration_agreements.pdf.

100 Article 31 of the TRIPS Agreement provides:

> Where the law of a Member allows for other use of the subject matter of a patent without the authorization of the right holder, including use by the government or third parties authorized by the government, the following provisions shall be respected: (a) authorization of such use shall be considered on its individual merits; (b) such use may only be permitted if, prior to such use, the proposed user has made efforts to obtain authorization from the right holder on reasonable commercial terms and conditions and that such efforts have not been successful within a reasonable period of time. This requirement may be waived by a Member in the case of a national emergency or other circumstances of extreme urgency or in cases of public non-commercial use. . . .

For additional perspectives on TRIPS, *see* Donald Harris, *TRIPS after Fifteen Years: Success or Failure, as Measured by Compulsory Licensing*, 18 J. INTELL. PROP. L. 367, 386 (2011); Jessica J. Fayerman, *The Spirit of TRIPS and the Importation of Medicines Made under Compulsory License after the August 2003 TRIPS Council Agreement*, 25 NW. J. INT'L L. & BUS. 257, 258 (2004); Divya Murthy, *The Future of Compulsory Licensing: Deciphering the Doha Declaration on the TRIPS Agreement and Public Health*, 17 AM. U. INT'L L. REV. 1299, 1307–08 (2001); Sara Germano, *Compulsory Licensing of Pharmaceuticals in Southeast Asia: Paving the Way for Greater Use of the TRIPS Flexibility in Low-and Middle-Income Countries*, 76 UMKC L. REV. 273, 294 (2007).

www.ingramcontent.com/pod-product-compliance
Lightning Source LLC
LaVergne TN
LVHW011702200926
848484LV00004B/1033

* 9 7 8 1 1 0 8 8 4 1 7 0 2 *